Wilhelm Dilthey:

The Critique of Historical Reason

MICHAEL ERMARTH is assistant professor of history at Dartmouth College.

The Critique

Wilhelm Dilthey:
of Historical Reason

Michael Ermarth

The University of Chicago Press

Chicago and London

The University of Chicago Press, Chicago 60637
The University of Chicago Press, Ltd., London

© 1978 by The University of Chicago
All rights reserved. Published 1978

Library of Congress Cataloging in Publication Data

Ermarth, Michael.
 Wilhelm Dilthey: The Critique of Historical Reason
 Based on the author's thesis, University of Chicago, 1975.

 Bibliography: p.
 Includes index.
 1. Dilthey, Wilhelm, 1833–1911.   I. Title.
B3216.D84E67   193   77–16223
ISBN 0–226–21742–6

MICHAEL ERMARTH is Assistant Professor of History
at Dartmouth College.

To the memory of my mother,

MARGARET ERMARTH

Contents

Acknowledgments

This work owes much to the influence and inspiration of my former teachers, especially Peter Celms, Karl Weintraub, and Paul Ricoeur. I would like to thank Dr. Christa Kirsten of the Akademie der Wissenschaften der DDR and Dr. Klaus Haenel of the Niedersächsische Staats- und Universitätsbibliothek Göttingen for their generous cooperation in researching the Dilthey Nachlass. Dartmouth College was unstinting in its support of my efforts; to Gail Patten of the History Department is due a special word of thanks for her patience and skill. Finally, I wish to express my deepest gratitude to Leonard Krieger, who epitomizes what Dilthey must have meant by the creative synthesis of understanding and immanent critique.

List of Abbreviations

Major Published Works

GS   *Gesammelte Schriften.* 18 vols. Stuttgart: B. G. Teubner, and Göttingen: Vandenhoeck & Ruprecht, 1914–77.

JD   *Der junge Dilthey: Ein Lebensbild in Briefen und Tagebüchern, 1852–1870.* Edited by Clara Misch, née Dilthey. 2d ed. Stuttgart: B. G. Teubner, 1960.

BDY   *Briefwechsel zwischen Wilhelm Dilthey und dem Grafen Paul Yorck von Wartenburg, 1877–1897.* Edited by Sigrid von der Schulenburg. Halle: Max Niemeyer, 1923.

ED   *Das Erlebnis und die Dichtung.* 14th ed. Göttingen: Vandenhoeck & Ruprecht, 1965.

VDM   *Von deutscher Dichtung und Musik: Aus den Studien zur Geschichte des deutschen Geistes.* Edited by Herman Nohl and Georg Misch. Leipzig: B. G. Teubner, 1933.

GPD   *Die grosse Phantasiedichtung und andere Studien zur vergleichenden Literaturgeschichte.* Edited by Herman Nohl. Göttingen: Vandenhoeck & Ruprecht, 1954.

LS   *Leben Schleiermachers.* 2d ed., rev. and enlgd. by Hermann Mulert. Berlin: W. de Gruyter, 1922.

Grundriss *Grundriss der Logik und des Systems der philosophischen Wissenschaften: Für Vorlesungen.* Berlin: Mittler, 1865.

Book Reviews

WM   *Westermanns Monatshefte.* Series 2–5. Braunschweig, 1859–85.

Unpublished Writings from the Nachlass

BNL   Manuscripts from the Berlin Nachlass. Literatur-Archiv der deutschen Akademie der Wissenschaften, Berlin. Cited by ms. folio number (new series), followed by page number, for example, *BNL* 24/68.

GNL   Manuscripts from the Göttingen Nachlass. Niedersächsische Staats- und Universitätsbibliothek, Göttingen. Cited as above for *BNL*.

BA   "Die Breslauer Ausarbeitung" (ca. 1880), from the Göttingen Nachlass. Cod. Ms. W. Dilthey, no. 2. Niedersächsische Staats- und Universitätsbibliothek, Göttingen. (Forthcoming as a volume of *GS*).

BE   "Der Berliner Entwurf" (ca. 1890–95), from the Berlin Nachlass. No. 179. Literatur-Archiv der deutschen Akademie der Wissenschaften, Berlin. (Forthcoming as a volume of *GS*).

LK   "Diltheys letztes Kolleg über das System der Philosophie," from the Göttingen Nachlass. Cod. Ms. W. Dilthey, no. 9. Niedersächsische Staats- und Universitätsbibliothek, Göttingen.

Wilhelm Dilthey:
The Critique of Historical Reason

Die Fragen der Wissenschaft sind sehr häufig
Fragen der Existenz.

—Goethe to Eckermann (December 30, 1823)

Introduction:
The Dilthey Problem

The thought of Wilhelm Dilthey has attained an extraordinary degree of influence. Although he died in 1911—well over half a century ago and prior to the inception of many cultural, social, and political developments generally linked with distinctively modern patterns of thought—his work continues to enjoy currency, not merely as an object of historical interest and appreciation but as a direct source of new ideas in the theory of the humanistic and social scientific disciplines, in specific branches of philosophy and criticism, and in the theory of knowledge in general.[1] Ortega y Gasset's assessment of Dilthey as the most important thinker in the second half of the nineteenth century has proved too restricted for some recent commentators, who see in Dilthey a major intellectual force in our own century, exerting an impact exceeded only by that of Kant and Hegel.[2] A partial list of prominent thinkers influenced by Dilthey's ideas would include Martin Heidegger, Max Weber, Karl Jaspers, Ernst Cassirer, Ernst Troeltsch, Max Scheler, Georg Simmel, Karl Mannheim, Raymond Aron, Ludwig Binswanger, Karl Löwith, Georg Lukacs, Eduard Spranger, Erich Rothacker, Rudolf Bultmann, Hans-Georg Gadamer, and Ortega himself. The formation of a full-fledged "Dilthey School" consisting of Herman Nohl, Georg Misch, and Bernhard Groethuysen also served to elaborate Dilthey's approach and bring it into wider view. It would require a large study in itself merely to trace the pattern of acknowledged influence, not to mention less explicit forms of intellectual filiation.

In the context of the perpetual "search for a method" in the social sciences and humanities, Dilthey is almost invariably invoked. Like the prodigious synthesizers Vico and William James—to whom he is sometimes compared—Dilthey constitutes a wellspring of provocative, if inchoate, ideas over a wide range of subjects. If it is true that there are signs of convergence among the various warring camps of phenomenologists, structuralists, behaviorists, functionalists, Marxists, and existentialists, then it seems likely that Dilthey's thought, which stresses mediation and represents a distinctive middle way among contending extremes, will continue to be of prime importance. At the very least it can be said that no serious effort to advance the theoretical discussion of the human sciences can afford to ignore Dilthey. It is the purpose of this study to establish this point by means of a comprehensive exposition of his thought.

The pervasiveness of Dilthey's influence and the continuing exploration of the implications of his work have given rise to an extensive and heated debate concerning the essential tendency of his thinking. For a number of reasons, a precise resolution of this crucial question is by no means assured. The very thinker who brought the theoretical problem of interpretation and "understanding" (*Verstehen*) to the forefront of methodological controversy himself presents a major problem of interpretation. His thought is notoriously enigmatic and has proven resistant to customary modes of classification and analysis. It has been viewed variously as a "philosophy of life," a theory of the humanistic and social scientific disciplines, an epistemology of understanding, a historically based "philosophy of philosophy," and a "hermeneutic" (methodical exegesis) of man's historical existence. These designations might be incidental except for the fact that the selection of one or another rubric has tended to predispose—often in a very one-sided fashion—the treatment of his thought as a whole. It is thus no exaggeration to speak of a "Dilthey problem" which exceeds the levels of complexity to be expected in most thinkers of abiding merit. After surveying this problem, Max Horkheimer aptly called the study of Dilthey "at once stimulating and boundless."[3] In a judgment which similarly mixed admiration with near desperation, Ortega was compelled to refer to the "secret" of Dilthey's thinking.[4]

The dimensions of the Dilthey problem are large and, owing to the present condition of the source materials, also shifting. There are both substantive and circumstantial factors behind the perplexing quality of his thought. He wrote an enormous amount, the full scope of which has only recently emerged from the exhaustive book-length bibliography compiled by Ulrich Herrmann.[5] Moreover, Dilthey occupied a position at the border of a number of disciplines and was not content to restrict himself to a single perspective. His fields of endeavor included history, psychology, philosophy (including epistemology, ethics, aesthetics, and pedagogical theory), theology, literary history, and literary criticism. Like many German thinkers he cultivated a style of thinking and writing which is at once cryptic and suggestive. Its virtues can prove to be sources of frustration. Dilthey did not go so far as his close friend and philosophical ally Graf Yorck von Wartenburg, who held that "paradox is a mark of the truth," but Dilthey did not feel bound by rigid rules of systematic consistency. He was not a systematic thinker in the usual sense: he deliberately rejected the *esprit de système* and "thinking in schools." His son-in-law, the philosopher

Georg Misch, observed that Dilthey should be likened to a geologist rather than an architect.[6] Indeed, his thought is more like a quarry that an edifice: it eschewed "absolute" beginnings and conclusions in the name of ever-renewed explorations. The dense yet allusive quality of his thought was noted by one of his most perceptive students, Bernhard Groethuysen: "There lay already in the thoughts which he expressed an element which led beyond these thoughts; there was in what he said a clue to something more, to something in the distance."[7] Graf Yorck (*BDY* 1) referred to the same characteristic in praising his friend for contributions which lay between the lines, as well as in what was explicit. Dilthey's suggestive power is widely acknowledged and has been encapsulated for American readers in his reputation as "the German William James." If, however, one is accustomed to ironclad and unequivocal formulations, his thought presents considerable difficulty. On the basis of the rather cursory critical treatment he is generally awarded in Anglo-American quarters it is perhaps too easy to concur with the recent judgment that Dilthey was "a poor logician and an impossible stylist."[8]

It is frequently said that Dilthey's published work is really a gigantic torso, lacking in full articulation. He wrote in diverse fields, and many of his studies were offered as tentative investigations, to be concluded after further scrutiny and revision. But in his characteristic "moving beyond," Dilthey was frequently taken up in new questions and did not return to complete what he had begun. In a letter written at the end of his life to Edmund Husserl he confessed that he was partly responsible for the misunderstanding of his work by allowing initial portions to be published while holding back later sections "for further reflection."[9] This quality earned him the unflattering title of "man of the half-volume" and "the great fragmentist"; it is said that he provided not introductions but "introductions to introductions."[10] His historical-philosophical introduction to the human sciences, his ideas on descriptive psychology, his intellectual studies of Schleiermacher and Hegel, his typology of world-views, and his poetics were all left open to future expansion and reworking. In works which are somewhat elliptical to begin with, Dilthey's habit of constant revision presents the student of his thought with special "hermeneutic" perplexities: he seems to invite both interpolation and extrapolation, yet the necessary controls on these procedures are difficult to establish.

The state of the published writings and other source materials merely compounds the problem. Dilthey himself published only a small fraction of his total production. Much of the *Gesammelte Schriften* was drawn together, sometimes hastily, after his death by a circle of faithful students.[11] The last 50 years have seen repeated assertions that the project had at long last been completed, or at least that the major theoretical writings had come to light. Such assertions have been premature; at the present writing, the published volumes run to 18 and are projected by a group of West German scholars to an eventual 20.[12] Obviously, in the light of the expanding corpus, pronouncements concerning Dilthey's thought in its entirety must remain somewhat provisional.

Aside from the reevaluation of published materials, continuing attention to Dilthey's thought ought to be assured by the extensive Nachlass which runs to well over 100,000 pages. The bulk of this unpublished literary estate is deposited in the Literatur-archiv of the Institut für deutsche Sprache und Literatur of the Akademie der Wissenschaften der DDR in Berlin; smaller portions were conserved by Misch and Nohl in the Handschriften-Abteilung of the Niedersächsische Staats- und Universitätsbibliothek in Göttingen.[13] Emerging from what Nohl characterized as "a jungle of papers written in an almost impressionistic handwriting," important but hitherto unknown portions of Dilthey's total effort are sporadically coming to light. These unpublished materials have been incorporated in this study and have influenced its conclusions significantly, oftentimes in a direction at variance with prevailing judgments. It should be noted that a truly complete and adequate critical edition of Dilthey's writings does not exist, and this fact must be borne in mind by any serious student of his thought.

Reactions among scholars to this fluid and complex state of affairs have varied. Some extreme critics have denied that there is any unity in Dilthey and have asserted that, if any such unity is to be supposed, it is not Dilthey himself but his readers who supply it. Others have alleged that there are no genuine conclusions in his thought. In an opposing vein, some interpreters find that Dilthey had only one fundamental idea, which he restated again and again in different formulations. A less extreme view insists that Dilthey's seemingly diffuse efforts are sustained by a unifying intention — that although a definitive systematic synthesis of his thought is not available in one concise formulation, it can be projected from existing sources. This projective view has been advanced by several careful interpreters, but it has been employed by less cautious ones as a license for unbridled speculation. Such projections and sweeping interpretations exist in abundance—indeed, they have unfortunately constituted the general image of the man. Employing a concept deriving from Dilthey's own theory of interpretation but brushing aside his restrictions, interpreters have attempted to understand Dilthey better than he understood himself. Frequently these efforts at "better understanding" culminate in what can only be called over-interpretation, based on very scant and highly selective textual support. Like that of his contemporary, Nietzsche, the entirety of Dilthey's work is too often flagrantly disregarded in favor of highly quotable snippets. It has been perceptively observed that "a process of vulgarization and diffusion had begun even before 1920 to transform Dilthey's complexities into a popular philosophy."[14] As a stringent corrective, more recent interpreters have called for a sober and painstaking "Dilthey philology" or "Dilthey hermeneutic" prior to further generalizations. Treating Dilthey "on his own terms" promises not only to rescue him from some of his critics but to save him from some of his disciples.

This study grew out of my bewilderment in the face of the vastly divergent interpretations of Dilthey and the highly polemical overtones surrounding his thought. The "Proteus Dilthey" offers grist for practically every conceivable intellectual mill. For better or worse he has become a focal point in a larger debate which exercises theorists in many disciplines. Quite often he functions as a kind of philosophical straw man; sections of his work are isolated and employed to bolster or attack a more generalized viewpoint. Although this dubious service has earned him a certain continuing notoriety, it hardly suffices as the basis for a serious assessment of his own work. His thought has been characterized according to an astonishingly varied and ill-sounding catalog of "isms": vitalism, neo-idealism, positivism, historicism, irrationalism, intellectualism, subjectivism, relativism, aestheticism, existentialism, "psychologism," "sociologism," "presentism," and a host of other variations. Not only are these terms woefully imprecise; many are glaringly contradictory. An embracing abstraction may be useful in fathoming a difficult thinker, but the lever should not be mistaken for the load. The interpretation of Dilthey has been hampered rather than promoted by the facile employment of such labels.

Dilthey constantly demanded that a thinker be treated on his own terms. Unfortunately this rule has not been applied rigorously enough to Dilthey himself. Instead of careful attention to his own words in their total context, he has been approached through presumptive, invidious, or anachronistic categories. The net result is that often his quite singular intellectual position is resolved into either a pale reflection of a prior Golden Age of German idealism or else a "genial" anticipation of later existentialism and phenomenology. In the attempt to place his thought under convenient or familiar rubrics, important distinctions and qualifications which he carefully maintained are blurred. Dilthey was neither prophet nor epigone; his position in intellectual history is not that of a mere afterthought of classical idealism nor an unwitting premonition of later phenomenology and existentialism *avant la lettre*. Nor is it sufficient to regard him—as is most commonly done—as a tenuous bridge between these two.[15] This study aspires to treat Dilthey on his own terms, without projective stylization or fluent but misleading parallels. While such a standard promises to recover some of the subtlety and originality of his thought, it also means presenting frankly some of its inner tensions and inconsistencies. By treating its subject on its own terms, this study hopes to dispel the lopsided but common view that the main value of Dilthey's work lay in preparing the way for subsequent positions—or that his thought may justly be considered to have been superseded by these later developments. Dilthey was a foundational, not merely a transitional, thinker; if he is freed from his customary transitional role, his foundations take on renewed theoretical importance beyond mere "preparation" and "anticipation."

A complementary principle requires setting Dilthey's thought in the intellectual context of his times. Treating a thinker on his own terms does not mean regarding his thought as *sui generis* and sealed off from the ideas of others. Dilthey's terms were of his times, and they cannot be comprehended without attention to the major intellectual controversies of his day. As the recent volumes of the *Gesammelte Schriften* and portions of the Nachlass show, the breadth of his reading in contemporary sources in all disciplines was staggering, and he garnered his ideas and insights from many quarters. The judgment that "Dilthey lived in the spiritual world of the 18th and early 19th centuries; the main part of his own century passed him by" is often repeated, yet it is clearly belied by his own writings.[16] Indeed, his thought becomes intelligible only in relation to the main intellectual currents of his time, and some of his murkier doctrines gain clarity only when set in this wider frame. Dilthey's many reviews, sketches, notes, manuscripts, and otherwise fragmentary studies are invaluable in the reconstruction of this context.

The Nachlass has been especially important in providing more detailed elaboration of points raised only in passing by the published texts. If such unfinished materials seem peripheral to an exposition of his final views, it is well to recall his own words concerning the "movement of thinking":

> The finished book says very little about the secret of its genesis. Plans, sketches, projected studies, letters—in all these breathes the living spirit of the person, just as sketches can reveal more than the finished picture. . . . Who can say what a single page might reveal when it comes under the right eye? . . . Where we can work out of the Nachlass of a great thinker or writer—there arises the most complete picture attainable in any part of history [*GS* 1:562].[17]

But, "right eye" or not, Dilthey's practice of continual revision obviously poses an acute problem of selection, emphasis, and internal criticism. What, one might justifiably ask, is really "finished" in his writings? What indeed is essential to the "most complete picture"? As successive editors have been compelled to admit, with Dilthey any reasonably selective compilation *is* an interpretation in itself. This present study proceeds by coordinating general premises with specific doctrines and applications, attending carefully to Dilthey's own terms and especially to what he called *"Mittelglieder,"* that is, the mediating concepts that were so important to his presentation of the human sciences. The principle guiding the choice of citations has been to choose the most inclusive or representative passages. Owing to its structure, certain portions of this study give greater weight to his later formulations, which generally display greater conceptual development, though sometimes in less polished style. It should be noted that all translations are my own and that no quotations have been rendered into composite form, as in some previous studies.

Employing these materials and guidelines, this study hopes to shed some light on the specific matter of the development of Dilthey's thought. The question of an early "positivistic" and later "existentialist" Dilthey has been nearly as decisive in the interpretation of his thought as in that of Marx—with the difference, one might suppose, that their respective phases were reversed. This aspect of the Dilthey problem is an especially important, though vexing, issue. On it hinges a number of crucial matters, including the precise relation Dilthey envisioned between the natural sciences and human sciences, the extent to which he regarded psychology and sociology as fundamental to the study of history, and the relationship between hermeneutics and epistemology. A careful tracing of Dilthey's intellectual evolution raises at the same time some substantive theoretical questions which go well beyond the specifically biographical sphere.

Several commentators have fastened on an assertion Dilthey made near the end of his life that his life's work was the execution of the plans of his youth (Foreward, *JD* v). This statement is often taken to mean that his ideas were fixed at an early stage and remained practically impervious to outside influence and confrontation with the views of others. It can also be employed to bolster the view that he remained unmoved by the shifting intellectual undertow of his age. But such a reading in terms of static *idées fixes* does not take into account other statements testifying explicitly to changes in his position and the palpable influence of other thinkers.

It is tempting to move to the opposite of the "stasis" thesis and postulate distinct stages in Dilthey's development. The proponents of the developmental thesis have discerned anywhere from two to six distinct periods in his work, each defined by a new theoretical departure or the impingement of other thinkers. A common way of treating Dilthey's development is to propound a "great reversal" in the years 1896–1904, during which time he is supposed to have radically altered his previous opinions. Those who regard Dilthey primarily as a precursor of existentialism are especially given to this approach. The fact that much of the interpretation of Dilthey has been undertaken through the darkening prism of existential philosophy (especially Heidegger's existential ontology) has particularly distorted the discussion of his development.

The view advanced in this study falls between those who see no development at all and those who perceive drastic reformulations and reversals. There is a high degree of continuity in Dilthey's thought, but it also manifests important shifts, stemming from his own reflections and the influence of other thinkers. He subjected his thought to the constant testing process of what he called "immanent critique," that is, critical judgment and revision in light of its own professed aims. One of the most confounding features of his thought is that the internal relations among component concepts and doctrines are modified — sometimes quite significantly — without a concomitant shift in the overall contours. What appears from one angle to be a radical change looks from another perspective to be a far less consequential adjustment or even a matter of nuance. Here Dilthey's peculiar attitude toward "system" is determinative; modifications in one area or at one level of his thought are not propagated with the logical consistency one might expect of a closely articulated system.

Although the modification of Dilthey's ideas is an exceedingly important matter, it is deceptive to portray this development in distinct chronological stages. By its very nature Dilthey's thought cannot be presented in serial fashion. A chronology of years is not necessarily an order of ideas, much less a "logic" of those ideas. In some respects Dilthey, like many other thinkers, came to "first" things last — at least in the sense of making explicit what previously he had simply assumed. There are transformations in his thinking which demand developmental treatment, but not in the sense suggested by reserving entire chapters for "phases" in his intellectual development. The chapter divisions in this study present topics or regions of his thought, and they necessarily reflect the dialectical relation of "reciprocal coherence" which is the hallmark of Dilthey's thinking. His terms really preclude neat divisions, so this study must often proceed by means of collateral soundings rather than linear synopsis.

Dilthey's thought evolved but also revolved. The structure and method of this work embody what he called the "hermeneutical circle," that is, the notion that, while the interpretive process must begin with a preliminary notion of the whole in order to integrate the parts, the evolving concept of the whole is constituted by an ever more probing analysis and synthesis of the parts. Such a procedure of circular exegesis entails a certain amount of recapitulation but has the virtue of remaining faithful to Dilthey's mode of thought. Perhaps equally important, it promises to provide a means of averting what has been called the commonest error of the intellectual historian: "to write about things he does not really understand — things he has not 'internalized' and thought through for himself."[18] Therefore, if this book succeeds in its design and exposition, it should be something more than the sum of its separate chapters. With the broad points conveyed in the separate chapters the reader is called upon to perform an interpretive circle of his own.

Chapter 1 surveys Dilthey's life and his intellectual context. He insisted that thought and expression arise from a cultural matrix as well as individual talent and act reciprocally upon this culture; hence, such a contextual approach seems mandatory. It is sometimes said that the biography of a man whose business is thinking should simply be the story of his thought. But if the subject matter of his thought is life, lived experience, and history, then that story must perforce extend beyond the strict confines of theoretical analysis. Dilthey held that life is the "prius" of thought, and we must acknowledge that his own life was the "prius" of his philosophizing. Here Dilthey himself furnished an appropriate principle—and caveat: "Especially since Hegel the connection between the character or life of a philosopher and his system has been emphasized—even to the point of overdoing it. It is *one* will which operates in both realms; it operates in the work of thought as well as in the formation of life (*GS* 14/1:463).

This study, however, does not purport to present a full-scale biography of Dilthey—a "Life of Dilthey" after the fashion of his epochal *Leben Schleiermachers*, a work which can be said to have inaugurated a new stage in the writing of intellectual history. This study is more theoretical and less specifically biographical in intent. It takes as a focus not the details of his life but his life-long project of a "critique of historical reason" or, to use less specifically Kantian terminology, a philosophical foundation of the human sciences. There already exist a number of accounts of his life, as well as his own autobiographical reflections, diaries, and extensive correspondence.[19] Although there can be no clear separation between "life" and "thought" in dealing with a thinker such as Dilthey—who constantly demonstrated their integral relation—the emphasis of this study rests with his thought.

Chapter 2 examines the deepest foundations of his thought, the concepts of "life" and "lived experience" and their role in distinguishing the human sciences from the natural sciences. The discussion of these "empirical" foundations leads directly to the problem of the "critical" foundations set forth in chapter 3, which is concerned with Dilthey's notion of a basic science of man and the relation of psychology and epistemology to the human sciences. Chapter 4 examines some crucial reformulations at the level of these foundations in response to allied and contending positions. Chapter 5 analyzes in depth and context the central Diltheyan concept of "understanding" (*Verstehen*) and examines alterations which this crucial notion underwent in his later period. This chapter treats Dilthey's specific reflections on the nature of history and its cognitive status. It also examines his actual practice of *Verstehen*, thus seeking to remedy the serious gap remarked by a recent German commentator: "It is characteristic that the historical works of Dilthey in the area of intellectual history have never been deeply analyzed from the standpoint of their actual method."[20] Dilthey practiced what he preached, but he did not always preach what he practiced; it is therefore necessary to coax certain theoretical postulates from his actual historiography. Such an examination should establish more clearly and concretely why he has been called "the true father of intellectual history" and at the same time dispel certain enduring misconceptions about the aims and assumptions of this field of history.[21] Chapter 6 deals with the controversial idea of the "world-view" and Dilthey's efforts toward a comprehensive analysis and typology of world-views. Contrary to the prevailing opinion that such a "science of world-views" actually represents the self-inflicted bankruptcy of science itself, this chapter shows that the doctrine of world-views represents a fruitful contribution to the human sciences. A concluding chapter seeks to draw these topics together in a general summation, suggesting some facets (and limits) of Dilthey's importance for present theorizing in the human sciences.

By way of a preliminary indication of the significance of this undertaking, it could be argued that the central issues of intellectual history change rather slowly; indeed, some observers would say that they hardly change at all. Many of the problems confronting philosophy and the human sciences today are arrestingly conveyed in Dilthey's thought. If contemporary thinking has gone beyond Dilthey on various fronts, his general problematic is still very much with us. It is well to remember that a body of knowledge which forgets its founders will not recognize when it is advancing or is merely retracing its earlier steps. An attentive study of Dilthey provides an object lesson in the kind of relevant intellectual history described by Merleau-Ponty as "that queer movement by which thought abandons and preserves its old formulas by integrating them as particular and privileged cases into a more comprehensive and general thought which cannot decree itself exhaustive."[22] If genuine history is the effort *reculer pour mieux sauter*, then one does not need to stylize Dilthey in order to disclose his meaning for the present. The crisis of scientific knowledge and culture he perceived around him has become an endemic fact of modern life. The imperatives of thought and life are still posed in uneasy tension by many belief-systems and philosophies. The "use and abuse" of history and the other human sciences are widely discussed. Establishing the difference between genuine science and illicit scientism has become a vital issue: anguished attention is paid to the dangers of the dehumanizing sort of reason and science which Dilthey attempted to banish from the study of man. The plea for an expanded, humane reason is heard on many sides. We are the heirs of Dilthey and the questions he posed.

When a body of knowledge is ready to become genuine
science, then there must necessarily arise a crisis.
—Goethe, *Maximen*

Our time has something of the character of the end of an
epoch. . . . A feeling of transitoriness again permeates this
hoary world.
—Graf Yorck to Dilthey, 1892

Dilthey and the
Crisis of European Thought
and Culture

Biographical Setting

In 1873, at about midpoint in a long lifetime, stretching from 1833 to 1911, Dilthey gave personal testimony to the deep impulse which dominated his life and work:

> The great crisis of the sciences and European culture which we are now living through has so deeply and totally taken possession of my spirit that the desire to be of some help in it has extinguished every extraneous and personal ambition [*JD* vii].

The tone of urgency and commitment sounded in this passage is repeated throughout his diary, personal correspondence, and theoretical writings. A protracted crisis of consciousness or "world-view" (to employ a useful term that has come into wide usage through Dilthey's own work) constituted the background of his thinking. As a student writing in the 1860s he found it "incredible and downright terrifying how all the problems of philosophy, history, and politics are now mutually intertwined" (*JD* 145). A decade later he characterized the situation of Europe as a ship on the high seas, moving in "the storm that rages all around us" (*LS* 798). This sense of crisis continued to deepen with the passage of time. Writing at the beiginning of the last decade of the nineteenth century, Dilthey portrayed his own age as a time of deep turmoil and uncertainty. He alluded to the "tangled problematic of modern thought" and ventured the judgment that never before in history had the ultimate premises of thought and action been so open to question (*GS* 10:14). To his friend Graf Yorck von Wartenburg he expressed the conviction that major catastrophes were approaching with frightening rapidity (*BDY* 156, 228). In an effort at historical analogy, he referred to "a shaking of human society and its foundations such as has not been seen since the declining days of the Greco-Roman world" (*GS* 6:246).[1]

It appeared to Dilthey that traditional cultural values were nearly exhausted despite feeble attempts by some thinkers to salvage them in an eternal canon. And while continuity with the past was increasingly disrupted, no sure beacons appeared on the horizon. Skepticism and "anarchy of conviction" had extended their power over more and more of the presuppositions and basic values of Western culture. In 1900, at the threshold of the new century, Dilthey reflected that the present age was more helpless in the face of the basic questions of life than any previous period. In contrast to the optimism of many of his contemporaries, Dilthey found the prospect of the new century "beclouded" (GS 8:193–94). A few years before his death he spoke urgently of "the task of giving security and strength to the life of the individual and society in the great crisis of the century" (GS 5:356).

Dilthey's thought cannot be understood apart from this context of prolonged, even endemic, crisis. The period through which he lived was marked by controversy and upheaval in almost all levels and sectors of existence. In none was the agitation more radical and far-reaching than in the realm of ideas. He lived through the *Hegelstreit, Religionsstreit, Materialismusstreit, Darwinismusstreit, Pessimismusstreit,* and the *Methodenstreit;* it was, as one observer noted in retrospect, "an endlessly strife-racked age."[2] The sense of crisis was all the more acute for the fact that it reached down to the very foundations of thinking and knowledge. Although the symptoms of crisis were often lodged in abstruse terms and intricate arguments, it was far from being a merely academic matter. The very nature of reason and knowledge were at stake and, with them, the prospects of a civilization increasingly shaped by their imperatives.

As Dilthey perceived it, the crisis of his age had been engendered by a fundamental discordance between thought and life. The growing separation between theory and practice threatened to culminate in the sterile extremes of "life-less" thought and "thought-less" life. On the one hand, intellectuals and philosophers for the most part continued to aspire to closed theoretical systems of eternal ideals and principles, while on the other hand men of practical affairs and researchers in the newer sciences vaunted their disdain of theory and any larger philosophical perspective for their accomplishments. Dilthey was deeply distressed that the normative philosophical disciplines such as ethics, aesthetics, jurisprudence, and pedagogical theory —the disciplines from which a culture draws its standards—were taken seriously on the academic podium but rarely in the hearts of ordinary men. Dogmatism prevailed in the lecture hall, while skepticism held sway in the streets. Formal thought and inquiry were out of touch with practical life and the conditions of a changing world.

Historical developments had brought this conflict into the lives of all thoughtful persons. In an essay of 1887 Dilthey sketched broadly the characteristics of the modern era:

With the French Revolution a new age began. A science which transforms life; an industry which is worldwide in scope; machines; work as the sole basis of the social order; war against the parasites of society, for whose leisure others have paid the cost; a new and proud feeling for the human mastery which has subjugated nature and promises to diminish the blind workings of passion in society: these are the basic traits of a world era whose dark and awesome outlines arise before us [*GS* 6:239].

But while the modern period showed the "rational control of all exigencies," it was torn by a deeper spiritual quandary. In contrast to the ample evidence of the power of reason and science to control nature and provide for the practical necessities of life, there were many signs of a general sense of the helplessness of the mind in regard to larger questions of meaning and purpose. The preeminent conception of *Wissenschaft* as specialized systematic knowledge seemed to be in head-on conflict with the human need for *Weltanschauung*, for a broader, integrative view of the world and life:

If the present age asks wherein lies the ultimate goal of action for the individual and the human race, then the deep contradiction running through our age becomes apparent. The present is no wiser concerning the great mystery of the origin of things, of the value of existence, or of the final value of our action than was a Greek of the Ionian or Italian colonies or an Arab at the time of Ibn Rushd [Averroës]. At this moment, surrounded by the rapid progress of the sciences, we find ourselves more helpless in these questions than in any previous time [*GS* 8:193].

In one of his last writings he isolated the deepest problem of modern thought and culture: "To understand life as it is lived by man—that is the aim of man today" (*GS* 8:78).

The result of this dilemma was a profound "pain of emptiness" to which many persons responded with either obscurantism and nostalgic invocations of an idealized past or apocalyptic prophecies of the future, predicated on a revolutionary break with the past. Although Dilthey was keenly aware of the urgency of the situation, he was skeptical of the facile solutions being offered on all sides. He especially wanted to avoid mere palliatives, which would in the end simply compound the deeper problem. In a review article of 1878 he noted that a "veritable abyss" had opened between the realms of theory and practice. This divorce between thought and life he deemed extremely dangerous. He attested that virtually everyone could recognize this crisis of thought and life but he went on to caution that "diagnosis is always easier than the cure" (*WM* 14[1878]:671).

The fundamental intellectual crisis which Dilthey was intent upon resolving was glaringly epitomized in the direct clash of various systems of thought stemming from the two traditions of idealism and positivism. For the sake of historical exposition, it can be said that idealism tended to dominate German intellectual life in the first half of the century, whereas positivism defined the intellectual development of the latter half. The revolutionary years in mid-century were an intellectual as well as political watershed. The conflict between these two positions had become acute by the 1870s and remained so after Dilthey's death in 1911. It had been building steadily since the period of his youth and had antecedents far back in the history of thought. The nineteenth century witnessed the continuing battle *in extremis* between the two tendencies of "spiritualization" and "naturalization."[3]

The idealists asserted that the human mind and its creations represent something wholly originative and unique in the universe—a supernatural, almost divine power transcendent to natural reality and experience. Mind, or "spirit" (*Geist*), for them constituted the universal condition of reality as apprehended in consciousness. The total, active power of mind defied any treatment analogous to that employed on natural or empirical reality. For the idealists, in Dilthey's words,

> the human spirit is a unitary formative power [*gestaltende Macht*], working from its own depths over the material of the real, a power which constructs the real in thought, ensouls it in the aesthetic capacity, and impresses it in action with the form of the ideal and freedom [*VDM* 332; see also *GS* 13/2:40].

The positivists, on the contrary, were convinced that certain and fruitful knowledge could come only from the extension of the model and methods of the natural sciences across the entire range of human behavior and expression. Dilthey defined positivism as "the preference for a method which interprets mental and historical reality from the standpoint of the study of the natural-external world" (*GS* 15:331). Positivism treated the mind and human consciousness not as the originary, formative power of the idealists but as a mere adjunct or epiphenomenon of nature. Though positivism cannot be identified with crude naturalism, its major premises tended to shade into the naturalist position.

The remedy Dilthey wished to provide consisted in mediating the barren opposition between a "soulless" naturalism and a "substanceless" spiritualism by means of a proper understanding of the human mind and its creations. He was convinced that the human sciences (*Geistewissenschaften*) offered a fruitful solution to the sterile dilemma which had impeded the growth of human understanding and threatened to undermine European culture. This body of sciences included history, psychology, theology, economics, jurisprudence, political science, philology, literary criticism, and other humanistically oriented disciplines. They furnished empirical and "positive" knowledge of man, but not of the same sort as the natural sciences. The human sciences necessitated special concepts, methods, and categories distinct from those employed by the natural sciences. The special character of the human sciences was the source of their unique meaning and practical potential for mankind, but this special character presented particular problems of theoretical definition and justification.

Dilthey was convinced that the human sciences could fulfill their potential only if they were placed on a secure theoretical foundation rooted in experience, avoiding both the Scylla of metaphysical speculation and the Charybdis of naturalistic positivism. The service which Kant had performed for the physical sciences in his *Critique of Pure Reason* remained to be undertaken for this other part of the *globus intellectualis*, of which Kant's theory had taken little or no account. With a general critical intent and terminology which in some ways reflected Kant, but with a subject matter vastly different from his, Dilthey designated his project as a "Critique of Historical Reason."[4] In his view, only such a critical founding of the human sciences could provide man with the certainty of valid knowledge and the confidence to face the unprecedented tasks of the future. A new form of reason and self-understanding were to provide the means of overcoming the crisis of the age and the "growing separation between life and scientific knowledge" (*GS* 5:145).

The broad outlines of Dilthey's life and career suggest the dimensions of his personal involvement in the crisis around him. In outward events his life was relatively calm, unmarked by any hint of cataclysm. Inwardly, however, his life reflected deep ferment and restlessness. Dilthey was born on November 19, 1833, in the small town of Biebrich am Rhein, near the city of Wiesbaden. His birth coincided closely with the "great caesura"—the passing of the last great luminaries of the classical period of German idealism, including Goethe, Hegel, Schleiermacher, and Wilhelm von Humboldt—and the inception of what came to be called the Silver Age or Alexandrian Age of German thought. For many Germans these designations marked off a shallow and jejune period from the incomparable luster and glory of the previous half-century. The intellectual legacy of this earlier period was of paramount importance for Dilthey's own project. Born at the end of what was widely perceived as the acme of German thought and culture, Dilthey was in no sense content to be an epigone of that earlier period. His temperament and training convinced him that the new age into which he had been born required new modes of thought and understanding.

With strong familial roots in the tradition of German pietism, Dilthey was initially bound for theological study and a career as pastor in the Reformed faith. His father and grandfather had both been Calvinist ministers with pronounced heterodox leanings. His father, Maximilian (1804–67), was court chaplain and councilor to the duke of Nassau and was more interested in politics and history than formal theology, which he regarded as the husk around the true core of religious feeling. His mother, Maria (1806–87), was the daughter of a renowned musical director and instilled in her son a love of music and a competence in performing it that were to last a lifetime and would even inform aspects of his philosophizing. Drawn to the expressive powers of music, the young Dilthey regarded listening to music as "a religious act" (JD 9).

The pantheistic and inward element in Dilthey's early religious training was very strong and was reinforced by his subsequent studies. Later in life he expressed a certain gleeful satisfaction at having a heretic and an Anabaptist in the family lineage (JD 306). These early pietistic and pantheist roots had a deep and subtle impact upon his mature thought, persisting beyond the point when he no longer considered himself a religious person in the conventional sense. Though on different grounds, pietism, like philosophical empiricism, militated against rationalist metaphysics and theology by stressing the necessity of direct inner experience of God and reality rather than deduction and abstract, logical proof. In a secularized form, *Erlebnis*, or lived experience, became the cornerstone for the entire edifice of Dilthey's mature thought.

Dilthey showed himself to be a dutiful if restive and intellectually ambitious student. He digested Kant while still a pupil at the Wiesbaden Gymnasium, from which he graduated at the head of his class in 1852. Despite a great love for poetry and music and a distaste for the minutely systematic, he showed a notable talent for following ancient, medieval, and modern thinkers through the most labyrinthine arguments. Throughout his life he was in the habit of pursuing his scholarly labors to the point of exhaustion, sometimes to the detriment of his health. To the end of his life he was in the habit of working 14 hours a day, still holding to his youthful desire "to multiply every hour by ten in order to grasp everything" (JD 27).

Although he had expressed a preference for law upon leaving the Gymnasium, Dilthey enrolled as a theological student at Heidelberg (1852–53) and then Berlin (1854–67), where he immersed himself in the methods of the humanistic disciplines, moving far beyond the confines of formal theology. Under the watchful eyes of August Boeckh, Franz Bopp, and Jakob Grimm, he studied philology, textual exegesis, and the newer theological criticism. He absorbed the painstaking techniques of the new, historically based philology, yet he remained dissatisfied with the remoteness and pedantry of the "philological spirit." In these early years of study he announced a kind of new instauration of humanistic learning: "I venture to assert the constitution of an effective religious-philosophical world-view which lies buried in the ruins of our theology and philosophy" (JD 140). With such pressing concerns in mind, Dilthey was repelled by both the sterility of much classroom learning and the swaggering "stupid routine" of university *Korpsleben* (JD 22, 46, 77). He took the state examination in theology and philosophy in 1856 (and gave a trial sermon at Biebrich) but was soon drawn in other directions. He suspended formal theological study for two years of teaching in Berlin gymnasia, in addition to free-lance writing and editing. His fluctuating religious convictions were gradually being translated into a new theory of knowledge:

> Christianity directs us back to ourselves and that which constitutes the presuppositions of our inner life. This is not meant as a defense of humanism in the strict sense: such a humanism forgets that there is nothing we know more certainly about man than we know about God. . . . There is, however, truth in one of the dogmas of humanism, namely that man is the one true beginning of knowledge, whether it is of the self or of the concepts in which we think. The certainty of our knowledge rests in us ourselves, and as we move away from ourselves, our knowledge becomes gradually less certain [*GS* 18:208].

An inspiring influence in these years came from Dilthey's intensive study of the thought of Schleiermacher, for whom he developed a life-long affinity. With all his empathic powers and exegetical training, Dilthey plunged into the task of mastering Schleiermacher's doctrine and of uncovering the wellsprings of that doctrine in his life and context. In 1860 Dilthey produced a brilliant historical-critical treatment of Schleiermacher's interpretive theory (or hermeneutic), which traced its genesis back through the idealist movement and Enlightenment to the exegetical conflicts of the post-Reformation period. This work manifested Dilthey's consuming interest in the theoretical problem of interpretive understanding and the historical-genetic approach to ideas. It demonstrated his belief that ideas are best understood by an examination of the process of contextual origin, transmission, and transformation. Dilthey's study was awarded the double prize of the Schleiermacher Gesellschaft. In this same period he coedited a volume of Schleiermacher's letters and unpublished manuscripts.

Dilthey graduated in philosophy at Berlin in 1864 with a dissertation on Schleiermacher's ethical principles; he habilitated with a related but more theoretical effort, "Versuch einer Analyse des moralischen Bewusstseins." Both of these early works reflect the primacy of ethical concerns in all of Dilthey's reflections; in them he attempted to secure a realistic basis for ethical action in the "knowable nature of man" and the results of the human sciences. His approach aimed toward a down-to-earth account of human nature without surrendering to sheer egoism or hedonism. In a logical treatise written in the following year, Dilthey continued to stress the link between the human sciences and the deepest premises of thought and conduct. With a youthful confidence which seemed to rival the boldest positivists, he expressed the conviction that the critical foundation of the human sciences would lead to a "conclusive and valid world-view" (*Grundriss* 3).

After his habilitation, Dilthey began to work on a comprehensive intellectual biography of Schleiermacher, the first volume of which was published in installments between 1867 and 1870. This sympathetic and critical account of Schleiermacher was set within the broader idealist movement of which he was a part. Although primarily historical and expository in format and content, the work adumbrated many of the theoretical problems pertaining to the human sciences which were to occupy Dilthey for the remainder of his life. In probing these questions Dilthey returned again and again to Schleiermacher for inspiration.

After considerable inner turmoil (and parental opposition) Dilthey began to move away from theology to philosophy and history, thus following a spiritual course which was characteristic of many German intellectuals in the nineteenth century. Already in this personal shift could be detected signs of the larger historical processes of "mundanization" (*Verweltlichung*) and secularization (*Entchristlichung*) which Dilthey found decisive in constituting the modern ethos of "worldliness" (*Diesseitigkeit*). In his diary Dilthey recorded a thought which was to become the cardinal principle of his own hermeneutics:

> Every effort of comprehension goes out from the world of the here and now; man, who constantly lives in this world and is moved to inquiry by it, does not live in the transcendent [*JD* 152].[5]

In his own development Dilthey moved from faith through doubt to the ultimate position that religion was simply a historical or "anthropological form of life," an enduring manifestation of existence which is of the same order as other forms, such as art and philosophy.

In 1870 Dilthey confessed, "I am not a religious nature," and characterized his attitude as "simple historical objectivity" (*JD* 279). He was later to avow to Yorck that he did not consider himself a Christian "in the specific sense" (*BDY* 126), and his last major study before his death was tellingly entitled "The Problem of Religion" (*GS* 6:288–305). This tension between historical consciousness and transcendent commitments was not merely a personal matter, for Dilthey regarded his own loss of faith as symptomatic of a larger cultural process: by the end of the century he offered the historical judgment that religion had all but disappeared as an active force in European culture (*GS* 10:17; see also 14/2:589). Although he affirmed the general shift toward "worldliness," with its attendant emphasis upon scientific knowledge and control of man's social and natural environment, he was deeply distressed by the preoccupation of his age with politics and natural science to the exclusion of spiritual concerns. In an age increasingly dominated by natural-scientific conceptions, the very concept of the human spirit required a new definition. At this juncture it was scientific reason rather than faith which stood in need of a kind of new Reformation.

Dilthey's academic training exposed him to critical indictments of the older forms of idealist *Geistesphilosophie* and provided the rudiments of a new orientation. At Heidelberg he heard Kuno Fischer subject the officially sanctioned synthesis of Hegelianism and Christian orthodoxy to corrosive attacks. Fischer's position provoked a furor and eventually brought his dismissal on charges of "pantheism," but not before he had exerted a lasting impression on several generations of students, including Dilthey, Wilhelm Windelband, and Max Weber. At Berlin Dilthey studied with F. A. Trendelenburg, the arch-critic of Hegel's speculative idealism and proponent of an evolutionary critical realism on Aristotelian lines. Coupled with his predilection for Schleiermacher, these influences instilled in Dilthey a novel type of immanent idealism, or *Idealrealismus*, which constituted a significant departure from the previous transcendental-idealist tradition.

A cardinal principle of the ideal-realist position was that the whole realm of thought and "mind," and specifically philosophy itself, had been viewed too formally and abstractly, that is, apart from its relation to the practical and experiential (or "lived") concerns of human existence. Caught up in its own theoretical postulates and intellectual constructions, philosophy chose closed, systematic architectonics over experience and the actualities of life. Dilthey's condemnation of such system-mongering was uncompromising: "We despise construction and love concrete investigation, remaining skeptical toward the machinery of a system. These forms of systematics and dialectics appear to us like a powerful machine operating in the void. At the end of a long life we are content to have but multiple paths of scientific investigation leading into the depths of things. We are content to die underway" (*JD* 87). In fulfillment of this program, Dilthey advocated a new kind of empirical investigation and philosophical reflection—a critical "philosophy of philosophy" which would disclose the deeper assumptions of thought and its relations with actual life and experience.

As a student Dilthey expressed the desire to grasp the ideal *in* life and actual experience. He mocked the sighing "Hyperion-types" whose idealism filled them with visions of a pristine realm beyond the pressing exigencies of mundane experience. The pathos of idealist "otherworldliness" repelled him as a form of escapism or mysticism. He characterized the dominant impulse of his time as "an insatiable desire for reality," and he constantly referred to the sober sense of reality (*Wirklichkeitssinn*) of the nineteenth century (*GS* 1:123; 4:305, 531, 562; 8:192). A lapidary formulation of his *Idealrealismus* appeared in one of his later ethical studies: "We must posit an ideality which is immanent in the world and science—or else none at all" (*GS* 10:54). He acknowledged only a "realizing" or practical idealism as the basis for actual comprehension and effective intervention in the real world. Along with others of his generation, such as Trendelenburg, Rudolf Haym, Friedrich Überweg, Eduard Zeller, and Franz Brentano, Dilthey preferred to define his own position as a brand of critical "realism" or "empiricism" (*Empirie*) in contrast to the reigning forms of transcendental idealism. But this was a realism in a special sense, one marked off equally from a reductive, nominalistic realism as well as from far-flung speculation. In insisting that thought take its content from experience and actual knowledge—including history and the human sciences as well as the natural sciences—Dilthey's thought belongs in the distinctive philosophical tradition of *Idealrealismus* which forms a mediating keynote in the complex intellectual counterpoint of the nineteenth century.

From the perspective of later years, Dilthey avowed that the dominant impulse of his philosophical thought had been, "in the spirit of the great Enlightenment, to hold faithfully to experiential reality as the One World of our knowledge" (*GS* 5:418). He often characterized himself as a hard-bitten empiricist, opposed to all soft-headed and sentimental speculation. Empiricism recommended itself because "one can get something underway with it" (*GS* 5:77; see also 13/2:78–79). The inner task of all theory of science he declared to be "the attainment of objectivism through the full employment of the empirical point of view" (*GS* 5:433). But the experience which Dilthey proposed to put at the basis of the sciences and philosophy was not the pale and dessicated "sensation" of conventional empiricism but rather the full content of mental life in all its manifestations. In one of the most crucial passages in all his writing Dilthey stated: "The basic conception of my philosophy is that up until now no one has put *whole, full, and unmutilated experience* at the basis of philosophizing, that is to say, the whole and full reality" (*GS* 8:171). In a phrase which defies translation he described his own position as "Empirie, nicht Empirismus," a genuine philosophy of experience rather than a narrow empiricism (*GS* 5:3). In a major unpublished draft he insisted that existing empiricism was not a "true philosophy of experience" but a "presumptive conceptual construction" which was no less abstract than transcendental idealism (*BA* 134; cf. *GS* 1:123). While holding to the basic impulse of the empirical position, Dilthey at the same time rejected its more dogmatic formulations. His *Idealrealismus* conceived experience as something quite different from the versions propounded by either conventional empiricism or idealism. He was convinced that a genuine "science of mind," based on the full fund of man's experience, would overcome the age-old opposition between theoretical reflection and practical life (*GS* 5:133). This full fund of experience had to be defined in such a way as to include man's history.

In an unpublished note from 1866, written during his shift from theology to history and philosophy, he asserted that "what is new in my method is the connection of the empirical study of man with his history" (*BNL* 47/260). With this pronouncement Dilthey was both mirroring and criticizing the preoccupations of his age. In the period after mid-century, as a feature of the process Dilthey called *Verweltlichung*, much of the prestige which previously had attached to theology and philosophy had passed to history and the emerging natural sciences. The nineteenth century was widely regarded as "the age of history," in contrast to the eighteenth century, which was seen as the age of philosophy. Dilthey came to define himself within this contrast; by taking a middle position between what were regarded as polar opposites, he sought what was valid and fruitful from both the "historical" and the "philosophical" consciousness. He often expressed his intention to undertake history "with philosophical intent" and to philosophize "with concrete historical content" (*GS* 5:35). History and philosophy were to be mutually corrective.

At Berlin Dilthey absorbed the methods of the German Historical School under the tutelage of Karl Ritter, Theodor Mommsen, and Leopold von Ranke. He participated in Ranke's famous historical seminar and came to regard him as "the very embodiment of the historical sense" (*GS* 5:9; also *JD* 30). The Historical School had emancipated history from the trammels of theology and moral philosophy, yet saved it from lapsing into a variety of *belles lettres*. In Dilthey's opinion this school had opened the way not merely to the factual richness of the past but to a whole new manner of looking at the world, the "historical consciousness." This new consciousness had promoted the profound discovery of man as "an essentially historical being" but, as a mode of thought, had not yet found its critical justification or precise sense of method (*JD* 124; *GS* 13/2:37).

But in crucial respects philosophy and history were no more satisfying for Dilthey than theology had been. On different accounts they lacked precision, depth, and comprehensive vision. Academic philosophy was still too much under the spell of abstract speculation, closed systems, and "dream idealism" (*Traumidealismus*), all of which accorded little with the conditions of modern life and the results of modern science. Philosophy was a "powerful machine operating in the void" which needed concrete empirical material. Dilthey looked forward to the reformation of philosophy through the human sciences: "Philosophy has wandered around long enough in the labyrinths of its own meditations. But now the scope of research has widened immeasurably; history, ethnology, and anthropology all offer an immense amount of material for true induction" (*GS* 11:212). The reformation of philosophy also depended upon a correlative reformulation of the human sciences, particularly the practice of history. If philosophy was too abstract and theoretical, history was too detailed and antitheoretical. Dominated by exacting philological methods, academic historiography was so taken up with minuscule detail that it failed to reflect critically upon its own foundations, and likewise failed to give insight into the general conditions of human life. While philosophy wandered among abstract ideas, history loitered in isolated facts.

As a student, Dilthey observed that "all questions concerning the method of historical knowledge have the greatest fascination for me" (*JD* 70); but, surveying the actual practice of history, he found more to censure than approve. He found much of it "formless," antiquarian, and insular— without vital links to either the general concerns of men or to the newer human sciences. In sum, history lacked a genuinely critical foundation. In an essay of 1875 devoted to the human sciences, Dilthey stated that "history most urgently needs a sharpening of its logical conscience" (*GS* 5:48). Without such a critical sharpening, history too often degenerated into an aesthetic portrayal of surface detail, to the neglect of broader synthesis, comparison, and the discernment of deeper causal relations. Dilthey was repelled by the pedantry of much current historical study: "I am perhaps too abstract, too little of a memorizer to do this kind of study . . . ; the grasping of characters and systems, of larger coherences and analogies in history is closer to my concerns" (*JD* 30; also 82). The task of history he described as seeing the general forms, structures, and laws in the manifold facts. Reacting strongly against speculative, aesthetic, and antiquarian approaches to history, the young Dilthey often sounded quite positivistic in calling for the determination of causal laws in history and the human sciences: "It will always remain my dream that history is now in the same undeveloped state as the natural sciences were when they were still merely a description of nature. Just as laws of movement rule all of physical nature, so mental life is ruled by laws of movement, though most certainly ones which are essentially different [from physical laws]" (*GS* 18:206). Although he came to revise this "dream" significantly as he worked through his critique of historical reason, Dilthey never wavered from demanding an approach to history which would bring it closer to life and a deeper comprehension of the world. Contrary to the prevailing antiquarian, fact-gathering spirit in historical studies, Dilthey saw a more vital and practical mission for history: "It would not be worth the while to study the past if it were not a means of grasping the world" (*JD* 81).

For Dilthey, history, like philosophy, had to serve the cause of practical reform and regeneration, not merely contemplation. In a preface intended for the Schleiermacher biography, Dilthey provided a pointed rejoinder to Ranke's ideal of self-effacing neutrality and plain narration of "how it actually was":

> I do not merely want to tell a story, but to convince. I want the reader of this book to have before him, when he closes it, the portrait of a great life, but also a coherence of lasting ideas, rigorously founded and pene-trating deeply into the scientific work and active life of the present [*GS* 13:xxxvi].

Elsewhere he asserted that

The mode of grasping things pursued by the Historical School, which only wanted to describe things and excluded intellectual guidance through scientific principles, is over for us. And happily so! For life imperatively demands guidance by thought [*GS* 6:189].

Dilthey's training and reflection led him to the conviction that neither philosophy nor history, as generally practiced, offered the resources or methods for genuine comprehension of the world, that is, the kind of knowledge which leads to action in the present and the formation of personal or social life-values. This negative judgment of prevalent philosophy and history was determinant in his positive conception of a critique of historical reason. There was a deep practical component in Dilthey's theory of the human sciences which was clearly reflected in his life. He was very much absorbed in the political and moral issues of his time and he belonged to a particular group of reforming, liberal intellectuals who wanted to give learning an effectual role in the practical life of Germany. His conviction that "man is not on earth simply to be but to *act*" disposed him toward a practical activism at odds with the contemplative spirit which dominated the fields of history and philosophy. Along with the other ideal-realists, Dilthey avowed that the problem of the will is "the greatest and most difficult problem confronting modern man" and affirmed that "only insofar as philosophical thought has an effect does it have a right to exist" (*JD* 6; *GS* 10:13; *BDY* 247).[6] It is noteworthy that he sometimes referred to the body of the sciences he was attempting to ground theoretically as the "sciences of acting man and the practical world" (*GS* 18:225). In speaking of Dilthey's conception of theory and theoretical foundation, one must bear in mind that for him and the other ideal-realists "every theory is a theory for *praxis*."[7]

Dilthey was intent upon having a practical impact beyond the cloistered realm of the university. He does not belong to the contemplative, tradition-ridden strand of German "mandarin-professors," which has been perceptively analyzed in a recent work.[8] His youthful motto was *Sic volo et jubeo*, and he later referred to himself as "old Praktikus" (*JD* 146; *GS* 5:lxviii). His activist temperament drew him to Lessing, Schlosser, and Schleiermacher, who had never allowed the Germanic ideal of self-culture to be pursued in contemplative isolation but had rather carried the cause of education out to the people through a crusading journalism. Like his mentors, Dilthey's commitment expressed itself in prolific journalistic activity. From the late 1850s into the last decade of his life, Dilthey contributed hundreds of articles, reviews, and notices to popular periodicals. A new genre of mass cultural journals had arisen in Germany, catering to the growing *Bildungsbürgertum*. The avowed purpose of these publications was to bring the spirit of learning and science into the daily lives of their readers.

Dilthey contributed primarily to *Westermanns Monatshefte*, the *Deutsche Rundschau*, the *Preussische Jahrbücher*, the *Berliner Nationalzeitung*, and the *Schlesische Zeitung*. The editor of *Westermanns Monatshefte*, Albert Glaser, who had been Dilthey's classmate at Wiesbaden and Berlin, announced as its goal "to make learning vital and thus to bring it into the lives of the many."[9] Rudolf Haym, the crusading liberal editor of the *Preussische Jahrbücher* and an intellectual ally of Dilthey, defined the purpose of his journal as "serving life by serving living knowledge."[10] Dilthey welcomed these new journals for "serving the needs for the historical and political sciences to take fresh and bold initiatives in the questions of the present and to turn beyond the narrow circle of university learning to the great body of persons who have become politically significant." (*GS* 16:66).

A survey of Dilthey's contributions conveys the immense scope of his interests and reading. He reviewed subjects ranging from the latest developments in optics to the Japanese novella. In addition to the established "greats" in thought and literature, he reviewed an astonishing array of contemporary thinkers, including Comte, Darwin, Marx, Engels, Feuerbach, Strauss, Mill, Lewes, Haym, Lotze, Renan, Spencer, Schopenhauer, von Hartmann, Lange, Riehl, Laas, Sigwart, Windelband, Ritschl, Ravaisson, Taine, Cohen, Eucken, Fischer, Fechner, Wundt, Steinthal, Lazarus, and many others. In the area of history he reviewed works by Burckhardt, Ranke, Droysen, Guizot, Buckle, Macaulay, Grote, Lecky, Mommsen, Giesebrecht, Sybel, Schlosser, and Gregorovius. In the natural sciences he surveyed studies by von Baer, Helmholtz, Liebig, and Schleiden. In the newer fields of anthropology, economics, and sociology he read Bastian, von Mohl, Roscher, Knies, Schäffle, Lilienfeld, Gumplowicz, and a host of lesser figures. His efforts in other areas are so numerous that it must suffice to say simply that Dilthey was anything but a cloistered academic tied down to a narrow specialty. In fact his reviews show clearly that he delved deeply into authors and areas of inquiry (including the natural sciences and newer forms of social science) of which it is often assumed that he was ignorant.[11]

Many of these reviews expressed his conviction that social and cultural conditions were changing faster than accepted forms of academic inquiry and philosophical reflection, thereby highlighting the breach between life and knowledge which he hoped to mediate in his critique of historical reason. The keynote struck by the reviews was the demand for "vitalized learning." In one particularly revealing piece Dilthey enunciated his program of a constructive, immanent critique: "It is not fitting for a thinker to indulge in impotent, cavilling complaints about the spirit of the times; his task is to conduct this spirit to earnest self-reflection—to educate and lead it with the insights of a deeper-seeing science" (*WM* 44[1878]:335).

The general ethos of "engaged" learning was alien and disturbing to many of Dilthey's colleagues. Although many of his earlier articles followed the convention of anonymous or pseudonymous authorship, it was more or less common knowledge among his associates that Dilthey was responsible for them.[12] In 1863 he was slated to become coeditor of the *Preussische Jahrbücher* but was forced to decline the position because of a worsening eye condition. In spite of the fact that these journalistic activities were viewed with consternation by his more detached colleagues, Dilthey pressed on at a furious and exhausting pace. He was impelled by the belief that in the context of the times the theoretical problem of the human sciences assumed immense practical importance.

In his desire to be efficacious, Dilthey was at pains to be politically active without being doctrinaire. Here too he sought a *via media* which complements his philosophical position. In many of his writings he professed a distaste for all apriorist systems and dogmatic ideologies, avowing of his generation: "we comport ourselves skeptically toward all transcendental propositions—and without these a political dogma can be neither constructed nor criticized" (*GS* 16:140). Yet he insisted that society in general and a political party in particular must have "an ideal core." The program of "reform without dogmatism" placed Dilthey in a circle of liberal intellectuals which included Rudolf Haym, Hermann Baumgarten, Ludwig Häusser, Julian Schmidt, Rudolf von Bennigsen, Rudolf Virchow, Theodor Mommsen, Franz and Max Duncker, and Max Weber, the father of the famous social scientist. In a letter to Baumgarten, Dilthey gave clear expression to his political affinities: "Both of us stand together on the extreme 'left' of the Constitutional Party."[13] This left wing of the Liberals remained close to the cosmopolitan *Vormärz* "Old Liberalism" of Dahlmann, Gervinus, and Schlosser. It was less willing than the supposedly hardheaded and "realistic" "New Liberalism" to forfeit individual liberties and political rights in return for German unity under Prussia. This refusal to exchange *Freiheit* for *Einheit* and *Geist* for *Macht* dictated a certain skeptical reserve toward Prussia, which was being heralded by the right wing, including Sybel and Treitschke, as the deliverer of all Germany. Although Dilthey looked to Prussia for leadership in German unification, he deplored the scare tactics of the Prussian government and its insidious policy of splitting the Liberals by presenting the false alternative of either radical democracy on the one hand or the anachronistic military-feudal state on the other.

Like many German (and European) liberals, Dilthey suspected that full-fledged democracy would evolve into a tyranny of the majority, subverting in the end the very freedom it purported to secure. On the potential of democracy he showed a curious ambivalence, insisting that "the feelings of every genuine and upright person are naturally democratic, but sober reason teaches us to endure a stringent monarchy" (*JD* 219–20). But throughout his life he held faithfully to the liberal ideal of the *Rechtsstaat* and affirmed that the basis for all political activity was "simple and undisguised abiding by the constitution" (*GS* 12:129). In his later studies of the Prussian *Landrecht*, he reminded his countrymen that it was based on natural law. His training with Trendelenburg had instilled a deep respect for natural-law tradition, which countered the "pure historicism" of the Historical School of Savigny (*GS* 10:103, 152 ff.).[14]

On questions of polity and society Dilthey aligned himself with the tradition of reforming moral individualism represented by Kant, Schlosser, Wilhelm von Humboldt, and Schleiermacher. This tradition rejected both the egoistic hedonism of utilitarian thought and the étatist, theocratic organicism of the Hegelians, which made the individual wholly subservient to the higher purposes of the state. There is little celebration of the state, or *Staatsfrömmigkeit*, in Dilthey's historical or theoretical writing. He regarded the tenets of the critical idealists as the authentic foundation of political liberty in Germany. Its most powerful adversary was, in his opinion, "Hegel's absolutizing and archaicizing concept of the state as an end in itself"—a view which apotheosized the state and lent itself to tyranny (*GS* 11:131).

Dilthey was neither an ideologue nor a revolutionary. He represented a political tradition of bourgeois liberalism which has been aptly called a kind of "liberal conservatism.[15] Such a hybrid combination offers a political parallel to his philosophical position of "ideal-realism." He rejected "radical theory" in politics, education, and social policy. His philosophical method of "immanent critique" was allied with a spirit of political gradualism. Like many Germans of his generation who lived through the failure of the 1848 revolutions, Dilthey deplored revolution on the somewhat surprising grounds that it was foredoomed to superficiality and usually issued in a worse despotism than the one it had set out to destroy. Revolution was seen as incapable of reforming the inner man. As in many other matters, Kant's views proved influential here. Though an admirer of the French Revolution long after his countrymen had turned against it, Kant had provided an "idealistic" argument against revolution which retained its cogency for many educated Germans through the nineteenth century: "Perhaps a fall of personal despotism or of avaricious and tyrannical oppression may be accomplished by revolution, but never a true reform in ways of thinking."[16] It was precisely such a reform in ways of thinking that Dilthey was intent upon, and he saw the pathway through an expanded conception of *Wissenschaft* and critical reflection, not revolution. In a review of a work on the French Revolution, Dilthey echoed the view of Kant, Goethe, and Wilhelm von Humboldt, which had been confirmed by the "liberal conservatives" de Tocqueville and Taine, and which had become an article of faith for most German intellectuals:

Revolutions do not change men. Stein and Gneist have conceived the important postulate that when a revolution topples the government, the control of society reverts to the same social organizations which previously possessed it; revolutions cannot create a new society. Thus it is with men. The individuals of the previous period behave in revolutions with their same characteristics. No matter how frequently the slogans of "Virtue," or "Brotherhood," etc., are invoked in such a time, the constellation of powers in the society does not change [*WM* 50[1876]:209].

The twin pitfalls of momentary excess and long-range inertia disqualified revolution as an effective means of social change. Dilthey avowed that his generation had lived to see the dissolution of the "republican legend" and that it now aspired to more lasting, evolutionary reform.[17] Such reform could issue only from the intensive and exact study of man in all his aspects. The human sciences would become instruments of rational and peaceful change in contrast to the convulsions of revolution. Dilthey even suggested that they could provide an antidote to revolution and its side effects:

In truth the on-going analysis of revolutionary movements will and must provide statesmen with the knowledge of the motivation and incitements through which revolutionary movements and terrorism arise and are maintained: then fear of them will diminish and the means of preventing them can be more clearly ascertained. Science must to a much greater degree than heretofore master those sudden concussions in society which now and again break out like epidemics with destructive force [*WM* 50 [1876]:215].

In his inaugural address at Basel in 1867, Dilthey affirmed that the task of his age was not the construction of remote ideals but the control of social processes and the immediate world of man. By 1883 he had become convinced that gaining a correct diagnosis of social problems and instability was "a vital question for our civilization" which could only be solved by a spirit of reform operating with the results of the human sciences (*GS* 1:4).

Dilthey's program for rational but fundamental reform was to be based on a comprehensive knowledge of man in all his aspects and manifestations. This program was to employ philosophy and history—but without embracing their ingrained defects. In pursuing these matters Dilthey gravitated for a time toward the newer disciplines which treated human thought and activity in an exact, empirical manner. After his partial disillusionment with philosophy and history, he immersed himself in the "positive" sciences of man: anthropology, psychology, physiology, and incipient forms of what later came to be known as sociology. He plunged into the physiological psychology of Johannes Müller, Wilhelm His, Adolph Horwicz and Hermann von Helmholtz. His excitement over these new researches was so intense that it deprived him of sleep. He drew upon sources of knowledge which were new and alien to the established tradition of German thought. He looked eagerly to British empiricism and French positivism for insights into the nature of man's knowledge of himself and the world. Here too Dilthey found disappointments as well as stimulation. Above all he wished to remain practical and empirical without divesting man of the traits of freedom, active striving, and individual worth which had been central to the idealist conception of man. A new synthesis of idealism and realism, of philosophical vision and empirical fact, was called for, one which avoided the two extremes of "barren skepticism" and "theological mysticism" (GS 5:142). To accomplish this ambitious synthesis in a deliberate manner, Dilthey set about articulating his own theories of knowledge, experience, and human action. He drew upon new developments in widely different fields, adapting and incorporating them into his own distinctive formulations. His quest for "living knowledge" and "reflective life" continued along the diverse paths of contemporary learning.

Dilthey's career took him to several different corners of the German-speaking world. After 1866, as Extraordinarius in philosophy at Basel, he was a colleague of the Swiss cultural historian Jacob Burckhardt. The renowned Burckhardt left a record of his vivid impressions of his younger associate:

> A sparking energy issues from him, as any conversation with him reveals immediately. He speaks not just intelligently—one feels that his thoughts about the world, history, literature, and art radiate from a luminous center. He gives the impression of a capacity which will accomplish everything he undertakes.[18]

At Basel Dilthey did not meet Nietzsche, whom he later came to regard as both philosophical ally and adversary, but during a summer excursion back to Berlin he did meet another man who was destined to become a more thoroughly compatible thinker—William James. They met at the home of Herman Grimm in 1867. Curiously, James reacted against Dilthey's rather unorthodox dress and table manners (Dilthey fell asleep at the table briefly, only to revive and launch into a new subject), but he found him to be a prodigious mind,

> . . . overflowing with information with regard to everything knowable and unknowable. He is the first man I have ever met of a class, which must be common here, of men to whom learning has become as natural as breathing.[19]

Dilthey and James parted after this unusual dinner with James desiring to become better acquainted with Dilthey, who had to return to Basel. Although they did not meet again personally, Dilthey later read James' work and was vastly impressed by it; indeed, he came to believe that he and

James were working on parallel paths in the theory of mind and the empirical study of man.

In his two years at Basel Dilthey immersed himself in the various specialized human sciences, including anthropology, economics, statistics, and all forms of psychology (social-, child-, medical-, and even criminal psychology). In addition to studying these new fields, he also found time to write major interpretive essays on Goethe, Novalis, and Lessing. This combination of attention to the most recent advances in science with an appreciation for the creative achievements of the past became characteristic of Dilthey's mode of thought; in his inaugural lecture at Basel in 1867 he called for unstinting efforts toward the attainment of valid empirical sciences of man but at the same time a deeper understanding of the "poetic and philosophical movement" of 1770–1800, which, if surpassed on several fronts, had nonetheless provided important insights into the nature of man and his mind. In his Basel period Dilthey seems to have achieved the basis for the theoretical consolidation he was working toward: "Almost without my will and deliberate exertion there is forming gradually in my head the components of a world-view" (*JD* 262). His attitude toward this new-found synthesis contained a characteristically self-critical note: "Against my will (for I do not ascribe much value to systems) there is arising something which appears like a system" (*JD* 274).

Despite the favorable judgment of his colleagues and unusually large classes, Dilthey was restive in the staid, patrician atmosphere of Basel. In 1868 he moved north to Kiel, where he finished the first volume of the *Leben Schleiermachers* (dedicated to Trendelenburg) and continued to lecture in philosophy, epistemology, logic, and psychology. The historical and systematic dimensions of his work continued to cross-fertilize each other. In an influential review of the Schleiermacher book Rudolf Haym hailed it not simply as a biography but as an "entirely new method" and "declaration of war" against the predominating "constructivist" histories of thought, which, in following Hegel, gave short shrift to the real factors in history in favor of the supposed "necessity of the inner dialectic of pure reason." Haym expounded on Dilthey's new method: "Our historian [Dilthey] is equally far from the twin errors of viewing mental life as a chain of external mechanical causes and from the speculative presumption of trying to show the process of individual thought as some absolute self-contained dialectic of pure reason." Haym praised Dilthey for his nearly perfect balance between the often competing claims of historical-biographical matters and philosophical-systematic concerns and went on to agree with Dilthey that the most urgent task of the present was the "mutual interpenetration of the historical and philosophical."[20]

After the publication of this work, which established his reputation by creating a new type of intellectual history, Dilthey moved east to the

University of Breslau, where his life assumed a new personal cast. In 1875 he married Katharina Püttman, the daughter of a Berlin lawyer. The three children of their marriage were not only a source of personal joy to Dilthey but also provided a further immediate "empirical" stimulus to his interest in the new fields of child psychology and systematic pedagogy. At Breslau Dilthey began a close and stimulating friendship with Graf Paul Yorck von Wartenburg (1835–97), a highly educated and opinionated East Elbian Junker, whose ideas functioned as both a goad and foil. A year before the publication of his major theoretical work, *Einleitung in die Geisteswissenschaften: Versuch einer Grundlegung für das Studium der Gesellschaft und der Geschichte* (published in 1883 and dedicated to Yorck), Dilthey was called to Berlin to fill the chair of philosophy which had been occupied before him by Hegel and Lotze. Dilthey's work proved worthy of his predecessors; half a century after its first appearance it was termed "epochal" in one of the most respected international forums of philosophical thought in Europe.[21]

During the nearly three decades he was at Berlin, Dilthey divided his energies between teaching and research. In 1897 he was inducted into the Prussian Academy of Sciences. He was a reserved but popular teacher, lecturing regularly in the Auditorium Maximum of 600 seats.[22] His scholarship continued to reflect his broad interests and synthetic intentions. It can be divided roughly into historical and systematic portions, though these areas cannot be separated too exclusively, for Dilthey repeatedly demonstrated that they cross-fertilized each other. Indeed, a primary impulse behind his theoretical endeavors was to show the grounds for this connection. It is characteristic of Dilthey's "circular" or reciprocal mode of thought that he should come to explicate the systematic thinking of Schleiermacher and Hegel only after he had articulated his own philosophical viewpoint—and yet his historical study of their work provided a continuing stimulus to his own systematic reflections. The historical and systematic sides of his thought were brought into closer relation in broadly conceived works on descriptive psychology, aesthetics, ethics, and pedagogical science.

His intensive study of Hegel, which culminated in the *Jugendgeschichte Hegels* (1905), added new conceptions to his evolving framework of ideas. Based upon hitherto unknown texts, the Hegel volume proved to be a powerful impulse to the revival of Hegelian studies in Germany by disclosing the concrete experiential roots of Hegel's thought—an interpretive technique previously employed for Schleiermacher. At the same time, Dilthey prepared for a new critical edition of Kant's writings and, together with Benno Erdmann and Eduard Zeller, founded the *Archiv für Geschichte der Philosophie*. Concurrent with his systematic inquiries into the foundations of the human sciences, he undertook historical studies of the role of the human sciences in the thought of the Renaissance, early modern, and Enlightenment periods. These projects manifested his conviction that actual historical practice is essential to any theory of historical reason—and of the human sciences in general.

But Dilthey gleaned from the immediate present as well as what he saw as the living past. His thought was enriched by new developments in contemporary logic, epistemology, psychology, and sociology. He studied the idealism of the German and French neo-Kantians, the vitalistic irrationalism of Nietzsche and Bergson, the new psychologies of Wundt, Stumpf, Lipps, and James, the sociological theory of Simmel and Weber, as well as the epochal phenomenological investigations of Husserl. As shall be shown later, his conceptions concentrated and deepened with the reception of these new impulses.

At the turn of the century Dilthey could take some satisfaction from the fact that the ideas he had been advancing for years in relative isolation were beginning to receive a wide and sympathetic hearing. He remained, however, quite critical of the form which this new "enthusiasm for life" assumed: as slogan gave way to slogan, he called for careful and critical analysis. After a period of illness forced him to retire both from regular lecturing and from theoretical work, he resumed after 1905 the task of his critique of historical reason. Major studies concerning the theory of knowledge and experience, expression and understanding, and the structure of the historical world were produced in this last period. Dilthey remained fully absorbed in a task which seemed to grow with the effort. His accomplishments brought public recognition in the form of several royal orders and the solicitations of high officials and famous thinkers, but to the end of his life Dilthey remained, even to his closest students, "the mysterious old one."[23]

Dilthey retired from teaching in 1907 to devote his full time to the completion of his project. Such a course must have been painful to him since he fervently believed that active teaching and research were inseparable. One of his last public stands was to enjoin against Kaiser Wilhelm II's project of setting up state-sponsored research institutes, where "pure" knowledge might be pursued apart from the responsibilities of instruction.[24] In keeping with his precept of the union of thought and life, Dilthey warned specifically against the dangers of theoretical rarification and affirmed that "The fruit and goal of all true philosophy is pedagogy in the broadest sense, the cultivation of man" (*GS* 9:7).

In striking fulfillment of his stoical admonition that the philosopher must be "content to die underway," Dilthey died on 30 September 1911 without fully consummating his life's project. In light of his own endeavors one could well agree with his statement that a thinker needs several lifetimes to complete his labors and that, ultimately, the true thinker, like the saint, exists only as an ideal. In his eulogy on Dilthey, the poet Hugo von Hofmannsthal characterized him in terms recalling those of Burckhardt and James, as "a German professor, the likes of Dr. Faust."[25]

If the final realization of his project eluded him, it remains to be said that Dilthey left much more than a mélange of provisional studies and fragments. It is often suggested by his critics that Dilthey spent so much time stating and restating his problem that he never got to the solution — or that he defined his problem so as to make it insoluble. Like so many judgments about Dilthey, these are half-truths which obscure as much as they illuminate. He never provided pat answers and closed formulations, but it is not true that "in Dilthey's work there are no conclusions."[26] There is a fundamental unity in his work, even if it is a typically Germanic "unity in diversity"—reflecting the fact that it was drawn from many different sources and was deployed in many different directions.

Dilthey's critique of historical reason was composed of many strands drawn from divergent intellectual traditions and combined in a unique pattern—a singular compound which not only differed from but clashed with its original elements. Dilthey was a master of selective or *critical* appropriation and novel recombination. Adopting one of his own key concepts, one could say that his attitude toward his intellectual inheritance was one of "immanent critique": he was both a product of his times but also a declared opponent of many of its reigning assumptions. His thought embodied both critical and conservative impulses. Because of his syncretism and zeal for synthesis, Dilthey does not readily fit into conventional philosophical categories; hence, it is especially important to treat him on his own terms. But as Dilthey himself demonstrated for Schleiermacher, Hegel, and others, every thinker—no matter how unique his terms—must still come to terms with the legacy of past thought. Before proceeding to a detailed examination of Dilthey's thought in its own terms, more extended treatment must be given to the general intellectual contours of the nineteenth century, for it is this context which posed the problems to which Dilthey's thought is a response. This context must be reconstructed from the vantage point of Dilthey's concerns but also in *its* own terms in order to provide a sense of the full horizon within which his thought moved. Such a recombinant perspective inevitably entails a certain distortion. Where possible, Dilthey's terms and those of his forebears and contemporaries have been integrated into a larger framework. If this framework seems somewhat schematic, it is because a great number of intersecting, reinforcing, and conflicting points of view must be treated as a whole.

Intellectual Background, 1800–1850: The Spiritualization of Reality

From the viewpoint of its leading thinkers, the nineteenth century presented a highly diversified picture, refracted, of course, through their own preoccupations. For the historian Treitschke it was "the richest century of the modern period," harvesting the fruits of all preceding epochs. For Arthur Schopenhauer it was a "philosophical century"—a century ripe for philosophy, indeed in desperate need of it. For the philosopher Friedrich Paulsen, however, it was the "century of history," in direct contrast with the "philosophical" eighteenth century. Kuno Fischer saw it as the "century of criticism," destroying cherished old myths and idols but lurching dangerously toward new and even more powerful ones. Perhaps Hermann von Helmholtz provided the most telling signature for the whole era in claiming that for both the man in the street and the researcher it was simply the "century of science."[27]

The profusion of descriptions has not been attenuated with the passage of time. The modern historian Friedrich Heer writes of the nineteenth century: "Everything in it was ambiguous, bearing the the past and future within itself. The problem of understanding the nineteenth century lies partly in this extraordinary ambiguity and partly in the difficulty of finding a proper perspective from which to look at it. Our anxieties and expectations prevent us from doing justice to this century in all its greatness and fruitfulness."[28] The fascination and frustration of Dilthey's thought lies in the fact that it combined all these impulses: history, philosophy, criticism, and science were all linked in a unique fashion. Friedrich Meinecke's judgment acutely distills the sweep of Dilthey's endeavor: "Out of his works as a whole the development of the modern mind comes to light in unmatched depth and fullness."[29]

In order to secure a general perspective on this complex development, it is useful to envision the course of nineteenth-century Europe in terms of a protracted and shifting conflict between idealism and realism—the positions which Dilthey was intent upon drawing into a new synthesis. From the outset, however, it must be noted that each term of this opposition included important subdistinctions, modulations, and attendant rivalries which were in some respects as striking as the primary polarity. Idealism included critical, transcendental, romantic (or "poetic"), and absolute forms; realism included positivistic, naturalistic, and materialistic forms. Some of these positions were primarily epistemological, others ontological in character—and these differences are, to say the least, considerable. Thus, one cannot portray the conflict of idealism and realism in a neatly dichotomous or dialectical fashion, although there is an undeniable dialectical quality to these conflicts and transformations. Hegel's insight that the development of thought proceeds by way of *Aufhebung* rather than by simple contradiction has proved remarkably applicable in intellectual history, even if his system became a mere artifact of that history. Finally, just as Dilthey traced the influences of three generations at work in Schleiermacher's thought, it is useful to project his own thinking against the triptych-like background of idealism, realism, and the revolt against positivism.

Part One: The Formation and Transformation Of German Idealism

Dilthey's thought is deeply rooted in the tradition of German idealism and *Geistesphilosophie*, which, as he repeatedly noted, was "the foundation of German national culture" (*VDM* 328). He is frequently classified as a "neo-idealist" or "neo-Kantian" in an effort to bring his thought into relation to the resurgent idealist movement which appeared in Germany in the last quarter of the nineteenth century. Indeed he is often called simply the "Kant of history." This classification is inexact and misleading, but it is just as misleading to say that "Dilthey's philosophy does not belong to the idealist family at all."[30] Dilthey's attitude toward idealism, in both its "classical" form and its later "neo-idealist" modification, was extremely complex and many-faceted. In general it can be said that he affirmed much of the inner impulse of idealism but rejected its formal, systematic elaboration. The inner tendency he regarded as fruitful, but the systems themselves he considered doctrinaire and otiose. Perhaps his pietistic heritage, which stressed direct inner experience rather than formal doctrine, was a factor in prompting him to make a separation between the living spirit and the dead letter of German idealism.

For Dilthey the transcendental idealism of Kant and his heirs had succumbed to the Platonizing metaphysical view of the world as a shadowy allegory or muddy "appearance" of a priori categories and eternal ideas. In the name of timeless truth and absolute certainty such high-minded idealism ended up overlooking reality instead of digging down into it and providing the means to change it. As discussed earlier, the highest vocation of thought for Dilthey was ultimately a practical, reforming one; thought was to be in the service of life. In becoming "thought about thought" rather than thought about life, German idealism had forfeited its true mission and ended in passive contemplation and remote system-mongering.

> In Kant and Fichte philosophy had immersed itself in itself, it tried to explain the world out of pure consciousness. An irremediable gap appeared between the philosophical consciousness in its own self-certainty and the ordinary view of things. The poets had conceived in the free play of imagination a distant world of aesthetic perfection; there was no connecting link between the free serenity with which they created these images and the confused, harried life of ordinary man. Philosoph-

ical idealism negated ordinary reality, poetic idealism forgot it. Its greatest task, however, was to reform it [*GS* 12:4].

In its internal transformation between 1780 and 1830, German idealism had disclosed important features and functions of the mind, but it had also obscured and obliterated other equally crucial aspects; its greatest error was to make pure consciousness into the "ground" of the world (*GS* 5:356).

The roots of German idealism extend far back in the history of Western thought to such figures as Plato, Augustine, Plotinus, Cusanus, Leibniz, and many others. But for interpretive purposes modern German idealism may be said to have begun with Kant. His philosophy accomplished what he termed a Copernican revolution in thought and prevailing conceptions of knowledge. It was a German revolution *par excellence*—a seemingly inner revolution in thought which could be said to have turned the world around and yet in a sense left it standing precisely as it was. This "revolution" was exceedingly significant in setting the terms for all further deliberations. Dilthey avowed that Kant "revolutionized German thought" and went on to note that Kant's critical course was susceptible to a double interpretation: one that led away from experience toward pure idealism and one that led toward experience and realism (*GS* 4:47 and 281). Between these two pathways, German thought in the nineteenth century was to alternate with striking regularity.

Before Kant, theory of knowledge had for the most part held to the seemingly "natural" view that the mind conforms to objects; but Kant held that objects as knowable reality must conform to the mind's own intrinsic operations. For Kant, the mind does not draw its forms and laws from nature or being but rather takes its material content from this reality and prescribes its own forms. The age-old notion of the mind's passive correspondence or "imitation" of things was supplanted by a conception of the mind's active, form-giving function. The mind may be said to know objects because it has "produced" them in a special sense of the word: not in respect of their real existence but in respect of their form. Cognition is precisely this process of prescribing form to the amorphous data of experience.

Kant's critical philosophy attempted to define conclusively the difference between mere thought and valid knowledge. His *Critique of Pure Reason* (1781) demolished in one colossal blow the possibility of traditional metaphysics and its claim to be valid knowledge. Whereas much of previous philosophy had endeavored to penetrate to an ultimate realm of essential truth apart from the subjective conditions of human perception— to grasp a "real reality" free from the intervening influence of the human subject—Kant proclaimed the impossibility of such an approach by establishing the logical priority of the mind's necessary and inalienable contribution to all knowing. What had previously been assumed to be a distorting medium or obstacle to knowledge of the "really real" was converted into the very precondition of valid knowledge. To be sure, such knowledge could no longer claim to be knowledge of ultimate and unconditioned reality; it had to content itself with being knowledge of phenomenal appearances. Kant held that knowledge of reality is conditioned; we can never know "things in themselves" because we are necessarily constrained to know them within the forms of our own mind. Reason has insight into that which it considers according to its own forms.

Kant's critique stressed both the constitutive, active power of the mind and the intrinsic and ineluctable limits of that mind. Such a doctrine embodied a double-edged principle, which, as Dilthey noted, was to prove a powerful stimulus to further reflection and development. In limiting genuine knowledge to the objects of sense experience, Kant did not deny the existence of a supersensible reality beyond experience; indeed, his whole system in a sense depended upon it. Rather, he insisted that traditional metaphysics could not reach this reality and was merely a "science of illusion" pervaded by contradictions. By those who saw knowledge in the old vein as necessarily rooted in God or metaphysics Kant was reproached as "the destroyer of all." However, for those who detected in his doctrines the germ of an entirely new world-view, he was, as the poet Hölderlin expressed it, "the Moses of our nation."

Kant's theory took existing physical science as the model of all certain knowledge and inquired reflectively into its logical presuppositions. His conception of knowledge was premised upon belief in the unimpeachable validity of Newtonian physics. The form of knowledge treated in the first *Critique* was the exact, physico-mathematical knowledge which had made such formidable advances since Galileo and Newton. His notion of what constituted truly scientific knowledge was neatly expressed in the famous statement that there is as much genuine knowledge in a discipline as there is mathematics. True to the scientific and cultural canons of his age, Kant's *desiderata* were logical universality and necessity: the measure of a science was the extent to which its content could be converted into mathematical formulation.

Kant's thought was "critical" and "transcendental," terms which were axial in his own system and which remained decisive for his successors, including Dilthey. They designate a manner of knowing the world and, in a sense, also reflectively "knowing this knowing" at the same time. By insisting that thought be "critical," Kant wished to avoid the twin pitfalls of dogmatism and skepticism. Critical thought therefore inquires into the proper limits of the faculty of reason and establishes the justified and unjustified uses of our mind: it neither dogmatically assumes from the outset what needs to be proven in the fashion of rationalist metaphysics, nor skeptically dissolves knowledge into habit or the play of personal opinion or prejudice in the fashion of Humean empiricism. Correspondingly, Kant's thought is "transcendental" in insisting that the theory of knowledge concern itself not with particular objects, or with the particular, personal consciousness, but rather with the logically necessary and universal formal conditions of knowledge as such.

Kant held that if there is universal validity in knowledge, then that knowledge must depend upon a priori forms, categories, and principles. These formal rules operate upon the flow of sense impressions or empirical data (*Anschauungen*) received by the mind. In a series of logical operations, perception is raised to genuine knowledge. The forms and categories of the mind must be a priori, not empirical or acquired, in order to guarantee the universal validity of cognition. Our knowledge begins with experience, but this is not to say that it is "grounded" in experience. Kant's theory of cognition supposes that the mind contributes something to knowledge which is necessarily different from experience.

Kant accordingly drew a sharp distinction between sense experience and judgment, or the faculties of sense intuition (*Sinnlichkeit*) and intellect (*Verstand*). He separated the mind's capacity for passive reception of impressions and its capacity for synthetic organization, but at the same time insisted that the mutual cooperation of both was necessary for knowledge. In the famous rendering of his words: "concepts without percepts are empty, but percepts without concepts are blind." Kant further stressed that all intuition is sense intuition of external objects: I cannot be conscious of myself except mediately. Only God, not human beings, is endowed with a faculty of "intellectual intuition," that is, a pure intuition, free of sense particulars. The synthetic unity of consciousness, or "transcendental subject," is not actually experienced as an object but is rather logically presupposed in all knowledge.

For Kant, experience cannot in itself furnish knowledge, which requires the intellect as "a faculty of rules" to impose its forms upon experience. The empiricist effort to derive all knowledge solely from experience is comparable to the attempt to make bricks without a mold. The investigation into the grounds of knowledge and experience cannot itself be empirical, for these grounds concern the possibility of experience in general, not any particular experience. The mind must be regarded as a synthesizing power regulated by a priori principles. The forms and principles of this activity cannot be approached empirically, for they are presupposed in every experience. Experience cannot of itself generate its own forms and rules. Kant, in sum, presupposes presuppositions—and ones of a special sort.

Kant's philosophy disallowed valid knowledge of things in themselves but it did not altogether preclude consideration of them. Indeed, it necessarily presupposed them. While we may not *know* certain things, we

can, and indeed must, still *think* them. Although the world of unconditioned noumenal reality is beyond our cognition, it functions as an eternal
task or "regulative idea" for the mind. This unconditioned reality is a
postulate of the moral will or practical faith. The transcendental ideas of
God, freedom, and immortality are not possible objects of experience or the
understanding; they function in a "regulative use" as incentives and guiding
principles for the mind in its capacity of willing. Here their use is as
necessary and justified for reason (*Vernunft*) as are the categories for the
scientific understanding (*Verstand*). Thus, although Kant barred metaphysics as science, he nonetheless recognized metaphysics as a "natural"
and ineradicable impulse of the human mind.

Kant made knowledge dependent upon something which is not itself
knowable: the "thing-in-itself" was retained as an indispensable limiting
concept (*Grenzbegriff*) which we cannot know, but must presuppose. His
delimitation of mental activity reserved an area of practical striving and
belief which was equally important as scientific certainty. Indeed, Kant's
statement that he had "to limit knowledge in order to make room for belief"
seemed to imply a path to the unconditioned which was neither that of
science nor of traditional rationalist metaphysics. But here Kant supplied
only an indicating marker rather than an explicit method.

In two subsequent critiques Kant extended his critical-transcendental
method to the realms of ethical and aesthetic judgment, thus completing a
survey of the mind's total activity. With the *Critique of Practical Reason*
(1788), the physical world of strict causal necessity constructed by the
scientific understanding was supplemented by a second, independent realm
of freedom and practical striving under the categorical form of the moral
law. The world of nature known by science is a world of strict causal
determinism, whereas the world of moral freedom is governed by the
autonomous principles which man prescribes to himself. The physical laws
of science and the moral laws of man's free activity were separated: man is
empirically determined but noumenally free. Pursuant to some parts of his
doctrine (but in apparent violation of other parts), Kant went on to hold
that the mind "naturally" seeks a connection between the realms of
necessity and freedom, of scientific cognition and moral will. His final
Critique of Judgment (1790) in a sense provided the lineaments of a
synthesis of the two realms. Here the necessity of scientific reason was
combined with the freedom of practical reason within a single teleological
framework. The vision of nature as a "whole" (as distinct from its scientific
analysis) and the appreciation of the work of art as a "total impression" (as
distinct from sense data) both showed analogously the synthetic unity of
mind at work in organizing partial contents together under the conception
of "purpose" or end.

In its separate aspects Kant's philosophy was preeminently a philosophy of formal precision and strict limits. The three *Critiques* provided specification and legitimation for the different capacities of the mind and its forms of judgment. Yet taken as a whole, the new transcendental method suggested (on some readings even *required*) a total world-view in which Kant's precise analytical distinctions would be overcome in the very synthetic unity which he regarded as the essential function of mind. If the basic work of the mind is active synthesis, as Kant suggested, then it was impossible to remain, as Kant appeared to remain, at the level of separate, even disparate, mental faculties. Kant was understandably interpreted as pointing beyond his own position. As Dilthey trenchantly observed, "There were coherences and contradictions in Kant which made it seem impossible to remain with him" (*GS* 4:45–46; also 49).[31]

Idealism after Kant assumed what is often loosely referred to as its "romantic" form, even though its major protagonists, Fichte and Hegel, were severely critical of the usual forms of romanticism. Kant's successors introduced into transcendental philosophy new conceptions drawn from poetry, religion, history, and the cult of nature. Fichte, Schelling, Schleiermacher, and Hegel each in his own way departed from Kant's cautious brand of formal and critical analysis. By turning portions of Kant's thought against other portions, they wound up reviving many of the ideas which he had laid to rest or placed beyond the scope of human knowledge. Kant's romantic interpreters insisted that they were merely removing implicit contradictions from his thought and converting its negative admonitions to positive results. As Dilthey expressed it: "They surpassed Kant by means of the consequences of his own system" (*GS* 4:201). Kant's critical philosophy was thereby converted to a way station on the route to the absolute and unconditioned.

The evolution of idealism beyond Kant began with the potent assertion that his very own method proceeded in violation of his tenet that knowledge cannot go beyond experience. His inquiry into knowledge was avowedly not empirical, but transcendental. It thus presupposed and demonstrated a kind of knowledge which is independent of experience. The movement of thought beyond experience, which for Kant resulted in insoluble contradictions and antinomies, became a positive, indeed necessary, method for his successors. They resolved his static dualisms, distinctions and antinomies into dynamic, dialectical unities. The "dialectics" which he had repudiated as "a logic of illusion" became the very key to the activity of mind and reality. The constitutive activity of synthetic unity which Kant had attributed to the mind became its very essence for his successors.

Fichte undertook the decisive extension of Kant by asserting that the unobservable and "insensible" transcendental activity of the mind *is* precisely the mysterious thing-in-itself. As Dilthey observed, Fichte regarded this profound emendation as merely "completing" Kant by bringing the three critiques into a unity (*GS* 4:50). The unconditioned absolute or "ground" of the world was explicitly thematized and located in the human mind. In grasping itself fully as free transcendental activity, the mind *becomes* the very thing which it could not attain in Kant's system. In the name of carrying Kant's critical method to its own conclusion, Fichte dispensed with the thing-in-itself as the final obstacle to a "consistent" idealism. With one stroke transcendental idealism was disembarrassed of its limits. Dilthey tersely noted this as "the first step in a fateful path" (*GS* 4:51).

Kant had stressed the synthetic activity of mind working upon materials given "from without" in sensation; Fichte went further in positing the "absolute ego" as the wholly creative principle of the world. He thus confidently attributed to the human mind what Kant had modestly reserved to Divine Mind. Fichte was, as Dilthey drolly observed, "a Spinoza in reverse" (*GS* 4:203). The ideas of reason were conceived not as facts (*Tatsachen*) but as acts (*Tathandlungen*); the objects of consciousness were to be viewed not as dead "things" but as mental creations. In Fichte, practical or ethical reason was elevated above theoretical reason and, indeed, subsumed it. Kant's transcendental method was thereby given a decidedly voluntaristic and evolutionary motif.

Fichte held that the knowing subject is most truly and authentically *Geist* only when it has as its object its own progressive activity. The mind is not limited by some circumscribed sphere of real objects of experience but rather by its conception of its own activity. Kant's logical conditions were converted into acts of "intellectual intuition." By turning away from things as natural, pre-given objects or metaphysical things-in-themselves, the mind is reflexively directed back to its own innermost transcendental activity. Without this unwonted return to itself and its activity, the mind is merely "lost" in objects, still "dogmatic," and not yet "critical." Realism is a form of slavish mental dependency; to be truly critical, the mind must escape from "naïve" realism and come to regard itself as the creative source of reality. In Fichte's radical form of idealism, reality is not merely organized by the mind, it is postulated by the mind and then realized in action; knowledge itself is a form of action. Will predominates over mere representation and the postulation of the "ought" (*Sollen*) has primacy over the passive apprehension of the "is" (*Sein*). Fichte's "conclusive" ethical idealism carried strong philosophical portents against the status quo, even though they remained lodged in inner consciousness.

Transcendental idealism took a different turn with Schleiermacher, who, like Fichte, thought of himself as Kantian in spirit. He is often placed at the center of the post-Kantian romantic movement, but in many ways he remained closest to the critical, anti-speculative spirit of Kant's philosophizing. It was the concrete richness of Schleiermacher's conceptions in combination with his aversion to speculative constructions which particularly attracted the young Dilthey. Dilthey judged that Schleiermacher alone among Kant's successors had held fast to the analytical method of Kant; he offered "not metaphysics, but phenomenology of consciousness" (*GS* 4:397). On the increasingly vexing question of "idealism vs. realism" Schleiermacher proclaimed "I am neutral" and he combined realistic premises with the transcendental method. Thus for Schleiermacher, thought and being are correlative but not identical, nor does one fully subsume the other. He avoided the dualism of Kant, the extremely subjectivist, even solipsistic idealism of Fichte, and the rationalist monism of Hegel by propounding a continuously creative interaction between thought and being, mind and nature, self and world. Contending that Kant and Fichte had given only *formal* autonomy to the subject, he aspired to put the full content of experience in the place of Fichte's "empty" transcendental ego. He rebuked existing forms of idealism for portraying *Geist* as active but essentially empty.

To furnish real empirical content for the reflective, transcendental consciousness, Schleiermacher posited an immediate self-awareness. This self-awareness is not pure thought but rather feeling—a comprehensive "self-feeling" which does not transcend or exclude the real world, but rather unites the self and the world in a patterned whole. This "wholeness" within man's self-consciousness became the ultimate criterion of reason. Not Fichte's all-subordinating will, which separates the self from its objects and directs it back on itself, but rather feeling becomes the core of *Geist*. In a philosophical turn which is likely to surprise anyone subscribing to accepted habits of reference, Schleiermacher employed feeling as a means of reintroducing objective, empirical content into an overly subjective account of the mind. Feeling is the synthetic unity of experience uniting the theoretical and practical, real and ideal, conditioned and absolute.

Yet, unlike his contemporary Schelling, Schleiermacher did not annul all distinctions into the ineffable whole of feeling, which Hegel ridiculed as "the night in which all cows are black." Schleiermacher put great stress upon the category of individuality in his theory of mind and other aspects of his philosophy. The synthetic unity of mind for him did not exclude distinction and differentiation. Schleiermacher propounded an ongoing reciprocal relation between particularity and universality, between the individual and community, between the subjective consciousness and the natural world. Unlike the other dialectical systems, Schleiermacher's did not allow the universal to subsume and cancel the individual. The human individual pursues his own particular view of the world and unique manner of conducting himself in it, though he is still in a relation of harmonious dependency with the whole. All unity is a unity-in-diversity, and God is the whole which harmonizes this diversity. Man's consciousness, as a feeling for this whole, is the seat of the infinite God; man is dependent upon this wholeness which is both outside and inside him. A religious feeling for the infinite does not diminish man but directs him back to himself. In this constant passage from the self to the whole and back, man realizes his true individuality and the true totality.

Of the German idealists it was Schleiermacher who came closest to the balance between thought and life that Dilthey aspired to. Schleiermacher did not slight experience for the sake of logical coherence. Dilthey termed his thought "epoch-making" and noted that it gave rise to a novel form of *Idealrealismus* carried on by Trendelenburg, himself, and others (*GS* 4:394).[32] Schleiermacher's stance was rooted in immediate feeling, yet it did not thereby exclude conceptual thought. Most important, reason and experience were much more integrally linked than in the other idealists. Thought was taken to be a representation of reality—different from its real correlate but not out of all relation with it. *Geist* achieves a partial unity with things, because it is not reflexive and self-contained but is directed toward the world and in touch with something outside itself. Unlike Fichte, Schleiermacher had achieved what for Dilthey was the proper synthesis of inwardness and outwardness: coordination, not subordination, was the keynote of his thought. His totality was not a uniform and indifferent identity, but a whole coordinating its parts.

Perhaps most alluring to Dilthey was Schleiermacher's conviction that the transcendental attitude cannot be reserved to a realm of pure thought but must be carried over into everyday life and its manifestations. Transcendental philosophy cannot be separated from history and man's concrete experience of the world; instead, it must be employed to illuminate art, religion, ethics, politics, language, and history. In this all-pervading form, the transcendental attitude engenders a sense for the perpetual mystery of the genetic development of the self and the world. In conjunction with the transcendental consciousness, Schleiermacher celebrated a historical consciousness which put the mind in touch with "that which is outside us and before us" (*GS* 4:261).

It is very revealing that Dilthey referred to Schleiermacher as his "god" and "scientific guide" and yet on several occasions strongly denied that he was a "Schleiermacheriener."[33] He maintained an attitude of "immanent critique" toward his mentor, finding him too "Plato-filled" (*GS* 5: 81).[34] Schleiermacher had elevated development as a central principle, yet he ultimately failed to grasp the true nature of man's concrete historicity (*Geschichtlichkeit*). As Kant treated experience, so Schleiermacher invoked history as a postulate to round out his philosophy without really taking it seriously enough as a concrete reality. In Dilthey's view, Schleiermacher was still too much under the spell of Platonic doctrine to recognize fully the influence of concrete conditions upon ideas. His idealist concept of individuality prescribed monad-like "canonical individualities" impermeable to analysis. Although Schleiermacher assigned a substantial role to earthly life and history in his thought, he did not dig down analytically into concrete manifestations. A truly concrete apprehension of things was in Dilthey's view precluded by the formal tenets of transcendentalism; idealism, even Schleiermacher's, viewed life from afar.

A markedly more romantic and poetic version of *Geist* was propounded by a group of thinkers who argued even more strongly than Schleiermacher that Kant's thought was abstract and formalistic. Dilthey observed that this group—which included Jacobi, Herder, Goethe, Schelling, the Schlegel brothers, and Wilhelm von Humboldt—all concurred that Kant had sacrificed life on the marmorial altar of theory, and what remained was only a "lifeless, lightless world of concepts" (*GS* 4: 53). Not abstract ideation and conceptualization, but concrete intuition was the rallying point for these thinkers. With somewhat different emphases, they all affirmed a human capacity for the objective "intellectual intuition" which Kant had reserved to God alone. This intuition did not wait upon the intellect to organize sense particulars into an intelligible order; it perceived everything holistically, penetrating directly to the living center of nature and history.

The advocates of intuition set out to expunge the subjectivist, reflexive, and "constructed" character of transcendentalism, but they did so only at the cost of a strong dose of irrationalism. Dilthey termed their thought "poetic idealism." With this turn of German thought, the irrational, as Dilthey noted, was given a large role; natural and historical reality were approached not in terms of causality, but in terms of analogy, allegory, myth, and symbol (*GS* 4: 265; 9:13). These thinkers held that reason, when it proceeds through concepts, categories, commensuration, and experimentation, is no longer in touch with the fullness of reality, but only with its own abstract constructions and contrivances. Kant's equation of science with commensuration resulted in a dessicated version of the knowable world; living reality was lost in "hollow" quantities. They demanded a new kind of science based upon concrete intuition and "wonder as a permanent state of mind" (*GS* 9:21).

In their rebuttals and "meta-critiques" of Kant, the defenders of intuition stressed that the objects of possible experience included more than the objects of Newtonian physics; art, religion, myth, and history were also legitimate sources and objects of knowledge, albeit of a different sort. Herder insisted that historical knowledge proceeded by way of an intuition of the "inner soul" of different epochs and cultures. Schelling held that aesthetic perception was superior to both scientific and moral reason, providing a key to the poetic and mythical dimensions of reality. Goethe rejected the formalized, mechanical, and "dis-qualified" Newtonian view of nature which Kant had taken as the point of departure for his theory of knowledge. Kant's preeminent concern with logic and the strict self-limiting conditions of knowledge had, in the view of these thinkers, confined the mind to a narrow band in the range of possible insight. Goethe's comment that "Kant puts the mind in a cage and then beckons it to look beyond the bars" pointed beyond scientific knowledge to another form.

From the perspective of later years, Dilthey came to view this phase of German thought as a "reaction of life" against an overly formal and intellectualized account of thinking. It was, thus, preparation for his own endeavors. He drew certain insights from these proponents of intuition, but he saw a major failing in their celebration of imagination, belief, and speculation over sober critical thought. Their mystical form of knowledge was for him often merely "dilettantish" or even "a leap into the indeterminate void" (GS 4:310–11, 317–19).

It was Hegel who proposed to carry the multiform aspects of post-Kantian thought to an "absolute" consummation. His thought represented a synthesis of critical, romantic, and rationalist phases of idealism. Against Kant's insistence upon the strict limits of reason, Hegel boldly asserted that to know a limit is to be already beyond it; the very essence of spirit is transcendence. He scorned Kant's critical modesty and envisioned reason as something absolute and unconditioned, developing and revealing itself in history. As Dilthey put it, Hegel's most characteristic urge was to grasp the world and history as an emergent totality of spiritual forces (GS 4:60).

All that is genuinely real is for Hegel a manifestation of *Geist*. Thought actually brings forth its own object; mind posits being. Whereas Kant's critical idealism had been epistemological, Hegel's was ontological and objective. The material or objective content as well as the form of the world is ideal. In contrast to the cautious formulations of Kant and Schleiermacher, Hegel made bold to assert that reality is fully comprehended in thought. True reality is not the opaque stuff of lowly, immediate experience but rather the ideal content which has been totally comprehended in concepts of thought. Reason comes to itself and to this "true" reality (which is also true ideality) by purging its own operations of contingent sensory content. Experience alone cannot fulfill the demands of reason; experience is both an "offense" and task given over to reason. The immediate reality of feeling and intuition celebrated by the romantics had to be transformed and transcended in the ideal operations of thought. Hegel abhorred mere subjective inwardness and saw the essence of mind precisely as its capacity to move outward and appropriate reality in concepts. Everything which has not yet been comprehended by mind is merely the "otherness" or alienation of mind. Nature is simply this preliminary "otherness" of mind waiting to be retrieved by the concepts of reason.

Dialectics for Kant had been a logic of illusion—a trap reason sets for itself in transgressing its own proper grounds. For Hegel, dialectics was the very living process and form of truth itself. Repudiating both traditional formal logic and Kant's transcendental-formal logic, Hegel's dialectical logic constituted yet another German "revolution" in thinking. It proceeded by throwing overboard—one might also say mobilizing—the most basic logical principle of noncontradiction. Dilthey's friend Rudolf Haym described Hegel's dialectical turn as "not only a powerful accomplishment in its own right but one of the most significant events in the history of German thought."[35] In contrast to static formal logic, Hegel devised a "logic of becoming" which purported to comprehend the movement of life and the activity of thought. This "logic of content" endeavored to show the actual process whereby thought comes into full identity with being. Hegel's logic was therefore not "merely logical" but also ontological and historical. In his study of Hegel, Dilthey defined the dialectical method as the "process that raises the ceaseless flow of life and development to conceptual knowledge. [Dialectics] was a method of conceptual thought that overcomes the fixity of concepts by making thought fluid and concepts concrete" (*GS* 4:236–37).

Hegel conceived the activity of *Geist* as a historical process. History was portrayed as the rational continuum along which the mind moves toward the attainment of absolute knowledge. History, which had previously been regarded by most secular thinkers as the sphere of contingency, chaos, and error, became in Hegel's system the very process of reason itself. In history the mind discovers and recovers the record of its own operation; it thereby comes to itself by overcoming its initial self-alienation. Needless to say, Hegel's view bestowed upon history an enormous significance and meaning; it became the royal road to pure, absolute truth—a kind of elaborate, temporalized syllogism in the mind of God.

To be sure, Hegel acknowledged that this absolute philosophical perspective was not the ordinary one of humble common sense. To comprehend historical development as the inexorable march of reason required a special vantage point superior to that available to those actually immersed in history itself. Hegel's perspective was that of the "whole" and of the "end." Neither sheer immanence nor transcendence, but rational "finality" constituted Hegel's vantage point on reality. What appears as happenstance and contingency to the immediate, "merely subjective" view of mortal eyes is really (that is, when seen in the final perspective of the whole) guided by what Hegel termed the "cunning of reason." Not the immediate experience of participants but the rational comprehension of the whole is the true content and reality of history. In Hegel's famous formulation, "the truth is the whole."

In his own estimation and that of many of his contemporaries, Hegel had spoken the last word in philosophy. To many it seemed as if he had indeed provided the whole truth. He had achieved the total dialectical mediation of all opposites, transcending all the polarities and tensions which had characterized previous idealism. His absolute idealism was the *non plus ultra* and final apotheosis of *Geist*. All separation and tension between subject and object, thought and being, spirit and nature, freedom and necessity, "ought" and "is" were transcended in the emergent identity of the absolute concept. A panlogical monism had displaced Kant's limited and dualistic conception of knowledge. Hegel had demonstrated that the real is the rational and the rational is the real—nothing further remained to be said. Pure rational thought encompassed all reality in a kind of metaphysician's immaculate conception. In Dilthey's dissenting view, "historical understanding was sacrificed to metaphysical schemas" (*GS* 4:249). Hegel's system, though it purported to begin in life, in the end extinguished life and experience in pure thought.

It would be difficult to overstate the impact which Hegel's thought had on the general intellectual life of Germany in the first half of the nineteenth century. A whole generation of students was captivated by his total synthesis. Dilthey referred to its "fascinating power over the youth" (*GS* 4:256). At Hegel's death in 1831 some of his most zealous followers likened his mission to that of Christ and foresaw his immediate ascent heavenward. All limits to reason seemed to vanish and all problems became transparent. The response of the young enthusiast, Wilhelm Vatke, who eventually became a prominent theologian on the Hegelian "Right," gave an indication of the almost magical powers attributed to Hegelianism:

> I can't express how joyous I am! All of the sciences have transformed and become clear to me. I now know toward what end History is striving; I now know how art forms itself and how religion attracts the human heart. I am constantly astonished that I know and I seek always to know more as a result of my astonishment.[36]

Such fascination was not confined to a narrow circle of directly inspired admirers. Owing to Hegel's close ties with the Prussian administration, his thought became the semiofficial philosophy of the Restoration in Germany and found imitators in most disciplines. His ideas were canonized in periodicals, curricula, academic methods, and official policies. His protégés undertook to show that all existing institutions and practices were comprehended in philosophy and were the realization of the ideal of perfect rationality. The sober naturalist Alexander von Humboldt observed skeptically that "the presumption of the times was to master the empirical totally through Ideas."[37] The urge to the rational All-One, and confidence in purely speculative methods, became accepted articles of academic and even wider public opinion. To many it seemed that Hegel had created a universal Empire of the Spirit incomparably more sublime and eternal than Napoleon's.

After disillusionment had already begun to set in, reaching a peak in the period of Dilthey's youth, Rudolf Haym attempted to recall the ambience of this period of Hegelian hegemony and "imperial idealism":

> For many of us today, the memory is still fresh of a time when all learning lived off the rich table of Hegelian wisdom, when all the other academic faculties waited in the antechamber of the philosophical faculty in hopes of appropriating something from the inspection of the Absolute and from the infinitely supple Dialectic—a time when one was either a Hegelian or a barbarian and an idiot . . . when, in the eyes of the Prussian educational and cultural ministry, it was almost a crime not to be a Hegelian. This then is the time one has to recall if one wants to perceive fully what the domination and total validity of a philosophical system means. One has to make present to himself that pathos and conviction of the Hegelians of 1830, who in full and bitter earnestness debated the question of what could be the further content of world history, now that the World-Spirit had attained its goal in Hegelian philosophy and true knowledge of itself.[38]

Virtually all the disciplines reflected the influence of idealism. Holistic *Naturphilosophie* was favored over a "vulgar" analytical and experimental approach to nature. Even medical studies were permeated with notions of ideal-forces and powers of spiritual attraction. Especially that area of inquiry which Dilthey was later to define as the human sciences was dominated by a kind of deductive, apriorist idealism which scanted empirical evidence in favor of grander schemes of the "totality." Speculative or intuitive methods were commended over observation, analysis, and experimentation. Early attempts by Johannes Fries and Friedrich Beneke at an empirical-psychological rather than transcendental and a priori approach to *Geist* were met with official ostracism and even outright repression; Beneke was dismissed from his post at Berlin on the grounds that any philosophy which did not deduce the real from the absolute-ideal was not worthy to be called a philosophy. As Dilthey later pointed out, Hegel had a direct hand in these pernicious dealings (*GS* 4:258). The normative or axiological fields of law, ethics, and aesthetics were particularly suffused with Hegelian assumptions. From a later perspective Dilthey portrayed Hegel's influence as that of an "absolute dictator" and observed that "there were only disciples and opponents" (*GS* 4:254–55). Hegel's idealism, despite its dialectical plasticity, had assumed a fixed, self-righteous character. In its pretention to absolute knowledge, idealism had transformed itself into a dogmatism which "relocated the center of life over into transcendence," leaving an even more oppressive hiatus between life and thought (*GS* 8:177). The fate of idealism in Germany was a powerful and lasting warning for Dilthey: it had begun as a philosophy of creative freedom and human autonomy but had evolved into a narrow orthodoxy and official apologia for the existing order. Idealism had "conquered" and comprehended reality only by forsaking it.

Part Two: Countercurrents, 1830–50:
The Resistance of Reality

In his study of Hegel, Dilthey pointed out that behind the dialectical mediations of absolute idealism there lurked "an inner ambiguity" which resolved itself into idealist-metaphysical and realist-historical positions (*GS* 4:249, 256). Since Dilthey's day, it has become almost a cliché of intellectual history that Hegel's system fell victim to its own dialectical self-subversion. The accusation which Hegel had once delivered against Kant—that critical idealism had provided merely an inert, formal skeleton in place of flesh-and-blood content—was turned upon Hegel himself. The grandiose system of absolute idealism called forth its opposite: an attentive concern for the real and the actual. Dilthey characterized the tone of this reaction as "a deep aversion to the flight of the mind into the world beyond, the conviction that new times were to be ushered in by the penetration (*Vertiefung*) of the mind into given reality" (*GS* 4:440). His own thought was steeped in this reaction.

The manifestations of this reaction were diverse; some took place within philosophy itself, but ultimately the most influential reaction came from the sciences. Classical idealism was subjected to a thoroughgoing critique and yet managed to emerge in a refurbished form. Idealism underwent "radical" and "reactionary" interpretations, in turn giving rise to new materialistic, positivistic, irrationalistic, and theistic positions.

In these complex developments we must be content to discuss several philosophical currents which had a palpable impact on Dilthey's thought. They include the "anthropological turn" of the Left Hegelians, the historical "Empirie" of the German Historical School, and the teleological realism of Friedrich Adolf Trendelenburg. The first was important in setting the tone for philosophy in the period of Dilthey's maturation, whereas the latter two currents had a directly traceable formative influence on his conception of the human sciences. These movements came into their own in the period 1830 to 1850, the crucial years of Dilthey's youth, which saw the erosion and dismemberment of rigid orthodoxy in philosophical and religious matters and the challenging of the reactionary political practices of the Restoration. As a whole, the period of Dilthey's youth in the afterglow of idealism was characterized by growing skepticism in theology and religion, by distrust of the pale abstractions of metaphysics, and by dissatisfaction with prevailing social and political institutions.

The Left Hegelians proclaimed a new Copernican turn of thought—a turn away from pure thought to "man incarnate" and the real conditions of his earthly existence. The fact that the turn began with theological doctrine only served to augment its impact. David F. Strauss's *Leben Jesu* (1835) inaugurated this transformation by showing internal contradictions in the Gospels and thereby resolving the Gospel story "dialectically" into verifiable history and purely mythical elements. By dissolving Hegel's fusion of faith and reason, Strauss's critical dialectic initiated a period of great intellectual ferment which, as Dilthey noted, one had to live through to appreciate. The work was "a meteor, which set everything in motion" and "the explosive spark that fell into the accumulated tinder of philosophical and theological contrarities" (*GS* 4:421). In contrast to Hegel's rationalizing dialectic, Strauss's critical dialectic ushered in a period of demystification and "Entdogmatisierung." Religion, and by implication much more besides, could be explained by natural and historical conditions, leaving the metaphysical remainder to collapse on itself.

The other Left Hegelians—Feuerbach, Bauer, Ruge, Marx, and Stirner—were even more radical in their employment of the critical dialectic. The period after Strauss's book saw what has been seen as a veritable cannibalistic orgy of successive "critiques of criticism"; idealism appeared to be devouring itself.[39] These critics held that idealism had substituted a deductive abstraction for concrete reality, divorcing man from his real world and real nature. The "anthropological turn" they advocated might be seen as both an extension and reversal of the original "transcendental turn" which had provided the impetus to the original formation of idealism. The original "transcendental turn" called the mind to turn away from the "naïve" or dogmatic conception of a world of pre-given objects in order to discover its own constitutive powers. The "anthropological turn" demanded that man turn away from speculative ideas, projections, and illusory constructions of thought in order to comprehend and reform the real conditions of human existence. Not the necessary and a priori preconditions of thought but the actual conditions of life became the prime concern of the Left Hegelians. They held that nature is the ground of man: the purely ideal or divine is opposed to man and, indeed, represents his self-alienation.

The Hegelian Left rejected Hegel's panlogical idealism and called for sober "realism" and the relentless demystification of the world. The primarily retrospective character of Hegel's thought was given a forward-looking orientation. Philosophy was reconceived as "transformative criticism" rather than docile accommodation to existing conditions. For these thinkers the real was not yet rationalized and the rational was not yet realized. Hegel's high-handed obfuscation of concrete reality had allowed him to postulate a premature identity of reason and reality. For these thinkers, genuine philosophizing was not the conjuring of eternal forms and absolute concepts, a means of reconciling the mind to reality, but as Marx put it in the last of his celebrated "Theses on Feuerbach," a means of

changing reality. Not contemplation and recollection, but active reformation and revolution became the keynotes of the new philosophy. True
dialectic—based upon the real conditions of man's existence—would culminate in the "realization" of philosophy; its disappearance in a fully
reformed reality rather than the disappearance of reality in the mists of
idealist philosophy.

These radical critics saw idealism as a thinly disguised form of Platonic-
Christian otherworldliness and a compulsion to look beyond man for the
sources of his meaning. Idealism was not the overcoming of the mind's self-
estrangement but its final expression, for idealism put man's essence outside
himself and beyond his own powers. It subordinated man to an idealized
construct of his own making, while reducing concrete existence to nothing
but a coarse reflection of divine mind. Idealism insisted that thought is the
"subject" and existence is the "predicate," whereas in reality things go just
the other way around; idealism bewitched the mind into acquiescing in an
inverted world.

By means of their "transformative method" the Left Hegelians claimed to
have set things aright by putting reality ahead (or "afoot") of thought,
standing philosophy on its feet instead of its head. Man thereby became the
"true subject" of philosophy, which is to say both the subject and the object
of thought rather than the mere vessel of divine thought. Man must
"reappropriate" himself by focusing upon his own concrete and embodied
existence. The mind and its ideas derive from the material world and man's
sensual nature. Thought does not generate reality; rather, reality generates
thought. The "subject" of the Left Hegelians was the concrete man of flesh
and blood, with needs, desires, and a body. The anthropological turn had,
in Bruno Bauer's words, "discovered man" by disengaging him from the
vaporous reveries of idealism. Not "ideal man" but "real man" or "natural
man" constituted both the point of departure and the destination of their
philosophical endeavors.

By many of their contemporaries the Left Hegelians were regarded as
sensualists and materialists. Nevertheless, their thought retained strong
idealist and voluntarist motifs in the form of the dialectic of consciousness.
Matter per se was not appointed the sole principle of reality, but was
conceived in a dialectical relation with human consciousness and the
transforming power of human action. Thus, although they revolted against
idealism, they still retained many of its premises—and, one might add,
many of its conclusions.

It was not long, however, before a school of nondialectical, mechanistic
or "scientific" materialism arose in Germany which simply dispensed with
mind altogether and reduced it to a composite of physical forces. This
development occurred after mid-century and will be treated later. Here it is
important to stress that the "anthropological turn" showed a tendency to
jettison consciousness and to pass into a crude "mindless" naturalism.

Dilthey could sympathize with the anthropological turn, but adamantly rejected its later extension. The same urge to concreteness informed his own thought, but he was not willing to identify concrete reality with "matter" or "nature" and separate it so drastically from the mental. His thought has a similar "anthropological" point of departure but he did not see such a departure as leading toward materialism.

A quite different turn of mind, which was also in part a reaction to idealism and yet perpetuated many of its premises, took place not in philosophy but in the field of historical study. It is often pointed out that the spirit of idealism lived on in the field of historical study long after it had been driven out of the principal position in philosophy. Indeed, one can speak of a form of "nonphilosophical" idealism suffusing the practice of historical writing in this period. The German Historical School of Barthold Niebuhr, Friedrich von Savigny, and Leopold von Ranke grew up in Berlin in opposition to the "Philosophical School" of orthodox Hegelians. Distrustful of all abstract and deductive frameworks, the Historical School resisted the wholesale importation of any system of rationalist *Geistesphilosophie* into the province of historical study. Although the Historical School repudiated the effort to force history into ideal forms and dialectical schemata, it conceived its own unique immanent *Ideenlehre* which incorporated many tenets of the idealist world-view. It was a latent or immanent idealism of historical "forces" rather than an explicit, conceptual idealism. The power of spirit manifested itself not in the constitution of a higher world of abstract forms and ideas but in the concrete world of particular historical events, individualities, personalities, and states. Instead of the rational system of Hegelian philosophy, the Historical School held to a belief in the dynamic plenitude of ideal forces in history. While protesting against systematic idealism in the name of historical science, the Historical School was allied with the Philosophical School in affirming a transcendent reality behind existing historical phenomena.

The views of Ranke were of particular significance in this regard. Ranke's idea of *Wissenschaft* owed much to the "poetic idealism" of Goethe and Schelling discussed earlier. Resisting the Hegelian mania for systematic, rational synthesis, Ranke distinguished sharply between history and philosophy. He assigned to each a distinctive way of knowing reality: philosophy proceeds by way of abstractions and conceptual reflection, whereas history advances through the careful investigation of particulars. Ranke regarded all "philosophy of history" as a blatant contradiction in terms. True philosophy and true history are distinct and can never come into conflict with each other. Ranke and his followers emphatically rejected any attempt at a speculative construction of history in the fashion of the Hegelians. Such "history a priori" was a rash and foolish intellectual monstrosity (*Unbegriff*).

The Historical School rejected not only abstraction but tended to be suspicious of theory as such. In his revealing and important short essay "On the Influence of Theory" (1832), Ranke expressed Goethe's view that all theory is marked by a hopelessly rationalistic bias which seduces its adherents into attempting to infer all reality from a set of first principles. Such attempts are bound to culminate in sterile illusions. Invoking the argument of the romantics and Goethe against all *raisonnement*, Ranke insisted that rational theory cannot produce or grasp the living reality. All theory is "gray"—deductive and purely formal—and therefore misses the vital center of things. Ranke averred that grammar cannot produce a language, aesthetics cannot produce poetry, and political science cannot produce a state. In sum, "theory" can be intellectually satisfying but the philosophical habit of mongering abstractions cannot account for the concrete phenomenon. Ranke affirmed the existence of a mysterious indwelling and inexplicable power present in every living reality and beyond the grasp of theory.[40] This power is ideal but not subject to rational conceptualization. In Ranke's historical studies the ideal power manifests itself in the particular phenomena of history—historic individuals, religious movements, and especially the "great powers," or European states contesting with each other in fulfillment of their intrinsic mission. No single mind or systematic formulation can encompass the manifestations of this ideal-power which is constantly displaying itself in particular individualities.

In this unsystematic and historicized *Ideenlehre*, spirit is present in each and every historical appearance. Like the "anthropological turn" of the Left Hegelians, the "historical turn" of the Historical School tended to collapse the distinction between essence and existence and bring the power of the transcendental down into the process of historical becoming. The historians affirmed that the nature of any particular phenomenon was entirely comprehended in its development. Development was taken to be the expression of the ideal, and each stage of history was to be judged by its own intrinsic norm. One might speak of an individualizing, "distributive" idealism in the work of the Historical School. Their aim lay not in comprehending diversity in a rational, conceptual totality, but rather in the devoted depiction of the constant evolution of ever-varied forms of individuality. No absolute criterion of rationality could be enunciated, for truth was immanent in every particular manifestation.

Rejecting both speculative and moralizing treatments of history, Ranke set down the task of history as showing "merely how it actually happened." When the Hegelian Heinrich Leo accused Ranke of a "barren empiricism" devoid of broader synthetic and speculative judgments, Ranke responded: "For our part, we have a different concept of history: the bare truth without any decking out in jewels—fundamental research into particulars, leaving the rest to God."[41] Such a modest conception of history sounded unpretentious indeed beside the philosophical claim that history was essentially the march of reason, the record of Providence, or the story of the moral betterment of mankind. But beyond this repudiation of "constructed" or "deductive" history lay the assumption that history embodied ideal forces. The "bare facts" of history reflected the ideas of spirit not in an explicit schematic and logical fashion but in an implicit and suffused form. The fastidious attention to particulars expressed the larger conviction that they manifested some portion of ideal or divine reality. Ranke, indeed, regarded the writing of history as "holy work" and likened the role of the historian to that of the priest.

Insofar as it could be said to hold to an explicit cognitive procedure, the Historical School favored the technique of "immediate intuition" invoked by Herder, Goethe, Wilhelm von Humboldt, and Schelling. Hegel had mocked this mode of thinking as logically indefensible and mired down in particulars, but what was for Hegel an offense to reason was a virtue for the Historical School. By means of an unmediated intuition of particulars, thought came into direct apprehension of the individual phenomenon without reducing it to a mere referent of some higher being or transitory stage in an overarching logical or ethical process. Ranke excoriated all higher judgment and mediation (*mediatisieren*) as implicitly reductive, and preached the "pure seeing of things" without praise or blame. Such pure seeing is possible "only if one evaluates everything according to its own standpoint and its own indwelling tendency" (quoted by Dilthey, *GS* 11:124). Thought must sympathetically "enter into" historical life and reality, not merely deduce it from a priori grounds.

The plastic, immanent idealism of the Historical School posited the individual as a self-contained and self-justifying whole. Ranke's celebrated saying, "each epoch is immediate to God," proscribed the subordination of the phenomena of history to any higher criterion or larger design, whether rational or ethical. General truth is apprehended directly in particulars without mediation. "Life carries its ideal in itself."[42]

By stressing the intuition of concrete particulars, the Historical School tended to bring history into close proximity to aesthetic appreciation. The rejection of all traces of moralism and rationalist construction (*Machen*) impelled the Historical School in the direction of a contemplative aestheticism. Reverential appreciation for each individual phenomenon in its own terms reflected a traditionalist spirit which was part of a larger political and cultural conservatism.[43]

Although he was more sympathetic to the immanent idealism of the Historical School than to the absolute idealism of the Philosophical School, Dilthey nevertheless found much to criticize in the assumptions and methods of Ranke and his followers. His attitude toward them was as double-edged as his regard for the older tradition of *Geistesphilosophie*. On the one hand, he felt an enormous debt to the Historical School for accomplishing the emancipation of history from metaphysics, moral philosophy, and the stranglehold of a priori abstraction. It had instilled a strong sense for concrete particulars and individualities in the study of the human world. It had contributed to the discovery of man as "an essentially historical being" (JD 124). But, on the other hand, the history of the Historical School, in eschewing all philosophy, theory, and conceptual formulation, threatened to become merely the barren narration of particulars; the "urge to the concrete" could easily degenerate into merely random recitation of surface detail devoid of general understanding.

Dilthey deplored the absence of a critical sense of method on the part of the Historical School; its indifference to epistemology and psychology—to theory, in short—was a serious failing. Fact-gathering and antiquarianism were at odds with Dilthey's conception of history with philosophical intent. Moreover, their manner of writing history was too narrowly political: it neglected the intellectual and cultural movements in history and their concrete setting.

Dilthey found that the Historical School promoted an attitude toward history which was "ocular" and aesthetic. Echoing certain of the objections brought by the Prussian School against Ranke's "anemic objectivity," Dilthey characterized Ranke as "all eye." "Ocularism" mirrored everything in faithful detail but became lost in the sheer contemplation of variety. History became an aesthetic spectacle and ceased to be a form of vital instruction, as it had been for the Enlightenment. Dilthey observed that the opposing positions of Schlosser and Ranke dominated the historical controversies of his formative period. He praised Schlosser's "enlightened" view, which kept history in close touch with ethical philosophy and regarded it as a means of practical instruction. The "ocular" and exclusively political method of the Historical School could not provide this guidance. It glided over the surface of things without digging down into deeper causal relations. Ranke's ideal of extinguishing himself in order to attain an Olympian conspectus culminated in a neutral, contemplative serenity which robbed history of its meaning for life.

It is interesting to note that Dilthey brought some of the same objections against the cultural history of Jacob Burckhardt: "He wanders through the world as though it were a museum."[44] While Burckhardt offered a corrective to the political emphasis of the Historical School, he neglected actual causal relations in history, merely grouping broad mental traits under general headings. For Dilthey such an approach had more artistic than scientific application. Burckhardt's cultural history lacked both empirical specificity and theoretical foundations; it sometimes became an arbitrary game with general concepts, unwittingly akin to Hegel. Dilthey alleged that Burckhardt's treatment of relationships in history was not probing and specific: his broad characterizations could apply equally well to other periods (*GS* 11:70–76).

In the field of philosophy proper, the most influential critique of idealism came from Friedrich Adolf Trendelenburg (1802–70), Dilthey's teacher and later friend. This important but neglected thinker dominated German academic philosophy after Hegel. Dilthey was but one of a distinguished group of thinkers, including Kierkegaard, Franz Brentano, Gustav Teichmüller, and Otto Wilmann, who credited Trendelenburg with "the greatest influence" over their thought (*GS* 5:7). Trendelenburg's *Idealrealismus* incorporated certain tenets of the Historical School, but it rested upon more critical theories of method and of knowledge. In many respects Trendelenburg might be called a more empirical Schleiermacher.

With his basic loyalty to Aristotle, Trendelenburg drew selectively on Kant and Hegel, but remained highly critical of both. He did much to destroy the philosophical hegemony of Hegel through his *Logische Untersuchungen* (1840), a devastating attack on speculative dialectics. In contrast to the idealist deprecation of experience, Trendelenburg based all thought and knowledge upon a self-correcting, open "Empirie" which he termed "the great teacher of humanity." Trendelenburg's notion of experience, however, stressed integration and anticipation rather than mere passive receptivity to sense impressions from the given. He insisted that philosophy must renounce closed systems and concern itself with "careful study of particulars" before flying off to the "totality" which can only be approached indirectly and progressively through experience.[45]

Like his teacher, Schleiermacher, Trendelenburg called for an "authentic fusion" of realism and idealism into what he called "transcendental realism" or "empirical idealism"; a realism which cannot issue in materialism because it takes seriously the constitutive role of consciousness and an idealism which cannot issue in subjectivism because it refers thought to a real "given." Trendelenburg protested against the rigid and artificial separation of thought and its object, which is the beginning of all strictly formal logic, but he also rejected Hegel's dialectical logic: "There is for us humans no pure thought. . . . Thought would kill itself, if it tried to divest itself of concrete perception."[46] Knowledge for Trendelenburg is always of something existing (*Seiendes*), but existing primarily in the sense of the ongoing historical process of articulate human experience. What exists in experience is disclosed in language, whose grammar constitutes a kind of "deeper logic." Trendelenburg regarded grammar and logic as "twins" which reciprocally learn from each other. From his insistence upon the open, ongoing nature of perception Trendelenburg was moved to assert that "all knowledge is interpretation, be it of the spoken word or of the meaningful phenomenon itself."[47]

Trendelenburg's *Idealrealismus* was rooted in the concepts of "life" and "becoming." As with the Left Hegelians, life was given epistemological priority over pure thought. Mind was conceived not as a realm unto itself separated from nature; it was continuous with nature but not identical to it. Trendelenburg rejected both the formal, static divisions in Kant and the mania for dialectical system in Hegel. He proposed to incorporate the concrete processes of both nature and history into a broad philosophy which he termed the "organic world-view" based upon the Aristotelian notion of entelechy. This world-view was to be teleological and holistic without falling prey to either irrationalism or self-enclosed systems. Philosophy, in Trendelenburg's view, had to concern itself not only with the critique of method, but also with a view of the continuous development of reality, including the history of man's attempt to grasp that reality. *Wissenschaft* could not be totally divorced from *Weltanschauung*; thought and being-as-becoming, mind and nature, science and world-view were conceived as continuous, not mutually exclusive.

Trendelenburg's stress upon concrete experience and the intensive study of past thought earned him the somewhat paradoxical title of "philosopher of the Historical School." He stressed purposeful becoming without crushing it into the confines of rationalist dialectic and he likewise protested the hypostatization of concepts and categories into eternal essences. For Trendelenburg something was understood only by knowing how it came into being; this genetic approach applied to philosophic thought as well as other natural and mental phenomena. A purely formal and static analysis of thought in the manner of Kant missed the origin and content of thought and created the illusion of a self-sufficient realm of pure thinking. Thought for Trendelenburg was functional, not purely "ideal." It exists only and always in relation to the world around it. From these premises Trendelenburg argued that philosophy must keep pace with the sciences and receive content from them; it cannot presume to lord it over the particular sciences and claim the right to dictate their method. By its very nature philosophy is relative, not absolute, knowledge. Trendelenburg did not, however, dissolve philosophy into plain history of ideas or the theory of the positive sciences. He was acutely sensitive to the genetic fallacy and denied that thought could be reduced to genetic causes—whether historical, biological, or psychological. His stress upon genesis and history was still far removed from a sheer historicism, and his functionalism retained transcendental elements which kept it from psychological reductionism.

The deep impact of Trendelenburg's thought upon Dilthey can be gleaned from Dilthey's own testimony. These declarations assume particular weight in light of the fact that Dilthey rarely made unqualified statements about the influence of others upon his own thought. Trendelenburg's functional and developmental approach to thought, his hostility to system-mongering, his stress upon life and becoming, his notion of the adaptive relativity of concepts and the reciprocal relation of philosophy and the sciences—all these factors made a lasting impression upon Dilthey and can be traced in his writings. Indeed, D. F. Strauss criticized Dilthey's treatment of Schleiermacher as being "too much in the spirit of Trendelenburg" (see *BDY* 242). For all his indebtedness to Trendelenburg, however, Dilthey desired to treat mental life in rather more historical and less biological terms than his teacher. In this respect Dilthey remained closer to the transcendental position and the immanent idealism of the Historical School. Up to his death in 1870 Trendelenburg remained opposed to the idealist monism of Hegel and the newer materialist monisms of the decades after mid-century. But like so many positions of the middle (including Dilthey's), Trendelenburg's thought proved to be doubly assailable, and it was frequently portrayed as a transition to the very naturalism he rejected. Such a rendering of his thought showed that on several fronts the decisive breach had been opened to a full-scale attempt at the "naturalization" of mind.

To those who brooked no compromise with new developments, the essential direction and continuity of German intellectual tradition appeared to be breaking up by mid-century. Many German intellectuals regarded the newer currents of thought as parlous and negative. By many accounts the period after 1830 was an age of *"Epigonentum"*—lackluster and derivative thought, living parasitically from the intellectual store of the past. Karl Rosenkranz, a prominent member of the Hegelian Right, prophesied at mid-century that the thinkers of the second half of the century were destined to be merely the "gravediggers and monument builders" for the great minds of the first half of the century. He posed the question whether Germany could ever again produce luminaries equal to those of the past, and concluded that "the talents of our own day do not seem capable of enduring."[48] The waning of idealism brought pronouncements of despair from other quarters as well. Burckhardt found that after 1830 the world had grown woefully "commoner." The philosopher and critic Henri-Frederic Amiel expressed the apprehension of many persons at mid-century:

> The old generation is passing. What will the new one give us? What will we give? Who is preparing himself to bear what is to come? Who among the dwarfs of the present are to be the giants of the future, the heroes of the second half of the century?[49]

Some took a very dim view of the imminent triumph of the positive sciences. Dilthey's teacher, August Boeckh, was notoriously exacting in philological method and a declared enemy of speculation, but he bitterly lamented the decline of philosophical spirit:

> Today many people take joy in what they see as the waning of philosophy and are jubilant that philosophy will soon be carried to its

grave: for me that means nothing other than taking delight in the fact that the light of the world will soon be put out.[50]

These Cassandra-like pronouncements of the impending end of great cultural accomplishments were foreign to Dilthey's mentality. Writing in the mid-1860s to counter the charge of sterile derivativeness, he observed of his generation:

> We are most certainly not the epigones of that great period, as is sometimes alleged, rather our gaze is fixed steadfastly toward the future, toward the colossal intellectual, political, and social events toward which everything is tending [JD 195].

A "philosophical restoration" or slavish imitation of the world-view of transcendental idealism was impossible; indeed, Dilthey specifically warned against the dangers of such backward-looking nostalgia:

> The rare and extraordinary appearances in the life of a people must be taken as a means of inspiration and incitement; they cannot, however, be imitated in detail, since in the light of the irremediable difference between times and conditions, such an attitude easily produces the very opposite of what was intended [WM 19(1865):256].

He cautioned further that "every epoch in the life of a people which cannot create out of itself and would rather live on the capital of a previous one is weak." The grand idealist world-view had served its function for its time and had provided unparalleled insights into man and his works. It had enriched all disciplines and facets of life. But a restitution of idealism was pointless and ill-taken, for changing times had brought new realities which the older idealism could not comprehend. In a review written in 1862, Dilthey noted the change in conditions:

> In the past half-century philosophy was like a powerful river which flowed over its banks and inundated the ground assigned to the empirical sciences; that river has now receded and has left the soil deeply enriched, so that the cultivation of it is doubly productive. This is especially true of the historical sciences [GS 16:396].

Intellectual Foreground, 1850–1900: The Naturalization of Spirit

Part One: Materialism and Positivism, 1850–75

In a thematic outline prepared originally in the late 1860s (and thereafter revised) for his general course in modern philosophy, Dilthey summarized the intellectual situation of the latter half of the century:

> The function of the philosophical spirit to guide life has moved from the

grand metaphysical systems to the work of positive investigation. Since the middle of the nineteenth century, various factors have led to the extraordinary decline in the influence of systematic philosophy on the sciences, literature, religious life, and politics. The struggles since 1848 for popular freedom, the consolidation of the nation-states of Germany and Italy, the rapid economic development and corresponding shift in the power of the classes, and finally international politics—these all have caused the interest in abstract speculation to diminish.[51]

The third quarter of the century witnessed vigorous reactions against the idealist synthesis which predominated in the earlier half. These currents were considerably more thorough in rooting out the last traces of idealism than those discussed previously. Hegel was said to be a "dead dog" and all traces of "Hegelei" were regarded with suspicion or contempt. The whole legacy of transcendental idealism was execrated as a futile excursus outside the real world. Idealism—even philosophy itself—was considered to be in hopeless contradiction with reality and the results of science. Kant was revived in a fashion conforming to the advances of the positive sciences; initially it was a "positivized" Kant who made an appearance in the neo-Kantian movement of the 1860s and 1870s. The great task of the new era was seen as the direction of practical affairs and the attainment of a new "realism" in place of the contemplative stance of "the age of poets and philosophers." Dilthey noted that "a new breed grew up which was in danger of losing touch with the great thinkers and poets of the past" (*GS* 9:234–35). G. S. Hall, who was to rank as the most famous American philosopher-psychologist after William James, observed in 1881 that "the old idealism is gone" and that philosophy had reached its "lowest ebb" in Germany.[52]

The transition from the age of poetry and speculation to that of science and practical realism was rapid and unsettling. A splintering of cultural life followed upon the demise of the great idealist systems. Karl Löwith has seen a true intellectual revolution in this period—one more portentous than the political revolutions of the time. Erich Rothacker isolates a "great turn" in the years after mid-century, as consideration of real particulars was substituted for the contemplation of ideal-universals.[53] Previous concern with the spiritual life of the "inner man" was replaced by concentration upon exact knowledge of the external world. *Realpolitik* in statecraft was but one aspect of a general reorientation toward the "real" and the "positive." Dilthey observed that the dominant thinkers after mid-century were "ruled by a spirit of a different time":

The philosophy of experience, as formulated by the French and English, was impressed upon them by Comte, Mill, and Buckle, and from this philosophy they formed their convictions. The rising natural sciences demanded close attention, if one wanted to arrive at sure results [*GS* 11:243].

The only real knowledge was conceived to be rigorously scientific knowledge. Previous claims for speculative knowledge, intuitive knowledge, poetic knowledge, and knowledge of faith were seen as riddled with contradictions. A reversal had taken place in the structure of the disciplines: whereas previously an overarching philosophical synthesis took precedence over the individual sciences, now the positive sciences relegated philosophy to a tenuous position of isolation and defensiveness. The opinion was widely voiced that philosophy was impotent and even superfluous. Some, like Dilthey and the other "ideal realists," looked forward to a rebirth of philosophy through cooperation with the positive sciences and acceptance of their results. Others anticipated the imminent extinction of philosophy, viewing it as premature speculation upon subjects which had not yet found a truly scientific basis. Philosophy would be revealed as a merely temporary historical episode in the march of scientific progress. A small embattled minority predicated the survival of philosophy on intransigent opposition to all the "little truths" of the particular sciences, demanding that philosophy continue in the grand tradition of metaphysics. Altogether it was widely conceded that the dominant task of German thought in the latter half of the century was to relate philosophy and the sciences to each other. But the precise nature of this relation was a very tendentious matter.

Dilthey was deeply involved in this intellectual transformation. As a student writing in the 1860s, he observed that "no stronger character is impressed upon our epoch than the interpenetration of philosophy and the empirical sciences" (*JD* 82). He affirmed that philosophy could no longer remain sublimely indifferent to the results of these sciences. He declared pointedly: "Thought is fruitful only when it is based upon the investigation of some aspect of the real" (*JD* 36). Writing exuberantly in 1865, he welcomed the empirical realism of science and the scientific spirit: "We know that the future belongs to it. We know that it is destined to change the world" (*ED* 219).

When Dilthey wrote these words, science had already done much to change the world and man's view of it. The general shift toward empiricism and realism in German thought in the years around mid-century stemmed in large part from the spectacular accomplishments of the natural sciences. To many it appeared that Hegel's confident assertion that "the real is the rational" was in fact capable of imminent realization—not through the perambulations of idealist dialectic or pure thought, but by means of the discovery of the incontrovertible laws of nature. Immense technical advances followed upon the exact formulation of the basic structures and laws of matter and natural reality. In 1842 Robert Mayer conceived the initial statement of the law of the conservation of energy. Over the next two decades it was established as a working principle in all fields of physics through the efforts of Hermann von Helmholtz and James Joule; it was further extended to the treatment of organic, living systems as well as physical matter. In chemistry the pioneering work of Justus von Liebig in organic and inorganic compounds was carried further by a distinguished group of disciples. Liebig and his followers called for an unswervingly empirical and experimental method, branding philosophical speculation as the arch-enemy of science and the "curse of the century."

Life itself was drawn into the domain of strictly scientific and experimental techniques. The artificial synthesis of urea in 1828 had laid a bridge between the inorganic and organic realms and the way appeared open to a purely chemical explanation of living matter. The cellular theory of plants was formulated by Schwann in 1838 and was immediately extended to animal tissue by Schleiden. A great advance in the analysis of all forms of matter came with the invention of spectroscopy by Gustav Kirchhoff. Johannes Müller brought the results of both the new chemistry and physics to bear on the problems of biology and carried out extensive microscopic studies of tissues and organs. A growing number of researchers arrived at the conclusion that all forms of life, including mental life, could be treated according to the laws of matter and energy. After his enormous discoveries in pathology, the crusading scientist-physician Rudolf Virchow came to the conclusion that "life is only a special form of mechanics, but, to be sure, one of the most complicated of that form." It was not a far step to the conclusion that the sphere of *Geist* itself, previously conceived as ideal and transcendental, was fully susceptible of empirical, scientific treatment.

In the 1840s the philosopher Hermann Lotze called for a strictly mechanistic treatment of organic processes, though he did not extend these processes to include the work of the mind and its products. But to many it appeared as if all processes of life, including the higher operations of thought itself, could be subjected to exact quantitative formulation. The laws of mechanics and the principle of the conservation of energy had established that there is only transformation, never creation, in the fixed quantum of force and matter. A constant quantitative relation was shown to exist between the antecedent cause and the effect which follows it. Holding to strictly scientific premises, the famous naturalist Alexander von Humboldt undertook in his *Kosmos* (1845) to describe the entire universe. This work proved to be immensely popular; in many different editions and translations, it was more widely read in Germany than any other book except the Bible. It initiated a new genre of popular scientific writing concerned with establishing a strictly scientific view of the world.

Although the active researchers in the new sciences generally pronounced themselves opposed to a materialistic rendering of their work—or any extension to an all-encompassing world-view—philosophies of mechanistic materialism enjoyed a remarkable vogue in the decade after mid-century. As Dilthey noted at the time in a review, materialism seemed to many persons simply the logical extension and "last word" of science (WM 41[1877]:548). Within the short space of several years, materialist tracts were published by Jacob Moleschott, Ludwig Büchner, Karl Vogt, and Heinrich Czolbe. Their works went through many editions and like Humboldt's were among the most widely read nonfiction books of the century. These materialists insisted that their position was merely the "consistent consequence" of the results of the sciences; theirs was not merely a "philosophical" materialism but a truly "scientific" materialism.

Moleschott attempted to show in his treatise Der Kreislauf des Lebens (1852) that biological and social life evince a constant circulation of matter and motion. The two forms of matter and energy account for all being possible in the world. The explanation for human behavior falls entirely under the concepts and methods of chemistry and physics. Even human thought can be resolved into the mechanical action of particles of matter. Such was the meaning of Moleschott's famous utterance: "Where there is not phosphorous, there is no thought." Three years after Moleschott's work, Büchner published Kraft und Stoff, which was termed the bible of German materialism. The author held that energy and matter stand in a fixed and necessary relationship. The inevitable corollary of this law was that mind is only a subsidiary product and property of matter. Just as the steam engine produces motion, so the organism produces a sum total of motion-like effects which have been subsumed under what were for Büchner the "quaintly anthropomorphic" categories of "mind," "soul," and "thought." Vogt came to similar conclusions from the basic premise that "all is matter and nothing but matter." The brain is the organ of consciousness and must be investigated like every other physical organ. In a formula reminiscent of the French materialism of the late eighteenth century, Vogt asserted that thought is a secretion of the brain just as gall is a product of the liver and urine a product of the kidneys.

In such dogmatic and uncompromising formulations, German materialism proved rather ephemeral. But it too underwent a process of internal transformation and modification just as the idealism of a half-century before. Under the impact of Darwin's evolutionary doctrine, scientific and philosophical thought seemed jointly to issue in an all-embracing naturalism, a kind of inverted image of Hegel's idealism. Dilthey testified in a review of 1877 to the immense impact of the Darwinian theory:

> Interest in Darwin outweighs everything else in the natural sciences. His hypothesis and its mode of generalization is a notable example of the way in which an *apercu* developed within the confines of a particular positive

science comes to condition the general intellectual orientation of an entire epoch [*WM* 40(1877):553].

The passage from Darwin's own cautious formulations to a full-fledged "Darwinism" was accomplished in many quarters, but nowhere more sweepingly than in Germany. Science appeared on the verge of the total explanation of things previously claimed by absolute idealism. Emerging in the 1860s and 1870s, Ernst Haeckel's evolutionary monism was to become the most influential statement of what Dilthey meant by a "general intellectual orientation." As Fichte had stood to Kant, so Haeckel believed that he was merely carrying Darwin's doctrines to their final and proper conclusion, thus realizing in a total cosmological scheme Darwin's own earlier prophecy that his theory would someday lead to a "complete philosophy." Haeckel's vast extrapolation of the evolutionary hypothesis filled Darwin with doubts, however, and he was moved to write to Haeckel: "Your boldness sometimes makes me tremble."[54]

Undaunted, Haeckel continued to insist upon drawing universal implications from Darwin. He avowed that Darwin had accomplished a "Copernican revolution" in science which removed the last traces of anthropomorphism and opened the way to a truly universal point of view. *Wissenschaft* culminated naturally in a total and conclusive *Weltanschauung*. In his crowning work *Die Welträtsel* (1899), Haeckel announced that the nineteenth century should be rechristened "the century of natural science," since the key to the riddle of the universe was now available:

> Evolution is henceforth the magic word by which we shall solve all the riddles that surround us, or at least be set on the road to their solution. But how few persons have really understood this password and to how few has its world-transforming meaning become clear![55]

Inclusiveness and uniformity of explanation, not exactness, were the keynotes of Haeckel's universal science. He worked from the basic "fact" that there is but one evolving substance in the universe and that this undergoes constant transformation according to strict causal necessity: "The great abstract law of causality now rules the entire universe—as it does the mind of man."[56] Haeckel avoided the charge of materialism leveled at Büchner and others by specifying that this single "world-substance" transcended the old dualism of matter and mind. His bold formulations attracted a significant number of followers that grouped together in the "Monistenbund." This movement was dedicated to the extirpation of all "anthropomorphic" and "spiritualist" traces from science and philosophy and to the propagation of evolutionary monism into every discipline. Hegel's emergent idealist monism had found its naturalistic antithesis.

A congeries of mechanistic, naturalistic, and evolutionary assumptions found their way into practically all the disciplines and sciences after mid-century. The swelling tide of Darwinism in the '60s and '70s even exceeded the impact of Hegelianism in the '20s and '30s. Psychology, anthropology, economics, geography, philology, ethical philosophy, and even episte-mology were remodeled on Darwinian lines. The idea of natural evolution came to dominate the thought of the later nineteenth century in a way comparable to the fascination exerted by classical mechanics in the seven-teenth century.

With evolutionary assumptions in mind, researchers pointed to the similarities between human reasoning and analogous processes in animals. The gulf which had been posited between the human mind and the brain of animals was bridged by wholly naturalistic theories of mental activity. Man was no longer to be conceived as a special creation, but part of the whole of evolving nature. Mind was but an epiphenomenon of nature, and human history was a tiny fraction of a larger natural history. Claims to the contrary were likely to be dismissed as vestigial "anthropomorphism," "idealism," or "intuitionism." In a short article of 1862 Dilthey summarized neatly the results of science in this period:

> Two general characteristics determine modern science: an infinite rich-ness of facts and the tendency to elevate the strictly natural and creaturely side of man over the moral side and to elevate necessity over freedom [GS 16:16].

The cruder forms of naturalism tended to coalesce and draw support from the philosophies of positivism and empiricism which gained ground throughout Europe after mid-century.[57] Both positions aspired to be strictly "realistic" and scientific in their approach, dispensing with all unobserv-ables and fictive "mentalistic" or metaphysical entities. Unlike the material-ists and monists, the positivists and empiricists tried to restrict their inquiry to questions concerning knowledge, rather than the nature of being. Kant, or aspects of Kant, proved to be of considerable support in this effort. But however ardently they desired to stay wholly within the realm of certain knowledge, both positivism and empiricism tended to assume the character of total explanations of the world—a peculiar sort of metaphysics modelled on physics.

Nineteenth-century positivism was an extremely complex movement with many internal variables and diverse manifestations. Its actual roots lie in the work of Auguste Comte in the earlier half of the century, but since its widest effects were not felt in Germany until after mid-century, it is discussed here along with the other movements with which it tended to coalesce. The chief impulse in positivism was the reformation of all branches of knowledge in conformity to the models of natural science. Positivism stipulated a rigorously scientific explanation of phenomena along lines defined by the physical sciences. An accompanying demand was for the final obliteration of all fictitious or "negative" philosophical speculation and concepts in order to pave the way for the practical reform of the world through truly scientific and "positive" knowledge. The means to this reform lay in a new conception of the order and development of the sciences. The hierarchy and structure of the sciences propounded by the positivists drew the human mind and human existence into an order of laws in the manner of physical laws.

The French philosopher Auguste Comte (1798–1857) had set down the principles of positivism in a series of immense volumes. He provided both a historical and logical treatment of the existing sciences which envisioned them leading up to a "final science." Comte believed that he had discovered the basic law governing the evolution of the human mind and of the sciences which it conceives on the way: the law of the three stages. These stages referred to both a logical and chronological order and actually designated distinct steps in the evolution of reason. In the "theological" stage, the mind is under the spell of supernatural beings and spirits and the world is explained in terms of the will of anthropomorphic gods and forces. In the "metaphysical" stage, conceptual abstractions are substituted for animistic beings, but these abstract concepts are merely fictional inventions and wishful projections. In the third stage of "positive knowledge," man recognizes that metaphysical knowledge is impossible and that the only truth is knowledge of the necessary laws of phenomena. This stage puts man fully in control of nature and his own social milieu by replacing fictional constructs with positive laws. Science leads to prediction and prediction to control, as celebrated in the positivist maxim: *Savoir pour prévoir, prévoir pour pouvoir.*

Overturning the ancient hierarchy of the sciences which culminated in metaphysics, Comte worked out an "encyclopedia" of the sciences crowned by the new discipline of "sociology." This final positive science was based upon the laws of human behavior and was to guide men toward the attainment of a perfectly scientific society or "sociocracy." The science of sociology achieved "positively" what negative metaphysics could only hope for in vain: ultimate and final knowledge.

Although Comte asserted that there are different sciences for different orders of objects, he insisted that there could be no independent and special science of the individual mind such as psychology. The subject matter traditionally conceived as psychology was apportioned between physiology and the new discipline of sociology. Comte never wavered from the conviction that the mind can discover its own laws only by modeling itself after the physical sciences. Introspection and self-intuition were barred as methods of inquiry because, in Comte's view, psychical phenomena cannot be enacted and observed at the same time and in the same act. Self-observation is an illusion. Not internal states of mind but the positive laws of behavior must be the objects of study, and these are gained only through studying the individual in the complex of his social relations.

Despite its hostility to philosophical constructions and its veneration for the factual, Comtean positivism was rather constructivist in its view of scientific method. Comte attacked both philosophical speculation and the sort of "trifling empiricism" which concerned itself with mere details. He drew a very crucial if cloudy distinction between particular facts and "general facts," the latter being the real basis for the laws of phenomena. Knowledge may begin in experience or observation, but it must proceed inexorably to the general laws of things. As knowledge advances toward the positive stage, it embodies less of common observation and more of the "general facts" and law-like generalizations of the physical sciences. Laws, not facts, are the ultimate criterion of science, and therefore the science of social reality must resolve its object into social laws. Comte eagerly anticipated the time when actual conditions of life might be contrived in conformity with these necessary laws. Reality and life—individual and social—could be redesigned by science. As in Hegel's system—to which Comte's bears a direct and traceable relation—rational thought would fully comprehend all life and history.

Despite certain eccentricities in Comte's later thought, which by making positivism into a religious cult seemed to bend the "positive" back into the "theological," the general doctrines of positivism spread widely throughout Europe. Gerhard Masur has argued that "in reality his philosophy became the ideology which blanketed most of the Western world in the years between 1850 and 1900."[58] This judgment is perhaps an overstatement, but it is indisputable that influential schools of positivist thought grew up in France and England. In Germany, positivism was never adopted in its unalloyed Comtean form (for one thing, it was branded as too Hegelian!) but in alliance with less constructivist strands of empiricism and naturalism, it joined the challenge to previous tendencies of thought. The refinements of positivism did not alter its basic assumption that the methods of physics could be extended to all ranges of behavior. Of this assumption Dilthey observed scathingly: "Coarse naturalistic metaphysics—that is the real foundation of Comte's sociology" (GS 1:107). Positivism was, in Dilthey's terms, anything but empirical.

Empiricism made its greatest headway in Germany after mid-century with the reception of John Stuart Mill's System of Logic (1843). Mill's work gave a powerful impetus to the hitherto weak cause of empiricism in Germany by putting it on a firm philosophical and logical basis. British empiricism had traditionally disdained abstract, deductive reasoning and demanded that every truth, principle, and demonstration be based upon empirical fact. Useful truths of fact, not comprehensive systems or grandiose world-views, were seen as the proper aim of human inquiry. (Mill, it might be noted, confessed to being nauseated by his reading of Hegel.) To be true and useful, knowledge had to be rooted in common experience and common sense. In his logic, Mill attempted to derive all logical and scientific propositions from observation and inductive generalization rather than from rationalist deduction or intuition. The true path of reason is not the high a priori road or intuition of wholes, but a modest induction which moves from particular to particular. Generalizations and abstractions were seen as merely the conceptual registers of a large number of particular cases. Even the axioms of geometry were shown to rest upon experience and sensory impressions received from the world. Unlike Hume, whose thoroughgoing empiricism landed him in skepticism, Mill was convinced that experience alone was sufficient to provide the grounds for the certainty of all judgments. He deplored reliance upon custom, untested authority, revelation, or intuition. Such nonempirical sources of conviction were merely hiding places for prejudice and unwarranted opinion.

Not unlike Comte's positivism, the ultimate ground for Mill's inductive view of scientific reasoning was the uniformity of nature expressed in the universal validity of the law of natural causation. Causality was seen as the extra-mental extension of the mental laws of association which link the sense data of experience. Mill based the case for scientific empiricism on the regularity of sensation and the fact that such regularity enables the mind to construct a world of "possible sensation" in memory and anticipation. Although critics questioned whether such "possible experience" was actually "real experience" and not a variant of the discredited forms of intuition or deduction, Mill insisted that his theory of knowledge was thoroughly empirical.

Mill's view clashed with both Hegel and Comte in its insistence that logic rested upon psychology: logical principles were conceptual formulations of the psychological laws which regulate the association of sense data. Mill affirmed that no matter how complex the phenomena which occur in the world, the laws of their sequence and coexistence result from the simple relation of their separate elements. Sense experience contains all the possible laws of relation. In the famous sixth book of this *Logic*, Mill called for the extension of inductive method into the realm of the "moral sciences," which had previously been dominated by intuition and deduction. This realm too was ruled by the law of uniform causality. Mill advanced the notion of an empirical psychology which would provide the foundation for an eventual science of man called "ethology." Although Mill rejected Comte's preoccupation with systematization and brusque exclusion of psychology, he conceived a structure for the sciences which was similar to Comtean positivism in carrying the methods and premises of natural science into the realm of mental activity. Although Dilthey shared Mill's dedication to the primacy of concrete experience, he insisted that Mill was still too much under the sway of natural scientific methodology; Mill had discarded Comte's grossest errors, only to retain the more subtle ones (*GS* 1:105).

Beginning in the 1860s a loose amalgam of positivism, naturalism, and empiricism was adopted by most researchers in German science as their programmatic and methodological framework. Previous adherence to the concepts of idealist *Naturphilosophie* seemed as benighted as alchemy. Idealist conceptions were not only excluded from the sphere of natural reality, they were being driven out of the study of human behavior, mental life, and its creations. By the early 1880s—when Dilthey published the *Einleitung*—"the positivist mentality had advanced mightily."[59] The insistence upon the discovery of laws in the realm of human activity and thought became the password of many disciplines. The positivist neo-Kantian Otto Liebmann argued in *Die Klimax der Theorien* (1884) that rational science, as distinguished from "childish superstition," depended upon the universal assumption of a strictly uniform causal nexus underlying all events, whether of the motion of stars and atoms, of the marketplace and exchange rates, of political decisions, ocean currents, or meteorological processes. Liebmann held that all norms and grounds could be resolved into strict causes and that rational science had no place for the problem of freedom.[60] In 1887, Wilhelm Bölsche expostulated on the "natural scientific foundations of poetry" in a book by that title. Similar assumptions pervaded the work of Eugen Dühring, who became a primary polemicist in Germany for a generalized "philosophical positivism." Dühring, like Haeckel, called for the complete eradication of all "mentalistic" presuppositions and the formulation of a true "philosophy of reality" (*Die Wirklich-keitsphilosophie*, 1875) which would constitute a total and exhaustive "world-schematism" free of all anthropomorphic elements. The laws of physical reality and the laws of human thought and action were seen as strictly identical. Such a position impelled Dühring back in the direction of the more simplistic materialism of the 1850s and was to be blisteringly satirized by Friedrich Engels as "vulgar-materialism."

In the name of scientific realism a combination of nominalism and determinism came to dominate the assumptions and methods of many fields of inquiry. The final task of science appeared to be the resolution of the complex patterns of human thought and activity into an order of laws derived from a hard substratum of simple fact. The new disciplines of anthropology, sociology, and physiological psychology applied these assumptions in a particularly uncompromising manner. Dilthey perceptively summarized the core of the positivist and empiricist positions:

> The precondition for a knowledge of the laws of thought and society is the connection of all phenomena according to the principle of causality.

Determinism is for them the necessary presupposition of a science of society. The self-active "I" is for them an illusion of the "intuitive" standpoint [*GS* 4:538–39].

Positivist and empiricist doctrines militated against the conception of any philosophical discipline superior to the existing positive sciences. Not only was metaphysics rejected, but so too was the critical inquiry into the conditions and meaning of knowledge itself. The results of the sciences were seen as "positive" and valid in themselves, needing no larger justification. The theory of knowledge was assigned to scientific psychology for its "definitive" solution. The sciences could be systematized and refined, but they could not be judged, for this implied some set of suprascientific values. Values were regarded simply as "unclarified facts" whose laws of genesis and relation had not yet been discovered. The positivists demanded the exclusion of normative judgments on the grounds that values do not express causal relations and are not a scientific form of judgment. The call for the extinction of all value judgments was reflected in attempts like those of Taine and Bölsche to write theories of art and ethics in which the words "beautiful," "good," and "right" did not appear. All traces of mentalistic "ideality" were to be expunged in deference to the truly "real": the factual and empirical. To the few remaining die-hard idealists it seemed as if the wellsprings of German thought had been poisoned by an unholy alliance of alien and indigenous currents.

It was in this context of a reigning positivism and empiricism that German neo-Kantianism made its appearance in the 1860s and 1870s. As might be expected, neo-Kantianism proved as protean as Kant himself; it was never a unified movement and recapitulated divisions and emphases within Kant's system. Authorities have isolated as many as seven different schools of neo-Kantianism, and each school propounded a substantially different version of the master. It is useful to distinguish between an earlier movement which arose in the 1860s and a later strand which began in the 1870s. Although both shared certain presuppositions, they were considerably different, even antithetical, in orientation. The earlier movement aimed toward accommodating the new results of physics, physiology, biology, and psychology to the general theory of knowledge, whereas the later group repudiated the implicit "naturalism" of their predecessors and came to stress the uniquely transcendental dimension of mind. The first group belongs more in the positivist camp, while the second was self-consciously neo-idealist and will be treated later as part of the reaction to positivism. A word of caution is in order, however: like so many of the intellectual currents of the nineteenth century, the relationship between these two schools was not one of simple antithesis.

The restoration of Kant's critical philosophy was announced from various sides, at first in the name of "realism." At the end of his corrosive study of Hegel (1854), Rudolf Haym called for the resurrection and purification of philosophy after a half-century of idealist speculation through a return to Kant's sober critical mode of thought. The physicist-psychologist Hermann von Helmholtz in the mid-'50s employed Kant's scheme of the forms of intuition to deal with the problems of visual perception. In the early 1860s Kuno Fischer published several works on Kant which attracted the attention of the philosophical community by pointing to Kant's continued relevance. Eduard Zeller provided a powerful impetus to the renewal of concern with the problem of knowledge in his lecture-treatise "Über die Bedeutung und Aufgabe der Erkenntnistheorie" (1862). This treatise was the first to employ explicitly the term "theory of knowledge"; it advanced a cogent argument for instituting this field of inquiry as the exclusive basis for all philosophizing. Philosophy was again admonished to concern itself only with what it can know with certainty, rather than what it might like to know. The full tide of the earlier neo-Kantianism was reached shortly after the publication of Otto Liebmann's *Kant und die Epigonen* (1865), which provided a comprehensive inventory of the fateful errors of post-Kantian speculation. After condemning each successive idealist attempt to pass beyond the certainties of strictly scientific *Verstand*, Liebmann repeated the vigorous exhortation "Back to Kant!"

The initial phase of the neo-Kantian movement tended to interpret Kant's thought in strictly psychological, even physiological, terms, purging it of the speculative extensions which had seemed so "necessary" to the idealists. There were precedents for this psychological reading in the doctrines of the "half-Kantians" Fries and Beneke. Although neo-Kantianism was partly a reaction against an earlier empiricism and positivism, as well as speculative idealism, it tended to continue the very preoccupations against which it was contending. It was in fact a stimulus to the internal revision of positivism and the formation of a critical "neo-positivism." The doctrine of the thing-in-itself, which had spurred the dialectical, intuitive, and speculative methods of the post-Kantians, was discarded as a gratuitous superfluity incompatible with scientific reason: Kantianism was put on a purely phenomenalistic and "positive" basis. The transcendental and quasimetaphysical side of Kantian thought was formulated in strictly psychological terms. Thought was certified as certain knowledge only insofar as it related the materials provided by sensations given to the mind in external experience. The truly "real" was given not in thought but in sensation. The upshot of many of these currents of thought was to underscore the urgent necessity of a truly scientific approach to mind and mental activity. The "science of mind" could no longer be conceived along the lines of Fichte's *Wissenschaftslehre* or the *Dialektik* of Schleiermacher and Hegel, but rather as rigorously empirical psychology.

The nascent discipline of psychology was enormously affected by the programmatic demands of positivism and empiricism. Indeed, it can be said that modern psychology, as opposed to older rationalist psychologies and variants of *Geistesphilosophie*, emerged only with the demand for strictly empirical methods and the discovery of laws of mental activity. From rudimentary and checkered beginnings in Herbart, Fries, and Beneke, German psychology flourished in the years after 1850 as a full-fledged experimental science. It attained independent status and was no longer merely the poor cousin and suppliant of philosophy, theology, or ethics. The critical idealism of Kant and absolute idealism of Hegel had been inhospitable to the very conception of psychology, but after mid-century the tables were turned: psychology tended to dissolve and digest the idealist systems. Borrowing assumptions and methods from the already established natural sciences, the new psychologies tended toward a rather crude physicalism. Yet in much of German psychology of this period, one is confronted by the paradox of a large group of thinkers who adhered to naturalistic and mechanistic premises but who also wanted to stop short of a fully mechanistic model of mental life. Psychologist-philosophers like Gustav Fechner and Hermann Lotze could affirm a strict physicalism and still arrive at a kind of pantheistic spiritualism by a *salto intellectualis*. Thus, Dilthey observed with considerable irony the simultaneous emergence of a school of "psychology without mind" and a school of "doubting and resigned" metaphysicians (*BDY* 20).

Initially this psychology developed under the sway of the physical sciences. Exact physiological research tended to define and dominate the field of psychological inquiry. The higher activities of thought, which in the traditional German philosophy of mind had been consigned to the mysterious realm of the transcendental a priori, were now drawn into an empirical order of natural laws. In the habit of the times "empirical" and "law-like" were considered synonymous or functionally equivalent.

The most influential figures in German psychology were Gustav Fechner, Hermann von Helmholtz, and Wilhelm Wundt. Dilthey reviewed their works and repeatedly referred to their thought in developing his own. All were deeply impressed by the results of the natural sciences and wished to introduce empirical exactness into the study of mental activity. Fechner approached psychology from the twin vantage points of the new physics and the older philosophy of nature. He demanded both exactness and inclusiveness in the explanation of mental life. The fulfillment of this dual demand depended, in Fechner's view, upon the broadest possible extension of quantifying procedures into the realm of the psychical. His researches culminated in the formulation of the famous Weber-Fechner Law establishing a definite quantitative equation between the intensity of an external stimulus and the intensity of the internal psychic sensation. This law was the first instance of a purely mathematical statement for the relation between a discrete cause in the "objective" physical world and a response in the "subjective" mental realm of perception. Fechner's widely adopted textbook, *Elemente der Psychophysik* (1860), extended the demand for exact measurement into all areas of psychic activity. "Psycho-physics" was defined as the exact empirical science of the relation between mind and body. The program of the new discipline called for the inclusion of higher mental processes such as attention and memory, but Fechner's researches focused solely upon forms of sensation.

Helmholtz, like Fechner, came from a background in physics and brought a preference for stringently inductive and mathematically formulated results into the field of psychology. In Dilthey's view, Helmholtz appeared as "the embodiment of the natural scientific spirit of the time" (*GS* 5:30; also 11:263). Helmholtz's study of mental processes issued in what seemed a rigorously empirical, indeed experimental, confirmation of Kant's theory of the a priori forms of intuition. He thus established himself as one of the principal figures in the movement which sought to give a precise psychological rendering of Kant's transcendental theory of mind. In a series of ingenious experiments, Helmholtz measured for the first time the exact speed of nerve conduction, which earlier speculations had fixed at the speed of light. Helmholtz's later work in the physiological processes of sight and hearing extended quantitative methods into the study of perception. From Helmholtz it was not a long step to the position that "real" experience was simply that which is susceptible to experimental verification. Mental reality was defined as that which could be reproduced and analyzed in the laboratory.

Wilhelm Wundt gained world-wide fame as the founder of the first psychological laboratory, established at Leipzig in 1879. He left his mark upon several generations of students and possessed an incredibly diverse intellect. According to Dilthey, Wundt was "the major founder and steward of empiricism in Germany" (*WM* 52[1881]:525–26). While insisting upon a high degree of analytical exactness, Wundt's notion of psychological science, especially in its later modification, went beyond the prevailing concentration upon sensation and elementary perceptual functions. In predicating the existence of dynamic, temporal patterns of consciousness, Wundt came to stress the creative and integrating function of the human mind. To account for the complex relations among mental contents, he designated a process of "creative synthesis," which translated Kant's "transcendental unity of apperception" into psychological terms. Indeed, Wundt revived the older Kantian notion of apperception to account for the manner in which new perceptions are integrated into individual consciousness. Thus, the "self" which had largely been banished from psychology in fulfillment of the positivist demand to pare away unnecessary hypothetical and "fictive" constructs, was reintroduced to explain mental life.

Significantly Wundt's interest extended beyond sensation to the higher forms of mental activity, including speech and the creation and interpretation of symbols. His demand for broader scope and synthesis in psychology was reflected in his call for a social psychology (*Völkerpsychologie*) to replace the earlier version established on constructivist, Herbartian lines by Moritz Lazarus and Hermann Steinthal. In addition to laboratory responses Wundt insisted that cultural products and symbols, as well as commonly observed behavior and introspective reports, were legitimate empirical subject matter for psychology. In his later works he took the decisive step of directing psychology toward content derived from history and cultural anthropology. Wundt's reorientation of psychology signalled its emancipation from strictly positivist premises and properly belongs to the same strand of *Idealrealismus* from which Dilthey's thought stemmed. In general theory of knowledge and many specific points they were treading parallel paths.

With a few notable exceptions, the general developments in the natural sciences, philosophy, and psychology in the third quarter of the nineteenth century had the net effect of banishing nearly all metaphysical, transcendental, and "mentalistic" conceptions. The concern for "ultimate" knowledge through speculation or intuition, which had been the hallmark of the first half of the century, was supplanted by exclusive concentration upon the ascertainment of the laws relating factual data. Knowledge was conceived almost exclusively according to the model of the physical sciences. Predictive laws became the *desideratum* of science. The positivist demand to bring the phenomena of social and mental life under the sway of causal laws was widely heeded, and opposing voices were usually dismissed as quaint vestigial echoes of a long defunct and discredited *Geistesphilosophie*. Even the operations of the mind itself were conceived in accordance with the determinate laws of coexistence and succession. Unobservable entities such as "idea," "value," "self," "mind," and many other general concepts were widely discounted as mere "illusions" and "anthropomorphic fallacies." The scientific realism and physicalism of this era seemed to dictate the final extinction of all conceptions which did not find conclusive demonstration in the exact procedures of the natural sciences. This intellectual situation has been perceptively formulated:

By 1860 or thereabouts the Enlightenment notion of conceiving the world on the analogy of a simple machine and describing its processes in differential equations and the universal law of attraction had attained the status of orthodoxy both in the popular mind and among theoreticians in non-scientific and semi-scientific fields in inquiry. This triumph of the mechanistic model for the interpretation of all phenomena, both social and physical, was largely the result of the confirmation of Newtonian principles of analysis in the fields of astronomy and geology and the discovery of the atomic mechanism in chemistry. The last refuge of anti-Newtonianism in science was biology, but the triumph of Darwinism soon reduced that bastion and permitted the description of living matter in exclusively objective, scientific terms. In fact, by the third quarter of the nineteenth century it was generally believed to be only a matter of time before the whole of life could be satisfactorily explained in terms of physiochemical processes.[61]

As seen earlier, Dilthey was personally much in sympathy with the general mood of realism dominating the years after mid-century. He found much to admire in positivism and empiricism, asserting that they provided grounds for getting research under way and admiring their scrupulous caution in fending off speculation and fanciful construction. But, as in the case of idealism, Dilthey made a separation between the inner spirit and the doctrinaire ritualization of realism. Genuine realism in his view was not to be equated with mechanism. Taking his stance in the middle—with an *Idealrealismus* in the tradition of Schleiermacher and Trendelenburg—he warned against the danger of lurching from one brand of "one-sidedness" to another. (*GS* 13/1:xliii). The realism of the second half of the century, like the idealism of the first half, tended to be carried along by the momentum of its own systematic formulations and thereby enticed into purblind constructions. In its urge to achieve a total explanatory system, realism betrayed itself in dogmas as remote from experience as earlier *Traumidealismus*.

Dilthey came to the judgment that the new realism in matters of thought and science passed all too readily at the popular level into a scorn for spiritual concerns and a cynical disregard of ethical values. He perceived grave dangers in a world-view emerging in the name of science which repudiated the idealist heritage in toto and opted for baser values congruent with immediate political and economic gain. Such a cynical realism could only result in the debasement of man's concept of himself and of human activity. Drawing a balance on the period, Dilthey was as acidly critical of certain forms of the new "worldly" realism as he was of the older "otherworldly" idealism:

> As superior as it would like to think itself, the general rejection of ideas and their philosophical expression on the part of the present bureaucracy and bourgeoisie is not a sign of a sense for realities [*Tatsachensinn*] but rather poverty of spirit [*Geistesarmut*] [*GS* 2:91].

Dilthey's critique echoed that of Rudolf Haym, who at the very onset of the era after 1848 had protested strongly against the "ideal-less realism" in the life and learning of the period after 1850.[62] Both men found much to admire in the spirit of active, practical striving in their contemporaries, but both cautioned against a wholesale break with the idealist past. Given at the peak of positivist enthusiasms, Dilthey's inaugural address at Basel, while affirming his adherence to Kant's critical program and the rejection of all speculation in favor of "an empirical science of mind," nevertheless insisted that the movement back to Kant could not pass silently and indifferently over the post-Kantian idealist philosophies, for these too had meaning and relevance for the present. For Dilthey a spirit of "joyful practical action" was to be preferred over "inner rumination," but he specifically cautioned against action without ideals. Dilthey perceived a kind of cultural self-alienation at work, hidden behind the newer currents of thought, and warned the Germans: "No people can flee from itself. The worst way to progress is to break with the results of a fruitful past." (*GS* 11:69).

Part Two: Countercurrents, 1875–1910: The Resistance of Ideality and Creative Subjectivity—Neo-Idealism, Neo-Romanticism, and Irrationalism

In a review written in 1877, Dilthey recorded that Kant was enjoying "an inestimable and constantly growing influence on the whole of Europe and has even surpassed Goethe in direct and perceptible influence." To drive home his point Dilthey cited a host of works, but especially the exceedingly influential work by the neo-Kantian Friedrich Lange, *Geschichte des Materialismus und Kritik seiner gegenwärtigen Bedeutung*. In the review Dilthey declared:

> Lange's book signals a crisis in our spiritual life. When it was produced, the thought of Vogt and Moleschott prevailed among the educated classes and materialism appeared to be the last word of science. . . . It [Lange's book] is and remains one of the books which mark the crucial changes of the philosophical spirit of our century [*WM* 41(1877):548–50].

For Dilthey and many others at the time, Lange's work epitomized the major intellectual problems confronting the last quarter of the nineteenth century. Lange had employed Kant's critical method to show that general philosophies of materialism and naturalism were as guilty of transgressing the proper bounds of human knowledge as the long-discredited systems of speculative idealism. By attempting to grasp the world "as a whole," these thought-systems ended up as metaphysical constructions or sheer "poetizing in concepts" (*Begriffsdichtung*). They were seen to be the product of mere emotional disposition (*Gemüt*), devoid of true cognition. The urge to wholeness and totality, no matter whether idealist or materialist in foundation, cannot result in valid scientific knowledge, which is necessarily limited to the order of sense experience. The desire to know things "synthetically," "wholly," or "as they really are" beyond the phenomenal order of science must forever remain an unfulfillable, if perpetual, yearning of the human mind. Metaphysics is devoid of knowledge, even if justified in terms of human needs and longings. Lange concluded his critical blast at materialist metaphysics with a sharp separation between the realm of certain scientific knowledge and the realm of personal ideals of life: *Wissenschaft* and *Weltanschauung* must forever remain cast in eternal opposition.

Lange's work employed a critical phenomenalism against the materialists and proponents of scientific realism. His form of neo-Kantian *Kritizismus* ushered in a period of drastic phenomenalism and scientific fictionalism, which, although intended to validate science against spurious extensions toward a total world-view, in the long run proved to be a stimulus to radical skepticism about science itself. Science was shown to be a symbolic construction of the mind, not the literal representation of an independent and objective order of real things. In grasping the world scientifically, the mind was shown to be confined to knowing things according to its own intrinsic forms and yet it was also portrayed as aspiring to think beyond these limits. The mind was represented as embroiled in an internal conflict with itself: valid scientific cognition was pitted against a total, synthetic view of life and the world. As Dilthey expressed it in a second review of Lange's epochal work, there is "a struggle between natural science and the higher demands of the mind. . . . Lange takes with one hand what he gives with the other. Although he has achieved a temporary balance, his viewpoint cannot satisfy in the long run" (*WM* 52[1882]:547). In striking fulfillment of Dilthey's prediction, the period after the appearance of Lange's work saw a strong reaction against not only materialism and physicalism, but also against the very phenomenalistic positivism which Lange himself propounded. Like idealism, positivism seemed to subvert itself through its own ambitions.

The reaction was as varied as the loose set of ideas and assumptions against which it was contending. Especially for the period after 1880 one must be wary of generalizations about a "temper of the times." There was an astonishing pluralization of assumptions and proliferation of positions, which Dilthey came to characterize as an "anarchy of world-views." Positions which seemed clearly opposed were often interrelated at a deeper level. In the course of the century the viable grounds for a single synthetic treatment of reality had eroded, so that by the end of the century those intent upon philosophical synthesis were left with precious little foundation and very unstable materials. The thought of the time had become, as Dilthey and Yorck constantly observed, "groundless" (*bodenlos*). With the old certainties of religion and philosophy gone—and with the new challenge to science itself—where was one to find a sure stand?

Probably only the most thoughtful persons perceived these problems in such terms. Certainly the vast majority of Europeans continued to marvel at science and its increasingly evident and momentous technological attainments. If they reflected upon it at all, they probably continued to believe that science had provided a view of the world which was indisputably "real" and objective. For many, "science" was the one and only possible *Weltanschauung*. But increasingly after 1880 intellectuals in many fields began to question the ultimate validity and grounds of scientific conceptions and came to challenge the effects which such conceptions had upon the conduct of life. In contrast to the earlier positivism, one is confronted with the singular spectacle of science brought to witness against itself. In some circles confidence in science began to wane and belief in the objective truth of science was questioned. Critical theorists of science came to challenge the naïve "scientism" of earlier positions. Science came to be viewed as a useful construct of the mind. It was not such a great step from this view to the view that science was a heuristic and hypothetical "fiction"—and thence to Nietzsche's unsettling conclusion that science was merely a "useful lie." The path seemed open to a whole set of "old" and "new" truths.

These decades witnessed various intellectual movements of revival and innovation which went under the various names of neo-idealism, neo-romanticism, vitalism, voluntarism, the "new irrationalism," and the "new metaphysics." In surveying them, one must be careful not to endow them with a spurious unanimity, for they were exceedingly diverse. Some were avowedly irrational, while others argued upon what were taken to be "ulterior" scientific grounds; some heralded the triumph of "life" and "will" over reason, while others called for a reformulation of reason in the light of new discoveries and new patterns of thought. There was a reaction against positivism from within the ranks of positivism itself. Positivism, through a process of internal and external criticism, transformed itself and became so highly phenomenalistic that it paved the way for a resurgence of the very sort of thinking it had originally opposed. It has been argued that the best critics of positivism tended to engage it on its own grounds, refuting it from its own premises (through what Dilthey would call an immanent critique) rather than resorting to the discredited metaphysics of idealism.[63] Yet in many cases the attack upon positivism either originated in a tacit form of metaphysical thought or else culminated in an avowed metaphysics. Many thinkers observed that the end of the century seemed to have come full circle, arriving back at many of the premises of its first decades.

More often than not, these intellectual movements did not share a common and precise definition of their philosophical foe, but they were united in opposing the "naturalization" of mind and consciousness which prevailed earlier. The various strands of Dilthey's thought—his conception of the human sciences, of a "historical reason," and of a "philosophy of life"—were deeply interwoven with these movements. He drew intellectual support from several of them and his thought as a whole is rightly regarded as part of this general revolt against positivism and naturalism. But he was very fastidious in his choice of intellectual alliances; as the tide turned against the simplistic fatuities of positivism, he was inclined to remind its enemies of its latent strengths. In an age which seemed to prefer extremes, Dilthey labored discerningly on behalf of fruitful mediation. Even when he found his own views in vogue, he was not swept along by intellectual fashion. This fact can best be seen in his attitude to the new idealism and new romanticism.

The most systematic reaction against positivism and naturalism came from the second wave of neo-Kantianism which followed upon the initial "return to Kant" discussed in the last section. The later schools of neo-Kantianism rejected the "psychological naturalism" implicit in the earlier positivistic versions of Liebmann, Lange, and Helmholtz. The later neo-Kantian schools of Marburg and Baden were adamantly opposed to a psychological rendering of Kant and argued that transcendental philosophy was antithetical to any form of psychology whatsoever. Whereas the earlier forms of Kantianism had tried to draw the transcendental into the orbit of the purely psychological, the later schools reversed the direction of pull and insisted upon the ideal, originary, and a priori nature of the transcendental. To their way of thinking, the true science of knowledge must begin not with the actual processes which go on in the individual mind, but with the logical presuppositions inherent in science itself. Not physiology or psychology, but transcendental logic provides the key to founding knowledge. Eventually the concept of transcendental logic was extended beyond the theory of the a priori norms of scientific knowledge and broadened into the problem of absolute transcendental values. Moving away from the psychological through the logical to the axiological, general theory of knowledge and science became "universal theory of value."

The Marburg School of neo-Kantianism, represented by Hermann Cohen and Paul Natorp, was intent upon a transcendental derivation of the pure forms of logic and mathematics. They countered all forms of positivist phenomenalism and naturalistic empiricism with a logical objectivism and rationalist idealism which bore a striking resemblance to the philosophies of Plato, Leibniz, and even Hegel. In opposition to the stress upon the sensing subject of critical positivism and "empirio-criticism," they placed the "thought-object" in the forefront of epistemology—not the empirical object of sense-particulars but the logical and mathematical object conceived by science. In addition to the exact physical sciences of nature, the Marburgers projected pure "philosophical sciences" of logic, ethics, and aesthetics. Kant's stress upon sensuous intuition was diminished and prime attention was placed upon the a priori logical grounds of all judgment. Not surprisingly, Dilthey found the idealism of this school to be helplessly "*bodenlos*," "an artificial logical web, spun from within, floating unsupported in the pure and empty air" (*GS* 5:50–51). Their logical objectivism promoted a radical turn away from psychology toward an uncompromisingly transcendental theory of mind. The realm of *Geist* was restored to its pristine preeminence only at the cost of placing it beyond empirical treatment.

The Baden School of Wilhelm Windelband and Heinrich Rickert constituted a different, but parallel case in point. They were concerned not with pure logic and mathematics but with the same body of historical sciences which Dilthey was trying to put on a secure theoretical foundation. In contrast to Dilthey, the Baden neo-Kantians termed these sciences not *Geisteswissenschaften*, which to them was too deeply imbued with faulty empiricistic and psychologistic prejudices, but rather *Kulturwissenschaften*, a body of sciences resting upon universal theory of value. Not ordinary human experience but transcendental values constituted the ground of man's knowledge of himself and his history. The Baden School was closer to Dilthey's subject area than all other schools of neo-Kantianism, and yet they were hardly allies. Indeed, he came in time to regard them as the chief adversaries and obstacle in his endeavors. Their thought was a kind of renovated Fichtean "postulatism" in his eyes. The details of their confrontation will be treated below, but it can be noted here that for Dilthey the Baden School had tried to rescue certainty in the human sciences by basing them upon absolute, transcendental values—at the cost of exacerbating further the split between thought and the experience of life.

The new transcendental idealism of these schools proceeded under the banner of opposition to all materialism, naturalism, empiricism, "psychologism," "biologism," "historicism" and all other positions that would make *Geist* dependent upon factors extrinsic to its own nature. The new idealism strove to vindicate a pure notion of rational truth, uncompromised by and irreducible to contingent factors of experience, conditioning, and milieu. Any complicity with those factors was for them an invitation to skepticism and irrationalism. Yet in order to make philosophical thought unconditioned and pure, they had purged it of real experiential content. In Dilthey's terms, the interpretation which they gave to the values in culture and history was so pure and rarified that it could not support life.

In a remarkably parallel repetition of the original transformation of idealism after Kant, the new transcendental idealism tended to pass over into a new romanticism. Pure abstract, logical form went begging for intuitive content. This ensuing "Neuromantik" was primarily a development of the period 1890 to 1910. Just after the turn of the century, Wilhelm Windelband noted that the "whole world" was taking cognizance of the new romanticism which was infusing philosophy as well as literature and art. He stated: "Out of the return to Kant, which was the motto for decades, there appears to be developing a return to Fichte, to Schelling, to Hegel.[64] It was "a hunger for world-view" which attracted the younger generation to the romantic idealists; not just the critique of scientific knowledge, but the constitution of a vision of the world was once again called for. In a 1910 lecture entitled "On the Mysticism of Our Time," Windelband stated that "in no epoch of history has the substance of the higher life of values been as much in flux, in dissolution and in reconstitution, as in our own." He went on to note that the same great turn in thought which had taken place in 1800 was repeating itself a century later: a turn from the rational to the irrational. "Once again the irrational is announced as the holy secret of all reality, as the fount of life lying beyond all knowledge."[65] The feverish revival of Boehme, Plotinus, Novalis, and Hölderlin was symptomatic of the new mysticism. Philosophies of the irrational will, the unconscious, and the ineffable were modish after the belated but extraordinary impact of Schopenhauer. The new mysticism and irrationalism were reflected in the widespread interest in theosophy and Buddhism. The disciples of Nietzsche, Bergson, Ludwig Klages, and Stefan George announced that rational thought and science were implacably opposed to life and true culture. It was widely held that life had been so debased by scientific reason that its only salvation lay in art, intuition, or will.

In many circles faith in science had given way to tonic doctrines of a "primordial will," "vital force," and the "poetic absolute." The critique of positivism had given rise to a general critique of science as such. Even its staunchest defenders expressed their doubts. The eminent neo-Kantian, Friedrich Paulsen, a colleague and friend of Dilthey's at Berlin, reflected upon the crisis in scientific circles:

> Everyone now works harder than ever before, but the inner necessity and rationale of the enterprise is not there; one has the feeling that the result for inner, personal life does not correspond to the expenditure of energy; the burden of a hundred camels that one tows along does not increase wisdom, it does not make one richer in the knowledge of human and divine things.[66]

Another of Dilthey's Berlin colleagues, the theologian and official historian of the Academy of Sciences, Adolf von Harnack, reported that "modern science has not emerged as the steward of life in the highest sense and has not given any great inner elevating impulse to life."[67] Wissenschaft had destroyed the grounds of the older certainties of religion and metaphysics but had proved incapable of providing grounds for a new vision of the world. Wissenschaft and Weltanschauung seemed pitted against each other, with science appearing less and less satisfying as the yearning for a world-view intensified under the unsettling conditions of the fin de siècle. New prophets and seers emerged in the wake of the disillusionment with science. The general "disenchantment of the world" accomplished by science promoted a reaction in new philosophies of vitalism and irrationalism. The two thinkers who were most symptomatic of this development and to whom Dilthey felt both attracted and repelled were Nietzsche and Bergson.

In a letter to Yorck in May 1897, Dilthey acknowledged that "Nietzsche has indeed really spoken the fearsome word of the times" (*BDY* 238).[68] In the last decade of the nineteenth century the thought of Nietzsche struck Europe like a thunderbolt—in just the manner that Nietzsche envisioned himself. Nietzsche's impact must be explained by the fact that he turned European culture back upon itself and called its deepest values into question. Perhaps retrospectively his efforts may be aligned with the venerable tradition of Socratic reflection or the Kantian notion of critique of values, but at the time Nietzsche portended rather a radical iconoclasm, a colossal "break" in every sense. In "philosophizing with a hammer" Nietzsche destroyed more than he created, even though, as Dilthey observed, his highest aim was creation. For Dilthey, who had a much deeper respect for Western historical values, the much-touted "overcoming" of nihilism was at base nothing more than "the great Nietzschean malady of an exaggerated subjectivity" (*GS* 9:210). In overturning culture and history, Nietzsche had not enthroned man or the creative self, but merely a gargantuan solipsism.

Nietzsche wove a series of vertiginous paradoxes into an immensely powerful and subtle body of thought. His thought combined elements of a quasi-Darwinian naturalism with a pragmatic voluntarism, derived in part from his reading of Schopenhauer. Schopenhauer's deeply pessimistic philosophy of the tragic struggle to negate the cosmic will-to-life was converted into Nietzsche's "joyful" and "gay" affirmation of the will-to-power. His notion of creation was deliberately *ex nihilo*—a brash counterpart and rejoinder to divine creation—which was to be accomplished after all values had been subjected to the acid test of their "usefulness to life." Vital values for Nietzsche were not based upon a priori norms or slow work of historical tradition, but were forged out of the spontaneous combustion of inherited culture.

Nietzsche, like Dilthey, was much concerned with the relation of thought to life, but he was a philosophical radical, not a mediator. In his view, most of Western thought had conspired to sicken and kill life. Traditional religion and philosophy had impelled the mind to seek solace in worlds beyond, thus breeding passivity, servility, and *ressentiment*. Nietzsche fulminated against "conceptual mummies," "numbing ideas," and "the moloch of abstraction." Excluding a few great "experimenters" (like himself), thinkers since Socrates had indulged in sentimental self-mystification leading to cultural sickness. Western rationality and science were but a part of the web of narcotic half-truths and "little lies" that added up to the "great lie" which was Western, and especially German, culture. Indeed, culture suffered under a congenital surfeit of rational thought, science, and "soft" and "feminine" understanding. In Nietzsche's view thought had to become "hard" and "hazardous" if it was to foster creative life.

For Nietzsche there is no single Truth—that indeed was the greatest and most pervasive lie of all—but rather only the many truths that man himself creates. Indeed there is no absolute "truth in itself"; rather, only interpretations rooted in life. Knowledge is conceived as a particular form of interpretation based upon the deeper will-to-power: "Wissenschaft" is at base a species of "Willenschaft," an expression of the primordial will-to-power. Synthesizing aspects of Darwinism and phenomenalism, Nietzsche held that truth is actually a "vital lie," "a kind of error without which a certain species of life could not live. The value for life is ultimately decisive." Relativism was for Nietzsche not only inevitable, it was positively invigorating. Reality is but an endless process of acts of will. Man for Nietzsche is not primarily rational but willful, the "not yet determined animal" that wills itself into perpetual being-as-becoming. Man's highest task is to overcome himself in the *Übermensch*. Such "overcoming" was not portrayed in traditional terms of the *askesis* of reflection or the enrichment derived from the compassionate understanding of others and of history; rather it came from a "love of fate" and an "everlasting yea" to the cosmic cycle of eternal return. Nietzsche's thought paradoxically combined a hyper-Fichteanism with an extreme fatalism.

Dilthey sensed deeply the power of Nietzsche's secular gospel of life and the impotence of those who, like Ferdinand Tönnies and Alois Riehl, tried to refute him on the basis of conventional philosophical grounds. But Dilthey came to deplore the substitution of paradoxical aphorism for critical thought and bombastic exclamation for logic: a series of lightning strikes did not add up to enlightenment. Both he and Yorck agreed that the modern style of thought was likely to become "Nietzscheanism"—experimental, daring, and anti-historical—but for them it was *"bodenlos"* and operating in a void. Nietzsche had not uncovered the texture of life, but merely peeled it away to a new set of arbitrary, subjective constructions. In contrast to Nietzsche's heroic egoism Dilthey's vision of life developed along historical and social lines. Whereas Nietzsche regarded history as "a poisoned well" and the "historical sense" as a symptom of sickness, Dilthey saw history as a vital source and a potentially curative power. For all its force, Nietzsche's thought was for Dilthey merely another symptom of the nihilistic disease of which it purported to be the cure.

Like Nietzsche in Germany, Henri Bergson in France placed the problem of life and thought at the center of his philosophizing. He too started with a critique of scientism and the scientific intellect and ended with an exuberant, irrationalist vitalism. Bergson was read more widely than any other philosopher of the day, including Nietzsche; "Bergsonianism" became a veritable intellectual wave which spread over Europe after 1905, having an impact in literature, psychology, education, and even military strategy. In the opinion of William James, Bergson was a new "Copernicus in philosophy," who had effected an intellectual revolution as great as Kant's.[69]

Bersgon drew a sharp dichotomy between the scientific intellect and direct intuition: the former is analytic and ratiocinative, serving a practical function in rationalizing experience through the construction of concepts and hypothetical models, while the latter furnishes direct inner consciousness of the concrete flow or "duration" of experience. There are two ways of "knowing" something: an outer and an inner way. The first implies that we merely "move around" an object; the second that we "enter into" it. All scientific knowledge is "external" and abstractive: it uses concepts, forms, symbols, and calculation to reduce the qualitative experience of objects to discrete elements already known. Concepts cannot capture the unique, the unforeseeable, and the truly creative—in short, concepts do not grasp concrete reality, but distort it. To analyze something scientifically is to express it as a function of something other than itself. Bergson held that not only scientific concepts but even language itself is a distortion and a petrification of this concrete duration. Intuition, on the other hand, is immediate and concrete. It makes an absolutely new effort for each object it encounters; it does not "mediatize" or distort, but "participates" in the real. All conceptualization is a departure from real experience: the "true empiricist" practices a silent intuition of the unbroken continuum of experience. It is not surprising that Bergson's fluid and eloquent doctrine provided a potent spring for the new mysticism and subjective metaphysics which many saw taking hold in Europe.

Dilthey shared Bergson's desire for a new kind of empiricism based upon concrete experience, but he did not share the latter's disdain for analytical concepts nor his unswerving faith in self-intuition. Bergson's error was to overestimate the gains to be derived from the intuition of the pure, indeterminate experiential flow apart from its structures, signs, and manifestations. Moreover, he exaggerated the disparities between experience and conceptualization, thus exacerbating the split between life and thought. As in the case of Nietzsche, Dilthey appreciated certain resonances between his own thought and that of Bergson, but there is no evidence to suggest that he felt even marginally indebted to Bergson.[70] Indeed, he berated the French philosopher for falsely dichotomizing life and conceptual knowledge; Bergson's rejection of science, logic, and formalizing procedures was far too extreme, inclining toward a romantic mysticism abhorrent to Dilthey. One did not gain life by sacrificing thought, as many slogans of the age exhorted.

It has been noted that the truly great thinkers of the late nineteenth and early twentieth centuries remained deeply skeptical of the modish new romanticism and sought to curb what romantic tendencies they discovered in themselves.[71] This judgment applies singularly well to Dilthey, who showed a growing revulsion toward the manifestations of excessive subjectivism and irrationalism which he saw on all sides. He attached great importance to the concept of subjectivity and the personal "attitude toward life" (*Lebensstellung*), but his notion of subjectivity was open and expansive rather than closed in on itself. Just as Rudolf Eucken and a host of other "philosophers of life" were heralding the turn to the twentieth century as a "turn to the subject," Dilthey countered with his own "turn to the objective" which will be treated below in detail.[72] He surveyed the spreading climate of self-enchanted *culte de moi* and mindless activism with grave misgivings and caustic rebukes. After 1900 he warned specifically against the dangers and futility of replacing the previously prevailing scientism with an equally fallacious subjectivism. The writings from the last decade of his life show that he condemned the new romantic irrationalism no less severely than earlier doctrinaire positivism. In one of his last lectures (from the year 1906, preserved as an outline in the Berlin Nachlass), he acknowledged that the "interpretation of life" (*Auslegung des Lebens*) constituted a deep impulse in modern thought which "in a fragmentary and arbitrary form" lay at the basis of the thought of Schopenhauer, Nietzsche, Bergson, the Wagnerites, and the circle around the poet Stefan George. Although he found this impulse to be legitimate and valuable, Dilthey objected vociferously to their actual methods and formulations, branding them as "subjective self-enchantment":

> There has arisen recently a subjective, limitless vortex of emotions. Every day more books appear which promise salvation through a subjective view of the world based upon some kind of introspection or self-immersion of the subject in itself. Everywhere the conviction is growing that objective, methodical knowledge is impossible.

Dilthey denounced this subjectivism as "balefully erroneous" and compared it historically to the hapless return to the irrationalism of Schelling: "I cannot warn strongly enough against proceeding along these dangerous and treacherous paths. This giddy rapture will prove ephemeral and fruitless— and more pernicious in my opinion than the formless swirl of the Schelling school" (*BNL* 49/218–20).

In attempting to understand Dilthey's thought in its full context, it is exceedingly important to recognize that as the ideas for which he had been crusading for years came into general currency by assuming an extreme and doctrinaire cast, he modified them considerably and even assumed a contrary attitude. What may seem to be equivocations and "reversals" on his part are, when seen in the entire context, part of an effort to establish a new balance. This sense of balance and mediation was central to his temperament and to his thought itself. As a mediator, Dilthey was more interested in balance and "unprejudiced vision" (*Unbefangenheit*) than in radical consistency. He recoiled from the extreme positions assumed by others who have come to be regarded as kindred thinkers. As in the case of the "realism" of the third quarter of the century, so in the *Neuromantik* of the years around the turn of the century he perceived a "new one-sidedness." (*GS* 5:302). As spontaneous intuition and unreflective will became the new keys to the "world-riddle" he came to stress deep reflection and objective understanding. As the partisans of the new romanticism mocked the Enlightenment, he came to its defense and called for a renewed appreciation of its basic values. And he continued to look askance at attempts to resurrect metaphysics as a means of shoring up the fragmented structure of the disciplines and attaining a "final" world-view. In the heady atmosphere of the turn of the century, he reminded his contemporaries of the classical maxim that "there is nothing great without limits" (*VDM* 430).

To the end of a lifetime which witnessed a tumult of surrounding intellectual changes, Dilthey remained faithful to the idea of an expanded *Wissenschaft*. He affirmed:

> The highest and most important task of all philosophy lies in the securing of valid knowledge. For the progress of mankind is conditioned in the modern period by its guidance through scientific knowledge; this knowledge must be secured against dark feeling and the arbitrariness of subjectivity—and the skeptical spirit which accompanies both [*GS* 4:200].

In 1900—on the symbolic occasion of the bicentennial celebration of the Berlin Academy and in the midst of rising chauvinist sentiments reflected in a Europe he described as "armed to the teeth"—Dilthey affirmed his commitment to the ideal of *Wissenschaft* as a source of international cooperation and cosmopolitan "consciousness of togetherness."[73]

In 1911—the year of Dilthey's death—a like-minded associate, the philosopher-historian Karl Joël, tried to assess some of the lessons and dangers of the past century of profound intellectual changes:

> As no other age, the nineteenth century experienced the dogmatic extremes of idealism and naturalism and left us at the end as someone who has been through two enormous debaucheries: "now, children, you know how things are, be prudent, judicious, and mature." We stand at present with all this hoary experience and youthful daring, but we do not know what to do. We understand every tendency of thought and are eclectic from sheer abundance of learning. We no longer endorse any tendency—we are thoroughly skeptical and critical. But such skepticism threatens to rob us of even the best legacy left by the nineteenth century: the sense of history.[74]

Dilthey grappled with all these polarities and intellectual shifts, trying to bring them into a fruitful synthesis which would engender not skepticism but a productive knowledge of history and understanding of human life. This sense of history and human affairs was to be based not on speculative constructs, nostalgic yearning, or sheer intuition but on genuine foundations secured by a critique of historical reason.

His project was directed toward history but also derived from it. He borrowed and adapted extensively from this legacy of ideas. Yet he was no epigone or imitator; he approached his age with a spirit combining broad understanding with searching criticism. He found much which was valuable in the many intellectual strands and schools of the century, but he saw major excesses, gaps, and dangers as well. His own thought reflected his time but also led beyond it. A contextual understanding of his life and thought demonstrates precisely his own hermeneutic principle that a major thinker mirrors his time and is conditioned by it, but that he is likewise capable of moving beyond it. Such a thinker not only reflects his age, but reflects upon it critically and creatively. In a favored German metaphor which aptly captures this element of creative tension, Dilthey might best be described as a "schaffender Spiegel."

2

The most astonishing phenomenon of all is one's own
existence. The greatest secret for man is man himself.
—Dilthey

The mysterious path lies inward.
—Novalis, quoted by Dilthey

The Empirical-Existential Foundations of the Human Sciences: Life and Lived Experience

The Problem of Foundations

From a biographical and historical vantage point, the preceding chapter outlined Dilthey's guiding philosophical preoccupation with defining a new relation between knowledge and human life, an issue which, however theoretical, was deeply conditioned by the exigencies of his *own* life and times. His project must now be explored fundamentally and systematically, yet with a constant eye to internal modifications. Dilthey's style of thinking led him to critical revisions and reformulations which, if divorced from these foundations, might suggest that he provided neither premises nor conclusions but a sinuous or circular argument beginning and ending in the middle. Although he sought a difficult middle way between existing philosophical extremes, this "middle" was based upon constant and discernible foundations which must be treated in their own right.

The effort to provide a theoretical basis for the human sciences thrust Dilthey into many of the most tangled controversies of modern thought—questions concerning the nature of consciousness, the role of experience and logic in knowledge, the nature of objectivity, meaning, and validity, the relation of values to culture, and a host of related issues. He could neither define nor defend the cause of the human sciences without delving into these matters, despite the fact that they sometimes seemed to carry him far afield. Yet however obliquely, he always returned to the central question: How is knowledge in the human sciences possible? The answer lay with a new critique of reason defined as methodical inquiry into "the capacity of man to know himself and the society and history which he has created" (*GS* 1:ix, 116. Cf. 5:9; 7:191, 278).

To be both fruitful and valid, such an inquiry would have to define the precise nature of the human sciences, disclose their experiential and logical foundations, trace the potentialities and limits of their cognitive procedures, show their interrelationship, and likewise their relation to the natural sciences. An additional task to which Dilthey attached cardinal importance was careful historical study of the human sciences themselves, for such historical understanding of their development was an essential aspect of their systematic treatment. The actual history of these disciplines had to be carefully considered in any genuine theory of their foundations and operations, since their historical emergence and differentiation had preceded attempts at their theoretical definition and justification (GS 1:39). To be useful and pertinent, a theory of the human sciences had to encompass their development and practice: "Insight into the historical development of the human sciences is the empirical foundation for a true understanding of their logical constitution. For the basic concern is not to construct new sciences, but to found a great, existing system of sciences" (BNL 191/76; see also GS 1:24 and 7:305). Both historically and conceptually the theory of the human sciences had to follow their *praxis*.

This peculiarity of perspective entailed a larger philosophical issue of prime importance. Dilthey's efforts toward a theory of the human sciences were guided by his often expressed admonition that in dealing with matters of the mind and human affairs, there is no "absolute starting point" or "presuppositionless beginning" (GS 1:419; 5:cx; BA 67). The theorist as well as the practitioner of the human sciences is "in" and "of" what he investigates. The special nature of this involvement presented exceptional perplexities for any "pure" theoretical treatment. After a lifetime of reflecting upon the problem of beginnings and foundations, Dilthey came to the conclusion that every beginning is in some sense "arbitrary" and that inquiry proceeds from a position in medias res by means of an interpretive process of circular clarification (GS 7:162; 1:419). It is worth stressing that any methodical exposition of Dilthey's thought must necessarily go over the same terrain from different angles if it is to reflect his characteristic conception of "foundations." As all genuinely critical thinkers who are in the habit of asking basic questions, Dilthey was a "perpetual beginner."

The Theoretical Definition of the Human Sciences

Although he may be said to have provided its "classic" formulation, Dilthey did not invent the term *Geisteswissenschaften*, nor was he ever completely satisfied with it. He settled upon the term gradually and with crucial qualifications which can only be explained by the fact that it was a true "Kampfbegriff," a concept perpetually surrounded by polemic. From clouded origins in the later eighteenth century it evolved through controversy in Dilthey's time and remains today not so much a neutral descriptive term as a constant source of contention.[1]

As early as 1861—notably before his shift from theology to philosophy—Dilthey distinguished between two great "systems of thought": (1) the "system of laws" (or simply "science") which has "unconditional validity," as distinct from (2) the "system of value-laden and meaningful existence" (also "world-view"), which is not "unconditional" but at the same time not simply personal (*JD* 141–42). This formulation conformed closely to the traditional separation of "physics" and "ethics" found in Aristotle and Schleiermacher, but modified through the neo-Kantian terminology of Hermann Lotze. Although Dilthey insisted upon the fundamentally conditional character of the "system of existence," such conditions did not altogether preclude knowledge of it: it was knowable in a manner different from the "system of laws" but not yet designated as any sort of "science." In a review article of 1863, Dilthey specifically brought this subject matter under the province of what he called *"geistige Wissenschaften"* and asserted that "in the area of the human sciences, of history and politics, a thousand signs point toward a revolution—one which is as profound as that which was accomplished in the natural sciences by Galileo and Newton" (*GS* 16:448).

The earlier distinction, which in Kantian terms might be said "to limit knowledge to make room for belief," was clearly reformulated in Dilthey's first logical treatise "Outline of the Logic and System of the Philosophical Sciences" of 1865, written after his shift from theology to history and philosophy. Here he contrasted the "sciences of mind" (also "sciences of culture") with the "sciences of the external world" (also "sciences of nature"). The former included philosophy, ethics, aesthetics, linguistics, and the sciences of history, law, state, and religion; the latter included physics, chemistry, geology, and biology. In this work Dilthey expressed his conviction that the "real sciences of mind" were united in a "fundamental science" (*Grundwissenschaft*) which he optionally termed "psychology" and "anthropology." From these premises he envisioned "an urgent practical vocation for this body of sciences in influencing the formation of society and culture" (*Grundriss* 2–5, 16). In this treatise of 1865, what had previously been designated rather vaguely as a "system of thought" beyond the scope of rigorous knowledge was henceforth brought under the auspices of a new kind of scientific knowledge on a par with the natural sciences. In notebook entries and reviews over the next decade, Dilthey often employed the terms "sciences of acting man" and "sciences of culture" to denote these disciplines.

By 1875 Dilthey had modified his terminology to differentiate on the one hand between the "sciences of social-historical reality," "moral-political sciences," and "sciences of man, society, and the state" as distinct from the "sciences of nature" (*GS* 5:31). These new, more loosely generic formulations reflected a concession to terms which had come into currency through the writings of Robert von Mohl, Karl Knies, and others. In 1876 he referred to the "sciences of the practical world" (*GS* 18:225). By the early 1880s, however, Dilthey settled again upon the previous term *Geisteswissen-*

schaften and adhered to it for the rest of his life, despite challenges from other philosophers and certain persistent reservations of his own. In the *Einleitung* of 1883, Dilthey entertained alternative terms such as "sciences of society," "sciences of culture," and "moral sciences," but rejected them as "too narrow." He found the term *Geisteswissenschaften* "least inappropriate" but stressed that the term did not exactly convey the true object of these sciences, since they do not separate the mental life of man from his psycho-physical life. In Dilthey's sense of the term these sciences do not investigate mental life in vacuo (*GS* 1:5–6. Cf. also 7:323).

Dilthey's initial variations in terminology should not be taken merely as vacillation in matters of verbal nuance: they stemmed from genuine philosophical issues, not philological ones. Despite unwieldy qualities, his earlier designations had the obvious and deliberate virtue of avoiding the problematic metaphysical connotations of the term "Geist," so freely invoked by the idealists. As indicated previously, Dilthey's attitude toward this idealist heritage was emphatically critical and he deplored its speculative excesses. But with the almost complete demise of speculative and transcendental idealism by the mid-1870s, the term *Geisteswissenschaft* had lost many of its arrantly metaphysical associations and could be employed without automatically summoning the chimera of Hegel's Absolute Spirit. It might be noted in this regard that in the same year in which Dilthey published the *Einleitung* (1883), the kindred psychologist-philosopher Wilhelm Wundt used the same term in his monumental *Logik*. As an experimental scientist, Wundt was no partisan of speculative thought and, like Dilthey, he tried to divest the concept of many of its idealist connotations. It is therefore questionable whether the very term itself "seems to imply an idealistic approach to the humanistic disciplines for which it stands."[2]

Beyond all such variations in terms, Dilthey insisted that there is a fundamental difference between the natural and human sciences, the two halves of the *globus intellectualis*. He was, however, intent upon avoiding specious and misleading grounds for this distinction, for such false grounds would return to distort both the theoretical definition and practical procedures of these sciences. After the mid-1860s he insisted that both bodies of knowledge should be considered "empirical," "objective," "factual," and "valid"—though in a manner constituted (*aufgebaut*) differently within each set of sciences. The distinction between these two bodies of knowledge rested finally upon differing "attitudes of mind," "orientations of consciousness," "standpoints toward experience," or "realms of experience." The separation could not be resolved into the dubious metaphysical assertion of two different kinds of "being," but rather stemmed from two different ways of experiencing the world *and* the manner in which that experience is elaborated in consciousness. The distinction was thus "empirical" in the broader sense of Dilthey's "Empirie": it derived directly from experience but was also the result of *reflection* upon experience. One misconstrues the grounds for Dilthey's famous separation unless it is realized that the difference between these sciences is both "given" in experience and "arrived at" in theoretical reflection.

At the basis of the distinction lay two different modes of experiencing reality: "inner lived experience" (*das Erleben, Erlebnis*, or occasionally *erlebende Erfahrung*) and "outer sensory experience" (*aüssere Erfahrung*). The human sciences are based upon lived experience and constantly have reference to it, whereas the natural sciences build their constructs and laws upon abstractions from sensory experience. Dilthey held that the human sciences have as their object an empirical reality given directly and "originally" (*originaliter*) to the mind as a coherent texture of relations and meanings. The natural sciences on the other hand have as their object the regular and uniform order of facts given from outside as phenomena related by the causal laws of coexistence and succession (*GS* 5:143–44).

It is crucial to grasp what Dilthey meant by the distinction between lived experience and sensory experience. Lived experience is the "originary" way in which we perceive reality. As living persons we have an awareness of things and ourselves which is immediate, direct, and nonabstractive. We "live through" (*erleben*) life with an intimate sense of its concrete, qualitative features and myriad patterns, meanings, values, and relations. It could be said that we "know" these features and relations more by tacit acquaintance than by explicit inference or discursive thought—but they are nonetheless real or empirical for being often below the threshold of conscious objectified attention. This lived experience Dilthey called the "primordial cell" (*Urzelle*) of the human-historical world and the basic empirical datum of the human sciences (*GS* 7:161). We are always aware of life as we live through it, even if its content often remains at the level of an unspoken awareness rather than explicit, formalized cognition expressed in discursive judgments. Such an awareness or immediate apprehension of experience constitutes the empirical foundation of the human sciences and the infrastructure of their cognitive procedures. It is lived experience which enables the human sciences to be constituted and certified as truly empirical sciences (*Erfahrungswissenschaften*) (*GS* 7:304).

The human sciences provide insight into human life by means of methodical cognition of the works and workings of the human mind and the human world. Man is the "starting point and endpoint of their analysis" (*GS* 1:388). These sciences explore the "mental world" (*geistige Welt*) or "social-historical world" of human experience as embodied in its processes and objectifications. This is the highly complex, though in a basic sense "familiar," world of human affairs, relations, values, and meanings which extends from the crudest implement to the most refined work of art or philosophy. This man-made world must be distinguished from the natural world; it is not definable in terms of sheer physical processes and objects *qua* "physical," although it clearly includes physical realities. Dilthey held that nature as a datum is "alien" and "closed" to us—not closed to scientific knowledge but rather to the immediate and concrete experiential awareness which makes us familiar with the social-historical world. Nature as a scientific construct has only an outer, not an inner side. In Kantian terms, the mind knows it only phenomenally through external sensory experience worked into an order of laws. The mental world of society, culture, and history, however, is known to us from "inside" as lived experience: "Nature is alien to us. It is only an externality, not an inner reality. Society is our world. We experience sympathetically [*erleben wir mit*] the interaction of social forces with all the power of our whole being, because we have within us the conditions and forces which make up the social system" (*GS* 1:36–37; also 7:58). In contrast to our sense of the natural world, we have an immediate, experiential sense of this "lived world" of social and cultural relations which is our normal context. Indeed Dilthey claims that this *human* world is more "natural" to us than the natural world of scientific conceptualization.

The human sciences are "empirical" like the natural sciences, but in a special sense which reflects their subject matter, methods, and general standpoint toward experience. Scientific knowledge of nature is phenomenal and constructed: its relations and regularities are constituted as "an order of objective phenomena governed by causal laws and independent from us" (*GS* 8:225). Nature as a scientific datum or construct, or as sheer physical appearance, is alien and unfamiliar to us, in a sense in which even a total stranger is not wholly strange to us. Dilthey asserted that among primitive peoples (and proponents of romantic *Naturphilosophie*) it was this quality of generic strangeness which prompted the animation and personification of nature. Such anthropomorphizing is an attempt to make nature intelleigible by projecting what is immediately familiar onto the otherwise incomprehensible processes of the environing world. From Galileo onward the study of natural reality became valid science to the extent that it freed itself from this type of projective ensoulment.

The human sciences, however, cannot dispense with such attributions of mental life, for "mind" is in fact constitutive of the human world itself. Knowledge of this world rests upon an experiential reality which is originally "lived through," not conceptually constructed. We know this reality first and foremost not by elaborate chains of inference and hypothesis testing, but by personal experience. The logical categories and methodological procedures of the human sciences derive ultimately from concrete structures and relations contained in the human world itself. The lived experience of the human world contains its basic relations as "given," whereas the data of the natural sciences exist only to be resolved into constructive, hypothetical relations. In the human world we do not find the same extreme split between knowing subject and object known which characterizes the scientific view of nature. Indeed the traditional dichotomy of subject/object cannot be applied in the same sense as with regard to nature, for in the human world the qualities and attributes deriving from the mental makeup of the observer are not neatly separable from the qualities of what he investigates. The special relation of subject and object in the lived experience of the human world defines both the special efficacy and problems of the human sciences:

> The human sciences have the advantage over the cognition of nature that their object is not mere appearance given in external sensation as the mere phenomenal reflex of something real but an immediate reality itself. And this reality, moreover, is given in the form of a coherence experienced from within. Yet the very manner in which reality is given in inner experience gives rise to great difficulties in apprehending it objectively [*GS* 5:317–18].

The "object" of the human sciences is not a physical object or physical processes (though it clearly may contain such objects and processes) but rather a mental reality given in experience: this reality is not resolvable into physical data. Dilthey provided a clear example of this difference: an economist may be interested in physical properties such as the make-up of the soil, but his interest is patently not identical with the chemist's. The economist concerns himself with such properties to the extent that they relate to lived-experiential realities such as "need, work, satisfaction—in short to what stands in relation to lived experience, to the understanding of experiences, or the content of lived experience expressed in judgments and concepts" (*GS* 7:311). The economist is thus concerned with "nature-for-man" and his lived experience, not nature per se. Unless some kind of special status can be assigned to man and his experience of the world, then Dilthey's claim that the human sciences are distinct from the natural sciences would be nugatory.

The natural sciences derive from a different "attitude of mind" or "orientation of consciousness toward experience." Their objects are physical process, not manifestations of mind. Experience for the natural sciences is strictly sensory experience, an "analytic minimum" stripped as far as possible of its secondary and "anthropomorphic" qualities (indeed of all "quality" as we ordinarily use the term), including value, purpose, and meaning. External sensory experience is merely the starting point for a process of abstraction, reduction, and formalization which issues in a construct or deductive hypothesis. The natural sciences must treat experience phenomenalistically and reductively, expunging its "lived" quality in order to arrive at testable hypothetical constructs and laws. These sciences do not remain at or return to the level of the concrete "sense of life" or "standpoint of life" which informs the human sciences; they arrive at their concepts, formulas, and *constructa* by intricate processes of postulation and experimental testing, rather than through immediate observation and ordinary awareness. Indeed, it is the deliberate splitting off of outer sensory experience from lived experience which is the inception for the process of abstraction which issues in natural scientific cognition. Such cognition must disregard the connections and relations inherent in concrete lived experience in order to establish another kind of connection: the order of strictly causal laws. Scientifically postulated relations are not those of the experiential world. The elements and analytic *minima* are homogeneous and equivalent; every element stands for a general class and can be submitted to exact measurement and experimentation. Though the human sciences also make use of abstractive and analytical procedures, the limits upon such procedures are considerably narrower, since these sciences derive their meaning and use from the fact that they have reference to the concrete reality of lived experience. Whereas the natural sciences must employ abstractive *minima* and elements, the human sciences deal with *individua* and concrete "wholes" (*GS* 1:29).

In spite of the fact that the natural sciences have advanced faster and more tangibly than the human sciences, Dilthey asserted that natural scientific knowledge was "derived" and "esoteric" in comparison with the human sciences—in the sense that its concepts and formulations are far removed from our daily experience of the world (*GS* 7:136; 8:175). He was, however, very careful to specify that by "derived" he did not mean to imply a value judgment concerning their cognitive validity: the natural sciences are no less true than the human sciences, they are simply true within the limits of their own procedures. It is entirely erroneous to suggest that Dilthey's separation of concrete lived experience and "derived" sensory experience implied some ultimate cognitive superiority of the former. He never maintained that the human sciences were more "real" or more valuable than the natural sciences: his point is rather that the human sciences remain closer to the ordinary sense of life and lived experience and that their content is "exoteric" and familiar in a way that the natural sciences are not. In the human world there is an experiential awareness of relations and meanings which is prior to scientific renderings: the objects of the human sciences are thus "objectively" familiar to us, even though they may not be "objectively" susceptible to physical identification and measurement. Therefore, reconciling the immediately given character of lived experience with the demand for scientific validity becomes a crucial problem for these sciences: "How are we to overcome the difficulty which everywhere weighs upon the human sciences—that of deriving universally valid propositions from inner experiences which are so personally limited, so indeterminate, so compacted and resistant to analysis?" (*GS* 6:107).

Dilthey maintained that we have an "originary" and fundamental experience of things in which "self" and "world," subject and object, are not separated as in the natural scientific rendering of experience. His words leave no doubt that lived experience is "of" the world: "What is given to us is never merely the inner life or the external world—both are not merely given together but interrelated in the most intimate bonds. This connection is first severed in the articulation of intellectual constructions" (*GS* 8:16). The "object" of the human sciences, then, is not some disembodied "mind in itself" or internal mental process, but the relation of consciousness *and* world. The "mental world" includes the "real" world as it appears to us. In the Nachlass Dilthey was even more explicit: "Here in the mental world the outer is given just as much as the inner—it is not superadded in thought." He went on to stress that self and world are strictly coeval and correlative: "A self without an other, or an outer without an inner—these are merely senseless words. All this finally boils down to the fact that there is no such thing as an 'enclosed self' from which the other or the outer could arise" (*BNL* 209/64). In the human world the "outer" is first and foremost an "other," not a sheer outer datum. It is only when Dilthey is referring to external objects as purely physical data that they function as constructions from sensory experience; as objects of lived experience, they too are implicated in a pattern of vital relationships. From the "standpoint of life," inner and outer experience operate conjointly, indeed inseparably, for the apprehension of objects is here not abstracted from its setting of lived relations. To drive his point home Dilthey spoke in his later essays of "the lived experience of outer perception." Lived experience is experience *of* the concrete world, not of an enclosed subjectivity (*GS* 7:20).

A point of great importance in Dilthey's thought is the fact that he rejects the Cartesian notion of pure knowing consciousness (*cogito*) as an arbitrary logical construct which does violence to actual experience. Repeating a theme stressed by Wilhelm von Humboldt and Feuerbach, Dilthey insisted that self and other are given together in a reciprocal relation which precludes any assignment of logical or genetic priority to one or the other. The notion of a "self without an other" evaporated into "merely senseless words"—a kind of purblind solipsism in which philosophy had immured itself in the name of logical consistency. In the 1890 study "On the Origins of Our Belief in the Outer World," Dilthey came to the notable conclusion that "the outer world is first given in other persons." From our first experiences other persons "have a higher energy of reality for us" (*GS* 5:110, 116). Although the notion "energy of reality" may seem no less assailable than the *cogito*, Dilthey was grasping for an exceedingly crucial idea: that the traditional "epistemological ego" or "transcendental subject" of European philosophy was a chimerical construct of pure thought devoid of precisely those lived relations which constitute the concrete world. Belonging to the sphere of life and of sovereign importance to the human sciences is the realm of other persons and their expressions. This world of "otherness," which is not ourselves and yet not wholly alien, provides the prime field of study for the human sciences. Here the "external world" does not stand over against us as something unrecognizable, but as a texture of relations and meanings in which we are deeply implicated. These relations provide the basis for the process of understanding (*Verstehen*) which is operative in both our daily experience and in the methodical inquiry of the human sciences.

Dilthey held to the distinction between the "mental world" of lived experience and the "physical world" of sensory experience in the steadfast conviction that it was a valid empirical distinction. It was both a philosophical judgment about experience and a sound inference from experience itself. In earlier works he contended that this difference was "given" in experience itself, but he gradually came to believe that for the difference to be given *in* experience, there had to be a kind of empirical *tertium quid* which grounded the difference. After the *Einleitung* he came to assert that experience is given *originaliter* as a unitary whole and that the distinction between "inner" and "outer" experience was itself the derivative result of reflective analysis. This distinction is at one remove from experience, while concepts such as "spirit" and "matter" are twice removed in abstraction. Thus, the difference of "lived" and "sensory" experience stemmed not from some primordial duality cleaving experience at the base, but rather from the different manner in which experience is clarified, elaborated, and modified in the operations of consciousness. After he had worked out the modes of lived experience and levels of awareness treated below, he defined lived experience and sense experience in relation to a single basic experience: experience in its primordial state is neither "inner" nor "outer," "lived" or "sensory," but is a basic given which tends to be developed along divergent lines.

Dilthey's wavering view as to whether experience is originally integral or dichotomous was influenced by the fact that the concept of experience had long been obliged to conform to narrowly physicalist and sensationalist premises: outer sensory experience was regarded as experience *tout court* and the remainder was consigned to a "nonempirical" realm of imagination, feeling, fancy, or pure thought. Dilthey's "Empirie" postulated experience as integral at base but twofold in its elaboration. In the important but unpublished "Breslauer Ausarbeitung" of 1880–83, which was to form the second volume of the *Einleitung*, Dilthey asserted emphatically that inner and outer experience were "two sides of the same experience [which is] viewed from different vantage points." When we abstract from this basic experience to arrive at natural scientific hypotheses "it is the same experience, which is here regarded from a different vantage point [*Es is dieselbe Erfahrung, welche hier unter einem verschiedenen Gesichtspunkt betrachtet wird*]" (*BA* 25). In the "Berliner Entwurf" of a decade later, written when Dilthey was rebutting charges of "logical dualism," he put the same point in even stronger terms: "There is only *one* experience which is accounted and applied in a double direction; thus arises the distinction between inner and outer experience [*Es gibt nur Eine Erfahrung, welche in einer doppelten Richtung verwertet wird, und so entsteht die Unterscheidung äusserer und innerer Erfahrung*]" (*BE* 12; see *GS* 5:434 and 18:97, 194).[3]

The two "directions" along which experience is "applied" are therefore constitutive of the natural and human sciences; our experience of the world is one, but it is elaborated differently in consciousness. The contrast of inner and outer experience in Dilthey's theory should not be construed (as it often is) as some radical metaphysical bifurcation or ontic dualism. Dilthey's careful use of phrases such as "attitude of mind" and "standpoints toward experience" to qualify the difference between inner and outer experience is meant to convey that this difference is always relative to consciousness and the way consciousness works upon and utilizes experience. The different "accountings" of experience derive from our way of being aware of it, not from some inherent difference in experience apart from our consciousness *of* it. The contrast hinges upon the manner in which experience is "there-for-me" (or there-for-consciousness), not upon some duality in experience "in itself." The notion of "experience in itself" apart from the interpretive work of consciousness was as mistaken in Dilthey's view as its rationalist counterpart of "thought in itself" apart from experience.

Thus it is not experience "in itself" but rather its accounting and application in consciousness which yields the relative distinction between inner and outer experience and between the human and natural sciences. Dilthey expressly warned against regarding this distinction as anything other than a contrast from the vantage point of the operations of consciousness. Only gradually did he come to a precise formulation of this exceedingly difficult point. In a note from the Nachlass written in 1897, he objected that neither "reality in itself" ("a useless abstraction") nor the "actual physiological configuration of man's sensory make up" ("sensoria") constituted the grounds of the distinction between inner and outer experience (*BNL* 17/79–80). After his intensive reading of Husserl's *Logical Investigations*, Dilthey affirmed in a set of notes written between 1907 and 1909 that the difference between inner lived experience and outer sensory experience was not simply logical or metaphysical but rather "phenomenological," that is, "pertaining to the manner in which experience is appropriated and elaborated in consciousness." Dilthey went on to express his strong agreement with Husserl that the distinction between the human sciences and natural sciences was "not a matter of some mystical abyss but of relatively independent realities." The distinction between these realities, Dilthey added, "must in the final analysis rest upon purely phenomeno-logical grounds and the proof of the distinction can only come through the actual progress of these sciences" (*BNL* 49/89–90).[4] Such "phenomenologi-cal grounds," while establishing the relative independence of the human and natural sciences, did not entail any a priori logical or metaphysical dualism.

Contrary to what many interpretations of his thought state, Dilthey did not posit the distinction of lived experience and sense experience—and *a fortiori* of the human and natural sciences—as some absolute, unbridgeable dichotomy. In an extended section of *Einleitung* he clearly insisted that the relation between the human and natural sciences was one of "relative independence" (*relative Selbstständigkeit*) rather than categorical separa-tion. He explicitly designated "points of intersection," of "mixture," and of "dependence" which linked the two bodies of science, insisting emphatically that "cognitions of both classes commingle everywhere." "The cognitions of the natural sciences intermingle with those of the human sciences." As examples he adduced the laws of tone formation in phonetics and music theory and the laws of ballistics in the study of warfare. "It can be seen further at this point that the knowledge of the conditions of nature developed by the natural sciences forms to a great extent [*in einem breiten Umfang*] the foundation for the study of mental phenomena." Indeed, Dilthey envisioned his task not merely as marking off the human sciences from the natural sciences in "relative independence" but as "developing the system of points of dependence [*das System von Abhängigkeiten*] by means of which they [the human sciences] are conditioned by the knowl-edge of nature." Such a task required recognition that "mental phenomena are the uppermost limit of the phenomena of nature, the phenomena of nature form the underlying conditions of mental life" (*GS* 1:17–19).[5] It should be noted that concurrent with his own efforts to define this relation of "relative independence" between the human and natural sciences, Dilthey was hailing attempts in anthropology and linguistics "to build a new bridge" between them (*GS* 17:467–68). Contrary to prevailing views of his thought, Dilthey did not maintain that there is an ontological chasm between mind and nature, nor an absolute epistemological cleavage between the human and natural sciences; the difference is emphatic, not absolute.

With regard to the distinction between the "physical" and the "psychi-cal," Dilthey remained cautiously circumspect and averse to far-flung metaphysical dualities. To avoid the suggestion of some mind-body dual-ism, Dilthey often used the term "psycho-physical unity" instead of "mind" and even "person" (*GS* 1:14–15, 17; 7:86–87, 159). He saw the proliferation of abstract dualities of body/soul, sense/reason, and the ultimate philo-sophical dichotomy of materialism/spiritualism as "fruitless hypotheses"

(*GS* 14/1:467–68). In a late manuscript written after 1908, Dilthey asserted that the "great facticity mankind" was the ultimate focal point of the human sciences but that they should eschew "one-sidedly spiritualistic accounts" of mankind. He struck a decidedly pragmatic note:

> What one usually tries to separate as the physical and the psychical is really inseparable in this phenomenon: it contains the vital coherence of both the physical and the psychical. We ourselves are nature and nature works in us, often unconsciously in dark drives. To be sure, this does not eliminate the possibility that the human sciences may make use of the distinction between the physical and the psychical where it advances their actual research goals. *But only insofar as they remain conscious of the fact that they are then working with abstractions, not with real entities, and that these abstractions are valid only within the limits of the standpoint from which they are set forth* [emphasis Dilthey's]; [*BNL* 17/74–75].

He reiterated this point in a subsequent published study, affirming that the distinction between the physical and psychical could be legitimately employed only if it is recognized that these concepts are "abstractions, not entities" and that "these abstractions have validity only within the standpoint from which they are conceived." He concluded that "both concepts can only be employed if we remain conscious of the fact that they are abstracted from the facticity mankind [*aus der Tatsache Mensch*]—they designate not full realities, but only legitimately formed abstractions" (*GS* 7:80–81).

Nor could the distinction between the human and natural sciences be wholly resolved into a simple matter of opposing logics or categories. Dilthey insisted that these two types of knowledge share in common certain elementary logical operations, formal categories, and cognitive procedures. In the formal sense, both use induction and deduction, classification, comparison, abstraction, and analysis—though the concrete application of these procedures is different (*GS* 7:121). It is not at the level of the separate, formal operations of thought that these sciences differ but in the concrete constellation of their operations in relation to an object. In a crucial passage written between 1897 and 1900, after he was accused of "logical dualism" by Wilhelm Wundt, Dilthey acknowledged the "identity" and "considerable similarity" of the formal categories and basic cognitive functions (*Erkenntnisfunktionen*) in both sets of disciplines. Dilthey went on to specify that the real logical difference between them rests not with opposing logical operations but rather in the actual "weaving together" (*Verwebung*) and "application" (*Anwendung*) of these operations in relation to specific contents (*BNL* 37/180–81).[6] Considered formally and abstractly, their elementary cognitive functions are similar, but taken in actual application as a total complex of operations, they differ. The real theoretical difference between the human sciences and natural sciences is, so to speak, a difference of "complex," that is, a difference in their respective actual "weaving together" of otherwise formally similar operations. Such a difference of "complex" (*Verwebung*) does not refer to any difference in comparative complexity, however, for Dilthey acknowledged both bodies of science to be highly complicated (*zusammengesetzt*) (*GS* 7:158). It is the concrete complex or "weave" of objects, methods, and logical operations together which accounts for the "relative independence" of the human and natural sciences. Dilthey insisted that the true logical relation of the human and natural sciences could be shown only if the false, abstract alternative of transcendental and empiricist standpoints was overcome (*GS* 1:20).

Opposed to competing views, Dilthey maintained that the human and natural sciences could not be neatly separated on the sole basis of either "object" or "method." He was skeptical of pat dichotomies and a priori logical distinctions. Indeed, for him object and method are strictly correlative and the attempt to separate them neatly leads either to false metaphysics or false epistemology. In distinguishing between the human and natural sciences there is no pure and simple *differentia*, but rather a combination or "complex" of grounds—grounds which are at once empirical, logical, epistemological, and methodological (or, in his later phrase, "phenomenological"). These two systems of knowledge are not defined by different types of being or material entities but by different standpoints of consciousness.

Dilthey contested the view that there is any inherent difference between natural objects and mental products "in themselves," that it, apart from consciousness: "A difference between natural objects and mental objects does not exist" (*GS* 5:248). In a passage in the Nachlass, he insisted that the human sciences could not be defined by "a special and determinate object in itself [*Gegenstand an sich*] but only by an attitude toward the object [*Verhalten zum Gegenstand*]" (*BNL* 17/79).[7] Accordingly, he defined the object of the human sciences by means of a cluster of terms: the "mental world," "mind and its products," "mental expressions and objectivations," "everything on which man has put his stamp," "cultural life," "the human-historical world," and most comprehensively as the "great facticity mankind" (*GS* 1:24, 27; 7:70, 81, 84). These terms are specifications of the fundamental concept of "life" (*das Leben*), which Dilthey declared to be the underlying reality which the various human sciences explore from different angles of vision. The manifestations of life tend to elicit a special kind of awareness (or "attitude"), which in conjunction with the operations of thought becomes a distinct method of knowing peculiar to the human sciences; this is the method of hermeneutic understanding (*Verstehen*).

There is a kind of intelligibility specific to the human world. Confronted with objects, actions, or expressions which are the products of mind, the mind of the observer moves from the sheer perceptual datum to the grasping of an inner meaning. Dilthey often characterized this grasping as a "movement from outer to inner"—a formula he recognized as misleadingly spatial and contestable from a strictly logical point of view, but for which there was not better substitute. As in defining the object of the human sciences, so too in defining their method Dilthey provided a cluster of designations. He termed it "understanding," "interpretation," "analytical grasping," "inner-genetic explanation," "extraction of mental content," and "seeing in coherence" (*GS* 1:94–95; 6:125; 7:131, 158, 163). These terms are grouped around the basic concept of methodical understanding (*Verstehen*), which will be taken up later in detail. In view of the variety of terms employed to designate the subject matter and procedures of the human sciences, it is apparent that he did not propose a single and rigidly exclusive object or method for them. Method and object are reciprocally conditioning; they indicate rather than dictate each other.

The human sciences are marked by what Dilthey termed a special "practical interest" and relation to the "*praxis* of life" (*GS* 1:22–24; 7:316). This is not to say that the natural sciences are devoid of practical and technical functions, but rather that this practical application has come, over time, to stand in a different relation to the theoretical foundations of these sciences:

> There is a far deeper reciprocal connection between the human sciences, whose object is man and human culture, and the transformations of this same culture than that which exists between the natural sciences and their practical results for subjecting nature to our purposes. This is not to say that the needs of practical life and technical discovery have no effect upon the natural sciences. Indeed, a factor essential to the rapid progress of the experimental natural sciences in our times is to be found in the twin conditions that work has become increasingly the province of the free citizen and the simultaneous linking of such free work with forms of knowledge. But in the human sciences there prevails a special fundamental relation [*Grundverhältnis*] such that we are living in society at once as an active agent [*wirkendes Element*] and also as aware of our effects [*unserer Wirkungen uns bewusst*] [*GS* 18:18].

The natural sciences gained their status as rigorous knowledge to the degree that they departed from concrete experience and *praxis* to deductively formulated theory. Dilthey pointed out that geometry became an axiomatic science in abstracting a body of principles and theorems for the original practical tasks of surveying and navigation. Likewise, mechanics and chemistry were constituted as genuine sciences in going beyond their practical roots in the "arts" of machine-building and smelting.

The human sciences, on the other hand, retained immediate and intimate connections with the "*praxis* of life"—connections which remain direct and pervasive; This practical aspect is constitutive of the human sciences even at the level of their most abstract, theoretical formulation. Dilthey found that the human sciences arose "naturally" from the needs and practice of life. They investigate "a world which the human mind made before submitting it to a scientific-theoretical formulation" (GS 7:70, 79; also 1:21, 60). In his historical analysis of the development of these sciences, Dilthey showed that grammar, logic, rhetoric, jurisprudence, history, and political theory all arose from practical, instructional purposes. They were intended to aid in the actual conduct of individual, social, and civic life. Even in their modern form they have not been divested of this practical interest: "They are essentially determined by influences which are different from our purely intellectual approach to objects—that is, by the nature and condition of nations, by the ideas of eras, by the turmoil in societies and states, and by the impulsive power of interests as voiced in public opinion" (GS 5:32). Human beings live in a world of their own practical devising before they submit it to theoretical reflection and scientific treatment. This practical involvement cannot be neatly prescinded as in the case of physical reality. The deep and subtle suffusion of practical interests in the human sciences constituted the source of their reformative power—but also of their potential abuse and distortion. The critical recognition and control of these interests was an important aspect of the critique of historical reason, for only then could they be marshaled for constructive tasks. Near the end of his life Dilthey echoed the practical reforming zeal of his youth: "The meaning of the human sciences and their theory lies first and foremost in helping us with what we have to do in the world—with what we want to make of ourselves, with determining what we can undertake in the world and likewise what influence the world has upon us" (GS 7:276). The human sciences remain rooted in what Dilthey termed the "standpoint of life." Their theory and methodology are ultimately based upon the individual's intimate and practical understanding of what it means to be a human being in the world.

The Standpoint of Life and Lived Experience

Stated in the most general terms the human sciences investigate "life" (*das Leben*) and take their departure from what Dilthey called "the standpoint of life," "standpoint of empirical consciousness," or simply "the natural attitude" (GS 5:136; 6:319; 7:261, 323; BA 216). These seemingly simple yet somehow nebulous terms were invested with a pointed, even technical meaning which belies their obviousness. In a passage from the Nachlass written between 1895 and 1897, Dilthey provided a striking, almost lyrical formulation of his conception of life:

The expression "life" denotes what is to everyone the most familiar and intimate, but at the same time the darkest and even most imponderable. All wonder, thought, and inquiry [*Alles Staunen, Denken, und Forschen*] arise from this most inscrutable of things. All knowledge is rooted in this most unfathomable of things. One can describe it. One can elucidate its peculiar and characteristic traits. One can, as it were, inquire after its tone, rhythm, and melody. But one cannot analyze it totally into all its factors, for it is not totally resolvable in this manner. What it is cannot be expressed in a simple formula or explanation. Thought cannot fully go behind life, for it is the expression of life [*BNL* 209/78].

For Dilthey, life is the primary and fundamental human reality and the sovereign datum of the human sciences. It is a cardinal concept in his thought and yet he insists that it is the kind of radically fundamental reality which eludes conventional conceptual treatment. This condition has prompted some interpreters to speak not of his "concept" of life but of his "idea" of life, thus invoking the special Kantian and transcendental sense of "Idea." This view, however, carries his notion in an idealist and metaphysical direction which is directly at odds with his intent. Life is a thoroughly empirical reality—the human reality which all of us "live through" and constantly refer to in ordinary speech; it is the human condition itself, not a transcendental Idea. There is no reality outside or beyond life, for everything we can think, perceive, or imagine is ultimately rooted in our existence. "Life is the first and primary thing—in it are woven all mental functions such as perception, ideation, and thought" (*BNL* 209/71). It is the overarching "great facticity" which encompasses all the particular facts and separate experiences which can be selected from it. Life is given to consciousness as an experiential reality through an awareness which does not necessarily proceed by way of explicit, conscious inference. It is a "sensed" reality, but not in the sense of the atomic "positive facts" of the positivists or the "ideas" of speculative philosophy. As Dilthey put it, "life is its own proof" and it has no more fundamental ground or reference (*GS* 5:131).[8] Given the primordial and encompassing nature of Dilthey's notion of life, it might seem plausible to equate it with the "Being" of metaphysics or with such concepts as Kant's *Ding an sich*, Goethe's *Urphänomen*, or Hegel's *konkrete Allgemeinheit*. Although there are certain undeniable resonances among these notions, Dilthey's specific conception of life cannot justly be regarded as the foundation for a metaphysics or ontology, for such attempts to grasp "Being in itself" are in his view foredoomed to failure. Life cannot be fathomed in a science fashioned either as physics or metaphysics.

Life is neither physical nor metaphysical but concretely empirical in Dilthey's sense of "Empirie." It is conveyed in perfectly commonplace and intelligible phrases such as "the life of Schleiermacher," "the life of the Christian sects," "life on the frontier," and so on. It is not "substance," "idea," or discrete "fact" but human reality as it exists for human consciousness.[9] It is a decidedly holistic notion but one which Dilthey insisted was within limits subject to analytical treatment. Life is experienced immediately or "lived through" by each person; thus one knows it not by a set of explicit inferences but through direct experience. It cannot be divorced from an "external" world or reality apart from consciousness: "The world is in us. Therefore it is woven out of the stuff of our self-consciousness" (GS 5:143). As it is present to consciousness, "life is there for us only as a coherence [Zusammenhang]" (GS 8:259). Life itself (das Leben selber) is the relation of self and world (GS 18:137).

Dilthey often referred to the necessity of "understanding life on its own terms." In this task he felt himself part of a larger current of modern thought which broke with both metaphysics and positivism but had not yet found its own standpoint and method. This movement of thought rejected both the airy constructions of speculative philosophy and the bare reductions of positivism in favor of a more direct "interpretation of life" (Lebensdeutung) as it is lived by concretely experiencing subjects: "somehow to understand life as it is lived by men—that is the will of modern man" (GS 7:121). Dilthey believed that the human sciences could furnish this understanding if they were placed upon a proper footing: this basis began in what he termed "the standpoint of life" or "standpoint of full experience."

Beside the more obviously indicative terms "standpoint of natural science," "standpoint of religion," or "standpoint of metaphysics" to which Dilthey often contrasted it, the phrase "standpoint of life" sounds like an inert generality or empty tautology—either far too vague or too obvious to occupy the pivotal role assigned to it. Yet Dilthey meant something quite specific by the term and he came to mark it off from several superficially similar positions. By "standpoint of life" Dilthey designated a mode of having and interpreting experience which grasps it in its original "raw state" (Rohzustand) of primary concreteness, prior to any abstractly scientific rendering (wissenschaftliche Bearbeitung) as accomplished in the natural sciences (GS 7:13). Such a standpoint does not find experience devoid of pattern and structure, but acknowledges it to be different from the abstractly formalized structure of natural scientific conceptualization. The standpoint of life, as defined by Dilthey, is akin to William James' "radical empiricism," Husserl's "phenomenological standpoint," and Alfred Schütz' "natural attitude."

The standpoint of life allows things to appear as what they are "for us" (für uns) in actual lived experience rather than hastily introducing conditions and constructs to account for the purported grounds and causes of such appearances. In contrast to both physics and metaphysics, the standpoint of life demands the fullest possible viewing and description of experience prior to the formulation of models, schema, and hypotheses. It practices the description of actual experience as it is "there-for-us" (Für-uns-

Dasein) as concrete subjects. This standpoint, as the point of departure for the *human* sciences of a *human* world, does not comply with the tendency of natural scientific conceptualization and explanation (and philosophies based upon them) to expunge the meaning from human experience by reducing lived experience to sensory experience, thereby stripping it of its specifically human "sense" and meaning.

From the standpoint of life, the perception of a tree is not simply a set of visual stimuli that can be resolved into optic and neural data but is rather the lived experience of the tree situated in a context of experientially implicit meanings, interests, and values, such as "blocking my view," "shade in summer," "fuel in winter," "beautiful," etc., which have reference to human life itself. From the standpoint of life these qualitative features and meanings are as real, factual, and objective as the purely physical processes involved in the perception of the tree. The tree is a "what" as well as a "how" for the understanding. The word "experience," as normally used, specifically encompasses these qualities and meanings of things—indeed, it refers first and foremost to this dimension of experience rather than what Dilthey called its "scientific rendering." For this reason Dilthey sometimes referred to the standpoint of life as "the natural attitude" (*GS* 6:319).

It might perhaps seem strange that a special exertion of thought is required to attain what is designated as the "natural attitude" or "standpoint of life." Are we not simply "in" it "naturally" and that is the end of the matter? Dilthey maintained that the long-standing preoccupation with abstraction and hypothetical constructs had so determined the very definitions of experience, of knowledge, science, and reason that the standpoint of life had been obscured; though "natural" to life, it had to be recovered by effort. His purpose was not to remain wholly at this level, but to integrate the standpoint of life into a wider conception of reason. In its initial function this "natural attitude" runs counter to the tendency of the "natural scientific attitude" (and must not be confused with "naturalism"), but for Dilthey it by no means connoted a repudiation of *Wissenschaft* or scientific knowledge as such. It was to provide the basis for an expanded conception of science which encompasses and raises to knowledge precisely what the narrowly physicalist and positivist conceptions of science ignore by exclusion.

Dilthey insisted that it was necessary to go behind conventional natural scientific assumptions and methods in order to secure a genuinely empirical foundation for the human sciences. The experiential reality investigated by these sciences was not the sort which could be reduced to purely physical or psycho-physical correlates. Using the term "metaphysical" in its original Aristotelian sense of "after the *Physics*" but not "beyond experience," Dilthey observed: "The full and unrestricted grasping (*unbefangene Auffassung*) of experience always shows experience to be referring to a real meaning and real coherence which is not meta-empirical (*nicht überempirisch*) but which is at the same time something metaphysical in its value and meaning" (*BDY* 92).[10] The meaning of lived experience, however, is not transcendent but is immanently constituted in the coherence of life itself: "life does not mean anything other than itself. There is nothing in it which points to a meaning beyond itself" (*GS* 8:234). In a curious phrase he spoke of a "natural metaphysic" of daily (*tagtäglich*) life which lies at the base of the human sciences (*GS* 18:192).

A cardinal tenet of Dilthey's thinking is that life is prior to conceptual thought and knowledge. In many different forms he repeated the basic observation that "life is the prius of thought" (*GS* 5:5, 136, 194, 196; 8:264). Thought operates in a wider life-coherence (*Lebenszusammenhang*) which is not of its own making but is rather its vital, ongoing precondition, both in the sense of source and presupposition. Thought is not autochthonic—it neither arises from nor begins with itself, but rather originates in life and ultimately refers back to it. Thought cannot "go behind" its source and reference to achieve a total and exhaustive grasp of this reality in the manner of Hegel's *Begriff*. Thought is limited to the interpretation and analysis of life: "We cannot reach life through a system but must rather proceed from the analysis of life" (*GS* 7:276). We are deeply engaged in life before we embark upon the attempt to know it; but rather than invalidating our inquiry, this existential precondition of "immanence in life" is at the same time the precondition of our knowing it. We must grasp life and lived experience from within.

There is no Archimedean point or presuppositionless position for the comprehension of life and the human world. Nor is there a timeless antecedent or static, eternal a priori of which life is the reflection or merely phenomenal manifestation. Dilthey rejected as a "contradictio in adjecto" the view that our actual experience of life is merely the phenomenal appearance of something more "real"—a view shared by both idealists and positivists despite their otherwise great differences. The ancient notion of pure thought or pure reason thinking itself free of all traces of experience founders on the condition that thought takes its departure from actual existence. Dilthey stated tersely: "It is an error of abstract intellectualism that thoughts arise purely and simply out of other thoughts" (*BNL* 137/83). Dilthey found that Herder, Schleiermacher, Humboldt, and others who had adumbrated the discovery of life as an explicit theme of reflection and study were led to conclude that we think in order to live, not vice versa. Dilthey, however, was far from taking "life" in a biological sense, which would make thought into a mere instrumentality of survival. All branches and forms of thought, including the abstract nodes of mathematics and formal logic, ultimately refer back to life, even though this reference may be enormously indirect and abstractive. The most general historical forms of life such as art, religion, philosophy, and science itself are all rooted in this fundamental reality, though their specific aims and perspectives are vastly different.

Life is not pure thought or pure consciousness, but it nevertheless includes consciousness as a constitutive feature. Life as it is lived through in experience is characterized by consciousness of itself or self-consciousness. Over the course of his reflections Dilthey came to stress more and more strongly that this self-consciousness is necessarily indirect and inseparably implicated with the "non-self." Life is not sheer brute existence, unreflective and wholly immersed in itself. However haltingly and imperfectly, human existence is disposed to a reflective awareness of itself, both at the level of individual experience and at the shared sociocultural level which draws these experiences together as a whole: "Every experience has a tendency to become conscious" (*BNL* 140/433–34). In the final analysis, "the world is *in toto* the making conscious of life" (*GS* 8:17). Man does not simply live; he leads his life with a more or less conscious sense of direction and pattern. In a suggestive (and somewhat Hegelian) turn of phrase, Dilthey defined life as "being which possesses itself" (*Sein, das sich besitzt*) (*GS* 18:166). This capacity for self-consciousness means that human life is not determined by purely immediate conditions or external necessity but to a certain extent chooses its own course. Man individually and collectively lives in a continuum of memory and anticipation: he has both past and future as integral conditions of the standpoint of life. The course of this life can be changed consciously in the form of action toward ideals and purposes. Though he rejected otherworldly notions of transcendence, Dilthey endowed human life and consciousness with a kind of immanent or empirical power of transcendence, that is, an inherent tendency to move by reflection and action beyond its immediate condition. Life shows reflective, anticipatory, and projective capacities which carry it beyond the here and now, yet always within experience. Human life always tends to move beyond a static present; it is inherently developmental.

Human life manifests a tendency to rise to ever higher levels of self-consciousness and conscious integration, but it never becomes wholly "spirit" in the sense of the idealists. Life retains an ineluctable basis in nature which is never fully transcended or overcome. On this point Dilthey's thought follows the *Idealrealismus* of Schleiermacher and Trendelenburg in rejecting the sharp separation between man's sensual-natural side (*Sinnlichkeit*) and his moral-cultural side (*Sittlichkeit*). Indeed one of the hallmarks of Dilthey's ethical, pedagogical, and aesthetic theory, as well as his historical writing, is the conjunction and interaction of these two realms. The mind does not create life; for the most part it reacts to it. At the most basic level the mind functions to provide for the needs of practical existence; here it operates in close conjunction with drives and instincts. When these needs are more or less satisfied, the mind moves toward other regions of more purely intellectual or aesthetic values and ideals. What the mind creates in this sphere often stands in tension with what transpires in the practical world, where the premises of its activity are to be found. This tension is the origin of the constant process of reciprocal interaction between "real" and "ideal," "nature" and "mind," which characterizes human life.

The natural basis of life (*das Naturell*) is composed of basic drives and impulses which constitute the "energetic core" of the human mind. Dilthey held that "man is first of all a system of drives" and in one of his few lapses into mechanical metaphor asserted that these drives are "the strong springs in the clock of life" (*GS* 5:95; 6:154). The basic drives for food, shelter, security, and procreation are in themselves neither good or bad. They can be limited and transformed in their effects but never cast off completely, for they are the natural foundation of all processes of the will: "We ourselves are nature and nature works in us unconsciously in dark drives" (*GS* 8:80). Traditional idealism, in its premature "haste to transcendence," put a one-sided emphasis upon man's rational and conscious capacities and thus promoted an oversimplified version of human behavior. Dilthey deplored the optimistic naïveté of this view: "Human nature has never been more egregiously misconstrued than in the benignant [*schönseelige*] aesthetic or intellectualist interpretation" (*GS* 10:50). Man has a kind of double nature: the "Naturell" of drives and instincts and a cultural "second nature" which has been produced gradually in history. Both sides are evident in the life-values and world-views which men create to organize reality. In contrast to the statically dualistic theories of man advanced by thinkers such as Kant and Pascal, Dilthey postulated a constant reciprocal inter-action (*Wechselwirkung*) between the spheres of nature and culture, leading to ever novel stages of historical development.

Life is not pure "spirit" but neither is it identical with its foundation in nature. Dilthey's view of man is close to that of Wilhelm von Humboldt, who held that "man must be regarded as a creature of nature and yet at the same time not altogether as a creature of nature." In a review Dilthey quoted Goethe on the same subject: "There is no spirit without nature, no nature without spirit" (*WM* 39[1876]:554). Dilthey was more in agreement with Humboldt than Goethe, however, for he did not conceive life in Goethe's biological or quasibiological sense, which was cosmically evolu-tionary without being truly historical. Life for Dilthey is preeminently a historical or biographical datum, not a biological phenomenon. Even though life cannot be entirely identified with consciousness, it is *conscious* experience over time which defines life in the human-historical world. It should be noted that after the emergence of various forms of "vitalism" around the turn of the century—including Bergson, Nietzsche, Hans

Driesch, and their popularizers—Dilthey stipulated emphatically that his use of the term "life" was restricted solely to the human world (*Menschenwelt*); such usage was "determinate and unequivocal" and did not apply to other organic beings (*GS* 6:314; 7:121, 229). The fashionable use of analogies from biology was no less subject to error than previous borrowings from physics. Such projections and importations (*Übertragungen*) tended to hamper rather than facilitate the understanding of life on its own terms. After discarding certain biological parallels and concepts carried over from Trendelenburg and Johannes Müller, Dilthey insisted that human existence has its own intrinsic categories and forms which derive from its own special standpoint. The "standpoint of life," though influenced by natural reality at many points, is not to be confused with the natural scientific standpoint: "If one takes nature as the sole starting point, one never gets beyond nature" (*WM* 39[1876]:559–60).

Life from its own "starting point" is the concrete course of experience-in-consciousness. It is not static substance or natural regularity but activity *sub specie temporalis*. Expressed metaphorically " it is a flame, not a being; energy, not entity" (*BNL* 209/80). Life is temporal and historical down to the level of its most basic forms and structures. To emphasize this quality of dynamic activity, Dilthey occasionally substituted the term *Lebendigkeit* for the more static *Leben*. Graf Yorck, who was attracted to the dynamic imagery of Heraclitus, insisted that it should be said of the human being not that he *is*, but rather that he *lives* (*BDY* 71). To stress further the difference between natural processes and human existence, Yorck posited a "generic difference" between what he called "the ontic" or "the natural" (*das Ontische*) and "the historical" (*das Geschichtliche, geschichtliches Leben*). Although Dilthey characteristically avoided such metaphysical distinctions in favor of empirical and phenomenological ones, both he and Yorck agreed that "historicity" (*Geschichtlichkeit*) and "temporality" (*Zeitlichkeit*) were fundamental categories of life (*BDY* 91; *GS* 6:314). From the standpoint of life man knows himself as a "creature of time" (*GS* 5:364). A distinctive trait of human life derives from the capacity of the mind to relate past, present, and future into a coherence expressing aims, values, and purposes. Through the entire body of Dilthey's work runs the insistent claim that this distinctively temporal-historical dimension of life had not been properly incorporated into the suppositions and concepts of the human sciences.

This condition stemmed from shortcomings in conventional logic and theories of knowledge—shortcomings which Hegel had perceived but ultimately exacerbated by his dialectical formulations. Because it is dynamic and changing, life manifests relations and features which appear to conceptual thought as elusive or self-contradictory. Logic insists upon clearly defined, self-identical concepts and propositions, whereas life manifests what Dilthey called "diremption" and "real-dialectical oppositions."

Life is "multifariousness, transformations into real oppositions, the conflict of real forces" (GS 8:69). In stressing such diremption and transformation, Dilthey seems to come close to some of Hegel's formulations, but whereas Hegel ultimately insisted upon the superordinate role of reason in these transformations, Dilthey emphasized that human existence and history are impelled not by an *Idealdialektik* of thought but a *Realdialektik* of concrete forces and tendencies in which thought plays a determining but not wholly determinative role. In analyzing the real-dialectical oppositions in life, Dilthey isolated the following pairs as especially significant in the formation of the human-historical world: (1) the time-bound and transitory character of life versus the strong impulse for stability and repose; (2) the great power of natural forces versus the perceived autonomy of human will; (3) the consciousness of the finitude and limit of human knowledge, cultural forms, and institutions versus the demonstrated human capacity to transcend what were previously perceived as limits. Such real-dialectical oppositions are not merely formal categories of thought, for they derive from actual conditions of concrete life. They constitute the core of what Dilthey called the "great mysteries" of existence: birth and death, reason and contingency, law and freedom (GS 8:80).[12]

The standpoint of life entails an intrinsic diremption which gives rise to reflection and knowledge. We are wholly "in" life and familiar with its forms, but it also retains an aspect of strangeness for us. Life as it is actually lived by men is not a simple or positive "fact" or "object," but a perpetually problematic situation which we are constantly led to reflect upon. This urge to reflection and self-understanding arises from a sense of incompleteness, the experience of frustrated effort, and the perception and revision of limits. One of the great impulses which moves us to reflect upon life is the consciousness of the ephemeralness of life itself. Dilthey designated this basic quality of life as its "corruptability" (*Korruptibilität*); it is the darker and more ominous side of man's historicity (GS 7:72). At the root of this consciousness lies the anticipation of death, which may be conscious or unconscious. Dilthey asserted that we know "about" death in a somewhat remote and external sense, but we cannot truly "understand" it as we understand life. We have a knowledge of the death of others, but our understanding stops short of really grasping our own, even though we know it to be inevitable. Death is thus a powerful presence—a constant, silent awareness of death conditions life and bestows meaning and sense upon it by impelling us to self-reflection. In a section of the "Breslauer Ausarbeitung" intended to establish a link between the conditions of knowledge and the conditions of life—between epistemology and anthropology—Dilthey referred to death in Socratic terms as "the great teacher," which by its threat of ultimate rupture conducts us to a more acute awareness of our connections with life and the world. Death makes life questionable to us and is at once the most fruitful and most fearsome influence or "presence" at work in life (*BA* 218). In his 1887 essay on Goethe, Dilthey spoke of "the deepest and most general relation which conditions our feeling for existence—that of life toward death [*das des Lebens zum Tode*]; for the limitation of our existence by death is always decisive for our understanding and assessment of life" (*ED* 162). A sense of death is silently at work in the standpoint of life and our understanding of the human world.

Although life is transitory and always changing, it is also characterized by relatively stable coherences and structures which can be elucidated by analysis. Life is "becoming" rather than static "being" but it develops in patterns and coherences. These patterns stem from the fact that experience is intrinsically synthetic: life is process, but coherent process. The coherence in experience pertains not to the "external" physical properties of experience but to its contents. The transitory occurrence of every experiential act or event is offset by the fact that the contents of experiences (which as mere "acts" may be vastly separated in time) are brought together in an inner relation and ultimately into an overall coherence of life (*Lebenszusammenhang*). Life is thus experienced as a dynamic coherence: it runs its course with the passage of time, but its experiential content is determined by structures which assimilate new experiences to the acquired coherence of past experience. "The whole course of life is a structural coherence of experiences widely dispersed in time, structured from within and bound into a unity" (*GS* 7:335). However paradoxical it might seem, Dilthey held that the dynamic unity of experience was a kind of "developing a priori" which conditions all future experience. Life has an immanent teleological structure of surpassing itself and moving beyond its present condition, but it does so within its acquired patterns: "there is always inherent in life the impulse [*das Moment*] which leads beyond it" (*GS* 7:266).

In his description of experience from the standpoint of life, Dilthey assigned a certain priority to the whole coherence over the parts, though his "holism" did not preclude analytical procedures. "Mental life does not arise from parts; it is not constructed out of simple elements. . . . It is originally and always an overarching unity. Mental functions have differentiated themselves from this unity but they always remain linked to this total coherence" (*GS* 5:211). A new way of thinking about experience was required to elucidate the nature of this coherence:

> If one proceeds from the total coherence of life, then all analysis aiming at the elementary and particular remains in the background: this coherence points toward the immanent teleology of life as the condition from which the elementary can be first understood as a component, but never as its original foundation [*BDY* 247].

Because it functions in a wider coherence of life, consciousness is always "directed," "disposed," "taking a position." The mind is not all-sided and omniscient but rather selective and oriented: it has a horizon and direction which are often subtly induced by concerns and interests of which we are only vaguely aware. In the "Breslauer Ausarbeitung," Dilthey stressed there are many levels of consciousness and we cannot analogize it as a *tabula rasa*, empty stage, or searchlight which illuminates everything equally (*BA* 75–83, 147; also *GS* 18:134–35). He even suggested that the breadth and depth of consciousness vary in inverse relation to each other. To illustrate the selectively focused nature of consciousness, he cited cases of listeners who shut their eyes to attend to what is heard—or of afflicted persons who forget their bodily pain when performing a demanding task (*BA* 160). Our perception of the world and of ourselves is led by our *Darinnensein im Leben*—the way we are "in" life and our "way of life."

Dilthey often characterized human existence as a radically immanent "being-in-life" (*Darinnensein im Leben*), stressing that we are "in" life in a special way: "this being-in-life accomplishes itself in stances taken toward life—that is, in the relations of life (*Lebensbezüge*)" (*GS* 7:99). Even though life is a comprehensive totality, we are obliged to take a position, attitude, or orientation. Our existence impels us to adopt a standpoint—both toward it and in it. This standpoint may be assumed with varying degrees of self-conscious awareness and inclusiveness, but it is assumed nonetheless by every person. We know life from within because we are vitally engaged in it. Our knowledge of this reality is not disinterested or neutrally "theoretical." Dilthey repeatedly criticized what he termed "ocularism" or "opsis," that is, an excessively detached and "spectatorial" account of our relation to reality. Modern thought tended to conceive of the human subject as pure thought for which the known world is not the perceived world of lived experience but a logical-mathematical construct endowed with pure and timeless certainty. The paradoxical result of this disjunction between abstract reason and concrete experience was that "since Descartes we have been taken up in building bridges to the external world" (*BDY* 55). But from the standpoint of life, "I am as certain of the outside world as I am of myself" (*BA* 49).

Life in the world is not "there for us" as a distant spectacle which we contemplate with Olympian aloofness. "What we call reality is something quite different from the dead and passive objectivity which resembles an image in a mirror" (*BA* 204). Dilthey insisted that "every lived experience is complexly compounded" (*GS* 5:373). Reality from the standpoint of life is a complex of vital interests and lived relations, not abstractive constructs: "Reality is what stands in relation to the totality of our consciousness in thinking, willing, and feeling" (*GS* 7:257). The conative and affective sides of mental life are constitutive of our experience along with the more strictly cognitive functions: "In lived experience the processes of the whole mind work together" (*GS* 5:172). The fusion of these mental functions means that reality appears as a texture of lived relations: they are not superadded to a more fundamental "pure" datum, but are constitutive of the experienced world: "Daily experience shows that the perception of objects is attended by feeling and willing" (*BNL* 243/77).

> There is no man and no thing which would only be an object for me and not a hindrance or help, a goal for striving or an instance of will, importance, demand for attention, closeness or opposition, distance or strangeness. The vital relation, whether momentary or lasting, makes men and objects into bearers of happiness, expansion of my existence, extension of my power—or they restrict the horizon of my existence, exert a restriction upon me, and lessen my potentiality [*GS* 7:131].

Thus the very perception of things accomplishes a kind of implicit interpretation from the standpoint of life. Everything we encounter is permeated with meaning for life and we experience things in terms of this tacit meaning. Such perception is an active and deeply practical affair: "the 'I' is not an onlooker who sits before the stage of the world, but is itself action and reaction" (*BA* 188). Our relation to life in the world cannot be "theoretical" in the original sense of *theorein*, a "godlike viewing." Yorck employed a striking image to convey the subtly pervasive nature of the lived relations: suggesting a corrective to the "ocular" bias of Western thought since the Greeks, he referred to "the hand which is implicit in the eye."[13]

By virtue of the selective yet synthetic nature of consciousness, each individual gradually acquires a particular but comprehensive interpretation of his life in relation to the world, which Dilthey terms the "world-view." This world-view is a combination of reflective, conscious awareness and pre-reflective interests and practical concerns. It relates one's own inner awareness to the world at large. The world-view is a meaning-structure which gives coherence to the individual's ongoing experience. It is a synthesis of the basic and recurring "lived relations" and vital coherences which the person finds himself in. It provides consistency, integration, and stability in the face of the constant influx of new experiences. The world-view, like the lived experience it synthesizes, is not simply the result of cognitive thinking, but of willing and feeling as well. All the capacities of the mind are brought together in a functional coherence—though Dilthey came to hold that one capacity tends to predominate, giving direction to the others. Pursuing this analysis further, he concluded that there is a typology of these world-views and a special discipline (*Weltanschauungslehre*) concerned with their historical and systematic explication. This particular facet of his thought is crucial to his understanding of life "on its own terms," but as a specific doctrine it is best examined in a separate chapter.

Through the process of acquiring and integrating new experience in a patterned life (and view of that life), human existence assumes the character of individuality. Dilthey found that the process of differentiation and individuation was a fundamental trait of human life and therefore of prime importance to the human sciences. Owing to tendencies operating within life itself, a major portion of the objects studied by the human sciences must be conceived as *individua* or relatively self-contained "wholes" rather than the abstract, homogeneous *minima* of the natural sciences. The individual, to be sure, manifests traits in common with other persons—to an extent that Dilthey often referred to a common "human nature"—but in addition to this universal set of attributes, the individual acquires a distinctive core of personality which is unique and irreducible. The individual coherence of personality is biographical and historical; it confounds all attempts to resolve it into a "natural" foundation. "I am history as well as nature" Dilthey observed of the individual, citing Goethe's injunction that one had to relive 3,000 years of history in order to understand oneself (*BDY* 72; *GS* 18:183). From the standpoint of life and from the perspective of the human sciences, the human being must be conceived as *ens positivum*, an irreducible and concrete reality. In this regard Dilthey's thought is closer to the pluralistic premises of Schleiermacher and Humboldt than the monism of Hegel, for whom the individual is not something final and autonomous but a "moment" to be overcome in the progressive emergence of the Absolute. Paraphrasing Humboldt's retort to all systems of thought which subsume the individual in some larger totality, Dilthey admonished: "Individuals are not merely more or less temporarily flourishing leaves on the tree of humanity, who grew out and then fall off in order to fertilize the soil of humanity" (*WM* 40[1876]:441).

A prime feature of the individual is that he has a will of his own. For Dilthey this will is "free," though in a special way which he was careful to distinguish from previous doctrines of free will. In both the published and the unpublished writings, Dilthey asserted that the will must be granted a wider role within the theory of mind in general and in the human sciences in particular. Whether they care to acknowledge it or not, the human sciences cannot help but operate with a notion of the will and they must take care to establish it critically. In a terse note in the Nachlass Dilthey judged that "the theory of the will constitutes the real working foundation of the human sciences—and such a theory is especially important to the handling of history" (*BNL* 168/66). In a later, more extended section he provided the outlines of such a theory of the will—not a primarily self-contained philosophical theory like the idealists' but one with direct bearing upon the aims of the human sciences. Dilthey insisted that the treatment of human will must avoid two traditional but tempting and treacherous extremes: (1) the assimilation of the will to the conception of the causal necessity of natural processes and (2) the portrayal of will as the "unconditioned *actus purus"* of Fichte's transcendental voluntarism. Between these two positions Dilthey stipulated that will is "free" in a quite special sense, not yet fully recognized in the practice of human sciences: not free *from* conditions, but free to *respond to* a multiplicity of conditions as mediated through consciousness and cultural forms. Freedom is thereby defined in terms of a range of possible responses and choices within a concrete situation. Taken together, these choices constitute the basis of individual character (*Charakter*). This character of an individual is not "fate" or "necessity" but a pattern of integrated responses and mediated reactions:

> The development of this inner pattern is the formation of character, which realizes itself in freedom, but this is not a freedom from conditions. This freedom is perceived in the inner experience of responsibility, the consciousness of accountability to one's fellows, and the possibility of regret for one's acts. Freedom as such cannot be known as discrete fact, since all such factual knowing must proceed according to the principle of sufficient reason. In the schema of science the will is not anti-logical but a-logical [*nicht antilogisch sondern a-logisch*] [*BNL* 191/68–69].

In dealing with individual will and character, the human sciences must acknowledge the limits of knowledge imposed by the peculiar nature of human freedom. From the standpoint of life, man knows himself to be at once "conditioned and unconditioned" (*bestimmt-unbestimmt*) (*BA* 99). These conditions derive not only from natural necessity but from society and culture.

The Social and Cultural Matrix of Life and Lived Experience

If life as "lived" is individuated and in some sense uniquely personal, it is also deeply implicated in a wider coherence composed of other persons and the patterns of society and culture. It is a matter of empirical fact that the individual stands in a complex texture of relations with others. In the *Einleitung* Dilthey asserted that "the connection of the individual with humanity is a reality"—or, as he put it later, "the individual life is part of life as a whole" (*GS* 1:100; 7:359). Such judgments were not simply moral postulates or pious wishes, but rather empirical facts of life to be explicated by the human sciences. Reflection from the standpoint of life shows that "we belong integrally to a total mental realm of which we are a part" (*GS* 5:35). "The foremost trait of the individual is that it lives in something which is not itself" (*GS* 1:30). Pursuing these observations further, Dilthey came to conclude that personal existence in fact becomes truly individual only in relation to this context of the "not-self" or "other." A critique of historical reason must also be a critique of "social reason" (*GS* 18:228).

In spite of the fact that society is our "natural" world to a much greater extent than nature is, it is one of the most complex and elusive problems for the human sciences. Like inner experience, our social existence is in many respects immediately familiar, but that does not mean that it is easily constituted as an object of scientific investigation. Indeed, the fact that it is so familiar to us from "inside" makes it difficult to objectify and analyze. In his essay of 1875 on the human sciences, Dilthey observed that the life of society was even more complex than the life of the individual person:

> Much more complicated and mysterious than our own organism, than even its most mysterious part, the brain, is society as it stands over against the individual as an object of investigation. We did not build this whole in which we stand as an element in reciprocal relation with other elements—and up to today we know only a few vague laws by which individuals act upon each other [GS 5:60].

The forbidding perplexities involved in apprehending this reality derive from the interrelationship of participation, action, and observation which characterizes all social phenomena:

> On the one hand the individual is an element in the interactions of society, a point of interaction but at the same time reacting consciously in will and behavior to the effects of these systems. On the other hand the individual is at the same time the intelligence which beholds and investigates all this [GS 1:37].

Both as inquiring subject and object of inquiry, the human individual is relative to others. The human subject cannot be treated as a "monad," for it is an entity existing in community by means of a pattern of relations which compose the common world of sociocultural experience. From the standpoint of life the "we-" relationship is given as a primordial condition of existence, not as something appended to a pre-existing self. As a sociocultural being, the individual functions in many different roles: he is a matrix or point of intersection (Kreuzungspunkt) of many different functions and systems of social interaction:

> There are many different persons in each of us—the member of a family, the citizen, the colleague; we find ourselves in a set of moral obligations, an order of law, in a coherence of life aiming at the satisfactions of wants. It is only in self-reflection that we can find the unity and continuity of life which binds all these threads together [GS 1:87; cf. 5:63, 151, 154; 7:278].

Every person, considered even at the farthest reaches of his individuality, is still a social and cultural being, for we experience life ab initio in common lived-relations (Lebensbezüge) with others. The concept of a single pure consciousness prior to society and history is a hypothetical construct which does violence to experience: "Man as a fact prior to society and history is a fiction of genetic-explanation" (GS 1:31). Descartes' rationalist cogito,

Kant's "transcendental ego," Rousseau's *bon sauvage*, and Adam Smith's "economic man" were theoretical postulates, not actual subjects. Dilthey found that the uncritical use of such abstractions, while at first glance providing a certain logical precision, ultimately tended to distort the inquiry of the human sciences rather than facilitate it.

Like many German thinkers, Dilthey defined society not as an aggregation of discrete elements but as a coherence in its own right which partially encompasses the individual: "individual life grows in this coherence [*Zusammenhang*] and persists in it." (*GS* 14/1:153). But at the same time he stood counter to the conspicuous German tradition of fusing the concepts of state and society into an "organism" or superordinate "totality" subsuming the individual and impervious to analytical treatment. Although the social-historical world is an overarching coherence, it is susceptible to analysis into lesser functional coherences and systems of interaction. These extend in a continuum from the individual through the family, "free associations," and temporary "movements," social organizations, states, epochs and generations, systems of culture, all the way to the "great facticity" humanity itself (*GS* 7:135). Both in his theorizing and historiography Dilthey devoted special attention to cultural systems and social organizations: they constituted two particularly influential social contexts. Dilthey, however, again reminded readers that they were useful analytical abstractions for the purpose of clarification, valid only within the limits in which they had been framed. They could not be hypostatized into self-subsisting entities, for life as a whole is a complex of many overlapping coherences.

Dilthey proposed a functionally differentiated and interactive view of culture: it is not a single "spirit" manifesting itself, nor a set of a priori cultural values. "Culture is first and foremost a texture of purposive coherences. Every one of these—language, law, myth, religion, poetry, science, and philosophy—possess an inner regularity which conditions its structure and this structure in turn reciprocally determines its development" (*GS* 5:7). The cultural systems are supraindividual in the sense that their basic coherence persists despite the fact that their individual constituents come and go over time. The systems thus generate a lasting structure of immanent values and ends which influence the persons who participate in them. The systems have a character of what Dilthey termed "massive objectivity" which is substantially determined by their participants and yet is partially independent of them (*GS* 1:51; 7:166). Though not wholly "spirit" in the Hegelian sense, Dilthey defined culture as "the distilled summation [*Inbegriff*] of component mental contents and the mental activities to which these contents are related" and he barred a strictly psychological approach to this content:

The perfected science of history would be the depiction and explanation of the coherence of human culture. . . . Culture cannot in any case be explained in a psychological manner—either in the fashion of Kant or the empiricists—but rather can be explained only in terms of intermediary historical structures [*Mittelglieder*]. The higher mental content arranged in these structures constitutes the range of cultural data.

In the same passage Dilthey went on to insist that to grasp this content fully the human sciences must "in a certain sense take up again the tendency of [Hegel's] phenomenology" (*GS* 5:lxxv–lxxvi; 18:152). This modified phenomenological and historical approach to cultural life would be capable of explicating its content and meaning without resolving it into purely psychological factors and causes.

Along with the cultural systems, life is "lived through" in social organizations. Dilthey specifically termed them "outer organizations of society" (*äussere Organisationen*), but "outer" here does not connote extraneous or "secondary" any more than "outer experience" is ancillary to inner lived experience. The outer organizations show the publically manifest, institutionalized aspect of social life and cultural content. They are collectively constituted "coherences of will" based upon generally accepted patterns for the distribution of social and political power (*GS* 1:67). They contrast with the cultural systems in accomplishing primarily practical social functions, but they often at the same time include cultural content. As social organizations Dilthey lists the family, state, church, army, class, and corporation. These organizations may be either deliberately designed and controlled or they may be in the sway of less consciously held interests and values. In comparison to the cultural systems, they are more directly rooted in the *Naturell* and hence more coercive: their function is expressed in the categories of "need, work, satisfaction, and domination" (*GS* 1:114). They may be transitory and subject to voluntary dissolution (as a holding company) or they may arise slowly and persist over long stretches of history (as a state or church); they show an almost infinite and shifting variety and, to a greater degree than the systems of culture, they are more directly responsive to changes in historical conditions. But Dilthey cautioned that the division of cultural systems and social organizations could not be applied rigidly, for some manifestations in the human world such as law and religion can be approached from either vantage point and in fact lie athwart this analytical distinction.

The cultural systems and social organizations exist only by virtue of the fact thay they are "lived through" by individuals, but their scientific study cannot be resolved into the experiences of individuals. The "massive objectivity" characterizing these systems extends through vast stretches of time and may not enter the awareness of their constituents. But while these systems bind and outlast the individual, they do not subsume him entirely. In the tradition of moral individualism deriving from Kant, Humboldt, and Schleiermacher, Dilthey insisted that there is always a portion of the person which remains independent of all social, legal, and cultural authority: "in his ultimate depths the individual is for himself [*für sich selber*]" (*GS* 1:74). Even the most searching analysis of his multiple roles will not exhaust the person; Dilthey repeated Goethe's admonition, *Individuum est ineffabile* (*GS* 1:29; 13/1:1).

While the cultural and social systems are more stable and enduring than the individual life, they too change over time. Life at all levels is historical and developmental, including its ideals, forms, and values. In Dilthey's most encompassing sense of the term, "life" does not come into being with *my* birth, for it is historically grounded and bears the imprint of past life:

Life is the fullness, the multiplicity, and the reciprocal relations which individuals experience. In its basic material life is one with history. At every point in history there is life. History consists of life of all kinds in the most diverse relations. History is only life grasped from the vantage point of the whole of humanity which forms a coherence [*GS* 7:256].

Individual life is not closed upon itself but merges with wider coherences up to the level of humanity as a whole. The various purposive and effectuating coherences (*Zweckzusammenhänge, Wirkungszusammenhänge*) of history and social life are continuous with the lived relations (*Lebensbezüge*) of individual existence, that is, they always have a reference to (or through) personal experience. But experientially continuous does not necessarily mean logically identical, as Dilthey came to stress more strongly in his later thought, for while we have an experiential reference for all relations in the human world, we cannot assume that their functions are entirely present in our actual experience.

The individual life operates according to an immanent teleology, not simply at the biological level toward its own self-preservation, but toward integration into the forms of social and cultural existence. Life has a double tendency to persevere in its own being (and its own perspective) but also to accommodate and appropriate the great objectivities of past life and tradition embodied in what Dilthey eventually came to refer to as "objective mind." The ongoing coherence of life relates personal lived experience to transpersonal experience in a wider reflective awareness:

This coherence of life is given in a double manner: in the self-reflection [*Selbstbesinnung*] of the individual subject through whose experience there is suffused a drive toward valid knowledge; and also in the historical reflection [*historische Besinnung*] which shows the same drive toward knowledge in mankind as a whole [*BNL* 243/168].

The specific relation of these levels of awareness—and their intermediate forms—must now be analyzed in greater detail in order to complete Dilthey's conception of the standpoint of life.

The Modes of Lived Experience and the Hierarchy of Reflective Awareness of Life

Dilthey's concepts of life and lived experience cannot be equated with that staple notion of German romanticism, sheer subjective "inwardness" (*Innerlichkeit*). Nor should the standpoint of life be confused, as it often is, with psychological introspection or the idealists' dream of "thought thinking itself." By rooting the human sciences in the standpoint of life, Dilthey did not restrict their content or methods to what is available in self-awareness or introspection. The standpoint of life discloses not a private, worldless "state of mind" spun out of its own subjectivity, but rather a complex set of relations constituted in close and continuous relation to the world—a social, cultural, and historical world. Indeed life in Dilthey's sense *is* this set of relations—not what might be left over if they could somehow be suspended in order to arrive at some pure "subjectivity." Dilthey left no room for doubt that lived experience encompasses external reality: "External objects are to be sure components of lived experience. As such they belong to the sphere of life itself" (*GS* 7:334). He became even more emphatic in making this point with regard to reflective awareness, insisting that "reflective" can in no sense be equated with "subjective": "The self is never given without an objective reality, an outer reality. All reflection upon the self is therefore at the same time a reflection upon its relation to an external reality and upon the origins and justification of determinations about that reality" (*GS* 8:39). "Self-consciousness and consciousness of the world are only two sides of the same consciousness" (*BA* 88–89, also 229). These two sides together are the standpoint of life.

In lived experience the object (*Gegenstand*) and state of consciousness (*Zustand*) are one; there is no independent object posited over against a subject. Reality is simply there-for-me: "Something which is there-for-me as a fact of consciousness does not contain a separate relation to an opposite object apart from my awareness. A pain as a fact of consciousness is not an object—I am simply aware of it." But the manner in which objects, persons, images, and mental meanings are there-for-me in lived experience is decisive: "The difference between physical objects and mental contents arises not from an 'objective' difference but from the difference in the way in which both are given in consciousness" (*BNL* 225/258). As Dilthey formulated it, the distinction between lived experience and sensory experience cannot be translated into the difference between the psychological concepts of "introspection" and "sensation," thereby splitting purely internal processes from externally induced ones. Dilthey held that conventional psychology had failed to come to terms with lived experience and that its usual assumptions were woefully inadequate to found the human sciences. Lived experience, as the foundation of our awareness of life, is never simply concerned with a private, subjective self as opposed to an external, objective world, but rather to their common and constant interaction. In trying to express this crucial point that lived experience refers to a *relation* rather than an "element" or "state of mind," Dilthey was running counter to some of the most deeply rooted conventions of European philosophical and psychological tradition; he was, as he put it in a letter to Yorck in 1890, traversing into "unknown land" (*BDY* 102). He required not only new concepts but new compass points.

The difference between lived experience and sensory experience cannot be resolved into the contrast of "subjective" and "objective," for lived experience is constituted in relation to the "outside" world of objects and other persons. The apprehension of lived experience is not subjective and inward in the sense of being divorced from perceived content of an existing reality. The reality is "lived through" as something concretely "there-for-me" or "there-for-consciousness" (*dieses Für-mich-Da-sein, Bewusst-Sein*) (*GS* 7:26). This "thereness" is not merely composed of bare sense data, but is the entire pattern of the object's (or person's) relation to our life. Objects and other persons are linked to the concrete, living self in what Dilthey called "vital relations" and "vital structures" (*Lebensbezüge*) which make up the pattern of actual experience; it is important to stress that they are "in" and "of" experience itself, they are not superadded as secondary attributes bestowed by the mind upon a more primary perception of things. These vital relations are not formal or logical relations but perceptual ones, originating in the whole mind as a perceiving, willing, feeling, and thinking consciousness. They do not falsify perception but make it possible in the first place by constituting experience as a coherence.

With some exceedingly important qualifications best discussed later in relation to his doctrine of expression and representation, Dilthey subscribed to the venerable but controversial view that what we have within our mind as inner lived experience is more concretely intelligible (not more "real") than what is outwardly observed and inferred from natural phenomena. Such a view might be described as the "privileged access theory of inner awareness," even though Dilthey consistently held that such awareness is by no means self-transparent—or self-evident to consciousness—and must be rigorously distinguished from introspection. Dilthey asserted that all intelligible reality is given in experience, including the relations constructed by thought. (At times he even suggested that *all* relations, including logical entailment and causal succession are rooted in the deeper vital structures of experience.) The patterns of coherence in the world and our scientific judgments about it rest upon the coherence of mental life given in our inner awareness. The patterns and structures of experience given in this direct awareness are more concretely familiar than the abstract thought processes of inference, generalization, and hypothesis which establish the laws and forms of the physical world. But although these patterns are given immediately, truly conscious and explicit awareness of them requires great exertions of thought and careful clarification. Nevertheless, Dilthey insists these patterns are "there-for-me" and as experiential realities they constitute the empirical foundation of the human sciences at every level of analysis and abstraction. In a passage preserved in the Nachlass, Dilthey offered a capsule summary of this matter: "The fundamental relations of history are processes which we actually live though [erleben] as reality in our self-consciousness" (BNL 237/27). At first sight such a view seems to suggest that everything which transpires in history and the world of human affairs actually takes place "psychologically" within our own minds; we are already, it would seem, everything we could possibly want to know.

Dilthey, however, was never a proponent of the view that mental life is entirely transparent or accessible to inner awareness or that such awareness contains the entirety of the content and forms of the human-historical world. Nor did he maintain that the basic awareness of life was identical with the methodical cognition of the human sciences. Rather he claimed that it was their necessary experiential foundation. The theory of lived experience established the empirical foundation of the human-historical world, but it did not thereby dispose of the problem of how this world is known in methodical cognition. He reminded his readers that "the very manner in which reality is given in lived experience gives rise to great difficulties in apprehending it objectively" (GS 5:317–18).

In many of his earlier writings Dilthey designated this primary awareness of life as "self-feeling" (Selbstgefühl), following the philosophical usage of Schleiermacher and Lotze. In the "Breslauer Ausarbeitung" Dilthey concurred with Scheiermacher's view that feeling must occupy this fundamental role because it alone encompasses the activity of the mind as well as its receptivity in perception; putting any other psychic process such as thinking or willing in this position would limit consciousness to the specific objects which these processes always refer to. Consciousness would thus be unduly narrowed, forfeiting the essential activity of consciousness always to be traversing "beyond" particular contents and discerning relations among the multiple contents of experience (BA 190–92, 200).

It is obvious that feeling assumed a definition and function in Dilthey's thought which differs markedly from its conventional meaning. Indeed it is employed by him in a sense which is the very opposite of what it has generally come to mean. Feeling is not merely subjective "emotion" or disposition (Gemüt), nor is it mere "affect" or "perturbation" of the mind. For Dilthey it has genuine epistemic status and objective content: it is the mind's active, self-conscious awareness of its "being-in-life" and perforce includes the experienced world. Like William James and Maine de Biran, Dilthey invested feeling with a comprehensive perceptual function which encompasses both thinking and willing. Feeling is the most basic form of self-awareness. Though often treated as "objectless," feeling has life itself as its constantly evolving object. In feeling the mind is most intimately in touch with its own dynamic operations.

Feeling makes possible the cognition of the self without spuriously reifying mental processes. In the Breslauer work Dilthey insisted that "the subject can never become an object to itself" (*BA* 197). All attempts to objectify the self or represent it as a "thing" among other things fall into an infinite regress: having defined the self as an "object," one is left with the endless task of adding to this object all the other qualities which constitute consciousness. But consciousness is not simply a summation of experiences; it is their total, ongoing coherence and for Dilthey this coherence can only be apprehended in self-feeling. This form of feeling is at the same time a feeling for others: "Feeling is, so to speak, the organ for the grasping of our own individuality as well as that of others—this grasping takes place by means of an empathic feeling into the nature of these individualities, which no conceptual knowledge can reach. Through feeling the depths which block knowledge are opened" (*GS* 7:52).

Feeling in this special sense is the mental function which most adequately apprehends the concrete fullness of lived experience. Dilthey held to this position throughout much of his writing. But after his close reading of Hegel and Husserl, he revised this stress upon feeling and retracted some of his earlier pronouncements. One detects in his new formulations a self-critique of his earlier position. He came to assert emphatically that inner awareness (*Innesein, Innewerden*) is not feeling and cannot be reduced to feeling, because such awareness is the work of the mind as a whole (*GS* 7:47). In a very late passage (1908) in the Nachlass, he protested against the frequent and egregious confusion of inner awareness with feeling and insisted that "feeling [*Gefühl*] must be clearly distinquished from the inner awareness [*Innewerden*] of experience, which is in turn the condition of inner and outer perception" (*BNL* 168/65). These late rejoinders were aimed at the objections of Wundt and Carl Stumpf, who had alleged that feeling was merely "subjective affect" and could not be taken as the basis of any perception of mental content. In order for Dilthey to maintain the objective reality and cognitive content of lived experience, he was forced to disengage it from its dependence upon feeling.[14]

Dilthey did not hold that lived experience was simply a self-evident given of immediate consciousness which thereby disposed of the problem of how we know it or formulate it. In his theory of mind, consciousness shows "grades," "modifications," "valences," and "interests" which are apparent in the different modes of observation, memory, reconstruction, supposition, imagination, dreaming, and even "thought experiments" (*BA* 90–92, 132). In the course of his investigations he became deeply occupied with defining the modes of experience in relation to reflective consciousness and cognition. The problem of knowing experience concerned not simply its "giveness" per se, but its clarification in thought. To stress the undisclosed depths of consciousness, Dilthey compared psychic life to the structure of a plant, of which only certain leaves are visible but whose roots spread out deeply in the earth. He consistently emphasized that while we do have an immediate perception of our lived relations, we cannot claim to know our "nature" or "essence" (GS 5:lx; 18:188–89).

Hesitantly and sometimes equivocally, he came to distinguish several levels of the awareness of lived experience which are analytically distinct but substantively related in a continuum. It should be stressed that the following register provides only an abbreviated, schematic version of a set of concepts and relations which Dilthey spent years trying to elucidate; he emphasized different modes at different points in his analysis of the human-historical world. Thus abstracted, they might appear as a prime case of philosophical pettifoggery or unnecessary "multiplication of entities," but they are crucial to his theory of the human sciences. In the "Breslauer Ausarbeitung" he asserted that the different levels could not be exhaustively defined but only experienced (BA 125).

It is important to stress that each level provides the experiential material for the next level, which "represents" it in a clarified, interpreted form. The progression through this scale is from initial "giveness" to full "clarification" and objective knowledge. The progression accomplishes not the diminution of content (except in the case of no. 4), but its more adequate representation by consciousness. The levels may be described as follows: First, the simple "having" of experience (Erleben) without conscious reflection, distinction, perceived relation, or sense of perspective. This most rudimentary level of experience is prior to the analytical separation of subject and object, self and world, form and content, inner and outer. It is pre-predicative and pre-reflective experience and entails no distinct awareness "of" itself or of some object. (Thus the term "experiencing" might be more adequate to Dilthey's meaning, since "having of" implies a distinction.) This is the "darkest" level of experience, which is never fully raised to conscious awareness, let alone comprehended in conceptual thought. Dilthey insists that there is nothing "behind" or "below" this experiencing. It simply is and has a certainty and validity of its own, which he came to define as the "consciousness of evidence"—thereby having to introduce an ulterior relationship to consciousness which seems to belie his initial premise (GS 7:126; BA 49). At any rate, this level contains everything which emerges into consciousness.

Second, the primitive awareness of experience (Innewerden, Innesein, Für-mich-dasein) which is accomplished in a process Dilthey called "silent thought." It, too, is pre-predicative, yet entails elementary acts of relation, association, reproduction, separation, comparison, gradation, and a crucial mental act Dilthey calls "typifying awareness." This level entails a "distinguishing attention" and "selective interest," but does not yet contain the separation between subject and object: "the awareness and that of which I am aware are one" (*GS* 7:28). This awareness is a "consciousness that-" but not a distinct "consciousness what-" Dilthey called it the "apprehension of mental reality" but marked it off from the "apperception" of traditional idealism, which is without empirical content.

Three, inner perception (*innere Wahrnehmung*), which is the accomplishment of deliberate acts of thinking and attending. This level attains a further "stabilizing in attention" (*Festhalten in Aufmerksamkeit*) and permits the separation between the acts and contents of mental life. This level of consciousness makes use of direct acts of thought and attention: it isolates stable, discernible, and self-identical contents of experience. Inner perception furnishes the empirical content for the special kind of knowledge which Dilthey called "objective grasping" (*gegenständliches Auffassen*), which raises to distinctive consciousness the content of what is given without changing the form of the given" (*GS* 7:122).

Four, inner observation (*innere Beobachtung*) or introspection (*Introspektion*) which by arresting and fixing the inner relations and patterns of experience raises certain isolated features of experience to deliberate attention. It predicates something of experience in terms of a preconceived question concerning what the introspecting subject is looking for. It thus tends to change the content of experience and has only a very limited use in Dilthey's view. In fact he became exceedingly skeptical of this kind of awareness and eventually excluded it altogether.

Five, memory (*Erinnerung*) as it functions in ordinary life (not as it would be "practiced" by deliberate effort), which is a normal form of awareness capable of skipping over vast reaches of elapsed experience to relate the separate contents in a meaningful coherence. Consciousness as memory is subject to the inevitably modifying influence of supervening experiences and even expectations of the future.

Six, methodical self-reflection (*Selbstbesinnung*), which articulates relations among experiences with one's ongoing existence and discerns their immanent value and meaning. This level explicitly introduces the consciousness of others into the realm of self-consciousness. It is at this level that the human sciences are explicitly constituted, for this level discerns the shared relations and common traits of life as a whole and analyzes the different contexts and world-views within which the more basic contents of experience have been formed (*GS* 8:79).

Seven, and lastly, there is "historical-philosophical reflection" (*historische Besinnung*) or "anthropological reflection" (*anthropologische Besinnung*), which interprets the contents of experience in the widest possible human perspective. This most comprehensive level of awareness has been schooled in all the human sciences and the manifold historical forms of life, life-values, and world-views; it can therefore relate individual experience to the accumulated patterns of culture and "objective mind" which human life has produced over the ages. Hypothetically this level of awareness is capable of conceiving of human experience in terms of universal history (BA 250).

It is apparent that this hierarchy of experiential awareness displays a heightening, refinement, and precision of content: each stage is reflective with respect to the preceding one, yet immediate and "foundational" with respect to the higher level. The human sciences draw upon all these levels of awareness and knowledge. The basic outline of Dilthey's analysis of mental life is quite close to that of his teachers, Kuno Fischer and F. A. Trendelenburg, though the stress upon higher synthesis shows a certain kinship with Hegel's phenomenology of mind—a method which Dilthey's friend Haym had criticized as "psychology confused with history and a history brought to derangement with psychology."[15] Whether it is psychology, history, or phenomenology is a question Dilthey came to ask himself, as will be treated in the next chapter. Here it is sufficient to stress that this process represents a step-like passage from "thoughtless" and immediate familiarity through cognition to re-cognition.

A tacit, preconceptual "awareness of life" is the experiential foundation and point of departure for the human sciences, but this does not mean that such awareness is their sole means of advance or their necessary point of arrival; it is their empirical pre-condition, but not their method or result. The human sciences make use of abstractive, analytical, comparative, and conceptual procedures which, though rooted in lived experience, nevertheless depart from it. This point is often obscured by critics of Dilthey who have collapsed these levels into one and then accused him of "irrationalism." They have drawn his "interpretive circle" too tightly. By mistaking the experiential grounds of knowledge for its results, these critics portray the Diltheyan conception of the human sciences as proceeding wholly at the level of lived experience, thereby divesting it of the mediating levels and conceptual procedures he insisted upon.

Dilthey carefully stipulated that the actual flow of experience as such is not susceptible to conceptual treatment; but he was just as insistent that the contents of experience could be excavated from their acts and subjected to elucidating conceptual procedures: "Reality can be subjected to thought only by means of the separation of single partial contents and by means of the distinct knowledge of these contents, for in its complex and immediate form reality is not available to thought" (GS 1:52). But these contents must always refer to some experiential reality, even if they do not "copy" it. The relationship which Dilthey drew between our ordinary awareness of lived experience and the methodical procedures of the human sciences bears out Goethe's maxim that "the sciences on the whole depart from life and return to it only by an indirect path."[16] Indeed, Goethe provided an almost perfect summary of Dilthey's position: "The sciences go forward not in a circle but in a spiral line in which the same content comes back again, but higher and in a wider coherence."[17]

The Special Role of Art in Representing Life

Dilthey attributed to art a unique capacity to reveal life in its concrete, relational aspect—as it appears from the standpoint of life. It is important to stress that his esteem for art did not stem from any temperamental "aestheticism" or cult of "art for art's sake" but was integrally linked to his project of providing a foundation for the human sciences. Indeed, he strenuously repudiated formalistic treatments of art and the various *art pour l'art* movements of his time, insisting that art always contains a deep and often unnoticed link to experiential content and "lived" meaning. Art is not simply the pleasing arrangement of forms according to canons of beauty but a constant "inducement to seeing" (*GS* 5:279).[18] Thus it accomplishes in a more direct manner what the human sciences achieve through mediating concepts.

However formally refined or imaginary, art draws its content and imagery from life. Even the most fantastic situations and inventions of the artist retain an experiential reference which is the touchstone of human meaning. Art can thus render human experience in a particularly vivid fashion because it is not tied to abstract schemas and discursive operations of thought. By virtue of its concreteness and capacity for synthetic "seeing," art has a power of disclosure which scientific cognition cannot match: "No scientific mind can ever exhaust, no advance of science can ever reach what the artist has to say about the content of life" (*GS* 5:274).

Dilthey could endow art with this particular explicative efficacy because he rejected the view (not altogether fairly attributed to Kant) that art is "beautiful appearance" (*schöner Schein*), a free construct of the imagination devoid of real empirical content. In the Kantian account, art is a pleasant illusion which contains no cognitive truth. Dilthey, however, argued against the position that art is contrived illusion or simply the outcome of forms, rules, and procedures which are divorced from concrete experience. At the beginning of his major aesthetic treatise he repeated Schiller's injunction that art should be judged ultimately under the criterion of *truth* rather than beauty (*GS* 6:243, 185). Art is not a fanciful world of pure images or forms but is continuous with life itself; it is a re-presentation of life which occasions a deeper consciousness of it, a consciousness to which no concept is entirely adequate.

Art is uniquely valuable as a resource for knowing man because it compells us to behold its images in a manner which directs us back to ourselves and radically recasts the abstractive relation of subject and object which is conventional to science. Though it represents experience, art is not the passive imitation of things but genuine creative synthesis from the content of life. Art has the effect of bringing man back from a world of merely "given" and "natural" objects to reflect upon himself and his own creative powers. In a citation which nearly perfectly captures his fusion of the "transcendental turn" and the standpoint of life, Dilthey quoted the observation of Fichte: "'Art makes the transcendental viewpoint into the commonly accepted one'" (GS 15:342). By this seemingly paradoxical observation Dilthey emphasized that art shows readily and "naturally" that reality-for-consciousness is not a stream of chaotic impressions or causal chain of mental associations but an organized, synthetic totality with immanent meaning. Art achieves the "seeing" and representation of wholes: it is intrinsically integrative and shows (rather than propounds) that we experience reality as a synthetic coherence rather than isolated elements or percepts. Art fulfills itself in leading us to perceive relations rather than abstracted units. The human world viewed from the standpoint of life shows this same relational configuration given to experience in a "pre-scientific" mode:

> The formation of a coherence is not a process which follows after the grasp of reality. Nobody perceives reality as a momentary image in isolation—rather we possess our image in a coherence through which we try to determine reality in a manner prior to all scientific concerns [noch vor aller wissenschaftlichen Beschäftigung] [GS 1:392].

Art interprets human experience by creating from it and rendering it in figurative form. Art is not merely subjective feeling—either in the individual artist or beholder—but an awareness of life containing a kind of tacit and concrete form of truth which the human sciences must acknowledge and incorporate. Dilthey's published works and Nachlass contain many passages stressing the peculiar truth-value of art: "Art, especially poetry, is closest to life—the truest, most comprehensive and at the same time most concrete representation of its coherence and meaning. Art is the organon for the understanding [Verstehen] of life" (BNL 225/163; GS 5:274). As evidence of this assertion, Dilthey pointed out in many of his historical studies that the poets, by staying close to the standpoint of life, anticipated in figurative and metaphorical forms what the philosophers and practitioners of the human sciences were only later able to transpose into conceptual formulation. For example, Novalis, Hölderlin, and Goethe provided many of the insights and perspectives on human experience which were subsequently formulated by Hegel or applied by the Historical School.

In the exploration of the human-historical world, art tends to anticipate more rigorous forms of knowledge (*GS* 5:273).

Dilthey maintained that art says something about life in general, not simply the creator's particular experience. In his inaugural addresses at Basel in 1867 and again at the Berlin Academy of Sciences in 1887, he emphasized that poetry contained "general truth"—albeit not in the form of abstract cognition—and that poetry could disclose the work of the mind in an especially lucid manner (*GS* 5:11, 17). In general he regarded art as a privileged repository of the understanding of life, and he often used music as a kind of analog of experience because of its concretely demonstrable "gestalt" quality (*GS* 18:206). But he was far from confusing poetry with science or attempting to revive the romantic notion that art and aesthetic intuition are superior to science. More "immediate" and "concrete" does not mean more adequate or valid for Dilthey. He emphasized that the great strength of art lies in its "pre-scientific" immediacy, but its limitation with respect to understanding human life lies in its lack of methodical rigor and precise articulation of the relations that characterize life (*GS* 7:240). In Dilthey's view the insights of art and the standpoint of knowledge should be complementary and reciprocal. The human sciences, while incorporating the "seeing" of life through art, must carry it toward methodical knowledge. In addition to drawing upon the content of the artistic representation of life, the human sciences could also selectively draw upon the more explicit and discursive interpretation of life contained in the tradition of thought which Dilthey designated as "life-philosophy." This tradition of thinking shared some of the virtues as well as limitations of art.

The Failure of Life-Philosophy as a Foundation for the Human Sciences: The Critical-Methodical Imperative

With his acute sense of history, Dilthey did not presume himself to be the first thinker to have uncovered the notion of life as concrete existence and lived experience. In fact, many of his historical studies are explorations of this theme in the work of others. He did, however, claim to be the first to open the way to bringing the concept of life into a fruitful relation to the theory and practice of the human sciences. Earlier thinkers and writers had insisted that man's concrete existence in the here-and-now was the starting point for all philosophical reflection and the source of all knowledge. Dilthey cited the Stoics, Montaigne, Lessing, Schopenhauer, Carlyle, Emerson, Ruskin, Nietzsche, Bergson, and Tolstoy as thinkers who eschewed the transcendent in order to remain close to life and its own immanent standpoint. All affirmed the autonomous value of worldly existence and were not led off into grand cosmological or metaphysical systems. They were impelled by a deep concern for man's active, ethical role and a desire to influence the conduct of life, not merely observe it from afar. Dilthey found their thinking to be marked by a high degree of seriousness and fidelity to the concrete features of existence—in this respect they pointed to what he called the standpoint of life.

But for the most part these thinkers provided merely genial intuitions and inchoate insights, untested by critical rigor and method. They allowed the standpoint of life to exclude the standpoint of science and disciplined knowledge. In their approach "aperçus were linked together in an un-methodical [*unmethodisch*] but provocative interpretation of life" (*GS* 5:370). For all their merits, these thinkers stood more in the tradition of rhetorical persuasion than methodical reasoning and scientific inquiry. They provided insights into man's condition, but in foreswearing the path of rigorous inquiry, they had to pay a serious price: their conclusions had the quality of sheer exhortation rather than careful demonstration. They relied almost exclusively upon self-intuition and introspection, often mistaking their private corner for the whole world. Consequently their insights were "arbitrary" and "dictatorial" and a careful examination of their *aperçus* showed that they "spoke only for themselves" (*GS* 5:370; 8:202).

Characteristically, Dilthey's response to this current of "life-philosophy" (*Lebensphilosophie*) was neither wholesale acceptance or rejection but a critical appropriation. After drawing the balance on their strengths and weaknesses, he set as his own goal "to seek within methodical science a more considered, sober, and less arbitrary solution of the task which the life-philosophers of the present have set for themselves" (*GS* 5:370). Dilthey aspired to combine their sensitivity for concrete existence with a methodical and disciplined (*wissenschaftlich*) treatment. His originality lay precisely in this joint demand for concrete insight into life and scientific rigor. He called for a critical and methodical "philosophy of life" (*Philosophie des Lebens*) as opposed to the murkier and arbitrary "life-philosophies" and "life-visions" (*Lebensdeutungen*) of the poets, essayists, *moralistes*, and "free interpreters" of life. Valid and useful knowledge of life was to be achieved not in spite of science but through the careful expansion of its concept and by employment of its rigorous methods. The hard-won heritage of empirical methods and critical inquiry which had freed man from specious forms of thinking had to be applied to the problem of life and man's understanding of himself.

The radical complexity and dynamic qualities of life pose special problems and limits to conceptual thought, which must proceed by means of abstraction. In treating the relation between life and thought, Dilthey left a kind of seminal ambiguity which has fostered charges that he was an irrationalist. In his published writings Dilthey often held that thought cannot fully comprehend life in concepts or capture it in conceptual formulations. Yet at the same time he insisted that thought analyzes and interprets life in the human sciences. In the unpublished "Berliner Entwurf" of 1892–96, Dilthey drew this fundamental ambiguity into a succinct passage: "This reality is thinkable [*gedankenmässig*], available to our thought, and meaningful in its vital presence—and yet it is unfathomable too. Life is at once thinkable and impenetrable. We all seek to express it, each in his own way. But the infinite cannot be expressed" (*BE* 52). In later published studies he referred to "immanent antinomies" between the content of life and the forms of thought (*GS* 5:173–75).

> It is as if lines have to be drawn in a continually flowing stream, figures drawn which hold fast. Between this reality of life and the scientific intellect [*Verstand*] there appears to be no possibility of comprehension, for the concept sunders what is unified in the flow of life. The concept represents something which is universally and eternally valid, independent of the mind which propounds it. But the flow of life is at all points unique [*überall nur einmal*], every wave in it arises and passes [*GS* 7:280].

Such passages leave the impression that thought and life are incommensurate functions, even full-scale antinomies.

These passages and others like them, however, cannot be taken as an ultimate avowal of skepticism or irrationalism on Dilthey's part. Here it is important to recall the deep antagonism between Dilthey's *Idealrealismus*, which propounds an ongoing, *provisional* understanding and the "absolute knowledge" of the Hegelians and "positive knowledge" of the postivists, both of which postulate "final knowledge." Dilthey was highly skeptical concerning ultimate and total claims such as the latter, but firmly believed that approximate and provisional knowledge was attainable in the human sciences. To deny this is to make a mockery of his whole critique of historical reason. In contrast to the Hegelian heritage, he held that reality could not be wholly subsumed in concepts, but he was equally insistent that the notion of reason and conceptual thought could be recast so as to provide valid cognition in the human sciences. His reference to "immanent antinomies" stood as a stern warning against a facile and final rationalism (whether metaphysical or positivistic); it was an exhortation that thought must remain in close touch with actual lived experience. Dilthey propounded not "absolute" reason but "critical" reason: "Here one must bear in mind the incommensurability [*Unangemessenheit*] of conceptual thought to the coherence of life. . . . All intellection concerning the experiences of life can only approach it within boundaries which must be critically established" (*GS* 10:43). A warning against rationalism is not the same as irrationalism. Life and lived experience retain an aura of mystery and perpetual problematic, but this condition does not preclude genuine knowledge. Human understanding can, within limits, interpret aspects of life with precision and validity, but it cannot exhaustively explain all its dimensions: life is more than it can know of itself. Dilthey's ambiguity on this point should be seen, not as a stumbling block to reason and the human sciences, but as a part of their generative impulse. Dilthey's perspective here is remarkably suggestive of that of Goethe, who observed that "it behooves man to accept something inscrutable but that does not mean that he has to put any limits on his investigation."[19]

In this investigation Dilthey wanted to avoid the suggestion of mysticism and speculation. During the last decade of the nineteenth century, which witnessed a sudden revival of spiritualist and vitalist life-philosophies of an avowedly mystical bent, Dilthey repudiated such a cast of mind and its often surreptitious religious ethos. In the "Berliner Entwurf" he proclaimed:

> We do not want to propagate mysticism. Our philosophy is broad in scope, clear, and lucid. It has nothing whatsoever to do with the nebulous ambience of a torpid religiosity. To show life as it is, that is what we are striving for. To describe life, that is our goal. Whether we live on after death we do not know. Whether there is a personal God, that too we do not know. This epoch of history demands only to know what is available to clear reflection and to conduct itself according to what is actually experienceable and knowable. But we also want to make life visible in its inexplicable depths and in its inexplicable coherence [BE 55].

As Dilthey was establishing life as the fundamental reality of the human sciences, other thinkers and writers employed it as a gnomic incantation to frustrate the claims of reason, logic, critical consciousness, and even language itself. Life came to be portrayed by the life-philosophers as instinctive, unreflective, and intrinsically irrational. Writing in the year of Dilthey's death, the neo-Kantian Heinrich Rickert asserted that the philosophical temper of the times could be summed up in the "modish slogan 'life'." Rickert concluded his stinging attack on the promiscuous use of this concept with the curt observation that "all science is necessarily something opposed to life."[20] Though Dilthey could not endorse Rickert's extreme opposition of science and life, of knowledge and concrete experience, he recognized clearly the need for critical reflection and rigorous knowledge. In one of the last passages he ever wrote on the relation of life and knowledge, Dilthey stipulated:

> In every sphere and area of mental life the demand for valid knowledge arises. To be sure, life itself precedes all methodical thought as the first and the most important datum [als das Erste und Wichtigste], but human life first becomes certain of itself in so far as it investigates and regulates itself according to valid knowledge [giltiges Wissen]. Thus man must transcend beyond the naïve consciousness of his immediate reality and its

qualities by means of critical knowledge. This process is essential and intrinsic to civilization itself. . . . The individual sciences of man accomplish this knowledge within their separate analytical frameworks. Finally, however, it is the function of philosophy to bring together in a comprehensive and validly grounded fashion this scientific reflection upon life [*BNL* 78/52–53].

Dilthey went on to specify the role of philosophy in relation to the human sciences: "Philosophy is the most strenuous and disciplined effort to bring things to full consciousness—as the consciousness of consciousness and knowledge of all knowledge [*als Bewusstsein über Bewusstsein und Wissen von allem Wissen*]" (*BNL* 78/57). It is to the specific elaboration of this critical program for the foundation of the human sciences which we now turn.

Before doing so, however, it is necessary to touch upon a crucial problem of the last half-century of Dilthey interpretation. It is often alleged by both his defenders and detractors that Dilthey's conception of the standpoint of life carried him not only beyond positivistic and natural-scientific conceptions of knowledge, but also beyond the human sciences as well—indeed "beyond science" altogether to a new interpretive "philosophy of life" or "hermeneutic of existence" (to use a term which is as modish today as "life" was in Dilthey's later years).[21] This view is a gross distortion of his thought concocted by highly selective quoting out of context. It is most frequently advanced by followers of Martin Heidegger for whom any trace of scientific commitments is at odds with truly "fundamental thinking," that is, ontology and "disclosure of Being." The fact that these interpreters constantly point out that Dilthey failed to make the "ontological turn" which is the source of "authentic" truth rather than the "little" truths of science should suffice to remind the careful reader that his commitments lay elsewhere. For Dilthey, insight into human existence must take the arduous path of the disciplined, methodical knowledge of the human sciences, not the high-road of the "new" twentieth-century metaphysics.

Consciousness is both the key and the lock to the world.
—Graf Yorck to Dilthey

The fact which must be grasped and analyzed in what is called
psychology is life itself.
—Dilthey

The Critical Foundations
of the Human Sciences:
Toward a Fundamental Science
of Man and Mind

The Idea of a *Grundwissenschaft*:
Fundamental Science, Not Final Science

In a commemorative article written in 1871 for a friend and kindred thinker, Friedrich Überweg, Dilthey asserted that "the fundamental and one of the most important tasks in philosophy today is the establishment of a valid theory of scientific knowledge" (*GS* 15:156). Throughout his career Dilthey labored at this basic task, approaching it from different angles but always with the same goal in mind. Showing at times varying degrees of confidence, he held to the conception of a foundational science of mind (*Grundwissenschaft*) which would provide a valid theory of knowledge and "grounding" for the human sciences. Although metaphysics (and its various intellectual heirs) had lost all legitimate claim to be "First Science" or "Final Science," the task of providing a foundational science remained to be fulfilled—in a discipline yet to be realized, whose form and content remained unspecified. The definition and elaboration of this *Grundwissenschaft* was to prove exceedingly difficult, so that tracing Dilthey's efforts here presents one of the most complicated problems in delineating his thought. Yet his efforts in this regard were especially important, for they concerned the deepest premises of the human sciences.

In the *Grundriss der Logik* of 1865, Dilthey linked together the two disciplines of "psychology" and "anthropology" to fill the role of what he called the "general foundational science of mind" (*Grundriss* 10). His choice of two disciplines to serve this function indicated that he was dissatisfied with the exclusive claims of any single existing "science of mind." He saw an uncharted area in need of a satisfactory disciplinary definition. Three years after the *Grundriss*—in a period when he was steeped in the new fields of "folk-psychology" (*Völkerpsychologie*) and anthropology—Dilthey expressed great hopes for the discipline of psychology, invoking the words of the prominent ethnologist Adolf Bastian:

Psychology is the science of the future, which alone can mediate the ever-growing gulf between faith and knowledge. But psychology cannot remain that narrow discipline which restricts itself to the self-observation of the individual. . . . Mankind as a whole—a concept which knows of no higher one—should be the starting point, as a unified totality within which the single individual figures only as an integrating part [GS 11:205-6].

This programmatic exhortation cited verbatim by Dilthey displays both the great expectations and trepidations he felt toward the formal discipline of psychology. He continued to hold both attitudes in a rather uneasy and shifting balance. In the 30 years between 1865 and 1895 his conviction concerning the crucial role of psychology as a *Grundwissenschaft* for the human sciences remained firm despite his growing disappointment with existing forms of academic psychology and the mounting frustration attendant upon his own efforts to reform it.

In his inaugural address at Basel in 1867, Dilthey provided further specification of the form and results he expected of this basic science of mind:

The task of our generation is clearly before us: following Kant's critical path, but in cooperation with researchers in other areas, we must found an empirical science of the human mind. It is necessary to know the laws which rule social, intellectual, and moral phenomena. This knowledge of laws is the source of all the power of man, even where mental phenomena are concerned [GS 5:27].

At this point in his thinking Dilthey envisioned a basic science of mind which was both empirical and capable of furnishing laws for the human-historical world. The concepts of rigorous science (including the *Grundwissenschaft*) and strict causal knowledge were integrally related. The decade following his call to Basel brought his closest rapprochement with the positivist ideal of knowledge and the zenith of his hopes for explanatory laws in the human sciences. While he continued thereafter to affirm the necessity of a new foundational science, he became less steadfast in the conviction that it could provide explanatory laws. After the *Einleitung*, the connection between "foundations" and "laws" was almost entirely reformulated.

In Dilthey's initial conception, the fundamental science of mind would incorporate philosophy and the results of the sciences, both human and natural. His reviews from the 1860s seem to suggest in a positivist vein that such a basic science would supplant philosophy altogether:

The foremost object of philosophy is the human mind. The most vital and palpable form of philosophy and the one which stands closest to the concrete sciences is anthropology. In it are combined the natural sciences, geography, history, and all the philosophical disciplines [GS 16:373].

A close reading of Dilthey's texts and reviews from this period indicates that he envisioned this "anthropology" in the manner of the "philosophical anthropology" attempted in Lotze's *Mikrokosmos*; such a fundamental discipline was both philosophical and empirical. In the *Einleitung* of 1883 and the massive unpublished accompanying study ("Breslauer Ausarbeitung"), Dilthey postulated a "general science of consciousness" which he continued to designate optionally as "Realpsychologie" or "Anthropologie" (*GS* 1:29, 34; *BA* 29 ff.). He assigned to it a function analogous to that which mathematics occupies in the natural sciences. After Wundt pointed out in his *Logik* that the more proper analogy lay with the "causal science" of mechanics and not the purely "formal science" of mathematics, Dilthey shifted his analogy to accommodate Wundt's objections: if fully realized in practice, such a psychology could be interpreted as the "mechanics" of the human sciences (*GS* 7:116–17).[1] As he continued to refine his notion of causality in the human sciences, however, Dilthey emerged with new objections to this analogy and ultimately rejected it. But while he came to qualify such comparisons with the role of mathematics or mechanics in the natural sciences, Dilthey continued to insist that without a fundamental science of mind the human sciences would exist only as a loose congeries of disciplines without coherent structure and logical organization:

> Just as the development of the single human sciences is linked to the constitution of psychology, so too the linking of these sciences together into a totality cannot be accomplished without an understanding of the psychic coherence of mental life. Unless some reference can be established between the human sciences and the mental coherence in which their relations are grounded, the human sciences are merely an aggregate, a bundle, not a true system [*GS* 5:148].[2]

To constitute an organized system, the human sciences, like the natural sciences, required an "organon" or *Grundwissenschaft*. But Dilthey's idea of such a fundamental science was at odds with the persistent philosophic ideal of a "final science" or consummating "absolute science"—whether based upon logical, metaphysical, or "positive" grounds. At the same time that he called for a "foundational science," he argued strongly against the seductive theoretic vision of an all-inclusive metascience which, in the manner of metaphysics, is expected to accomplish in a closed system what in fact can only be accomplished gradually by a group of related sciences. Therefore, providing a critical foundation of the human sciences did not mean transmuting them into an overarching super-science, metaphysical or otherwise, which would somehow supplant their specific inquiries (*GS* 17:7–8).

Even at the level of the most basic grounds of knowledge, truth is given to the mind in different forms and grades. While the human sciences required a "science of grounds," it could not be accomplished in some grand "science of the whole" such as Leibniz's *scientia generalis*, Hegel's philosophy of history, or Comte's sociology. Indeed philosophy itself could not claim superiority over the separate sciences. It was a means of clarifying their operations and results, not a substitute for their actual work. As the "reflective science of the sciences" or "reflective self-consciousness of mind," philosophy was constrained to perform its clarifying task alongside existing bodies of knowledge, thought-systems, and forms of human experience. The belief in a "total science" or "master science" rested upon a colossal fallacy of misplaced finality. Scientific knowledge for Dilthey is ipso facto relational: the idea of absolute knowledge is a contradiction in terms— perhaps laudable in intent but ultimately a vacuous attempt "to square the circle" (*GS* 1:95). Dilthey compared Hegel's speculative philosophy of history and Comte's positive sociology to the phantasmagoria of medieval alchemistry: "Philosophy of history in the hitherto existing sense of the term is a charade—like philosophy of nature, it is an attempt to reach a level of synthetic knowledge for which we do not have the means at our disposal" (*GS* 5:36, 47). In the *Einleitung* he cautioned: "If we speak of philosophy of history, this can be nothing but historical inquiry from a philosophical standpoint and with philosophical aids" (*GS* 1:92). Drawing the balance upon all such dauntless enterprises of "final science," Dilthey assented that "we have seen that we are not granted a knowledge of the whole concrete coherence of historical-social reality except through analysis of it into separate single coherences, that is to say by means of the single sciences" (*GS* 1, 113).

Dilthey rejected the tenacious assumption that where there is no *one* science there is no genuine science. The rejection of the noble dream of a total unifying science did not, however, dispose of the need for a fundamental science to provide clarification and critical reflection concerning the procedures and results of the individual sciences. The relation between the fundamental science and the separate sciences must be a reciprocal one. The "positive-practical" results of the individual human sciences must be validated through "critical-theoretical" reflection, but at the same time this general form of reflection should synthesize and order these results in an emergent science of man. The two directions implicit in Dilthey's notion of a foundation (*Grundlegung*) must be held as complementary: scientific results must go through the test of critical-theoretical reflection, but this reflection must take its content and criteria from the actual results of the sciences, not from some "higher" point of reference. A *Grundwissenschaft* cannot mean final foreclosure upon the growth of knowledge itself, but rather the theoretical clarification of its premises and development.

In pointing to a form of psychology (or indeed any empirical science) to fulfill the role of *Grundwissenschaft*, Dilthey was contravening the strong current in German idealist tradition which was implacably opposed to allowing psychology any sway in matters of *Geist*. His persistent attempt to elaborate a fundamental science of mind in empirical and psychological terms rather than purely logical or transcendental ones marked *his* "ideal-realism" off clearly from the basic tenets of idealism. Dilthey in fact concurred with many of the idealist's objections to psychology, but he found that such objections were not sufficient to disallow psychology altogether. The important task was not to dismiss psychology high-hand-edly, but rather carefully to examine "the critical possibility of psychology" in such a manner as "to expand it to its true concept"—thus making it capable of its tasks (*BA* 239, 254–55).

Dilthey's attitude toward psychology has aptly been designated as the most tangled and controversial aspect of his thought.[3] Like all features of his thinking, it is an aspect which cannot be treated in isolation or at only one level, for it stood in reciprocating relation to other features and levels. Moreover, it was transformed in the course of his own reflections and the criticism of other thinkers. It would seem that the only plausible solution to the enigma of Dilthey's stance toward psychology lies with a double perspective of theory and practice. On the one hand he insisted upon the *theoretical* necessity of a unifying "mental science" which would organize and ground the separate human sciences. On the other hand he became increasingly convinced that all existing *practical* efforts (including portions of his own) to provide a substantive formulation of this discipline were inadequate to the initial theoretical demands. The upshot of this predica-ment was that Dilthey's adherence to a foundational psychology remained a necessary theoretical premise of his thought, while its actual realization as a definite and circumscribed discipline was seen to be more and more a practical impossibility. The growing divergence between theoretical de-mands and practical possibilities engendered an "immanent critique" of his own premises and an internal shift in his position, bringing certain sides of his doctrine into sharper focus, while diminishing those aspects which were closely tied to psychology in the strict sense. Not surprisingly, a close study of Dilthey's attitude toward psychology shows the same kind of "inner dialectic" which he was fond of pointing out in the thought of others: his notion of psychology seems to point beyond itself.

In explicating the function which Dilthey assigned to psychology in his critique of historical reason, it is necessary to emphasize the utterly inferior place (or outright ban) assigned to it in idealist accounts of "spirit." Since their gradual separation, psychology and philosophy have traditionally conducted border wars and confiscatory raids over what seemed to be the same territory. These conflicts were all the more heated in German thought, as psychology defined itself as stalwartly empirical, and philosophy re-trenched to a resolutely transcendental position. From the standpoint of idealism (both classical and "neo-" forms), psychology was denied independent status or classified as a natural science. Either way, it had little or no role to play in the examination of matters of *Geist*, let alone as the foundation of the *Geisteswissenschaften*. Idealist tradition was hostile to all efforts to employ psychology in relation to the "ideal content" or "ideas" which were supposed to form the basis of logic, theory of knowledge, and cultural-historical phenomena in general. Kant's view of psychology as merely a "physiology of the understanding" incapable of grasping the transcendental grounds of reason proved to be vastly influential. Later idealists adopted Kant's premises and further identified psychology with the "pragmatic" method of the eighteenth century, which reduced "higher" historical events and actions to the "baser" self-serving motives of separate individuals. Hegel insisted that this method destroyed all reason in history:

> In the psychological-pragmatic view of history, the great events and manifestations become merely products of petty or powerful passions and individuals in their actions are viewed as ruled by merely subjective interests, so that history in this way sinks to the level of being a play of personal activity and incidental occurrences without ideal content.[4]

There can be no true "history" or "phenomenology" of spirit at this level of individuals and their private, personal motives: psychology furnishes the stuff of physiology (or the "natural history of the body") and the novel, but not of true history and philosophy. Hegel stigmatized psychology as *"subjektive Menschenkennerei"* and in his scheme of progressive spiritualization he placed it in the sub-basement below the rudimentary level of the "subjective spirit" which is dialectically transformed into "objective" and "absolute" spirit. Not at the trivial personal level (*Verkleinerung*) but only at the level of suprapersonal generalization (*Verallgemeinerung*) did Hegel encounter genuine history as the manifestation of spirit: "The mere particularities of individuals are far removed from the real object of history."[5] Schelling, too, rejected "this so-called science 'psychology'" as "barren empirical science of mind," because it attempts to subsume all free spiritual manifestations under a causal order of necessity. Under the "knife of psychology," all that is great and free is reduced to mere mechanical caricature or subjective illusion.[6] Wilhelm von Humboldt departed somewhat from this uniform deprecation by allowing psychology a role in historical study—but only with the proviso that it be conceived intuitively as "insight into the human condition" rather than mechanistically. In his famous essay "On the Task of the Historian," he cautioned that the psychological interpretation of history was the "least universal" for it wrenches the individual out of his whole context and tends toward "trivialization" (*Verkleinerung*) and the extinction of content.[7] Following in this same tradition, Johann Droysen put stringent limits upon any psychological approach to matters of the spirit. In his *Historik* and lectures, psychological method was treated as inherently reductionistic and alien to the true subject-matter of history.[8] It is noteworthy that Dilthey praised Schleiermacher for putting "empirical psychology" at the basis of his account of mind. But Dilthey went on to observe that Schleiermacher ultimately permitted psychology only a provisional role as "Seelenkunde" (analogous to "natural description" rather than "ethics"), which was to be transcended in the dialectic of mind. Empirical psychology was merely "preparatory to philosophy" (*GS* 14/1:465–66).

In Dilthey's own time, the Baden neo-Kantians represented the culmination of the idealists' disdain for psychology. They held that philosophy grounded in transcendental logic and value-theory was the sole legitimate basis for the study of mind and all its genuinely "spiritual" accomplishments, including scientific knowledge. Psychology was a natural science and could not claim competence in matters of the spirit. Psychological and transcendental methods were entirely divorced. Indeed, they could neither meet nor conflict, for they were not on the same plane (and if they seemed to conflict, it was owing to a logical confusion). Windelband classified psychology as a "nomothetic" science of necessity and empirical facticity, not freedom and ideal-values. Following earlier precedents, the neo-Kantians distinguished between empirical psyche (*Seele*) and true spirit (*Geist*) or reason, which is universal and ideal. Windelband's student, Heinrich Rickert, elaborated this distinction in a manner which was to become immensely important in the ensuing debate over the human sciences:

> Spirit means something principally different from all psychic being, indeed something independent of it, what Hegel called "objective spirit" in contrast to "subjective spirit"! The merely "unspiritual" life of the soul can be reckoned to nature.[9]

Confined solely to the consideration of facts and laws of causality, empirical psychology could not deal critically with matters of value and meaning central to the human sciences; these were reserved exclusively to transcendental philosophy or theory or value.

Dilthey regarded the long-standing idealist disdain for psychology as "speculative haughtiness" (*GS* 14/1:419). Their transcendental *hauteur* prevented these philosophers from seeing that psychology was capable of much more than brain physiology and calculation of specific energies of nerve conduction—that indeed it had more to say concerning the actual workings of "mind" than could be contained in a transcendental logic or theory of value. A genuinely "unrestricted" (*unbefangen*) and empirical psychology would shed much light on the "mental world" of culture, society, and history and provide the necessary foundation for the human sciences. But the psychology he envisioned to fulfill these aims was far removed from all existing psychologies. Practically without exception

Dilthey rejected every extant form of psychology as inadequate to a full grasp of mental life. In an early essay he echoed the complaint of Novalis: "The psychology of today belongs to the species of false idols which have taken places in the holy temple where authentic divine images should stand." Borrowing Novalis' terms, Dilthey called for a "real-psychology" (*Realpsychologie*) or "content-psychology" (*Inhaltspsychologie*) which would treat the actual "inner" content and meaning of mental images and ideas, not merely the "external" and formal order in which they are related (*ED* 300; *GS* 13/1:380). Formalistic and mechanistic assumptions had come to dominate the discipline of psychology, producing a distorted account of the mind's operations. In an outline of 1879 bearing the motto "Empirie nicht Empirismus" Dilthey summarized his allegations against current forms of the discipline: "Psychology has up to now elaborated forms and laws of the psychic process, but the contents which in the first place determine the meaning of our existence are excluded from consideration" (*GS* 5:lxxvii; 18:193). Such psychology cannot possibly fathom the meaning of mental contents, for it regards them as simple, causally-linked elements devoid of integral, "lived" relations to the human subject. Dilthey came to be highly skeptical of the various "laws" which had been isolated by psychologists from elementary neural processes and then employed to "explain" higher mental functions such as thought and speech. He insisted that psychology should develop "laws" or "coherences" of content which would encompass symbolic and cultural meaning. He specified the error implicit in the conventional notion of law: "Psychological laws are only laws of form; as such they do not have anything to do with the real content of the human mind, only with its formal aspects and processes. They are, so to speak, merely the syntax and meter of the poem" (*GS* 6:43). Dilthey's general judgment concerning existing psychology was drastically negative:

> Contemporary psychology is an expanded doctrine of sensation and association. The fundamental power of mental life falls outside the scope of psychology. Psychology has become only a doctrine of the forms of psychic processes; thus, it grasps only a part of that which we actually experience in mental life [*GS* 9:183].

One might be led to wonder why, given his almost uniformly negative assessment of existing psychology, Dilthey could invest it with the crucial function of *Grundwissenschaft* for the human sciences. The answer lies in his underlying conviction that it could be reformed and expanded "to its true concept" in a way which would allow it to fulfill this fundamental role. For all its shortcomings and accumulated errors, psychology seemed potentially more fruitful and fitting for this task than existing epistemology, which in its own way was as dogmatic as the metaphysical systems it replaced.[10]

Epistemology and Critical Theory of Knowledge: Critique, Not Criticism

Since Dilthey referred to his own project in Kantian terms as a "critique of historical reason," one might expect that he would insist in Kantian fashion that epistemology should assume the crucial role of fundamental science of mind. For reasons which will become apparent, this was not precisely the case. Dilthey did not regard epistemology—at least as conventionally conceived—as an autonomous and self-contained discipline capable of founding the human sciences. In his view the narrowly conceived discipline going under the name "critical theory of knowledge" must perforce pass into broader inquiries of psychology, intellectual history, and the philosophy of life and culture. Conventional theory of knowledge (*Erkenntnistheorie*), as it had come to be defined since Kant, must be taken up into the larger tasks of philosophical and historical "reflection on life and consciousness" (*Selbstbesinnung*).

In the broadest sense, Dilthey may be said to have subscribed to the transcendental-critical spirit of Kant's philosophy. He is frequently aligned with the various neo-Kantian movements of the latter nineteenth century. But it must be stressed that he differed immensely with Kant and the neo-Kantians on fundamental matters. If he may be legitimately (if loosely) described as "the Kant of history," it is equally true that "though Dilthey maintained a profound admiration for Kant, he cannot properly be described as a neo-Kantian."[11] As was his habit, Dilthey discriminated between the "spirit" and the "letter" of Kant's philosophy: he subscribed to the living impulse of Kant's thought, while dissociating himself from its doctrinal particulars.

In his Basel address, Dilthey avowed that Kant had set down the basic problem of philosophy for all time, that is, "How is valid knowledge possible?" In one of his many review of the proliferating literature on Kant and "*Kritizismus,*" he judged that the *Critique of Pure Reason* was "the greatest philosophical work ever produced by the German mind" (*WM* 47[1879]:126). Kant had effectively demolished the copy-theory of knowledge and replaced it with the doctrine of the primacy of consciousness, thereby establishing the mind itself as the key to the problem of knowledge:

> It is the highest and most universal problem of all inquiry: In what form is the world given to us, a world which is there for us only in our perceptions and representations? Through what processes is constituted from the disparate and constantly in-streaming impulses which meet the senses the picture of the external world in which we live? And likewise out of inner intuitions the picture of the mental world [*GS* 5:12; cf. *BNL* 48/341]?

The leading impulse of the transcendental-critical approach was to trace all phenomena back to a creative source in the human mind. This method had broad ramifications for the study of man and the entirety of his works: "In all areas German transcendental philosophy brought into clear recognition the creative capacity of human nature" (GS 6:268). All fields of inquiry must ultimately return to critical consideration of the nature of the human mind, for all rigorous knowledge (*Wissenschaft*) is the disciplined self-consciousness (*Selbstbesinnung*) of man. All possible phenomena are "there-for-consciousness" and have as their original basis the creative capacities and restrictive limits of that consciousness; hence consciousness cannot be conceived as merely a reflection or epiphenomenon of nature but as the creative source and limit of all reality. Kant's decisive recognition of the constitutive role of mind was the core of the critical approach to reason. Quoting Goethe's formulation of Kant's critical imperative, Dilthey affirmed that "in the apprehension of things as well as in action, we must separate that which is attainable from that which is not; otherwise we will do little in science as well as life" (GS 1:124).

Yet in the final analysis Kant was not critical enough. For all his stress upon *Kritik*, he fell victim to his own brand of dogmatism—one which became even more pronounced in the *Kritizismus* of his disciples. In his last seminar on Kant, Dilthey expressly avowed the critical method of Kant but purged of its "nativistic inclinations" (LK 3). Kant's transcendental a priorism was not in keeping with his own intention to provide a full account of human knowledge. Under the precept "no Kantianism, but, to be sure, a recognition of what Kant really accomplished," Dilthey attempted to submit Kant to a kind of immanent critique, separating the dispensable dogmatic content from the true and lasting achievements (BNL 49/250). Kant had set the crucial problem, but he had not provided the definitive answer. His true followers were therefore not his slavish imitators "who wish to install him everywhere in direct relation to the present but those who regard him with a healthy historical sense and thereby feel the need to move beyond him" (WM 47[1879]:125–26). In this effort of immanent critique, Dilthey felt that he was truer to the real critical thrust of Kant's philosophizing than the self-proclaimed neo-Kantians, since "Kant always supplemented his original frame of questioning [*Fragestellung*] with another frame of questioning" (BNL 49/136).[12]

Kantian *Kritizismus* was not critical enough in the sense that it did not examine its own assumptions in the light of the actual process and growth of knowledge. It was abstract, formal, and highly peremptory and therefore unable to do justice to the full scope of mental life and the true content of knowledge and experience. Kant's theory of knowledge, despite abjuring metaphysics, was still taken up in the quasimetaphysical enterprise of introducing absolute forms and principles from a transcendent *Hinterwelt*. Kant had maintained that the inquiry into the validity of knowledge must be independent of experience in order to secure that knowledge on apodictic grounds: the "grounds of science" and the critical "science of grounds" must both be transcendental in character.

Dilthey, in contrast, insisted that "knowledge of knowledge," for all its second-order claims of superior jurisdiction, is itself an empirical inquiry and that it too must rely upon an extended concept of experience for its "proof." Kant was correct in positing the primacy of consciousness, but wrong to take an abstract and formal approach to his own discovery. The knowledge which we have (including the knowledge of mind itself) is not the result of a deduction of transcendental forms, but the distilled product of man's cumulative experience. The proper critical approach to consciousness is not only empirical but historical, for knowledge is developmental in character. Dilthey was intent upon providing an empirical and historical rendering of the transcendental approach to the mind and its works, including knowledge itself. Unless one has acknowledged this seemingly paradoxical position—which in one breath suggests both Mill's empirical psychology and Hegel's phenomenology of mind—Dilthey's theory of knowledge will remain unintelligible.

Kant's errors, like his positive accomplishments, were systematic and closely interrelated. He adopted hard and fast disjunctions and formal dichotomies rather than reciprocal relations leading to higher levels of synthesis. Thus his greatest and most pressing problem came to be "defining the relation of what he originally held apart in abstract opposition" (*BNL* 49/238). By insisting upon the sharp separation of perception and conception, content and form, experience and thought, Kant was forced to adopt the "whole apparatus" of the transcendental a priori to bring them together. Kant adopted a truncated Humean notion of experience as "sensation" and then alloyed it with an abstract, a priori notion of the understanding. In the name of apodictic certainty Kant resorted to transcendental "logicism." First he disordered experience and then attempted to re-order it with the transcendental-logical forms. He emerged with a "logical subject" and a "logical object" of scientific knowledge, but the real objects and subjects of experience were left in "pure transcendence." The sharp contrast of a chaos of impressions on the one hand and the logic of thought on the other could be mediated only by a *vinculum substantiale* of transcendental postulates. As a result of this tenuous bond, Kant's theory of knowledge tended to break apart into phenomenalism or metaphysics, as evidenced in subsequent lines of development of his doctrine (*BNL* 49/244–50).

A true theory of scientific knowledge must begin with the problem posed by Kant, but can solve it only by employing a much more encompassing notion of experience and a more dynamic conception of the reciprocal relation of experience and higher intellectual functions. "Kant's negative doctrine of the unknowability of things in themselves will thus be transformed into the positive doctrine of a genuine knowledge which progresses stepwise within certain limits [*einer innerhalb gewisser Grenzen stufenweise fortschreitenden wahrhaftigen Erkenntnis*]." This new critique of reason aspired "to go beyond Kant in experience" (*GS* 15:156). In direct contradiction to Kant, Dilthey postulated what he termed the "immanence of order and form in the material content of our experience" (*GS* 5:79). And in most un-Kantian fashion, he asserted that this immanent form is not static and a priori, but developing and historical.

Dilthey found that Kant was "not truly critical because he was not historical." Kant's urge to absolute certainty blinded him to the historical nature of knowledge itself. Thus he took a stage of natural scientific knowledge and elevated it as universally valid. Dilthey went on to insist: "The analysis of the present state of our knowledge is necessary and important, but only preliminary" (*BA* 74). The character of knowledge as *developing* certainty was more adequately explored by Schleiermacher and Trendelenburg, who gave up the notion of a static a priori. Hegel, too, began with this great insight but hastily moved on to speculative construction rather than careful historical reflection with philosophical intent. Surveying these post-Kantian developments, Dilthey insisted that the valid portion of transcendental-critical philosophy and his own historical analyses were "digging toward the same depth" (*GS* 2:496).

The Kantian theory of knowledge produced an inversion of things: it uses thought to "explain" experience in the service of scientific certainty. The result is a distorted account of experience and a static view of knowledge. Dilthey suggested that these errors stemmed from the fact that, despite all protests to the contrary, Kant ultimately confronted knowledge as an "object" rather than a process. It was Schleiermacher's great insight to have seen that second-level "knowledge of knowledge" is not an "object" but rather, like primary knowledge, an ongoing process of "becoming aware" (*BA* 81a). Dilthey carried this doctrine further in claiming that conventional critical and neo-critical theory of knowledge would take its place within the "epistemological epoch" which was simply a passing phase in the larger process of ongoing *Selbstbesinnung* (*GS* 7:334). Such reflection would, in Dilthey's view, "bury" existing epistemology (*GS* 5:lxxxv).

Kantian *Kritizismus* was caught in an insoluble dilemma which stemmed from an exaggerated demand for absolute and apodictic certainty in scientific knowledge. If it was not critical enough on some points, it was hypercritical on others—and, as a result, pure logic was taken as the canon of knowledge. Kant's epistemology endeavored to investigate the formal and logical conditions of the possibility of knowledge independent of actual knowledge itself, whereas a genuinely critical examination of knowledge must proceed from the ongoing practice of the sciences, not from some abstract, hypothetical model: "An epistemology which is divorced from the single sciences yields problems but no solutions" (*BNL* 48/345). In attempting to attain a priori "knowing of knowing," this abstract form of epistemology involved itself in the implausible task of employing thought to examine itself for validity, while at the same time purporting not to assume its validity from the outset. Such a tactic either begged the question through its original model of knowledge or else culminated in the fruitlessly formal exercise of constantly honing the critical knife without getting down to the practical work of slicing the roast. Dilthey's objections to the hypervigilant logical formalism of *Kritizismus* in many respects paralleled those of Hegel, whose strictures against a purely critical and formal approach to knowledge were given notably careful treatment in Dilthey's study of the young Hegel. For Hegel, Dilthey recorded, a purely critical theory of knowledge always threatened to become trapped in the vicious and ultimately reflexive circle of assaying the formal validity of knowledge, while holding its actual application in suspension. In a famous passage specifically cited by Dilthey, Hegel compared this gingerly scholasticism with the desire to learn to swim without going into the water (*GS* 4:233; cf. 18:228). A "consistent" *Kritizismus* ends up in the thin air of abstract, schematic formalism, in which thought has sacrificed empirical content for certainty of form.

For Dithey, the theory and practice of knowledge, as well as its form and content, cannot be separated, for they are linked in the real source of our knowledge—experience in the broadest sense. We cannot hope to get fully outside the actual experience of the mind in order to test the formal validity of its operations. In contrast to the Kantian postulate of a rational ego or transcendental consciousness, we must recognize that there is no higher consciousness which validates our thought. We can never arrive at a Kantian *Bewusstsein überhaupt*, for consciousness is always immersed in the actual experience of the world. In an essay, Dilthey cited Fichte's observation that "pure theory cannot lead beyond the facts of consciousness"; consciousness is always experiencing, even when it is reflecting upon itself and the grounds of its knowledge (*ED* 259).

The true *Grundwissenschaft* must begin with the full reality of experience as given to consciousness—otherwise it becomes lost in a labyrinth of mirrors or "eyes behind eyes but no seeing." The real contents of experience are the world-for-us—the "thing itself"—and it is fruitless to seek eternal grounds outside experience. Experience contains real and objective relations and does not need recourse to transcendental forms to produce knowledge. "Experience is not just perception, it is knowledge on the basis of perception. Perception as such is not yet [genuine] experience, which consists in judgments and contains an expansion of knowledge of facts" (*BA* 36). Certainty is thus not the accomplishment of some superordinate "faculty of rules" but is in experience itself. Dilthey's epistemology stipulates the "objective reality" of lived experience. Every judgment refers to something contained in experiential reality. Even where this relation seems to disappear (as in mathematics and formal logic), it is only "very mediated" (GS 5:84–85). Mental life consists first and foremost of relations, not elements; and abstractions are for Dilthey "signs of relations" in which the perceptual content remains "dark" (GS 18:140).

The critical vigilance of epistemology must be moderated by a certain pragmatic "belief" in the evidence of experience; otherwise thought ends in equally sterile extremes—in closed a priori formalism, in skepticism, or in phenomenalistic "bridge building," which suspends the world of experience only to reintroduce it as a logical postulate. In experience we "know" many things tacitly and practically without being able to offer a perfectly articulated and exhaustive account of the grounds of this knowledge. A formal "critique of reason" can never entirely analyze or account for this knowledge, though it can shed light on its foundations and procedures. In one of his reviews Dilthey expressed agreement with Goethe's objections to Kant's position that "before we can claim to have knowledge, we have to bring it to court" (GS 17:59). Pointing to an antinomy at the heart of neo-Kantian Kritizismus, Dilthey referred to "the irresolvable problem of examining the possibility of knowledge prior to or independently from knowledge itself" (GS 7:277–78).

Dilthey's corrective to the reflexive formalism of Kantian theory of knowledge is the plain "naïve" conviction of practical common sense and what he called "belief." In an arresting passage in the "Breslauer Ausarbeitung," he drew the seemingly "uncritical" conclusion that "all scientific knowledge begins in belief, that is, with the acceptance of presuppositions" (BA 266–267a; also 49, 59, 67). This assertion however, should not be interpreted as a way of smuggling some form of religious faith into the theory of knowledge, as was attempted by the "metacritical" thinkers Hamann, Herder, and Jacobi. Rather, as William James was later to insist, Dilthey was simply calling attention to the fact that all knowledge contains a fiduciary element which can never be proven on purely rational or logical grounds. On the basis of ordinary experience we "know" that we have knowledge of reality and we do not generally need the arcane and elaborate arguments of epistemology to furnish us with guarantees. Ultimately one has simply to suppose the validity of knowledge without any exhaustive prior demonstration of absolute criteria. Dilthey broke out of the regressive circle of Kritizismus by endowing experience with an indigenous certainty of its own which is tested against other experiences in a reflective process which goes on as new experience is integrated with the old. The actual "critical" test of knowledge does not come from some prior logical proof, but from the actual process of seeing it at work. We must be content with the practical "proof" of experience, which provides only a "relative certainty" (komparative Allgemeinheit) rather than a purely rational, apodictic proof (*denknotwendige Allgemeinheit*) (*GS* 15:157). Dilthey developed this conception further in stipulating a scale or gradation of certainty which is furnished by differing levels of reflection upon experience and different types of intellectual representation (*BA* 123 ff.). This doctrine of a scale of relative certainty deriving from the reflection upon experience owed much to Schleiermacher and Trendelenburg—and quite likely to J. S. Mill.

Dilthey's experiential and pragmatic approach to the problem of knowledge is strikingly manifest in his treatment of the problem of the status of the "real." For him the real (*das Wirkliche*) is the effectuating (*das Wirkende*). This fundamental tenet of *Idealrealismus* had been indicated by his mentors Schleiermacher, Trendelenburg, and K. Fischer long before the emergence of a full-fledged pragmatism in the latter part of the nineteenth century. The most pointed reference to this doctrine occurred in Fischer's *Logik*:

> Reality [*Wirklichkeit*] here means the same as effectiveness [*Wirksamkeit*]. What does not work is therefore not real in the strictest sense of the term. Only the effectual is the truly real, knowledge of which is the aim of philosophy.[13]

Reality is *in* consciousness, but not in a passive or neutral sense. The manner in which reality "works" in the mind is not merely a matter of passive, theoretical ideation or representation but the volitional and affective engagement of the entire consciousness.

Dilthey's identification of reality with what is practically at work in the mind forms the key to his treatment of the age-old problem of the proof of the external world. This thorny problem had occupied thinkers ever since the ancient skeptics, but had become especially acute since the Cartesian reduction of the world of experience to the purportedly indubitable certitude of the pure, rationalist *cogito*. The progressive attenuation of consciousness to pure thought was primarily responsible for the proliferation of phenomenalist positions which put the status of the external world in profound doubt. Dilthey held that in assuming a purely "theoretical" attitude, the mind was led to doubt the existence of an external world, but the same path of pure theoretical intellection could not reestablish the world as real. A more adequate theory of consciousness based upon the full content of experience would show this problem to be the artificial conundrum of abstract thought gone amok. It is only by ignoring experience that the world becomes "external" and theoretically problematical.

Characteristically, Dilthey foreswore the attempt to furnish a purely logical or rational proof of the external world: the demand for a strictly rational proof can only lead to further enervating skepticism or a purely formal construct. The mind is saved from skepticism not by logical proof but by the "proof" of lived experience as tested through time. In keeping with his principle that knowledge always entails an element of "belief" which critical reason itself cannot penetrate, Dilthey spoke not of a "proof" of the external world, but of the "origins of belief" in it; not logic, but experience, must be the arbiter of our knowledge of reality (*GS* 5:90 ff.).

In actual experience—that is, before any purely intellectual and theoretical attitude toward the world—we are bound to the world by a complex coherence of lived relations. These relations are practical in a sense which is prior to all theoretical reflection. Theory can only elucidate the practical relations implicit in the standpoint of life. As discussed previously, the "standpoint of life" shows us to be engaged in the world with all our mental capacities—not just thinking, but willing and feeling as well. The mind in its practical-volitional function resolves the problems posed by its purely theoretical-thinking function. It is from volitional experience that we derive our conviction of the reality of the external world. The world is originally and primordially a lived experience for us, not a matter of rational demonstration. From our first experiences we come to know the world through the dynamic and reciprocal processes of the exertions of our will and the resistances (*Hemmungen*) which these exertions encounter. The experience of frustrated effort gives us a sense of the independent status of an "outside" reality. The experience of a successfully executed effort gives us grounds for believing in our own independence. We come to realize that we are "we" and not "it." Indeed it is out of this practical experience of exertion and resistance that the theoretical distinction between subject and object arises. Reciprocal action and reaction through time instills the conviction that reality is "there for me." Self and world are thus coeval in experience; neither can be conceived as a starting point before the other. "I am as sure of the outside world as I am of myself" (*BA* 49). Dilthey's argument, echoing that of Fichte and Maine de Biran, is based upon the *praxis* of will in action and reaction, impulse and inhibition. Reality is an effectuation in consciousness and this effectuation is shown from the standpoint of life to be the mutual process of action and restriction of our willing efforts. Existence is known to us by resistance. In the "Breslauer Ausarbeitung," Dilthey asserted bluntly that from this vantage point "reality and resistance are identical" (*BA* 237).

In what might seem a paradox, Dilthey held that a truly comprehensive theory of knowledge must give up a purely "theoretical" view of reality and knowledge. Such a theory must be more than a transcendental deduction of the forms of knowledge employed in the physical sciences. It must be broadened to include not only cognition in the strictest sense (*Wirklichkeitserkenntnis*) but also other classes of human experience and knowledge, including the positing of values (*Wertsetzung*) and the setting of rules (*Regelgebung*). The real subject of this broader inquiry is not Kant's "transcendental ego" or some other "logical subject" but concrete, "anthropological" man:

In the veins of the knowing subject that Locke, Hume and Kant constructed runs not real blood but the diluted fluid of reason as a merely intellectual function. Historical as well as psychological concern with the whole man has led me to put this willing, feeling, ideating being in the multiplicity of its powers at the foundation of the explanation of knowledge and its concepts (such as the external world, time, substance, causality), regardless of whether knowledge and its concepts appear to be woven merely out of the stuff of perception, ideation and thought [*GS* 1:xviii].

In the "Breslauer Ausarbeitung" there appears a sentence which might properly stand as the quintessence of Dilthey's theory of knowledge and mind: "We begin with the whole and it is with this whole that we are constantly concerned" (*BA* 224). The "whole" which Dilthey alluded to was not Hegel's whole of the Absolute Concept, but the concrete whole of lived experience. This experiential whole is the precondition of thought and the perpetual object of philosophical reflection and historical inquiry. It is gradually disclosed in the process of man's self-understanding, which is much more than a merely formal "knowing of knowing" in the sense of *Kritizismus*.

Dilthey's theory of knowledge occupies a position between the conventional designations of empiricism and a priorism. His description of Schleiermacher's views provides a useful key in determining his own position. For Schleiermacher, neither the eternal, innate ideas of the rationalists nor the sensory chaos of the empiricists provides an adequate account of mental operation. All thoughts in the mind are the result of the dynamic relations between the action of outside objects and the concomitant working (*Mitwirken*) of the mind's own operations:

Every separation of an a priori in the sense of a condition of consciousness which precedes the act of thought is impossible. The functions expressed in the categories, the rules of thought, are not an a priori separable from the material of our thought, which would somehow be already contained in consciousness. They arise in the interaction of both factors. "Matter of thought" and "form of thought" do not appear in real thought. All real thought is conditioned by the reciprocal interrelation [*Aufeinanderbezogensein*] of both functions [*GS* 14/1:112].

The forms and categories of experience must be brought down from their transcendental heights into the dynamic process of experience itself. Dilthey firmly insisted that the forms of experience are not static and immutable but are subject to change in the course of man's historical experience. In the "Breslauer Ausarbeitung," he gave testimony to the seemingly contradictory doctrine of a "historical a priori":

The a priori of Kant is fixed and dead. The real conditions of consciousness are living historical process and development; they have a history and the course of this history is accommodation to the ever more exactly and inductively known manifold of experiences. The life of history in its powerful flux has engulfed the apparently static forms under which we think. Life is here, as everywhere not just form, which is only an abstraction [BA 269].

What the Kantians gained in certainty by focusing upon pure a priori form, Dilthey was willing to compromise in order to do justice to the open, dynamic, and self-correcting qualities of knowledge. The project of a critique of historical reason entailed not merely the notion that a special variety of reason is employed in historical thinking but also that reason itself is historical and developmental. Thus, the burden of his theory of knowledge was borne not by static forms and categories, but by the ongoing and self-integrating process of knowledge itself. Reviewing the logic of the neo-Kantian Christoph Sigwart, Dilthey asserted that the conditions of knowledge are "mutable" and that new categories are constantly being produced in science: "The conditions in which we try to comprehend reality undergo constant correction and transformation in the history of the sciences" (WM 50[1881]:525; see also GS 6:204). Such a position clearly entailed a special conception of logic and the relation of thought to experience.

The Role of Thought and Logic in the Human Sciences: Logic, Not Logicism

Dilthey regarded the neglect of the full scope and content of experience and a preoccupation with formal logic as the twin failings of existing epistemology. In the "Breslauer Ausarbeitung" he tersely stated a proposition which is found in many forms in the published writings: "All reality is given in experience. Thought is the analysis of this reality." He went on to state that we have "reality itself" in this experience and that while thought and logic cannot *add* to the reality of this experience, it can *explicate* it and raise it to clearer consciousness: "All the work of thought, science, and reflection can only serve to bring the unknown meaning of these experiences to consciousness" (BA 58–59). The upshot of this "Empirie" is that experience is not, as for the Kantians, categorically or materially distinct from thought and knowledge, but is their ground and presupposition: "All knowledge is an analysis of experience" (GS 5:434). Experience and thought are co-determinative, and ultimately rooted in life: "The fundamental conditions of knowledge are given in life and thought cannot go behind them" (GS 5:136). Dilthey's doctrine entailed an extensive revision of the very notion of the function of logic, rules of thought, concepts and categories in such a manner as to comprehend the manifold nature of lived experience. Such a basic logical reformulation was crucial to the foundation of the human sciences (GS 7:281).

Dilthey insisted that the human sciences were "empirically" grounded in lived experience and the "praxis of life," but he was no less insistent that they qualified as genuine sciences only with the employment of the operations of thought, including conceptualization, abstraction, analysis, and the determination of "law-like" or "structural" relations and regularities. It is important to establish this point, since Dilthey is often erroneously portrayed simply as a proponent of an anticonceptual "intuition," or some mystical notion of "knowledge-as-raw-experience" or "feeling." In holding that all science and knowledge derive from experience, he was far from identifying knowledge with unmediated experience. Unlike the Kantians, he did not neatly separate experience and thought (and thus could not provide the kind of formal or transcendental logic of the human sciences which presents itself once this separation is admitted), but he always insisted that the operations of thought are necessary for the transformation of lived experience into knowledge. Knowledge in the human sciences is not the mere having or "living through" of experience, but is the methodical ascertainment of structures, uniformities, and patterns in human experience as a whole. Lived experience and thought are reciprocally related in a steplike arrangement in which thought explicates what is contained in experience. Thought is the interpreter of lived experience, not its author or judge of its reality. It apprehends and clarifies relations contained in experience; it does not produce these relations. Thus, it is obliged to represent the content and relations of experience, but in a clarified and patterned manner.

Thought cannot "produce" experience—or substitute for it—but it is nonetheless necessary to clarify experience and provide certainty in the "nexus of concepts" (*GS* 7:3). In his essay of 1875, Dilthey provided an admonition which is too often overlooked by his critics: "Without the mediation of thought—that is, in its sheer immediacy—we cannot grasp any reality, not even our own mental states, in a clear, distinct, and orientated framework" (*GS* 5:85). He underscored the same point in the *Einleitung*, insisting that the cognitive aims of the human sciences can be reached only through the intervention of thought in the form of concepts, judgments, analysis, and abstraction (*GS* 1:27). The necessarily selective nature of these intellectual operations means that the human sciences have as their scientific object only the "partial contents of a complex reality," not the whole of reality itself. We are therefore both empowered and limited by the operations of thought: limited in the sense of excluding some features of perceived reality in order to clarify and order other features.

Dilthey conceived logic as an aid to thought, not its result. He often termed it the "conductor" or "guide," rather than the supreme arbiter of science. He did not provide an independent systematic logic of the human sciences as was attempted by Rickert, Wundt, and later by Erich Rothacker and Ernst Cassirer. This omission stems not so much from temperamental bias or intellectual failings, but from his very conception of logic itself.[14] Logic is the "art of discovery" (*Kunst der Erfindung*) or part of the "doctrine of method of thinking" and thus relative to the specific problem (and objects) of inquiry. As an aid to inquiry it cannot be conceived as a closed set of formal rules devoid of experiential content (*BNL* 140/396; see also *GS* 1:116). As the clarifying guide of experience, logic is not its a priori condition or ultimate judge: it rather brings the aids of thought to the contents of experience. In actual inquiry there is no logical operation without experiential content and a "working" logic must stay in touch with the results of observation. Dilthey denied that formal or transcendental logic could provide grounds for an adequate account of actual knowledge. Such logics sacrifice the content of experience in order to set up chains of shadowy concepts and deductions. Dilthey regarded the hypostatization of logic into "logicism" (*Logismus*) as a residual effect of the ancient urge for a "first science" of things: "Metaphysical philosophy, with its cult of reason in the sense of abstract thought, has played a role here in establishing logic as the judge over experience" (*GS* 6:145). He went on to point out that from the standpoint of pure logic a madman can be "formally" (*formell*) correct, while an experientially-based notion of reason would find him "materially" (*materiell*) in error. Logic is not sufficient to itself, nor can it stand as the summation (*Inbegriff*) of reality, as in Hegel's grandiose scheme. Logic must regard itself critically as a refining instrument of thought, not a substitute for the fullest possible empirical viewing of reality. In an evocative image in the "Breslauer Ausarbeitung," Dilthey compared the proper role of logic to the process of climbing a look-out tower: the rules of reasoning are like the steps of the tower—in their proper sequential pattern they are indispensable to the climbing, but they are not the "seeing" itself (*BA* 42).

A working logic must rest upon the apprehension of the contents of a given reality, which remains its true ground. It clarifies and interprets experience by representing its content in categories, judgments, and systems of inference. To stress the intimate connection of basic logical functions such as comparison, contrast, and gradation to the contents of experience, Dilthey called them "perceptions of the second degree" (*GS* 7:302). These functions link logic to psychology and epistemology. By itself, logic neither produces experience, nor can it alone determine the truth-value of judgments in the sciences. In actual inquiry it stands not by itself but as a "mediating member" (*Mittelglied*) between the general discipline of epistemology (or more properly *Selbstbesinnung*) and the single sciences. Logic is linked in two directions: to the critical theory of knowledge on the one hand and the actual ongoing work of knowledge on the other. Positioned between the "theory" and "practice" of knowledge, logic is superior to neither but indispensable to both. Dilthey asserted that if logic were to fulfill its proper task, it would mediate between philosophy and the individual sciences, tearing down the "artificial walls" which had been erected from both sides (*GS* 1:117). At times he proposed that a genuine philosophy of experience or a truly empirical psychology would encompass the realm of logic:

> If psychology proceeds from the totality of life—if it grasps the inter-action of the processes of will and representation, then it does not have to split the play of representations off from logical thought and postulate above the capricious and random processes a higher form of mental life [*GS* 6:145].

Whether conceived formally or transcendentally, logic in itself cannot provide a genuine foundation for the human sciences. To a great extent the operations of logic are an extension of relations implicit in experience. Lived experience remains primary, the formal operations of thought secondary, in any theory of knowledge attempted for these sciences. Experiential content provides the material and formal coherence of thought and judgment (*GS* 5:86). Dilthey stressed this point over and over: "That which is experienced in life and the understanding of every kind of experience are the foundation of all the judgments, concepts, and cognitions which are characteristic of the human sciences." And again: "The human sciences and their logical-epistemological foundation presuppose everywhere a knowledge of lived experience. The condition for this knowledge is contained in lived experience itself" (*GS* 7:71, 318).

In contrast to Kant and in keeping with Trendelenburg's evolutionary *Idealrealismus*, Dilthey regarded logic not as the final inventory of the a priori forms of thought, but as a set of integrated and refined reflections upon the body of accumulated human experience. His dispersed observations upon logic follow sporadically the ambitious program he enunciated in his youthful diary: the replacement of "closed systems of logic" and "logicism" with the "doctrine of the evolving forms of the human mind" (*JD* 124). In his program the rules of logical reasoning are conceived as the distilled results of human experience in the broadest sense. The formal axioms of thought cannot be vested with ultimate judgment of what is given as real in experience, for not all meaning and knowledge can be fully subsumed in logical rules. Logic must follow the actual results of the sciences rather than presuming to dictate to them according to its own formal canons. To be fruitful, logic must take its material from the accomplishments of science; it must renounce all ontological claims to be a "science of being" and content itself with the more modest role of "science of method" for the particular sciences. As did Trendelenburg, Dilthey conceived of logic not rationalistically as "the science of thinking" as such, but pragmatically as general inquiry into specific inquiries; logic becomes a range of sublogics or field-logics conceived as "methodo-logics."

Dilthey's logical tenets are deployed throughout his writings in accordance with his conviction that the fruitful form of logic is not a self-enclosed, uniform system in itself, but a multiform "doctrine of method" elaborated in relation to specific topics of inquiry: "Logical analysis embraces all the accomplishments of thought, stretching all the way from pre-discursive thought to the ultimate level of a theory which takes thought itself as an object" (*BNL* 22/26). He condemned both extremes of "logicism" and "misologism" and insisted that the study of the development of logic was invaluable in disclosing its proper use in actual investigation. Logicism reverses what Dilthey called the "natural relation" of experience and thought; the immediate certainties of experience are forced to conform to the necessary axioms of thought rather than letting thought guide and clarify experience (*BA* 46). To make formal logical coherence the primary criterion of knowledge results in a "phenomenalistic shadow-world." Misologism, on the contrary, tries to dispense with the ordering work of thought and concepts in favor of an unmediated intuition of particulars. It results in a purely aesthetic rhapsody of immediate qualities. To correct both extremes, Dilthey called in successive writings for a new and expanded concept of logic which would focus upon the relation between thought and experience by penetrating behind the formal axioms of discursive thought to the coherence of mental activity which lies at the basis of all judgments. This "analytical logic" would, if conceived in relation to descriptive psychology, issue in a new doctrine of categories and judgment for the human sciences. Although he never pursued this conception of an analytical logic to a finished form (a form perhaps unattainable, given his conception of logic), Dilthey did sketch out many of its facets.[15]

The human sciences form a coherent body of disciplines, but they do not constitute an "integrated totality of logical constitution" analogous to the natural sciences (*GS* 1:24; 5:53). The clearly articulated, block-like structure of the natural sciences is lacking in the human sciences; they overlap and sometimes even show conflicting perspectives upon the same object or body of evidence. Each of the human sciences employs a different constellation of experiential content, conceptualization, analysis, and abstraction. In their ultimate reference to the human world, therefore, they are incorrigibly relative to one another in a manner which distinguishes their logical structure from the logical structure of the natural sciences. Dilthey insisted, however, that this relativity does not vitiate their results, for it promotes constant new refinements of analysis and synthesis (*GS* 1:28).

As an open-ended and relational system of knowledge, the human sciences are constituted by means of analysis and abstraction, but their truth-value and validity can be judged only with reference to the experiential reality contained in their judgments. All concepts and analytical or abstractive judgments in the human sciences ultimately refer to a relation or content contained in human experience. Even where this content seems to disappear into abstractive formulations, it is only very mediated. It is the general "fit" of concepts and experience which determines the general validity (*Allgemeingültigkeit*) of the human sciences. This fit is not merely a matter of logical form or coherence.

Thought clarifies, amplifies, and fixes the contents of experience in valid concepts and judgments. By means of intellectual operations, thought emancipates itself from the plethora of experiential contents in order to concentrate upon the significant relations in the total content. After adopting the crucial phenomenological distinction between the "acts" and "contents" of experience (a subject which will be taken up later), Dilthey concluded that cognition and cognitive judgments pertain to the contents not to the acts of mental life. Inquiry in the human sciences refines but never entirely transcends experiential reference; it must constantly return to experience—not in the sense of a literal re-enactment, but rather as a clarification of experiential content.

This work of thought is aided by the fact that our perception and experience are suffused with relations which Dilthey called "elementary operations of silent thought." "These elementary operations permeate the whole area of both inner and outer perception. They differ in form from discursive judgments. They constitute the silent thought which is our original grasping of the world [*originäres Auffassen der Welt*]" (BNL 225/623). From the standpoint of life and actual experience, there is no such thing as "raw experience"—the unpatterned flux of impressions assumed by empiricism—for the elementary operations provide a form of intellectual synthesis in experience itself. In terms which would confound any Kantian, Dilthey referred to these operations as the "intellectuality of perception" and rejected the notion that experience required a transcendental power of intellectual synthesis to organize itself into knowledge. The operations of logic are simply refinements of operations implicit in experience. As relations in perception rather than objects of perception, these operations do not fall within the direct ken of perception or introspection and must be read off from perceptual accomplishments by means of analytic logic and descriptive psychology. But here critical reflection and analysis encounter a difficulty—indeed, an apparent antinomy similar to Kant's, since thought is called upon to represent these pre-logical operations of silent thought with the logical concepts of discursive thought. This antinomy is partly overcome by the fact that the operations of silent thought may be inferred from the resulting contents, but Dilthey warns that the full elucidation and enumeration of these pre-logical operations is impossible. Discursive thought can "guide" experience and bring it to a refined and integrated awareness, but it cannot provide it with exhaustive rules and iron-clad criteria of validity.

The human and the natural sciences both employ the same elementary logical operations and rudimentary cognitive functions, including induction, deduction, subsumption, analogy, description, identification, comparison, abstraction, and analysis. But the actual integration of these operations is distinct and hence the final results are manifestly divergent. In answer to the charge that he was a "dualist" in logic, Dilthey reiterated again that both bodies of science use the same "elementary conceptual and logical aids [Hilfsmittel]" but added that "these aids taken in themselves must not be confused with what is attained by means of them in concrete investigation." The ultimate orientation and goal of the sciences remain different: "The natural sciences disclose an order of appearances according to the strictest explanatory law, whereas the human sciences teach us to see [sie wollen sehen lehren]" (BNL 237/19–20). At the elementary level of formal operations the sciences are undeniably similar, but the level of practical application is the true test—and such application always implies a specific object of research. An inventory of formal logical operations cannot add up to a genuine method.

> The human and natural sciences are different first and only in the application [Anwendung] of the elementary operations as conditioned by the nature of the object. By method we mean the manner and way of applying the aids of thought to the material-content of experience. This material-content of experience is conditioned by the special nature of the object, the knowledge of which is the goal of the inquiry [BNL 237/26].

Dilthey's notion of logic as the "doctrine of method" entailed a special conception of the function of categories and judgments. Although the human and natural sciences share certain basic categories and forms of judgment, there are significant differences at the "material" or objective level. Dilthey held that working categories should be defined with reference to predications about objects and relations in the world of experience, rather than as self-subsistent "modes of being." Such categories are therefore the most general forms of perception and cognition, not of "things in themselves" or "thought in itself."

> In the predications which we make of objects there are contained modes of conception [Arten der Auffassung]. I term "categories" the concepts which designate such modes. Every such mode carries in itself a rule of relation. The categories in themselves constitute systematic relations; the ultimate categories designate the highest standpoints for grasping reality. Every such category thus designates its own world of predication [GS 7:192].

In a note in the Nachlass written in conjunction with the above definition, he underscored the experiential relation which is implicitly contained in all categories: "Categories are conceptual expressions for relations in the given;

the relation taken by itself—apart from what is given in experience in the broadest sense—is an empty word" (*BNL* 209/28). Once again siding with Trendelenburg against Kant, Dilthey suggested that the categories of thought are not a priori forms of a universal reason but derive from the grammar of the "developed Western languages" (*BNL* 49/242–43). He returned to this fundamental insight into the grammatical roots of logic to stress the need for a genetic-developmental treatment of the categories of thought; "analytic logic" and intellectual history "with philosophical intent" complement each other.

Categories can be classified as "formal" or "real" according to their relational properties. Formal categories concern the nature of thought itself abstracted of any particular object of empirical content. Dilthey called such categories "modes of conception above all reality" or "abstract expressions for logical operations." He cited identity, difference, gradation, relation, and distinction as such categories (*GS* 7:197). They apply to the conceptual ordering of all reality in general and constitute the formal conditions of knowledge in both the human and natural sciences.

Of more specific interest are what Dilthey called "real categories," which render into conceptual form something given in experience. However far they seem to depart from actual experience, their foundation remains experiential. They are logical modes of grasping empirical content and hence must represent the fullness and diversity of experience. As the most general representations of human experience, they are essential to the understanding of life: "Life is to be understood in its peculiar essence through [real] categories which are foreign to the cognition of nature. What is crucial here is that these categories are not applied to life in a priori fashion as from outside but that they lie implicit in the nature of life itself" (*GS* 7:232).[16]

The real categories of the human sciences may also be termed "categories of life," for they represent life and its dynamic lived structures. They are not categories of "being" in general but of *human* being and the tacit knowledge we have of being human. These categories are plastic, indefinitely numerous, and mutually related: "We can neither delimit a precise number of categories, nor bring their mutual relations into a definitive order" (*GS* 7:302). Dilthey's scattered efforts to define and order the categories of life seem to reflect the intractable, mutually implicated quality he attributed to them. He isolated various ones, including temporality (*Zeitlichkeit*), historicity (*Geschichtlichkeit*), reality (*Wirklichkeit*), possibility (*Möglichkeit*), potency (*Kraft*), part and whole (*Ganze und Teile*), coherence (*Zusammenhang*), reciprocal effect (*Wechselwirkung*), augmentation (*Steigerung*), drive or instinct (*Trieb*), structure (*Struktur*), development (*Entwicklung*), value (*Wert*), purpose (*Zweck*), meaning (*Sinn, Bedeutung*), essence (*Wesen*), type (*Typ*), configuration (*Gestaltung*) and a special kind of causality (*Kausalität*) peculiar to the human world. In different periods of his thinking Dilthey changed the priority and order he assigned to these categories. Not only did he alter the relation among the categories, but he even shifted the definition of individual categories, especially those of causality, meaning, and value. Convinced that the fundamental categories of thought undergo transformation along with the development of the sciences, his own thinking provides a case in point.

Knowledge in the human sciences makes use of special categories and is also expressed in particular kinds of judgments. Dilthey expended considerable effort in specifying the logical form of these judgments. Against the skeptical consequences of subjectivistic accounts of judgment, he maintained that a cognitive judgment is an act of a subject, but its content "is and remains objective" (*BA* 204). In the *Einleitung* he provided a classification of the three types of judgment characteristic of the human sciences: (1) "judgments of fact," or predications about events and phenomena as something "real," that is, given in perception, either inner or outer. Dilthey termed these judgments the "historical" or "descriptive" component in knowledge, that is, something particular given directly in experience, not arrived at by abstraction; (2) "judgments of law" (also "theoretical judgments" and "theorems"), or predications about recurrent regularities, arrived at by abstraction. Dilthey designated these judgments as the "abstract-theoretical" component of knowledge in the human sciences; (3) "judgments of norm, value, and rule," or predications about the standards and ends which govern the relations of the human-historical world. Dilthey termed these judgments the "practical" component in the human sciences (*GS* 1:26).

These three types of judgment—descriptive, explanative, and normative—are logically distinct, but in actual inquiry they are almost always related in an "inner coherence of judgment" characteristic of the human sciences (*GS* 1:20). Indeed, it is the close interrelation of these forms of judgment (Dilthey sometimes calls them "tendencies" of judgment) which defines their actual working procedures and methods. The human sciences are constituted by a weaving together (*Verwebung*) of these judgments into a coherence of representation. One type of judgment may predominate in a particular human science (such as "facts" in history, "laws" in linguistics, or "norms" in aesthetics) but they are always found operating together in what Dilthey called a "structural coherence" of inquiry. As will be shown later, this structural coherence defines Dilthey's method of interpretive understanding or *Verstehen*.

In the actual practice of the human sciences there is no necessary ground for isolating one form of judgment from the others. Norms and values may be treated "factually" in the human sciences (that is, without their validity being presupposed). Likewise, a pattern of norms can provide the basis for a judgment of law or regularity; or, conversely, a judgment of law might be traced back to a set of values. The practitioner of the human sciences never operates with simply one class of judgments, for he finds them closely intertwined in his material and constantly weaves them together in his account. In a passage conserved in the Nachlass, Dilthey emphasized that contrary to the Kantians there can be no cut-and-dried logical schema for the "weave" or coherence of judgments which characterizes the human sciences: "We cannot bring the judgments of reality, law, value, and rule into a purely logical schematism which would fully account for the structural coherence of judgments in the human sciences" (*BNL* 191/26). All judgments (*Ur-teile*) are "parts" or "partial contents" of a basic coherence (*Ur-zusammenhang*) which is given in experience, but clarified in thought.

Dilthey maintained that the forms of judgment, like the categories and logic itself, are part of the general doctrine of method. He was exceedingly conscious of the importance of method, yet at the same time he warned against overemphasizing the formal doctrine of method as an end in itself; a critical approach to method must also be on guard against a kind of "methodism" or "methodolatry." He demanded the most careful, self-conscious reflection upon method, insisting that "an empiricism without the right method ceases to be a science" (*GS* 16:105). But he also saw practical limits to the theoretical formalization of methodologies, as attempted by the neo-Kantians. One of his cardinal theoretical postulates (which also informed his writing of intellectual history) is that *praxis* precedes formal theorizing, that use is preliminary to demonstration. This tenet is rooted in his view that experience of life is prior to reflection upon it: mankind tends to "do" before it "thinks" and when it thinks reflectively, it perforce thinks about this doing. This peculiar relationship is preserved in the development of knowledge itself, as illustrated in the fact that the use of machines preceded and promoted the development of mechanistic cosmology and that the practical tasks of statecraft preceded the development of *Staats-wissenschaft* (*BNL* 137/86–87). Knowledge in general and the forms of human science in particular are inevitably contextual and practical. The ultimate adequacy and validity of knowledge is determined not by its logical form but by its use. There can be no ultimate and universal method abstracted from specific objects and subject matters. This crucial point is conveyed pointedly by a late note in the Nachlass in which Dilthey expressed his full agreement with the proposition of the young Max Weber that "methodology can only be reflection upon the intellectual means which have been preserved and tested in *praxis*." To Weber's statement Dilthey added a corollary for historiography directed against the neo-Kantian position: "The validity of historical method never has its presupposition in a particular a priori philosophical conviction" (*BNL* 242/437).

To all forms of a priorism in method Dilthey reacted with a pragmatic injunction: "Whether a knife is sharp can be discovered best when one cuts with it. The fruitfulness of a method can finally be determined only by whether one makes discoveries through it" (GS 5:42–43). Although he is often said to have advocated an exclusive method of "empathic understanding" (Verstehen) for the human sciences, he in fact proposed under this rubric a range of methods including description, analysis, comparison, and a special kind of explanation. He rejected methodological monism as vehemently as metaphysical monism and instead adopted a kind of pragmatic pluralism on the assumption that methods would prove their usefulness by their results. This same practical attitude extended to the most basic disciplines concerned with the critical examination of knowledge itself:

> I compare epistemology, logic, and psychology with tools or aids [Hilfs-mittel]. I see in these sciences not only a body of insights which can be brought to the other sciences, but I also see that they, like mathematics, constitute methods and conventions of mental inquiry which, though attained only through the probing investigations of the special sciences, can nevertheless be extended beyond these special sciences. This is what is meant by the philosophical spirit [GS 5:48–49].

Method, like logic, should be "guiding" (anleitend) and heuristic; it should not be allowed to become an end in itself. Method should set the terms but not the results of inquiry and it must stay in close touch with experience rather than running off into its own constructions. Dilthey's attitude toward the role of method in inquiry in some respects parallels that of Goethe, who held that "only one who is tired of careful empirical study [Empirie] is driven to method."[17] Method in the useful and practical sense begins as reflection upon experience, not a set of theoretical prescriptions set down in advance. Indeed all theory of method must be on guard against the nearly incorrigible tendency to fix the terms of inquiry in a manner which narrowly predisposes the outcome. Again one encounters a peculiar ambivalence on Dilthey's part. While he stressed the importance of conceptual thought, logic, and method in the human sciences, he at the same time insisted that they remain in close touch with lived experience in order to check their presumed tendency to become enthralled in their own constructions rather than guiding us to "see." In Schleiermacher's typology of methods (the "rhapsodic"—an impressionism concerned with the qualities of particulars; the "dogmatic-deductive"—a systematic deduction from abstract first principles; the "heuristic"—a constant coordination of principles and particulars in an emerging synthesis), Dilthey adopted the view of method as heuristic. Method is so deeply constitutive of the process of inquiry that it must be "guiding" and yet constantly open to the evidence presented by new experience. In a Nachlass note Dilthey tried to capture this relation of coordination between theoretical method and experience: "The development of knowledge accomplishes itself in a process in which theories and appropriate methods are brought to explain the expanding and broadening body of human experience" (*BNL* 168/62).

Descriptive Psychology as the Foundational Science of Mind: Psychology, Not Psychologism

Dilthey was convinced that the valid elements of empirical and transcendental approaches to mind could be synthesized in a new form of psychology to provide the *Grundwissenschaft* of the human sciences. The total coherence of mental life constituted the real basis of the process of knowledge and of human consciousness in general. Genuine theory of knowledge cannot therefore simply be deduced from abstract principles, but must be construed from the relations and contents of this psychic coherence. A full and unprejudicial (*unbefangen*) description of this psychic coherence must remain at the foundation of epistemology. Such description, far from tracing the mere adventitious "surface" changes of mental life, actually provides the grounding of the fundamental science.

> The basis of epistemology is contained in the living consciousness and the valid description of its psychic coherence. Epistemology does not require a totally complete psychology, but all fully executed psychology is only the completed scientific form of what also constitutes the basis [*Untergrund*] of epistemology. Epistemology is psychology in motion— in motion, to be sure, toward a specific goal. The basis of epistemology lies in a self-reflection [*Selbstbesinnung*] which encompasses the entire, unmutilated content of psychic life. Universal validity, truth, and reality are determined in their meaning first and foremost from this basic content [*Befund*] [*GS* 5:151–52].

Dilthey maintained that epistemology presupposes some form of psychology, whereas the orthodox Kantians held just the reverse—that psychology (and all empirical science) presuppose epistemology. Dilthey's coupling of epistemology with psychology for them represented a sorry confusion of empirical fact and transcendental norm, of specific material content and ideal form. As simply one among the empirical sciences, psychology could not by its very definition provide a generally valid standard of what can pass as knowledge. An example of scientific knowledge is not the same as a formal norm concerning what constitutes knowledge as such.

As indicated previously, Dilthey challenged these Kantian separations and insisted that empirical psychology could encompass what Kant's followers reserved to transcendental philosophy. But in order to do so, psychology had to be made adequate to concrete experience and the full content of mental life. Because it was under the spell of natural scientific methods and models of knowledge, Dilthey rejected prevailing psychology as "psychology without a soul" (GS 5:159). Such a psychology did not start with the full fund of lived experience given to the mind but with an abstract and formalized caricature of experience drawn from physics and mechanics. Existing psychology was infected by three related errors: associationism, atomism, and constructivism. Empiricism in psychology was narrowly taken to mean adherence to deterministic associationism—the very opposite of what Dilthey meant by *Empirie*. Associationism conjured up a picture of mental life as a mechanical process of racking up billiard balls. Analytically isolated "percepts" (*Vorstellungen*) and "sensations" (*Empfindungen*) were linked together by mere contiguity, not by structural coherence of their lived content and meaning. Dilthey found that the "sensations" of conventional psychology, which were taken to be the ultimately "real" fundament of experience, were in truth abstractly conceived hypothetical *minima* made to stand in for experience: "So-called 'sensations' are merely the partial and abstract contents of genuine experience, which are then hypostatized" (BNL 244/461–62). The relation postulated among perceptual units had nothing to do with the actual content of what was perceived (and the mind's ongoing relation to this content), but was merely a formal and "external" arrangement in time and space. The process of association was mechanical not synthetic, for it moved from discrete datum to discrete datum without an emerging structure of formative coherence. The mind was viewed as the mere sum of separate perceptions and was divested of any independent organizing power. Psychology thereby fashioned a "homunculus in a retort" rather than practicing true description of experience (GS 16:447). Dilthey could become almost abusive on the subject of associationism in psychology: "The whole reigning conception of associationism and psychic atomism is a psychological castle in the air" (BNL 209/71). A real viewing of experience shows that "for consciousness there is no simple 'percept.' All perceptions are in consciousness as a relation of part to whole. A simple percept is an abstraction. There is a tone only in relation to a scale" (BA 164; also 234–35).

The idealists' determination to introduce a transcendental unity of consciousness had merely served to perpetuate a forced alliance of physicalist and metaphysical assumptions which overlooked the coherence in experience; such an unnatural compound tended to come apart under scrutiny. The rationalist psychology implicit in Kant's view of the mind was no more immune to conversion to a crude naturalism than was plain associationist psychology. This fact could be seen in the psychology of Herbart, which dominated German theorizing for decades. Experience was resolved into elementary, formal units (deceptively termed "*Realen*") which could be formulated mathematically and mechanically. These atoms of perceptual data were susceptible to quantifying treatment but violated the "standpoint of life and experience:" "Psychological mechanics sacrifices that which we are aware of in inner perception to reasoning built up with the analogies of external nature" (*GS* 1:378).

The natural scientific bias in psychology was also entrenched in the doctrine of psycho-physical parallelism, according to which every psychic process was assumed to be accompanied by a perceptible physical event whose correlata were experimentally ascertainable. Psychologists presumed to infer from "observable" neural functions (i.e., experimentally) to conclusions about the higher mental activity. This parallelism tended to be converted to a kind of unilateral causation, from physical "cause" to psychic "effect." After Herbart, the influential Fechnerian school attempted to found psychology wholly upon physiology. Dilthey objected that the supposed parallelism was simply a hypothesis which is not actually given in experience but extrapolated hypothetically. "The physiological can never be introduced as an explanation for the psychological" (*BA* 93). The primary relation in mental life is not between physical facts and psychic acts but among mental contents. Mental phenomena are, to be sure, accompanied by physical processes, but the former cannot be reduced to or explained by the latter. Mental processes have an "independent vital course" (*selbst-ständige Lebendigkeit*) and unique coherence of content which is distinct from any causal succession in nature (*GS* 10:44). A true psychology of experience discloses complex mental phenomena such as the consciousness of self and others, of memory and expectation, of duty, sympathy, and a special kind of freedom—for all of which there are no verifiable physiological correlates.

Dilthey's corrective to the doctrines of associationism and parallelism was not the Kantian "unity of apperception" or a metaphysical concept of "soul," but the developing and acquired coherence of mental life. He avoided the controversial term "soul" but freely invoked the terms "psychic coherence" and "psychic structure." His position partly accommodated and partly rebutted the notorious conclusion of Ernst Mach's empirio-criticism that "the self cannot be salvaged." In the name of a genuine *Empirie*, Dilthey reaffirmed what Mach and others were banishing from scientific psychology: "We must introduce into psychology the consciousness of the coherence of mental life, which is then raised to scientific clarity. But here too we remain at the level of empirical consciousness." This coherence of mental life does not evince strict causal laws of regular succession and uniformity, but, rather, "typical" patterns and processes: "It is not causal uniformity but rather the typical process in a whole [*typischen Verlauf in einem Ganzen*] which constitutes the goal of our empirical reflection (*BNL* 141/433–34). Using such reflection, psychology must be reconstituted to grasp what Dilthey called "relative wholes" of "qualitative content (*BA* 109–11, 113).

Perhaps most significantly of all, this "typical process toward relative wholes" includes the capacity to project ourselves into a future situation and into the situation of other persons. In a Nachlass passage, Dilthey provided a model description of both cases: "We are facing a decision. In this situation we ponder existing conditions and those which might arise in the future: with all our vitality and experience we project ourselves testingly [*versetzen uns probierend*] into these conditions." In this manner an expected state of affairs becomes a very real and functional part of our experiential coherence. A similar but more complex process is involved in the perception of other persons: "Even more complicated is the process whereby we perceive the actions of another person with whom we have to reckon. Here too we put ourselves into the situation from which the person will act. And here too it is our vitality [*Lebendigkeit*] which is brought into play. But here there arises between us and the other person a certain type which the person represents to us, which type colors and conditions our perceptions of his expected actions." Dilthey insists that there are limits to this projective process and its failures are experienced as much as its successes:

> Let us say that we are attending a play and we feel frustrated in that we cannot reconstruct in our own minds what is going on—then everything has the character of improbability. This frustration shows very clearly how we bring our own vitality into play from certain given circumstances and always within certain limits corresponding to the person involved [*BNL* 141/437].

By neglecting these reciprocal processes involving whole situations (and other persons), conventional psychology showed another of its errors—its methodological "individualism." "The science of psychology developed as individual psychology; in dead abstraction it tried to approach the problem of the original constitution of the individual severed from the historical trunk of society and its interactions" (*GS* 5:63). While Dilthey's theory of the human sciences assigned great importance to the category of individuality, he conceived of individuals as something quite different from self-contained units or monads. In the 1860s he had been attracted to the nascent field of "folk-psychology" (*Völkerpsychologie*) as a means of overcoming the artificial isolation of the individual mind. An ancestor of social psychology, sociology, and anthropology, this field purported to study the mind in its social context and web of social relations. The manifesto of its founders, Moritz Lazarus and Hermann Steinthal, proclaimed psychology incomplete so long as it focused exclusively on the individual mind. Their folk-psychology was to correct this neglect by ascertaining "the wholly special psychological relations, events, and creations which do not pertain to the individual mind and do not derive from it." These relations, while specifically social and cultural in nature, were nevertheless conceived on a strictly mechanical, Herbartian basis: "What psychology is concerned with is essentially the same as what the natural sciences are striving for and attaining, namely, to dissolve things into lawful relations."[18]

Though initially drawn to folk-psychology for a broadly contextual approach to mental life, Dilthey was ultimately put off by its exclusive reliance upon Herbartian assumptions and its overblown pretensions to provide rigidly explanatory laws of cultural and historical life. In the final analysis, folk-psychology treated society, culture, and history as simply the individual writ large and approached them promiscuously in terms of the "laws" which had been proven in physiological psychology. Dilthey's ultimate judgment of this endeavor was largely negative: "It is the error of the modern school of folk-psychology to believe that it can undertake to explain history, that is to say the sum of human life up til now, on the basis of psychology, a science of the forms of mental life" (*GS* 6:43; also 18:218, 224). This passage conveys clearly the tension which Dilthey came to feel more strongly and urgently between the real content of historical life and the abstractive, formalizing methods of psychology. But he continued to hold to the "critical possibility" of a genuinely social and cultural psychology (often termed "anthropology") which would encompass specifically social relations such as loyalty, work, love, deference, and a host of other relations which he subsumed under the concept of "social bonding" [*soziale Bindung*]. In the *Einleitung* he insisted that true anthropology was not merely the reflection of the subjective ego upon itself and in a subsequent note of 1886 he spoke of "the urgent necessity of a psychology of the other self" (*GS* 1:32; *BNL* 49/90).[19]

Dilthey's hopes for a psychology adequate to experience and to the "founding" of the human sciences came to center upon the realization of a *descriptive* psychology. Such a psychology would be free of both metaphysical and physicalist hypotheses concerning the nature of the mind. It would be truly empirical and "unbefangen"—free of distorting influence of speculation, hypothesis, construction, and false models of explanation. Dilthey's avowal of descriptive method runs like a leitmotiv through all the major and minor writings concerned with psychology and theory of mind. In an early (1862) review of Schleiermacher's psychology, he struck the note which came to dominate his later reflections:

There where psychologists undertake to grasp the *total extent of the mind* (of which Herbart treated only the simplest, lowest manifestations)—there they must now combine the *descriptive* with the explanatory method [emphasis, Dilthey's; *GS* 16:372].

In the "Breslauer Ausarbeitung," description is called the method of "pure experience" (*reine Erfahrung*) which is capable of "putting the psychic process back on its feet" (*BA* 88–90, 264). The descriptive method simply "tells what it finds" and is thus a prime prerequisite of "unrestricted science" (*unbefangene Wissenschaftlichkeit*) (*GS* 5:221; 6:246).

According to a student, Eduard Spranger, who later became a very influential German psychologist, Dilthey's seminars over the years were frequently punctuated with the exclamation "Analysis and description! Analysis and description!"[20] It might be noted that after about 1875 the injunction to "description" became a precept in many sciences—both natural and human—including biology, linguistics, economics, and even physics. Like "empiricism," with which it was often coupled, it proved a very elastic term, stretching to cover a multitude of often diametrically opposed meanings. Thus it meant something quite different to the positivist Ernst Mach from what it meant to the neo-realist Franz Brentano. Mach employed it as a stringent antidote to deductive reasoning, teleology, value judgments, "multiplication of entities," and even "theory" as such, whereas Brentano invoked it in a broader sense to reinstate the mind's immediate awareness of its own acts. Dilthey's notion of psychology is close to Brentano's and there is clear evidence that he relied upon Brentano's *Psychologie vom empirischen Standpunkt* (1874) to specify the role of description in the study of consciousness. In Dilthey's view Brentano had conclusively refuted the pervasive error of assuming that perceptual content can be reduced to physiological correlates, but at the same time Brentano's classification of mental functions was rejected as "sheer fiction" (*GS* 18:139, 147–49, 234). Brentano was not descriptive enough: in the end he sacrificed the "standpoint of experience" for construction.[21]

Dilthey's important treatise of 1894 entitled "Ideen über eine beschreibende und zergliedernde Psychologie" contained the lineaments of his own descriptive psychology. It was an avowedly provisional but path-breaking effort which had a considerable impact on German psychology by pointing beyond prevailing practices and suppositions. In this work Dilthey distinguished description from strictly causal explanation. Such explanation orders phenomena into a determinate causal order by means of a limited number of simple elements. The causal order is not actually experienced but is hypothesized or constructed. To explain mental processes, psychologists propounded innumerable hypotheses, so that a "war of all against all" prevailed in psychology as in metaphysics. Dilthey acknowledged that not all hypothesis or explanation could—or should—be eliminated from psychology, but cautioned that it must be postponed until the most careful observation and description of experience have been accomplished.

The great error of explanatory psychology was "the premature mixing of theory and observation"—what Goethe had similarly deplored as "the overhasty transition from appearance to theory" (*BA* 86). In its haste to provide a systematically predictive account of the mind's operation, psychology dispensed with a full tracing of experience and instead hurried to the construction of a theoretical model. The scientific predilection for the most "economical" account of the data forced the reduction of the inherent richness and complexity of experience into hypothetical models. As revealed in the "Ideen," Dilthey's attitude toward the role of hypothesis in inquiry is a very complicated matter and it must be viewed in a context somewhat wider than the "Ideen" itself. It might seem that his warnings against hypothesis and "construction" presuppose a kind of ineffably concrete Bergsonian empiricism incompatible with all generalizations, assumptions, or even preliminary questions about mental life. But his strictures against hypothesis were directed against the abuses of "construction" stemming from the speculative methods of the idealists and the reductive methods of the positivists: both allowed their hypotheses to pass uncritically into rigid hypostatizations, whether of rarified ideas or irreducible analytic *minima*.

Such hypothetical construction was barren in Dilthey's terms. Yet beginning with his early study of Schleiermacher's hermeneutics, Dilthey acknowledged the necessity of a preliminary question or framework which provisionally sets the terms of the inquiry without predisposing the results; this kind of preliminary orienting "thesis" is essential to all inquiry, including textual interpretation. Dilthey's general attitude toward the function of hypotheses was reminiscent of Goethe, who—following Bacon's aversion to "anticipations of nature"—found them likely to hinder "seeing." They are necessary, but too easily become idols of the mind: "Hypotheses are scaffolding which one uses to construct a building and takes away after it is done. As such they are indispensable, but one must not take the scaffolding for the building."[22]

Most hypothetical models of the mind were static and formal, whereas true description would reveal that mental life is dynamic and replete with real content: "What is needed is a psychological science in which the whole content [*ganze Inhaltlichkeit*] of mental life finds room" (*GS* 5:156). If psychology refused to recognize this content, it would remain inferior to the plain "experience of life" (*Lebenserfahrung*) and unsystematic insights of great poets and writers. Indeed, pursuing his earlier injunction that psychology must come to terms with materials which it had previously rejected out of hand, Dilthey advocated that descriptive psychology concern itself with the reflections of thinkers such as Seneca, Augustine, Montaigne, Pascal, and other "life-philosophers," for they contained an understanding of man in his full experiential reality: These thinkers indicated a valuable way to the full content of life, even if their more intuitive understanding remained to be raised to methodical and rigorous knowledge. By contrast the narrowly explanatory psychologies of Herbart,

Hartley, the Mills, Taine, Fechner, and Helmholtz were unable to fathom the content of mental life because they conceived it as analogous to natural processes and in natural scientific categories. Among the Germans only Wilhelm Wundt had, in Dilthey's estimation, departed from this reductionist proclivity; he saw a power of "creative synthesis" at work in the mind which is not accountable in terms of psycho-physical parallelism or the principle of the conservation of energy. Dilthey also singled out for praise the new psychology of William James, which made an even stronger and more studiously empirical case for the free and creative features of consciousness (*GS* 5:167).

The "Ideen" went on to insist that if we approach experience descriptively rather than hypothetically, we find that whereas the connections in natural processes are arrived at through constructions departing from experience, those of the mental world itself are given from within as immediate reality and "living coherence *originaliter*" (*GS* 5:143). This lived coherence is the primary reality, while all "elements" are derived. Mental life is actually there-for-us as a lived coherence, not a constructed causal sequence. The faithful descriptive tracing of this coherence, not its construction or explanation from putative elements, is the most urgent task of psychology. (Dilthey did not say "ultimate" or "only" task; the "Ideen" were directed to the state of psychology at the time.) A psychology which fulfilled these requirements would be fundamental and useful to epistemology and the human sciences, for both need empirical knowledge of psychic life. Dilthey was careful not to claim that psychology could substitute entirely for epistemology, but rather referred them both to a deeper reflection (*Selbstbesinnung*) on the full content of mind.

Psychology should begin with the fully developed mind and the whole range of its functions, including memory, speech, imagination, and volition, not simply elementary processes such as sense perception. From the coherence of mental life psychology must then isolate recurrent psychic relations and analyze them clearly. Analysis is always linked to description—indeed they are mutually dependent. Both synthesis and analysis must be employed to provide an adequate account of mind. Synthesis shows the depth and breadth of the mind's operation, whereas analysis yields clarity and distinctness. Psychology must move from the whole to the analytically isolated parts and back to the whole again. Dilthey suggested that this method of investigation retains a good deal of the more intuitive process of *Verstehen*, which cannot be reduced to strict explanation (*Erklärung*) by simple, distinct concepts. The attempt to fix the concrete operations and coherences of mind in univocal concepts encounters what Dilthey called "immanent antinomies" in man's self-knowledge (*GS* 5:175).

Only a descriptive science of mind can adequately grasp the interweaving of fact and value in the human world: "Since facts and norms are inseparably connected, the linking of both permeates all the human sciences" (*GS* 5:267). Description discloses coherences of value (*Wert*), purpose (*Zweck*), and type (*Typ*) in mental life. Dilthey provided an interesting example to illustrate the mutual dependence and interpenetration of perception and judgment, of fact and value: When we see a skater or a dancer, the perception of actual movements is inseparable from some notion (held with varying degrees of self-consciousness) of the appropriateness or perfection of those movements. The apprehension of the "real" (*Sachvorstellung*) is bound up with a notion of value (*Wertvorstellung*), which need not emerge as a formal concept and is most certainly not a priori. This immanence of the value or norm in the "fact" is not restricted to artistic production, for Dilthey insists that "in every portion of human expression there arises a type which represents their most appropriate execution. This type designates their norm, since it lies between deviations on both sides" (*GS* 5:269).

This concept of "type," which became exceedingly important in the writings after the "Ideen," was the mediating member bridging the realms of fact and value. The researcher in the human sciences must learn like the artist to "see typically" (*typisch-sehen*) in order to make his material intelligible. Such seeing in types is not an innate function, since this capacity is generally augmented in the course of life through the self-integrating work of the psychic coherence: the acquired coherence of the mind not only integrates a "self" but integrates this self's perceptions of the world according to its developed types. Such "seeing" is a thoroughly empirical form of perception but it contains its own inner standard of judgment. Critics such as Rickert—who were hostile to psychology and who asserted that Dilthey provided a psychological theory of experience but never arrived at a logical theory of judgment—have failed to acknowledge the role of "seeing typically" and the "intellectuality of perception" in his doctrine of experience.

Since the whole coherence of mind does not fall directly under the purview of consciousness and cannot be entirely fixed in concepts, psychology must look at the mind indirectly through its creations and expressions, in which, as Hegel observed, it has become "objective" and stands fast for repeated examination. The "massive objectivities" of history, art, literature, language, myth, religion, even science itself are material for this comprehensive psychology. In a passage which summarizes his skepticism toward a psychology limited strictly to introspective or experimental methods, Dilthey insisted: "What man is he experiences surely not by ruminating over himself and not in psychological experiments, but through history" (*GS* 5:180).

By employing the full content of mind derived from inner awareness, literature, and history, Dilthey insisted that descriptive psychology could become a productive science, thus overcoming the stultifying separation of theoretical knowledge and practical life. He suggested that descriptive and analytical procedures would provide a basis for a clearer understanding of individual character, the differences of the sexes, national character, and the forms of social life. Indeed, he confidently re-asserted that such a psychology might provide a foundation for the human sciences as mathematics does for the natural sciences (GS 5:193). But he cautioned that this psychology must always have for its object the fullness of experience and its concrete coherences, not constructed, purely formal relations.

> The living coherence of mind is life, which is prior to all knowing [das Leben, das vor allem Erkennen da ist]. Vitality, historicity, freedom, and development are its characteristics Our consciousness of the world as well as our consciousness of ourselves has arisen out of our own vitality [Lebendigkeit]; this is more than ratio [GS 5:196].

Dilthey concluded the "Ideen" with the admonition that the entry into the life of the mind must proceed through many diverse passages. Descriptive method in its very nature is pluralistic not monistic. A descriptive psychology must forge links to other disciplines, subject matters, and methods which conventional psychology has excluded. Psychology must compensate and balance the intrinsic limitations of its various procedures. It must coordinate various approaches—the perception and observation of the self, the understanding of other persons, the study of children, and the analysis of pathological, abnormal, and unconscious phenomena. It must employ comparative methods as well as introspection and experimentation. And a very important complement to all these methods and materials is the understanding of the "objective products" of mind, to which the inquirer can return again and again. Dilthey ended his sweeping program with an indication of the immense tasks which still lay ahead:

> What a task it would be to build a bridge between psychology as it has been practiced heretofore and the understanding of the historical world! Only if one adds to existing procedures that of the study of historical products and that of experimentation directed at determining the psychic differences of individuals will we be able gradually to near such a goal [GS 5:237].

4

From the fact that basic psychological relations constitute everywhere the material [of the human sciences] it follows only *that one can understand nothing without psychology but not that one understands anything by means of psychology.*
—Dilthey

The operation of *Verstehen* lies at the deepest foundation of descriptive psychology.
—Dilthey, "General Thoughts on the Human Sciences"

Critical Confrontations
and Revisions

New Directions and Influences

In the decade after the "Ideen" (1895–1905), Dilthey became embroiled in a series of philosophical encounters and conflicts which together might be called the period of the "shaking of the foundations." These controversies involved not only the cognitive status of psychology and its suitability to serve as *Grundwissenschaft* of the human sciences but also concerned the nature of the human sciences themselves. It is difficult to offer a precise characterization of the transformation of Dilthey's thought in this period. Perhaps the best way would be to mix images from architecture and archeology: Dilthey discovered a more original foundation below the one which he had been laboring to set down. This "new" foundation, the "simple" operation of human understanding or *Verstehen*, had been there all along—in fact it had been both presupposed and stipulated in Dilthey's previous work—but it required new efforts of philosophical excavation and clarification to bring it into full view. And once disclosed, it was granted a new status in keeping with its more fundamental and original position. The operation of *Verstehen*, which had been treated in the "Ideen" as a supplementary aid to the other methods of descriptive psychology, was elevated to the position of principal method of the human sciences. The change in Dilthey's thinking was more a "deepening" or "thinking through" than a reversal; he uncovered a foundation below the plane of his own psychological investigations, yet he continued to remain within the sphere of the empirical consciousness or standpoint of experience. Furthermore, his mediating position of *Idealrealismus* was attacked strenuously from both sides, by realists and idealists. These confrontations had the effect of forcing a reestablishment of his position—but on a basis even further transformed and adjusted. The science of psychology no longer qualified as the *Grundwissenschaft* of the human sciences, for it was only one large chamber, at once confining and interconnecting, in the general site of the mind and mental world. The reconstruction and analysis of these fun-

181

damental changes must rely heavily on Dilthey's Nachlass, as it provides a more complete record of his thinking in this period than do the published writings.

In this ten-year period of intense intellectual ferment, Dilthey suspended his theoretical writing, concentrating mainly on historical subjects: studies of Schleiermacher, Hegel, and the intellectual history of the seventeenth and eighteenth centuries. Various reasons can be cited for this apparent interruption and shift of focus. Graf Yorck's death removed a major source of philosophical stimulation and dialogue. Dilthey's health seems to have deteriorated markedly in this period, particularly his chronic eye problem; this may have impelled him back in the direction of familiar historical ground. Nonetheless, the historical studies of this period were "history with philosophical intent"; anyone who reads them can discern their direct bearing upon the development of his theoretical position. His comment on his own treatment of Schleiermacher is revealing in this regard: "It was possible to fathom completely his inner work only after I elaborated my own basic direction" (GS 14/1:32). His intensifying concern with the theoretical status of psychology is reflected in passages of his works on Hegel and Schleiermacher; it is also indicated more fleetingly in his treatment of Hume's "psychologism" and the opposing "logical realism" of Bernhard Bolzano.[1] In trying to reconstitute and secure the foundations of the human sciences, Dilthey continued to draw upon past as well as contemporary thinkers.

This chapter, however, follows the evolution of his theoretical position vis-à-vis more strictly contemporary influences. The full range and impact of his reading in these sources can be gauged only from his unpublished papers. He read (and re-read) Heinrich Rickert, Edmund Husserl, Wilhelm Wundt, Max Weber, Ferdinand Tönnies, Georg Simmel, William James, Henri Bergson, Theodor Lipps, Carl Stumpf, Franz Brentano, Alexander Pfänder, Alexius Meinong, Hans Cornelius, Oswald Külpe, Rudof Eucken, and even some of the earliest writings of Ernst Troeltsch and Ernst Cassirer. Of this rich variety of contemporary thought we can treat only certain lines of impact and readjustment, specifically concerning the status of psychology and its role in the human sciences.

Some interpreters have regarded Dilthey's change of views between 1895 and 1904, that is, between the "Ideen" and later "Aufbau" studies, as an abrupt break or "reversal" issuing from the combined force of the neo-Kantian critique of psychology and Edmund Husserl's devastating attack on "psychologism" in logic and the general theory of mind. While these influences (along with several others) undoubtedly served to crystallize Dilthey's lingering doubts into outright revision of his views, it should be stressed that he had always harbored strong reservations concerning psychology. His training with Trendelenburg and Fischer had imparted a sensitivity to the dangers and fallacies of psychologism long before the full-scale assaults of the Neo-Kantians and Husserl. In his 1860 essay on hermeneutics, Dilthey explicitly condemned a specious "psychologizing" (*Psychologisieren*) which reduces mental activity to bits and pieces. Such an approach results in a "scattering" (*Verzettelung*) of mental life and a false view of history (*GS* 14/2:705). In his analysis of the moral consciousness of 1864 he referred to "the general difficulties of psychological empiricism." Following Lotze, he cautioned that an altogether psychological approach to the mind cannot grasp values and norms: "Psychology knows only of psychic processes. . . . [It knows] nothing of what could be a value to the mind" (*GS* 6:29–30). This brief judgment anticipated the entire neo-Kantian critique of psychology, as did the following one from 1866: "Culture cannot in any case be explained psychologically, neither in the fashion of Kant [viz. Kant's *Anthropologie in pragmatischer Hinsicht*] nor the empiricists, but rather only by means of genuinely historical concepts" (*GS* 5:lxxv). In a sketch of 1874 he observed that "the foundation which we expect of science for both history and practical life could only be provided in an anthropology which would have a much broader basis than our current psychology" (*GS* 5:432–33). Shortly thereafter he noted that many of the concepts of psychological science seemed to derive from a more original and ordinary form of consciousness which he called "reflection of life in language" (*Reflexion des Lebens in der Sprache*) (*GS* 18:135).

Even as Dilthey set about formulating his own psychology, his reservations seemed to grow steadily. In the "Breslauer Ausarbeitung" he asserted that the adoption of the "principle of consciousness" (*Satz des Bewusstseins*) yields an inexhaustible field of investigation but at the same time does not in itself provide a determination of the *specific* science or scientific framework within which to approach consciousness. The *Grundwissenschaft* of the human sciences must analyze consciousness but it does not yet have a satisfactory determinate form. After expatiating upon the vast dimensions of the field of mental life, Dilthey added: "Finally psychology must be subordinated [*ist unterzuorden*] to a developmental-historical approach which grasps mental processes in their coherence" (*BA* 27–28; also 239). In an essay of 1889 he stipulated that the coherence of mental life is "always historical": "The historical nature of man is his higher nature as such"— and psychology has not been able to explain it (*GS* 4:559–60). Five years before the publication of the "Ideen" Dilthey warned of the "immanent cognitive limits of psychology" and of the "antinomy in psychology" (*GS* 10:46; *BNL* 62/158). In the unpublished "Berliner Entwurf" sketched between 1890 and 1896, he included a major section entitled "The Limits of Psychological Knowledge" (*BE* 57).

Dilthey's double standpoint toward psychology contained all along in virtual form the elements of its own transformation. This transformation had more the character of a semi-dialectical *"Aufhebung"*—both a cancelling and preserving at a different level—than an outright reversal. Although his earlier work contains suggestions of such a change, the actual shift seems to have been precipitated by the strong polemic delivered against Dilthey's descriptive psychology by his erstwhile friend and colleague at Berlin, the internationally renowned psychologist Hermann Ebbinghaus.

The Critique of Dilthey's Descriptive Psychology

In an article entitled "Über erklärende und beschreibende Psychologie" (1894), Ebbinghaus accused Dilthey of being out of touch with the current state of psychology and guilty of setting up straw men. As a member of the vanguard of German psychology, Ebbinghaus responded to Dilthey's "Ideen" as if it constituted an indictment of all forms of psychology. After summarizing Dilthey's arguments, Ebbinghaus pronounced them a mixture of vague generalities interspersed with astonishing trivialities. Dilthey was censured for demanding much but delivering little. The much-touted field of descriptive psychology was scorned as broad in scope but lacking content and a specific object of inquiry. Ebbinghaus doubted that the "Ideen" even qualified as psychology in the first place, since most of its examples were drawn not from "psychology proper" but from literature, philosophy, and personal experience. (Ebbinghaus based his objections on precisely the distinction which Dilthey was at pains to revise.) Moreover, Ebbinghaus found Dilthey's assessment of explanatory psychology to be grossly misleading, as it rested on a blithe ignorance of the major innovations in psychology during the last 50 years. The "constructivist" Herbartian procedures which Dilthey deplored had long since been surpassed in newer psychologies already well-established. Ebbinghaus explained the reliance of earlier psychologists upon strictly natural scientific methods as a result of the fact that natural science had accomplished the emancipation of knowledge from "childish anthropomorphism." Dilthey, in short, was flailing in thin air and attacking phantoms—his arguments were judged to be confused, redundant, and ultimately pointless.[2]

The crux of Ebbinghaus' scathing critique concerned the doctrine of the self-givenness of the psychic coherence. Such coherences are there, to be sure, but they are not directly and immediately given in experience, but are imputed or "constructed"—just as in the hypothetical procedures of the explanatory sciences. Even in the case of attending to its own inner psychic life, consciousness must construct out of partial contents what is not fully given. The psychic coherence is not "lived through" directly—as Dilthey insisted—but is superadded (*hinkonstruiert*) and retroactively inferred (*rückwärts erschlossen*).[3] Since this degree of hypothesizing cannot be denied or averted, there is no such thing as "pure description" and "pure experience." Ebbinghaus found that the difference between description and explanation was more apparent than real, for Dilthey's psychic relations turn out to be as hypothetical as any explanatory schema. True knowledge does not admit such a disjunction between description and hypothesis. Hypothesis and explanation are as necessary in psychology as in any other genuine science. Ebbinghaus concluded: "What Dilthey recommends is already in practice and what he attacks has been long since abandoned."[4]

This devastating critique seems to have had a deep effect upon Dilthey, both personally and theoretically. He had previously delighted in frequent "philosophical walks" with Ebbinghaus and considered him the pre-eminent psychologist at Berlin. After the article appeared, Dilthey declined to attend an international psychological congress to which he had been personally invited by Theodor Lipps and William James because he could not bear to sit in the same room with Ebbinghaus. His reaction was far from mere personal pique, however. Indeed, it appears that Ebbinghaus' assault had a wide effect in scholarly circles. Both Edmund Husserl and Karl Lamprecht were initially dissuaded from reading Dilthey by Ebbinghaus' article. After 1895 Dilthey stopped lecturing on psychology (giving most of his courses to Carl Stumpf), and concentrated instead upon recent philosophy, from which he attempted in part to reconstruct his position.[5]

Dilthey's own efforts at defense were sporadic and somewhat inconclusive, despite the fact that he received support and advice from Brentano, Stumpf, Riehl, Lipps, and others.[6] Surveying the field of contemporary psychology, he found constructivist tendencies still very much alive; although rigidly explanatory schemata had been overcome "in principle" on some fronts, many basic constructivist assumptions remained in force despite Ebbinghaus' confident assurances. Dilthey even reprimanded William James for a residual constructivist bias and went so far as to chastise himself for allowing such distorting premises into his own position: "I am not the Pharisee who believes only himself to be pure" (*GS* 5:lxx–lxxi). In an unpublished manuscript "On the Problem of Explanatory Psychology" written in response to Ebbinghaus, Dilthey continued his campaign against the "haste for explanation." It is not because psychology abstracts but because it abstracts *wrongly* that Dilthey disqualified it. Under the sway of natural scientific models, it abstracts always toward discrete elements and quantifiable relations rather than toward structures, types, and configurations; explanatory psychology imposes a genetic-causal coherence of "laws" on the mind which does not appear in consciousness or reflective analysis (*BNL* 171/104). Rejecting every approach to mental life which "tries to show how it is made," Dilthey reaffirmed that "the productive point of departure for the sciences of culture and for their inner philosophical connection into a fruitful whole lies solely in a descriptive content-psychology" (*GS* 5:lxxi; 14/2:370). Nevertheless, his position continued to be disputed.

Following Ebbinghaus' argument rather closely, another psychologist,

Theodor Elsenhans, objected to Dilthey's distinction between descriptive and explanatory methods. A pure description which attempts to do away with hypothesis and explanatory procedures is impossible in any science worthy of the name. Elsenhans pointed out that no matter how unprejudicial and ingenuous we try to be about our mental life, we must still employ terms and concepts which are "specifically psychological." When we describe mental processes, we perforce do it with words and notions drawn from formal psychological science: "We speak of sensations, representations, feelings, and drives and we thereby order the processes in question under psychological concepts."[7] Elsenhans wished to defend formal psychology from its threatened dissolution into merely inchoate descriptions of experience, real or imagined.

As Georg Misch has observed, Dilthey's response to this deepening theoretical quandary was increasingly to draw a distinction between the "psychic" and the "psychological" (GS 5:lxxx). The realm of concrete mental life was redefined in terms of an objective content, whereas the province of psychological science in the strict sense receded into the background. The mental content disclosed by the human sciences cannot be comprehended by the incorrigibly reductive procedures of conventional psychology. In Dilthey's later writings "human understanding of things human" (Verstehen) is more and more sharply demarcated from the usual methods of psychological science. Dilthey found that there was "no agreement in psychology concerning the most important questions" and whatever agreement existed was almost hopelessly at odds with the standpoint of life and the understanding of life (LK 2). Although the distinction between the psychic and the psychological seemed to suggest a move in the direction of transcendental idealism, Dilthey believed he was remaining solidly on the standpoint of the empirical consciousness. This conviction defined his relation with the Baden neo-Kantians, another party with whom he grappled over foundations.

Neo-Kantian Philosophy of Value and the *Kulturwissenschaften*

It is important to realize that Dilthey's encounter with the Baden school began over a decade earlier than has previously been assumed. Existing scholarship has placed Dilthey's confrontation with Windelband in the period following the latter's famous rectoral address "Geschichte und Naturwissenschaft" of 1894, the same year Dilthey published his "Ideen." A careful reading of both thinkers shows that they were engaged with each other long before the mid-90s. In an article entitled "Genetische oder kritische Methode" of 1883 (the year of the *Einleitung*), Windelband declared in an obvious and unmistakable reference to Dilthey that a "critique of historical reason" was indeed a worthy project, but that it could not be executed "without a notion of what reason actually is." Windelband insisted that contrary to Dilthey's premises, this proper notion of reason cannot be attained solely on the basis of history itself or the "genetic-empirical method," for a purely empirical method issues only in "bare facticity" not "general validity." There is vastly more to reason than mere experience, even the collective experience of mankind in history; one must pursue a truly critical-normative or transcendental method in order to arrive in the temple of reason. Experience alone cannot show the way, for it does not and cannot furnish a criterion of judgment; all reason, including "historical reason" is necessarily a matter of judgment based upon transcendental norms. The true conception of reason can be reached only via a critical method which presupposes transcendental values as the a priori forms of all experience. While lauding Dilthey's ultimate goal, Windelband pronounced his method nugatory.[8]

In an interesting strategic maneuver, Dilthey employed Kant against his own disciples by asserting that the master had in fact stressed synthesis where they saw only logical distinctions. In an 1885 review of Windelband's *Präludien* (which contained the article on method treated above), Dilthey invoked Kant against his professed followers:

The basic premise of Windelband's position is that through all areas of mental [*geistigen*] life there permeate norms, whose validity is independent of their origins. The method which explicates the relation of these norms to the functions of mental life and its goals is the critical one. It must necessarily appear questionable whether this conception of the task of the critical method can legitimately invoke Kant, who throughout his development did not separate the validity of these norms from the problem of their genesis [*WM* 57 (1885):290–91].

Although Windelband was eventually compelled to grant that Kant himself did not reject all consideration of the genetic origin and empirical conditioning of mental forms, he continued to rail against any confusion of the transcendental and the empirical.[9] Surveying the course of nineteenth century thought, Windelband again acknowledged the central importance of a critique of historical reason, but found that Dilthey's version remained "stalled in the timidity of psychological relativism, which does not have the power to advance from the flux of historically and anthropologically conditioned values to eternally valid contents."[10]

As indicated previously, the Baden neo-Kantians had a considerably different conception of the human sciences and the nature of their foundations. They preferred the term *Kulturwissenschaften* to *Geisteswissenschaften* because, under the pervasive influence of a false and "uncritical" empiricism, "*Geist*" was being increasingly confused or elided with em-

pirical *"Seele"* and even *"Gehirnfunktionen,"* or experimentally determinable brain processes. Taking Kant's position as a "whole," the Baden
School asserted along with Dilthey that true transcendental *Kritik* must not
restrict itself to natural scientific cognition but must take the entire cultural
content of humanity as its object. But they held that the foundation of this
content could be found only in transcendental values, not in experience;
hence the fundamental science of culture must be an absolute philosophy of
values or transcendental axiology (*Normwissenschaft*) rather than psychology, anthropology, or any other empirical science (*Tatsachenwissen-
schaft*). Building upon Kant's separation of the *quid juris* and *quid facti*, the
neo-Kantians proscribed any muddling of the strict dichotomy of empirical
and transcendental. The transcendental science of "consciousness as such"
or the "knowing self" must not be confused with any empirical science of
the "self that is known." The neo-Kantian conception of the human sciences
was grounded, not in Dilthey's "One World of our experience," but in the
ideal and professedly "unreal" (*irreal*) realm of transcendental values.

The crucial difference between the natural and cultural sciences derived
not from a difference in subject matter or "objects" but a difference in
formal method. The form, not the content, of these disciplines provided the
desideratum of their status as scientific knowledge. Windelband insisted
that "every science produces its own objects initially with its concepts."[11]
Contending against all forms of "naïve realism" and transcription theory of
knowledge, Windelband and his followers maintained that knowledge can
never offer a complete copy (*Abbild*) of reality but rather a highly selective
conceptual construction (*Umbild*) of it on the basis of a priori forms.
Knowledge, like action, accomplishes an alteration of reality, not an
imitation of it. Consciousness does not and cannot represent "things in
themselves" but must satisfy itself with cognition of those aspects of things
which can be brought under the a priori forms of consciousness. The mind
gives its own form to the things which it knows: hence true science is not
merely the random "information" of experience, but the categorical "put-
ting-in-formation" of experience through the transcendental forms.

To account for the difference in formal method between the natural and
cultural sciences, Windelband recalled Kant's distinction in the *Critique of
Judgment* between the two "interests" of reason: the one "generalizing" and
the other "specifying." By a logical extension (not provided by Kant, but
developed by the neo-Kantians) these two "interests" came to qualify as
full-fledged, independent "methods." The natural sciences proceed according to a generalizing method which issues in general laws: these sciences
are "nomothetic" or law-positing—their results appear as general apodictic
judgments. The cultural sciences proceed according to an individualizing
method which Windelband termed "idiographic." Not general laws but
detailed depiction (*Darstellung*) of individuality is the aim of history and
the other cultural sciences—their results appear as singular, assertoric

propositions constituted under the form of a cultural value. The same content—for example, the explosion of a bomb—might be subjected to either method with entirely different results. The nomothetic method would by definition attend to those aspects which are common to *all* explosions, that is, its physical and chemical laws, whereas the idiographic method would focus upon the presentation of the unique particularities of this *specific* explosion—posing such questions as Who planted it? To what end? In what circumstances? and so forth.[12]

Windelband was careful to stress that the difference between these two methods as actually practiced in the sciences was relative: all sciences use features of both methods in their actual procedure. But for the theoretical purposes of logical clarity, the division according to method was "absolute"—even if it seemed to issue in the paradox of a body of sciences provided with one method by logic and another by actual practice. The natural sciences seek abstract laws of causation, whereas the cultural sciences seek concrete, individual configurations (*Gestalten*): "The uniform and repeatable law and the singular event remain opposed as the ultimate and incommensurable measures of our view of the world."[13] Both of these forms of knowledge have their own logic as well as method. Windelband explained the historical preponderance of the nomothetic method on the basis of the long-standing preference (or "interest"), originating with Greek thought, of attending only to the constant and abiding in the flux of appearances. The Baden School demanded a "logic of individuals" based upon universal values to fend off the hegemonial claims of the generalizing natural sciences. In combining Kant's transcendental method with history, Windelband was brought to a position patently reminiscent of Hegel:

> Historical research attains the scientific character of generally valid knowledge only insofar as we regard history as the progressive realization of rational values, only as the process of culture, in which the universal values of spiritual life [*geistiges Leben*] struggle to consciousness and realization out of the confusion of human interests and passions.[14]

Windelband's most famous student, Heinrich Rickert, set out to be even more stringently logical than his teacher. In an effort to stem what he regarded as the growing confusion of reason and experience, value and fact, he carried the distinction between the form and content of knowledge even further than Windelband. In his giant treatise *Die Grenzen der naturwissenschaftlichen Begriffsbildung* of 1896, Rickert counseled that the theorist of the sciences must "look at the method not the material":

> We attempt always to secure science not through the concept of its object but the other way around: to secure the concept of the object from the concept of the science which treats it.[15]

Reality is not reproduced in knowledge. Critical analysis shows that the natural sciences are no more capable of grasping reality as it "really" is than are the cultural sciences: naïve natural scientific realism must give way to the critical recognition that both bodies of knowledge are equally valid within the limits of their respective rules of concept-formation.

Rickert held that it is logically fruitless and empty to define the natural sciences as sciences of "objects" and the cultural sciences as sciences of "subjects." A "science of subjects" is a meaningless concept since self-perception is a contradiction in terms: it belongs to the very definition of perception that the perceiver must be separate from that which is perceived.[16] By its method and concept formation, psychology is an empirical science of laws (i.e., a natural science by *method*) and therefore cannot be linked with the values of the cultural sciences. To do so is to fall into the grievous fallacy of "psychologism," that is, the more subtle and surreptitious form which naturalism was compelled to assume after cruder forms of materialism had been driven from the field by earlier brands of Kantianism. If given competence in matters of "spirit" and culture, psychology leads necessarily to relativism and skepticism, since by definition it cannot provide criteria for valid knowing and judging. The "must" of natural processes has nothing to do with the "should" of values. If the historian or student of culture may be said to employ a "psychology," it must be considered in an informal, unsystematic sense:

> The historian is a "psychologist" only in the sense that he needs knowledge of determinate individual psychic processes in specific persons; he has not justification to transpose this knowledge into a general theory of the life of the mind. Indeed such a general theory would destroy precisely that which he has in such knowledge.[17]

Rickert was even more insistent than Windelband upon the strict separation between generalizing and individualizing methods; the concept of "historical law" he pronounced a *contradictio in adjectivo*, for in history the general always functions as a means not an end.[18] This distinction was carried further in Rickert's division between valuing and nonvaluing modes of thought. History and the other cultural sciences are constituted by an individualizing method which rests upon universal values. The individualizing method is divorced from the generalizing method of the natural sciences but is nonetheless founded upon universal values. Such values do not derive from empirically given reality, but rather the other way around: what can be given as an object of knowledge derives from transcendental values. The essence of such values is not their real existence (*Sein*) but their ideal validity (*Geltung*): "Empirical material can appear only as an example for clarification [*Verdeutlichung*] of previously determined logical principle." The mind grasps values, not existence.[19]

The validity (or truth) of values does not depend upon their actually being held or the circumstances in which they may be held: a thought is not true because *I* think it or experience it as true at this time or another. Factual existence and ideal values must be strictly separated. Transcendental values are the a priori of history; they are not real and "historical" in the sense of being part of historical reality, they are the original grounds of the possibility of historical knowledge. "They are suprahistorical, because without them there can be no history which we could grasp. In them history finds its limit, as in every true a priori."[20] The cultural sciences must rest upon a system of eternal values which are not historically conditioned but are valid in themselves like mathematical theorems. The separate cultural sciences have as their ultimate ground an absolute and universal philosophy of value which is purely formal and has nothing whatsoever to do with psychology or any empirical science.

True to the rigid separation of form and content, Rickert did not undertake to specify the content of the values which are presupposed by every judgment in the cultural sciences. The separation between form and content was paralleled by an equally sharp separation between theoretical and practical modes of apprehension. Science as theoretical knowledge must be carefully distinguished from the practical situations of life. Rickert deplored any blurring of the categorical distinction between science and life, that is, between methodical knowledge (*Wissenschaft*) and actual experience of life (*Erlebnis*). Dilthey's efforts toward a methodical and critical "philosophy of life" was in Rickert's terms a monstrous misconception. The sheer immediacy of experience cannot furnish knowledge but only confusion, for "real" concrete experience is wholly irrational and "dumb" (*nichtssagend*), a welter of percepts without concepts. Neither experience nor reexperiencing (*Nacherleben*) can offer valid grounds for scientific knowledge, since there is no such thing as a science based upon pure induction and description; such a science is a bizarre nonconcept (*Unbegriff*), "a science which does not take it upon itself to erect standards of what can pass as science."[21] In disallowing any notion of a science grounded in lived experience, Rickert was entirely consistent in accusing Dilthey of reducing the faculty of judgment in the human sciences to mere irrational "feeling" and "intuition": only the pure value forms can marshall experience into true knowledge.

In clarifying his own theory of judgment, Rickert was compelled to carry his distinctions even farther. As sciences, the cultural sciences do not take the practical stance of actually evaluating (*wertende Betrachtung*), but a theoretical attitude of "relating values" (*wertbeziehende Betrachtung*). The method of "relating values" and "understanding values" is "intermediate" between the practical evaluating which is accomplished in life itself and the value-free (*wertfrei*) method of the natural sciences. History and other nonsystematic cultural sciences are based upon a form of judgment which relates and examines values "theoretically" without evaluating in the practical sense. This form of judgment exposes and relates values without concurring with them.[22]

Rickert's systematization of neo-Kantian *Kritizismus* and value theory became so formal and theoretical that knowledge seemed deprived of any immediate or functional relation to existence and experience. The "absolute" separation of existence and validity brought some awkward consequences, even in theory. Rickert had to remind his readers that although cultural values are formal and "irreal," they are held by "real men." After excoriating Dilthey for the "cloudy mysticism" of the doctrine of self-intuition, Rickert, had to resort to some of his own to formulate the manner in which values appear in history. According to his position transcendental values "inhere" (*behaften*) in the concrete individual.[23]

After Dilthey and others pointed out that critical value-philosophy was exceedingly formal, that is, lacking specific determination of the status of cultural values and any point of synthesis between value (*Wert*), valuation (*Wertung*), and reality (*Wirklichkeit*), Rickert allowed that transcendental values were the *form* of culture and experience its *content*. Though continuing to rail against all forms of psychologism, historicism, and the "concept-less, pre-scientific standpoint of *Erleben*," Rickert made what would seem to be some major adjustments in the status of the a priori values. After accusing Dilthey of basing the cultural sciences upon a "naïve empiricism" and "irrationalist life-philosophy" rather than rigorous conceptual thought, Rickert was compelled to admit that these sciences rested partially upon an experiential awareness of life, but he vigorously denied that this awareness could be examined in psychology; indeed, it does not qualify as any form of genuine knowledge whatsoever. Adapting one of Dilthey's most crucial terms, Rickert conceded: "the life-experience (*Lebenserfahrung*) which we require for a genuine world-view must be experience of historical life as a whole. Prior to the problem of the world stands the problem of values and prior to that stands the problem of history. Certainly, however, philosophy does not dissolve into history."[24] Addressing the problem of how formal values come to "inhere" in experience, Rickert asserted that they are united in a "third realm" of meaning (*Sinn*).[25] With this rather vague *tertium* Rickert seemed to gloss over all the careful "absolute" distinctions of ideal/real, value/fact, form/content, theory/practice which his logical treatment had erected. It is interesting to note that in the third edition of the *Grenzen* Rickert asserted that Dilthey was moving closer to his own position; given the changes in that position it is not so clear who was moving toward whom.[26]

Dilthey's response to the Baden neo-Kantians was a mixture of praise and deeper criticism. As early as 1880 he commended Windelband for adapting a standpoint which "brings philosophy into relation with general culture—the only possible standpoint" (*WM* 48[1880]:293). In his "Essence of Philosophy" of 1907 he credited the neo-Kantians with forging a link between what Kant had called the "school-concept" and "world-concept" of philosophy. But in the final analysis they chose the wrong foundation on which to legitimate the human sciences. By placing reason, culture, and values in realm of sheer transcendence, they reverted to the old paralyzing two-world theory. They rightly stressed the function of values in the human sciences, but they then hypostatized these values into eternal forms. Dilthey found that their exposition of the cultural sciences contained a lopsided and indemonstrable assumption concerning the essentially "ideal" content of culture and history: among other effects it fostered an "all too optimistic interpretation of mankind—in whom dark instincts toward subjugation and destruction play a very considerable role" (*GS* 5:358; 7:323).

Transcendental formalism was for Dilthey the "death of history" and all genuine science. Neo-Kantian logic of values "saved" history from the natural sciences only at the double cost of severing all connections with generalizing methods and destroying an essential attribute of history itself—its historicity and development. This "Fichtean faction" of neo-Kantians attempted to ground history not in its own real contents and categories but by a pure deduction of values. They thereby transfigured history into a very formal species of ethical idealism teaching by example. Moreover, the hyper-formalism of this position invited the very consequence it was intended to avert: the skeptical outcome of subjectivism, phenomenalism, and a purely "constructed" account of knowledge.

> The Kantians hold that in this sphere of cultural-historical relations there must finally be something which grounds and which is not itself grounded, which is presented, but not itself represented. Thus in this view there is something posited absolutely by means of these relations which does not itself contain a relation. This "something" is not available in actual experience but rather constitutes the foundation of the very limit of experience [*BNL* 225/31]

Transcendental logic extended to the sphere of values could not, in Dilthey's view, suffice for a genuine critique of historical reason. The Kantian urge to eternal validity propelled logic beyond its proper bounds and issued in an impoverished account of historical-cultural content: by turning away from actual experience of existence to the ideal-logical "conditions of possibility," the Kantians produced a "forcible separation" (*Losreissung*) of history from the other sciences (*GS* 5:258).

In Nachlass notes recorded between 1902 and 1904 Dilthey observed that Rickert was on first reading more systematic and consistent than Windelband, but further examination showed him to be "mired down in barely concealed infinite paradoxes and an incredible confusion of concepts."

Rickert's whole position rested upon a "one-sided derivation of knowledge from its dependence upon a transcendental value," which leaves both the subject and object of knowledge "hovering in a haze of transcendence." Rickert adopted consciousness only as a formal *Grenzbegriff*, a necessary supposition or logical condition which cannot be experienced: his epistemological subject is not a vital reality but a theoretical construct (*BNL* 245/71).

Likewise the "new Fichtean" account of the relation of the subject to reality is one of mere postulation, not experience. "The should is given priority over existence [*das Sollen ist vor dem Sein*]." For Rickert, "being arises only in judgment, not in perception and in every such judgment a value is acknowledged but not given." Dilthey went on to assert that Rickert totally neglects "the moment of givenness or evidence in judgment which has been deeply explored by Husserl." For Rickert the object is constructed in judgment according to a kind of epistemic ethics; this view, Dilthey insists, is vastly different from his own position and that of Husserl, for whom the object is always "founded" (*fundiert-sein*) in an immanent being-in-consciousness. Dilthey offered a perceptive résumé of Rickert's system:

> Theoretical knowledge is in every step a recognition of value without any attention to how values are actually given. Whoever searches for truth puts himself under a "should," just as much as the person who obeys his duty. Logical standards and the norms of will are parallel. Consequently, the ultimate and final basis of knowledge is conscience. This "should" gives truth—reality is a value concept [*BNL* 244/272, 471, 492, 517].

Dilthey gave credit to Rickert for emphasizing a crucial component of any critique of historical reason, that is, the intimate connection between value and historical judgment: "Without the determination of values in the historical material and the historical process, neither historical reality nor historical study are conceivable." But at the same time as he acknowledged Rickert's contribution, Dilthey underlined its limitations: "But such values are not transcendental values, but life-values (*Lebenswerte*)" (*BNL* 78/58). These values are not a priori but the lasting deposit of the ongoing process of reflection upon experience accomplished in the course of historical life itself. The great error of Windelband and Rickert was to interpret Kant's categories as a priori "objective-teleological" values rather than historical-cultural manifestations which assume the character of general validity (*Allgemeingültigkeit*) from their actual effectiveness (*Wirkung*) in meeting the total needs of human life over time (*BNL* 49/133).

Dilthey found the weak point of Rickert's theory to be the "problem of the actual relationship between the ideal-value and the historical manifestation of value." Rickert was correct in stressing that history—both as past fact and as present knowledge—rests upon values, but one cannot draw these up in a table of eternal a priori ideals. Turning Rickert's own premises against him, Dilthey judged that Rickert came perilously close to forfeiting his much vaunted critical position: in holding that history can be understood only in terms of universal values, Rickert stopped just short of saying that history "realizes" these values—which would be to succumb to the old substantive or "material" philosophy of history which his critical position excluded. The crux of Rickert's theory remained its weakest point: the notion of the "inherence" of universal values in the individual. The question of how these values come to reside in the individual—whether by pre-formation or by education—met with no response other than the postulate of a transcendental ego (*BNL* 242:448).

Dilthey also found Rickert's logical division to be misleading: history makes use of generalizing knowledge—indeed it adopts some insights from the natural sciences; likewise, the natural sciences make individualizing judgments of a "formally historical" nature. The neat dichotomy of generalizing and individualizing methods is "fruitless and inaccurate," a case of formal logic trying to preempt genuine science. The human sciences actually contain a "double direction" (*doppelte Richtung*) of grasping individualities and general regularities; indeed the "most characteristic trait" of these sciences resides in "the connection of the general with the individual" (*GS* 7:312; 5:xlix). In answer to Rickert, Dilthey insisted that the human sciences could serve the interests of mankind only if this double direction is carried forward through mediating concepts (*Mittelbegriffe*). Although the two directions of reason toward "singularity" and "abstraction" can be isolated logically, the actual process and results of inquiry show both tendencies to be conjoined (*BNL* 191/77–79). The same applies to the rigid separation of fact and value, for in the realm of life and the human sciences that which "is" cannot be isolated from that which "should be." *Sein* cannot be split off from *Sollen* and *Gelten* by logical postulates:

> That which *is* shows itself to be inseparable from its *value* or what it *ought to be*. Thus, to the facts of life are attached its norms. . . . The truths of fact cannot be separated from ideal-representations and norms. This separation into two classes of propositions, in which one contains what is and the other says what should be, robs knowledge of its fruitfulness and divests the ideals and norms of their coherence and function [emphasis, Dilthey's; *GS* 5:268].

Dilthey went on to assert that evaluation and a teleological "relation to a purpose" are immanently contained in every system of factual judgments. Thus the writing of history always includes factual description, knowledge of causes and more general relations, and critical judgment; indeed, "judgment of what has happened is in and of itself inseparable from the presentation of it." Rickert's fine distinction between the "theoretical" and "practical" relation of values cannot be maintained, for genuine understanding (*Auffassung*) is intimately linked to evaluation (*Wertung*). Dilthey was equally critical of the disjunction of "psyche" (*Seele*) and "spirit" (*Geist*): "It appears plausible like all neat separations. But the question arises whether what is separated in theory is separated in reality." Rickert's whole system of tidy divisions is a "postulation *in abstracto*" (*BNL* 244/272–73).

Rickert regards the Should as the one true "object" of knowledge: it is the transcendental norm which allows all empirical objects to appear. But, ironically, Rickert has confused the notion of the *object* of knowledge with the *criterion* of knowledge: What we see or judge is not identical with the norm of our judgment. The "evidence of givenness" is not reducible to the criterion (*Rechtsgrund*). Such *Kritizismus* turns our experiential world upside down in the sense that reality is not given as evidence-in-consciousness but is pushed over into the "hither-realm of the validity of the transcendental Ought" (*BNL* 244/273–74).

The Baden position was deeply suffused with the Fichtean tendency to bend critical thought back into reflexive self-gazing by emptying thought of its real experiential content. In contrast, Dilthey re-affirmed that the subject always remains linked to the world in lived relations which not only permeate perception but also judgment. In valid judgments, the mind accomplishes the discursive formulation of an objective grasping of reality; judgment is always "the predication of being" [*die Setzung eines Seins*) in which the mind maintains "an attitude of attending in which consciousness looks away from its own individual configurations to a given reality." Reversing the neo-Kantians, Dilthey insisted that reality as evidence (*Evidenz*) is prior to formal value and evaluation: "The being of the object is the presupposition through which relations are first constituted." Dilthey went so far as to assert that the very concepts of transcendence and the transcendental are themselves drawn from a "relation of being" (*BNL* 244/468–74).

For all his chiding of Rickert, Dilthey was considerably impressed with Rickert's critique of psychologism. Admitting all psychological conditions and determinations about the knowledge process, this knowledge *qua* knowledge still contains something further, not contained in these determinations. Epistemology cannot be entirely dissolved into psychology, for this would destroy the grounds of validity. Indeed, Dilthey claimed over Rickert's objections that he himself had not lost sight of this distinction. Epistemology and *Wissenschaftslehre* must establish genuine grounds of validity (*Rechtsgründe*) not merely facts (*Tatsachen*)—but this can be done only on the basis of the "phenomenological analysis of experience, as Husserl has shown" (*BNL* 244/284–88). The criteria of knowledge must be drawn from experience itself, conceived as an ongoing process of self-correcting perception, assertion, doubt, and critical testing against contrary empirical evidence. "Experience is vastly more than what the empiricists and Kantians have portrayed under that name." When this "more" is acknowledged, the nexus of judgment can be drawn down into experience itself and not consigned to the abstract realm of transcendental value-theory:

> Rickert wants to arrive at reality as a transcendental object solely through inference on the basis of mere logical relations of an epistemological subject—and he finds that this will not work. This is the error of his method. The real method must proceed from the empirical consciousness. This method recognizes that it is futile to undertake constructions on the basis of abstract concepts. It also recognizes that reality cannot be constructed or be fully demonstrated logically, but only made plausible. [*BNL* 244/288].

It can hardly be argued that Dilthey and the Baden neo-Kantians were saying the same thing with different local emphases. Their differences concerned grounds, not details; Dilthey did not subscribe to their notion of the transcendental a priori and they did not admit his concept of experience. It is, however, possible to discern certain signs of mutual adjustment: Rickert made concessions to Dilthey's concept of "experience of life" and his critique of logicism, whereas Dilthey accommodated certain aspects of Rickert's value-theory and his critique of psychologism. Dilthey was moved to draw a sharper distinction between the "acts" of experience and the "contents" of knowledge in order to secure a firmer concept of validity for the human sciences. But he continued to seek these foundations wholly within the realm of the "empirical consciousness." In support of his effort at a true *Empirie*, he was strongly drawn to the fresh stimulus of Edmund Husserl.

The Phenomenology of Edmund Husserl: The Bridge between Psychology and Epistemology—and Beyond

It has been widely recognized that one of the principal factors which brought Dilthey back to his theoretical labors after the turn of the century was his reading of Husserl's new study in logic, the *Logische Untersuchungen* of 1900. Dilthey immediately hailed it as "epoch-making" and "the first great step forward which scientific philosophy has made since Kant's *Critique of Pure Reason*" (*GS* 7:14).[27] Dilthey was the first prominent German philosopher to use Husserl's work in his own courses, prompting Husserl to initiate a personal contact. After this contact Dilthey proved quite supportive of Husserl, who felt he was swimming against the tide of accepted academic philosophy in Germany.[28] Although the general influence of Husserl's thought upon Dilthey can be partially inferred from the published record, its full scope and specific character emerge only from Dilthey's Nachlass.

A recent observer has testified to the profound impact of Husserl's work:

> Without exaggeration it may be said that the appearance of this work in 1900 and 1901 gave a new direction to the life of the European mind. The *Logical Investigations* acted as a turning point in the history of the theory of knowledge, logic, and philosophy.[29]

Within a relatively short time this initial direction broadened immensely, so much so that one of its adherents was moved to proclaim that "the phenomenological movement, which originally appeared merely as a reform of the least popular philosophical field of logic, has developed into a full-scale revolution within the whole of philosophy."[30]

It is impossible to do justice to Husserl's extremely rich and complex work; here it must suffice to stress some of its major insights. Perhaps the single most influential doctrine propounded in the *Logische Untersuchungen* concerned the "intentionality" of consciousness and its experience. Husserl insisted emphatically against all subjectivistic and phenomenalistic accounts that consciousness is always consciousness *of* an "object" (*Gegenstand:* physical or mental) or "objective content." The doctrine of intentionality had earlier been enunciated by Husserl's teacher Franz Brentano, but Husserl gave it a more radical and far-reaching statement. Mental experience is not primarily immanent and subjective—that is, self-contained and self-referring—but is a dynamic, transitive process directed toward an ideal unity of content which both transcends and "fulfills" individual psychic acts. Experience is more than a series of subjective-psychological acts or occurrences, for it necessarily intends ideal-objective contents. Husserl announced summarily: "I do not see sensations of color, but colored objects"—a trivial enough sounding observation, but one which entailed a wholly new conception of what it means to be "scientific" about experience and its contents.[31] The world is composed of real objects, not sense data or abstract physical *correlata* with labels attached to them.

Experience goes to "things themselves" and philosophy must do likewise by means of analysis of the primary experience of meaning. There is nothing mystical or abstrusely metaphysical in this turn of thought: Husserl's celebrated "turn to the object" restored (if in roundabout fashion) the commonsensical view that there is no experience without "meant" objects. Husserl affirmed that the preeminent tendency of consciousness is to be directed intentionally to "things themselves"—hence his philosophical motto, "Zu den Sachen selber." Consciousness is first and foremost primary awareness of intentional meaning, *not* awareness of psychological processes. The mind's original intentionality and conventional psychology are, so to speak, going in opposite directions. Therefore, in phenomenological analysis "one thinks *in* the meanings instead of *about* them."[32] Because the type of explanatory-genetic method presupposed in conventionally "empirical" science (and especially psychology) expunges precisely this primary experience of meaning, it must be excluded from phenomenological description. This radical alteration stems from the crucial distinction between the acts and contents of experience: the acts may be defined as "empirical" and "psychological," but the contents are "ideal and objective." Psychology by itself cannot suffice to establish logic, science, or indeed any apprehension of meaning, for it provides only causal laws and not the grounds for grasping of the objective contents constitutive of experience and knowledge. Husserl therefore inveighed in his first volume against all brands of psychologism in logic and epistemology: logic must be based upon ideal laws of essence (*Normgesetze* and *Wesensgesetze*) which are independent of empirical-factual laws of psychology (*Naturgesetze*).[33]

Lest this program sound like a mere restatement of Kantian transcendental logic, it should be stressed that Husserl insisted strongly in the second volume that, while logic must be purged of psychologism, it is rooted in experience of a special kind which must be elucidated in a "descriptive psychology" or phenomenology of logical and cognitive experience. Logic alone will not clarify the full work of consciousness, nor does logical form exhaust the world of intentional meanings. Like Hegel's logic, Husserl's *Untersuchungen* pointed beyond the formal axioms of thought to a realm of experienced *realia*. (The neo-Kantians contended that the second volume contradicted the first.) Logic therefore cannot rest with a fixed set of rules, for the categorical relations treated explicitly in logic extend beyond language itself and are implicit in pre-discursive experience. The categorical rests on the perceptual and points toward a sphere of nonverbal, experiential meaning which remains to be clarified in phenomenology.[34] Husserl's logic pointed toward a new "transcendental realism" with a strongly ontological proclivity, which became even more marked in his later deliberations.

Husserl insisted that all knowledge "begins" (*fängt an*) in experience, but it does not wholly "originate" (*entspringt*) or "conclude" in experience—at least not experience conceived in a nominalistic or "psychological" sense of the term.[35] In meaningful acts of consciousness such as expressions, judgments, and signs in general, consciousness signifies something about what is, not about its own makeup. While the act of meaning may be empirical, temporal, and relative, the content of meaning is ideal and "essential"; thus, all possible acts of collecting are not identical to the concept of number and cannot "explain" it. In our ordinary attitude we attend to the objects of consciousness and not to the constitutive acts of consciousness, but through an "unnatural" alteration of attention the mind can be brought to attend reflectively to its own acts of intending the ideal-contents of the world:

> Instead of becoming involved with the actual performance of the mani-fold of acts constructed upon the basis of each other (and as a result naïvely to posit, so to speak, the objects meant by their meaning as existing and to determine what they are), we shall rather "reflect," i.e., make these acts themselves, along with their immanent meaning-content, into objects for investigation.[36]

This "phenomenology of inner experience" represents a new approach to the whole field of mental life, which in freeing itself from naturalism and psychologism opens the way to treating the actual contents rather than the purported "causes" of mental experience. Husserl's phenomenology called for a vigilant "seeing" of the mental meaning given in experience prior to its formalization and certification in logic, epistemology, or scientific con-ceptualization.

In the process of thinking, Husserl distinguished three levels: the *object* we intend, the *content* of the representation (or the totality of the characteristics which are thought), and the *act* of thinking itself. The object and the contents are not necessarily identical, but are clearly related "internally" in a manner which is not simply "causal." In the process of knowing, the contents and the object approach a relation of identity or full adequation, so that knowledge is "perceived" as the fulfillment of a meaning-intention. All mental contents (e.g., a melody or design in a carpet) are given in perspectival profiles (*Abschattungen*) which are filled in by subsequent psychic acts which have an ideal-structural (not causal) relation to previous ones. These profiles are coordinated by a structure of anticipation into a unity of content. The ideal limiting case of knowledge is the full disclosure of the "sense" of the object through an "all-sided seeing" or total intuition, which Husserl called a "categorical representation" or *Totalanschauung*. Truth is the experience of full evidence.[37]

Husserl's distinction between the acts and contents of consciousness established an ideal-objective reference to acts of meaning, so that one can say that he understands the meaning (*Sinn*) of another's wish without literally "wishing along" with him in the same acts (*Erlebnisse*).[38] The grasping of the "meant" is not identical with repeating the "actual" acts of meaning themselves. Husserl agreed with the neo-Kantians that meaning is ideal, not "factual" in the sense construed by the physical sciences. The key to the understanding of meaning is not the discernment of causal relations along a chain of psychic acts, but the grasping of the ideal-structure which unites them into a whole content. By means of these structures the mind can "represent" contents which are not themselves directly presented in sense perception. The understanding of meaning is not a single flash of intuition but a gradual filling out of mental structures. Phenomenology is pre-eminently concerned with these structural relations, which Husserl insists are "eidetic" or essential and cannot be "explained" (*erklärt*) but only reflectively elucidated (*aufgeklärt*). The mind is capable of a vast variation of these structural relations: act and object may be varied independently— the same object may be entertained in different psychic acts (as judging, desiring, doubting, supposing) or the same act can have different objects. In these variations Husserl underscored the intentional unity of meaning deriving from the manifold subjective experiences in which the meaning is actualized.

The mind, as it were, is always moving beyond itself (*hinausmeinend*) in the process of constituting its world of meaning.[39] Mental life has an immanent *telos* of intentionality which must be explored by phenomeno-logical analyses of the different modes of intending reflected in logic, grammar, science, religion, even philosophy itself. Of all existing philos-ophies, Husserl's phenomenology came closest to a viable, broad-ranging synthesis of transcendental and empirical standpoints. Its appeal for Dilthey must have derived in considerable measure from its roots in the tradition of *Idealrealismus* of which he felt a part.

Dilthey was deeply impressed with Husserl's work. Not given to casual hyperbole, his use of terms like "epoch-making" and "first step" must be taken in relation not only to general philosophy but to his own project of a critique of historical reason. Before treating their specific affinities and disagreements, however, more must be said of their personal relationship. The actual contacts and encounters of the two men constitute something of a mystery, which in the light of their later positions deserves deeper investigation. Certain basic facts are known, but they seem to raise more questions than they settle.

Dilthey credited Husserl with creating a new philosophical discipline and hailed him as a "genius of philosophical analysis." In an important epistemological study of 1902 Dilthey paid homage to Husserl and ex-pressed his outright indebtedness:

> In seeking here to build forth my foundation to a realistic or critical-objective theory of knowledge, I must once and for all indicate *in toto* how much I owe to the *Logical Investigations* (1900–1901) of Husserl, which are epoch-making in their application of description to epistemol-ogy [*GS* 7:10; cf. 13–14].

The significance of this passage is underscored by the fact that Dilthey rarely testified so explicitly to any direct intellectual inspiration. Dilthey used this new work in his last seminar on logic at Berlin; the unpublished notes for this seminar, collected by a student, contain laudatory references to Husserl's use of description in the theory of knowledge (*LK* 13). References to the *Logische Untersuchungen* appear in numerous places in Dilthey's later published studies. And Husserl figures so frequently in the pages of the Nachlass that his name is shortened to "Hus." and finally to "H." From a letter written to his daughter in 1900, it emerges that in the search for a successor for the world-renowned neo-Kantian philosopher Friedrich Paulsen, Dilthey held out strongly for the relatively young and still unknown Husserl.[40] In the light of these facts it is necessary to revise H. A. Hodges' judgment that Dilthey "borrowed certain words from Husserl . . . but never borrowed Husserl's doctrines, and he left his adverse opinion of them on the record."[41] Indeed there is substantial evidence to support Dilthey's avowal of deep indebtedness, even if he ultimately assumed a more critical attitude stemming from a thinly disguised attack on Dilthey by Husserl coupled with a basic shift in the definition of phenomenology.[42]

Dilthey initially regarded Husserl's thought as a "profoundly new and original realism" which would provide an antidote to both the formalistic idealism of the neo-Kantians and the reductive psychologism of the empiricists (*BNL* 244/153). Husserl provided a rigorously logical and objective foundation for the "standpoint of life and experience," which had hitherto been largely couched in terms of religious or poetic sentiment, as in Schleiermacher, Goethe, and the *Lebensphilosophen*. Husserl had, in sum, made the concept of lived experience logically and scientifically credible. Although both thinkers started from vastly different points (Husserl from pure mathematics and Dilthey from history), they discovered a considerable area of common ground and shared assumptions. They both agreed upon the constitutive role of consciousness and the original and underivable nature of inner experience. Husserl confirmed that mind cannot be conceived as a natural object but as an intentional structure which cannot be "explained" causally but can be elucidated in reflection and description. After reading Husserl, Dilthey underscored more emphatically the difference between causal explanation and phenomenological description, or between "genetic" and "foundational" accounts of the knowledge process. The reception of Husserl was decisive, not because it gave Dilthey entirely new ideas but because it gave him the logical foundation for ones he had all along. It should be noted that he did not rely entirely upon Husserl for the twin concepts of intentionality and mental "objectivity": "The doctrine of the object-directedness [*Gegenstandsgerichtetsein*] of thought has been thoroughly worked out by Brentano, Stumpf, Meinong, and Husserl" (*BNL* 209/27). (The fact that Dilthey at this time was also immersed in Schleiermacher's *Dialektik* may have added further support, for Schleiermacher had insisted that "in every thought some object outside thought is assumed. To think means not only that there is a determinate thought, but that there is a relation of it to something assumed to be outside it.")[43] The doctrine of intentionality provided a means of breaking out of the phenomenalism in which modern thought was imprisoned: consciousness is, so to speak, not merely "pushed from behind" by a causal sequence, but "led from ahead" by intentional structures of anticipation and fulfillment.

Husserl's demonstration of intentionality vindicated Dilthey's theory that inner experience is transitive and "immanently teleological." In studies written under the influence of Husserl, Dilthey emphasized that all psychic experience is directed toward objectivities (*gerichtetsein auf Gegenstände*) (*GS* 7:38, 42, 127–28). Analysis of this experience must focus not on the genetic-psychological "how" (*Wie*) of experience but on the objective "what" (*Was*) of the meaning of experience. The understanding of mental life belongs first and foremost to these objective meanings or contents, not to putative or inferred relations among psychic acts. It is in the elucidation of this kind of meaning that Dilthey relied most heavily on Husserl: "The laws of thought are founded in relations of meaning. We know what meaning is in a sense as immediate as what we know color and tone to be. It cannot be further defined, for it is something which is descriptively final [*ein deskriptiv Letztes*]. Whenever we understand an expression, it means something to us, we accomplish its sense" (*BNL* 209/109). Husserl had demonstrated that we live in a world of primary meanings and significations—and it is this world which we understand by means of the human sciences: "In real understanding we do not have the bare presentation [*Vorstellung*] of a word, but its meaning and this meaning is objective and identical through different contexts" (*BNL* 191/21). The otherwise bare "word" becomes "world" through the meaning-content implicit in experience.

The distinction between act and content introduced a decisive change in Dilthey's treatment of meaning. What is grasped in the understanding of meaning is a content, not a set of mental acts or events (e.g., when I try to "think through" some of Dilthey's ideas, I think the contents of those ideas, I do not somehow replicate a set of psychological acts or events which went on in his head). Attention is originally and primarily directed to mental contents, not acts; therefore the understanding of meaning is best described not as a re-en*act*ment of psychological processes but a "re-*content*-ment" of what is meant. When Dilthey spoke of understanding as "re-experiencing," he did not mean it as some sort of literal repetition of psychic acts. The next chapter will show that Dilthey's fully developed concept of understanding (with its correlative theory of expression and representation) owed a great deal to Husserl.

The standpoints of phenomenology and the human sciences concur in focusing upon experiential contents which are "given as meant." This phenomenological standpoint is not phenomenalistic: it does not dismantle the world of mental contents in order to transmute it into a more basic or "real" substratum of elements or atomic facts. After reading Husserl, Dilthey asserted with new assurance that the relations which characterize mental life are not causal relations among psychic acts but structural relations among the contents of those acts. Perhaps most significantly, Husserl provided a new kind of critical test for the validity of cognition which avoided the strictly formalistic logical coherence of the Kantians: cognitive experience assumes its own "evident" (not merely formal) validity in the inwardly perceived and progressive "fulfillment" of its own intentional structures. In the Nachlass, Dilthey avowed that his view concerning the relation of empirical reality and objective validity "corresponds perfectly with that of Husserl." The "reality" of experiences which lie at the basis of all judgments is given immediately, but the "objectivity," as a system of valid judgments, remains a *terminus ad quem*. The evidence of immediate experience must be taken up in a wider coherence of mediated evidence and integrated into a system of judgments (*BNL* 209/88–89).

It is noteworthy that Dilthey increasingly employed the term "phenomenology" where he would previously have used the term "psychology." In the Nachlass, "psychology" is often struck out in favor of Husserl's term.[44] In passages in the later, published studies, Dilthey referred to the "phenomenology of philosophical systems," and he even came to regard his treatment of metaphysics in the *Einleitung* as "phenomenology of metaphysics." This shift of emphasis is not merely a matter of words but is—from the standpoint of phenomenology—a matter of true content. Psychology, by its very nature, cannot explain or otherwise grasp the meaning constituted in mental life or the objectivity of its contents. Psychological science considers the mind and its processes analytically and anaclastically, that is, devoid of the intentional relations to an object which constitute "natural" meaning. Phenomenology concerns itself with the intentional "consciousness-of," thereby taking the mind as intrinsically and essentially related to an object. The "science" of this primary consciousness which is always in possession of a real world of meanings is phenomenology. Although Dilthey did not restrict his conception of phenomenology as narrowly to "logical" experience as Husserl did initially, he regarded Husserl's program as a decisive contribution to a new foundation of reason, with specific merit for his own critique of historical reason.

In an unpublished manuscript entitled "Natural Science and Human Science," Dilthey drew support for his basic position from Husserl's analysis: the difference between these two bodies of knowledge is not a matter of metaphysical "substances" but of phenomenological contents. Citing Husserl's text, Dilthey insisted that the distinction was "descriptive but still fundamental": "If one works his way clearly through the difference in both classes of sciences, so I am again mainly in agreement with Husserl."

Husserl is praised for demonstrating that "what is given is given as meant" and that all meaning is inseparable from sense data, but not reducible to it. Dilthey further praised Husserl for showing that the "I" is not a meta-physical entity but a "unity of relations" or "complex of lived experiences"—just as the distinction between the natural and human sciences, the "I" is not a metaphysical but a "phenomenological finding" (*phänomenologischer Befund*). Husserl had provided a stringently logical defense of inner per-ception against Rickert's charges: "Inner perception is a grasping of what is contained in experience—insofar as this content is a qualitative meaning." After stressing his agreement with Husserl, Dilthey went on to note a crucial and surprising difference: "My view presupposes epistemology" (*BNL* 49/89–92).

Dilthey was not uncritical of Husserl's position, even before the turn their relationship took after Husserl's *Logos* article of 1910 discussed below. The new phenomenology had great strengths but also limitations. In calling attention to these limitations, Dilthey showed the same double attitude toward Husserl that he took toward the neo-Kantians (and, one could add, increasingly toward psychology). Indeed at the same time he invoked Husserl against their position, he seems to employ some of their arguments against Husserl! He insisted that phenomenology is a necessary but limited and provisory part of a larger "method of foundation":

> The phenomenological method has its indubitable value in the fact that it clarifies the sense which concepts and words have in ordinary thought and in the developing sciences. But the simple accomplishment of such phenomenological clarification would not contain a definitive determina-tion of the legitimating grounds [*Rechtsgründe*] of such concepts and judgments. For the latter, one would have to move on to a foundational method.

Dilthey went on to assert that a "true procedure of methodical under-standing or interpretation must combine *both* phenomenological and foundational methods" (emphasis, Dilthey's; *BNL* 208/39–42). It is evident from this passage that Dilthey looked to a new hermeneutic method to combine phenomenology and epistemology.

Dilthey proclaimed Husserl to be "a genius in the discovery of funda-mental principles" but "too scholastic" in the application of them. After distinguishing correctly between the act and content of knowledge, Husserl went further to distinguish between the content and the object of knowl-edge, which is somehow presented in the contents but which is itself not really known. Dilthey judged that with this extra distinction Husserl for-feited part of the gain of his critical realism and fell back into the "transcen-dence of the object," like the Kantians. There is an almost insupportable tension in Husserl's thought—a tension which verges into contradiction.

"From the standpoint of logic he [Husserl] distinguishes sharply between act, content, and object and then, from the standpoint of phenomenology, he proceeds to elucidate their relation." In fact, Dilthey asserted, lived experience contains act, content, and object in a "differentiated, structural totality" (*BNL* 244/163).

Husserl's need to reify his distinctions stemmed from his failure to follow his own discovery. Despite his own realism, Husserl assumed a residually nominalist view of *Erlebnisse* as psychological-neural processes (or events) separated from their intentional meaning. Thus, in analyzing the perception of a die, Husserl endeavored to separate its "empirical" content (white planar surface with dots) from its intentional content (its location on the table, its "place" in a winning strategy, its determinable but hidden sides, etc.). Using portions of Husserl's investigations against other portions, Dilthey affirmed that the intentional content is given with the original experience; Husserl had forsaken the profundity of his own insight into experiential meaning (or experience-as-meaning) by allowing a residual separation of "intendedness" (*Gemeintsein*) and "experienced-ness" (*Erlebtsein*). Using the same tactic he had employed against the Kantian distinction of *Seele* and *Geist*, Dilthey found that what Husserl treats as "ideally" (*ideell*) separable and distinct is "really" (*realiter*) mutually dependent. (*BNL* 244/163–65; see *GS* 7:51, 123).

Tracing the impact of Husserl's thought upon Dilthey has been complicated by the turn which their relationship took after Husserl published (in the respected international journal *Logos* in 1911) a searing indictment of all forms of relativism, historicism, psychologism, and "world-view philosophy" in his famous article "Philosophie als strenge Wissenschaft." This article forms the link between what has often been termed the "pre-transcendental" position of the *Logische Untersuchungen* and the full-fledged "transcendental phenomenology" of the *Ideen* of 1913. The most surprising aspect of these developments was that Dilthey seems to have had a hand in impelling Husserl toward the very position from which Husserl indirectly denounced Dilthey's thought as "relativism" and "historicism." Dilthey's acquaintance with Husserl was not limited to the *Logische Untersuchungen*. Husserl revealed in a letter to Georg Misch in 1929 that he had had a series of conversations with Dilthey in 1905 which furnished an impulse leading from his earlier work to the *Ideen*. Husserl expressed the desire to clarify the content of these conversations, but begged off for the moment.[45] Some inkling of the gist of these conversations may be gleaned indirectly from the record of conversations which Husserl had with one of his students, W. R. Boyce Gibson, who later translated the *Ideen*. Boyce Gibson reported in his diary that an American "realist" at Göttingen, Walter Pitkin, had informed Husserl that Dilthey was holding a seminar at Berlin on the *Logische Untersuchungen*. Husserl went to Berlin and spent several days "in earnest conversation" with Dilthey and came away "vastly impressed." Gibson reported that prior to this visit Husserl had considered himself a positivist (!) who shared Ebbinghaus' caustic view of Dilthey's psychology, but that through these conversations he was moved to a "sympathetic and lively interest" in Dilthey and came to adopt Dilthey's position on the role of "absolute spirit" (*absoluter Geist*).[46]

Evidently what Husserl and Dilthey meant by "spirit," however, came to diverge sharply, for Husserl employed this concept in his *Logos* article of 1911 to propound a transcendental phenomenology as "absolute science of the spirit," a new *mathesis universalis*. Husserl attacked psychologism, historicism, and world-view philosophy as covert forms of naturalism and relativism. Dilthey was not actually named, but the implication was unmistakable. All these doctrines were judged guilty of the genetic fallacy, that is, the erroneous conclusion that the empirical circumstances in which a judgment arises determine its truth or falsity. Genetic considerations were seen by Husserl to be psychological and historical, not logical and transcendental: they cannot arbitrate questions of truth. The world of empirical facticity can never furnish the way to the world of truth and essences. An absolute science of essences is available in transcendental phenomenology, which has nothing whatsoever to do with psychology, history, or any other science which predicates the empirically conditioned nature of consciousness. Phenomenology, in its proper transcendental guise, treats a self-sufficient realm of pure rationality.[47]

As a life-long antagonist of pure and lifeless *ratio*, Dilthey was not long in taking up the cudgels against this new and unexpected turn in Husserl's thought. In a marginal note to the *Logos* article, he reproached Husserl as "Pure Plato who first fixes the flowing, becoming things in concepts and then adds on the concept of flowing as supplementation" (*GS* 5:cxii). There followed a cool, if courteous exchange of letters between the two men.[48] Dilthey adamantly denied the characterization of his position as "historicism" and expressed their fundamental mutual agreement upon the existence of a valid theory of knowledge (*allgemeingültige Theorie des Wissens*): "So I cannot be called a skeptic or even brought into any relation to skepticism." Dilthey acknowledged that he denied the possibility of a metaphysics which tries to express validly the coherence of the world in a fixed set of concepts, but this did not thereby qualify him as a skeptic: "I am not a philosopher of intuition [*Anschauungsphilosoph*], nor an historicist, nor a skeptic."[49] Husserl's consuming ideal of a pure rational science of essences impelled him to find skepticism and relativism among positions otherwise compatible with his own.

Husserl responded somewhat equivocally by asserting that his indictment was in fact not directed at Dilthey and that "serious differences do not really exist between us." But he went on to postulate an a priori realm of ideal-laws (*Idealgesetze*) which constitute the "meaning of being" (*Sinn dieses Seins*). Truth is to be apprehended from the ideal content of its pure presuppositions, independent of "anthropological-historical facticity." Thus, all "true and possible religion as such" has nothing to do with its positive-historical manifestation. "The historical-factual serves as an example, if we are oriented toward the pure ideal [*das rein Ideale*]." Every science of positive existence [*Daseinswissenschaft*] transforms itself *eo ipso* into metaphysics when looked at from the viewpoint of phenomenological doctrine of essences. Husserl concluded that what Dilthey fought as metaphysics was not the same as what Husserl meant by that discipline.[50]

Dilthey, however, was not convinced. After again lauding Husserl as a "genius of philosophical analysis," he went on to allow that their differences might have to remain until further clarification from Husserl. Dilthey would welcome such clarification:

> For the misunderstanding is not only mine, but is shared from many different and important sides. Perhaps my work on the structure of the human sciences would give you a natural and appropriate opportunity, since in it there emerges clearly my orientation toward a universally valid foundation of the human sciences and the objectivity of historical knowledge.[51]

Dilthey's last comment upon the dispute with Husserl came in the Nachlass as an affirmation of "a general scientific perspective which depends upon philosophical investigation"; such a perspective must be "objectively valid knowledge, which stands above all unprovable world-views" (*GS* 6:303). There remained for Dilthey a higher scientific perspective above the level of world-views, but it did not take the form Husserl had lately advocated.

Like Husserl, Dilthey did not equate knowledge with the natural sciences. Both thinkers were striving toward a expanded concept of *Wissenschaft* which would accommodate the unique nature of human consciousness. But although he too rejected naturalism, positivism, and a narrow empiricism, Dilthey could not follow Husserl to the opposite extreme of an a priori "absolute science" of pure essence and its suggestion of a new metaphysics. Resisting all such platonizing impulses, whether very old or very new, Dilthey continued to hold to experience (or *Empirie*) as the key to the problem of knowledge. His exchange with Husserl after the *Logos* article, when read in the light of his later studies, seems to suggest that, while they shared much common ground, they were moving in different directions. Perhaps one could say that in the search for new foundations, they moved back to their own disciplinary origins. Unlike Husserl's later thought, in which experience points intentionally beyond itself to a realm of rational essence independent of all "historical facticity" and almost mathematical in its purity, Dilthey's concept of experience remains firmly rooted in history.

Indeed it is precisely the conjunction of history and experience which constitutes one of the signal motifs of Dilthey's later thought. Individual experience is formed and expanded in constant relation to transindividual coherences and contexts of meaning which endow experience with a relative validity. In analyzing the historically and culturally conditioned nature of experience, Dilthey came to stress even more strongly the inadequacy of psychology to grasp experience and its meanings.[52]

The Limits and Antinomies of Psychology

In a key passage written sometime after 1903, Dilthey ventured a sweeping judgment which can be taken as indicative of the impact of these confrontations: "The whole of psychology is problematic for the indefinite future" (*BNL* 200/114). The factors producing this state of affairs—and thereby rendering psychology doubtful for the foundation of the human sciences—have already been treated in part: disagreement on the very nature and definition of psychic "facts," the narrow limits of psychological methods, insufficiencies in the treatment of psychic relations, failure to consider relations of meaning and value, and the inability of psychology to provide criteria of cognitive validity. Dilthey's judgment bespoke a theoretical "war of all against all" in German psychology in this period; William Stern, an acute observer of the proliferating schools and escalating disagreements, likened the psychological map of Germany to its teeming political map before unification.[53]

The crux of the controversy concerned the question of what precisely is given or presented in human consciousness—is it sense data and "percepts," rudimentary "idea-units," whole contents and ideas, determinate relations, or some nonpareil "relation of all relations" which eluded either description or experimental verification? If there was any general tendency in German psychology as a whole in this period, it was a new critical sophistication with regard to the limits of both introspective and experimental methods.

It is clear that after 1895 Dilthey became increasingly attentive to the difficulties of a direct, objective knowledge of inner experience and more specifically of transposing mental content into the concepts of a scientific psychology. His previous doubts, coalescing with the strictures of Ebbinghaus, the Baden neo-Kantians, and Husserl, brought about a broad shift in his thinking. It is, however, difficult to say whether this shift represents a difference in kind or simply in degree, for he had always distinguished inner experience from introspection. Dilthey had previously often emphasized that the course of experience and mental life does not stand still for analysis but rushes onward: "as it is in itself we can neither grasp it nor express it." He insisted that the investigator can only fixate certain partial contents and aspects of the human mind and its experience—but added the confident assertion that these partial, fixating procedures could themselves be corrected and controlled (*BA* 54, 94, 141, 160). In a set of notes written after Ebbinghaus' critique, Dilthey emphasized that the treatment of inner experience in psychology falls heir to some of the same problems of perspective and selection which pertain to the cognition of external objects:

> There is no doubt about the relativity of every single cognition of the external world. But this same difficulty appears in a different form in the study of the inner world. The concept formation and application of psychology are always relative, for they are always conditioned by their connections to a whole, which can be raised only gradually to greater clarity. Thus one can only try to bring system into the fluctuating condition of consciousness [*GS* 5:lxxxiv].

After 1900 Dilthey showed notably less confidence in the capacity of psychology to compensate for its own limitations of method; its "antinomies" prevail over its potentialities. He stressed more emphatically what could be called a kind of indeterminacy principle of mental life: that close inspection alters the phenomenon observed. In his hermeneutics article of 1900 he stated that the way in which mental reality is given in inner experience is attended by "great difficulties" for any attempt to grasp it objectively. Experience is a process which inevitably covers it tracks and thus conceals itself to inner perception. Dilthey suggested that lived experience remains the touchstone of our understanding of the human world but that the apprehension of our own inner states cannot be called understanding (*Verstehen*) in the genuine sense (*GS* 5:317–18). Our primary lived awareness, while disturbed and altered by secondary acts of conscious attention (and more so in subsequent psychological conceptualization), goes to work directly and "naturally" in the understanding of signs, expressions, and objectified meanings. The interpretation of expression is more "true to life" or veridical than any supposed direct observation of inner states.

Introspection is inevitably predisposed and biased: "Only under very restricted circumstances does experience remain present to inner observation" (*GS* 7:19, 194–95). There are insuperable difficulties in this procedure:

> I experience something which by its intensity stands out in my consciousness. That which took place previously is also there. I am pained by the death of my nephew; I remain localized in space and the temporal process. Through introspection I now make this process an object of my observation. Can I base a science on this?

Dilthey went on to point out a basic, if subtle difficulty intrinsic to introspection:

If I want to express this observation in words, I find that they belong to a linguistic usage which is conditioned in many ways. The observation itself is conditioned by the questions which I pose. [For example,] if I ask myself or another person whether the aesthetic impression of a mountain scene contains an element of sympathy, then this feeling is immediately put there [by suggestion] [*GS* 6:316–17].

Introspection is foiled by the imprescriptible inherency of linguistic usage in our experience.

Our most careful observation is at odds with what we are trying to perceive. The more careful we become, the more we are susceptible to interfering with experience; hence we must be careful about being careful—and so on, in a kind of infinite critical-methodological regression. Dilthey implies that there is an ultimately intractable (i.e., antinomous) form of the subject-object problem lodged at the basis of introspection which is more vitiating than that contained in the "natural" understanding of meaning objectified in expression. He in fact came back to cite Kant and Comte against the possibility of inner perception and any science based upon it. At the same time he insisted that "the antinomy of psychology can be solved only in the hermeneutic understanding of expression" (*BNL* 62/158; cf. *GS* 7:319). The hermeneutic standpoint acknowledges that the mind comes to know itself not by transparent self-consciousness or inward intuition but by indirect inference from its own concretely objectified operations in the world. The mind grasps itself not by privileged insight into its own immediate, evanescent being but by interpreting what it manifests in expression. Hermeneutic understanding is not introspection or self-notification but the interpretation of publicly manifest meaning.

Dilthey's growing mistrust of introspection was most certainly bolstered by admonishments from both inside and alongside the field of psychology. Following Brentano's distinction of inner perception and introspection, Husserl pointed to "the disturbing influence which secondary acts of reflection exert upon the phenomenological content of primary acts."[54] He went on to dispute the claim that either inner perception or introspection could furnish a plain and immediate perception of mental acts "as what they are and not as what they are taken to be or interpreted." Husserl insisted that interpretation enters into everything which appears to the mind, whether internally or externally: "I perceive my own psychic phenomena by way of interpretation [*interpretierend*]."[55] Phenomenological reflection cannot be equated with introspection *simpliciter*, for it recognizes levels and structures of perception contained within experience itself but excluded by conventional psychology.

In successive editions of his *Logik*, Wilhelm Wundt tried to manage these predicaments somewhat differently—without undermining psychological science and without recourse to some special mode of mental reflection. Following Kant, he claimed it was "impossible and naïve" to hold that we can "live through" an experience and observe it at the same time; the having and observing of experience are two separate acts that cannot be conducted together, for the very contents one wants to observe are altered or suppressed in self-observation. Like Dilthey, Wundt spoke of an "immanent antinomy" in introspection, but he believed it could be overcome through the aid of other techniques such as experimentation, comparison (with animals, children, pathological cases), memory, attention to "unexpected" and "unintentional" experience, as well as something he termed the "historical-psychological method" which studies "the objectivated productions of human consciousness." This latter method is exceedingly close to Dilthey's hermeneutic understanding, but Wundt insisted that it is not identical with history per se, since it translates historical relations into psychological relations of causality and tries to extract psychological laws. Very much like Dilthey, Wundt in turn came to acknowledge that beyond experimental situations psychology was caught up in logical aporias and circularities; unhappily, its power of illumination seemed to dim in precisely those regions where it was most needed.[56]

It is no coincidence if American readers should find certain similarities between Dilthey's and Wundt's doctrine of immanent antinomies and William James' treatment of the fallibilities of introspection and the "psychologist's fallacy." It has been generally recognized that Dilthey was much in sympathy with James' general approach to experience and mental life. In the "Ideen" he expressly praised James for "the astonishing, realistic power of his capacity for inner perception" and he later proclaimed him a "psychological genius." But apart from Dilthey's superlatives and general commendation of James' descriptive approach to experience, no specific lines of agreement or influence have been established.

Dilthey's papers contain interesting references in this respect, showing that he employed some of James' insights to argue not only against introspection but against psychology itself. James' *Principles of Psychology* had been recommended to Dilthey by Stumpf in a letter of 7 November 1890 as "an excellent work, the best we have, which makes Wundt look sorry by comparison" (*BNL* 140/240–42). Notes written after the "Ideen" show that Dilthey returned to the *Principles* (most probably to rebut Ebbinghaus) and was especially taken by those sections which dealt with the potential pitfalls of introspective analysis. Dilthey adopted the surprising strategem of converting James' diagnosis of a tension in the introspection of feelings into a full-scale, radical antinomy in the standpoint of psychology itself and then replacing it with the hermeneutic understanding of expression:

The antinomy in psychology has been pointed out by James: that one can never grasp a feeling as such in self-observation. Such a feeling is always something very complex and compacted, which can be partially reduced to its parts but not taken whole. However, one can overcome the standpoint of James through the relation of expression and understanding [*BNL* 209/158–60].

Dilthey was referring to the tension running throughout James' treatment of the "stream of thought"—a tension between the dynamic, "transitive" tendency of experience itself and the static, "substantive" tendency of observation, conceptualization, and indeed any verbalization of experience. Like Bergson, James held that "no state once gone can recur and be identical with what it was before"; he concluded that "experience is remoulding us every moment, and our mental reaction on every given thing is really a resultant of our experience of the whole world up to that date."[57] Postulating (or rather discovering) a dynamic "whole of experience," James faulted traditional psychology for finding only discretely definable units commensurate with its own yardstick:

> The definite images of traditional psychology form but the very smallest part of our minds as they actually live. The traditional psychology talks like one who should say a river consists of nothing but pailsful, spoonsful, quartpotsful, barrelsful, and other moulded forms of water. Even were the pails and pots all actually standing in the stream, still between them the free water would continue to flow. It is just this free water of consciousness that psychologists resolutely overlook.[58]

James employed these insights to stress certain failings in psychology which were summarized in his famous statement of the "psychologist's fallacy": "The great snare of the psychologist is the confusion of his own standpoint with that of the mental fact about which he is making a report."[59] With the kind of striking image so characteristic of his thought, James compared the introspective predicament with the effort of turning up a light quickly "to see how the darkness looks."[60] But if he paid heed to the arguments of Comte and others against introspection in particular and psychology in general, James ultimately affirmed that inner observation was invaluable in the scientific study of mind. James found that "introspection is difficult and fallible" but that this difficulty "is simply that of all observation of whatever kind."[61] Thus, for all his critical recognition of the fallacies, fallibilities, and distortions to which psychology is liable, James nowhere discerned an "antinomy" in psychology: one does not ordinarily write a classic work of giant proportions in a field of inquiry in which one has first discovered an insuperable antinomy! Dilthey, in sum, had interpreted certain of James' arguments and caveats in such a manner that they appeared to render psychology more fundamentally problematic than James himself admitted. The greatest psychologist in America was invoked to testify against psychology itself (*BNL* 62/158). Dilthey's reading of James was so obviously slanted in the direction of Dilthey's own concerns that it might best be termed a case of the wavering psychologist's fallacy!

Another thinker writing on the problem of psychology who had a demonstrable influence on Dilthey was the renegade neo-Kantian Wilhelm Schuppe. Dilthey read Schuppe's article "Begriff und Grenzen der Psychologie" after his confrontation with Ebbinghaus, and the Nachlass contains an entire section devoted to it.[62] Schuppe was not as categorical in his rejection of psychology as the Baden neo-Kantians, but he repeated several of their arguments in order to show the intrinsic limits of psychology. Schuppe insisted that the manifold forms of knowledge require other foundational sciences besides psychology. As the "science of individual consciousness," psychology cannot provide the standards of certainty and validity necessary for logical and scientific thinking. Knowledge arises in the individual subject but is not wholly dependent upon it, or referrable to it. As concrete subjects, we do not actually "experience" the necessary relation in an inference. There must be formed in every individual mind a "general world" defined by logical, cognitive, and normative properties which cannot be constituted from individual experience. Thus, there is in addition to the individual consciousness a broader "species consciousness" (*Gattungsbewusstsein*) and most importantly a "consciousness as such" (*Bewusstsein überhaupt*) which is the ultimate ground of thought.[63]

Rejecting psychology as the "prius" of thought, Schuppe argued that psychology presupposes logic, epistemology, and the other "normative sciences" of ethics, aesthetics, and philosophy of law. Knowledge must presuppose a logic and ontology which is distinct from psychology and individual acts of consciousness. "Individuality" is not the ground of knowledge but its consequence, for we do not think the specific qualities of an object but its generic properties. Reversing the "natural attitude," Schuppe claimed that "when I think the color red, I do not mean this or that red object." But when one says "I," what is meant is something concretely specific, that is, not something ideal and generic but "lived" as a specific experience. The "I" as a unity of consciousness can arise only in reflection, not in experience. The "social and objective world" could never arise in the specifically conditioned experiences of individuals. In examining the mind, one must distinguish between what is objectively given and what is subjectively given: "This distinction is clear and unavoidable. If psychology is not the science of the total consciousness and its contents but rather of those which belong to individual consciousness, then the norms of thought and the concepts of objective reality and truth can never be developed from it."[64] Schuppe seemed to reach a predictably orthodox Kantian resolution in affirming that every psychology presupposes a criterion of objective truth and reality defined by logic and epistemology. This objective world is not "given [*gegeben*] in experience" but "given as a task [*aufgegeben*] to thought"—"the goal of a striving"; "Thus psychology is not the fundamental science."[65]

Schuppe, however, took a somewhat more qualified stance than Rickert in allowing what he termed "concessions" to the empirical point of view. Since we cannot get out of our skin—either as persons or philosophers—we must begin with experience, even while we recognize that its basic conditions, objects, and laws cannot be given in experience itself. Psychology cannot by its very nature be the sole foundational science of mind, but it is "still the most important field, in which everything emerges and to which everything refers." Philosophy cannot be reduced to psychological knowledge, but it cannot operate without this knowledge.[66]

Some indication of the impact of the searching critique of psychology being waged after the turn of the century may be drawn from the observations of Wilhelm Wundt. Even the greatest of German psychologists felt thrown on the defensive by the mounting skepticism concerning psychology. In the third edition (1907) of his *Logik*, he insisted that despite its "backwardness" psychology was still "the natural and indispensable foundation of the human sciences."[67] Wundt, however, was led to admit that the practitioners of these sciences were "still far removed from the general recognition of such a foundational science" and added that "only a dwindling minority" still believed psychology could fill this role.[68] Wundt's observation was clearly and quickly borne out in the position of Georg Simmel, who maintained in his *Soziologie* of 1908 that the claim of psychology to be the master science of mental life could not be sustained on either logical or empirical grounds. The complex nature of mental reality demanded approaching it from different standpoints and with different sciences: "The scientific study of mental reality is not necessarily psychology."[69] Dilthey read Simmel's pioneering treatise and defended it on grounds which are more properly treated later; it seems likely that Simmel's critique of psychology aroused further qualms concerning its efficacy as fundamental science.

There is a great deal of ambiguity in Dilthey's treatment of psychology after 1900. On the one hand he insisted that a descriptive psychology would, if properly realized, contain the "necessary preliminary concepts" (*Vorbegriffe*) for the foundation of a valid *Wissenschaftslehre*. But at the same time he found that in psychology "there is no agreement on the most important questions" and that putting psychology at the foundation of knowledge would yield only uncertainty. The theory of knowledge cannot be based upon psychology because "it is in itself a science and as such needs justification. It is impossible to found a theory of knowledge on a not yet legitimated psychology" (*LK* 2–3, 13). Dilthey came to see that psychology exacerbated rather than resolved many of the very shortcomings in traditional epistemology which had impelled him toward psychology in the first place. The problem of knowledge could not be satisfactorily stated, much less confronted, within the framework of psychology: "Thus psychology refers already at its point of inception to the logical-epistemological" (*GS* 7:319). While writing the "Aufbau" studies (1904–6) concerned with the cognition and structure of the "historical world," Dilthey granted a portion of Rickert's point:

> If Rickert were correct in holding that historical thought has no connection with systematic psychology, then the exclusion of the latter from the complex of the human sciences would be justified. One must grant him that it is an open question whether such a psychology can be produced with sufficient certainty [*GS* 1:418].

Five years hence Dilthey was even more dubious, yet kept the door open to a future possibility:

> What can be regarded as certain in psychology is not sufficient to explain the deepest manifestations of the human mind. The foundation of a true content-psychology will have to await the connection of psychological description and analysis with the analysis of historical reality [*GS* 8:15; also *BNL* 243/154–55].

The more he came to stress the specifically intentional-objective and the historical-cultural nature of mental life, the more Dilthey grew wary of the limits of psychology. Two motifs in his later thought which carried him beyond psychology were the new concepts of mental "structure" and of "culturally-mediated experience of life."

The Primacy of Structure in Dilthey's Later Theory of Mind

In the period after his "Ideen," Dilthey increasingly came to stress the notion of "structure" as the defining characteristic of mental life. In a passage preserved in the Nachlass he exclaimed with a sense of discovery: "Structure is everything!" (*BNL* 78/21).[70] Whereas previously the concept of structure had been invested with the quasibiological qualities of a "trope," after 1900 it is recast in terms which resemble closely Husserl's phenomenological intentionality.[71] Structure is the very hallmark of the mental:

> Psychic life is knowable by means of the particular structure. Therein lies the truth of the metaphysical proposition carried over since Plato which sees the difference between the physical and the mental in the coherent

unity of the mental, in which a manifold is integrally related. The mental world is constituted in a uniquely peculiar class of relations which arise originally [*primär*] in the relation between modes of mental acts and their contents [*BNL* 78/50].

Mental structure has no analogies in the natural world and Dilthey specifically warned against any attempt to compare it to the causal relations in nature: "This inner intentional relation is an utterly unique characteristic of mental life" (*BNL* 195/10). At times Dilthey suggested that it is so unique and yet so universally constitutive of our experience as to evade all specific definition: "It can only be experienced and indicated, but not defined." Structure is a unity which cannot be grasped by introspection nor fully expressed in concepts (*GS* 7:16; 9:230; 8:22).[72]

With this proviso, Dilthey nevertheless provided a kind of definition by example. In a portion of the Nachlass he is found to say "I shall now attempt to arrive at a conceptual determination of what is meant by structure." He offers the following example: A man passes a restaurant and decides to eat—this looks simple enough on the surface and could easily be "explained" (*erklärt*) in purely psycho-physiological terms by the elementary "constant" of "need to eat." But the actual mental structure in this situation is not so simple, for it encompasses many different "effectuating coherences" (*Wirkungszusammenhänge*). The seemingly "elementary" need to eat is deeply implicated in a pattern of means, expectations, and memories. The physical need is related to other needs; for example, saving for his family or for the future. Or the need may be conditioned by habit or social convention (it is "time to eat"). This superficially simple experience contains outer perception ("Here is a restaurant"), inner perception ("I am hungry"), judgment ("This restaurant offers food at the right price"), and the positing of values and ends ("Eating here will not strain the budget; there will be funds for Sunday's outing"). Dilthey concludes that all lived experiences are "woven" (*verwebt*) out of many such effectuating coherences which are in turn bound into a structure which cannot be reduced to any isolated psychic datum:

> In structure we are concerned not with a viewpoint under which mental processes are explained but rather with the structural relation among different effectuating coherences. This relation is not identical with the concrete and very complicated mental process in which a certain mental condition passes into another by means of impressions [*Eindrücke*]—rather, it concerns only the inner structural relation among different coherences.

Dilthey went on to specify this viewpoint:

> The state of consciousness which perceives reality, evaluates, and posits

goals contains in itself an order of levels [*Schichten*] in which every mental relation provides a foundation for one built upon it in a particular manner. Here we do not have elements but structure—and the progression through the levels within every mode of relating manifests its own structure. This structure of step-like order can be disclosed only if one looks away [*absieht*] from the shifting conditions which stem from bare impressions and psychic processes and attends to the relations and acts of thought which determine these relations [*BNL* 196/7–9, 22–24].

In other words, the structural viewpoint "looks away" from bare impressions to the contextual framework in which they are constituted as meaning: experience always has reference to a whole situation which must be gradually elucidated. History, as man's *collective experience*, is constituted from similar structural relations, but of a suprapersonal sort.

Dilthey employed the concept of structure to refine his basic notion of lived experience and to mark it off clearly from the formless flow of "pure duration" of Bergson, for whom inner experience is ineffably concrete, indistinct, and without symbolic manifestation. Yet Dilthey did not thereby reach for the timeless, a priori forms of the Kantians:

> The qualitatively determinate reality which constitutes lived experience is structural coherence. To be sure, it flows in time and is experienced as a process—its temporal qualities are apprehended. But what is preserved, so to speak, as a force in the present, even though past in time, receives a peculiar quality of presence [*Präsenz*] through this structure. Although lived experience is a flowing process, it is a dynamic unity—and not only objectively but for our consciousness [*GS* 6:315].

Experience is not simply an indistinct "process" but a productive process with a product: it consists not merely of sensed qualities but of objective contents which are expressed. Bergson's error is to portray mental life as purely self-directed internal flow (*BNL* 197/17–19). The concept of intentional structure carried Dilthey beyond psychology, away from the sheer immanence of psychic process to a mental world whose contents are "partially transcendent" to the immediate awareness of mind, yet which can be reflectively brought to consciousness. The human sciences are concerned with mental contents not "psychological" processes. The *Grundwissenschaft* of the human sciences is concerned with "mind" but not as conceived in conventional psychology.

The basic "unit" of mental life is defined in terms of structure: "Lived experience is first and foremost the structural unity of mental acts and contents. . . . Every lived experience in fact has in it the act of living though and that which constitutes its content [*das was dessen Inhalt ausmacht*]. Thus lived experience cannot be wholly separated from its content—it has objectivity" (*BNL* 208/21–27; cf. *GS* 7:325). If lived experience cannot be divorced from its contents, these contents can nevertheless be analytically isolated from the mental coherence and attitudes in which they arise:

> In every lived experience an intended content is present. "Content" here designates everything which is contained in a comprehensive mental coherence and yet can be separated from it. These contents are immanent in lived experience; they have their being in it. But lived experience also consists in the taking of an attitude toward these contents. Such attitudes may vary independently of the content. I perceive, feel, judge, hate, desire: always there is a "what" [*ein Was*] to which these attitudes relate [*BNL* 78/66].

As experienced, these contents contain an "ideal unity of meaning" which belies all separation of the form and matter of thought (*GS* 1:420; 7:73, 269). These contents, however, must not be construed as Platonic essences existing entirely apart from their experiential acts. Dilthey's concept of structure did not permit the distinction between act and content to be stretched so far as to allow a self-subsisting world of ideal-contents. The contents always exist as "consciousness of-" or "as experience—if this word is taken to mean less the life process itself (*Lebensvorgang*) and more the manner in which it is there for us" (*GS* 7:26).

The role of lived experience remains central to Dilthey's project, but there is a shift in emphasis from the engendering acts to the resultant contents. What is preserved over time by the mind is the deposited content of experience. "The primary insight consists in this: that everything which arises in life, experience, and the empirical sciences is founded in lived experience. But every lived experience is a relation of a mental attitude to a content" (*BNL* 210:233). The contents of experience are structurally related in two dimensions of "depth" and "breadth"; different contents are structured in depth (*Vertiefung*) as stages in the grasping of a single object, or a single content may be related to other objects in a structure of breadth (*Ausbreitung*). The "ideal sum" of these structural relations would be the scientific "concept of the world": "Every science concerns a delimited objectivity [*abgrenzbare Gegenständlichkeit*] in which its unity lies; the coherence of the disciplinary region gives coherence to the propositions in that area" (*GS* 7:127). Dilthey further specified the nature of these contents but left open the question of the ultimate derivation of the acts in which they arise:

> The content can be abstract or concrete. It can have the character of givenness as such, as in a perceived object, or, as in the case of the object of a wish, the character of irreality [*Unwirklichkeit*]. In every case there must be a mental process in which this content arises. And thus we come to the question of how the processes in which the content is produced actually work. Here we find ourselves in the face of an alternative: either

we try to arrive finally at simple processes in which these contents are produced (and thus conclude that there are psychic processes which do not consist in the relation of act to content, but rather act to act) or there must occur in these processes themselves a special "relating to" [*Verhalten*] in which the act is not separated from its object. Here the method of description meets its own limit. Questions arise which at the present time and perhaps forever can only be resolved hypothetically [*BNL* 78/80–81].

After posing the question "Where does the knowledge of the structural coherence come from?" Dilthey added pointedly "The answer self-observation is not sufficient. The knowledge of the structural coherences is a matter separate and distinct from self-observation. These coherences are, as it were, the a priori, to which an objective philosophy must return. And to be sure in the genuine Kantian sense of that which lies at the basis of knowledge" (*BNL* 78/87).

The concept of structure must be distinguished from causal genesis and laws of explanation: "Our investigation is not at all concerned with genetic relations but with relations of structure" (*BNL* 255/28; cf. *GS* 7:16, 44). If lived experience is viewed in terms of its content rather than as a psychic act, then its relation to the ongoing coherence of life is more closely analogous to the meaning-relation of a word in a sentence rather than to an event in a causal succession; these relations must be analyzed contextually not atomistically. Using Husserlian terms, Dilthey drew a sharp distinction between the structural relations which "found" the content of experience and all causal relations which might be adduced to "explain" the relation among acts: "To be founded [*Gegründetsein*] does not mean genetically conditioned. In the structural relation there is always a mode of relating to a content. The relation exists only as such a relating to a content" (*GS* 7:44). Moreover, the mental content constituted by the structures cannot be apprehended directly from within, but must be grasped indirectly through the interpretation of expression:

> The concrete content of these structural relations is not provided in the observation of the self, but rather in the understanding of expression, that is, mental creation. Here lived experience shows a specific and characteristic feature. What it lacks in initial exactness is compensated by the fact that it shows constant repetition [*BNL* 209/158].

The structures of mental life can be ascertained only from its accomplishments (*Leistungen*), but not captured in psychological terminology: "I avoid psychological terms for these accomplishments, since these terms are open to many objections, and instead substitute the *products* of the psychic process such as object, value, norm, and goal" (*BNL* 195/10). Dilthey's emphasis shifts from psychic acts to meaning-contents (or "products"): "We live and move not in a sphere of sensations but of objects presenting themselves to us, not in a sphere of feelings, but of value, meaning, and so on" (*GS* 6:317). The intelligibility of such contents for different subjects is due not to some purported identity of psychic processes or "universal mind" but to common experiential structures: "Structure is the basic form [*Grundform*] of the common consciousness" (*BNL* 191/106). The reflective clarification of structure concerns shared experience in general, not merely the experience of a particular personal subject. Such clarification, Dilthey observes, is an endless task (*GS* 7:19, 32).

Dilthey insisted that full recognition of the role of mental structure would preclude the separation of the "form" and "matter" of experience and thought. Yet at the same time he continued to employ the distinction between the act and the content of experience. While insisting that structure constituted an utterly unique kind of coherence indigenous to mental life, he proceeded to draw it apart or polarize it into acts and contents. At times he stressed the unified result or "product" of mental life; at other times he emphasized its act- or process-like character. He seemed to contradict himself (as he had accused Husserl) by first stipulating that structure is "phenomenologically irreducible," and then portraying it analytically as a relation of constitutive "accomplishments": "The fundamental structure of mental life can be conceived only as a relation of accomplishments [*Leistungen*]." Mental accomplishments are always acts-towards-contents; they are neither self-contained neural events or different mental faculties. Dilthey hammered on the point that the notion of mental accomplishments has nothing whatsoever to do with the older conception of "faculties": "Structure is an immanent-teleological relation of accomplishments. Structure does not at all mean the separation and ordering of mental powers or faculties but rather a relation of mental accomplishments" (*BNL* 78/62–72).

In their spontaneous coherence, such accomplishments produce a mental "attitude" (*Verhaltungsweise*). There are many such attitudes:

> They present themselves to us in a vast multiplicity which cannot be reduced to a specific number. Questioning, opinioning, supposing, asserting, feeling, wishing, desiring, and willing are modifications of the psychic attitude. Between these various modifications there exist affinities of different grades. And, to be sure, in the case of a change in external conditions one such modification can pass over into another.

This "passing over" cannot be conceived as a causal relation, for the attitudes are always related to a content in a special manner:

> The mental attitude is directed to its content, but not in a simple temporal or logical relation. There does not occur, so to speak, different layers of mental conditions running parallel as discretely separate acts and contents; on the contrary, an inner relation exists between both. This inner

relation can be designated as "structure" and thereby clearly differentiated from causal succession, the sequence of psychic components, or the logical relation of ground and consequence. This structure, then, is *sui generis* [BNL 78/49–50].

In another passage he reiterated: "The relations set up in the mind contain vastly more than can be subsumed under the concept of causal law or formal-logical entailment" (BNL 232/82). There are many attitudes, but three "typical" ones: knowing, feeling, and willing. Each is characterized by a different intentional relation of the mind toward the given: knowing—to an object (*Gegenstand*), feeling—to one's own existence (*Eigendasein*), and willing—to a condition yet to be realized (*Verwirklichung*). The concepts used to discriminate these relations cannot explain them, but only convey their function. We cannot speak in any precise sense of a temporal or logical priority in the attitudes of mind, for they are always found operating together as mutually implicated. The results of one attitude become the conditions for the appearance of another:

> The structure in which the three attitudes are bound together designates neither a genetic relationship nor a separation of provinces of psychic life. *It is the unity of psychic life which is decisive.* It is an act of arbitrarily schematic thought to isolate such provinces of psychic life and one should be totally free of this tendency. [emphasis, Dilthey's; BNL 243/133; cf. LK 28].

The relation(s) among the psychic acts which go into "making" a judgment is not the same as the relation judged, nor the relation among judgments. In a rather subtle and tortuous maneuver, Dilthey insisted that the subjective acts of judging are linked to the contents judged in what he termed a "valence-relation" (*Valenzverhältnis*): they can neither be entirely separated, nor entirely identified. Every judgment falls in a valence between the two poles of pure subjective act and pure objective content (BNL 210/164).

To be sure, logical form does not exhaust meaning, nor can there be pure forms of judgment apart from both contents and context. A factual judgment made in actual discourse or investigation does not fall simply under the criterion "true/false" but also under the value judgment "important/unimportant"; likewise a value judgment is not simply "valid/invalid" but contains factual judgments about reality. The forms of judgment are not self-evident but must be subjected to a wider interpretation. A change in logical form (i.e., from factual to value judgment) may indicate a different empirical content or a different object of thought—or it may not. One must constantly insert the judgment in a coherence of mental acts and a coherence of objective contents to see through its logical form to its actual meaning. A mental act can be objectified in such a way as to divest it of its relations to a subject, even though this relation remains "silently implicit" in the judgment. Dilthey instanced the following forms of judgment: (1) "I want to make this biography my life's work"—a judgment of goal or purpose; (2) "This biography should be done"—a judgment of value; (3) "This biography is possible to do"—a judgment of fact. In these different forms of judgment, the immediate quality of willing and evaluating has been changed into a factual judgment by dropping or suppressing the reference to a concrete personal subject; all of them, however, rest upon the same experiential basis (*Wert- und Wirklichkeitserlebnisse*). Logical form is not a sufficient condition of intelligibility; we must take our departure from "reflection on the meaning in language" (*die Besinnung über Sinn in der Sprache*) (*BNL* 191/11–13). This reflection must begin with the recognition that "judgment is never isolated but is always oriented by its relation to a total coherence of thought" (*BNL* 210/164). This coherence encompasses subjective acts and objective contents in a valence relationship. Within this valence we determine whether a judgment is primarily factual, emotive, or evaluative, even though we know in actual meaning that it is rarely exclusive or pure.

Acknowledging a level of meaning (and interpretation) beyond logical form does not vitiate the conditions of objectivity but keeps the "object" in objective judgments: "The judgment intends something objective. This means nothing else than that it brings something given in perception to expression. This is a relation of representation [*Repräsentation*]." Representation is neither a concrete perceptual image (or "picture"), nor pure logical form; it is the "evident" union of content and form brought about by the structures of experience. "The unique nature of the structure of cognitive experience is that of adequate representation in concepts and judgments of something experientially given." This representation is not a mirror image or literal transcription of the primary acts of experience; it is the transformation of the contents of experience into a "second mental world" which, however, is not reducible to pure logical form. Dilthey judged that Husserl had demonstrated conclusively that the mental structure presupposed in all judgments is not reducible to logical form: "In exploring this relation of representation and judgment, Husserl has clearly portrayed the fallaciousness of the theory of Rickert" (*BNL* 225/239–40; cf. *GS* 7:307).

Dilthey came to the view that for the purposes of the human sciences the most fruitful direction in logic lay in the phenomenological description of the structural relations of mental acts and contents read off from the manifold forms of linguistic usage. Such a notion of logic stood opposed to the stringent formalization and "mathematicizing" of logic attempted by Alois Riehl and William Stanley Jevons. Though Dilthey had previously taken up the cause of an analytic logic to replace Kantian transcendentalism, he now felt compelled to distinquish carefully between his own interpretive logic and this variety of strictly formal analytic logic: "The means and results of such an analytical logic, as shown in the example of Jevons, is the elimination of all content—and correlatively the elimination of the grammatical element—from logic itself" (*BNL* 244/238, 244). The dependence of logic upon grammar—indeed of all forms of thought upon the structure of language—was a consistent theme in Dilthey's thought. It stemmed from his training with Trendelenburg and was manifested in his interest in Husserl's project of a pure grammar.

Extending his concept of structure into the sphere of discursive judgments, Dilthey ultimately came to reject both psychologism and transcendentalism in logic. Husserl's notion of a "phenomenology of logical experience" served to mediate precisely these untenable extremes, represented by Benno Erdmann and Rickert. Dilthey was caustic towards both: "Much in Erdmann is descriptive and therefore important; but Erdmann proposes a psychological doctrine of judgment alongside the grammatical and logical approaches—in the end he confuses rather than founds logic" (*BNL* 210/203-4). In extreme contrast to Erdmann's employment of concepts drawn from psychology, Rickert attempted to base logic upon an absolute "value-inherence" (*Wertanhaften*) and "shouldness" (*Sein-sollen*). In Dilthey's view "the justificatory grounds of judgment have nothing to do with such an absolute 'should'" (*BNL* 244/273).

Dilthey clearly distinguished between a judgment (*Urteil*) and an expression (*Ausdruck*): "A judgment is distinguished from the expression of a mental attitude in a sentence by the fact that the coherence of words in a judgment intends an objective, universally valid, and necessary state of affairs" (*BNL* 195/23). But expressions have an intentional object (and not simply an expressing subject) even if they are not judgments.

> And here I link myself to the terms of Husserl, Lipps, and Erdmann in designating everything which is grasped in attention, even mental states, as an object. With such usage we have a term for the cognitive state in which something is grasped in attention. The grasping of such mental objects is knowledge of a special kind. . . . The world of objects constitutes the presupposition of judgment as well as discursive thought. This world of objects is constituted in an objective grasping [*gegenständliches Haben*] which is prior to judgment [*BNL* 195/25].

It is sometimes alleged that Dilthey's theory of mind (and his critique of historical reason as a whole) cannot discriminate between truth and error because it is rooted exclusively in immediate lived experience—that it is not a theory of judgment but a "psychologistic" theory of experience. In fact, however, he addressed himself specifically to the problem of error:

> A judgment is false when it proposes a reality which does not exist. Now every fact of consciousness is as such true. Error therefore first arises

when thought perceives a relation among the facts of consciousness, or a relation of these facts to the self, or to the outer world, which does not correspond to reality [*BNL* 209/67].

There are several classes of delusions (*Täuschungen*) and errors peculiar to lived experience which may be carried into expressions of experience—or predications about experience in the human sciences. Two of the most common are distortions which arise from the arbitrary severing of our lived relations with the world (Dilthey seems to imply that a good deal of philosophy rests on this methodological error) and the warping of our time sense. But the most common delusions concern our own motives, about which we are often deceived. They cannot be determined from within in self-observation but only through others' observations of our manifest conduct (*BNL* 209/60). Our judgments about ourselves, about others, and about human life in general can be validated only through a process of reciprocating interpretation and reflection. Human experience is woven from and into structures which are deeply social and cultural, so that genuine reflection (*Selbstbesinnung*) is not analysis of the mental process but of cultural meaning and content. Rebutting the erroneous identification of reflection and introspection, Dilthey repeated: "Where does our knowledge of structural coherence come from?—the answer self-observation is not sufficient" (*BNL* 78/87).

From Lived Experience to Culturally Mediated Experience

Brought on by changes in his own thinking and the combined criticism of other thinkers, the most pressing problem emerging in Dilthey's later thought was the problem of mediation between the immediate qualitative content of lived experience and the general propositions of science. He refused to concur with Rickert that "knowledge is necessarily something opposed to life"—least of all when this knowledge is about human life and human experience. In place of Rickert's transcendental values Dilthey held fast to experience but transformed it in such a manner as to meet charges of psychologism and intuitionism. After seeing his concept of *Erlebnis* misunderstood as purely inward intuition, subjective feeling, or introspection, Dilthey shifted his theory of mind and re-centered it upon the understanding of expression. Experiential meaning is always mediated though expression and therefore inflected with historical-cultural forms. It is not simply immediate "individual" experience but mediated experience. The "filled self-consciousness" is first and foremost historical and must be approached by a method which takes into account the historical nature of experience itself (*GS* 7:187).

In addition to the relation of structure and content treated above and the relation of expression and culture to be taken up later, two of the most important mediating features which Dilthey introduced in his later thought were the allied notions of "reflected experience of life" (*Lebenserfahrung*) and "life values" (*Lebenswerte*). Taken together these conceptions mark a decisive transformation of the doctrine of *Erlebnis* at the core of his psychology and epistemology. Experience in the broadest sense continues to provide the armature of his thinking, but with the significant difference that personal "psychological" experience has been taken up into cultural, "inter-subjective" experience. These new concepts serve to link the concrete immediacy of *Erlebnis* to the general sphere of meaning and values which the neo-Kantians and Husserl had rightly emphasized but wrongly construed in a transcendental manner.

The shift in Dilthey's concept of experience is, as might be expected, more a dialectical "*Aufhebung*" than a clean break, much less a reversal. He had employed the concept of *Lebenserfahrung* in earlier writings but not with its later, specific meaning, which is distinguished from both *Erlebnis* and *Erleben* (GS 6:55, 170, 185–87). The distinction between these two differing but overlapping kinds of experience is not merely a matter of semantic nuance but of substantive grounds. *Erlebnis* is immediate and unreflected experience, whereas *Lebenserfahrung* is reflected and articulated experience, embodying insights into "life in general" which have been clarified, tested, and evaluated in reference not only to the experience of other persons but also to the past experience of mankind. With the concept of *Lebenserfahrung*, Dilthey introduced a new form of "experiential thought" (*erfahrendes Denken*) which is more compatible with the objective and historical character of his later thought as a whole. From the published writings it appears that this new concept was most fully specified in the period 1907–11, but unpublished sources indicate that Dilthey began elaborating it about five years earlier—and in direct relation to his concepts of "structure," "content," "value," and "meaning." The crucial new idea has scarcely been mentioned in existing scholarship; this omission is particularly serious, since Dilthey's later concept of experience provides the means by which he bridged the sphere of personal existence with the larger realm of culture and "objective mind." It is precisely this "gap" which critics have seen as the weak point in his thinking. [73]

Dilthey explicitly emphasized that *Lebenserfahrung* is *mediated* experience: it is personal *Erlebnis* which has been elevated "through the communal to the universal" (GS 7:141). [74] Such experience is not the "living through" of life in its subjective "mere particularity" but the reflection and articulation of experience in terms of the general, the essential, the meaningful, and the valuable. It arises in a process which Dilthey claims is "equivalent to induction" and it issues in special kind of a general knowledge of man. Through this process *Erlebnis* has been clarified, expressed, interpreted, and brought into relation to shared values and transpersonal criteria: "The coherence of processes through which we explore the values of life and the value of things I call experience of life." Such experience is both reflected and discursive. It is personal experience "raised to reflection and expressed in language." So mediated, Dilthey stresses "it is not immediate but still objective" (*GS* 5:lxii, 374; 7:132–34). This experience takes the form of statements which are not equivalent to strictly scientific propositions, but nonetheless "proven" in a special manner:

> By experience of life I mean these propositions [*Sätze*] which constitute themselves in a collective circle of persons. They are statements about the nature and course of life, judgments about what has proved to be of value, rules of living, and determinations of goals and goods. Their hallmark is that they are creations of a community. And they apply just as much to the life of the individual persons as to the life of the community. As morality, tradition, and public opinion they exercise a decisive power over the individual person. The certainty of this general experience is relatively greater than that of the individual view-point.
>
> The certainty of experience of life is different from that of scientific validity. For the process of generalization at work in such experience is not accomplished methodically in the strict sense of the word and cannot be brought into fixed formulas. But nevertheless the individual viewpoint which adheres to strictly personal life is corrected and refined in general experience of life [*BNL* 144/323–25; cf. *GS* 7:132–34].

These predications about life cannot be calculated or fixed in formulas; rather they assume the character of sayings, imperatives, "lore," and practical wisdom. In sum, *Lebenserfahrung* is characterized by reflection, articulation, repetition, general acknowledgment (within a community or tradition), and its own peculiar forms of method and proof. Can there be any doubt that this new conception of experience represents a significant alteration of the "pure experience" (*reine Erfahrung*) of Dilthey's earlier writings?[75]

The newer notion of "experience of life" does not take the place of the familiar "lived experience" but redefines it in terms of a wider context and deeper historical content. Evidently Dilthey concluded that his original notion of experience was still too subjective and "psychological" to encompass the real content of the mental world. His later view of experience is purged of the residual "brute datum" quality which he detected in Husserl's sense of *"Erlebtsein"* and revised so as to incorporate culturally imparted meaning. Dilthey comes to insist that there is an interpretive "moment" in experience itself, which is not secondary to some purportedly more original, elementary process, but is constitutive of experience as such.

To be experiencing is already a kind of proto-interpretation, for we do not exist *de novo* out of our own immediate subjectivity but rather "live through" life in a vast network of accumulated meanings and life-values. In what might seem a paradoxical or logically circular move, Dilthey suggested that such general experience of life is not only the pre-condition of human understanding, but also its result. Experience of life and understanding are mutually implicated and work together reciprocally to promote ever-higher levels of consciousness:

> *Erlebnis* first becomes *Lebenserfahrung* through the fact that understanding [*Verstehen*] leads beyond the narrow confines of personal experience into the region of the whole and the universal [*GS* 7:143].

It is interesting—and at first sight puzzling—to note that Dilthey elaborated the concept of experience of life in direct relation to the thought of Husserl. In a manuscript entitled "The Standpoint of Husserl and That of the Human Sciences," Dilthey stressed the *telos* leading from immediate experience to general experience:

> As in all knowledge and the ordering of conduct, thought in the human sciences moves forward from the incidental, particular, subjective, and relative in lived experience [*Erlebnisse*] to still yet imperfect and partial generalizations which then are gradually improved. I call this later aspect of experience "experience of life" [*Lebenserfahrung*]. Its objects are the values of life [*Lebenswerte*].

Dilthey proceeded to stress the role of social context in the formation of this kind of experience:

> The shared experiences gained in society make themselves felt as valid. Law and morality, which bring these experiences forth, have as their background concepts of value which are defined out of such experience. Thought and experience are inextricably linked here. This experiential thought [*dies erfahrende Denken*] makes its initial appearance as unmethodical lived experience. But impelled by the disappointments of momentary desire, boundless passion, and the subjective will of the heart, such experiential thought produces ever more refined, adequate, and higher insights into the stable values of life.

An "inner dialectic" transforms immediate experience to reflective experience:

> In reaching its own limits—indeed in falling into an inner dialectic which stems from the lack of stable foundations—such unmethodical lived experience raises itself to methodical experience of life. Its goal is a system of life-values of a generally valid character. These values are immanent in so far as they apply to a condition of the subjective mind. But they are external in so far as they come to us from without, from that which has

a capacity to produce life-values. The most important and deepest experiences of life we constitute in ourselves but always with this reference to without. Every lived experience [*Erlebnis*], insofar as it includes a life-value, is such an experience of life [*Lebenserfahrung*] in the general sense [*BNL* 191/29–30].

This articulated and reflected experience constitutes the common stock of practical knowledge about human existence deposited through time. Introspection and psychology most certainly do not have the means or methods to apprehend this kind of experience of life: it is neither purely personal nor universal, but cultural. It has a certainty and "validity" of its own but not in the sense of scientific judgments. Dilthey stresses that experience of life stems from a kind of continuous reflection but there is no single discernible method by which this reflection proceeds. Nor is there one science, such as psychology, which comprehends it, for it is contained in all the human sciences. The certainty and content of this experience grows as individual points of view are "mutually coordinated" (*gegeneinander ausgeglichen*) in a kind of *Realdialektik* of perspectives (*GS* 7:34, 132, 197).

In his essay "Das Wesen der Philosophie" (1907) Dilthey highlighted the difference between life in the immediate sense and reflective experience of life:

Life is the inner relation of psychic achievements in the coherence of the individual person. Experience of life is the growing consciousness and reflection upon life. Through it the relative, subjective, contingent, and singular in the basic forms of behavior are raised to the level of insight into what is valuable and in keeping with ends [*GS* 5:408–09, also 379].

Such generalized experience is achieved only through the mutual relation and communication among individuals in social existence, whereby personal life is mediated through forms, conventions, and shared values. In many different passages of the later writings, Dilthey reiterated that such experience arises only with reflection and relation to values (*GS* 2:508; 7:79, 143, 201; 8:197).

Experience of life in Dilthey's sense embodies "life-values." These values are made and applied by men: they are not transcendental and a priori. But neither are they personal and subjective, for they have a general validity which extends beyond the personal subject. The historical becoming of the life-values is slower than the becoming of the individual life, and they thus appear to be a priori; they are valid but not "in themselves," that is, apart from lived relations among living subjects. It has been said that Dilthey's value-theory is "subjectivistic" and "psychologistic"—that he acknowledges valid values and precepts within particular spheres of activity but denies objective and unconditioned norms of conduct. This judgment is wide of the mark, for it misses Dilthey's way of mediating between the personal and the absolute. He portrayed life-values as arising from separate coherences of life but went on to stress that their validity was not confined to the original source, whether personal or social: "The characteristic feature of life-values is the coherence of life itself—meaning the linking of attitudes by which an objective content is linked to different subjects" (*BNL* 199/281). The coherence of life is implicitly contained in the value judgment but not intentionally expressed in the judgment. Dilthey employs Husserl to make his point: the subject is "given with" (*mitgegeben*) the value judgment, but its intentional object is what is meant. "Its logical quality derives from its intended object [*das Gemeinte*]" [*BNL* 191/281]. Thus, value judgments assume a meaning and validity which is relatively independent of the psychic acts of judging. A sphere of values arises beyond the specific, individual life-values:

> Beyond the sphere of specific life-values there stretches the region of general values which originate within the coherence of life but which become independent of it. Every value which originates in a life-coherence can be scrutinized to see if it possesses a value [*Eigenwert*] independent of this coherence [*BNL* 199/282–83].

Values are, so to speak, "released" from the circumstances of their origin into an independent valence: "Objective value persists independently of the variability of the valuating subject" (*BNL* 199/165). In contrast to the neo-Kantians, however, Dilthey finds an empirical foundation for this independence. As paradoxical as it may sound, Dilthey insists that we actually *experience* (or "live through") the condition that the value judgment is not merely "subjective" experience:

> This independence is actually experienced and such experience endows the object with a value independent of the valuating subject. We do not have to adopt the notion of a "universal consciousness" of a priori value. For experience itself makes manifest the character of objectivity in the judgment. The term "objectivity" means only the independence of the objective value from the variability of valuating subjects and valuating acts. So a judgment can be pronounced without the restriction of its validity to certain valuating subjects [*BNL* 199/166].

Dilthey clarified the seeming contradiction of "my" experience of objective value independent of "me" by adverting to Husserl's "intentional fulfillment" and Meinong's "realization":

> The judgment predicates a value of an object, not a subject. What is intended in the judgment must be distinguished from a feeling. The value of the object, as posited in the judgment, is not identical with the psychic act of evaluating. The value judgment is not the simple expression of the act of evaluating. It follows from this that the objective value judgment is not founded in the momentary, subjective acts. To such foundation

belongs not just lived experiences as acts but also the fulfillment of what is predicated in the content of the judgment itself. This fulfillment is a process of "realization" [*Realisierung*]. This realization is a broader form of experience which founds the judging acts and to which they are structurally related [*BNL* 199/177–79].

This process of "realization" entails recognition that other persons also make the same predications as I do; through this ongoing reciprocity of recognition there arises a transpersonal, interactive pattern of objective values. In the final analysis Dilthey rejected both transcendentalism and historical relativism in his theory of values:

> History itself realizes values, whose validity arises from the explication of relations contained in life. Such a relation is exemplified in the binding quality of a contract and the worth of every individual as a person. These truths are universally valid [*allgemeingültig*], because they make possible an order of rule [*Regelung*] at every point in the historical world [*BNL* 200/66].

As permeated by such historical values, experience of life is not a passing state of mind or feeling but a settled attitude toward life which has been integrated and adjusted by reflection and interaction with others. It rests not simply upon the "acquired coherence" of the individual personality but upon the acquired coherence of culture—what Dilthey called "objective mind."

Dilthey's "experience of life" is not personal experience but a specification of the concept "experience in general" which he broached first in the "Breslauer Ausarbeitung" (p. 25) and elaborated upon later in his explorations of mental structure. It might be considered "human experience as such" or *Erfahrung überhaupt* in some ways akin to Husserl's paradoxical notion of "transcendental experience." Indeed in a brief passage written after the "Ideen," Dilthey postulated a third form of experience (besides inner and outer experience) which he designated as "transcendental experience" (*GS* 5:247; cf. 7:19). Like inner experience, it is "mental" in character but not subjective in the same sense. His use of "transcendental," however, referred here not to a logical or axiological a priori transcendent to experience but to the synthetic tendency *of* experience, whereby it apprehends reality in integrated accomplishments. The contents of these accomplishments in turn become the foundation of further experience. Dilthey continued to insist that there is no formal a priori in either *Erlebnis* or *Lebenserfahrung* (though it can be argued that he came to a kind of "material a priori" in his conceptions of culture and objective mind). His new categories of experience and value met the objections of the transcendental idealists without surrendering the demand for a consistent *Empirie*.

Under the mutually reinforcing impact of the contemporary critique of psychologism and Hegel's attack upon subjective mind, Dilthey expanded and deepened his concept of experience to include its tendency toward expression, its intentional directedness toward objective content, its saturation with meaning, and its deep implication in sociocultural life-values. The internal transformation of Dilthey's concept of experience provides a perfect case in point of Ernst Troeltsch's cryptic but utterly incisive observation that where philosophers are concerned "there is sure to be a difference between experience and experience."[77]

"Final" Foundations: Hermeneutic Reflection and the Human Sciences

The alteration in Dilthey's concept of experience had wide repercussions for his notion of the foundations and *Grundwissenschaft* of the human sciences. The focus of his thought moved away from the subjective acts of experience to the intersubjective and mediated contents of experience, which are not primarily psychological but cultural and historical. The question arises: Does this kind of experience still fall under the scope of psychology—or any single discipline? Dilthey was not sure—as Hodges notes, he was prey to "conflicting tendencies" and did not provide a precise resolution of this question.[78] In several passages of his later writings he rejected "problematical psychological reasoning" (*problematisches psychologisches Raisonnement*) for the interpretive grasping of meaning in expressions (*GS* 7:284). He insisted upon the understanding of objective meaning-complexes in place of "psychological analysis" (*psychologisches Raffinement*) (*GS* 7:260). This understanding of objective content has little or nothing to do with the postulation, imputation, or discovery of specifically psychological processes. With a touch of self-criticism, Dilthey observed that "it is a common error to put the actual psychic processes or science of psychology in the place of our knowledge of this inner side of man" (*GS* 7:84).

In sum, Dilthey differentiated ever more sharply between interpretive "knowledge of man" and the science of psychology (or scientific knowledge of the psychic process). Our native, yet ongoing and reflective knowledge of life and experience (*Besonnenheit des Lebens, Besonnenheit psychischer Erfahrung*) cannot be equated with the methods and results of psychology. He stipulated emphatically and repeatedly that this knowledge of life is not "intentionally psychological." Therefore it would seem that the organon of the human sciences is no longer psychology but rather this special understanding of life which resists full systematic and theoretical formulation. Dilthey asserted that if such understanding could be raised to the level of theoretical science, it would have to be called "anthropology" or "anthropological reflection" not psychology (*GS* 7:239, 266, 269). But to stress its altogether concrete and variegated perspective, he affirmed that it is "akin to poetry" (*GS* 6:305). The already amorphous term "anthropology" receded even further into the general notions of "understanding of life" and "recognition of man": "Anthropology is always simply the look of the artist into the soul of man, the inducement of artistic configuration, a seeing which discloses individuality, epochs, and nations." Dilthey seemed simultaneously to preclude the possibility of a fundamental science, yet to keep it as a heuristic condition of inquiry:

> The life of the mind is inexhaustible. There is no single science of this inexhaustible thing, which always shows new expanses and infinitudes. There are different attitudes of knowing it. That which would be closest to it is an anthropology which would penetrate into the concrete phenomena of life as it shows itself through the interpretation of mental creations and history [*GS* 7:331].

In most of his later studies Dilthey concluded that such general reflection upon life is not the special province of psychology but rather the implicit basis or ground of all the human sciences:

> Such self-reflection is accomplished by every individual and constantly renews itself in different grades. It is always present and expresses itself in ever-new forms. It is present in the verses of Solon as well as in the reflections of the Stoics, in the meditations of the saints as well as in the life-philosophy of modern times. It alone makes historical insight possible. The power and breadth of one's own life and the energy with which we reflect on it are the foundation of historical vision [*GS* 7:200–201].

The arrangement of the human sciences is not a two-tiered structure with psychology at the base, but rather what Dilthey called a relation of "circulation" and mutual dependence. All the human sciences exist and progress in mutual relation: no single one can be isolated as specifically fundamental. Psychology, like all the others, is simply a facet of "the search for man" (*GS* 7:278, 142–45).[80]

In the final analysis it can be said that Dilthey both mooted and transmuted the problem of a fundamental science for the human sciences. The notion of a critique of historical reason based upon psychology led to fundamental critique of psychology itself: psychology was seen as part of the problem rather than the solution. In developing his own position, Dilthey was led beyond psychology (or in the light of certain statements he was led back "before" psychology). The concept of a distinct fundamental science faltered upon the very condition it was intended to secure: the deeper historical, social, and cultural implication of all mental life and psychic contents. Dilthey insisted that both psychology and epistemology must become historical—but how then can they "ground" history? So reconceived, they tend to be transformed into history itself. They must somehow presuppose and assimilate what they are called upon to validate critically—but they are thereby taken up in what Dilthey called the "circle of thinking." The evolution of his theory of a *Grundwissenschaft* described its own kind of circle or spiral, for in the end he came back to hermeneutic understanding as the key to the human sciences and their critical foundation. In the circle of Dilthey's thinking the notion of a fundamental science becomes a kind of "regulative idea" or *Grenzbegriff*, logically necessary but not fully demonstrable. It is something we must presuppose but cannot fully formulate, for it is so basic that it cannot be altogether elucidated. The *Grundwissenschaft* is itself an essentially interpretive discipline like the individual human sciences but having those sciences for its objects: it is a hermeneutic of the human sciences.

In his quest for an adequate foundation for the human sciences, Dilthey strained so far beyond the bounds of existing psychology and epistemology that one is provoked to ask whether what he had in mind is still a coherent discipline in any sense of the term. He himself was not certain and his terminology reflects this central ambiguity. He retained the older terms "real-psychology," "descriptive psychology," and "anthropology," but also came to speak of "structural psychology," "phenomenology of consciousness," and "comparative anthropology as fundamental science" (for example: *BNL* 191/73). All of these terms were comprehended in what he called "general self-reflection." In a passage entitled "Realpsychologie" in the Nachlass, he isolated the prime mission of the field: "Psychology should portray the processes from which historical relations arise—the relations which are simply life itself. The test of its capacity lies here" (*BNL* 191/98; cf. *ED* 213). Such a "psychology of historical life" seems ambitiously to combine both Husserl's and Hegel's conceptions of phenomenology. Indeed, Dilthey in the Nachlass designated his hoped-for form of fundamental reflection as "phenomenology" and specified his own equivalent of the "phenomenological turn" within the empirical consciousness: "Just as in the realm of logical judgments, so in the whole field of the human sciences, the researcher must accomplish the revolutionary turnabout [*revolutionäre Umwälzung*] which leads from the empirical attitude through reflection to the grasping of the phenomenologically given reality" (*BNL* 225/345; cf. *GS* 7:306).

In a set of notes written in 1904 which are laced with references to Husserl, Dilthey asserted that both conventional psychology and epistemology rest upon a deeper foundation which can only be approached gradually by the method of "description of the contents of consciousness." He explicitly rejected the term "psychological science" for this method, calling it instead "the phenomenology of knowledge, value, and ends." Phenomenological description of contents does not refer to any specific individual person but neither does it find its ground in "universal consciousness *an sich.*" Husserl is praised for having charted the dark region between the untenable extremes of the "pure" individual subject and "pure" universal subject. Dilthey averred that one form of phenomenology had advanced significantly beyond the others: "The phenomenology of knowledge has progressed the furthest, for here the components and relations are easier to differentiate. Here especially I refer to the *Logische Untersuchungen* of Edmund Husserl" (*BNL* 78/66, 75).

But Dilthey's earlier hopes for psychology did not completely turn into disillusionment. The judgment of some older German and more recent American interpreters that Dilthey ultimately rejected psychology *in toto* cannot be sustained.[81] While revising his theory of mind to make it more "hermeneutic" and phenomenological and less dependent upon the science of psychology, he also attempted to transform his descriptive psychology into a structural psychology. As outlined in his last writings this psychology begins with the premise that all mental acts are directed toward a totalizing accomplishment, a "whole" of content. Every experience contains along with immediate perceptual data less palpable structures of memory and anticipation—all linked together in an ongoing coherence of interpretation. In the course of our actual experience an implication of past, present, and future is constantly being realized. This complex structural coherence eludes direct self-observation but can be disclosed through phenomenological reflection and through the interpretive understanding of expressions:

> In an unrestrictive [*unbefangen*] manner we bring experiences which have been fixed through expression into a coherence—a coherence in which the structural relation of those experiences to the coherence of memory, a plan of life, and the totality of life is accomplished.

These structural relations are constitutive of our workaday understanding of life and other persons; they are expressed in conversations, poetry, and what might be called our informal "life-philosophy." The understanding of mental life through its expressions is "more originary and natural" (*älter und natürlicher*) than the procedures of psychological science:

> This procedure is more originary and natural than resorting to psychology. Experience obtains [*erhält*] expression. This expression represents experience in its fullness. It exhibits something new. It takes place without the construction of psychological concepts and does not require them [*GS* 6:317; cf. 7:322 ff.].

In all expressions a structural relation between the condition (*Zustand*) of a subject and an object (*Gegenstand*) is contained and given with the expressed content. These various modes of relation can be grouped and studied according to type, but only by means of expressed meaning: "So, while a stable delineation was not possible from the experiences themselves, that is, as unexpressed, such a determination can be demonstrated through the expressions and objectivations." Dilthey went on to remark that this "indirect procedure which goes by way of the expression" had already been employed "within certain limits" by Brentano and Husserl (GS 6:318). The phenomenological program of a pure description of experience is not possible apart from the cultural embodiments of these experiences, especially in language. This crucial recognition carries Husserl's phenomenology more in the direction of Hegel's notion of phenomenology.

Language enables man not only to transmit experience but to store it, so that this body of knowledge becomes a social-cultural heritage, a kind of heredity of experience which appears "a priori" because it is immemorial to the individual mind. Language is a medium which expresses the contents of experience in what must be considered a general (or at least "common") form in reference to a common world. It is not *my* experience or *your* experience but *our* experience which is expressed. Dilthey held that the forms of language reflect and condition the structures of our intentional "experience-of" and he showed a special interest in Husserl's project of a "pure grammar" to elucidate these general structures of meaning. The stress upon meaning rather than causation has important consequences for a critique of historical reason. As Ernst Cassirer points out, "The rules of semantics, not the laws of nature, are the general principles of historical thought. History is included in the field of hermeneutics, not in that of natural science."[82]

With a spirit of critical caution and distrust of all pretense to "absolute" science, Dilthey expressed guarded hopes concerning the future uses of hermeneutics. In his article of 1900, which inaugurated a revival of philosophical interest in hermeneutics, Dilthey judged that "Taken in relation to the epistemology, logic, and methodology of the human sciences, the theory of interpretation [i.e., hermeneutics] becomes an important link between philosophy and the historical sciences, a major component of the foundation of the human sciences" (GS 5:331; cf. 2:115). A short time later he reaffirmed that "hermeneutics offers a beginning of highest value for the modern foundation of the human sciences." Indeed, in his last writings Dilthey maintained that hermeneutic interpretation is not only the working *method* of the separate human sciences but also the key to providing them with a provisory critical-theoretical *foundation* in lieu of an agreed-upon theory of knowledge: "Thus the foundation of the human sciences is first and foremost interpretation of the concepts which are constitutive of the human world disclosed in the human sciences" (GS 7:309). The method of hermeneutics applies not just to the original expressions and objectivations of life but to the second order scientific concepts *about* those expressions as well. The foundation of the human sciences must take the form of critical exegesis of their major concepts, categories, and methods rather than the form of a single, systematic science.

Regrettably, Dilthey did not specify whether he had in mind two essentially different types of hermeneutic, the first more phenomenological and the second more epistemological and logical in character, but this "valence" distinction seems implicit in his previous comments upon the limits of phenomenological method. He stressed that his own projected hermeneutic of scientific concepts was a provisory stage (and still in its beginnings), but that its replacement (or consummation) in a full-fledged theory of science was nowhere in sight: "The foundation of the human sciences can be nothing other than such an interpretation [of their concepts and procedures], for the general philosophical foundation which posits wider and higher goals has not yet reached any finished form. A generally accepted *Wissenschaftslehre* as a whole does not yet exist" (*GS* 7:310; cf. 1:405; 7:10). A hermeneutic of the sciences must stand in for this as yet unrealized comprehensive theory of knowledge, since there is as much disagreement in epistemology as there had been previously in metaphysics. Dilthey had earlier isolated the crucial factor necessitating a hermeneutic approach to the human sciences rather than a simple systematic *Wissenschaftslehre*: "The object of the human sciences is itself constituted only gradually before the eyes of the developing sciences" (*GS* 1:109; 7:145). A systematically-conceived and completed theory of science would be in danger of not keeping pace with the actual sciences and might block their advance. A hermeneutic approach is best able to comprehend the actual working of the human mind and also the dynamic process of science itself.

It should be obvious that Dilthey's theory of mind and knowledge cut across the frontiers which separated the established and emerging forms of psychology, epistemology, logic, and phenomenology. His developing notion of a *Grundwissenschaft* moved in regions beyond and between these disciplines and cannot be neatly assigned to any of them. This condition accounts for his tendency to combine them (as in linking psychology and anthropology), to coin new terms (as *Realpsychologie* and *Inhaltspsychologie*) to invest rather ordinary terms with new technical meaning (as *Selbstbesinnung*), and to look to new disciplines emerging under older, even ancient names (as "phenomenology of consciousness" and hermeneutics). It must be said that here Dilthey's reach exceeded his grasp; the profusion of terms suggests a confusion of premises—and at a fundamental level. Even more so than in his definition of the human sciences, Dilthey's groping variation in defining their *Grundwissenschaft* derived from his dissatisfaction with the assumptions prevailing in all fields which might claim this fundamental position. As Rickert and Husserl observed, his detestation of all a priorism, dogma, and "Befangenheit" tended to work against the very idea of theoretical foundations. At this level Dilthey was better at suggesting new directions than in following any one of them through to finished conclusions.

One primary feature, however, emerges with unmistakable clarity:

Dilthey was intent upon a fundamental transformation of existing theory of knowledge. Although he was not entirely successful in showing precisely how this new theory of knowledge would synthesize psychology, anthropology, phenomenology, and epistemology into a coherent *Grundwissenschaft*, he nevertheless stipulated that it would not merely provide a complement to existing theory of physical science but would work a change upon all theory of knowledge as such. This feature of his project makes it quite inaccurate to charge him with some kind of ultimate epistemological dualism or with positing a rigid and "final" separation between the natural and human sciences. He never reneged on the judgment of the *Einleitung* that the independence of the human and natural sciences was relative. In his last writings he alluded to the future possibility of a "general theory of knowledge" which would encompass both bodies of science (*GS* 7:119–20, 276–77, 306). If his theory of the human sciences was directed toward more proximate tasks in one region of the spectrum of knowledge, he did not foreclose the future possibility of establishing links or "valences" among these areas of inquiry. In fact, viewed broadly, his whole theory requires just such relations.

For Dilthey no philosophy, no science, and no "foundation" is final, though they can and do attain a relative certainty. Dilthey is perhaps one of the few philosophers in history who took a historical-critical perspective on his own thought as well as that of others. In a complete passage written in 1904 and preserved in the Nachlass, he summarized his position in a form which deserves quotation as a whole, complete with his emphasis:

> There is no presuppositionless philosophy. If the individual makes the Cartesian determination to shake off all presuppositions, this is a fundamental epistemological error. We can encompass and master the developing totality of human intelligence only in a comprehensive historical self-reflection. And only in such reflection can be founded the function, direction, and rules of knowledge. We can only bring to consciousness that which is contained in the *cognitive coherence of humanity*, in which we ourselves are inextricably involved. Such a consciousness, however, does not merely consist in the logical principles and forms of abstract thought, but in the empirical conviction that there are objects and persons—and that these latter contain the relations which yield *valid knowing*.
>
> We must begin then with a type of thinking which directs itself to consciousness and the phenomena which are contained in that consciousness. If we encompass these phenomena in their entire scope, then we see something arising which is of utmost importance to the theory of science: the emergence of a valid empirical science of the human consciousness. This is the fact which constitutes the true center and firm foundation of the sciences.
>
> The foundation of philosophy is not concerned with a mere comparison of consciousness—as consciousness occurs as individual conscious-

ness; it is not *my* consciousness and its individual phenomena which comprise the starting point for epistemology. If I take this starting point and analyze the way in which perception is true, concepts and axioms are necessary, then I cannot from these determinations of how knowledge arises in *my* consciousness make inferences about an independent reality. This was the erroneous way of the English, especially Hume. This great thinker believed himself able to make inferences on the basis of pure facts of individual consciousness. This is a path which leads to no result. Rather, the starting point lies in my consciousness insofar as it contains a coherence of knowledge which is in agreement with *other consciousnesses* perceived by me—a coherence therefore which extends beyond my own consciousness. I say only: the coherence of all knowledge from which all efforts at foundation must proceed stretches beyond the thought of separate persons and contains the inner necessity of a scientific conclusion. This is given in my consciousness—I do not have to transcend my own consciousness to find it—for I find in my consciousness the coherence of an objective knowledge which is the same in every possible consciousness and encompasses all members of humanity: every one thinks with me, every author I read thinks with me.

How this coherence arises—this coherence of the totality of knowledge —that is what we must search for; it offers the basic foundations for a true theory of knowledge. We must get away from looking at the kind of formal logic which takes thought in itself separated from its accomplishment. Such a formal logic is an unfruitful abstraction; all thought consists only in the relation to reality. In all mental activity and judgments—including comparing two works, determining ends, and relating ends to means—in all this there is a relation to reality. At this point I should take note of the presently much-favored emphasis upon *norms* as such, independent of reality, which are supposed to lead a higher life above reality. This emphasis upon norms of thinking, willing, and aesthetic feeling, etc., conceives them as independent of their effect in the subject in which they appear and independent of the objects to which they relate. It is unfruitful to make such a pure theory of values the starting point for knowledge. There is an objective thought which we call knowledge, and knowledge provides its own self-demonstration in the empirical sciences.

But this objective thought [*gegenständliches Denken*] extends much farther than has been previously assumed. Everyone possesses in his consciousness objects, memories of objects, but also images of other persons, images of their speech and of various encounters with them. These persons stand in relation to the individual, who sees the same objects as they do and who communicates with them about this world of objects. And it so happens that all these images which he has of other persons and of their images can be grasped so to speak as conditioned in a perspectival manner but derived from one and the same objective order. There is no perspective without an objective order. This is the fact which is finally the guarantee for the objective and real validity for our knowledge [*BNL* 208/337–45].

At every point understanding opens a world. Transposition
is transformation.
—Dilthey

All understanding is interpretation, be it of the spoken word
or the meaningful phenomenon itself.
—F. A. Trendelenburg

The Theory and Practice of *Verstehen*: Hermeneutic Understanding and History

Conceptual Background

Undoubtedly Dilthey is best known for his controversial doctrine of *Verstehen*. Ever since his theoretical statement and practical employment of this concept, it has occupied a central place in discussions concerning the methods of the humanistic and social scientific disciplines. Although he was by no means the first to employ the concept, he brought it to the forefront of theoretical debate. Through the tangled course of his reflections (as well as in this exposition) the concept was there from the outset, but it received thorough and systematic treatment for the most part in his later studies. Primarily owing to these later formulations, the two concepts of *Verstehen* and the *Geisteswissenschaften* have become so closely intertwined as to be simply identified: they stand or fall together.

Both partisans and detractors frequently assert that *Verstehen* constitutes the sole and exclusive method of the human sciences—and moreover, that it is a method of a radically subjective and mysterious sort akin to an ineffable "art of intuition" or even an "act of faith." With this reading *Verstehen* appears more poetic and aesthetic than conceptual and logical in character. At best it provides "immediacy" but not validity; at worst it becomes subjective fantasy and sheer feeling. If *Verstehen* is conceived in this manner, the specific character of the human sciences as methodical knowledge is called into question or shackled to the bogus notion of an "unmethodical method." The fact that *Verstehen* is often assimilated to the romantic conception of "intellectual intuition" (or to variants such as Bergson's concrete intuition or Croce's "lightning-flash" of historical insight) has seriously distorted the sober examination of this concept. In the vast literature on *Verstehen* the "intuitive" and "divinatory" aspects have been stressed to the exclusion of Dilthey's equally strong emphasis upon methodical rigor, empirical evidence, and general validity. As a result, the lopsided view has arisen that *Verstehen* is not a method at all but rather some neo-idealist *gnosis* best left to telepathists and clairvoyants. It is alleged that such a "method" reduces the human sciences to a ghostly communion of spirits or some sort of social science seance. It is no wonder that *Verstehen* has been called "the murkiest of the many dark corners of German social science."[1]

Dilthey's theory and practice of *Verstehen* were much more "critical," more carefully articulated and qualified, than many second-hand expositions would indicate. It must be said that his notion of understanding is, ironically, one of the most *mis*understood concepts in the theory of knowledge and the sciences. There has probably been more arrant nonsense written on this subject than on any other key concept of modern thought and inquiry. In the face of such pervasive misunderstanding, this chapter seeks to provide a detailed examination of *Verstehen* in Dilthey's specific sense and practice of the term. An accurate treatment of *his* concept of understanding must attend closely to qualifications and stipulations, many of which have been neglected or distorted in its subsequent reception. From the outset it might be noted that many of the most stringent objections brought against *Verstehen* were clearly anticipated by Dilthey himself. If he left some dark corners, he certainly provided more than a methodological "night in which all cows are black."

Dilthey's interpreters have often lost sight of the fact that for him the human sciences are nonetheless sciences for being distinguishable from the natural sciences. His emphasis upon critical rigor and method in the human sciences is all too often obscured in both existentialist-phenomenological and logical-analytic treatments of *Verstehen*. The former school is inclined to invoke *Verstehen* primarily as a "ground of existence" or "way of being," while bracketing the human sciences entirely (or, alternatively, assigning them the role of mere preparation for deeper ontological matters). The latter school is in the habit of regarding *Verstehen* as merely preliminary to full-scale "explanation sketches" (or, alternatively, dismissing it altogether from the company of the sciences). In keeping with his conviction of the convergence of knowledge and life, Dilthey was not inclined to sever the scientific (viz. "epistemological") and existential (viz. "ontological") dimensions of *Verstehen* in order to elaborate one side in isolation. Though his middling position leaves him vulnerable to attack from both sides, it is likely to prove the most fruitful for the human sciences as a whole.

In one of the most salient passages in the whole of his writings, Dilthey isolated what he considered a fundamental characteristic of the growth of knowledge: "Often a method arises in the mind of its discoverer without being accompanied by a full consciousness of its logical character and scope: this consciousness then arises only later" (*GS* 7:126).[2] These words define precisely the situation in which Dilthey found himself in regard to *Verstehen*: As a method it had already been widely and successfully practiced without "full consciousness of its logical character and scope."

Despite the efforts of many predecessors, the practice of human understanding was still without firm theoretical foundation; a method long in use
remained in need of critical justification. Dilthey's entire critique of
historical reason may be said to center upon the philosophical vindication
of *Verstehen*. As will be shown, this vindication proceeded along several
lines which have not been properly traced by his interpreters.

Before undertaking a detailed examination of Dilthey's theory of *Verstehen*, it is necessary to stress that his formulations drew upon and extended
an intellectual heritage which had to a great extent set the terms of
treatment. With remarkable unanimity thinkers such as Vico, Herder,
Baumgarten, Winckelmann, Ast, Humboldt, Goethe, Schleiermacher, and
Droysen all acknowledged a special form of cognition for human and
"mental" phenomena. Thanks to one of Dilthey's most astute followers,
Joachim Wach, this tradition has been thoroughly elucidated.[3] But in the
crucial study "Das hermeneutische System Schleiermachers in der Auseinandersetzung mit der älteren protestantischen Hermeneutik," we have
Dilthey's own specific account of the development of *Verstehen* (*GS*
14/2:597–787. cf. *JD* 87–95). Though more abbreviated than Wach's later
treatment, Dilthey's *Preisschrift* of 1860 on hermeneutics sheds a great deal
of light upon his specific conception of the status and development of
Verstehen prior to the point at which he set about providing it with critical
foundations. In a dual sense, this work provides the proper historical
backdrop for his theoretical treatment of *Verstehen*.

The *Preisschrift* argues in detail that the two interpretive criteria of
scientific rigor (*Wissenschaftlichkeit*) and vital meaning (*Lebendigkeit*) were
the outcome of a long and twisting historical development; the history of
hermeneutics discloses its modern premises in the most palpable manner.
The development of hermeneutics evinced a shift from sacred, classic, or
otherwise privileged texts to human expression in general; not just the
sacred "Word" but "Life" itself was seen to require careful exegesis (*GS*
14/2:724). With the reduction of the distance between sacred and profane
realms since the reformation, a transition was accomplished from special
and dogmatic hermeneutic systems to the idea of a general hermeneutic.
This transition showed intervening stages of "accommodation theory" in
which sacred and profane claims were mingled. The sense of religious awe
and devotion felt toward divine things was gradually transferred to life
itself and the sphere of *Diesseitigkeit*: the secularization of the divine Word
was paralleled by the consecration of the human world and its creations.
Human life emerged as a kind of universal text behind all special texts. The
true mystery and meaning of the world were seen to reside in its immediate
presence, not with an invisible transcendence.[4]

In this process Dilthey focused especially upon the transition from
rationalist and formalist hermeneutic systems, based upon purely gram-

matical or logical treatment of the text, to the psychological-historical hermeneutic first emerging with Schleiermacher. As the "Kant of hermeneutics," Schleiermacher aspired to raise a body of scattered ad hoc precepts and practices to the status of truly critical science; to him belongs the distinction of aligning interpretation theory with the critical theory of knowledge (*GS* 14/2:689). Hermeneutics was recast in the spirit of the transcendental turn, emphasizing the creative powers of human consciousness. For Schleiermacher every expression must be referred to an active generative source in the human mind, not simply to a set of formal rules of composition. The objectivations of mind consist neither of atomistic units nor of imitations of foreordained rules: they are genuine creations unified by an inner form. In such a psychological-historical hermeneutic "the viewpoint under which the work is considered is that of the unity of individuality; its goal is to grasp the whole of the work as an act [*Tat*], genetically in all its parts" (*GS* 14/2:755). Dilthey commended Schleiermacher for providing the closest approximation of a general hermeneutic, even while falling short of the mark. It is significant that Dilthey remained quite critical of specific aspects of Schleiermacher's system.

Ultimately Schleiermacher failed to be truly historical in his hermeneutic. His adherence to Platonic *Ideenlehre* in the form of the doctrine of germinal synthesis (*Keimentschluss*) fostered a view of all human creation as "pre-formation." The "idea" of the work is alleged to be implicit from the beginning of the creative process and all creation is merely the unfolding of this germinal principle. The work comes thereby to be viewed as a self-contained, individual Idea, divested of interaction with its world—it is the reflection of a higher world. The monadic individuality of the author and text is so rigidly circumscribed as to exclude the surrounding context; with such a closed conception of individuality history is sacrificed for internal coherence. Dilthey judged that "Plato-filled" Schleiermacher alternated "without real mediation" between the poles of universality and individuality, unable to envision the concrete development of ideas and actions in a truly historical manner: "The presentation of the historical becoming of human culture is transformed into static and timeless forms. Becoming is viewed *sub specie aeternitatis*" (*GS* 14/2:692). Though Schleiermacher's hermeneutic represented a real advance over previous systems, it was by no means definitive, since it remained tied too closely to idealist assumptions and eternal or sacred forms.

In Dilthey's critique of Schleiermacher, one can discern the lines along which a more adequate hermeneutic should develop. It must combine both the critical-transcendental and empirical-historical standpoints, viewing meaning not in an "ideal" textual isolation but in the concrete context of reciprocal historical relations. Dilthey's earliest systematic treatment of *Verstehen* stipulated that it must eschew the barren alternatives of sheer universality or individuality for a reciprocating mediation. Thus, hermeneutics and dialectics are not opposed but convergent: both seek to facilitate the movement of the mind toward the truth through the reflective grasp of the mind's own concrete creations.[5] Dilthey discerned two levels of interpretation: (1) the "philological," which grasps the literal meaning of a work in a strictly intrinsic sense, and (2) the "historical," which encompasses the wider context of the work and discloses its extrinsic relations to the surrounding milieu. There are thus two directions of understanding, intensive "immersion" (*Vertiefung*) and extensive "comparison" (*Vergleichung*). A truly adequate hermeneutic must coordinate both levels (*JD* 151–53).

In the *Preisschrift* Dilthey stipulated that the science of hermeneutics— "the science of the art of understanding"—concerns that portion of understanding which can pass as true knowledge. By designating Schleiermacher as the "Kant of hermeneutics," Dilthey indicated that a new level of critical consciousness and standard of general validity had been attained for interpretation. Schleiermacher accomplished the breakthrough to a "general hermeneutic" which could go beyond the special interpretive systems hitherto provided for classical and sacred texts. Dilthey's endeavor can in a sense be regarded as an immanent critique and extension of Schleiermacher's program toward a specifically human scientific understanding (*geisteswissenschaftliches Verstehen*). Dilthey reconceived hermeneutics so that it was no longer simply a literary or philological technique for special and sacred texts but rather the fundamental science of all methodical interpretation. In this form it undergirds his critique of historical reason—as well as his entire conception of human *Selbstbesinnung*—and has assumed a very prominent position in many departments of modern thought.[6]

Verstehen and Its Modes

For Dilthey, *Verstehen* is both an ordinary or "natural" (i.e., unreflected) form of human awareness and a method of inquiry in the human sciences. The former sense of the term could be designated "ordinary understanding" (Dilthey sometimes calls it *Menschenkenntnis*, a kind of knowledge by familiar acquaintance). The latter sense of "methodical understanding" is the province of the human sciences. These sciences accomplish the transition from a largely tacit *Kenntnis* to a methodical *Erkenntnis* (*GS* 5:437).[7] These two senses of understanding—the more commonplace and the more technical—can be distinguished but not entirely divorced. Perhaps more clearly than any other facet of his thinking, Dilthey's theory of *Verstehen* shows the continuity and reciprocal influence of *Leben* and *Wissenschaft*. Human understanding is not fully resolvable into logical, methodological, psychological, epistemological, or ontological prescriptions: it may be approached from all these vantage points but cannot be assigned exclusively to any one of them. Schleiermacher had seen that hermeneutics straddles the traditional divisions and schemas of knowledge. It is related to logic, rhetoric, dialectic, philology, and psychology—but not reducible to any single discipline. Therefore, *Verstehen* seems especially elusive and intractable because it cuts across the very differentiation of philosophical areas which have largely set the terms for the definition of knowledge.

Especially after his confrontation with the Baden neo-Kantians Dilthey repeatedly stressed that the human sciences do not simply deal with a special object, that is, human life as distinct from nature, but that they employ a special method or "attitude" (*Verhaltung*) toward that object (*GS* 7:84, 118). Method and object, however, condition each other reciprocally and can be separated in analysis only with the proviso that they operate in synthesis. Understanding is not an act without a content, nor a result without a process of arriving there. *Verstehen* is a "natural" or practical attitude in life which, by means of critical controls and refinements, becomes the method of the human sciences. But this condition poses special difficulties for a theoretical critique of historical reason. For the sake of direct experiential clarity (though not necessarily for purposes of logical analysis), Dilthey often expressed the difference between the human and natural sciences by drawing a sharp distinction between understanding and explanation: "We explain nature, we understand mind" (*GS* 5:144). Referring more specifically to the mental attitudes pertinent to each body of sciences, he observed: "We explain through purely intellectual processes, but we understand through the cooperation of all our mental powers" (*GS* 5:172). *Verstehen* is knowledge of the inner mental life of man, whereas *Erklären* is knowledge of the laws of the causal order of natural phenomena. We understand only man, his actions, and his works: "In the whole circle of things it is only man who is comprehensible [*verständlich*] to man; everything else we understand by way of an analogy" (*JD* 141).

Understanding is an ongoing approximative process: it has no absolute beginning or final end: "We understand life only in a constant process of approaching"—therefore "all understanding remains always relative and can never be fully completed" (*GS* 7:236; 5:330). But if understanding is necessarily relative, it is not simply a medley of perceptions or perspectives, for it shows a progressive refinement toward general validity. Dilthey specifically reserved the term "interpretation" for the "disciplined elevation of understanding to general validity" (*GS* 7:265). The critical theory of such methodical interpretation is hermeneutics—and it is thus inseparably linked to general validity.

Its task is to furnish, in opposition to the continual threats of romantic arbitrariness and skeptical subjectivism to the field of history, a theoretical vindication of the universal validity of interpretation, upon which all certainty in history depends [*GS* 5:331].

To stress both its exacting and yet provisional qualities, Dilthey referred to such methodical interpretation as "an intellectual process of the highest difficulty, which can never be completely realized" (*GS* 7:227).

Dilthey insisted that the human sciences are preeminently hermeneutic in character: they interpret objectified meanings within a coherence of contexts. But this is not to say that they have a single and exclusive method: *Verstehen* is carried out as a scale of accomplishments within different coherences of meaning (*GS* 5:319). *Verstehen*, like all forms of human awareness, shows different "grades" and "valences"—and, as shall be shown below, at certain points Dilthey judges it to be, at some levels at least, convergent with *Erklären*. It is an error to collapse the different levels and contexts of understanding into a single, invariant procedure. As a young scholar weary of the hegemonial claims of idealists and positivists, Dilthey observed that the assertion of one true method was "petty scholasticism" (*JD* 178).[8]

Dilthey called attention to the ubiquity of *Verstehen* and the interpretive situation: understanding reaches across a range of meanings from the stammering of a child to *Hamlet* and the *Critique of Pure Reason* (*GS* 5:318). Life itself—as we live through it—is a constant pattern of interpretive efforts at many different levels. Following Humboldt and Schleiermacher, Dilthey distinguished between the elementary and higher levels of understanding. Elementary understanding arises in practical situations and functions "in the interests of practical life" (*GS* 7:207). Most often we do not notice it as a conscious process or method, as it requires no great deliberative or reflective effort. Elementary understanding concerns itself with the meaning of simple signs and expressions in an immediate and largely conventional context of reference. Here we must make certain "inferences" in order to understand, but these patterns are so familiar as generally to transpire unawares. (Thus, a workman at a construction project raising his hammer ordinarily signifies certain aims; we do not have to "reconstruct" in conscious inference the whole situation to understand that "construction is going on.") The higher forms of understanding build upon the elementary forms but are distinguished by the degree of complexity, the scope of their coherence of meaning, and the "inner distance" between the sign and its ultimate significance. Higher understanding places the manifestation in wider contexts of meaning and entails more general and often more remote patterns of signification. (What does the "type" of the hammer swing signify about the workman? What will this construction project do to the neighborhood? Etc.) Higher understanding is the province of the human sciences. The expression (or patterns of expression) here refer to wider segments of experience and therefore permit inductions to an entire coherence of life. These higher inductions are more encompassing and more "significant," yet often less determinate, than those of elementary understanding.

The ordinary attitude of elementary *Verstehen* is implicit in the standpoint of life; we orient ourselves to others and to situations by means of a largely tacit process of interpretation. The notion of *Verstehen* is difficult to bring to light not because it is so mysterious, but because it is so commonplace and familiar. *Verstehen* is so fundamental to our way of being that it is constantly presupposed and hence goes unnoticed and unrecognized. It illustrates Hegel's maxim that "The familiar is not known, precisely because it is familiar." Normally we are unaware of everyday understanding: it is as "natural" and unobtrusive as the air we breathe and we notice this kind of understanding more in its absence than its presence. Such understanding is implicitly and "silently" at work in the perception of every human situation and human manifestation.

We can understand without a theory of understanding. As it occurs normally in the practical exigencies and familiar coherences of life, understanding is pre-theoretical. We have this native understanding not because we reflect upon it or engage in formal systematic inquiry but simply because we are human beings in human situations. In day-to-day living we practice an informal kind of understanding which is neither deliberately methodical nor assigned to critical proof. Our common experience of life is replete with myriad acts of understanding: "Knowledge is there [in *Verstehen*]; it is bound up unreflectively [*ohne Besinnen*] with experience" (*GS* 7:18). We are thoroughly at home in this world of familiarly understood meanings: "Every square planted with trees, every construction in which seats are arranged is understandable from childhood on, because human purpose, order, and valuation as a whole have assigned every object in the room its place" (*GS* 7:208). Understanding and experience are not separate but reciprocally related. Only by a process of theoretical abstraction can the specific results of understanding be disengaged from the process of experiencing. *Verstehen* is thus largely tacit but it is the very opposite of esoteric or private. On the contrary, it is so pervasive and commonplace as to lack the definite limits which would make it specifiable by contrast. *Verstehen* is not a mystical or abstruse process reserved to adepts, for it is "exoteric" to human existence itself. Thus, Dilthey can assert that the interpretation of a drama by a sensitive but untutored person may show as much depth and adequacy as the most erudite scholarly analysis. Most of the objects of the human sciences are "understood before they are known"; we are aware of them as meaning something, though this meaning may not be held in distinct consciousness. Following Wilhelm von Humboldt, Dilthey defined understanding as the "knowledge of that which is already known"; it is both direct cognition and reflective *recognition* (*GS* 1:109, 120).

In his restless effort to give a concise but comprehensive theoretical statement to a concept which by its very nature is very resistant to such treatment, Dilthey provided a profuse variety of definitions, specifications, and analogies. As with the definition of the *Geisteswissenschaften* as a whole, Dilthey was never fully satisfied with definitions of *Verstehen* and he reminded his readers that all such attempts were "rough and schematic" or "schematic and symbolic" (*GS* 5:277; 7:213). The characterization cited most often designated *Verstehen* as "the re-discovery [*Wiederfinden*] of the I in the Thou" (*GS* 7:191). Originally coined by Wilhelm von Humboldt, this formulation reflected the humanistic premises of idealism concerning the ultimate community of all persons. The community of human subjects engenders a special cognitive relation which cannot be resolved into the dichotomous subject-object model of conventional epistemology—though of course there is an "object" for *Verstehen* as for *Verstand*: "Here [in *Verstehen*] the subject of knowledge is one with its object and is repeated at all levels of objectivation" (*GS* 7:191).

Objectivation, or expression, is crucial to understanding, for without it there would be nothing to understand. "We term 'understanding' the process in which we come to knowledge of mental life through expressions given to the senses" (*GS* 7:82). Expression includes nonverbal forms such as action and gesture, but Dilthey was especially concerned with expression in language: "Only in language does mental life find its fullest and most exhaustive expression, one that permits an objective comprehension" (*GS* 7:217). Such understanding must of course begin with sense-perception but it moves "naturally" from outer sign to inner meaning. We understand an expression not as a sheer physical datum or analytic minimum but as a sign or symbol of something mental. The expression is "resubjectified" into the life-forces (*Lebenskräfte*) and life-coherences (*Lebenszusammenhänge*) which gave rise to it. *Verstehen* is thus knowledge of the acts, contents, and conditions of mind (*Geist*: both individual mind and what Dilthey came to call "objective mind"); it is "the extraction [*Herausholen*] of the mental from the different expressions of life" (*GS* 7:131). There is thus a crucial difference between objectivity in the human sciences and objectivity in the natural sciences: "If the mind places itself over against its own creations as something merely objectively empirical and analyzes them according to the external natural scientific method, then there occurs a self-alienation of mind in regard to its own creations" (*GS* 6:126). *Verstehen* accomplishes the "re-translation [*Zurückübersetzung*] of the expression back into the mental life from which it issued" (*GS* 5:265). This mental life, however, is not pure disembodied consciousness in the manner of the transcendental idealists, but rather the "working content" of the mind in concrete situations.

Verstehen is the ordinary mode of the empirical consciousness (or standpoint of life), but Dilthey also links it to his own special version of the transcendental standpoint. Paradoxically, *Verstehen* embodies a "natural" transcendental turn in which the mind moves spontaneously from the physical manifestation to the mental life which produced it and the mental content to which it refers. For Dilthey, human understanding stands in a special relation to "making." Like Vico, he assigned a privileged status to knowledge of what is made by man. We know the mental world of human meanings in an especially intimate way because we have in a sense produced it. The conditions of historical knowledge are rooted in the conditions of historical life, that is, carried out through active involvement and "lived" participation in common patterns of existence:

> We are first of all historical beings before we are inquirers into history, and it is only because we are the former that we become the latter. . . . The first important factor for the solution of the problem of historical knowledge is revealed: the primary condition for the possibility of historical knowledge lies in the fact that I am a historical being, that one who studies history is the same one who makes history [*GS* 7:278].

In a formula reminiscent of Vico's famous *verum et factum convertuntur*, Dilthey maintained that "only what the mind has made does it fully understand" (*GS* 7:148).[9] Cognition and creation are here integrally related. Indeed, the artist's work is paradigmatic for all formative activity (including lived experience and understanding), for our original involvement in experiencing the world is "artistic" and transformative. *Verstehen* is implicitly transcendental, but this transcendental aspect pertains not to pure ideal forms of thought but rather to relations in life itself, shared by living subjects.

To convey the nature of understanding, Dilthey employed terms such as "transposition," "projection," and "resubjectification," which connote a process of empathic identification. The German terms (*Gleichsetzen, Sich-hineinversetzen, Sich-übertragen*) suggest the adoption of the life-position or world-view of another and seem to presuppose that complete identification with another subject or total situation is possible. The accent is upon concrete immediacy. Indeed, Dilthey often referred to *Verstehen* in terms which suggest virtual re-enactment of mental processes: "We understand only that which we allow to happen over again (*nachgeschehen-lassen*) in ourselves" (*ED* 45; *GS* 9:258). Understanding is a "reconstruction" (*Nachkonstruktion, Nachbildung*) of mental life. In certain passages Dilthey implied that *Verstehen* is sheer empathy or "love," as conveyed in Goethe's maxim that "one only understands what one loves": "We understand a man only in feeling with him, reliving his impulses in ourselves; we understand only through love." Thus, understanding is "dependent upon the degree of sympathy— we do not understand completely unsympathetic persons" (*GS* 6:74; 5:277).[10] As vivid and "sensible" as these attempted definitions may be, they are also highly problematic, as Dilthey himself was well aware.

By its very nature, *Verstehen* proves exceedingly resistant to purely logical analysis. It cannot be reduced to univocal logical rules and forms: "In all understanding there is something irrational, even as life itself is irrational; it cannot be represented by any formulae of purely logical functions" (*GS* 7:218; also 5:319). Understanding thus retains something mysterious and divinatory about it. Dilthey acknowledge it to be "a mysterious matter . . . something like an *Urphänomen*" (*GS* 5:277). But this is not to say that it is essentially mystical or irrational, but rather that it cannot be fully rendered into logical rules; here as elsewhere in Dilthey's thought we are confronted with a question of degree. *Verstehen* is by no means illogical or a-logical simply because it cannot be completely resolved into logical form. Dilthey himself provided the rudiments of such a logical analysis in his unpublished notes on "the logical problem of hermeneutics": "Expressed in our current logical terminology, the logical side of *Verstehen* consists in the cooperation of induction, the application of general truths to the particular case, and comparative procedure." He went on to add that "the immediate task would be the precise determination of the special forms which these logical operations and their connections assume in *Verstehen*" (*GS* 5:330; see also 7:174).[11] An important aspect of the analysis of *Verstehen* concerns not simply the determination of psychic structure but also linguistic structure, that is, "theory of language, specifically grammar" (*GS* 5:335). A broadly conceived theory of *Verstehen* must recognize that both our ordinary awareness of life and our scientific knowledge contain an element of "symbolization" and symbolic meaning which, contrary to positivist presumptions, can never be eliminated (*GS* 7:213). Indeed, Dilthey observed: "in a certain sense all knowledge, like all poetry, is only symbolic" (*JD* 147).

Human understanding is not pure *ratio*, for it embodies all the capacities of mind operating together. From a phenomenological standpoint, *Verstehen* quite literally "makes sense," but from a strictly logical standpoint it seems riddled with circularities and aporias. *Verstehen* shows neither an absolute beginning nor ending; it is neither purely inductive nor deductive but both at once, for it involves a to-and-fro movement from part to whole and back to part again. There are no simple "elements" or indubitable starting points in the comprehension of the human-historical world. Any particular act of understanding depends upon a vast fund of prior understanding. Interpretation in the human sciences proceeds by means of a complex of previous acts of understanding which remain in the twilight of consciousness and past experience: "Here we know and understand immediately in order to know in the strict sense" (*GS* 1:109). *Verstehen* is thus a complex of experiential and cognitive content which paradoxically is both possessed from the start and augmented in the process of understanding itself: the object is understood in a tacit sense before it is known in the fullest sense.

Dilthey asserted that "we always understand more than we know" (*GS*

1:119–20). This initially puzzling statement suggests that the mind has a kind of global and primordial "sense" of its world which it brings to explicit consciousness. What the mind grasps through this primary understanding the sciences raise to knowledge by means of analysis, clarification, comparison, and verification. But the methodical procedures of the sciences are dependent upon this original "sense" of the world and must constantly return to it. Knowledge as *Verstand* will never exhaust this primordial understanding: "The formal knowledge which is operative in the sciences will never wholly master the lived experience which is present to the whole mind in immediate knowledge" (*GS* 1:131).[12]

As he probed more deeply into *Verstehen*, Dilthey came to emphasize not only its different levels but also its inevitably circular character. The circularity which is an offense to logic is quite functional to understanding. The "hermeneutic circle" pertaining to all interpretation is irresolvable in theory, but in practice it proves to be a productive rather than vicious circle. A considerable portion of Dilthey's later reflections was devoted to the problem of this interpretive circle, which had been designated by Schleiermacher, Lotze, and Sigwart. Knowledge in the human sciences appears to involve a procedure which is logically circular: generalizations can be formed only by abstracting from the data those traits and relations which belong together. But this procedure presupposes a prior notion or criterion of what we are looking for. Selection, abstraction, conceptualization, comparison, and classification all demand an initial criterion of judgment; thus, it is impossible to be purely inductive or descriptive in method, for thought always demands such a prior determination.

> Description, which is based on observation, demands the construction of concepts; the concept and its definition presupposes a classification of the phenomena; if this classification is to be an orderly totality, if the concepts are to express the essence of the facts which they represent— then they presuppose a knowledge of the whole. There arises a circle here. At base, it is an artistic process in which the power, the universality, and the objective character of the intuitions determine the value of the results [*GS* 11:258].

For example, Dilthey points out that in writing a history of philosophy "it appears that one has already to know what philosophy is, if one begins with the formation of the concept on the basis of the single facts" (*GS* 5:343). Every description and analysis depends upon an anticipatory determination of what the thing is. Yet actual empirical investigation works back to revise the original conception. Thus, interpretation begins with a provisional or "shiftable" hypothesis (*verschiebbarer Richtpunkt*) and a constant shuttling process takes place between this initial predetermination and the results of closer investigation. All interpretation entails an anticipatory measure or idea (*Massstab*) which functions as a heuristic guide for the selection of traits, definition, classification, and comparison. This preliminary standard conditions the procedure and results of the inquiry, but it is not fixed and "a priori" in the conventional sense, for Dilthey insists that it is modifiable; we use it and modify it at the same time (*GS* 8:99).

The interpretive circle could be easily resolved by assuming with the neo-Kantians that our general concepts derive from fixed a priori norms, ideas, or essences. But the actual course of knowledge shows no such mental skyhooks and we are thrown back upon the fact that all knowledge (except mathematics) appears to move in a circle and thus contains a certain degree of "Alogie": "This circle pertains to all human thought" (*GS* 8:160–61; 7:179). There is no Archimedean point or presuppositionless beginning in understanding, but only this continual shuttling movement of elucidation.[13]

Although an avowed foe of fixed a priori notions, and a staunch advocate of *Empirie*, Dilthey nevertheless came to emphasize what can be considered a certain a priori aspect in all interpretation. His a priori, however, concerns "silent" and "shiftable" meaning-relations in the contents of experience, not pure forms of reason: our immediate understanding from the standpoint of life functions as the precondition of our methodical scientific knowledge. In this regard Dilthey repeated Humboldt's observation that "in order to understand, we must already in some sense have understood" (*GS* 5:336).[14] This prior, native understanding, which remains silent and unnoticed, is the foundation of further understanding. It remains the presupposition of the more methodical cognition of the human sciences and can be elucidated in reflection (*Selbstbesinnung*), but it can never be fully formalized in a specific discipline. Dilthey's later writings contain indications of a new attitude toward the role of the a priori, as reflected in language and the ideal content of all acts of signification (*GS* 7:262; 14/1:435).

At first sight Dilthey's exposition of *Verstehen* seems to entail the precedence (or "a priority") of self-awareness and immediate self-understanding, for he claims "We understand only by means of transposition" (*GS* 1:318). Or more pointedly, "We have lived experience firsthand only in ourselves; into the interior of other individuals we penetrate only with the light of analogy" (*GS* 5:67). In the "Ideen," Dilthey went so far as to assert that "experiencing oneself and the reconstructive understanding of another are alike in the core of their processes" (*GS* 5:276). Numerous passages portray *Verstehen* as similar to an inference by analogy (*GS* 5:110, 277; 7:207; 8:82). Thus, a schematic rendering of the understanding process would go as follows: I perceive an objectivation; I have lived through (and "know" by inner awareness) situations in which such an objectivation was produced; I infer by analogy that a similar lived-experience must lie behind this objectivation; I reconstruct or reexperience such an experience and therefore understand it. If we understand others solely or primarily by means of analogy with ourselves in the literal sense of projection and transposition, then *Verstehen* would seem to entail a prior knowledge of ourselves; we understand others to the extent that we re-live or recognize experiences in them which we ourselves have already undergone. But it is obvious that such procedure rests upon a circular *petitio principii* which precludes what it is trying to demonstrate, for it reduces *Verstehen* to a barren identity: we understand in others only what we first understand in ourselves. If other minds are known to us in the same way as our own, we do not encounter the other, only ourselves, for we have to be already what we want to know in the other. By invoking analogy the interpretive circle is reduced to a sort of solipsistic vanishing point.

After pursuing this tangled issue, Raymond Aron has maintained that Dilthey gave up his "banal" theory of analogy in his later writings.[15] Although there is some basis for this claim, a close reading of the earlier writings shows that Dilthey's treatment of analogy was from the outset more reciprocal and "dialogical" than his critics have admitted. It would seem that his use of the term "analogy" was itself only a "rough and schematic" analogy and that later critics have erred in taking it too literally.[16]

Before the *Einleitung*, Dilthey had stipulated that our experience of others is as original as our own self-awareness; consciousness of self and consciousness of other are coeval and inseparable. "The most important and central perception, that of the 'I' . . . exists only by virtue of the notion of the 'Thou'" (*BA* 211). It is a travesty of Dilthey's position to bend it back on itself, as if he claimed that we experience and understand only our "inner" selves. Overturning the reflexive, "bridge-building" tendencies of epistemology since Descartes, he insisted "We posit a self only in positing a world and the most important access to its formation lies in the representation of another self [*ein fremdes Selbst*]" (*BA* 211). Even immediate self-awareness rests upon shared and interactive experience. The fully developed notion of *Lebenserfahrung* betokens precisely this state of affairs.

After the "Ideen," the tentative analogy-model of *Verstehen* was qualified even further: neither logical nor analogical schemas proved sufficient to elucidate our actual understanding. Dilthey's increasing emphasis upon the specific attributes of expression and objectivation tended to erode the theory of analogy, so that in his final formulations Dilthey seems to have gone around "full-circle and a half" to arrive at a new position: He claimed that in the proper and strict sense of *Verstehen* we do not really understand ourselves. "We have experience of ourselves, but we do not understand ourselves" because understanding necessarily refers to an otherness embodied in an objectivation (*GS* 7:225; also 86, 220). Considered as sheer immanence, our inner experience would be "*selbstverständ-*

lich" and lacking the requisite quality of objectivated otherness. Ultimately Dilthey suspended the question of logical or temporal priority: "The basic relation [*Grundverhältnis*] of experience and understanding is one of reciprocal determination. This relation specifies itself further as one of gradual elucidation." Experience and understanding exist only in a *Doppelverhältnis* (*GS* 7:145, 86). It is quite beside the point to object that the analogical model of *Verstehen* is reflexive or solipsistic, since Dilthey insists that an individual's experience is in fact constituted in constant interaction with others. *Nacherleben*, like *Erleben*, is experience of the world and self together, not self alone, and one misconstrues his theory by resolving it into a form of introspection or sheer inner feeling. Dilthey did not contend that *Verstehen* is a "doubling of egos" nor did he maintain, as some critics would have it, that understanding history is simply a matter of private awareness, analogous to experiencing a toothache!

The further Dilthey departed from the inadequate analogy model of *Verstehen*, the more it was portrayed as a graduated series of idealizing accomplishments. Without surrendering his stress upon reexperiencing, Dilthey's later analysis of *Verstehen* emphasized its ideal-logical component and thus accommodated the objections against subjectivism and psychologism. Though understanding constantly draws upon the lode of actual experience, it proceeds by way of ideal representations. To the subjective, experiential side of *Verstehen*, Dilthey added a new stress upon objective content as distinct from psychic acts (*GS* 5:335; 6:304). Discerning a "reversal from historicity to logicity in the theory of propositional acts," Paul Ricoeur has perceptively attributed this departure to the influence of Husserl:

> After 1900 Dilthey himself made the utmost effort to introduce into his theory of meaning the kind of ideality which he found in Husserl's *Logical Investigations*. In Dilthey's late works, the inner connection [*Zusammenhang*] which gives to a text, to a work of art, to a document, its capacity to be understood by another and to be fixed by writing is something similar to the ideality which Frege and Husserl recognized as the meaning of a proposition. If this comparison holds, then the act of *Verstehen* is less *geschichtlich* and more *logisch* than the famous article of 1900 "Die Entstehung der Hermeneutik" had claimed it was. The whole theory of *Geisteswissenschaften* was affected by this important shift.[17]

Though Ricoeur's use of "reversal" seems somewhat drastic, he is perfectly correct in pointing to a shift in "valence" from mental acts to mental contents. Dilthey offered a cogent example of the function of such ideal content in an ongoing process of interpretation: When we interpret a debate, we must constantly ascertain from what standpoint and interests a debater grasps the intentional object of the debate. We judge the debater's performance constantly in relation to this object (*diesem Gegenstand gegenüber*), not in relation to any particular experience of the debate itself. This intentional object is ideal in Husserl and Meinong's sense (*GS* 7:226).[18]

The ideal objects and ideal meaning structures contain and represent experience, yet are "partially transcendent" to it (*GS* 7:87 ff.). Thus my actual experience of the law does not exhaust the meaning of the law as a general object of understanding; nor could the sum of such actual experiences encompass this meaning. Our experience is always referential to an ideal content which is the distilled whole (*Inbegriff*) of real and possible experience. The comprehension of such contents derives from experience but cannot be reduced to any particular experience. Thus, there are objects of understanding which strictly speaking are not found in direct experience.

Understanding properly belongs to the content not the specific mental acts of others. Although the term "reexperiencing" suggests an actual reenactment of processes, one can understand a mental content without sharing in it oneself. Even before reading Husserl, Dilthey had distinguished between interpretive reconstruction and such enactment:

> There is a reconstruction [*Nachbildung*] of the feeling and willing processes of others which is to be distinguished from actual experiencing just as sharply as the mental representation [*Vorstellung*] is from the perception [*Wahrnehmung*] [*GS* 6:134].

Husserl underscored the same point: "It is undeniable that the wish of another can be understood exactly and grasped experientially [*urteilend nacherlebt*] by someone who does not share the wish itself."[19]

In elucidating *Verstehen*, Dilthey was confronted with an extremely knotty problem for which traditional logical and epistemological conceptions were inadequate. The analogy model proved deficient—it was itself merely a rough analogy. A similar difficulty pertained to the definition of understanding as "reexperiencing" and here, too, Dilthey responded by introducing important qualifications. Frequently Dilthey implied that *Verstehen* accomplishes an actual repetition or reproduction of the mental process or mental life going on in the mind(s) manifest in expression. Certain passages define a very immediate, almost identical, relation between the original productive process and the subsequent act of understanding:

> Understanding is in itself an operation inverse to the productive process itself. A perfect sharing of life depends upon the condition that our understanding shall move forward in the line of history itself. Advancing continually, it moves on with the course of life itself. Thus, the process of transposition is ever-widened. To relive is to create along the line of history. So we move forward with the course of time [*GS* 7:214].

By itself this passage suggests that Dilthey held a crude transcription or correspondence theory of knowledge founded upon an utterly uncritical realism. Rickert, in fact, accused him of holding precisely this position. Though he sought to counter the excessive formalism of the Kantians with a strong dose of realism, Dilthey was far from holding that *Verstehen* entailed the total recapitulation of another's mental life. Other passages make clear that *Verstehen* cannot furnish a "copy" of the whole of mental reality. Dilthey's stress upon individuality and the passage of time would make such a complete identity impossible. Hence Dilthey argued that interpretive understanding does not aspire to a full copy (*Abbild*) of the mental world but rather a structural representation (*Repräsentation*) or constitution (*Aufbau*). The intelligible pattern to be understood is not the original temporal order as lived; the interpreter does not grasp every experiential detail but rather a set of relations formed into an "ideal order" (*GS* 7:255). The grasping of this order begins with reexperiencing (which for Dilthey is already a structure), but proceeds through different levels of conceptual representation. The greater the scope of our understanding, the more it is emancipated from the original sequence of events, and the less it resembles a replication of what went on in another mind.[20]

Reflecting its background in *Idealrealismus*, Dilthey's theory of understanding took its position between the uncritical realism implied by immediate reexperiencing and the critical idealism of the neo-Kantians. Rickert and his followers accused Dilthey of erroneously identifying understanding and experiencing, thereby divesting cognition of any logical criteria and ideal forms; in their view Dilthey's theory inevitably gravitated toward "psychologistic empiricism." Genuine understanding for them concerned ideal cultural contents, not "dumb" factual experience, for just as experience requires categorical formation to qualify as knowledge, so understanding depends upon the presupposition of a priori cultural values. On the basis of Rickert's argument, Dilthey's conception of understanding as reexperiencing has often been distorted (and then dismissed) by misplaced literalism and nominalism. His later concept of experience would indicate that reexperiencing does not mean that the interpreter literally reenacts the psychic processes transpiring in another's mind. In the first place, experience is phenomenologically "there for me" as a "what" of structured *content*, not as psychological acts. From the standpoint of life we live in a sphere of meaningful contents; thus, *Verstehen* might be better termed a "re-contentment" of these contents than a reenactment of psychic processes. Understanding is of something "inner" but this inner cannot be construed as psychological processes going on in the mind of the originator. The crucial phenomenological distinction between mental acts and contents establishes a kind of objective referent to mental life, so that one can say one understands the meaning of another's wish without thereby wishing along with him. Thus, Dilthey insists, we can understand Wallenstein's actions without wishing to carry them out ourselves; the content understood is not the same as the act of understanding.

By neglecting this distinction between act and content, critics of *Verstehen* have construed it as an implausible "vibration" or "imitation" theory based upon literal recapitulation of acts. Thus it is widely but erroneously maintained that Dilthey restricted understanding to the subjective acts which compose the expression, thereby reducing its meaning-content to psychological processes. The grasping of meaning becomes *seelische Identifikation* or *Gleichsetzen* of interpreting subject with expressing subject. Dilthey is alleged to have confused the meaning which is understood with the psychic process of expressing (or the process of understanding) and thereby falls into "psychologism" and the genetic fallacy.[21] In a Nachlass entry Dilthey seemed to anticipate precisely such a specious rendering of his concept. Specifically contrasting his own position with Theodor Lipps' *Einfühlung* and Karl Groos' *innere Nachahmung*, Dilthey stated:

> The distinguishing marks of the process of understanding are: (1) that it does not contain merely formal relations but the content of that which is [*was in sich ist*]; (2) that it is accomplished by means of the totality of the mind's powers; (3) that it does not separate inductive and deductive procedures—nor does it separate the particular and the general—but rather it represents a kind of subjectivation within the experiential limits of the general [*ein Subjectieren in erfahrenen Grenzen des Allgemeinen*] [*BNL* 137:88].

In spite of his efforts at clarification, it is still widely contended that Dilthey's *Verstehen* either presupposes or aspires to some sort of concrete identity of feelings, that is, an interpersonal sympathy (or empathy) which has nothing to do with logic, concepts, judgment, or any patterns of generalization whatever. Rickert accused Dilthey of reducing the faculty of judgment to mere "intuitive feeling" and this charge has dogged *Verstehen* ever since. Yet even before Rickert's critique, Dilthey emphatically rejected the view that *Verstehen* was simply a matter of sheer empathy or feeling. He never subscribed to Yorck's view that "historical reality is a reality of feeling" and he remained decidedly cool to earlier romantic and later Bergsonian conceptions of intuition, insisting that one could legitimately speak of an intuitive apprehension of a phenomenon only on the condition of the mind's protracted and studious occupation with the object (*BDY* 113).[22] The *Preisschrift* of 1860 stipulated that true *Verstehen* is by no means simply a matter of emotional projection or the reconstruction of a subjective state of mind (*Gemütsstimmung*). The attempt to base interpretation solely upon intuition was deplored as "aesthetical mysticism" and "enthusiast obscurity" (*GS* 14/2:650–58; *BDY* 146). Though Dilthey insisted that the human sciences stand in close proximity to art, he expressly denied that they could be subsumed under the category of art. After Theodor Lipps had popularized the concept of empathy (*Einfühlung*) through his aesthetics, Dilthey insisted that *Verstehen* must not be confused with empathy or sheer affect (*GS* 7:125). In the Nachlass Dilthey sometimes referred to understanding as "intuition" but of a very special sort which "always and everywhere proceeds from the interrelation of personal experience (*Erleben*), general experience of life (*Lebenserfahrung*) and an understanding of the objectivations of life" (*BNL* 196:327).

Most expositions of *Verstehen* dwell upon its so-called "intuitive" or "divinatory" aspect and neglect Dilthey's repeated insistence that human scientific understanding must be represented in valid concepts and judgments. Knowledge in the human sciences is grounded in everyday experience and understanding, but it involves a great deal more: "The content secured from experience and understanding is then represented in concepts and judgments. These latter are founded in experience and understanding. Thus arises a complex of knowledge [*Gefüge des Wissens*] in which experience, understanding, and their representations are mutually connected" (*GS* 7:331; also 3, 280). Dilthey leaves no doubt that the tacit "sense of life" embodied in everyday understanding is the beginning but not the end for the methodical understanding of the human sciences. He expressed full agreement with Wilhelm Wundt's insistence that analysis and abstraction are essential to all interpretive understanding—a point which he himself emphasized in the *Einleitung* and later Aufbau studies (*BNL* 137/189; *GS* 1:94; 4:251). "The order of concepts in which these lived experiences are brought to knowledge arises only with the work of the mind in producing a second mental world, which is founded in the first but created only by means of the understanding, judgment, and conceptual thought that belong to the mind" (*GS* 7:307). *Verstehen* in the human sciences, like our primary awareness of life, entails a hierarchy of accomplishments in which each level furnishes material for the next and for the work of other researchers:

> The human sciences are concerned with objective knowledge of their object. All researchers are united in this striving; their work combines in this tendency. The human sciences establish facts; in the light of the full meaning of these facts, the human sciences seek to reexperience in understanding [*verstehend nachzuerleben*]; they grasp [*erfassen*] the coherence in this happening; they analyze [*analysieren*] it; they separate [*sondern*] on the basis of this analysis by means of abstraction [*Abstraktion*] the systems of partial contents and bring them to conceptual knowledge [*begriffliche Erkenntnis*]. From this analysis there originate new means of grasping more deeply what has happened [*GS* 7:313].

All understanding in the human sciences must combine reexperiencing with intellectual conceptualization: "The task of the human sciences is to relive the manifestations of life and to grasp them intellectually [*denkend zu erfassen*]." There is a constant reciprocity of reexperiencing and representation in conceptual formulations:

> The human sciences show the constant reciprocal interaction of lived experience and the concept. These concepts find their fulfillment in the reliving of the individual and collective structural coherences, while on the other hand immediate reliving itself is raised to scientific knowledge by means of the general forms of thought. If both functions of the inquiring mind are brought to correspondence [*Deckung*], then we grasp the essential in human development [*GS* 5:340–41].

This concept formation entails selection at every stage of inquiry: "When an account is made of a historical process, this always takes place by means of a selection from what is handed down in the sources, and this is always conditioned by an assessment of the value of the facts" (*GS* 7:5). Selected traits and relations are grouped around a "type" or "ideal case" which represents those relations in an "ideal order" of coherent presentation (*GS* 7:188, 255).

In his treatment of conceptual representation, Dilthey made it clear that the order and function of the expression in the original *generative* coherence of life is not the same as the order of the representation in the *cognitive* coherence of the interpreter. The latter is selective, abstractive, analytic, and synthetic. It examines the mental content or meaning of expressions in a variety of contexts of which the expressing subject may have been unaware. The system of interpretive knowledge is not identical to the coherence of acts, thoughts, and experiences which it is "about"; it is an ideal-order, or "second world" which furnishes a new perspective upon the given content. The experiential reference for the procedures of the human sciences is given in ordinary life, but their concepts and results are reached by complex intellectual operations. (Dilthey's position is quite similar to that of Husserl, who insisted that representation does not take place in a "single flash" but always in a partial and step-wise fashion toward the ideal unity of the "given" and the "represented.")[23]

Dilthey insisted that understanding both employs and produces "representations of the mental world in general concepts" (*GS* 7:145). Yet perhaps because he did not treat these representations at length in any one portion of his published works, critics have lost sight of this stipulation and reduced *Verstehen* to a nonconceptual intuition or "feeling." The Nachlass provides more extensive and concentrated analysis which should serve as a corrective. In unpublished notes, Dilthey emphasized that understanding must make use of forms of conceptual representation which go beyond the perceptual grasping of the particular. There is a scale of such representations proceeding from the sheer perceptual datum to the most general concepts. Dilthey calls for a "logic of representation" to examine the cognitive validity of each level and of transitions from level to level. "With concepts and judgments we enter the sphere of discursive thought. The process of objective grasping must take place in words, which are the representation of a prior perceptual representation." This new "re-representation" is not simply immediate intuition: "The relation of the subject and predicate in the judgment—or relation of *characteristica* in concepts— belongs to a sphere which is separate from that of the perceptual grasp of particulars. And yet in continuity from this initial perception up through the highest stage of abstract knowledge, there is a progressive system of ever-higher forms of representation" (*BNL* 142/324; cf. *GS* 7:44). This progressive system culminates in "ideal forms" and "ideal subjects" such as states, religions, organizations, and concepts like "the romantic temperament"; but unlike pure intellectual constructs, these ideal subjects are "representations in which the original significant empirical contents and traits are preserved and highlighted." In support of his position Dilthey adduced Husserl's notion of "adequate evidence":

> In every representation there must be an accompanying consciousness of evidence, which shows that the representation is founded in acts which bring the given content to adequate expression. The initial consciousness of givenness as such is transformed into a consciousness of adequate representation [*BNL* 142/326].

Thus *Verstehen* proceeds by way of psychic acts but operates with representations of mental content, not psychological acts. Understanding does not remain at the level of the particulars (*Einzelheiten*) but proceeds toward higher levels of generalized representation. Each level is related to the next higher by a relation of "founding" (*Fundiertsein*). The concepts and judgments of the human sciences must be adequate to the content of original experience. The interpretive judgments of the human sciences show a peculiar relation of "foundedness":

> Every judgment expresses directly or indirectly, that is, through possibly many intermediate steps, the givenness of a state of affairs or a relation to an objective reality. But one must be on guard against the tendency to take the judgment in isolation and instead see it in the many relations which constitute it. My statements about Juno or Zeus express something given in the objective reality of Greek mythology: they have a relation to an object. This same relation to a particular object is found in all systematic thought.

Dilthey concluded that this process of conceptual representation can move to ever-higher levels of abstraction, but must always refer back to a structure of experience (*BNL* 142/327–28; also 22/281; 243/84).

The process of representation in the human sciences is something quite unique (*eigenartig*), like intentionality in lived experience. It cannot be construed simply as a logical, causal, or temporal relation. Employing Husserl against the neo-Kantians, Dilthey asserted that it is not an imitation or transcription:

> The relation of representation to what is represented is an intentional one, established in the process of knowing; it is not a relation of imitation [*Abbilden*], but is unique to this sphere of cognitive operations. A judgment is true insofar as correct perceptions are brought to representation in valid intellectual judgments. Then the judgment is the objective expression of perceptual content [*BNL* 78/36–37].

There are different orders or "grades" of meaning and understanding—and different ways of representing these contents: "From experience a direct line of representation leads to the order of concepts in which it is grasped intellectually" (*GS* 7:139).

One form of representation to which Dilthey devoted considerable attention is the type (*der Typ*): it is a key concept linking his later notion of experiential structure to his typology of world-views. Both everyday understanding and the human sciences operate with such types. Following Goethe, Dilthey held that we tend to see the world in terms of types as composite organizing images of our experience. We do not see discrete particulars or bits and snatches of sense data, but relative "wholes" or types; the type is not superadded as a construct of thought, for typification operates in concrete experience.[24] The human sciences refine these everyday types and provide them with greater exactness, certainty, and fruitfulness. Even when the historian is dealing with a single individual, he does so in terms of a type, which must be constantly controlled, adjusted, and broadened:

> A type of human nature always stands between the historian and the sources which he wants to bring to life. And likewise such a type stands between the political thinker and the reality of society, whose rules of development are sought. Science intends only to give validity and fruitfulness to subjective type. Science aspires to provide general propositions, whose subjects are the individual phenomenon and whose predicates are all judgments fruitful for the understanding of history and society [*GS* 1:32].

The type characterizes but it does not determine in the sense of a physical law; it represents a "convergence of traits" rather than a necessary sequence of events (*GS* 1:51; 5:279–82). The type does not conform to the neo-Kantian distinction between nomothetic *Gesetz* and idiographic *Gebild*; Dilthey insists that it assumes a function "between that of law and that of the ideal" (*GS* 8:73; 5:cvii).[25] Thus, the type embodies a teleological aspect which organizes and "fills out" experience. Unlike Max Weber's ideal types and Husserl's essences, Dilthey's conception of types was primarily as empirical representations rather than ideal forms, yet he acknowledged an implicitly idealizing element in all types which is very close to Husserl's notion of the "ideating abstraction" operative in experience. In a paradoxical formulation Dilthey referred to the type as "a way to overcome experience by means of experience, so that it is felt more intensely than in the truest copy of reality" (*GS* 6:172). The type is neither purely logical nor aesthetic; it informs the humblest of everyday experiences, but is most clearly manifest in artistic creation:

> Artistic creation produces types which raise and intensify [*steigern*] the manifold of experiences to an image and thus represent it. Thus, the opaque and mixed experiences of life are made comprehensible [*verständlich*] in their meaning through the powerful and clear structure of the typical. That which is elevated and connected in the type, what is seen to be necessary to the coherence of life from the vantagepoint of the life of the creator—that we can call the essential [*das Wesenhafte*].[26]

We recognize these types because they assemble and intensify the largely tacit meaning contained in experience. After Dilthey had sketched out his doctrine of types, Graf Yorck hailed it as "the key which opens the subtlest and most difficult of locks" (*BDY* 191). Dilthey's specific typology of world-views remains to be treated separately—here it is important to stress the central role of the type in his general theory of understanding. Because they retain the meaning-content of experience even at the highest level of abstraction, historical concepts are not purely intellectual constructs or laws but types (*GS* 7:188).

Dilthey always advocated comparative methods to expand and complement an "inside" understanding of a phenomenon. In contrast to the Historical School's concern for individuality and uniqueness—which was reinforced logically by the neo-Kantian stress upon idiographic method—Dilthey continued the less conspicuous strand of German thought which demanded comparative treatment. He insisted that the human sciences "can never do without a comparative treatment in relation to the individual" (*GS* 7:226; also *BNL* 17:68). This demand brought the disapproval of Yorck, whose radically immanent theory of knowledge militated against all forms of what he termed *Mediatisieren*—including generalizing, explanatory, and comparative methods. For Yorck, true understanding proceeded solely by way of a concrete intuition of the unique phenomenon, free of any abstractive and generalizing conceptual constructions (*BDY* 101, 256). The critical objections which are usually brought against *Verstehen* apply more properly to Yorck's version than to Dilthey's, in which "depth" (*Vertiefung*) is coupled with "breadth" (*Vergleichung*).

Verstehen in the human sciences entails general knowledge at every stage of its operations—even when focusing upon individual persons. If understanding presupposes general knowledge, it also aims at general knowledge. Against the Baden School Dilthey argued:

One misconceives totally the interest which the inquiring mind brings to the historical world when one sees the formation of concepts in this realm only as an auxiliary device employed in order to reproduce and represent the singular as it is in itself. Beyond all reproduction and stylization of the factual and singular, thought strives to arrive at knowledge of the essential and necessary: it strives to understand the structural coherence of the individual and social life. We only gain control over social life to the extent that we grasp and employ regularity and coherence [*Regelmässigkeit und Zusammenhang*]. The logical form in which such regularities are expressed are propositions whose subjects are general, just as their predicates [*GS* 5:341–42].

In a note captioned "Rickert and the Logical Problem of History" Dilthey insisted:

History seeks true *and* general propositions. "General" of course has different meanings. The totality of the historical process per se is of course not general. But insofar as its very determination and comprehension depends upon the knowledge of general traits, this totality contains a general knowledge within it.

Dilthey concluded by taking the side of the sociologist Ferdinand Tönnies against Rickert in arguing that general concepts are not merely the means but also the ends of historical inquiry (*BNL* 242/453; also 459).

Verstehen in the human sciences, then, depends upon abstraction, conceptualization, and representation. What is understood by reexperiencing must be represented in conceptual thought. We cannot have the whole phenomenon through some privileged intuition: "We penetrate into history from different sides through analysis and abstraction" (*GS* 4:251). While ordinary understanding may proceed at the nondiscursive level, understanding in the human sciences is defined by a hierarchical scale of intellectual operations directed toward valid representation (*allgemeingültige Repräsentation*). Employing the Husserlian term, Dilthey avowed that the totality of these representations would ideally constitute the scientific concept of the world (*Weltbegriff*). But while these concepts derive from intellectual operations and function in an ideal order, Dilthey stresses that they are derivatives (*Abkömmlinge*) of experience, not pure a priori essences of some ghostly transcendental subject: "So the fullness of experience reverberates in even the most abstract propositions of this body of science" (*GS* 7:145; also 127).

It is only by regarding *Verstehen* as a scale of accomplishments that one can begin to comprehend Dilthey's critique of historical reason. He insisted the "levels of methodical certainty in understanding are dependent upon the development of general truths through which this process secures its foundation" (*GS* 7:142). The object of the human sciences is not simply the unique individual, as constituted by the idiographic method of the neo-Kantians, nor is it strictly causal laws, or absolute values. For Dilthey, it is precisely the interrelation between individual and general which constitutes the human-historical world and is therefore the hallmark of *Verstehen*. There can be no strict separation between the singular and the general, for both appear in reciprocal dependence (*GS* 7:152). The individual always and as such presents itself within a more general reference:

> Life-expressions are in reality something general; we infer from them insofar as we subordinate them to a type of gesture, or action, or to a circle of linguistic usage. In the inference from particular to particular, there is present a relation to something general which is represented in each case [*GS* 7:219].

The understanding of an individual person or phenomenon is possible only on the basis of general knowledge: "The human sciences do not attempt a copy of the singular . . . Every one of their cognitions depends upon general concepts" (*GS* 7:316). Meaning in the human-historical world is constituted in various coherences of purpose, effectuation, and causation (*Zweck-, Wirkungs-, Kausalzusammenhänge*). Individual objectivations, as well as persons and sequences of behavior, have reference to several coherences at once and cannot be resolved into a single coherence. Dilthey provided an enlightening example from his own lived experience:

> When a scholar writes a book, this process may be a link in the sequence of truths which make up a science; at the same time it is the crucial link in an economic process which culminates in the preparation and sale of copies of the work; it also has a legal aspect, as fulfillment of a contract, and it may be an element in the professional functions of the scholar as laid down by the administrative system. Thus the writing of every letter of this work is an element in all these systems [*GS* 1:49–50].

Meaning is thus multiform and polyvalent. *Verstehen* does not grasp The Meaning as some inward essence or quality but as a pattern of relations. Dilthey instanced the effort to understand Bismarck: We have a fund of documents and records which refer to Bismarck—but only through the general coherences (*Zusammenhänge*) which integrate the person Bismarck into wider categories such as Prussian noble and landholder, Christian, father, European statesman, and ultimately mankind itself. Bismarck is, to be sure, an individual (and his inmost personality is irreducible), but he is also a point of intersection for numerous coherences such as family, state, religion, legal system, class, generation, and culture, which define his role as historical agent (*GS* 7:316). To understand Bismarck, we must have general knowledge of these historical coherences, which in distinction to actual persons, Dilthey calls "ideal subjects."

History is "life," but not simply the individual life writ large, for it encompasses patterns and structures which are not identical or isomorphic with lived experience or the relations in individual life. The understanding of history is grounded in lived experience but is by no means accomplished through some fanciful "historical introspection." Dilthey insisted that historical knowledge required the employment of an extensive set of specifically historical concepts and ideal-subjects such as social organizations, cultural systems, and epochs. The individual life of the concrete subject participates in these ideal-subjects but is not congruent with them. The cultural systems and forms of life do not arise from different sides of human nature but are "specifically historical constellations [*Gebilde*]" showing diversity and development through time (*BNL* 137/85). Every historical epoch develops a "life-horizon" within which personal existence and the collective patterns of social life adapt mutually. The epoch shows a "self-centering" (*Selbstzentrieren*) in which separate spheres of activity— economic, political, legal, religious, artistic, and cognitive—come into a particular constellation, sometimes loosely called *Zeitgeist* (*GS* 7:170ff). Dilthey used the concept of *Zeitgeist* in a carefully qualified sense, and cautioned specifically against its misuse (*GS* 14/2:666). It is not an "ideal cause" or even a univocal concept but a pattern of tendencies and responses: "It is not a unity which could be expressed in a fundamental thought, but rather a coherence among tendencies of life which establishes itself in the course of historical life" (*GS* 7:185). Thus, there is no single "idea" of the Enlightenment such as reason, critique, or progress, but a structural coherence which includes countertendencies as well. History is neither sheer flux nor a strict causal sequence, but a structure of overlapping coherences. These coherences make history intelligible:

> Whereas we can find no law of development in the concrete course of things happening, the analysis of it into single, homogeneous coherences opens the view into a sequence of conditions—determined from within and each presupposing the other, so that higher levels are built upon lower levels and in such a way as to lead to increasing differentiation and integration [*GS* 7:169].

There are causal factors in each coherence, but as a "relative whole" it cannot be subsumed under strictly causal laws. Such coherences "produce" (*erwirken*) and "condition" (*bestimmen*), they do not "cause" in the physical sense: "An effectuating coherence differs from a causal connection in producing values and realizing ends according to the structure of mental life" (*GS* 7:153). Though we cannot speak of "laws" of history, we can speak of patterns and structures:

The apparent meaning of history must first of all be sought in that which is constantly present, constantly recurring in structural relations, in the effectuating coherences, in the formation of values and ends, in the inner order in which these are related—from the structure of the single life to the ultimate embracing unity: that is the meaning which history has at all time and everywhere—resting upon the structure of the single life and manifest in the structure of the complex coherences of the ob- jectivations of life. This regular structure has conditioned development up until now and will condition the future [*GS* 7:172].

In treating Dilthey's conception of meaning in history it is necessary to recall that for him mental activity and experience are defined as a pattern of relations and transactions, not some inner, self-contained essence. When we grasp meaning, we trace our way through a complex of relations rather than inserting ourselves into some interior core of the "soul" as a noumenal datum. *Verstehen* for Dilthey remains the elucidation of functional and structural relations rather than an intuition of essences—whether in the fashion of Schleiermacher or Husserl. The human sciences trace these relations through multiple coherences and systems of interaction. Therefore the only meaning available to them is structure or coherence, not a purely internal aspect or "state of being." "We understand only coherence. Coherence and understanding correspond to one another" (*GS* 7:257).

Excursus: *Verstehen* in Practice in the *Leben Schleiermachers*

Dilthey's historiography was not only consistent with his theory of understanding but in a real sense provides its best demonstration and proof. It is perhaps a measure of their success that his histories cannot be easily dissected into tidy components: the attempt to unravel them reinforces his observation that human understanding is a complex "weave" of operations and that structure in the historical world (and in historiography) is more readily experienced than defined and analyzed. Of the many sustained applications of Dilthey's method of historical understanding the *Leben Schleiermachers* deserves first place, both conceptually and chronolog- ically. This work became the model for much of his later historiography and the original lode for his theory of history and the human sciences—and in a way which literally bears out his dictum that "theory follows *praxis*." His later studies of Leibniz, Frederick the Great, and Hegel were to follow much the same pattern as the Schleiermacher volume. At least in a virtual sense it contains all the fundamental categories of Dilthey's theory of the human sciences such as lived experience, type, world-view, acquired coherence of personality, generation, social organization, cultural system, and others.

The work was based upon extensive research in many kinds of sources: published writings, letters, diaries, notes, book lists, journals, novels, poems, liturgies, sermons, scientific treatises, and newspapers. Not all the sources are literary or specifically "textual" in nature: Dilthey employed figures for population growth, marriage rates, budgets, and enrollments in presenting conditions in the towns, courts, and universities. Altogether Dilthey's understanding of Schleiermacher and his age rested on a great deal more than "congenial intuition" or "inward speculation." From the premise that "the center of biography, as in life itself, lies in the relation of the individual to the whole [*Gesamtheit*] in which he develops and upon which he acts in turn," Dilthey aimed for an "approximative, objective understanding [*annährend objektiv verstehen*]" (*GS* 13/1:xxxiii; 13/2:261).

Dilthey's method might be schematically, if clumsily described as one of "ex- and concentric circulation," that is, moving through different but overlapping contexts of Schleiermacher's life from a shifting center. The narrative is constructed around the multiple coherences of this life, ranging from immediate and lasting (such as his family) through the more transitory and partial (such as student clubs at Halle and the *salon* culture at Berlin) to the most general and inclusive sort (the Enlightenment and Romantic movements). Each context is described and analyzed, then translated into a typified "life-attitude" or set of "life-stances" (though Dilthey is careful to admit qualifications and divergences). These different orbits provide focus, but are not permitted to function as self-enclosed and exclusive constructs, since Dilthey dwells upon their points of intersection. Throughout the work these different contexts are integrated with Schleiermacher's life by means of direct citations from his writings. Dilthey's narrative strategy thus embodies the reciprocating interpretive directions of "immersion" (*Vertiefung*) and "extension" (*Verbreitung*) defined in his hermeneutic study of 1860. Although it would be impossible to trace out all the coherences in the work, selected major ones can be highlighted.

The first coherence is Schleiermacher's family, which is traced back two generations along both paternal and maternal lines. Along with direct personal descriptions, Dilthey provides an account of the beliefs and practices peculiar to the brand of pietistic Reformed Protestantism to which the family adhered. Besides such "spiritual" concerns, however, Dilthey attends to aspects of Schleiermacher's "Naturell," notably his poor health and crippled side which necessitated special care. Without interjecting any explicit theory of personality, Dilthey quite plausibly suggests that Schleiermacher's later notions of religious dependence and community owe something to this early experience of vulnerability.

The next coherence is constituted from his early education at the hands of the Herrnhuter Brethren at Niesky and Barby. A stern religious code instilled a deep desire for grace and inner piety, but at the cost of stifling curiosity and contact with the secular world. Schleiermacher's increasing interest in science and art could not be fulfilled by the severely inward religion of the Brethren; after considerable tension with his father, Schleiermacher left the Herrnhuter school, intent upon formulating a more "exoteric" view of religion as the fullest participation in the world. By exploring these tensions, Dilthey is able to show why Schleiermacher later described himself as a "Herrnhuter of a higher order" (*GS* 13/1:395).

Dilthey coordinates his subject's widening horizons with a corresponding change of context: after treating with almost tactile vividness Schleiermacher's initial experiences at the University at Halle and a rural parish at Schlobitten, the narrative breaks off in favor of compact and lucid analyses of the German Enlightenment and "Poetic" movements, the two great strands of his more mature throught. In an effort to avoid a confusing pastiche-like approach, Dilthey defines the former primarily through Kant's critical philosophy and the latter through Lessing's writings. Thus, a thematic center is clearly defined and other figures are employed to round out the coherence.

From the plane of ideas, Dilthey turns to sketch the transformation of Berlin in the second half of the eighteenth century from a bleak garrison town dominated by Frederick's court and bureaucracy to a much larger city with an educated but politically powerless bourgeoisie. Announcing that "there exists an important and hitherto not yet scientifically examined connection between the great directions of society and those of intellectual creation," Dilthey attempts to relate population growth, rising prices, and levels of consumption to the emergence of a new pattern of social life (*Geselligkeit*) outside the courts (*GS* 13/1:217). Seemingly trivial matters such as card playing, mahogany furniture, paved streets, and a flourishing scandal literature take on unsuspected significance in this light. The change from the old autocratic regimen, in which Frederick's heavy hand had left Berliners with "only the right to mock," to a new urban society proved especially conducive to the formation of literary-philosophical clubs and journals. Dilthey points out that the Monday Club of Lessing, Mendelssohn, and Nicholai grew up outside the circles of the courts, ducal pensions, and university learning. The new journals served the cause of civic enlightenment by combining free learning with a sense of public responsibility and involvement (*Öffentlichkeit*). (Dilthey's special interest in the function of such journals is apparent throughout his works and undoubtedly derives from his own endeavors.)

These various coherences are carefully articulated, both internally and externally. Considerable attention is devoted to the details of ecclesiastical, municipal, and academic governance. For example, Dilthey explains how the organization and funding of the Berlin Charité (the hospital where Schleiermacher assumed a chaplaincy in 1796) promoted deplorable conditions and practices, such as having selected patients cook the food in order to keep down costs and pay for their own cure. In this situation Schleiermacher's "exoteric" notion of religious service assumed the form of public letters of protest and broadsides against the Ministry for Indigents. In a similar vein, Dilthey shows how academic administration at the different German universities contributed to the growing rift between "old" (rationalist-Wolffian) and "new" (critical-Kantian) modes of thought.

Throughout the work Dilthey tries to disclose the experiential dimension of Schleiermacher's ideas and teachings. The reader is shown how his friendships and social relations contributed to his philosophical doctrines of community, love, individuality, and humanity. From letters and diaries Dilthey reconstructs Schleiermacher's enduring friendships with Henriette Herz, Dorothea Veit, and Rahel Varnhagen—relationships which kindled his progressive views on the emancipation of women and Jews and promoted his vision of a potential humanity beyond the most deeply inscribed social distinctions. From his many friendships and broad learning Schleiermacher contrived a concept of individual self-formation based not upon narrow self-seeking and social hierarchy but on the "compendium mankind" (*GS* 13/1:406). For all his ideals, however, Schleiermacher is by no means transubstantiated into pure spirit. Dilthey returns repeatedly to his physical and financial problems. Though not employed as distinct causes to "explain" his life and thought, they are adduced as influences. Thus, for example, Schleiermacher's constant state of near poverty is cited as a factor behind his prolific reviewing activity and even some of his major works, including his famous Plato translations.

The technique of interpreting ideas in the light of actual experience is not confined solely to Schleiermacher. Dilthey, for example, shows how Friedrich Schlegel's cardinal concept of "irony" reflected a life lacking in firm and unequivocal commitments. The reader is led to reflect upon the manner and extent in which intellectual and artistic creation (*Dichtung*) is a re-creation (*Umdichtung*) of life (*GS* 13/1:500). It should be noted, however, that Dilthey avoids the sort of biographical reductionism which tries to explain all ideas in simple reference to individual experiences. Consonant with his (and Schleiermacher's) hermeneutic principles, Dilthey analyzes not only the genesis (the "how" or *Wie*) of various central doctrines and texts, but also their objective content (the "what" or *Was*), as well as their eventual impact. Thus the reader is provided with a careful exegesis of the form and style of several notable works (e.g., Schleiermacher's *Reden* and *Monologen*, Schlegel's *Luzinde*) along with an account of their public reception.

The overall tone of the work is celebratory and hortatory, but not uncritical. Schleiermacher emerges as the herald of new ideas, a "reformer after the Reformation," whose thinking may be "held up to criticism but not contempt" (*GS* 13/1:xlii). Trying to interpret this legacy of ideas for an age priding itself upon realism, Dilthey insists that its true meaning resides in anything but narcissism, escapism, or subjectivism. Whatever one may think of Dilthey's final judgment of Schleiermacher, his method of arriving there through *Verstehen* deserves to be largely exonerated of these latter charges. This task requires returning to his theoretical elaboration of that method.

Expression and Objective Mind

All understanding must proceed by way of an objectivation or expression, that is a perceptible sign of meaning such as a gesture, a written text, an action, or a tool. Understanding in the human sciences concerns single objectivations and entire patterns of objectivation; it attends to both intentional-deliberative and unintentional expression. It would be difficult to overstate the crucial role which expression—and most particularly in language—plays in Dilthey's later thought. He came to define the human sciences in terms of the triad *Erlebnis-Ausdruck-Verstehen*. Contrary to the charges of some of his critics, Dilthey did not isolate one component of this relation as more "fundamental" than the others—for example, reducing the latter two terms to forms of the first; this would have amounted to finding one side of a triangle more important than another. While retaining his emphasis upon lived experience, Dilthey at the same time came to stress more and more the importance of mediation, insisting that man understands himself "only through the detour (*Umweg*) of understanding others" (*GS* 7:87). His later thought is consonant with Hegel's observation that the true path of consciousness is the "detour" of mediation through objectivation. "In everything wherein mind has objectified itself, there is contained something common to the I and the Thou" (*GS* 7:208).

The special function of expression is reflected in the fact that Dilthey came to define history itself in terms of objectivation: "It is through the idea of objectivation that we first gain insight into the essence of the historical" (*GS* 7:147). History is not ineffable *Leben an sich* but *objectivated* life, manifested in the forms and patterns of wider sociocultural participation: "History is the realm of life, grasped as its objectivations in the stream of time, that is, the structure of life grasped according to the relations of time and effectuation. It is a whole which is never completed" (*GS* 7:241; cf. 246). History, thus, is not simply the past as such but the surviving past, the past expressed in the life-category of *Präsenz*. History is given only as the summation (*Inbegriff*) of the objectivations of life. These objectivations may be construed as "mind" but not in the purely subjective-personal (or psychological) sense, nor in the pure, disembodied sense of absolute spirit or transcendental mind.[27]

Dilthey distinguished three classes of expressions and an order (and criterion) of understanding pertaining to each: (1) scientific and theoretical judgments; (2) practical actions; and (3) expressions of lived experience (*Erlebnisausdrücke*) in a direct and specific sense. All three classes are "expressions of life" (*Lebensausdrücke*) in a general sense and hence cannot be entirely exclusive; but there are expressions of life in this wider sense which are not necessarily expressions of lived experience as designated by the third class.

The first class is composed of logical and scientific propositions, including the concepts, categories, laws, and larger thought patterns of the sciences. Their content is theoretical and purely intellectual. These judgments are self-identical and valid regardless of the time, place, or persons in which they arise; they are knowledge in the strict sense and their content is independent of lived experience. They are understood and judged according to the criterion of truth and falsity. The understanding of this class of expressions does not show relative degrees but rather strict formal validity: "Here understanding is directed solely to the intellectual content; this content is the same in every situation and thus understanding is here more complete than in relation to any other expression of life" (*GS* 7:205). The understanding of these judgments is complete and perfect, but in a sense "shallow" in that they do not refer to experience from the standpoint of life. Dilthey's analysis of the first class shows that he was far from contending that logical and scientific judgments were merely subjective manifestations or excrescences of a world-view; though science and logic are "forms of life," they contain objective truth.

The second class of expression is voluntary action (*Handlung*). These expressions arise from human purpose and intention but their original mode of intention is not to communicate something directly but to carry out an aim or end. Although it may "say" something to observers, the action of a man chopping down a tree is not ordinarily undertaken to communicate something, but rather to accomplish something. Although the action is manifestly purposeful, Dilthey finds its meaning to be unintentional and involuntary, that is, derived from its direct accomplishment. Therefore, we understand actions by an indirect process of re-creating the aim which the action intends to fulfill. For a specific action, grasping this aim is not to be confused with understanding the entire mind or state of mind of the agent. In contrast to theoretical judgments, actions are judged according to the criterion of success or failure in attaining their end. Dilthey cautions that the understanding of action may be full and complete so far as the specific, discrete action is concerned but that such functional understanding is "partial" and does not by itself allow us to make inferences to the broader context of the action or the coherence of personality behind the action. We can understand an action without understanding the agent—though an intelligible pattern of actions would begin to meld into an understanding of the agent. Actions thus verge upon expressions of lived experience.

The third class of expressions Dilthey terms "expressions of lived experience" (*Erlebnisausdrücke*), which he employs in a sense both specific and wide-ranging. They are direct manifestations of inner mental life; they may be largely conventional, unconscious, or involuntary—gesture or exclamations, for example—or highly reflective and deliberative in character, as a work of art. These expressions disclose the deepest recesses and resources of the human mind—indeed, they may reveal more about a person than he himself is conscious of. The interpretation of this class of expressions is often the most complicated and tentative but also the most revealing of individual life and human life in general. The shallow and partial (yet precise) qualities of classes one and two do not pertain to these expressions, for they manifest the full range of mental life. These expressions are judged not according to the standard of truth or falsity, success or failure, but authenticity. Dilthey observed that expressions in this class could be distorted, feigned, or delusive, but even so, they retain a reference to life. This reference must not be narrowly construed as direct reference to the life of the expressing person, for often a great work of art or literature creates a meaning which extends far beyond its engendering experiences. In his own particular endeavors in intellectual history Dilthey was most concerned with this last class of expressions and the type of understanding appropriate to it, but he never claimed that it was the sole province of the human sciences as a whole.

The human sciences clearly make use of all these forms of expression. What can be separated for purposes of theoretical analysis is found operating together in the actual practice of the sciences. In the Nachlass Dilthey cautioned against mistaking these distinctions for the actual objects of understanding. Although the "specific structure of each region of expression is different," they all rest upon "common achievements of thought" which underlie every mental manifestation. Dilthey suggests that there is a kind of deeper logic of these common achievements—a logic subtending all these regions of expression. He went on to insist that "an expanded and comprehensive logic in the manner of Husserl" would elucidate these achievements in their actual coherence (*BNL* 225/23–26). Dilthey, however, did not clarify a crucial point: to which class of expressions do the judgments of the human sciences belong? They have in part the logical form of class one, but they interpret material in classes two and three. The methodical interpretation of any human manifestation must employ judgments akin to the first class, while retaining qualities of the second and third. We are left to conclude that "an expanded and comprehensive logic" would show that judgments in the human sciences are a compound of all three. Although such judgments are rooted in lived experience, they cannot be taken simply as expressions of lived experience per se. Contrary to the charges of some of his critics, Dilthey emphatically stressed the logical difference between the *judgments* of the human sciences and the *expressions* about which these judgments are made: "It is important to establish first of all that all statements [*Aussagen*] which occur in religion, art, world-views, and metaphysics must be sharply distinguished from those which valid science [*allgemeingültige Wissenschaft*] makes about those configurations" (*GS* 6:304).[28] This critical distinction shows patently that for Dilthey scientific judgments cannot be swallowed indiscriminately into the category of world-views or mere expressions of life.

Dilthey's repeated observation that *Verstehen* shows different grades defeats objections that he never clarified the logical status of the "what" which is understood. Echoing Schleiermacher's view that "hermeneutics should go after the phenomenon itself and not its shadow," Dilthey insisted that we always understand an objective "what" as well as a genetic "how" (*GS* 14/2:710; 3:260; 15:342). We do not, however, understand only pure essences, or ideal objects but a whole range of meanings, including persons, propositions, dispositions and states of mind, and complex patterns of social behavior. Dilthey did not separate "subjective" mental processes from "objective" contents, nor did he conceive of meaning solely as the internal coherence of experience "behind" the expression, that is, as the relation of parts to whole in the experience of the signifying agent. Particularly after his reading of Husserl, he extended his notion of meaning to include the relation between the sign and the thing signified and stipulated that what is signified cannot be resolved into experiential components or configurations. *Verstehen* is thus not simply the "resubjectifying" of objectivations in a "backward" movement from the objective expression to the immanent subjective experiences of the expresser, but also a "forward movement" from the sign to its intentional object. To use the metaphor of the flight of an arrow, one could say that Dilthey's later theory of meaning alternatively shifts the emphasis from bow to target—from the *a quo* to the *ad quem*. In contrast to any purely subjectivizing view of understanding, Dilthey maintained that an expression always refers to something general which is neither psychological nor available to piecemeal inferences from part to part (*GS* 7:219). An expression is referential in two directions: toward the experiential acts or process which produced it but also toward an objective meaning. The former valence may be considered more psychological, the latter more logical in character—though these aspects are not neatly separable and work together in any actual process of interpretation. An expression is not simply an external sign of a psychic state.

Dilthey fully acknowledged the sense in which an expression or work has objective autonomy apart from its originator or original context. *Verstehen* need not rest upon the "reexperiencing" of authorial experience and may have no reference to it. Dilthey stated that though one form of higher understanding traces the relation of end result (*Erwirkten*) and producing agency (*Wirkenden*), another form of understanding concerns the relation of the expression (*Ausdruck*) to the "what" expressed (*Ausgedrücktem*), which may have no direct genetic relation to the actual experience of the author. Such understanding concerns the inner coherence of the work, that is, the coherence in which the parts of the work (not of the author's experience!) form an integral whole. There is no specific reference "outside" the text to any engendering process. Thus Dilthey is led to stress that a theatergoer can understand a play without ever thinking of the author, for his understanding moves in the autonomous mental world of the play itself, not in the mental world of its author. The meaning grasped is more or less objective and self-contained, severed from the actual experience of its originator, though founded upon "general experience" of life. Likewise in lyric poetry we may re-create a coherence of experience, but this is not the actual one which stimulated the poet but one which he has put in the voice of an "ideal speaker" (*GS* 7:214). In "understanding" a piece of music we do not grasp something psychological going on in the composer's mind but something "musically objective." Dilthey insisted that this form of objective and formal interpretation is "of utmost importance and must be developed in its autonomy" (*GS* 7:211). It might be noted that these frequently overlooked passages anticipate much of the formal and "textualist" program of the New Criticism of the twentieth century—that very school which reacted so strongly against what was taken to be Dilthey's "historicism" and "contextualism."

Dilthey denied any transcendent source of meaning, insisting upon the "immanence of meaning in that whose meaning it is" (*GS* 5:lxxxiv). We have the beginnings of all human meaning in our own awareness of our experience, but we must perform many interpretive efforts to follow it through. Meaning has both a subjective and objective "valence" and in developing his notion of *Verstehen* Dilthey tried to combine the subjective-personal emphasis of Scheiermacher with the objective-impersonal emphasis of Hegel.[29] Husserl's phenomenology seems to have provided the proper account of this "double direction." In a section of the Nachlass entitled "Phenomenology" and obviously indebted to Husserl, Dilthey expanded upon the difference between objective *Bedeutung* and subjective *Kundgabe*:

Let us distinguish two ways in which signs are related to what is given in them: (1) in a judgment we grasp from the signifying verbal coherence something given objectively. This operation can be performed upon lived experiences: either we describe experiences in judgments or we predicate certain constantly recurring objective features of such experiences; (2) or the signs can function purely as expressions of lived experiences given directly. The grasping of what is given in these ways is *Verstehen*. *Verstehen* is correlative to what is given and only this given can be understood [*BNL* 191/515].

Dilthey added that most signs and objectivations contain both propositional and expressive components; while logically separable, impersonal "judgments-about" and personal "expressions-of" are empirically most often found together. (Thus, the judgment "Dilthey was a poor logician" says something about both Dilthey *and* the critic, as well as entailing a general or "typical" notion of logic itself.) Though meaning must imply something meant as objective, Dilthey rejected the attempt to build a new metaphysics upon meaning, to proceed from *Sinn* to *Sein*, as Husserl proposed in his letters. Dilthey insisted that "meaning [*Bedeutung*] and sense [*Sinn*] are simply correlates for the results of understanding. As far as understanding reaches, so far extend meaning and sense" (*BNL* 144/44).

A prominent feature of Dilthey's theory of interpretation is his doctrine of "*Besser-Verstehen*," that is, that the interpreter can understand the author of a work (or agent of an action) better than that author understands himself. This seemingly brash presumption derives from several quite commonplace conditions: (1) the role of unconsious and unintended factors in all human action and creation; (2) the fact that the interpreter may view the expression in contexts and coherences unknown to the author; (3) the use of new sources of information and knowledge likewise unknown to the author. Meaning cannot be restricted to the *mens auctoris* or its generative experiences and contexts, for the expression as "fixed and enduring" is cut loose from its immediate context and may be interpreted in reference to new ones. The very nature of expression engenders an ongoing process of interpretation, which may disclose the meaning of the expression to be something different from its original intention. Most forms of expression contain a valence of meaning beyond the originator's subjective consciousness.

Dilthey's account of expression culminated cogently in the concept of objective mind (*objektiver Geist*), which forms a synthetic keynote in his final views. This concept, which appears very prominently in the writings after 1903, brought together many of the disparate strands of his previous lines of thought. In stressing objective mind Dilthey shifted the content of understanding from immediate experience to culturally mediated experience. Folowing the hermeneutic circle, Dilthey concluded that objective mind is both the precondition and end of human understanding. Hence he came to define the entire body of the human sciences by means of this concept: these sciences study human life, but life now reconceived as objective mind. While this new resolution is amply evident in the published writings, the Nachlass contains Dilthey's clearest statement. After enumerating the partial and unsatisfactory definitions of the human sciences such as "sciences of the subject," "sciences of real experience," and "sciences of culture," Dilthey concluded: "I draw all this together: the human sciences have as their comprehensive reality [*umfassende Gegebenheit*] objective mind" (*BNL* 114/398).

Objective mind is the vast sphere of cultural content preserved in lasting manifestations. It should not be confused with the romantic doctrines of "folk-soul," or "group mind," which Dilthey regarded as sheer personified abstractions. Although it is not necessarily rational or consciously entertained, Dilthey insisted that there is nothing mysterious or preternatural about objective mind:

> I understand by the concept of objective mind the diverse forms in which the community among individuals objectifies itself in the sensible world. In objective mind the past is a constantly persisting present for us. Its province stretches from the style of life, the forms of intercourse, to the coherence of goals which society has posited, to morality, law, state, religion, art, science, and philosophy [*GS* 7:208].

It is a domain of meaning which concerns neither the sphere of physical things nor psychic events transpiring in individual experience. Dilthey's concept, however, is not identical with the *Kultur* or *Kulturgut* of the idealists, as he insisted that it contained not simply "high culture" but practical life-values, sublimated drives, and technical arrangements. His concept of objective mind cannot be equated with the culture-concept of the neo-Kantians precisely because he grounded it in historical existence rather than transcendental norms. There can be no doubt that Dilthey borrowed the term directly from Hegel, but he gave it a significantly different application in his thinking. By bringing art, religion, and philosophy into the realm of objective mind, Dilthey attenuated Hegel's final dialectical resolution i.e., from objective into "absolute" spirit) and brought its content back down into the purely human sphere of culture. Objective mind is a cultural coherence which "is contained in its lasting products." It is a cultural possession (*geistiger Besitz*) and also a kind of "pre-possession" in which the individual is immersed from birth yet constantly appropriates:

> From earliest childhood on, our self receives its sustenance from this world of objective mind. It is also the medium in which the understanding of other persons and their expressions takes place. For everything in which mind has objectified itself contains something common to the I and the Thou. . . . The child grows up in the order and way of life of the family, which it shares with other members; the guidance of the mother is absorbed in this coherence. Before it learns to speak, the child is

already immersed in this medium of common forms [*Gemeinsamkeiten*]. It learns to understand the gestures and miens, movements and exclamations, words and sentences only because they reappear constantly in identical form and in the same relationship to that which they mean and express. Thus the individual orients itself in the world of objective mind [*GS* 7:208–9].[30]

Objective mind is, as Dilthey put it, the "atmosphere" of meanings in which we live: it is easy to overlook because for the most part we take it for granted. Yet we understand primarily through this common medium of shared experience and culture. It is not an a priori table of ideas, categories, or values, but a developing yet binding fund of meaning revealed in the unity of reason, sympathy in feeling, and mutual obligation in moral duty and the law. This common fund of sociocultural meanings is not reducible to a psychological process or a datum of psychological science. It is disclosed through the hermeneutic understanding of law-codes, literary texts, sayings, and other forms of objectivation. From the most fleeting gesture to the most enduring system of law, every objectivation represents something shared in this realm of objective spirit:

> Every word, every sentence, every gesture or politeness, every work of art, and every historical action are only comprehensible because a community binds the expresser with the interpreter; every person lives, thinks, and acts constantly in a sphere of community and only in such a sphere does he understand [*GS* 7:146–47; also 209].

Language is the example par excellence of this community of objective mind; it is the largely unnoticed medium which links the individual to a common world of meaning. Dilthey stressed throughout his career that language conditions experience just as much as experience conditions language. Language presents a uniquely fundamental instance of the reciprocity at work in mental life. Like Vico, Humboldt, Herder, and Schleiermacher, Dilthey saw language as constitutive of our world-view and as a condition or our perception: "Man fulfills himself only in the perception of all forms of human existence—and no other organ is provided for this [perception] than language and writing" (*JD* 88). The *Preisschrift* emphasized that language is a form of mediation (*Ausgleichung*) between the individual and the general. Humboldt had observed that "man lives with the objects such as his language brings to him . . . the learning of a new language means adopting a new view of the world." This same insight was refined by Schleiermacher, who observed that "language both leads and accompanies [*leitet und begleitet*] man in his historical development" (*GS* 14/2:749, 787). In a review entitled "Language" published in 1863 Dilthey continued this line of thought:

The reciprocal effects which language works upon the thought of the individual and which the thoughts in turn exercise upon the form of the language are incomprehensible if we view language as simply a product of human arbitrariness or a natural process. Thinking does not fit itself in the same mold in every language. Translation is frequently possible— and especially with difficult thought—only through a re-thinking [Um-denken] [GS 16:425].

In a passage from the Nachlass reminiscent of Trendelenburg, Dilthey observed that "the a priori and eternal categories which Kant inscribed on the tablets are in actuality deeply embedded in the development of the European languages" (BNL 49/242). In the Einleitung he further observed that "metaphysics only carries further what language has already begun" (GS 1:83). The effect of language is at once utterly pervasive and yet especially intractable, as we cannot suspend it in order to explain it or reconstitute it anew. We do not "make" language in the same sense that we "make something" or "make something happen," yet language makes our world of meaning. Especially in his later thought Dilthey called attention to this constitutive function of language, which cannot be fully explained (erklärt) but only elucidated. By 1907 Dilthey insisted that language is more resistant to analytic treatment than the psychologists and linguists were willing to admit: "We cannot reconstitute in ourselves the processes in which mind is at work in language." Linking language to his later notion of experience and hermeneutics, Dilthey opined that in ordinary experience we are unaware of the deep effects which our language exerts upon us: "The productive force in this area [of language] runs its course unnoticed in processes which cannot be fully reconstructed. We have only its products" (VDM 30; cf. GS 10:80–81). Along with the structural coherence of experience, language accomplishes tacitly what the reflective-consciousness tries painstakingly to unravel. In the Nachlass he specifically linked Husserl's project of a pure grammar to Humboldt's idea of a universal grammar; such a discipline analyzes the syntactical structures of language and relates grammatical sense to experience, thereby providing a bridge between syntax and semantics (BNL 83/243). In several instances Dilthey tried to combine such a linguistic approach with his phenomenological analysis of lived experience, finding that the prepositional forms of "auf," "über," "vor," etc., reflect recurrent structures, typical mental "attitudes" and vital relations. Pursuing his earlier insight that "all language is to some extent an anthropomorphizing," he tried to link grammatical forms to modes of consciousness. In all this Dilthey seems to have come close to the contemporary view that the structures of language in a sense anticipate and engender our view of the world. The "facts" of experience are incorrigibly relative to the forms of language and hence our interpretive concepts cannot be resolved into a pre-linguistic fundament of pure experience. Though a declared adversary of idealist "pre-formation theory" and the a priori, Dilthey seems to have shown leanings to a kind of linguistic a priori.

In a late fragment Dilthey insisted that expression alone is capable of manifesting the full content of lived experience:

> Lived experience is not silent and dark. The inner can come to complete expression where it goes into expression involuntarily, unhampered by reflection. Mankind in the full scope of its inner life is there for us only in expression. What is in this life appears only in the content of expression [GS 5:lxxxvii].

The expression is not a paltry facsimile or "mere appearance" of mental life but its truest being, for the expression manifests more than any direct inner scrutiny can ascertain. Thus expression discloses what is unavailable to direct, immediate self-consciousness:

> In lived experience alone our own self is not graspable, neither in the form of its development, nor in the depths of all that it encompasses. For like an island, the small province of conscious life arises out of the impenetrable depths. The expression, however, arises from out of these depths. It is creative. And thus life itself is available to us through understanding, as a reconstruction of the productive process [GS 7:220; also 8:78].

The expression is "creative" because its meaning may exceed the intended meaning of the author: its meaning for us is not identical to its meaning for its originator. *Verstehen* in the human sciences, therefore, entails more than approximating the author's self-understanding of his own actions, intentions, or works. Any expression assumes a form which is set free from the immediate experience and awareness of its agent. The expressions are in a sense autonomous and carry their own "life and law" in themselves. Expressions do not simply "present" or "re-present" experience as it is lived; they stand in an inner dialectical relationship to the mind which produced them: "The mind objectivates itself in expression—this objectivation is external to mind and yet its own creation" (GS 7:329).

This growing recognition after 1900 of the importance of expression and objective mind constituted a departure from some of Dilthey's earlier pronouncements. Over the twisting course of his reflections one can detect a subtle but unmistakable shift in his attitude toward the nature of human expression—a change which might best be characterized as a gradual movement from the "poverty to the plenitude" of expression. Although it is difficult to specify precisely, this shift was probably engendered by his reaction to some of the more extreme subjectivistic implications of his notion of *Nacherleben* in conjunction with his intense study of Hegel and

Husserl. His emphasis is transposed from the immediate awareness of experience to its articulation and interpretation.

In many of the earlier writings Dilthey emphasized the insuperable limits and shortcomings of verbal expression (see, for example, *JD* 122, 190). The full content of lived experience undergoes a truncation and deformation in passing into discursive language. Most notably as a young man, Dilthey seems to have subscribed to the typically Romantic notion that the reality of inner life can never find adequate representation in verbal "objectivation"; language exacerbates rather than mediates the estrangement of subject and object, of subject and subject. To the musician Bernhard Scholz he repeatedly confessed that he found words an inadequate vehicle for his thoughts and that he had to resort to music—especially instrumental music, as the purest form—in order to do justice to his immediate experience.[31] In his only published piece of original literature, a trite sentimental novella entitled "Lebenskämpfe und Lebensfriede," the major characters Heinrich and Helene experience such great surges of immediate feeling that they are left entirely speechless. Distrustful of all words, Heinrich adopts music as the sole authentic form of communication (*WM* 22[1867]:241–65).[32]

These misgivings about language were not limited to personal musings. In the hermeneutics study of 1860, Dilthey faulted Schleiermacher for adopting the premise of *Identitätsphilosophie* that "being goes without remainder into appearance and thought goes fully into language" (*GS* 14/2:749 ff.). Dilthey posited a gap between inner and outer modes of existence and stressed that there were dimensions of inner life which cannot find expression in language. He specified this point by means of the curious principle that the immediate richness of experience is inversely related to the tendency toward expression (*JD* 190). In the "Breslauer Ausarbeitung," Dilthey maintained that although experience has a "natural tendency" to pass into expression, this expression can never be fully identical with the immediate awareness of experience. While expression may be natural, it is partial and wanting in comparison to the ineffable fullness of lived experience (*BA* 36–37).

The critique of language as a traducer of inner experience has been a persistent theme in Western thought and was particularly prominent in the Pietistic tradition which Dilthey absorbed as a youth. Opposing all forms of rationalistic doctrine, this tradition propounded a "negative theology" which held that all concepts and discourse must inevitably fall short of their divine object; plain silence or music were regarded as more profound forms of witness than spoken prayer or doctrine. So marked was their veneration of silence that the Pietists were known as the "quiet ones" (*die Stillen*).

The distrust of language came to be a fundamental tenet of romanticism and was continued through many strands of German thought. Expression (*Äussern*) was regarded as form of alienation (*Veräussern*) issuing in a dead artifact of inner life. Even Wilhelm von Humboldt, who regarded language as a "miracle" and who stressed the indivisibility of consciousness and speech, nevertheless contended that words could only partially accord with that to which they refer. German *Sprachskepsis* found its most radical statement in Nietzsche's view that language is the "first lie." It should be noted that Yorck espoused a particularly radical and uncompromising form of subjective, Pietistic *Innerlichkeit* predicated on the "necessary inadequacy" of all expression: "It can be regarded as the inevitable tragedy of all historicity that it is impossible for life to bring itself to full and complete expression, because its medium imposes a particular limitation. The Word captures Life as little as does the Deed." Yorck, like Bergson, held that the immediate reality of life always contains "something secret, unexpressed, and inexpressible."[33]

Sometime after the mid-1890s, after Yorck's death and during his intense study of Hegel, Dilthey's attitude toward the potentialities of expression underwent a notable change. It is not the limitations of language which receive primary emphasis but rather its positive accomplishments. Expression in language shows itself to be not merely adequate to experience but bountiful and productive of ever-new meaning in the process of history. This new attitude is conveyed in a late passage which has a distinctly Hegelian ring: "Objectivation is eternalization" (*GS* 8:12). Not the duplicities and antinomies, but rather the potential plenitude of language assumes first place in Dilthey's treatment, in a manner directly opposite to his treatment of psychology and introspection. A Nachlass passage conveys what in comparison with his youthful remarks seems like an about-face on Dilthey's part: "The full content of life only becomes what it is in expression" (*BNL* 203/41).[34]

Gradually expression was invested with a special function and accent in Dilthey's later theory: it is not simply the confining integument of a deeper reality but the very form and content of that reality given together. Through objectivation, lived experience takes on a general cultural form of manifestation which renders it fixed and lasting, but also located in a general matrix of meaning shared by others. Expression is expression "of" and expression "for:" It is quite literally the condition and the mark of the translation from *Erlebnis* to *Lebenserfahrung*, from immediacy to common meaning. Lived experience is not falsified in being expressed but rather augmented and made available to communication and interpretive knowledge:

A significant augmentation of lived experience—by means of which the richness and coherence of mental life first rise to knowledge—is contained in the fact that something inner obtains expression and then can be understood from it in a regressive movement of thought.

It is in language alone that the mind finds "its complete, exhaustive, and objectively intelligible expression" (*GS* 5:319; cf. 14/1:298–301, 314). Language does not traduce experience, but induces and conduces it.

Dilthey's revised view of expression most probably derives from his excogitation of Hegel's objective idealism. Passages from Hegel suggest precisely the "objectivizing" line of thought which Dilthey pursued in his later reflections. In the *Philosophie des Geistes*, Hegel mocked the romantic pieties of ineffable inwardness and all "torpid subjectivity":

> We know only our thoughts—real determinate thoughts—when we give them the form of objectivity, of difference from our interiority, which is to say the form of externality. To be sure, such an externality at the same time carries the stamp of the highest inwardness. . . . The only such inner outwardness [*innerliches Äusserliches*] is the articulated tone, the Word. To want to think without words, as Mesmer once tried to do, seems therefore to be unreason. . . . It is ridiculous to regard the necessary connection of thought to words as a lack or misfortune for thought. For although it is common to hear it said that the ineffable is far and away the most excellent, this opinion, which arises in haughtiness, has no grounds, since the ineffable is in truth only something dark and turgid, which gains clarity only in coming to expression.[35]

To Hegel's influence must be added the complementary impact of Husserl's theory of the ideal-objectivity of meaning. Dilthey adopted Husserl's definition of expression almost verbatim and likewise stressed the "intentional objectivity" of meaning. The relation between the physical sign and its meaning is not a mere coinciding or causal relation but an inner intentional unity:

> The character of expression is defined by the fact that when we experience it, we experience not the presentation of the word itself [*Wortvorstellung*] but exclusively its sense, its meaning [*seines Sinnes, seines Bedeutens*]. Our attention belongs to the intended object [*Unser Interesse gehört dem gemeinten Gegenstand*] [*GS* 7:40].

When we understand expressions "naturally," we accomplish their meaning in being directed to the "what" which is expressed. This "what" is an objectivity, not simply a set of engendering psychological acts. But it is a "mental" or "intentional" objectivity. Dilthey's exposition is unmistakably Husserlian: "The direction of understanding goes from the word and the sentence to the object which they express." *Verstehen* is a "relation to an intended object" (*Beziehung auf ein gemeintes Gegenständliches*). This relation characterizes not only logical or scientific propositions but poetry and music as well (*GS* 7:124, 214).

Dilthey's new sense of the actualizing and augmenting function of expression prompted him to revise portions of his previous works. In the

1905 version of his study of Goethe (originally published in 1877), he made a decisive alteration by adding the following passage:

> We are not at all concerned here with the observation of inner processes and the subsequent portrayal of what is observed. What we experience by means of self-observation is always restricted in narrow limits, and even the scientific study of mental life conducted on this basis attains much less than is commonly supposed. For in turning our attention to our inner states, all too often we find that they have disappeared. The manner of the poet, who expresses personal inner experience is totally different from this. It rests on the structural coherence between the lived experience and the expression of what is experienced. What is experienced goes fully and totally into the expression. No reflections separate its depths from their portrayal in words. The total modulation of the life of the mind is made available to understanding through the expression. In expression depths of the mind are opened which are not available to observation [*ED* 165–66].

The full content and meaning of the expression—and therefore genuine understanding of the expression—cannot be encompassed in psychological concepts:

> Infinitely much is contained in the realm of expressions of lived experience and their proper concepts—an infinite amount which goes beyond the content which is available to the deliberately psychological determination [*GS* 7:319].

The particular explanatory concepts of psychological science and the actual understanding of meaning are at variance. The rejection of "deliberately psychological" concepts cannot be taken as referring to concepts altogether, however, for Dilthey expressly called for proper ones, which would highlight meaning by elucidating the relationships between lived experience and the content expressed. *Verstehen* proceeds through these concepts but it is not about these concepts. There is a sense in which such understanding remains "psychic" or "mental," but it is not specifically and formally psychological. Contrary to some interpreters, Dilthey never repudiated the notion of some kind of psychological foundation for *Verstehen*; to do so would have meant surrendering the decisive advance signaled by the "psychological-historical" hermeneutic of Schleiermacher and his successors. Again it should be stressed that when Dilthey is speaking of the existing psychological science of his day, he places it in contrast to hermeneutics; but when he refers to a psychology projected to "its true concept," he sees psychology, history, and hermeneutics as complementary.

Dilthey often asserted that *Verstehen* presupposes not only the community of individuals in the patterns of objective mind but also its ultimate foundation in a common human nature:

In the process of understanding, the individuality of the interpreter and his author do not stand over against each other as two incomparable facts; both have developed on the basis of a common human nature and herein is made possible the community of all men for speech and understanding [*GS* 5:329].

Ultimately human expression is understood on the basis of something universally human (*Allgemeinmenschliches*). This basis, however, is not a static or a priori identity but is rather a relation of "community":

The whole framework of the mental world is permeated with this basic experience of community, in which the consciousness of the self and that of similarity with others, of the identity of human nature and yet of individuality, are linked together [*GS* 7:141; see also 151, 259].

In treating human nature as a relation, Dilthey chose a median position between an extreme essentialism and an extreme historicism. On the one hand he seems to confirm the eighteenth-century view of a common human nature, and on the other hand he seems along with the nineteenth century to find the "essence" of this nature in history. This view was clearly defined in his essay on Schlosser of 1862:

It is the essence of man that he is historical, that is, he accomplishes his moral task only in the continuity of culture. This essence cannot be captured in anthropology, which deals with the empirical existence of the individual, nor in moral philosophy which legislates the "ought": it is captured only in philosophical history, which has as its object the life of the human race itself [*GS* 11:140–41].

Mankind therefore is an emergent community of recognition. Like Droysen, Dilthey insisted that human nature is a *historical* nature and that this "essence" is determined first and foremost by what man does and makes of himself. Epigenesis, not preformation, defines the nature of man. Therefore Dilthey holds that mankind is "only an unfixed type" and that history dissolves any fixed notion of the "type mankind" (*GS* 7:159). Such a viewpoint, however, raises the vexing problem of the relationship between human essence and historical existence, between uniformity and historicity:

Here we touch upon the most profound fact of the human sciences: the historicity of mind, expressing itself in every system of culture which mankind brings forth. How is the unity of our human essence, which expresses itself in uniformities, linked with its variability, its historical being [*GS* 6:108]?

This "most profound fact" is lodged at the basis of *Verstehen* itself; an absolute identity of human nature would make understanding superfluous, while an absolute difference would make it impossible. In the final analysis Dilthey seems to define human nature in terms of the relation of identity-indifference which permeated German thought ever since Nicholas of Cusa: it is a *Grenzbegriff* which we must assume but cannot demonstrate conclusively. In Dilthey's thought the concept of human nature remains a somewhat clumsy, even incongruous way of providing a fundamental and unshakable basis for objective mind and mutual understanding.

In a few passages in his later studies, Dilthey stated that the differences among persons can be reduced to quantitative differences in the apportionment and intensity of certain mental traits and processes (*GS* 5:229–30; 329–30; 7:315). These assertions have given rise to considerable controversy, since they imply that individuality is basically a matter of quantitative combination of traits, reducible to measurable elements. This notion was roundly attacked by a number of thinkers (notably, Georg Simmel) as an "artifact" of the Enlightenment which had been dispelled by the idealist notion of personality; such a mixture-makes-the-man theory seemed to contradict virtually every one of Dilthey's other doctrines. Two of his closest students, Misch and Landgrebe, have treated it as an unfortunate and thoughtless lapse into "positivistic" models of explanation. The doctrine of quantitative differences was seen as basically incompatible with his conceptions of structure, coherence, lived experience, and *Verstehen* itself.

Dilthey attempted to meet these criticisms by quite literally "qualifying" his position. In a set of comments written between 1904 and 1907 he insisted against Simmel that "quantitative determinants [*Bestimmungen*] constitute an important and entire dimension of mental life," but added the significant proviso that "such determinants are all individually constituted" (*BNL* 191/86). This passage suggests that there are different levels of "determination," just as there are different levels of awareness. Quantitative factors may be isolated analytically but they *function* qualitatively in an individual coherence and thus are largely "understood" at this level. By "quantitative differences" Dilthey meant something other than psycho-physical units in the fashion of the Herbartians; he was probably referring to variations in intensity and scope of perceptual experience. Although his thinking tended to move wholly within the sphere of the descriptive and qualitative (i.e., the phenomenological), Dilthey also insisted that quantifiable factors enter into the constitution of the lived-experiential world and are necessary to understanding. His doctrine of quantitative differences seems a somewhat feeble and contrived means of stressing that differences among persons are not final and absolute but relative and susceptible to analysis. If one recalls his view that *Verstehen* takes place on a relative scale between pure identity and difference, then the quantifying doctrine seems more plausible as a means, albeit a crude one, of envisioning these scalar differences and preserving the possibility for comparative treatment. Nevertheless, it must be admitted that the quantitative doctrine does not accord readily with the larger notion of objective mind.

The more Dilthey stressed the role of objective mind in history, the less importance he assigned to the sphere of the strictly personal and psychological. Again, however, one is presented with a question of emphasis rather than any sudden reversal of perspective. At the start of his training he had insisted that "history is neither the depiction of personalities in their subjectivity, nor a treasure chest of catchy anecdotes" (*JD* 89). After finishing the *Leben Schleiermachers* he defined *Verstehen* as "objective immersion [*Versenkung*] in a cultural tendency" (*JD* 289). In an 1876 review of a biography of Rousseau, Dilthey faulted the author for a lopsided psychological interpretation which presumes to explain Rousseau's accomplishments and ideas by tracing them back to early influences (*WM* 41[1876]: 330). Genuine understanding comprehends human experience in a wider, ongoing sociocultural context, not simply as a psychological datum. This condition operates even in the field of biography, in which the purely personal-subjective level must be distinguished from the historically significant: "There is a curious inclination in our time to disregard the boundaries which lie between what is historically significant in a man's life and what is a purely personal matter. Yet I think these lines can be drawn clearly" (*GS* 11:167). The psychologizing approach in history and philosophy tends to reduce ideas, ends, and values to functions of merely personal motives and immediate experience, whereas in truth the tendency of mental life is the other way around (*GS* 9:68).

History is neither the play of purely individual activity nor the work of supraindividual forces and institutions but the reciprocal relation of both. Dilthey characteristically affirmed that in the long-standing dispute between the so-called "pragmatic" historians, who regarded history as the stage for the enactment of personal ends, and the Hegelians, who saw it as the sphere of the self-realization of suprapersonal ends, both parties have a portion of the truth. The pragmatic school was correct in asserting that everything accomplished in history is the product of human will and desire, but the Hegelians were right in insisting that this will stands under general imperatives and ends which are not resolvable into personal acts. The pragmatic method looks at persons as discrete elements in a predictive sequence:

> Let us focus on the essence of this method. Its characteristics are: an orientation to causal knowledge, recognition of individuals as the sole true, that is, empirically demonstrable causes, and the consideration of the individuals not from the standpoint of unconscious energies but from the standpoint of deliberate intention and plan—in short, from an intellectual capacity which is based in self-interest. Consequently it is characteristic of this method that it is devoid of a concept of the relation of persons in society which would be given along with their separate existences—devoid of a concept of people or state as original historical entities [*GS* 9:265–66].

Such abstract methodological individualism overlooks many of the less accessible relations and coherences which constitute the human-historical world; no less than in the panlogical system of the Hegelians, history is reduced to a pallid schematism. Dilthey cited the work of Ludwig Spittler: in his history of the early Christian church, everything is treated as the result of deliberate planning: "His [Jesus'] relation to the disciples approximates that of a professor on the podium in Göttingen to his students" (*GS* 9:266). The pragmatic method was best illustrated in Hume's *History of England*, "the first basic pragmatic history of a modern period in the grand style," in which historical relations are summarily read off from a general theory of the human passions and human nature rather than from careful research in the sources (*WM* 31[1866]:136).

In several later writings Dilthey averred that the search for individual motives was largely illusory and could only result in historical skepticism. The innermost realm of personal-subjective motivation is closed to the historian, whose real concern lies with objective meaning not "psychological refinement." History, as it were, inquires after publicly manifest effects not private affects. The meaning of an action or expression is not reducible to the motives of the agent and may differ from its intended purpose as well. Following Trendelenburg and Fischer, Dilthey distinguished between purpose and motive—excluding the latter from exact understanding.

Just as he provided for the relative autonomy of the expressed meaning apart from the lived experience of its author, so too Dilthey allowed a level of historical meaning apart from the intentions of an agent. Subjective purpose and objective meaning do not necessarily coincide; nor is the understanding of the interpreter tied to the self-understanding of the subject. Historical agents are limited by their horizon and life-coherences; they act for proximate purposes, not for a theoretical totality or "for" history. Often the effects of these actions are at variance with their intended purpose. Rejecting Hegel's notion of a "cunning of reason," Dilthey refused to impute an ulterior rationality to this quite commonplace historical occurrence: "There is nothing mystical here; one does not have to see a providence at work, much less a goal toward which history is striving" (*GS* 7:341). Dilthey's doctrine of unintended consequences is quite similar to Wundt's "heterogony of ends." Both notions encompass a level of meaning distinct from originating purpose—or the agent's awareness of purpose. The ramifications of an action, just as the meaning of a text, may change with the ongoing process of history. History shows a "centering" in certain epochs, styles, world-views, and movements, but this centering is accompanied by "duplicity of effects": "It is in the nature of finitude of all historical forms that they are marked by hindrances and servitude, by unfulfilled yearning" (*GS* 7:186). This duplicity gives rise to further development beyond the existing cultural forms. There is development in history, but Dilthey resists the ascription of "progress": "We can describe developments, but we do not know that something higher proceeds out of this striving" (*GS* 8:69).

In the *Einleitung*, Dilthey observed that history constituted "the ultimate and most complicated problem of the human sciences" (*GS* 1:380). By grounding historical knowledge in our tacit understanding of existence, he could claim that "the first problem of grasping and presenting historical connections is already half-solved by life itself" (*GS* 7:200). He was, however, equally cognizant of the obverse side of the special nexus between history and life.

Dilthey acknowledged that "the horizon of the historian is conditioned and limited by the standpoint which is his by virtue of contemporary history" (*GS* 11:70). Historical knowledge remains provisional and relative, without, however, disqualifying itself as true knowledge: "There is no last word in history which expresses its true meaning—any more than there is in nature" (*GS* 1:92). He dismissed the "false idea that there is a point in history from which history would no longer be historical" (*JD* 191). Inevitably "what we set as our future goal influences our determination of the meaning of the past" (*GS* 7:233).

> Every cognitive effort is conditioned by the relation of a knowing subject and his historical horizon to a specific group of facts which is also conditioned in scope according to a specific horizon. For every attempt at understanding, the object is there only from a specific standpoint. Therefore, it is a specifically relative way of seeing and knowing its object.

Unlike the resigned skeptics or "heroic" relativists of his day, however, Dilthey neither despaired nor gloated over this state of affairs. In a phrase which has a distinctly Hegelian ring, he went on to assert that "[it is] precisely this limit which provides the energy" (*GS* 1:413–14). The knowing mind, in recognizing its perspectival limits, is impelled by an inner dialectic to move beyond them. In acknowledging our own particular horizon, we are not thereby justified in settling down within it, but are enjoined to reflect on it critically and to broaden it outwards.

History, inevitably, must be rewritten, but this process of revision testifies not primarily to the incorrigible limits of knowledge but to the growth of knowledge itself. Thus, in a review of Sybel's study of the French Revolution, Dilthey found that, beyond the influence of ideological factors and changing contemporary attitudes, the history of this crucial epoch was revised in the light of new documentary evidence and new forms of knowledge (*WM* 44[1878]:554). While recognizing the ineluctable impact of the present on the study of the past, Dilthey deplored sheer "presentism" as "the attempt to adapt the history of past times according to the mode of the present, either by making it more familiar through the viewpoint of the moment or to bring it into an artificial proximity (*künstliche Nähe*) by employing modern terms (*WM* 52[1882]:278–79). A narrowly restrictive (*befangen*) view of development leads to a captious form of understanding (*Ruckübertragung*) whereby "each age finds in the prior one a disguise of the forms which come to full expression in its own" (*JD* 188–89). He deplored the facile form of *Ungeschichtlichkeit* in which the past appears as a kind of imperfect version of the present; to this way of thinking "everything becomes a Today" (*GS* 8:129).[36] In a review of Ludwig Häusser's *Deutsche Geschichte*, he reminded his readers of Aristotle's observation that the poet is free to create his object after his own imagination, whereas the historian remains bound by his materials even in forming them into an object of knowledge (*WM* 19[1865]:258). He condemned the tendency to substitute intuition for prolonged study and exact analysis, noting that "to throw overboard the so-called 'ballast' of exact sources and citations in order to have easier passage—this tendency is the real scholarly sickness of our time [*Zeitkrankheit*]." He went on to pillory the author of a work on D. F. Strauss for attempting to contrive a total view of his subject without sufficient basis in the actual materials; the result was a mere tissue of subjective guesswork (*Heraussublimieren*) with no objective foundation (*WM* 43[1878]:669; cf. *GS* 1:155).

The fact that the interpreter is limited in perspective by being "in" history —just as his subjects were limited in perspective—does not cancel the possibility of historical objectivity for Dilthey. Objectivity is a matter of asymptotic approximation rather than full identity or "synopsis *sub specie aeterni*" (*GS* 8:129). There can be no Final Word, unless history itself should come to an end. But the absence of a total or final perspective, such as Hegel's stage of Absolute Mind, does not nullify the degree of truth we attain through the human sciences. Although relative and approximate, *Verstehen* provides genuine knowledge of man, not simply a Nietzschean welter of interpretations:

> Understanding continues to increase our historical knowledge by making use of historical documents, by going back into parts of the past hitherto not understood, and finally by the very process of history itself, which produces new events and thus enlarges the field of understanding. This enlargement demands that we find new general truths to penetrate this world of unique events. And this widening of the historical horizon allows us to form more and more general and fruitful concepts. Thus, at any point and at any time in the work of the human sciences, there is circulation between experience, understanding, and the representation of the human world in general concepts [*GS* 7:145].

Historical knowledge must keep abreast of its constantly developing subject, mankind's historical existence:

Such is the inner law of the historical sciences: just as the historical world develops through time, so too develops the scientific understanding of the historical nature of man. For man does not understand himself by subjective self-brooding [*Grübelei*], from which springs only the great Nietzschean misery of an exaggerated subjectivity: man comes to consciousness of himself and his capacities—in good and bad—only by understanding the historical reality which he produces [*GS* 3:201].

Against the skeptics and relativists of his day, Dilthey concluded that "the historian sees truly" (*VDM* 341).

Verstehen and the Realm of Facticity: The Role of the Generalizing Human Sciences

It is a serious and common error to regard Dilthey's hermeneutic (and indeed his entire theory of the human sciences) as simply a refurbished version of German *Geistes-* or *Ideenlehre*. He constantly insisted that the basis of history was not ideas but a stratum of resistant "facticity." Many interpreters have insisted that Dilthey made "an absolute distinction, as does Hegel, between the world of history and the world of nature."[37] Yet he himself repeated again and again that "there is no chasm [*Kluft*] between nature and mind" (*GS* 9:182; also 1:6, 14; 5:61, 246 ff.; 7:80, 119, 122, 146, 311, 323). He quoted Goethe approvingly: "The Germans make life harder rather than easier with their Ideas which they inject into everything. . . . Do not think that everything is in vain just because it cannot be put as an abstract thought or Idea" (*GS* 6:206). Not ideas in themselves but the dynamic relation between the human mind and its total set of conditions— including physical, social, and political ones—constitutes the fabric of history. Dilthey scorned *"Traumidealismus"* and faulted the Idealists for their neglect of the influence of *Realfaktoren* and *das Naturell* in life and history. He criticized the Idealist tradition for "acting as if the world of lower drives and motives did not exist" (*JD* 188). In the Nachlass he observed that "it is a grave error of intellectualism to believe that thoughts are purely and simply born out of other thoughts" (*BNL* 137/83).[38] Because his own variety of *Geistesgeschichte* attended to these factors, he differentiated it from the more Hegelian *Begriffsgeschichte* of Rudolf Eucken and Gustav Teichmüller. His historical writing, consonant with his theory of mind, was undertaken in the spirit of concrete "anthropological reflection," focusing in large part upon actual human needs, drives, and interests. One of his last pronouncements stipulated that "the facticity of race, geography, and power relations constitute the foundation of history, which cannot be spiritualized" (*GS* 7:287–88).

In his historical writing Dilthey concerned himself with the mutual interaction of the mind and its conditions. Neither "spirit" nor "facticity" assume priority; rather, the specific relation between them is the true object of history. In a programmatic section of his Novalis study, Dilthey isolated two factors which condition the culture of an epoch: the content of received tradition which must be mastered (*bemächtigt*) and "the conditions of environing life—factual relations, social, political, and other infinitely diverse conditions." The intellectual historian has to select from these conditions and can thus claim "only a very approximate validity" (*ED* 188). This qualification has been overlooked by those critics who accuse Dilthey of excessive "intellectualism" (this was precisely the same charge *he* had leveled at the previous generation of Idealists). Thus Frank Manuel has asserted that Dilthey's *Erleben* was "lived experience as a closeted Wilhelmine professor of philosophy conceived it. . . . [In Dilthey's history] nothing below the navel was mentionable. Economic and social reality may penetrate the narrative but only as part of a world-view, and political revolutions are quickly transformed into abstract ideas." Manuel concludes by accusing Dilthey of "neglecting the whole man" and writing "elitist intellectual history."[39] In a similar vein Fritz Ringer accuses him of "insulating" the intellectual world.[40]

It is obvious that Dilthey was neither a Freudian nor a Marxist, and his distrust of reductive models would not have disposed him favorably toward the grander claims of these theories. But he cannot be said to have neglected the "real factors" in history, including material and instinctive ones. He stressed instincts and drives in his view of man and history, insisting that man at the core is a bundle of drives (*BDY* 92; *GS* 10:49–58). In a review he asserted that "the dignity of history is not demeaned by paying attention to the physical factors which condition the facts, which are unfortunately all too little known to us."[41] His historiography dealt specifically with Schleiermacher's crippled condition, Herder's hypochondria, and Schlosser's poor health as factors relevant to their outlook or world-view.

Dilthey was by no means unaware of Feuerbach's "discovery" of man's sensuous nature, Schopenhauer and von Hartmann's stress upon unconscious will, or of Marx's doctrine of economic determinism. But Dilthey was pluralist, not a monist. His hermeneutic may seem disarmingly eclectic in its theoretical statement, for he posited multiple causes and determinants, not single causes and overall determinism. As a mediator and *Idealrealist*, Dilthey was as far from materialist determinism as he was from rationalist determinism; both were for him cases of illicit metaphysical hypostatization which violated empirical science.

With his demand for "unrestricted science" (*unbefangene Wissenschaft*), Dilthey repudiated all monocausal interpretations of history. This fact largely defined his attitude toward Marx. It has been widely assumed that Dilthey knew nothing of Marx and was simply blind to the question of economic conditioning in history. Georg Lukacs has asserted that modern sociology and economics were "totally unknown" to Dilthey and that his doctrine of *Verstehen* revolves upon a wholly irrationalist "identity of feelings." Hajo Holborn has correctly discerned that Dilthey paid attention to economic, social, and political factors, but has asserted that Dilthey "never found it worth his while to discuss Marx." Other interpreters have contended that Dilthey had no knowledge of Marx and have taken this as a sign that one of the foremost intellectual currents of his period passed him by.[42]

These views rest upon a partial reading of Dilthey and a misconstrual of *Verstehen*. Dilthey had read the older "constructivist" sociology of Comte and Spencer and also the newer sociologies of Adolf Schäffle, Paul von Lilienfeld, Paul Barth, Gabriel Tarde, and Georg Simmel. He had studied the economic works of Schmoller, Roscher, and Knies. In a review of Schmoller's *History of Economics* he asserted that economics was one of the most important of the human sciences and designated it as the key factor in analyzing "the dangers which surround contemporary Europe like storm clouds" (*WM* 40[1874]443). He regarded economics as "the most important of the human sciences for present-day action" (*GS* 11:254). Most interesting of all, however, is the fact that Dilthey read and was impressed by Marx; he even seems to have adopted certain facets of Marx's critique of capitalism.

In an unsigned review of "New Literature" in the area of the human sciences written for the May 1878 edition of *Westermanns Monatshefte*, Dilthey called attention to the "growing significance which the problem of Social Democracy has assumed for disciplined learning" and cited Franz Mehring's *Die deutsche Sozialdemokratie: Ihre Geschichte und Lehre* and Marx's *Das Kapital* as "most instructive." Of Marx's work Dilthey wrote:

> If one wants to instruct himself in a disciplined [*wissenschaftlich*] manner on the basic thoughts of the new German socialism, then one must always turn to a book which is more often mentioned than studied and which must be designated as the main and fundamental book of socialism: *Das Kapital* [*GS* 17:186].

In his review Dilthey faulted Marx for the onesided and abstract character of his labor theory of value, a fault which he atrributed to Marx's continued subservience to Hegelian *Begriffsphilosophie* and Ricardo's abstract principles. Dilthey contested the exclusive stress Marx laid upon labor as the source of value, for this view tended to overlook the real needs of individuals and the relation of these needs to scarcity. "As a result he [Marx] misconstrues the meaning of the enterprise which fits labor to needs: that of trade." In Dilthey's view, Marx's theory of value, contrary to Marx's own claims, represented a relapse into an unhistorical way of thinking ultimately inimical to a proper notion of value. Under the spell of Hegel's objectivist metaphysic, Marx attempted to derive the value of a good in absolute terms, irrespective of perceived cultural or psychological wants, on the basis of the purported "objective" standard of the amount of labor embodied in the product. Although the labor originates with man, the value for Marx is "an sich" and subsists apart from the actual wants and needs of man. Marx's theory of value succumbed to the very unhistorical form of apriorist metaphysics which he reviled as mystification.

Although Dilthey faulted Marx for his abstract value theory, he found his philosophy of history "most interesting and original." He judged that Marx's examination of the progressive concentration of capital in the hands of the few was carried through "in an exceptionally brilliant manner" (*GS* 17:187). Although Dilthey never again discussed Marx at any comparable length, there are several references to Marx and Engels in Dilthey's later reviews and essays.[43] These passages indicate that Dilthey was familiar with the doctrine of the "material" determination of ideas. In light of Dilthey's admiration for Marx's analysis of the concentration of capital, the following passage, which concludes a treatment of the intellectual history of the post-Renaissance era, was in all probability influenced by his reading of Marx:

> Within the economic sector the naturalistic system of the human sciences brought forth the awesome and terrible result of capitalism. As it once had been under the regime of the Roman Imperium, mobile capital under the modern system of law is unrestrained in its power. It can let fall what it will and seize what it will. It is like a beast with a thousand eyes and tentacles, which is devoid of conscience and can turn wherever it will [*GS* 2:245].[44]

Careful study shows that Dilthey did not neglect the role of economic and social factors in history and that his historiography is replete with perceptive, if elliptical, observations in this regard. In the Nachlass he stated clearly that the differentiation of the cultural systems of art, religion, and science from their original condition of fusion was predicated upon economic developments, specifically a greater productivity in agriculture which in turn stimulated greater efforts toward the control of natural processes. Altogether, man's basic needs exert a determining influence on culture and systems of thought: "For how man stands in relation to his needs is the primary factor [*Denn wie der Mensch sich zu seinen Bedürfnisse steht, ist das Erste*]" (*BNL* 138/84). Specific examples of this premise abound in Dilthey's intellectual history. He asserted that the "Socratic Revolution," which "moved minds so deeply as no other change in ideas since the rise of exact knowledge itself," was to be explained partly as the result of changes in economic and political conditions in Greece (*GS* 1:174). He attributed the rapid rise of the Sophists to the dissolution of the ancient constitution of the Greek city-states, which destroyed confidence in the self-evidence of truth and put a premium upon the rhetorical arts of persuasion. Political changes thereby engendered changes in logic, science, and the organization of the disciplines (*GS* 1:219). Although he did not provide any detailed elaboration of these relationships, Dilthey discerned parallels among the processes of specialization in labor, social differentiation into orders and classes, and the differentiation of the sciences.

In his essay on the modern epochs of aesthetics he emphasized that "here again it is a reformation in the social order—the English Revolution of 1688—which is the foundation of a changed attitude of man and this attitude worked simultaneously on the arts and aesthetic theory" (*GS* 6:254). In a rather profound insight into the social foundations of knowledge, Dilthey marked the great influence of the urbanization process upon modern science and isolated a crucial difference between the modern and Greek ideal of science, which he related to the social order: the modern ideal of science is practical and applied, aiming at the alleviation of work, whereas the Greek ideal of science could remain preeminently pure and theoretical because slaves did all the taxing physical labor (*GS* 3:10). Likewise he perceptively showed the impact of war and slavery on educational ideals (*GS* 11:21 ff.). Without assigning any causal priority, he posited a link between the preeminence of natural scientific thought in the eighteenth century and the ferment leading to the French Revolution. And he went on to make a telling point that has recently been explored in detail: that the emergence of the human sciences in the nineteenth century was partially conditioned by antirevolutionary sentiments (*GS* 1:xv)[45] In an insight which seems especially noteworthy in light of his own philosophical position, Dilthey argued that "philosophers of life" such as the Stoics, Bruno, Montaigne, and Nietzsche came into prominence in times of rapid, unsettling social and political change (*GS* 2:51, 253, 287–90). In short, Dilthey eschewed any simple, unilateral historical idealism. While recognizing a measure of truth in the view that "it is not just the case that man has ideas but also true that ideas have men," he rejected as preposterous the view that the ideas of the Enlightenment produced the French Revolution or that Luther's and Zwingli's sermons and writings brought about the peasant wars and insurrections of the sects (*GS* 2:71). Ideas may provide the direction and legitimation of social and political action, but they do not often constitute the direct impetus. Dilthey's historiography remains in keeping with his epistemology: thought alone does not produce reality.

In regard to the German scene (where one might expect a certain implicit "idealization"), Dilthey was equally alert to the effect of nonideal factors. In his discussion of the sects in the *Leben Schleiermachers*, Dilthey pointed to the reciprocal influence of Protestantism and capitalism, though he did not analyze it as thoroughly as Weber and Troeltsch were later to do. He stressed the importance of political and social developments in fostering the "inward turn" of German thought and the rise of transcendental idealism. He explained the cultural ideals of the German middle classes partly as a result of their exclusion from the political life of the state. Indeed, Dilthey provided a kind of curious yet apt historical exemplification of his theory of the practical origins of the mind's belief in the external world. In his studies of Schleiermacher, Hegel, and the German Enlightenment, he observed that German transcendentalism was partly to be understood as a reaction to the frustrations of political life. Denied the opportunity to work changes upon a sociopolitical reality vested largely in the hands of the aristocracy and state bureaucracy, educated Germans turned inward to transform themselves. The German ideal of "self-culture" stemmed in part from the absence of opportunities for public participation.

In his path-breaking analysis of the intellectual life of eighteenth-century Berlin, he underscored the effects of Frederick the Great's "autocratic and inquisitorial regime" upon the exchange of ideas and forms of communication. A literate society which is denied an active role in the state takes to the private discussion of political matters in clubs and fraternal groups (*GS* 13/1:209–14). In the same vein Dilthey's reviews reflect the demand for the close relationship between the realm of ideas and the concrete interests and facts of society. His review of Georg Brandes' monumental *History of Literature in the 19th Century* lavished praise upon the author for accomplishing the "integral connection of literary developments with political facts" (*WM* 39[1875]:616). It can hardly be said that Dilthey treated the Revolution of 1848 as "an abstract idea." In his article on Dahlmann, it figures both as personal *Erlebnis* and as a social upheaval of first magnitude (*GS* 11:175 ff.). *Der junge Hegel* was original on several accounts, one of which was because it took Hegel's early politics as seriously as his early theological writings. In contrast to both Rudolf Haym and Theodor Haering, Dilthey insisted that Hegel's reaction to the French Revolution was not to be dismissed as a mere student fad.

Dilthey was by no means blind to the role of class in history. He criticized Dahlmann for his intransigent and exclusive belief in the sole historical mission of the middle classes and his neglect of the working classes, whose importance had been pointed out by Gervinus and demonstrated in developments in France (*GS* 11:185). In his discussion of Schleiermacher's theory of constitutions Dilthey found the theory lacking in appreciation for the influence of economic and class factors (*GS* 14/1:390, 410). He even related the rise of science in the early modern period to class structure:

At the same time a decisive change of the economic life and the social orders took place, and this resulted in a total shift of intellectual interests. The work of the bourgeois classes in industry and commerce appeared as an independent force in the midst of the feudal and ecclesiastical orders of life. It directed the mind toward this world. Thinking probed into man and nature. The significance of reality and the autonomous value of family, work, and the state were felt and recognized [*GS* 3:8].

Even literary forms and genres were related to social and economic factors. After interpreting the epic as a reflection of the social dominance of the warrior-class, Dilthey anaylzed the social conditions behind the rise of the novel:

Insofar as this task [of finding an appropriate genre] is attainable in an epoch of industry, commerce, science, and advanced civilization, the modern novel was called upon to fulfill it. The society needs such a form and searches for it. This task reflects the nineteenth century, which was steeped in social reality. The same epoch which brought forth sociology —the analysis of society into its various cultural systems and filled with the consciousness of the inner coherence of all phenomena with this whole—also brought forth the social novel. Without the needs, questions, and scientific tendencies of this time, the novel would not be conceivable [*GPD* 306].

In an unpublished manuscript on "Social Structure," Dilthey outlined the emergence of class interests within the modern Prussian state in terms of the transition from a feudal to money economy, a tendency which created a "social gulf" between a closed aristocracy rendered functional by state offices and a relatively powerless bourgeoisie. This gulf was only partially and ineffectively bridged by the new class of bourgeois officials, who tended to ape the aristocracy and assume its special interests and prerogatives. Dilthey judged that this "demoralizing process" reached its peak under the personal rule of Frederick the Great and left a deep cleft in German society (*BNL* 54/219–50).

Dilthey's method was, as he observed of the nineteenth century itself, "steeped in social reality." It is ironic that he is often reproached for a narrow "idealism" and "intellectualism"—precisely the charges he leveled against many of his fellow Germans. In his own time he was accused of making too many concessions to postivistic *Milieutheorie*, whereas today he is widely accounted as a proponent of a narrowly "idealistic" intellectual history. After being identified with Trendelenburg's naturalism, he is now often identified with Hegel's idealism. These associations, often more distorting than illuminating, have obscured his historical method and practice. His actual histories demonstrate his principle that "history proceeds through the reciprocity [*Reziprozität*] of idea and facticity" (*GS* 11:51).

It is often claimed that the method of *Verstehen* (and its concomitant conception of the human sciences and history) excludes generalizing techniques, such as comparison and quantification, and further that it is antithetical to generalizing disciplines such as sociology. Although a few interpreters see Dilthey taking the first tentative steps "from history to sociology," the prevailing view is that he refused to acknowledge sociology as a legitimate discipline and confined the human sciences to a narrow "historicizing" method. In point of fact, he neither dissolved sociology into history, nor excluded sociology from the human sciences. As in the case of psychology, his assessment of sociology changed over time; but it changed, so to speak, as sociology changed.

It is true that he rejected sociology as it was conceived by Comte and Spencer, that is, as a totally encompassing and final science of the social-historical world, a new substantive philosophy of history. Such a sociology was for Dilthey simply a new "social metaphysic," an ill-fated, uncritical attempt to erect another First Science upon the principles of natural science. It is a serious error, however, to construe Dilthey's attacks upon this form of sociology as a rejection of sociology as such. In a clarifying passage written in 1909 and intended for a new edition of the *Einleitung*, he made it clear that his polemic against sociology was directed at its earlier excesses. He went on to say that he "naturally" recognized as legitimate and necessary the new sociology of Georg Simmel, which rather than attempting a total synthesis, contented itself with careful analysis of the multiple forms of social grouping and relations. Dilthey even suggested that he could claim some credit for having anticipated Simmel through his analysis of the "cultural systems" and "outer organizations" of society (*GS* 1:420–21).

H. A. Hodges has suggested that "Dilthey himself held opinions which can only be called sociological, though always refusing to recognize them as such" and that "Dilthey's reasons against the possibility of a sociology amount to a sociology in themselves."[46] Restating this point in a later study, Hodges concluded that "as Dilthey grew older, the sociologist in him grew weaker and the historian grew stronger. The sociologist in him never died."[47] These comments have the merit of indicating that Dilthey's attitude toward sociology was by no means simple and uniform; at the same time, however, they raise more questions than interpreters have been able to answer on the basis of the published texts.

It is only in the Nachlass that Dilthey's views emerge with more clarity. One finds that his attitude toward sociology was quite similar to his double view of psychology: He rejected the "constructivist" tendencies characteristic of its incipient phase but insisted upon the possibility of a genuinely critical and empirical sociology, which he saw emerging in the work of Simmel, Wundt, Weber, Tönnies, and others. By no means did he simply annex sociology to history (or to psychology). While stressing its reciprocal relations with the other human sciences, he tried to specify its special characteristics.

In an extensive section of the Nachlass captioned "On Sociology" and written between 1905 and 1907, Dilthey sketched certain principles for the discipline. Specifically rejecting Spencer's "psychologism," he insisted that "the organizations of society cannot be derived by means of psychology. For psychology is concerned only with the regularities of individual mental life." Dilthey went on to assert that the social relations into which the individual is woven cannot be disclosed by reference to the individual self-consciousness. Such a method results merely in arbitrary constructions masquerading as a universal theory of social phenomena. He added: "These objections, of course, do not apply to a sociology in the sense of Wundt or Simmel." True sociology will emerge not from premature synthetic systems based on analogies from other sciences such as psychology or physics, but only from careful research (*Einzelarbeit*) into particular spheres of social life: "Sociology is the progressive continuation of empirical research into defined and particular areas, seeking out the ultimate relations between social coherences and organizations." The fruitfulness of this more limited and precise conception of sociology was evident to Dilthey in the recent studies of Simmel and Tönnies, but also Gabriel Tarde and Paul Barth (*BNL* 141/32–50; cf. *GS* 7:138, 212).[48]

In another section of the Nachlass (which unfortunately cannot be dated with certainty) Dilthey attempted to define a set of theoretical guidelines for sociology on the basis of its own specific historical development. After discussing the conditions which hampered its emergence (such as the identification of state and society and employment of specious concepts such as "group-mind"), Dilthey concluded that "the formation of a basic science of the societal life of man had to follow necessarily upon the recognition of the correlative problem of the distinctively social nature of man himself." The particular forms of political and ecclesiastical organization had to be studied before any general doctrine of social life could emerge; these general theories were largely based upon biological premises carried over from Aristotle, Cuvier, and Buffon. It was only very gradually that the notion of society was disengaged from that of the state: "Only very slowly then did one arrive at and delimit the problem of socialization itself [*die Gesellschaftung selber*]—that is, those processes in which socialization is realized and the forms which it produces—as a special object of study."

Dilthey went on to evaluate the strengths and weaknesses of various approaches to this still nebulous object of study. "One cannot say with certainty that any of the investigations which arose in these conditions have produced a thoroughly satisfactory treatment of the problem." The German national-economists made signal contributions in isolating key economic relations, but they erred in defining these relations too abstractly, that is, apart from the actual context of economic activity. They asked the proper questions concerning the forms of "socialization and stratification" (*Ver-*

gesellschaftung und Schichtung), but their base was far too narrow. Dilthey proceeded to repeat the same charge against the folk-psychologists, but on different grounds: "Their empirical base is too narrow: one cannot infer the forms and processes of social life—in language, in the creation of symbols, in relations of property and domination—from purely psychic processes." And while their premises are too narrowly psychological, their aim is too far-flung and hegemonial, for they want to explain all social life and culture on the basis of psychological laws. In overreaching themselves, they come inevitably into conflict with the other human sciences. In drawing the balance on all these attempts, Dilthey severely reproved the spirit of methodological monism; the unity in the human sciences remains a unity in circulation.

> There is no other way: actual historical life can only be know empirically —through analysis, combination, and comparison—methods which naturally have in psychology one of their most important tools. In the present state of these matters we must be content to develop the processes and forms of social life to their full extent as they have arisen from the concrete coherences and conditions of life [*BNL* 169/151–79].[49]

It is significant that Dilthey included quantifiable factors among these "concrete conditions." His abiding interest in statistics has unfortunately never come to light. The conventional view of the human sciences as based solely upon an act of subjective intuition or personal identification between "I and Thou" seems to preclude any application of quantitative methods. This view is misleadingly partial—at least in respect to Dilthey, for he saw *Verstehen* as a complexly differentiated process which deals with a range of objects and sources, including quantifiable ones. Ever since his early exposure to the work of Adolphe Quetelet, the Belgian "father of statistics," Dilthey was greatly intrigued by the field and could be considered a pioneer in calling for the application of statistical methods to provide exactness in certain areas of the human sciences, including notably his own field of *Geistesgeschichte*.

Dilthey's interest in statistics began early in his life and lasted throughout his period of active reviewing. Some interpreters might be tempted to dismiss it as a transitory manifestation of his early affinities for positivistic *Erklären*, but this is a dubious judgment, since his later, expressly hermeneutical view of *Verstehen* does not in the slightest preclude a quantitative formulation of certain aspects of the materials to be interpreted. Indeed, in some respects, it expressly requires it (*GS* 4:555). In an early article "Der Mensch und die Zahlen" (published anonymously in 1862), he showed a marked enthusiasm for the employment of statistics:

> Statistics belongs to the newly-founded sciences and more especially to those which have enjoyed a great upsurge. And what a discipline! If one

opens one of these books, one finds instead of words—those deceptive expressions for dubious thoughts—nothing but numbers, the unequivocal expressions for incontestable facts. . . . In every disputation the proper use of statistics will carry the day. Numbers prove [*Zahlen beweisen*]! [*GS* 16:134].

Looking at Mephistopheles' words:

> Im Ganzen haltet Euch an Worte,
> So geht Ihr durch die sichre Pforte
> Zum Tempel der Gewissheit ein.

Dilthey substituted "unequivocal numbers" for "deceptive words" and reformulated Goethe's wisdom as:

> Im Ganzen haltet Euch an Zahlen,
> So geht Ihr durch des Zweifels Qualen
> Zur Ruhe der Gewissheit ein.

Dilthey foresaw the likelihood of careless abuse of this new discipline, but adamantly refused to join "those weak and illusioned souls" who wanted to turn science around and divest it of quantification in order to put it back under the tutelage of theology or speculative metaphysics:

Statistics is above all a science which in its present state all too easily leads one astray to the denial of freedom of will, or more exactly to denial of moral self-determination, and for that reason is subjected to the theological ban. Thus, it is certain that statistics is a science which is still in its beginnings; as every half-truth misleads one to error, so it is true that many erroneous conclusions and doctrines can be derived from present-day statistics. But the path to truth and clarity lies not in a return but in a forward movement. . . . Only insofar as every science presses forward on its own does it come closer to the common goal of all sciences, the truth [*GS* 16:136–37].

In his 1875 essay on the human sciences, Dilthey found statistics to be a "natural aid" to history. (He had employed population and budget figures in his Schleiermacher study.) After acknowledging a paucity of data for many periods of the past, he called for a statistical approach to intellectual movements in order to show how ideas and individual works are related to a much broader pattern of popular attitudes and opinions. Using the records of libraries and academies, this new approach could demonstrate whether the great intellectual transformations usually traced back to isolated individuals were in fact the outcome of larger movements of opinion: "The application of statistical methods to the collections of libraries makes possible the exact quantitative determination of the scope and intensity of certain intellectual movements, the pursuit of specific branches of inquiry, and the spatial distribution of the same." The careful use of statistics, combined with the interpretation of documents relating to the genesis of a work, would show

> . . . how widely dispersed elements of a culture, which are given through general conditions, social and moral presuppositions, and the effects of predecessors and contemporaries, are reformulated in the workshop of the individual mind and are combined into an original whole which in turn works creatively back upon the life of society [*GS* 5:40–41].

Again in the *Einleitung*, Dilthey asserted that statistics could provide exact "numerically determined insights into the facts of society" and he specifically called for the use of graphs to represent these statistical findings (*GS* 1:25, 115). He remained particularly intrigued with Gustav Rümelin's attempt at a statistical profile of generations.

Although he rejected its hypostatization into a "social physics," Dilthey welcomed the new field of statistics and reviewed many works in this area. Properly and critically employed, the quantitative and statistical approach does not "mediatize" the individual into a mere function of mass forces. Dilthey deplored

> the prejudices and fantasies of those childish enthusiasts of freedom [*Freiheitsschwärmer*] who believe that the responsibility and specifically moral qualities of man can only be secured by regarding every personality according to a wholly individual self-determination or by taking every act of will as spontaneous creation [*WM* 40(1876):440].

In a review of Emilio Marpurgo's *Die Statistik und die Sozialwissenschaften*, Dilthey lauded the author's effort to employ the theory of probability to mass behavior and extolled his contribution to the nascent field of social statistics. Similarly he praised a statistical monograph by Holtzendorff on "Wesen und Wert der öffentlichen Meinung" as "the first attempt to treat this matter in its psychological origin, historical development, and its meaning for the political life of the present" (*WM* 45[1879]: 226; 49[1880]:140). Dilthey showed himself a pioneer in these pronouncements: most German philosophers and historians regarded statistics and sociology as "antiindividualistic," "deterministic," and "naturalistic" sciences.[50] The narrowly subjective view of *Verstehen* as the "reliving" of inner mental experience would seem to banish quantitative methods from the human sciences. But Dilthey's concept of understanding specifically encompassed the situation in which meaning is constituted, since for him there is no "text" without context. He conceived this context as wider sociocultural "coherences," and there is clearly a role for statistical analysis in the determination of the character and influence of these coherences. While Dilthey might have concurred with the view that "social relations really exist only in and through the ideas which are current in the society" and that in the final analysis the actual grasping of meaning is primarily a matter of qualitative experience, he acknowledged that the larger setting of mental meanings can be illuminated by quantitative treatment.[51] Depending upon the set of the interpreter's compass, statistics may be a legitimate and even indispensable part of the hermeneutic process.

Dilthey extended the scope of hermeneutics beyond its original textual locus to encompass other, nonverbal forms of meaning. He insisted that hermeneutic method applied to cultural systems, social organizations, and systems of scientific or philosophic concepts. In a revision of the "Aufbau" essay entitled "Hermeneutic of Systematic Organizations" he observed:

> A rigorous hermeneutic of social organizations is needed in addition to single textual works. . . . Hermeneutics is possible here because between a people and a state, between believers and a church, between scientific life and the university there stands a relation in which a general outlook [*Gemeingeist*] and unitary form of life [*Lebensform*] find a structural coherence in which they express themselves. There is here the relation of parts to the whole, in which the parts receive meaning from the whole and the whole receives sense from the parts; these categories of interpretation have their correlate in the structural coherence of the organization, by which it realizes its goal teleologically [*GS* 7:265].

It should be noted that Dilthey's claim to apply hermeneutic method to society does not rest upon any implicitly mentalistic doctrine of the "World as Word." He assumes structural coherences in all *Lebensformen* and he posits ideal ends for *some* of these forms, but nowhere does he claim that the coherences are ideal in nature, nor did he contend that one science can grasp them altogether. Dilthey did not view history in splendid isolation as the crowning achievement of the human sciences. He insisted upon its links with economics, sociology, psychology, and the other sciences in the process of disciplinary circulation. The relativity of each science is offset by the ongoing relation among all of them.

Understanding and Explanation in the Human Sciences

Dilthey repeatedly stressed that the human sciences aspire to causal knowledge, yet his distinction between *Verstehen* and *Erklären* has been widely interpreted as a rigidly exclusive dichotomy which entirely precludes explanation in the human sciences. A recent judgment is typical: "In Dilthey's view historical understanding has nothing to do with scientific explanation."[52] A careful study of Dilthey's position, however, shows that he was by no means so rigidly exclusive with this distinction. His concept of understanding is not only compatible with but to a certain extent convergent with a form of explanation—a condition which he explicitly recognized in some of his last writings. Not only did his own concept of causal explanation show changes over time, it showed an accommodation to alterations in the general notion of explanation evident around the turn of the nineteenth century. As explanation "softened" from strictly physical models of necessary and predictive laws, Dilthey came to stress not the divergence but the connection of explanation and understanding in a gradation of cognitive accomplishments. His views in this matter have not been subjected to careful analysis; this is a serious omission, since such analysis would meet objections that his theory of the human sciences hinges solely upon some mystical power of mental projection or some ultimately metaphysical "identity of Mind." His actual position emerges as considerably more acute and tenable than is often acknowledged.

It should be noted that the tradition of *Idealrealismus* of Wilhelm von Humboldt, Trendelenburg, Fischer, Haym, Lotze, and Wundt (as well as Herder and Ranke) had a distinctive conception of "law" which differed from both strict natural scientific causality and the Hegelian dialectic of ideas.[53] This notion of law incorporated two related features of human behavior: a purposive, teleological element in human activity, and reflective consciousness (or "apperception") of that activity. In the human world things do not just happen, they are *perceived* to happen as activity toward ends and this perception influences the outcome. The apperceptive activity of mind is not merely another "fact" in some inexorable causal chain but a dynamic factor which, to a greater or lesser extent, influences the resulting state of affairs: man is an agent of his effects. In contrast to the more uncompromising position of classical idealism, however, the ideal-realists portrayed mind as a codetermining but not as the exclusively determining influence, since for them empirical reality is never wholly resolved into ideal forms and forces. The synthetic activity of mind which makes causal judgments possible with regard to physical reality tends to militate against the unmodified application of the same form of "external" causality to the mind itself. The activity of the mind is partially free and yet partially determined by its own reactions to that which it brings about. Although it is not always apparent from his statements, it is this dynamic and reciprocating notion of law which emerges in Dilthey's treatment of explanation. Therefore he can claim that while there is no natural scientific causality in the human historical world, there are still "laws" or "rules" of behavior (*GS* 7:197).

His first formulations simply equate "causality" and "law-like," regardless of any distinction between mental and physical phenomena. In the early 1860s he defined the primary task of science as causal knowledge: "The task of science is not simply to see [*anzuschauen*], but rather to investigate the causes of things, to develop *causas cognoscere rerum*, to explain and to understand" (*GS* 16:427). In subsequent writings he postulated "laws of society," the "lawful metamorphosis of images" in the imagination, and "explanatory laws of style" (*GS* 16:403; 15:100; *ED* 42). He even attempted to invoke a kind of psychological causation to explain our understanding of other persons. In a note of 1866 written during his study of the physiological psychology of Fechner and Horwicz, Dilthey referred to the perceptions of other persons as "causes" and "causal complexes"—a view which seems to contradict the premises of his earlier essay on hermeneutics (*BNL* 237/25). In his Basel address he insisted that "knowledge of laws" constituted the source of all human power over the world, including mental and social phenomena (*GS* 5:27). And in a writing from the same period which weighed the relative merits of Schlosser and Ranke, Dilthey praised Schlosser for viewing history in terms of "the most basic historical category: sober causality." Ranke was berated for interpreting history in the quasi-Hegelian categories of "concentration" and "dialectical construction," which issued in ideal-images and spiritual agencies. Yet Dilthey went on to affirm that Ranke had a measure of truth in his method. Schlosser's form of causality was basically mechanical and therefore had serious limitations in regard to the meaning of cultural phenomena; with such a mechanical causality "everything is seen solely in terms of its origins and effects, we never get to the phenomenon itself" (*GS* 11:150). Such narrowly conceived causal analysis produces a truncated view of the historical object, missing its specific meaning and value. After further reflection Dilthey cautioned against taking causality in the sense of strict "lawfulness" as the sole criterion of knowledge:

> It is a dire error to regard the most abstract knowledge we have, i.e., the knowledge of laws, as the only valuable kind. This is comprehensible in a Mill or a Buckle, but with us is denied from the start by the orientation of much significant German investigation [*GS* 13/1:200; also 249–51].

Nonetheless, Dilthey continued through the 1870s to demand a causal treatment of the "law-like relations" in the human-historical world (*GS* 5:47–48). In a lengthy essay of 1876 on the Japanese novella, he envisioned literary criticism to be on the threshold of "strict science" and called for a comparative method to isolate recurrent "elements" and laws of formation: "As does culture everywhere [literature shows] certain basic characteristics. Just as chemical elements in certain proportions always and everywhere produce the same compounds, so the passions, the imagination, and perceptual activity in man all hold sway in a uniform manner and produce something commensurable" (*WM* 40[1876]:577). Extending the same program to the thought-systems and world-views, he looked forward to a morphological treatment which would demonstrate the law-like evolution of these systems. In 1888 he affirmed that "all knowledge in the strict sense is causal knowledge" and in 1892 he repeated that "science has taught us to grasp the lawful sequence in the real. Today we understand man only in the natural, social, and historical coherence in which we find him conditioned" (*GS* 15:5–6; 6:285). These formulations suggest that Dilthey insisted upon the cardinal importance of causality and law, yet at the same time reserved a special conception and use for them in the human sciences. It should be stressed that even during his closest convergence with positivism, Dilthey insisted that the laws of history and the human world must be "essentially different" from those of nature (*GS* 5:li; 18:164, 206). Only gradually, however, was he able to specify the character of this difference. His continuing insistence upon causal treatment must be considered as a realist's reaction to the idealists' disdain for causal knowledge and their narrow preoccupation with "idea" and "essence." Dialectical, organicist, and emanationist logics and theories of knowledge had virtually eliminated causality from the human sciences. Although he demanded that causation in the human sciences be distinguished from physical law, Dilthey insisted to the end of his life that some form of causal explanation was indispensable to these sciences.

Especially in the 1880s Dilthey began to distinguish more carefully between two different kinds of causality—one wholly naturalistic and deterministic and another which is "geistig" or "effectuating" in a mental sense. This latter mental causality is reminiscent of Kant's "causality of freedom" and entails a direct relation to ends and values, as well as the determining conditions of circumstance. Natural causality is blindly mechanical and uniform, whereas mental causality is dynamic and purposive. In natural causality the effect is strictly contained in the cause: the rigid equation *causa aequat effectum* defines this relation. As invarying and determinate, this relation may be reduced to quantitative formulation, with a mathematical equation to cover both terms of the sequence. Dilthey maintained that this form of causality is "external" and hypothetical; we do not actually experience it ourselves, but rely upon an indirect inference to relate its terms. Indeed he suggested that this form of causality—far from being an innate category of the mind as Kant maintained—is derived by analogy from the more basic and immediate "effectuating causality" which we "live through" as agents. The human form of willed effect is experientially prior to natural causality (*GS* 8:260; 5:142–44).

"Human" causation is more immediate and familiar to us but also more complex and difficult to grasp conceptually and logically. The strictly mechanical order of succession obtaining in nature is contrasted to a complex pattern of willed effort operating toward an end or multiplicity of ends. As teleological and purposive, no equation can be applied, for "here the basic law [sic] of productive augmentation [*Steigerung*] applies." More is contained in the effect than was contained in the cause; this "more" cannot in any case be reduced to the mechanical transformation of existing elements and forces, for it manifests genuine development. The additional content in the resulting "effect" is the outcome of action undertaken toward the attainment of ends. "The extra element in the effect is the work of freedom, and this is simply a kind of 'bringing about' that is, a setting up of connections" (*GS* 9:182–83; cf. 5:66, 74). The result is directed by innumerable intervening and guiding acts of will, so that the *effectum* may be said to be the purposeful outcome of the workings of mind(s), but not devoid of codetermining physical conditions.[55]

Human causation is marked by "augmentation" and "complication," by which Dilthey meant a reciprocally determining relation between formative acts conducted by a more or less conscious agency (not necessarily an individual person). This very special kind of lawfulness Dilthey compares to the progressive formation manifest in the composition of a melody line; the initial choice of signature, key, and opening notes exercises a peculiar "determinate-indeterminate" relation upon the further development of the melody (*ED* 179). He later came to define this kind of causality as "inner lawfulness" and "structure" to differentiate it from physical causation. It prevails in the realms of language, myth, poetry, social action, and ethics.

Although he never provided a truly thorough analysis of this concept, Dilthey postulated a general relation which would combine the causal and teleological modes of thought. With characteristic hyphenation he termed it a "new teleological-causal approach" and anticipated that it would be of great use in the human sciences (*GS* 9:179–80; 6:66–74; 5:176; 3:39).[56] His later historical studies were organized upon this principle. Both in theory and practice Dilthey resisted any identification of his concept of human causation with the "final causes" of the neo-Aristotelians and neo-vitalists: the "end" of human causation is proximate and immanent to human action.

As one follows his thinking on this subject, it becomes clear that Dilthey's use of "law" and "lawfulness" in the human sciences meant something quite different from the laws of physics, biology, and even psychology. The laws which hold in the human sciences have the looser character of patterns and general rules of associated traits rather than predictive explanations. As he refined his views on the subject of explanation, Dilthey substituted the looser terms "structure," "regularity," "function," and "rule" for the stricter term "law." But here, too, it is misleading to speak of a distinct break in his thinking. In the "Breslauer Ausarbeitung" (1880), he maintained that an empirical law in psychology is "nothing but the expression for the relation between the general conditions of life and the appearance of certain analytically isolated facts of consciousness." He hastened to add that such laws do not refer to "true causes" (*verae causae*) in the natural scientific sense (*BA* 91–92).[57] There are general patterns of intelligibility in the human world which accommodate the perceptual awareness of the agents; these patterns cannot be assimilated to strict causal necessity but are nonetheless rule-bound in some sense. These patterns embody our expectations of the expectations of others. In the *Leben Schleiermachers* the term "empirical law" is used freely to refer to historical patterns such as the intensification of family solidarity over several generations and the mutually conditioning relation between changes in ethical thought and religious conceptions (*GS* 13/1:3). A much stricter conception appears in the *Einleitung*, in which Dilthey cites Grimm's Law in linguistics, Thünen's Law in economics, and Comte's Law of the Three Stages as instances of laws in the human sciences. But again in a freer sense, he employed the term "causal sequence" to refer to the evolution of Schiller's character Wallenstein under the impact of circumstance (*GS* 5:297). And in treating the formation of world-views, he posited a "general law" of the development of consciousness according to which the mind directs itself to the objective world of things before it discovers itself (*GS* 8:128). These instances of "law" are hardly *verae causae*!

In many of the writings which appeared after the turn of the century, Dilthey preferred the dynamic "real-category" of reciprocal action (*Wechselwirkung*) for unilateral "formal" causation. The difference is decisive:

> There is no natural scientific causality in the historical world, because "cause" in the natural scientific sense necessarily entails the production of effects according to laws, whereas history knows only the relations of effecting and of being affected, of action and reaction [*GS* 7:197].

The categories of law and causality were subordinated to those of meaning, structure, and type, so that a "law" in the human sciences becomes a pattern of acts tending to produce a unity of effect, content, value, and significance —what Dilthey called a *Wirkungszusammenhang*. After Rickert asserted that "historical law" was a contradiction in terms, Dilthey substituted "coherence" and "structure." These coherences have no predictive power, for they merely elucidate relations which may change with altered circumstances. They are descriptive and retrodictive:

> Every empirical and comparative procedure can only extract a rule from the past, whose validity is historically limited; it can never bind or determine what is new or may appear in the future. This rule functions only backwards and does not contain a law of the future.

In such historical coherences there are only "moments" of lawfulness: "It is futile to seek laws in the course of history. But at the same time it is clear that every purposive coherence carries within it elements of lawfulness [*Momente der Gesetzlichkeit*]" (*GS* 7:219).

On the vexing subject of "causality and value" in the *Methodenstreit*, Dilthey assumed a characteristically mediating position. History cannot be properly elucidated with either of these categories by itself:

> The causality of history has an immanent-teleological character. History

does not cause, it creates [*Die Geschichte verursacht nicht, sie schafft*]. It creates because the structure of life is at work in the acts of knowing, evaluating, setting of goals, and striving for ends. Man, operating under the conditions of nature, brings forth the objectivations of mind in history. History constantly shows this creation of values and goals—and all concepts in the human sciences are only reflections of this activity—but these values derive from and operate upon experience. Therefore the meaning of history cannot be elucidated from pure concepts of value. But neither is history simply a repertorium of set conditions, for it [history] is the active expression [*Sichauswirken*] of man under the conditions of nature in a variegated manner. History has a meaning only because it shows the realization of values and goals, only because its form of causality works teleologically, only because its subjects create [*BNL* 198/326].

It should be stressed that these modifications were not intended to nullify the concept of causality but to broaden it and provide it with experiential content, thereby fitting causal treatment to the human-historical world. In one of his last notes on causal knowledge, Dilthey cited the position of Max Weber that *Verstehen* and *Erklären* share a common logical ground which can only gradually be occupied and explored through the refinement of concepts:

> The logical ideal of the real sciences of man is to arrive at the separation of that which is essential and meaningful in the individual phenomenon from that which is purely incidental and meaningless—and to bring the former to clear consciousness. The need to place the individual phenomenon in a coherent and valid order of concretely intelligible causes and effects compels these sciences to ever more refined constitution of concepts which can encompass the individual reality through the selection and synthesis of characteristic traits [*BNL* 242/445].

The rigid separation of understanding and explanation was not Dilthey's final word on the subject. In trying to make sense of what seems to be his equivocation, it is crucial to underscore his own observation that his ideas were developed in the context of the struggle waged in the 1870s and 1880s against the excesses of positivism and physicalist modes of explanation. After the celebrated "crisis of causality" of 1895–1905 had provoked thinkers such as Poincaré, Hertz, Duhem, Tönnies, Simmel, and Weber to propound more refined and diversified notions of explanation, Dilthey came to portray the relation of explanation and understanding not as an absolute disjunction but rather as a graduated, step-like arrangement (*Stufenfolge*) of cognitive achievements. In notes appended to his last essay on hermeneutics, he claimed that "between explanation and interpretation there is only a graduated difference, not a fixed boundary." Indeed, he specifically postulated an ideal case in which the initial meaning apprehended in understanding could be resolved into a discernible complex of causal factors. In these rare and special cases one might legitimately speak of a complete explanation in the human sciences. Although he implied that such a pure case was unlikely owing to the vast complexity of the human world, Dilthey did not posit an unbridgeable chasm between understanding and explanation: "At the extreme limit understanding is not separate from explanation; explanation has as its presupposition the full accomplishment of understanding" (*GS* 5:334–37). This passage suggests a position somewhat akin to (and perhaps derived from) Max Weber's notion of a "*verstehende Erklärung*," a method which combines subjective meaning with causal imputation and empirical verification.

But even if the differentiation is provisional and relative in Dilthey's final reflections, one must conclude that any full congruence of understanding and explanation remained an ideal limiting case—much as in the case of his vision of a general theory of knowledge for both the human and natural sciences. In this regard Dilthey admonished the young positivist historian Kurt Breysig that in matters of knowledge one must distinguish between the ultimately and ideally attainable and the more proximately attainable.[58] Given the existing and foreseeable state of science, the distinction between understanding and explanation was valid and useful, though by no means ultimate and absolute. For better or worse, Dilthey was not inclined to posit absolute distinctions—and the separations he did make did not rule out future cooperation and adjustment.[59]

The Ethical Dimension of Historical Understanding: Immanent Critique and the Vitalities of History

Dilthey's theory of understanding, in addition to its epistemological and methodological aspects, embodied an ethical component which is pervasive, yet difficult to specify. Like Humboldt, Schleiermacher, and Droysen, Dilthey regarded the act of understanding as deeply anchored in the nature and ideals of man. We understand in the light of what we are and what we want to become. The human sciences are not value-free, nor merely value-related. They are inextricably bound up with evaluation and moral judgment. Dilthey insisted that *Wissen* and *Gewissen*—science and conscience—cannot be neatly separated in the study of human affairs. Therefore, the ongoing interpretation of the human-historical world is implicated in a larger vision of humanity and what it ought to become.

Verstehen must be "open" in order to grasp the particular human manifestation. Paradoxically this openness is attained only with the cultivation of an attitude of studied ingenuousness or "disciplined naïvete." While everyday understanding originates and remains at the level of practical interests and immediate "lived relations," the methodical understanding of the human sciences proceeds beyond these subjective-personal interests to the level of "general human" interests (*Allgemeinmenschliches*) (*BA* 255).[60]

Verstehen presupposes the full experience of the living subject; all cognition in the human sciences is in a sense the re-cognition of human life. Consequently, Dilthey concluded that Ranke's desire to efface himself before the object would be tantamount to removing the vital precondition of understanding itself. A pure *cogito* or *ich-loses Subjekt* cannot provide the grounds of comprehending the human world, for such a conception suspends precisely the web of lived relations which link the subject and object in this sphere. The researcher must not (and could not) eradicate these lived relations and interests, for they provide the impetus to the investigation and constitute its preconditions. These subjective and affective factors cannot be removed but rather must be raised to consciousness and thereby controlled, broadened, and compensated for. *Verstehen* arises from vital bonds and interests, but it qualifies as genuine reason to the extent that these interests assume a "generally human" rather than specifically personal stamp: "At the deepest level one could say that we understand to the degree that we form our inner world universally" (*GS* 5:283; cf. 14/2:729).

Following Goethe and Schleiermacher, German thought often postulated a distinction between two kinds of knowledge: knowledge as control (*Wissen als Herrschaft*) and knowledge as receptivity or "awe" (*Wissen als Hingebung*). Natural scientific *Verstand* was assigned to the former type, for it aims to control the phenomenon by bringing it under a predictive order of causal laws; human scientific *Verstehen* was linked with the latter type, as it treats its objects as living subjects, that is, as ends rather than simply as means. Although Dilthey did not wholly subscribe to this dichotomy, it does inform his conception of the ethical import of *Verstehen*. In a review, he furnished an example of the morally pernicious effects of allowing covertly manipulative forms of science to dominate the study of culture. Referring to the unrecognized practical motives pervading current anthropological theory, he reminded readers that "the Western nations stand in a practical relation to the primitive peoples of the world: these peoples are not merely the objects of a purely theoretical consideration. The influences of *praxis* have misled some American and British researchers to some very curious theories." One such theory, Dilthey found, was propounded by Louis Agassiz, who in the name of "positive" anthropological science concluded that the "higher" white races were called upon to be masters over the "lower" dark ones since these latter peoples could never attain a higher cultural level (*GS* 16:374). In this debased version of human science, knowledge is not truly "open" to its object, but merely subordinates or controls it on the basis of prejudices and preconceptions.

Dilthey's entire program of thought emphasized the reciprocal relation of theoretical *Wissenschaft* and practical *Leben*, and he was naturally sensitive to challenges and dangers to this delicate balance. As a young activist disgusted with sterile pedantry, he had demanded knowledge in the service of life and *praxis*. In the agitated atmosphere of *fin de siècle* Europe, however, he witnessed the unbalancing of this relation and the aggrandizement of "life" and its alleged correlates of "action" and "will." This tension surfaced in the German *Methodenstreit* in the conflict between those who demanded immediate effectiveness (*Wirkung*) and those who held to stringent, objective validity (*Gültigkeit*). Dilthey reminded his contemporaries that there is a difference between the truly practical and the merely expedient: the path to genuine and lasting effectiveness lay with the hard-won objectivity of scientific knowledge (*GS* 7:137–38). Dilthey's later writings contain strong condemnations of those misguided followers of Nietzsche who would convert *Wissenschaft* into *Willenschaft*.

Dilthey insisted that *Verstehen*, as the understanding of human purposes carried out in the name of human purposes, stemmed from a deeply practical concern: "The coherence of scientific thought is not abstract, hovering above life—rather, it grows out of life itself and increases with the power of practical interests" (*LK* 26). But genuine *Verstehen* cannot be conducted under the sway of narrow, practical purposes of its own. A peculiar double ethic on the part of the interpreter is required: deep concern and interest, even "love," are necessary, but an impersonal attitude is also requisite. The interpreter must draw upon all the resources of his own experience and personality and yet not fall victim to narrow subjectivism. Understanding depends upon a double movement of immanence and transcendence, a going within and going beyond: in short, what Dilthey termed "immanent critique."

The concept of *Verstehen* as immanent critique is one of the most profound ideas developed in his theory of the human sciences. Although it is explicitly mentioned in relatively few places, it animates the entire body of his work; it is a principle which emerges more in actual demonstration than in theoretical specification. Contrary to many accounts of the matter, Dilthey's theory of human understanding preserves a normative function which saves it from precisely those vitiating and "de-moralizing" consequences often attributed to it. *Verstehen* contains a normative property which has been obscured by exclusive attention to its logical and epistemological status. As Kant's theory of natural scientific *Verstand* pointed toward the transcendental ideas of moral reason, so Dilthey's theory of human scientific *Verstehen* points toward immanent values of historical life and culture. However much he railed against "two-world theory" and transcendental notions, Dilthey's hermeneutic maintained a tension between the actuality and potentiality of all human phenomena. This relation is embodied in his view of meaning and development, as indeed it informs his whole conception of *Idealrealismus*. The conception of immanent critique provides a fundamental point of convergence for many facets of his thought which might otherwise seem unconnected: it links the concept of "seeing typically," the relation of fact and value, the motive force behind intellectual development, and the whole program of "history with philosophical intent." Because human understanding is at once immanent *and* critical, it is capable of normative evaluation and reformatory influence.

Understanding is not an "all-forgiving," antinormative, and uncritical (or "meta-critical") mode of thought. Nor does it culminate in the boundless relativism of *tout comprendre, tout pardonner*. Dilthey never admitted the strict separation of fact and value, of scientific and normative judgment, in the human sciences. History in particular acknowledges no such clear distinction:

> To be sure, history will always combine description, causal knowledge, and judgment: not an exclusively moralistic judgment but one which proceeds from the values and norms of all vital human capacities. . . . Judgment concerning what has happened is in and of itself inseparable from the presentation of what has happened [GS 5:268].

This integral relation of presentation and evaluation is conveyed in Yorck's memorable formulation that "all history which is truly living history—and not merely picturesque and colorful—is critique" (BDY 19).

Dilthey regarded his own historical studies as conducted in the spirit of immanent critique. In his letters and diary entries he explained that his understanding of Schleiermacher was critical as well as sympathetic, negative as well as affirmative, for Schleiermacher was judged to have fallen short of his own mark. In a letter to Wilhelm Scherer in 1870 Dilthey defined his method:

> When I explain a world-view or life-view out of the actual inner life of certain larger cultural attitudes, then naturally I must move on to a critical estimation of its value and thus supplement the explanation with a methodical, scientific critique.

But he went on to caution that such critical evaluation must be based upon a thorough understanding of the subject at hand: "the final assessment of value [*Wertbestimmung*] can only be the end result" (JD 286–87). The same point was repeated in a study of 1904: "real and productive critique arises only from the combination of great masses of different studies, from which new and fruitful combinations arise to illuminate an area of study" (GS 4:424). As in all fruitful theoretical endeavor, true critique is the result of prolonged and careful "inside" study, not of the hasty urge to refutation.

Although there are indications of the idea in his early diaries (JD 23, 151, 186), it was in the *Leben Schleiermachers* that Dilthey first articulated and employed the notion of immanent critique. Here the reader is brought to reexperience a point of view in order both to understand it and to go beyond it. The interpreter places himself inside a coherent set of premises and values (world-view) in order to perceive its strengths—but also its shortcomings. Immanent critique is possible only because human action and expression—as indeed the whole of the human world—embodies an immanent teleology from the actual to the yet-to-be actualized. Every more or less purposeful human phenomenon—a system of thought, a constitution, a program of action—can be measured by its own yardstick of aims and values. But since this measure implicitly contains a tension between what is realized and what is indicated as possible, the phenomenon is found wanting by its own standards. Immanent critique is thus an interpretive attitude which entails a double movement of immanence and transcendence on the part of the interpreter; it is an internal tracing through and re-thinking of a human phenomenon but also a surpassing (*GS* 14/2:526). (Lest this seem puzzling, one has only to think of the task of reviewing a book: it must be judged on its own terms and yet this inside-view does not preclude the possibility of criticism—precisely because the terms include unrealized possibility.) In Dilthey's view, such an immanent critique differed decisively from the mode of critique practiced by the Enlightenment, which was generally "external" and devoid of empathy, because its sole standard of judgment was abstract rationality. Genuine critique must judge, but by the standards of what is being judged. Dilthey regarded this kind of interpretation, which goes "beyond" by going "within," as the particular gift of all truly great thinkers. It was the method Aristotle employed on Plato, Leibniz on Spinoza, and Schleiermacher on Kant (*GS* 13/1:130). This was precisely the stance Dilthey assumed toward his subjects, including Schleiermacher, Kant, Hegel, Leibniz, and the Enlightenment and Romantic periods.

Perhaps the most obvious and compelling example of Dilthey's combination of "inside" understanding and critical judgment is to be found in his treatment of the development of the human sciences. Here his efforts at *Verstehen* culminate in a "methodical, scientific critique," not merely appreciation. Dilthey made it clear that an immersion (*Versenkung*) in the course of intellectual history is preliminary to a judgment (*Urteil*) regarding the foundations of scientific thought. But the judgment must emerge from careful historical understanding. Thus, the history of metaphysics is its own critique: "Mankind will fully overcome this great intellectual phenomenon only insofar as it understands it" (*GS* 1:126). In a revision intended for a later edition of the *Einleitung*, Dilthey stressed the paramount importance of a "historical-critical form of thought" which would constitute an "immanent critique" of man's efforts to fathom his own intellectual development and would provide the necessary propaedeutic to future systematic thought (*GS* 1:417). In all interpretation, fidelity and critique condition each other reciprocally (*GS* 8:124).

Like *Verstehen* itself, the concept of immanent critique has a long and variegated background which shades off into obscurity. A full exposition would exceed the scope of this study, but a few salient points can be elaborated in order to highlight Dilthey's use of the idea. Stemming from the conflict of Kant and Herder, German thought in the early nineteenth century tended to divorce the intellectual dispositions of "immanence" and "critique," as in the separation of "awe" and "control"; the inside-subjective and outside-objective viewpoints were seen as mutually exclusive. Dilthey's hermeneutic theory, however, mediated this opposition. As one might surmise from its implicitly dialectical character, the concept appears to have been thought through first by Hegel and employed by his philosophical heirs. For Hegel true knowledge was not simply scientific *Verstand*, that is, "a monochrome formalism, which only arrives at distinction in the matter it has to deal with, because this is already prepared and well known." Such abstract reasoning issues in "a skeleton with tickets stuck on it," a caricature of concrete, "living" reason:

> Instead of making its way into the inherent content of the matter at hand, *Verstand* takes a formal survey of the whole, assuming a position above the particular existence about which it is speaking, i.e., it does not see it at all. True scientific knowledge, on the contrary, demands abandonment to the very life of the object.[61]

Knowledge in Hegel's sense of awe or abandonment must strive to become one with the inner content and life of its object; such concrete knowledge stands in contrast to the critical formalism of Kant's *Verstand* and the censorious judgment of Enlightenment *raisonnement*. Such spurious forms of reason are "merely" critical, or critical in an external sense: "*Raisonnement* in the first place adopts a negative attitude toward the content apprehended; it knows how to refute it and reduce it to nothing." External critique treats it subject matter as "alien and external," whereas true knowledge is the "living experience of the subject matter itself."[62]

But true knowledge as "living experience" is not a simple barren identity with the object or uncritical "adoration" and "belief"—both of which Hegel stigmatized as mere romantic "feints at thinking." As dialectic, true knowledge retains a critical element, constantly assaying limits and moving beyond them. Cognition is neither sheer "inside" affirmation nor "outside" negation, but recognition deepened by critical contrast. Thought proceeds by opposition, refutation, and reconciliation. The critical impulse however, must emerge from within and in terms of the object itself, otherwise the opposition is sterile fault-finding—quite literally beside the point:

> If the refutation is complete and thorough, it is derived and developed

from the nature of the principle itself, and not accomplished by bringing in from elsewhere other counter-assurances and chance fancies.[63]

Following Aristotle, Hegel specified genuine critique as one which goes into and grows out of the subject at hand, following the *telos* of its content: "True critical refutation must penetrate into the power of the opponent and adopt a position within the circle of his strengths; to attack him where he is not and thereby believe oneself to be in the right does not further truth."[64]

Another likely source of the concept of immanent critique was Kuno Fischer, Dilthey's mentor at Heidelberg, who practiced just such an attitude with respect to the teaching of Hegel. In his *Logik*, Fischer articulated the conditions of genuine critique:

> There is a genuine critique which meets its object [*Sache*] and a false one, which remains external to the object. Both judge the value of the object, both need a measure for judgment. The genuine critique compares the object with its own inner aim; the false critique compares it with an alien one, which does not concern it.[65]

Immanent critique depends upon the discernment of a norm against which the object is judged. This norm, however, is not an abstract postulate but rather the extrapolation of tendencies which lie within the phenomenon itself. The phenomenon is measured against its own aims and purposes. All genuine interpretation follows the intentionality of the phenomenon but in so doing, it judges the phenomenon against its own terms. As Dilthey stressed: "To arrive at results, lasting results—that means to judge . . . but real judgment rests upon deep acquaintance with the object [*Sachkenntnis*]" (*GS* 11:96). Wilhelm Wundt also insisted that critique was an integral aspect of interpretation, and like Dilthey he held that such critique must derive its standards from its own object: "All criticism must therefore be an immanent criticism; just as with understanding, so too the evaluation must derive first and foremost from the object itself." The object is always situated in a pattern of general relationships, which become criteria of reflective evaluation: "Immanent critique cannot therefore think of its object as divorced from the fullness of relations in which it belongs to the general development of mental life. . . . In this inevitable projection of the single object upon an encompassing mental background, the immanent form of critique passes naturally into the transcendent form of critique."[66]

Although it was elaborated primarily by German thinkers, it is R. G. Collingwood who has provided the best summary statement of immanent critique. Collingwood's affinity with Dilthey has often been pointed out, and on this matter their agreement is close indeed. Collingwood's trenchant and arresting analysis warrants full quotation:

> It [understanding] is not a passive surrender to the spell of another's

mind; it is a labour of active and therefore critical thinking. The historian not only re-enacts past thought, he re-enacts it in the context of his own knowledge and therefore, in re-enacting it, criticizes it, forms his own judgment of its value, corrects whatever errors he can discern in it. This criticism of the thought whose history he traces is not something secondary to tracing the history of it. It is an indispensable condition of historical knowledge itself. Nothing could be a completer error concerning the history of thought than to suppose that the historian as such merely ascertains "what so-and-so thought," leaving it to someone else to decide "whether it was true." All thinking is critical thinking; the thought which re-enacts past thoughts, therefore, criticizes them in re-enacting them.[67]

The critical element essential to *Verstehen* distinguishes it from the sheer empathic exegesis of the true believer or the awestruck appreciation of the antiquarian. Dilthey was conscious of the pitfalls as well as vistas of *Verstehen* and the modern historical consciousness. Like Nietzsche, though without his strident iconoclasm, Dilthey saw the potentially stultifying effects of an "all-understanding" sanctification of the past and the need for critical history written from the standpoint of its "value of life." *Verstehen* cannot be merely antiquarian appreciation or recollective justification of the past. Dilthey insisted that the past must be studied on its own terms but this is not to say that it is studied for its own sake. History, like philosophy and the other human sciences, points toward the "generally human," whose grounds are not transcendental but given in general experience of life. Historical understanding, in grasping the past, provides the means beyond it toward active creation of the present and future.

Although the nineteenth century is often characterized as "the historical century" and German thought seems especially marked by the consciousness of history, Dilthey's belief in the vitalizing function of history was by no means unchallenged. There ran through the period an influential current of antihistorical thought which reached its crest at the end of the century. Some of the century's most celebrated thinkers displayed a deeply ambivalent and even hostile attitude toward historical study and historical consciousness. Aspects of Dilthey's theory of historical understanding were formulated to meet these objections. As Schleiermacher had once defended religion, so Dilthey defended history from its "cultured despisers" and "most recent detractors" (*GS* 7:216).

Goethe had judged that history, even the best, always harbored "something corpse-like." History, as methodical inquiry, was incapable of grasping life in its fullness and individuality; obsessed with final outcomes, it often wound up with a *caput mortuum*. Whereas nature was open to "objective seeing," history was "legendary" and "symbolic" due to its incorrigibly anthropocentric character. Goethe therefore remained quite skeptical of the worth and objectivity of historical knowledge.[68] Even

Hegel, in identifying reason and history, was far from an unqualified "historicism." He distinguished "reflected" or philosophical history from mere "historical history" and avowed that the aim of Spirit is first and foremost to be *true*, not to be historical; "What Spirit does is not history; it is concerned with what is true in and of itself—not something past, but something simply present."[69] Authentic history for Hegel is concerned with the "emergently eternal" or the "actual," not with the "merely historical."

Hegel's grand dialectic of truth and history was fatuous wishful thinking for Schopenhauer, whose revulsion from all "*Hegelei*" entailed an indictment of history and historical consciousness. Time itself is a mere subjective illusion and history is the "confused dream of humanity" constructed *ex analogis hominem*—that is, the prime source and symptom of man's inflated anthropocentric view of things. History is neither meaningful nor knowable in any genuine sense; a science of history is a contradiction in terms, for history deals only with particulars, whereas science and philosophy aim at the universal. Schopenhauer dismissed history as "meaningless caterwauling" and reviled the historical sense as a symptom of mankind's preening self-fascination. In one of his early studies Dilthey cited Schopenhauer's bitter allegation that historical knowledge is neither true, significant, nor edifying:

> I do not know of any more perfect objection against the value of historical study than the question directed against the historical pedant: "And had I lived before all these things happened, would I necessarily have been any less wise?" [*GS* 16:366].

The vituperative positivist Eugen Dühring likewise viewed history as elaborately contrived but useless baggage, "shadow-games played with ideas which are directed backwards." Historical understanding was vilified as illusory, vain, and stultifying.[70]

The hostility toward history reached its peak in Nietzsche, who called for willful "forgetfulness" and heroic emancipation from history. Nietzsche postulated such forgetfulness as the "vital condition" of creative will. History, as conventionally practiced, was for him antithetical to life in the present: it issued in an indiscriminate "taste for everything" which is in truth a taste for nothing. Nietzsche regarded the much-vaunted historical consciousness as a furtive form of resentment (i.e., obsessive "feeling again") and "cud-chewing." Thus, it was basically just another symptom of European sickness and nihilism. The unrestrained historical sense encourages the cult of facts and "*faitalisme*"—the uprooting of the future and the "dead burying the living." As a corrective to this auto-mummification of culture, Nietzsche called for the cultivation of the "unhistorical" and the "superhistorical."[71] Whether justly or not, Nietzsche's exhortations were taken as a call to will over "petrified" knowledge and life over "dead" history.

In 1898 Dilthey noted the pervasiveness of Nietzsche's doctrine: "The voices are growing loud which complain bitterly about the heavy burden of the past which we carry with us. It is recommended that once and for all we throw off this burden and lighten the load with which we enter the new century" (*GS* 4:528). A few years later, in 1906, Windelband repeated the same point in strikingly similar words:

> This present generation has come to feel that tradition, the great histor-ical schoolbag of modern man, is a burden and it believes that it can cast it off easily, while boasting of the originality of its own efforts. At pre-cisely the moment in which we Germans have begun to make history, we do not care to know anything about it.[72]

The pervasive feeling of a surfeit of history and historical consciousness continued to grow. Max Nordau, whose pessimistic treatise *Entartung* was widely read in the years before WWI, impugned the concept of scientific history as a contradiction in terms: history was "subjective illusion" or "*roman á thèse*, nothing more" based upon man's self-infatuation and "natural tendency to exaggerate the importance of his species in the universe." Following here his arch-antagonist Nietzsche, Nordau denied that "great conquerors, rulers, or law-givers ever possessed what is called the historical sense," and he derided the "disproportionate value attached to pre-occupation with the past."[73] In the midst of the war which was to prove the undoing of much of European history, the young Ludwig Wittgenstein gave utterance to the revulsion against history. With a kind of touching yet disquietingly deliberate obliviousness, he furnished what seems to have been the motto of a significant portion of a new generation of intellectuals: "What has history to do with me? Mine is the first and only world."[74]

The ethical and pedagogical value which Dilthey attached to historical understanding led him to counterattack against this new strand of thinking. Like Burckhardt, he regarded disdain for history as a sign of barbarism. Along with Nietzsche, he recognized the historian's proclivity to an enervating "all-sided receptivity which verges into impotence," but he was deeply disturbed by Nietzsche's glorification of the "naïve consciousness" which lives unreflectively in the present (*GS* 8:204). The assault upon historical understanding, whether in the name of science, art, myth, will, or even "life," was symptomatic of a deeper erosion of shared human values and of a dangerous subjectivism:

> What the human spirit is can be revealed only by the historical conscious-ness of that which the mind has lived through and brought forth. It is this historical self-consciousness of mind which alone can make it pos-sible to arrive gradually at a scientific and systematic knowledge of man. . . . What man is only history can say. If the mind chooses to lighten its load by casting off history, then it forfeits its means of living and work-ing. The rejection of historical inquiry is tantamount to foreswearing

knowledge of man himself—it is the regression of knowledge back to a merely genial and fragmentary subjectivity [*GS* 4:529].

Dilthey cautioned self-styled Nietzscheans that history was not a skin which could be peeled off like an onion. Confirming the historical humanism of Humboldt, he counseled that mankind "becomes" itself only by appropriating and building upon its historical legacy; willing the future *ex nihilo* without knowledge of the past was merely the heroism of folly. And he warned that Nietzsche's end in lonely madness was symptomatic of his voluntaristic subjectivism and narrow, a-historical *Lebensphilosophie* (*GS* 5:379; 8:199–201).

The accusation that historical consciousness represented an incapacitating estrangement of man from himself and his present was for Dilthey the disingenuous ploy of a shortsighted, even narcissistic perspective. Proceeding by the strenuous path of "otherness," *Verstehen* remains the principal mode of man's self-consciousness. What the idealists had designated as "otherness" (*Anderssein*) fulfills a profoundly positive function. In understanding "otherness" man surrenders himself (or his immediate preoccupations), only to rediscover himself at a deeper level. Though it is rooted in our primary existence, historical understanding provides the possibility of what Dilthey called a "second existence" (*zweites Dasein*) whose vistas are wider than those of personal life; the transposition of the self into the other accomplishes the transformation (*Umformung*) of the self in the process of understanding (*GS* 5:262). The self has been formed into a coherence by its own experience, but this coherence can be widened and enriched by understanding. Such understanding extends one's world-view, not by effacing but by enlarging the self:

> The course of life produces in everyone a constant determination by which implicit possibilities become realized and limited. This formation of one's existence conditions all future development. In short, one constantly comes up against the fact that the range of new perspectives on life and inner possibilities of personal existence is a limited one, whether in the matter of sheer circumstance or the larger form of life. It is understanding, however, which opens up a wide area of possibilities which are not immediately present in the determination of one's actual life [*GS* 7:215; also 13/2, 155].

Historical understanding leads the self beyond the circle of attitudes and experiences in which it is immured: it constitutes the prime means of widening our horizons, enriching our perceptions of the world, and quickening our human energies. As a young man Dilthey had contended that "the proximate aim of historical study is the knowledge of the internal and external connections of events and ideas" but went on to insist that "history should work ethically too, in arousing enthusiasm for the ideas which raise the individual from his isolation to participation." Writing near the end of his life, when historical understanding was being impugned as inimical to will and action, he proclaimed a broader, even universal ethical aim for history:

> The understanding of the past must become an energy to shape the future. . . . The historical consciousness must contain the rule and energy which will allow us, in contradistinction to all past happenings, to turn freely and sovereignly toward a unitary goal of human culture [*GS* 8:204; cf. 16:91].

The last word of the mind which has traversed through all of the world-views is not the relativity of them all, but the sovereignty of the mind in relation to each single one of them, and also the positive consciousness of how, in the different forms of mental attitudes, the one reality of the world exists for us.
—Dilthey

A Science of Aspects:
The Doctrine of
World-Views

Wissenschaft and Weltanschauung

After Kant's Copernican revolution, the problem of subjectivity and perspective became increasingly acute and enormously widespread in European thought. Indeed, it might be seen as the more or less explicit preoccupation of almost all thinkers of the nineteenth and twentieth centuries. If the mind is regarded as capable of knowing only what it considers according to its own prescribed plan, then there can be no pure "subject-less" knowing, a strictly objective apprehension of things as they are in themselves. The outcome, as Dilthey observed, was "the subjectivity of the modern way of looking at things" (*GS* 1:413). As long as there remained something like a "universal subject" or "transcendental consciousness" equipped with universal and timeless categories, then the problem of subjectivity found ultimate resolution in the assumed identity of knowing subjects. The unity of knowledge was maintained by positing a rational and unitary subject.

But when consciousness was particularized and conceived concretely as a specific reflection of culture, society, history, circumstance and even unconscious factors and interests, then the unity of the world threatened to break apart into a welter of world-views. To the general principle of phenomenality was added the corollary of the individual subject: as Dilthey stressed, the world is only "there for me." The knowing subject—now conceived concretely and historically, not abstractly and logically—seemed to subvert knowledge itself. Hegel's celebrated transformation of "substance" to "subject" was deflected to the very form of "bad subjectivity" which he found arbitrary and irrational. The result has been aptly distilled: "After doubts about things, we have begun to doubt consciousness."[1]

Much of German intellectual history of the modern period may be said to center upon the properties and perplexities of the notion of world-view. For countless thinkers following Kant there was no longer a *Welt an sich* but only a *Welt-ansicht*. In a somewhat desultory fashion the problem of

world-views received treatment in the works of Leibniz, Goethe, Schleiermacher, Hegel, Trendelenburg, Teichmüller, Schopenhauer, and others.
German thought after Hegel continued to propound the notion of an
actively formative consciousness, but this consciousness was less and less
defined in transcendental or universalistic terms and more in terms of
partial and circumscribed world-views. It seems likely that, in addition to
the romantic stress upon concrete individuality, the sense of accelerated
historical change was instrumental in highlighting the problem of world-
views. Dilthey designated the historical consciousness as the "organ of
sight" which brings the world-views into focus and makes them specific
objects of analysis. The sheer pace of historical development—in conjunction with the historical sense—seemed to require that each age create anew
its organizing vision of the world. Dilthey was not alone in announcing that
even the categories of thought itself were historical and changing. The
vaunted nineteenth-century "sixth sense" of history seemed to lead inexorably to the consciousness of world-views.

> Each epoch is conditioned in its deepest experiences by the life-perspec-
> tive [Bewusstseinsstellung] and further by the implicit presuppositions of
> thinking and feeling; men breathe, feel, think, and will within this per-
> spective. This insight is essential to all genuinely historical thought [GS
> 2:204].

Although his work was prefigured in a number of predecessors, it was
Dilthey who raised the problem of the world-views to a comprehensive
theoretical statement. In this area he pioneered and mapped intellectual
terrain which was later to be explored by students in many different
disciplines. His writings provide a full-scale treatment of the genesis,
articulation, comparison, and development of the world-views. His doctrine or "science" of the world-views (Weltanschauungslehre; often Wissenschaft der Weltanschauungen), which is frequently treated as a marginal
dimension of his thought, is in reality one of its fundamental elements and
requires careful analysis in its own right. Here again it must be stressed that
Dilthey was hardly as careless and heavy-handed in his use of this doctrine
as many of his interpreters.[2] As in the case of Verstehen, there is a great deal
of polemic surrounding this facet of Dilthey's thought: what he regarded as
a breakthrough for the "historical reason" of the human sciences his critics
have often taken to be the breakdown of reason itself.

Dilthey maintained that the process of living requires an over-arching
orientation or interpretation: life engenders an attitude toward life (Gesamt-
lebensgefühl) which in turn conditions our further conduct of life (GS
18:175). A person is drawn to make sense of his own existence and
surroundings by synthesizing his experience into a coherent whole. There is
a tendency toward a world-view already in the "naïve" consciousness. The

mind demands a stable framework to meet the baffling multiplicity, contingency, and imponderability of life—and especially the open prospect of the future. Life presents us with ceaseless change, and yet for that very reason it requires constancy and steadiness on the part of the living subject. Dilthey used a variety of terms to suggest the encompassing function of this mental disposition; it is a "fastness" (*Halt, Festigkeit, Lebensverhalten*), "ground" (*Boden*), or basic mental stance (*Grundstellung, Bewusstseinsstellung*). "Every mental attitude strives for a point which is beyond relativity" (*GS* 5:415). Persons tend to confront the awesome variegation in life by means of the formation of a world-view. This formation takes place over the course of a lifetime and is never "completed," yet it manifests consistency and wholeness. The world-view is the more or less articulated and "objectivated" form of the acquired coherence of personality which otherwise remains tacit and unreflective.

We cannot live our life without adopting a stance toward it and we do this from the vantage point of our own individual consciousness. At times Dilthey seems to imply that life itself, not the particular individual, is the agency at work in the creation of the world-view: "Thus life creates its own world from out of every individual" (*GS* 8:79). The world-view is a total complex of meanings which arises from our "being in existence" (*Darinnensein im Leben*). It is a coherent interpretation of our total experience. The world-view is at one remove from reality—it is not reality itself, but an interpretation of reality (*GS* 5:379). This interpretation is not merely an aggregate of separate experiences but tends toward an integrated whole (*Gebilde, Gefüge*). The world-view is not given to us like a discrete fact or object in the world; it is a total outlook compounded of experience, reflection, and interpretation. It is not purely theoretical, scientific, or "philosophical" in character; it is not constructed like an argument or hypothesis—though it is not therefore irrational. It contains unconscious attitudes and deep presuppositions, but these are not wholly inaccessible, since lived experience is permeated by incipient elements of silent thought and reflection. The world-view unites different levels of meaning and integrates different aspects of experience. In H. A. Hodges' apt phrase, it is "the response of the whole mind to our experience as a whole."[3]

The world-view is not knowledge, science, or "theory" in the strict sense: it might best be called a belief-system. It is not simply the construction of purely rational thought, for, as Dilthey stresses, man does not think, let alone live, by sole means of theoretical reason. The world-view is not a logical system of judgments but a configuration which integrates cognition, volition, and affection; it is a synthesis of facts, values, and ends. Compounded of both subjective and objective conditions, the world-view arises from the perception of factual states of affairs but also from the deepest attitudes of personality, which Dilthey sometimes called "moods of life." The term *Lebensstimmung* might better be translated "mode" than "mood," however, for it is the very opposite of a momentary state of emotion (*Laune*). These "moods" are the deepest dispositions of consciousness. Following a philosophical usage after Schopenhauer, who discerned "an absolute need for the interpretation of life," Dilthey sometimes classified the two most fundamental "moods" as optimism and pessimism. But he was quick to point out that these dispositions were specified in many different forms. The world-views are products of history, not just inner life, for they reflect the influence of cultural tradition, nationality, and epoch. Dilthey stressed that they are conditioned by the milieu in which they arise, but in opposition to Taine and German exponents of *Milieutheorie* he rejected the notion that the world-views could be explained solely from these conditions. There always remains an elusive and unfathomable personal factor in the formation of any world-view, but no world-view is wholly individual, for it is constituted in relation with other persons and other world-views.

Inclusive of ideals and ends, the world-view is not merely a knowledge of what is, but a postulation of what ought to be; the world-view is in Dilthey's words "creative, formative, and reformative" (*GS* 8:84). All capacities of the mind cooperate to form a world-view, although one may come to predominate over the others. Since the world-view is not produced solely by scientific reason, the attempt to grasp it solely with reason entails an antinomy. Using Dilthey's own relative distinction, it could be said that, whereas science "explains" the world analytically, the world-view "understands" the world synthetically, seeking to give a more general meaning to our life in the world. The connection between *Verstehen* as a method in the human sciences and the intrinsically or "silently" *verstehende* operation of the world-views underscores the fact that the human sciences are continuous (but not identical) with life as directly presented in lived experience. The comprehension of any world-view is not some vague, objectless "intuition"; rather, it is "insight-into-an-outlook" composed of many lived relations, life-values, and mental contents.

The world-views are not necessarily held self-consciously, nor are they even explicitly formulated and objectified. Transparent to those who hold them, the world-views require a great effort "underground" in order to be brought into view. This is the task of the hermeneutic science of world-views—a science extending beyond the conventional bounds of epistemology and even philosophy itself. While he was still a theological student, Dilthey proposed what he termed a "philosophy of philosophy," a second-level inquiry based upon "philosophical-historical self-reflection" (*JD* 80). Philosophy becomes the object of its own reflection in such a "meta-" discipline. The science of world-views combines phenomenology, hermeneutics, and intellectual history. It studies the recurrent patterns of "pre-scientific" meaning manifest in the major thought systems and works of the mind. It must be stressed strongly that the science of the world-views is not conducted on the same level as the world-views themselves. It is the confusion of these two levels which has brought upon Dilthey the charges of unmitigated relativism and historicism. In this connection one must recall Dilthey's crucial distinction between the direct experiences and expressions of life on the one hand and the scientific judgments made *about* those expressions on the other hand (*GS* 6:304; also 5:408).[4] Although continuous with and related to the "understanding" accomplished in the world-views, the methodical interpretation conducted by the human sciences is not identical with such ordinary understanding. Knowledge of an outlook is not identical with the outlook itself.

The theory of world-views constitutes a special case of methodical *Verstehen* in the human sciences, involving description, abstraction, analysis, typification, comparison, and generalization. It attempts to reproduce or re-evoke at the conceptual level the original content of what is "there for us" in lived experience, but goes on to examine this phenomenological content in relation to sociocultural forms and certain typical patterns of thought. Dilthey came to insist that the human sciences as such do not directly make up a world-view—though they may presuppose one or contribute to its formation. It is a wholesale misreading of his position to assert that he regarded *Wissenschaft* as simply one of the world-views, existing and functioning upon the same plane. A properly differentiated, scalar notion of *Verstehen* remains the only corrective to this pervasive distortion, which arose in part because Dilthey did not provide a precise formulation of the relation between his theory of knowledge and the theory of world-views. These two levels of Dilthey's theory of mind are clearly related but not identical; it sometimes appears as if he developed them in a carelessly disjointed fashion, thus opening him to the charges of skeptical relativism first leveled by Rickert and Husserl.

Surveying the course of his exposition of world-view theory, one finds a discernible alteration in tone and substance. Some of his earliest pronouncements showed confident hopes for a full-fledged synthesis of the human sciences *and* the world-views, whereas after the *Einleitung* he became more "critical," contenting himself with developing a particular science *of* the world-views. This discipline was first propounded in the '60s and '70s as an explanatory psychology of "thought-elements" but was gradually reconceived after his cooling toward psychology as a hermeneutic of typical life-perspectives. The tone of caution and critical reserve which the older Dilthey expressed toward his own brain-child contrasted strikingly with his earlier confidence in its explanatory certainties. As a student, he proposed, after the manner of Goethe, Trendelenburg, and Johannes Müller, a "morphology" or "true logic" of the world-views, which would uncover the precise law of their formation on the basis of simple elements. This morphology of world-views was considered analogous to the morphology of plants and crystals: the science of world-views was expected to provide explanatory laws of their formation and transformation. Such laws would necessarily resolve (*auflösen*) the world-views into simple factors, but the young Dilthey considered such reduction to be the proper form of comprehension. Writing in the early 1860s he judged that "the richness of the world arises out of simple, even primitive elements, laws, and basic forms combined through endless combinations." Shortly thereafter he insisted on the existence of "primordial constitutive elements" in the formation of all world-views (*JD* 89, 124).

With the increasing stress upon objective mind and structure, the recognition of the "circle of thought," and the insistence upon the dynamic and reciprocal determination of mental life, Dilthey dropped this belief in elementary units. As the conception of the genesis and transformation of the world-views became more diversified, he ceased to use the term "law" (*GS* 6:63 ff., 176 ff.). The doctrine of the world-views, as a subdiscipline of the human sciences, could no longer be conceived in such close analogy with the categories of the natural sciences. In a Nachlass passage from the mid-1880s, Dilthey observed: "Certain regularities [*Regelmässigkeiten*] can also be found operating in the area of the world-views, just as in every other area of mental life. But a total resolution [*Auflösung*] into regularities is impossible" (*BNL* 191/107). Hermeneutics, not psychology, emerges as the key to the comprehension of the world-views, for the regularities in the structure and development of the world-views are more properly analogous to the sphere of language than that of nature: "It [the doctrine of world-views] stands to the history of philosophy as comparative philology stands to the history of language—and if anyone cares to go beyond the separation of the two, I will be the last to oppose him" (*GS* 8:232).

The science of the world-views is an interpretive discipline which penetrates down to the level of basic assumptions and uncovers the sources of creation, development, and diffusion. It attempts to grasp the conditions and structures of certain typical ways of interpreting reality from different standpoints of life. It is a methodical "interpretation of interpretation," that is, a kind of meta-interpretation or general hermeneutic of life-attitudes. Dilthey stressed that it is not a science of strictly causal laws, but a science of vital relations and structures; nevertheless, it is capable of valid generalizations and conceptual knowledge. It is not psychology, much less a "psychology of philosophy," for it studies not only the single mind but the general complex of common attitudes in history, culture, and society. This kind of historical-philosophical reflection is no easy matter and is alien, even repugnant, to many:

There is a powerful potentiality in this self-reflection which bores into the depths, directed down to the presuppositions of consciousness: a kind of labor underground, a strange endeavor which is suspicious to most men [GS 8:38].

Hand in hand with philosophy and the other human sciences, such critical reflection is "the highest power to make conscious"; it accomplishes the "bringing to highest consciousness, founding, judging critically, and relating in the broadest coherence" (GS 5:407, 413).

The Typology of World-Views

Employing the plastic notion of type carried over from Goethe and Trendelenburg, Dilthey excogitated a general typology of the major philosophical world-views. He discerned three basic forms: naturalism (or positivism), subjective idealism (or the idealism of freedom), and objective idealism. Each type reflects not simply rational thought but a total attitude of life. In their formation all mental capacities are involved, though one may be uppermost and lead the others. The world-view is coherent and stabilizing but not self-enclosed and static, for it is attended by an "inner dialectic" which compels the revision of premises.

Naturalism takes as its foremost reality the physical world given in sense-perception. The tangible facts of this external world, especially the "Naturell," occupy the center of attention. Naturalism's canon of understanding is the lawfulness of physical reality. Mental phenomena are regarded as mere interpolations or epiphenomena in the regularity of the physical world. Mind or spirit is derivative and subsidiary—merely the passive register of external reality. Naturalism and its variants tend to deny the spontaneity of mind, free will, and the reality of values and ends. This world-view is manifest at different levels, specifically as materialism in metaphysics, hedonism in ethics, sensationalism in epistemology, and realism in art. Dilthey asserts that after the critical turn in philosophy, naturalism tended toward phenomenalism, or materialism. But freed from certain metaphysical assumptions, it showed new life in a new critical brand of positivism. Dilthey maintained that positivism could not be "nailed down to the errors of Comte" (GS 4:544). Positivism thus showed a development away from a total metaphysic and philosophy of history toward a critical theory of knowledge.

In its historical development, naturalism is impelled by an inner dialectic toward a recasting of its original premises. This inner dialectic arises from the recurrent tension between the perception of nature and the self-perception of consciousness. All matter appears for consciousness and one cannot derive consciousness solely from that which appears for it. Just as surely as the mind is conditioned by nature, so too can the mind exert its control over nature. This inner dialectic forces naturalism in the direction of the other world-views. As representatives of naturalism and positivism, Dilthey classed Protagoras, Epicurus, Democritus, Hobbes, Locke, Hume, Bentham, Condillac, Comte, Destutt de Tracy, Feuerbach, Büchner, Moleschott, Mill, Spencer, Haeckel, Mach, and Avenarius.

Subjective idealism (or the idealism of freedom) was the creation of the Athenian spirit and was reformulated and conserved in Christianity. Indeed, Dilthey went so far as to characterize subjective idealism as the "official philosophy" of Christianity (*GS* 4:550). It asserts the primacy of free consciousness and the moral will and is grounded in an activistic life-attitude. Mind or spirit is seen as superior to natural reality and therefore able to impress its forms upon it. Spirit is regarded as an originary force (*Kraft*), capable of creation apart from physical causality. Thus, Christianity posited a creation *ex nihilo*. Subjective idealism postulates the "independence of all spirit from givenness" (*GS* 8:109). This world-view tends to conceive spirit in terms of personal agency (either mortal or divine), and thus comes to exalt the creative power of personality. It also tends to be consistently dualistic, conceiving the world in terms of polar oppositions such as mind and matter. It presupposes the priority of the ideal over the real, the "ought" over the "is." In religion this form appears as personal theism; in art it appears in the epic and dramatic forms; in philosophy it manifests itself as transcendentalism and voluntarism. Dilthey designated Anaxagoras, Socrates, Plato, Aristotle, Cicero, Corneille, Bayle, Voltaire, Jacobi, Kant, Schiller, Fichte, the Scottish moralists, Fries, Herbart, Maine de Biran, Cousin and the French spiritualists, William Hamilton, Ranke, Guizot, Carlyle, Treitschke, Renouvier, Lachelier, Nietzsche, Bergson, and William James as subjective idealists.

The inner dialectic in subjective idealism emerges from its postulation of the "unconditioned" nature of mind: *Geist* is not wholly sufficient to itself and the attempt to validate this standpoint leads to revision of its principles. Subjective idealism is an intrinsically unstable world-view, for by beginning and ending with the mind as "self" or "subject," it furnishes only a tenuous basis for the sociocultural world. It must fall back upon nativist or a priori assumptions which do not bear the test of experience. Subjective idealism thus is impelled to accommodate a resistant reality conveyed by experience. Without such accommodation, subjective idealism tends toward a subjective solipsism like Fichte's, who mistook the pure ego for the ground of things (*Weltgrund*): "The world is for Fichte only a ball which the I has thrown and caught" (*GS* 5:356). If naturalism tends to reduce mind to natural reality, subjective idealism tends to collapse reality into mind.

Objective idealism is based upon a universal apprehension of mind and reality as an integral "whole." It is grounded in a predominately contemplative and aesthetic attitude of life. Dilthey held that this world-view constituted the major portion of traditional metaphysics. Primary attention is given to the intuition of the wholeness of things. The self or subject is seen as united with the universe in an evolving whole. The universe is regarded as a work of art to be appreciated in awe and apprehended in its unity. This world-view tends to resolve particularities into functions of an overarching whole; it tends to be ultimately monistic, yet each separate individuality may be credited with its own value and the capacity to reflect the whole. It is opposed to analytical differentiation into homogeneous elements, for it conceives of parts only in relation to meaningful wholes, as words in a sentence. In religion this type is manifest in varieties of pantheism and panentheism in which the distance between the divine and the mundane is collapsed into oneness. As implicitly monistic, objective idealism is "beyond" tragedy, pessimism, irony, and a critical attitude. Its basic mood (or mode) is awe or affirmation (*Bejahung*), not judgment (*GS* 2:284). This world-view envisions the expansion of the self through participation with the universe. (Although Dilthey himself does not spell it out, one is struck by the affinities between the attitude of objective idealism and the method of *Verstehen*, though Dilthey's conception of *Verstehen* includes a distinctively critical-judgmental component which brings it closer to subjective idealism.)

The inner dialectic of objective idealism originates in the tension between what the mind aspires to conceive as a whole and what it can grasp in particular. Try as it will, objective idealism is forced to recognize that the whole remains only a symbol or postulate, not a fully comprehended reality. But it nevertheless tries to attain this whole. As objective idealists, Dilthey grouped Heraclitus, Parmenides, the Stoics, Nicholas of Cusa, Ibn Rushd, Bruno, Spinoza, Leibniz, Shaftesbury, Herder, Goethe, Schleiermacher, Hegel, Schopenhauer, Sigwart, Bradley, and Green.

As with most facets of his thought, Dilthey provided a more carefully qualified application of his views in actual historical practice than in some of his programmatic statements. His theory and practice together show that he never regarded the doctrine of the types of world-view as a kind of philosopher's stone or open sesame for all problems of interpretation. He always insisted that the types serve to elucidate history, not vice versa. More conscientiously than perhaps any other thinker of his time, Dilthey struggled against being bewitched by his own methods. After subjecting his earlier views to an immanent critique, his later *Weltanschauungslehre* is more heuristic than explanatory in character. As typological method became modish around the turn of the century, Dilthey never tired of repeating that all types and typologies are only provisional aids to inquiry, not fixed and final results in themselves. Throughout his later writings there appear warnings against a simplistic application of world-view theory: the types serve as a "provisory aid to see deeper historically"—and all such "seeing" must struggle to keep itself open to new insights and refinements. Dilthey was exceedingly cautious in this respect:

> In these matters intellectual inquiry must, in relation to its results, constantly keep itself open to every possibility of a transformation [*Fortbildung*]. Every theoretical judgment is only provisional. It is and must remain only an aid to see deeper historically [*GS* 7:86; also 8:99–100, 150, 160].

With his suspicion of narrow "methodologism" and reification of abstractions, Dilthey cautioned against the hypostatization of the world-view types. Because of the "circle of thought" implicit in all forms of classification, even the concept of the world-view can not be determined univocally (*GS* 8:165). He warned specifically against the dubious procedure of trying to abstract an entire world-view from individual works or actions (*LS* 194). It is especially ironic that in the area in which Dilthey counseled the greatest degree of caution—that of artistic creation—the doctrine of world-views was later applied most indiscriminately. He stressed that art always contains more than general truths and world-views and that the truly creative mind tends beyond the confines of any particular world-view (*GS* 5:397). The doctrine of world-views, like all methods, is an aid to seeing, not an end in itself.

Although separable for expository purposes, the three types never appear as pure forms but rather as organizing centers. The basic types manifest many specific intermediate forms (*Zwischenglieder*) and the actual belief-system is often of this mixed nature (*GS* 4:548–53). It has been alleged that despite his objections to Herbartian atomism and Brentano's "scholastic isolation" of mental faculties, Dilthey himself fell victim to that very trap when he came to classify the world-views. It is true that the classification of naturalism, subjective idealism, and objective idealism seems to imply alignment with the respective "faculties" of intellect, will, and feeling. But this reading is rather arbitrary and selective, for he insisted that psychic life was a complex which could not be resolved into elementary faculties (*GS* 8:83). Indeed, it is this complex which is the originating force behind the formation of world-views, so that the attempt to resolve the complex into separate faculties would remove the very precondition of their existence. After Dilthey had formulated the concept of objective mind, he was able to carry forward the theory of the world-views, since this concept provided the means of surmounting the a-historical building-block assumptions of prevailing anthropology and psychology. After tracing the interaction of objective mind and the world-views, Dilthey insisted that they cannot be identified and explained psychologically (i.e., in terms of the predominance of one or another mental faculty), for they arise from the totality of culture and work reciprocally upon it (*GS* 4:558).

The world-views are not static and exclusive, but show shifts and development. There are rarely sharp borders where the mind is concerned with "seeing deeply" into itself and its own works. Here too Dilthey deplored the "platonizing" emphasis upon pure form to the exclusion of historical development and dynamic change. The frequent accusation that his typological method is ultimately incompatible with *Verstehen* and a genuine sense of historical development is very wide of the mark.[5] In his later thought Dilthey persistently stressed the inner dialectic of world-views which impells them toward reformulation and further development. There is nothing mysterious or suprahuman about this dialectical development. The tendency of life toward a coherent world-view is constantly counteracted by the opposing claims of what has been excluded or suppressed from view. Life constantly confronts us with new and intractable situations which the mind struggles to integrate into its general view of things; this view must be changed in the process. Dilthey insists that consciousness is perspectival, but not statically so. This process of inner dialectic is much more complicated and enmeshed with nonideal and nonlogical factors than Hegel's *Idealdialektik*:

> The inner dialectic which is contained in these problems drives from one standpoint to another. . . . The difficulties which are contained in a standpoint drive beyond it; but it is erroneous to posit with the school of Hegel that they lead neatly and directly to the following standpoint [*GS* 2:312].

Ernst Troeltsch has argued that many nineteenth-century thinkers rejected Hegel's dialectical construction of history only to revert to it in a modified form to portray the dynamics of actual change.[6] This insight is highly pertinent to Dilthey, who, despite his early aversion to Hegel's hollow dialectical schemas, nevertheless fastened onto dialectical form after attempting to fill it with concrete experiential content.

Dilthey provided specific examples of the inner dialectic at work in the world-views. Descartes for example passed from naturalism to subjective idealism and yet continued to partake of both positions. Fichte, who in many respects might stand as the epitome of subjective idealism, also showed traits which brought him into proximity to objective idealism. Victor Cousin is classified as a subjective idealist and yet in his analysis Dilthey treats Cousin in terms of the effort to mediate between subjective and objective forms of idealism (*GS* 4:537–38). To underscore the limits of his classification, Dilthey cautioned that a relation of general similarity of type is not to be construed as a relation of dependence or even of necessary agreement (*GS* 4:550). Thinkers grouped within a general type can be found in contention against each other, as in the cases of Schopenhauer and Hegel or Comte and Mill.

One of the endemic errors of Dilthey interpretation has arisen in reaction to the promiscuous application of world-view theory by later thinkers: the heedless sins of the sons are ascribed to the more cautious position of the father of this doctrine. Following Dilthey's lead but often forgetting his admonitions, researchers in the fields of art, religion, psychology, psychiatry, sociology, and philosophy propounded vast and inclusive typologies. Thinkers such as Eduard Spranger, Karl Jaspers, Josef Nadler, Rudolf Otto, Wilhelm Worringer, Herman Nohl, and Oswald Spengler adopted the theory of world-view types as a means of overcoming "atomistic empiricism," monocausal explanations—and, indeed, any consideration of causality whatsoever. Unfortunately many of these typologies of culture, style, character, and religion, came to be regarded as final, exhaustive, and sacrosanct. Typological method, originally conceived to combat doctrinaire empiricism, acquired its own brand of dogmatism. This orthodoxy of types, which for a time suffused many branches of the human sciences, stood in marked contrast to Dilthey's insistence that all types are only "provisory" and heuristic. When interpreters attempt to categorize Dilthey on the basis of his own typology, he is generally classed as an objective idealist.[7] The basis for this classification is derived from his critical attitude toward naturalism and subjective idealism and the fact that he contrasted his objectivism with Yorck's subjectivism (GS 8:233). Yet this exercise, which purports to pin Dilthey down to his own terms, in fact disregards some of those terms. Such a classification neglects the fact that Dilthey was highly critical of objective idealism and it does not square with his own stress upon the will as the vital center of the human mind. If Dilthey is to be snared in his own typology, then he can only be regarded as representing a combination of all three—with the major constituents being objective and subjective idealism, but with a considerable dose of naturalism. But such a characterization has only limited value at best, since Dilthey the catechist of the world-views is beyond any one of them. Or perhaps it is more adequate to say that his interpretive posture is one of immanent critique: he is both immanent and transcendent to them.

Relativism and the Inner Dialectic of World-Views

It has become almost habitual to portray the theory of world-views as the ultimate signal of Dilthey's grudging but somehow inevitable capitulation to relativism and skepticism.[8] The matter is not quite so simple, however. For him the theory of world-views represents the extension not the abdication of knowledge, for it is knowledge of their limits which provides the spur beyond them. The world-views are indeed relative, but the positive knowledge of them is not relative in the same sense. Dilthey was very explicit on this point: "It is the task of the world-view doctrine . . . in opposition to all relativism to present the relation of the human mind to the mystery of the world and life" (*GS* 5:406). The methodical examination of the world-views is conducted on a plane which is not simply immanent to the world-views themselves but partially transcendent to each of them (*GS* 5:380; also 13). The world-view doctrine must be considered the prime example of immanent critique, whereby the positions of consciousness become objects of understanding but also incentives to "a movement beyond." It was precisely this positive dimension of the theory of world-views which Husserl failed to see in his polemical *Logos* article. To understand the world-views is not merely to appreciate them from "inside" but also to perceive their limitations and to move beyond them.

The contention that all criteria of knowledge and truth necessarily dissolve in the doctrine of world-views is patently false. To say that perception is perspectival is not to say that nothing is perceived or that we ultimately perceive only ourselves. Here it is perhaps necessary to recall Dilthey's unequivocal statement that "There is no perspective without an objective order" (*BNL* 208:345).[9] Objectivity is not denied, though it is rendered more complex and arduous. And to grasp a perspective reflectively is not the same as simply having it in the first place. It seems almost too obvious to stress that a world-view cannot be viewed *as* a world-view unless it is taken as a particular and partial formulation within a more comprehensive perspective, even if this latter cannot be fully articulated in one system. Raymond Aron is perfectly right when he asserts that Dilthey safeguarded valid knowledge, science, and exact philosophy both *prior to* and *after* the world-views.[10] Dilthey's science of the world-views has a clearly ancestral relation to modern sociology of knowledge and theory of ideology and is integrally related to his method of *Verstehen* as immanent critique. This latter relation is indicated in Dilthey's work, but only rather faintly. If Dilthey had spelled out this relationship more clearly in his published works, he might have exonerated himself from the charges of relativism and historicism which he was notably loathe to accept, but which always accompany his name. His notes in fact contain the rudiments of such a defense.

In a section of the Nachlass written after 1905 entitled "The Transcendental Standpoint and the Problem of Relativism," Dilthey defended the position of Georg Simmel from the charge of Rickert that it issued in a dangerous relativism. Like Husserl and Dilthey, Simmel had asserted in his theory of judgment that predications about reality implicitly contain a set of unacknowledged perceptions about the existing self and the situation in which it perceives. Simmel held that objectivity was functionally related to *Existenz* and that the logical forms of judgment were linked to "subjective dispositions" and "interests," especially that of "usefulness to the subject." In rebuttal Rickert turned the tables and retorted that any reflections concerning this subjective or personal *Existenz* must logically presuppose an objective judgment about it by a "pure judging self" (*urteilendes Ich*) or transcendental ego. Rickert found Simmel's concern with the existential reference of judgments to be erosive of truth and Simmel's entire position was judged "inane and contradictory."

Dilthey's spirited defense of Simmel offers a telling insight into his own position. He insisted that the philosophical observation that the forms of judgment have arisen selectively over time according to their usefulness for ordering human experience does not ipso facto open the door to "boundless relativism" (*grenzloser Relativismus*) but rather entails the recognition that "their validity is restricted to the general historical subject mankind [*Menschheit*] which made them." After substituting the "historical subject mankind" for Rickert's transcendental ego, Dilthey went on to rebut a further charge. Rickert had alleged that Simmel's "functional" view of truth in effect reduced it to the "view of the majority," ascertainable only by polling that majority. Here Dilthey turned the tables back on the neo-Kantian: "Rickert confuses the origin and scope of the forms of judgment with their actual substantive employment in an ordered system of contents." Truth is always relative to both a subject and an object but this relativity does not add up to a nullifying relativism unless one holds to a purely transcendental criterion of truth (*BNL* 244/277–78).[11]

It is widely assumed that, as Dilthey probed more deeply into the formation and structure of the world-views, he ended up in a position of sheer relativism. By denying any elementary units, a priori forms, or other "Archimedean points" his doctrine could only culminate in a thoroughgoing skepticism. Although Dilthey distanced himself equally from positivistic notions of law and neo-idealistic transcendental values, he nevertheless retained a special conception of order and coherence which is embodied in the concept of the inner dialectic. The common portrait of Dilthey "the Relativist" or "Resigned Skeptic" emerges only by arbitrarily severing the portion of the theory of world-views which concerns their multiplicity from the equally crucial sections which treat the inner dialectic of world-views. The twin concepts of inner dialectic and immanent critique provided Dilthey not with a stable and timeless Archimedean point "outside" history but rather with a shifting point of perspective and evaluation which is both in and beyond the world-views. Karl Heussi, following the crucial and neglected distinction of Karl Mannheim, rightly argues that Dilthey's position is really a "relationism," not a relativism.[12] The investigator in the human sciences does not have the detached Olympian objectivity of the natural scientist, for he is in a sense a participant in the life he is examining, but this does not mean that he is bound merely to a single "inside" perspective. It is precisely the consciousness of historical relativity which provides the impulse to objective knowledge beyond the world-views.

In his famous essay "The Dream" (1903), Dilthey acknowledged that the initial effect of historical consciousness was to disclose an "anarchy" of philosophical systems and world-views. History seems to contain a powerful impetus toward skepticism—more powerful than all the formal proofs of the avowed skeptics. Taken on this level, intellectual history and the theory of world-views seems to reveal only a vast field of ruins. The great systems of thought have fallen victim to the corrosive vicissitudes of time. Whereas Hegel could see in this apparent contradiction a deeper dialectic of the progressive revelation of Reason, Dilthey sees "untranscendable antinomies": each system is true in itself, but one-sided. "The pure light of truth is given to us only in broken rays" (*GS* 8:224; also 18:200).

There is something tragic in the antinomy between the claims of the world-views to universality and the astringent effects of the historical-critical consciousness. The mind aspires to encompass the totality, but is limited; its reach exceeds its grasp. The critical-historical consciousness seems to conspire toward deep disillusionment and the recognition that the absolute is unattainable. Dilthey faced this recognition squarely and concluded that the contradiction between the claims of the world-views and the historical consciousness was "the deepest, silently-borne pain in present philosophy" (*GS* 5:364). The tension between the urge to absolute truth and the historical consciousness constituted the most basic "irony of history" (*GS* 6:60).

But on deeper examination, the antagonism of the world-views and historical consciousness contains more than tragedy, irony, and pain. In several of his last writings Dilthey asserted that the historical consciousness can heal the wounds which it has struck. This conviction was not merely desperation disporting itself as confidence, for in the intellectual tradition of *Idealrealismus* from which he drew inspiration, a special sort of relativity was directly linked to knowledge and truth. The human mind and its creations are conditioned and relative, but this "conditionedness" is the very source of their intelligibility and truth, for truth is a relation among conditions rather than the absence of such conditions.[13]

To say that the truth is given to us in broken rays is not to say that there is no truth, but rather to remain vigilant against dogmatic foreclosures, partiality, and complacency. Dilthey was decidedly no skeptic. He regarded skepticism as the "dark companion" of the spirit of dogmatic metaphysical systems; both erect an impossible standard of certainty. Once this unattainable standard is surrendered, skepticism, like traditional metaphysics, loses its hold over the mind. Dilthey cited the traditional Socratic argument against skepticism which was given currency in the latter nineteenth century by Lotze: that skepticism is self-refuting. In order for doubt to arise in the first place, the doubter must have a standard of truth; therefore he cannot doubt everything (*BA* 46a).

The historical consciousness has the initial effect of instilling skepticism, but for the persistent mind it serves to disclose the emergent quality of knowledge and truth. The mind cannot have a single systematic Universal Science in the fashion of Hegel and Comte; it is constrained to know conditionally and provisionally. In stressing the process-like quality of knowledge and science, Dilthey went further in healing the "wounds" of the historical consciousness than he is usually given credit for. By the inner dialectic of thought, the historical consciousness leads toward a constantly emerging universality:

> There lies therefore in the process of thinking about the way in which a coherent structure solves the tasks set before it an inner dialectic which lets thought progress through historically conditioned orientations—and the formulas which correspond to them—to a universality which is everywhere and always tied to historical thought. Thus, here, as everywhere, the historical consciousness is itself creative, in that it raises the capacity of man in society above the limits of time and place [GS 5:338].

In his extended study "Das Wesen der Philosophie" (1907), Dilthey suggested that the investigator takes his position above and beyond the world-views by virtue of the historical-comparative method which is the legacy of the historical consciousness (GS 5:380).

At the end of his life Dilthey reaffirmed that the conditioned nature of thought, as revealed in the doctrine of world-views, was countered by an "urge toward the unconditioned." The metaphysical systems as systems are seen to be historical products, but the metaphysical consciousness behind them Dilthey deems "eternal" (GS 2:497; 8:218). Although at first sight it would seem that the metaphysical consciousness and the historical consciousness would be forever deadlocked, for Dilthey they ultimately point toward a common condition: that the human mind is the author of its own truth and that, in its own "conditioned sovereignty," it is ever-productive of new truth.

To think life, that is the problem; the consciousness of life in itself would be the same thing as the consciousness of what is man.
—Hegel

Conclusion:
Hermeneutics and Historicity:
Dilthey's Historical Humanism

On the problem of assessing the stature of a thinker, John Stuart Mill wrote:

> A great thinker can only be justly estimated when his thoughts have worked their way into minds formed in a different school; have been wrought and moulded into consistency with all other true and relevant thoughts; when the noisy conflict of half-truths, angrily denying one another, has subsided, and ideas which seemed mutually incompatible, have been found only to require mutual limitations.[1]

With respect to many facets of Dilthey's thought, the process of assimilation and accommodation, which Mill described as a kind of gentlemanly dialectical consensus, has advanced beyond the stage of barren polemics. Major aspects of his thought have been subjected to careful examination and continue to demonstrate their usefulness and validity. The concepts of lived experience, understanding, world-view, and history as a complex of coherences of interaction have become working doctrines for many researchers in the human sciences. It is safe to say that there are many practicing "native" Diltheyans who may never have heard of the theoretical source of their concepts. Wilhelm Wundt suggested that the latter nineteenth century might well be called the "age of the human sciences" because this period saw relatively greater conceptual advances in these sciences than in the natural sciences.[2] If disagreement remains as to whether Dilthey should be considered the "Bacon" or "Kant" of these developments, there is no doubt that he played a preeminent role in an intellectual transformation whose effects are still felt today.

But there is still remarkably little consensus regarding Dilthey's thought as a whole. Indeed, there remains a great deal of controversy as to whether it constitutes a whole in the first place. To say the least, it is difficult to offer a final appraisal of someone so wary of "final words." A primary purpose of this study has been to treat Dilthey on his own terms, and these terms militate against neat conclusions. Dilthey's elaboration and development of his ideas contrasts strikingly with his description of Schleiermacher:

When we penetrate Schleiermacher's intellectual development more deeply, we notice behind the amazing versatility of perfect accomplishments a tenacious steadiness; we could say a parsimony of spirit which has its roots in keen self-consciousness, firm comprehension, and clear sense for order. He had to take back almost nothing, not even of those matters which he had considered privately for himself. His development is a cautious, steady advance [*LS* 285; also *GS* 13/1:270–71].

After tracing Dilthey's more tentative and digressive development, one would rather be inclined to say of him what he said of Goethe: "For him everything was a problem; every solution contained a new problem— nothing left him in rest" (*GS* 16:217). Though sprawling and diffuse, his thought shows an underlying coherence, but it is, to use one of his own categories, a "dynamic coherence" rather than a formal-systematic one. His concepts and categories are not "clear and distinct" but dynamic and dialectical, embodying movement, internal tension, and reciprocal relations. His key notions such as "part-whole," "structure," "teleological causality," and "immanent critique"—all designate relations which are difficult to define precisely, yet are nonetheless illuminating. Dilthey found that life, unlike logic, does not always follow the law of the excluded middle; the mind tends toward abstract dichotomies but experiential reality seldom conforms to these schema. Therefore, the keynotes of his thought remain the relations of mediation, gradation, circulation, and reciprocation. It is no wonder that thinkers with a strong commitment to the view of philosophy as systematics have tended to view Dilthey not as the "rescuer" of philosophy but as one of its assailants.[3]

Anyone attempting a summation of Dilthey's thought is left in a difficult position, out of which there appear less than satisfying strategies: to wrestle his thought into a familiar school or world-view, to hedge it around with a set of "isms," to resolve it into a manifesto of his personality, or to portray it as a restless "inner dialectic without end" in search of a world-view. Altogether his project eludes most conventional rubrics, yet he continues to be mustered out as an idealist, positivist, skeptic, irrationalist, historicist, existentialist, or metaphysician *manqué*. Close study, however, tends to undermine such designations and recent interpretations have been marked by a tone of almost gingerly caution and reluctance to employ sweeping labels. One such work begins by warning that the student of Dilthey cannot proceed carefully enough; another concludes that after hundreds of studies and successive waves of adulation and reproach Dilthey is still the most misunderstood thinker of the nineteenth century.[4]

Owing to the formidible scope and format of his writings, he continues to be approached more often by hand-me-down reputation rather than head-on. Husserl's observation that he was "much more a man of genial and comprehensive intuitions than of analysis and abstract theorizing" has become the common judgment of philosophers.[5] The term "creative instability" has been applied to his personality and critics are inclined to treat his thought as merely the "life-expression" of this personality.[6] He would not have denied Fichte's dictum that "one's philosophy in the end depends upon what sort of person one is," but he was equally aware of the psychologistic fallacy of confusing personal temperament with philosophical judgment.

Certainly with a thinker like Dilthey it is impossible to quarantine his thought and explicate it in isolation, but it is too easy to move to the opposite extreme and appraise it ultimately as a matter of personal *Gemüt* and/or historical *Zeitgeist*. Unfortunately his more famous expositors adopted this approach without seeing its limitations. Ernst Troeltsch found him to be perpetually torn between "two souls," the romantic and positivist.[7] Max Scheler judged him to be "as problematic a nature as Nietzsche," driven by a romantic yearning which "undertakes much but fulfills very little." At the root of this yearning lay "the touching childishness of a man, who in being constantly oppressed by the rich experience of historical life, cannot express it."[8] Ortega likewise concluded that "it is characteristic of Dilthey that he never succeeded in thinking through to the end, in shaping and mastering his own intuition."[9] It remains true that "no one felt more sharply or suffered more deeply the intellectual contradictions of nineteenth-century cultural life"—but must we then conclude with Max Horkheimer that "Dilthey's failure proceeds inexorably from his intention to reconcile the irreconcilable—an intention which is highly characteristic of all German thinkers of that time"?[10] Must the final word on the Dilthey problem be, in H. S. Hughes' phrase, "a synthesis too great for the human mind"?[11]

It has been said that one of the dominant and most fruitful motifs of Western intellectual history has been the effort to find mediating concepts (*Mittelbegriffe*) between contending extremes.[12] Recent observers have noted the emergence of an "epistemology of convergence" which promises to reconcile some of the same polarities with which Dilthey struggled. Although he has been called a "worshipper of immediacy" (*Unmittelbarkeit*), his project was carried out not under the romantic shibboleth of immediacy but in the cause of a new kind of mediation or convergence.[13] He was intent upon revising the traditional dualities of real and ideal, content and form, experience and thought, practice and theory, and a host of others. He shared his generation's sense that while philosophy had busied itself spinning out tidy systems of a priori or speculative ideas, the realities of human experience threatened to elude the grasp of reason. The complacent "dream of absolute philosophy was over and done with": the range of knowledge had to be expanded and grounded anew in order to come to terms with a changing world (*GS* 14/1:222). In contrast to the sluggish orthodoxies of idealism and the narrow tenets of positivism, Dilthey ventured a synthesis of his own.

The ultimate significance of Dilthey's thought lies in its attempt at synthesis, and a just assessment requires that it not be explained away as merely a temperamental or historical manifestation. Although we may see his synthesis as "conditioned" in many respects, this does not mean that it ceases to bear upon present-day issues. Conversely, to argue for its value does not mean cutting away its original conditions but showing how these conditions continue to inform ongoing investigations. His thought is best viewed not as a holdover from the past or harbinger of the future but as a synthesis in its own right, reflecting its own times. But to say that Dilthey is of his time rather than ahead of or behind it is not to deny enduring significance to his achievement. Hegel observed that ideas do not set out in the first place to be "historical" but rather to be *true*: if we are to view Dilthey historically, it should be in the spirit of what he called "history with philosophical intent." He himself provided the proper guideline in insisting that historical understanding activates rather than abrogates the value of past ideas, actions, and works, by showing their continuing efficacy through time.

It is in this sense that Dilthey can be located in the German tradition of *Idealrealismus*, an important nineteenth-century current of thought which deserves closer study than it has received. Its inspiration came not from the absolute idealism of Hegel but from the critical realism of Schleiermacher and Trendelenburg. *Idealrealismus* was a deliberate hybrid: a realism which could not be converted into materialism or naturalism because it accepted mind as real along with sensible objects; an idealism which could not become a subjectivism because it held that mind must always follow the binding evidence of what is given in experience. In this modification of traditional realism, thought is a representation of reality, which is not identical with its correlate but not out of all direct relation to it. The mind is neither wholly active nor wholly passive, nor can its functions be deployed to separate faculties. The mind both reproduces and imposes an order on things; apriorism is excluded because reason must always remain open to correction and expansion through experience. A strong measure of functionalism is characteristic of the ideal-realists, who subscribed to a graduated scale of certainty rather than an exclusive standard of truth, either idealistic "coherence" or realistic "correspondence." Their conception of logic included ends as well as grounds, for reason is conceived not as conformance to a body of rules but as a self-realizing practical function. Man's sociocultural experience becomes his own "a priori" and the future is given a certain epistemic priority.

Ideal-realism represented a reaction to the idealist propensity for reified abstractions and disembodied ideas, yet it sought to salvage the potentiality of thought and action by anchoring the transcendental powers of *Geist* in the concrete, living subject. The ideal-realists wanted to realize the ideal, not just contemplate it from afar; reason, ideals, and values were not removed to a pristine sphere of pure consciousness but function rather as practical instrumentalities in the world. Above all, they held that thought and life, philosophy and experience, must interact and reinforce each other.

From this philosophical "middle" informed by a sense of history, Dilthey was able to survey problems and vistas closed to more conventional positions. He saw European thought moving in the direction of a new secular-scientific culture. While intent upon preserving aspects of the idealist heritage, he remained critical of thinkers like Rudolf Eucken and Albrecht Ritschl, who sought to arrest this development by forcing it onto the old tracks of quasitheological idealism. He likewise came to see that neo-Kantian value-theory and Husserl's transcendental version of phenomenology ultimately resorted to the same old Platonic containers. Dilthey showed few regrets for the lost certainties of "absolute philosophy" and he was scathingly critical of successor forms of "absolute science." While hostile to doctrinaire positions and dogma of any stripe, he retained a deep respect for Western values and did not intoxicate himself in Nietzschean fashion with the infinity of world-views opened up by unbridled subjectivism and relativism.

He felt himself to be moving into new intellectual territory, an "unknown land" demanding new forms of thought and reason. This unknown land was human experience itself, but in a vastly fuller sense than had been acknowledged in existing philosophy and psychology: experience as "lived through" immediately, as shared with others in the common medium of culture and language, and as interpreted through its objective manifestations. In a Nachlass passage Dilthey recorded: "Reality is there for me as lived experience. Philosophy is only the interpretation of this state of affairs" (*BNL* 210/186). Not the nominal sense-experience of the positivists and Kantians but the whole of lived experience, including its reflected and culturally mediated forms was the keynote of the critique of historical reason.

Dilthey's concept of experience remains rooted in critical realism—it is not to be equated with subjectivism or phenomenalism. Experience provides access to reality, not a pale register of impressions. It is intentional experience "of" something. Because of its intentional structure, it is prepredicative knowledge displaying "a special kind of universality" (*GS* 7:42). As developed in his thinking, experience is both individual and cultural, both immediate and reflected. Our "raw" experience is permeated by mental structures and transpires in sociocultural coherences. It is constituted not within the private confines of pure consciousness but within the cultural medium of objective mind. As he probed more deeply, Dilthey became convinced that conventional psychology remained blind to the most basic coherences and contents of human experience, as manifested directly in its objectifications. He shifted from a psychological to a hermeneutical foundation for the human sciences which could more readily accommodate man's symbolizing activity. History, while still dependent upon the critical foundation provided by "anthropological reflection," is less beholden to psychology proper: "Psychology must go to the school of history and not the reverse."[14] The method of hermeneutic understanding is more revealing of man's full mental life and its patterns of meaning than the psychological techniques of introspection or experimentation.

Dilthey's stress upon experience may leave no special impression with Anglo-American readers because they are so accustomed to it. What could be more obvious and commonplace than the "primacy of experience"? Yet Dilthey's position was controversial in his day and remains so today precisely because of the continuing clash between what he termed *Empirie* and *Empirismus*, the broader phenomenological and narrower sensationalist readings of experience. Dilthey's decisive departure lay not simply in the primacy of experience but the primacy of intelligible structure *within* experience. The novelty of this position prompted Ortega to observe in 1918 that "the manner in which Brentano and Dilthey, especially the latter, were empiricists continues today to be the future of philosophy."[15] After a half century of philosophical development since Dilthey's death, Jean-Paul Sartre felt compelled to reassert the demand for a conception of reason founded upon the dynamic unity of experience: "Because no one has been willing to establish this rationality *within experience*—I state as a fact— absolutely no one, either in the East or the West, writes or speaks a sentence or word about us or our contemporaries which is not a gross error."[16] These words might have been written by Dilthey a century before; in fact, his concept of *Verstehen* is quite similar to Sartre's "dialectical comprehension" rooted in "full experience" and proceeding by "continuous cross-reference" and "reciprocal involvement," which is intended to bring existentialism into closer relation to the empirical sciences of man. If there is one feature which continues to make Dilthey's philosophical program indelibly distinct from others, it is the effort to establish a new form of reason within experience, thereby linking our common awareness of life to the methodical inquiries of the human sciences.

It has recently been said that "above all Dilthey's achievement was to have called attention to the fact that life is in itself hermeneutical."[17] So stated, such an achievement may seem at once obvious and obscure—such that the term "achievement" sounds ill-suited in denoting something fixed and definite, whereas its real meaning ramifies on many different levels. The recourse to hermeneutics to found the human sciences has some notable consequences. It should not be confused with a pan-spiritualism which takes life and history together as some ultimate "text of texts" to be interpreted by intuitive "divination," for it is altogether more down-to-earth and soberly critical. Dilthey established that the process of interpretation is not something secondary to a preexisting reality but a primary attribute of being alive; interpretation is the original condition of life itself, not the subsequent refraction of an antecedent reality. The world of our experience comes to us as already interpreted. Man, as concrete living subject, is implicated fore and aft in his own knowing. He cannot bracket or relinquish one component of the experiential coherence of self and world in order to grasp the other in isolation. We cannot step outside life to see it in discrete parts or all at once—anymore than we can divest ourselves of language in order to talk about it. We begin our understanding of the human world in the middle, for we cannot reconstitute our object *de novo* from simple elements and still retain its qualities of meaning. These meanings are both "for" a subject and "of" an object and they take place within a larger field of cultural meaning. There cannot be any pure, immediate intuition of self, but only the coordinate understanding of different levels of expression. There is no presuppositionless knowledge of man entirely free from the influence of perspective; method is never purely "neutral" to its object and enters into the formation (or deformation) of that object. A hermeneutic theory of knowledge entails recognition that the researcher is not pure rational consciousness but a subject living in a set of contexts. There is an inevitable perspectival component in all knowledge and this recognition demands vigilant critical controls. And in the final analysis the ultimate methodological presupposition of knowing man is our own concrete existence (*BDY* 256).

Dilthey restored hermeneutics from the obscurity to which it had been relegated since Schleiermacher by reconceiving it so that it was no longer simply an interpretive technique for special texts but a general method for the human sciences. He broadened its field from specifically textual meaning to include all forms of signification in the human world. His departure has been pursued in many directions and has proved fruitful in philosophy and the human sciences. It must be stressed that the focus of Dilthey's hermeneutics remained the sciences of man and the critical reflection upon those sciences rather than a new philosophy in its own right. Owing to Heidegger's and Jasper's influence upon recent thought, it is common to find hermeneutics treated not primarily as a method in the human sciences but as a new bridge to the old promised land of ontology and metaphysics. On this reading the interpretation of man's historical existence is taken to be merely "preliminary" to the disclosure of Being as such. Hermeneutics is enlisted in the effort to transcend science, epistemology, and methodology in the name of "recovering" and "uncovering" Being. In the face of these efforts toward a "post-critical" and "post-scientific" conception of hermeneutics, it must be stressed that Dilthey viewed hermeneutics not as a means of transcending science and epistemology but of broadening them; he continued to insist that "in the whole field of reflection and hermeneutical operations, the epistemological question must be given primary importance" (*GS* 8:128). To reintroduce metaphysics in the guise of hermeneutics is alien to his fundamental purpose of founding the human sciences: man may desire to go beyond himself to some unconditioned truth of Being, but in the end this, too, is a truth about man. Dilthey's hermeneutic conception of knowledge bars the way to "absolute philosophy" of Being but opens the way to critical-methodical knowledge of man's being.

As fruitful as Dilthey's ideas have proven to be, they are problematic in the form in which he left them. With due regard to his frank admission of the gap remaining between his aims and accomplishments, it is within the spirit of his thought to submit it to an immanent critique, that is, to judge it by its own standards. And by these standards Dilthey must be said to have fallen short of his own mark. His thought is sometimes unnecessarily ambiguous and opaque. In "going beyond" he too often leaves his previous assertions behind without clarification. Admitting his preference for "coherence" over "system," he still falters at crucial points. He was impartial to the point of contradicting himself and he glossed over many problems, seeming to prefer open-ended reconnoitering and interim reports to steadfast judgments. It is characteristic that he regarded all methodological monism as "impoverished scholasticism" and often remarked upon his propensity to see all sides of a question (*JD* 68, 76). He is sometimes so kaleidoscopic and "all-sided" as to seem lacking in a point of view of his own. The interpretive criteria of "openness" and "fidelity to experience" are not without costs: they too easily lead to a wayward impressionism, lacking formal unity and closure. Dilthey's prodigious capacity for the understanding of others made it difficult for him to present his views clearly and consistently. It sometimes seems as if his primary intent was not to give his *own* conclusive interpretation but rather to show that *interpretation as such* is everywhere and irrecusable. The recognition that life itself is hermeneutical may lead to critical self-consciousness but also to a kind of formless wonder—or as Cassirer observed, an attitude of "sheer perceptual awe."[18] The famous hermeneutic circle can be illuminating, but also downright allocentric.

Dilthey's middle sometimes degenerates into a muddle and many of the dichotomies he claimed to have overcome in "full experience" were merely postponed to later appearance. His mediations were supposed to be accomplished "silently" in lived experience by way of pre-reflective, tacit knowledge. But he could not furnish a fully convincing account of the structural relations in experience without leaving the plane of experience itself. He rejected the a priori formalism of the neo-Kantians and the essentialism of Husserl and wound up claiming that much of what is a problem for thought somehow ceases to be so for the concrete experience of life. He sometimes portrayed conceptual thinking and lived experience as antinomies, yet his whole project is predicated upon their cooperation in the cognitive procedures of the human sciences. The endeavor to go beyond Kant by means of experience comes close to Baron Munchhausen's fabled effort to pull himself from the swamp by his own topknot. Too often Dilthey invokes "life" and the "standpoint of life" as a philosophical *deus ex machina* to rescue himself from competing theoretical claims.

Availing himself freely of this standpoint, Dilthey criticized others for conjuring up empty verbalistic or logical schemes with no real empirical content; by reverse token, however, he can be accused of imputing more cognitive efficacy to such a standpoint than it can provide, regardless of his postulate of "general experience." His censorious remark concerning the "analytical scholasticism" of Brentano and Husserl was ill-taken: a keener analytical effort on his own part would have made his own synthesis more cogent. Too often analogies and metaphors do service for careful, sustained analysis—a reflection of the fact that Dilthey cared more for concrete relations than theoretical conceptualization. It remains difficult to determine whether his distinctions are distinctions of degree or of kind. His critique of historical reason would be more persuasive had he provided careful taxonomies such as Husserl's for the different forms of experience, Simmel's for social relations, and Meinong's for mental objects.

Despite his differentiation of "act" and "content," Dilthey did not distinguish properly between lived experience as an object of understanding and as a constituent in the process of understanding. As a result, his theory of knowledge seems to shift its ground. He failed to provide a sufficiently coherent order of life-values and categories for the human sciences; his treatment of the separate categories does not proceed convincingly to show their joint articulation. He was fond of invoking Goethe's formula of the natural "systole-diastole" of analysis and synthesis in all thinking, but it must be said that he was not fully proficient in maintaining this rhythm. He undoubtedly poses significant questions—but too often seems to prefer rephrasing them at a different level to answering them straightaway. Like many thinkers in the nineteenth century, he had a problem of Hegelian dimensions, but without a Hegelian solution. Although his thought contains more conclusive results than he is often given credit for, there is some truth in the judgment that his merit lies more in what he began than in what he finished.[19] In this respect, his observation that "openness to experience" is historically a transitional intellectual phenomenon which tends to occur between the perishing of one conceptual framework and the emergence of a new one might be seen as testimony to his own sense of deficiency (*GPD* 30).

Despite these shortcomings, Dilthey's thinking most often departs from and returns to a position of what might be called, for want of a better term, "critical-humane common sense." Its faults come in train with the corrective reaction to positions which were overly speculative, a priori, and peremptory. The inchoate quality of his thought seems more commendable when contrasted to the doctrinaire certainties of the major "school standpoints" of his time. For all its diffuseness, there is an experiential richness in Dilthey's thought. In reading him one often has the feeling not so much of encountering an entirely new philosophy but of recognizing what one knows from experience and yet finds lacking in most philosophy and theory.

In a central passage of his ethics, Dilthey contended that "there is no theory which could influence life which has only theoretical origins" (GS 10:27). Thought follows life and life is first of all not a theoretical matter for us, no matter how dispassionate we wish to become. The stress upon concrete experience, lived relations, and "praxis of life" was not intended to nullify reason but to widen its scope and deepen its foundations. Dilthey was allied with other thinkers following Kant who discerned a kind of practical reason dimly lodged behind the clearer profile of theoretical reason. But this does not put him in the camp of irrationalists who viewed cognition as a reflex of will and philosophy as some sort of involuntary memoir. He gave the irrational its due, but he did not cede it the field by reducing reason to the subordinate instrument of a blind, unappeasable will or life-force. Dilthey's conception of life owes nothing to Schopenhauer's "will-to-life," Nietzsche's "will-to-power," or Bergson's elan vital. Although his thought is often treated as foreshadowing the twentieth-century rift between existence and reason, his basic aim lay rather with their mediation. He inveighed against logicism and intellectualism, but in the name of an expanded concept of reason. His adversary was not science but scientism, not reason but the kind of rationalism which restricts reason solely to the methods of physical science and then extends these methods to all forms and features of reality. Reason for Dilthey is not only the abstract ratiocination of Verstand but man's total capacity for Besonnenheit, that is, awareness of himself and the world. Merleau-Ponty has provided a judgment which might stand in testimony for Dilthey's position: "The most effective defenders of reason in practice and even in theory are not those who abstractly make the strongest claims for it."[20]

Dilthey's concept of historical reason was "grounded" in lived experience and concrete awareness of life. Although he recognized that the prevailing tendency of scientific method lay in the direction of commensuration and the resolution of experience into abstract schemata, he proclaimed a critical limit to this tendency in the human sciences. His critique of historical reason entails a fundamental recasting of the assumptions which lie behind the scientific crusade against "anthropomorphic," "symbolic," and "teleological" modes of thought. To exclude lived experience from the logic and method of the human sciences is tantamount to constructing these sciences without man. When "disinfected" of lived experiential content, scientific objectivity and validity become literally meaningless. If the human sciences try to efface the level of lived experience, they have purchased an allegedly "higher" objectivity at the cost of basic intelligibility. This is not to say that the human sciences can arrive only at a kind of subjective or "personal" truth, for lived experience remains common to human life as such. The human sciences are anthropomorphic but not in a subjectivistic sense; in Cassirer's apt phrase, they embody an "objective anthropomorphism."[21]

Nothing could be more misleading than the view that Dilthey's thought culminated in skepticism or irrationalist *Lebensphilosophie*. He was a relativist at the level of the world-views but not at the level of science and critical reflection. Only with stringent qualifications can Dilthey be classed as a proponent of *Lebensphilosophie*, which he often criticized as a "mood without a method." He distinguished his way of thinking from these sundry irrationalist currents by aligning it with "philosophy of experience" and "philosophy of man" (*GS* 14/1:464). The standpoint of life was inseparably linked to the critical-scientific spirit of the human sciences. In his essay "The Dream," which is often selectively cited as proof of his "relativism," he reemphasized his faith in science:

> The empirical sciences of nature have transformed the external world; now the world-epoch has dawned in which the sciences of society and man will gain increasing influence upon the world [*GS* 8:225].

In one of his last sketches he postulated the steady progress of these sciences and the formation of a "general international coherence of scientific knowledge" which would overcome the barriers of time and space (*GS* 7:346).

It has often been alleged that the nineteenth century began by rationalizing history with Hegel and ended by historicizing reason with Dilthey, thereby bequeathing to the twentieth century an anarchy of world-views deprived of the arbitrating authority of reason. The notion of a critique of historical reason is said to resolve itself into a "historical critique of reason" which degrades scientific reason to the status of a mere stage or world-view in the history of thought. Since he interpreted consciousness and thought in historical rather than static, a priori terms, Dilthey is often assigned to the company of irrationalists and relativists on the grounds that his emphasis upon history vitiated his commitment to reason.[22]

This study has deliberately avoided applying the label of "historicism" to Dilthey in the belief that it obscures more than it illuminates. It is a term with vastly different meanings, exceedingly polemical overtones, and many different ideological valences. Like many "isms" it has come to mean so much that it is in danger of meaning nothing at all.[23] Many of the meanings propounded for historicism are not merely incompatible but even diametrically opposed. Some interpreters stress its emphasis upon concrete individuality, some its emphasis upon "wholeness," and others its assertion of historical laws and predictability. By some accounts it is realistic and "factualistic"; on others it is idealistic and "holistic." It has been seen as a circumscribed method, a total world-view, an outright metaphysics, and a political ideology. It is no wonder that one authority who has investigated the term carefully has suggested that it be avoided altogether.[24]

Despite the vagaries of the term, Dilthey is almost invariably linked with historicism. Ernst Troeltsch claimed that he was "the most spirited, discerning, and vital representative of pure historicism." He has been called "the philosopher of historicism" and "the first to make fully clear the consequences of historicism." A recent work, after stating that "no conclusive definition of historicism is at present possible," nevertheless goes on to find that "Dilthey, though he would have indignantly disclaimed the label, is the historicist's historicist par excellence."[25] Like many capsule judgments of Dilthey, this one sets off in the right direction but goes astray in neglecting the full range of his terms. He frequently used the term "historicity" and isolated it as a category of life, but he explicitly rejected the characterization of his thought as historicism. Although according to his own hermeneutic theory we may be in a position to understand Dilthey better than he understood himself, treating him on his own terms may also mean accepting outright his assertion to Husserl that he was *not* a historicist. There are several reasons for taking his own self-assessment at face value.

Dilthey regarded the historical consciousness and transcendental consciousness as two complementary aspects of the same general intellectual transformation: man's understanding of himself and the appropriation of his own creative capacities. History, as the arena of man's self-discovery and self-creation, is endowed with great significance; indeed, Dilthey sometimes referred to the "joys of historical becoming" and "joys of historical seeing" (*GS* 11:218; also xvi–xix). But this is a far cry from postulating some grand substantive meaning in history à la Hegel. Dilthey was not inclined to deify history or to regard it as the extension of religion or metaphysics by other means. If historicism has come to mean an all-encompassing relativism, an interest in the past for its own sake, or the belief in some overarching meaning or direction in history, then Dilthey cannot be accounted a historicist. Even if it denotes simply a commitment to the view that human affairs are best comprehended in terms of individualities in a unique process of genetic development, then Dilthey still does not qualify as a "pure historicist," for he always insisted upon the importance of generalizing, typifying, and comparative methods, as well as the "circulation" among all the human sciences. In fact, he might be properly considered as one of the first architects of the program "historical science beyond historicism" which has recently drawn so many adherents.

He did not resolve science, religion, philosophy or other cultural forms wholly into history. To claim that history is the primary mode of intelligibility for the sociocultural world is not to deny the necessity of systematic theoretical inquiry. At the conclusion of the essay "Das Wesen der Philosophie," Dilthey ended not with rounded historical pronouncements but with a call for further theoretical endeavors:

> The history of philosophy hands over to systematic philosophical work the three problems of the foundation, validation, and ordering of the single sciences—and the task of confronting the unceasing need for ultimate reflection upon being, ground, value, and end and their connection in the world-view, whatever the form and direction this investigation might take [*GS* 5:416].

If philosophy is no longer Absolute Knowledge, neither is it merely the history of world-views or piecemeal service at the table of the positive sciences: "Philosophy is the mind's reflection over all its capacities, down to their last premises" (*GS* 5:358). Or as he put it in the "Berliner Entwurf": "It is philosophy alone which can give individual scientific investigations coherence, foundation, and ultimate intelligibility—and this only through a fuller and deeper consciousness of reality" (*BE* 25). The reciprocity of philosophy and history and the "circulation" of the human sciences as a whole precludes any "pure" historicism.

Historicism is often said to be an ideology of the status quo, resting upon an implicit "historical faith" or optimism, a quasi-religious and quietistic affirmation of the past. It is branded as a contemplative, uncritical, and morally indifferent "retrospective theodicy" grounded in the view that "whatever was, is right." A recent critic of the German historical tradition has asserted that its exponents, deeply imbued with this numbing faith, were utterly unaware of the cultural crisis around them:

> The suspicion that modern civilization was approaching a profound crisis was shared by many thinkers and artists by 1870, but there were strikingly few historians among them. . . . Nor did German historians in the years 1870 to 1914 reflect the fear that modern European civilization was in a crisis.[26]

It was precisely this crisis which provided the impetus behind Dilthey's theory and practice of history. Though he refused to join in the chorus of cultural pessimism, Dilthey was no historical Pangloss, leaving history to take some foreordained course. In 1907 he wrote:

> Present-day reflection upon human existence fills us with the feeling of the fragility of all life, the power of dark instinct, of human suffering

because of dark forces and illusions, and of the finitude of all life—even there where the highest attainments of social and cultural life arise [GS 7:150].

One of his major differences with the neo-Kantians lay with his view that history included dark forces, powerful illusions, and sinister behavior as well as *Kulturwerte*. And unlike the neo-Hegelians, he refused to translate these forces into unwitting agents of a cunning of reason, world-spirit, or *raison d'état*. If Dilthey can be said to have had a faith in history, it was of a piece with this faith in reason and mankind itself: it was a critically chastened and reformatory faith.

The twentieth century has brought a succession of pronounced reactions against historicism, even to the extent of attacking it with its own methods. It has been interpreted as a transitory manifestation in European thought traceable and explainable in terms of certain specific historical conditions. This "historicizing of historicism" sometimes proceeds under the banner of reestablishing as "absolute" the moral values so grievously abused and compromised in this century. A considerable number of philosophers (including Karl Löwith, Leo Strauss, Gerhard Krüger, and Leszek Kolowkowski) have portrayed historicism as logically specious and morally pernicious, ultimately reducible to an "all-understanding, all-forgiving" relativism. Löwith has provided the strongest indictment of historicism:

> If the history of the recent past can teach us anything, then it is that history is not something by which one can orient his existence. To want to orient oneself to history when one is in the middle of it, is like wanting to hold onto waves in the middle of a shipwreck.[27]

Without bothering to ponder the problem of *post hoc, propter hoc*, Löwith and others have invoked the "shipwreck" of the twentieth century to discredit the historical consciousness of the nineteenth century. Whatever its logical and moral basis, such an argument it still profoundly historical in nature and partakes of the very historical sense which it calls into question. Another recent judgment of historicism is indicative:

> By reducing history to the study of the past for its own sake, concerned with understanding rather than reshaping reality, the German historicists sowed the intellectual seeds of a philosophical and ethical nihilism which prepared the way for Hitler. Far from reflecting the triumph of the German spirit, historicism was a monument to the abdication of the educated, liberal bourgeoisie, the flight into an inner world of contemplation which had been its reaction to every crisis since 1848.[28]

If this study has accomplished anything, it must have shown that for Dilthey "understanding" was inseparable from "reshaping" and that human thought cannot be divorced from the outer world of concrete conditions and actions. If Dilthey is to be viewed as a historicist, it must be in a very special sense of the term—a sense which seems largely lost to its more recent interpreters.

This special sense of historicism has been maintained by two German thinkers who can hardly be accused of any abdication from the cause of critical reason. Early in the debate Karl Mannheim emphasized that historicism is not a specifically German form of "metaphysics in disguise," extolling the past for its own sake, but an indispensable method of the human sciences:

> Historicism has developed into an intellectual force of extraordinary significance. . . . The historicist principle not only organizes, like an invisible hand, the work of the cultural sciences, but also permeates everyday thinking. . . . Historicism is therefore neither a mere fad or fashion; it is not even an intellectual current, but the very basis upon which we construct our observations of sociocultural reality.[29]

Likewise, Ernst Cassirer has cautioned against the fallacy of misplaced iniquity, and the common habit of viewing historicism only in the light of its allegedly destructive aftereffects. In the course of the fragmentation of knowledge in the nineteenth century, when every group of facts seemed to constitute an individual science, historicism, far from inducing relativism and nihilism, provided a synthetic perspective upon mankind: "Historicism found Being no longer in God or in the Absolute Idea, and wanted to hold fast to it in the human mind and the totality of humanity."[30]

Dilthey was averse to describing his thought in terms of "isms" and he would be surprised by the company to which he has been consigned by many of his interpreters. But along with the term *"Idealrealismus"* there is much to recommend the designation of his thought as a "transcendental historicism." He regarded the combination of the transcendental and historical points of view as the great legacy of the early nineteenth century and the point of departure for his own thought (*GS* 14/2:538). As coefficients in the process of human "self-reflection," these two standpoints combine when the mind ceases to take itself and its surrounding world for granted and initiates the methodical search for its ground and background. He believed that the genuine impulse of transcendental philosophy and his own historical studies were "digging toward the same depth" (*GS* 2:496; 8:10).

Transcendental historicism may be considered a philosophical position which regards history as the prime perspective upon man and the chief means of disclosing the conditions of man's possibilities for self-realization.[31] History, therefore, can be said to provide the indication of something absolute and eternal in man—not in the sense of a priori norms or fixed essences, but as potentiality for the truly human. For Dilthey, this transhistorical absolute was the creative capacity and sovereignty of the human mind, defined not as an ethereal "Idea" but displayed in concrete life and its conditions. If the term "transcendental historicism" seems to step beyond Dilthey's own terms, his phrase "history with philosophical intent" amounts to the same thing. "History for history's sake" was alien to his concept of human knowledge: hermeneutic understanding aims not at antiquarian fact-gathering but re-creation and re-formation in the service of life in the present and future. Nietzsche's notorious disjunction of history and life, which has been incorporated into modern existentialism, represented the contradiction of Dilthey's entire program.

Dilthey's transcendental historicism must be marked off from "pure historicism," but it must also be distinguished from twentieth-century existentialism. It has often been observed that certain forms of historicism found their continuation in modern philosophies of existence.[32] Although Dilthey's hermeneutics of historical life is an obvious antecedent of such philosophies, one must not overlook the differences. For Dilthey, man's historicity is integrally linked with social and cultural conditions; human existence submits itself to positive examination in the human sciences and is ultimately comprehended in universal history and philosophical anthropology. The concrete individuality of the human subject does not obliterate the fact that man is a social and cultural being whose experience is always beyond an enclosed self. Nothing could be further from Dilthey's view of man and human experience than the lonely cry of Zarathustra which became the credo of existentialism: "In the end one experiences only himself."

Man for Dilthey has an "open" nature, particularly open to communication with his fellow man. Following the "circle of thought," one might say that Verstehen is the basis of human nature just as much as human nature is the basis of Verstehen. Dilthey had a functional and transactional rather than purely essentialist or existentialist view of human nature: history must be concerned with constancy as well as change, the typical as well as the unique. It is noteworthy that Dilthey stopped short of Yorck's concept of "absolute historicity," which had such a great effect upon Heidegger; he even invoked Plato's critique of Heraclitus against the views of his friend (BDY 71–72). Thus, Dilthey's historicity is quite different from the radical all-corrosive "naughting" historicity of the existentialists, who have portrayed life as the dreadful freedom of "thrownness," devoid of cultural tradition, continuity, and communication. Dilthey's historically grounded Leben shows fundamental differences from the a-historical Existenz of these thinkers. The solitary, encapsulated "für sich" and "en soi" of Heidegger and Sartre bear slight resemblance to Dilthey's notion of life as participatory "being with" (Mitsein) in human understanding. The historicity of man is defined within the community of mankind, so that human life shows rootedness, not just uprootedness. Dilthey's insistence upon the "binding power of historical tradition" stands in marked contrast to the historicity of the existentialists (*GS* 4:403). This insistence puts him closer to the universalistic liberal humanism of the Renaissance, Enlightenment, and Idealist epochs than to the radically subjective individualism of the existentialists, which makes much of historicity but nothing of history.[33]

It has been said that contemporary thought is in the initial stages of a new Eleaticism or "essentialism," a new (yet old) scientific paradigm set up in reaction against the vertigo induced by earlier preoccupations with genetic development and history. Much recent work in the human sciences has abandoned historical perspectives and methods in favor of synchronic and structuralist modes of thought. Theorists of this new dispensation speak of the "death of man"—meaning the death of the concept (or construct) of historical and existential man devised by the nineteenth and early twentieth centuries. The conviction that man is the source of his own meaning and the agent of his own development has been dismissed as the last fading idol of a blinkered, vainglorious humanism. Although these new modes of thought might serve as a valuable corrective to the shortcomings and complacencies of a "bad historicism," they also show signs of theoretical rigidification and a certain hardening of the categories, which threatens to wind up in the position of reason without life and of human science without man. Between the extremes of "historicity" and "synchronicity"—the formless flux of existential phenomenology and the lifeless form of certain recent forms of structuralism—Dilthey's position might best be reviewed with an eye to discovering grounds for fruitful synthesis rather than the pendulum-swing between philosophical extremes.

Dilthey yields no easy prescriptions, no comforting prospect of a closed system of explanation culminating in a Final Word. Truth for him was a process, not a proposition: *"Die Wahrheit ist in keiner Formel"* (*GS* 9:176). In his Lessing study Dilthey reminded his readers: "The genuinely human is never totally realized and yet is everywhere. It cannot be fully exhausted in concepts and yet all ideals of mankind and views of life disclose a side of this inexhaustible reality" (*ED* 129). Man's self-interpretation is always *"unterwegs"* with his own history. But through the turbulent spectacle of history Dilthey offered a broadly humane vision. In the year of his death the international journal *Logos* affirmed that "a deep belief in mankind lies at the basis of every line Dilthey wrote."[34] He urged his contemporaries to use their eyes for themselves; he did not tell them what to see. Many fixed conclusions about Dilthey are wide of the mark—but in the end his words on Lessing provide an unsurpassed summary of his own intellectual impulse:

As over against all systems, he propounded a freedom which was not mere vacuous emptiness but rather reflected the creative tendencies of the human spirit. He conducts us up to a tower to an unobstructed vista. He does not just point out what he sees, he makes us see [*JD* 187].

Notes

Introduction

1. Recent theoretical works which show an indebtedness to Dilthey are H. P. Rickman, *Understanding and the Human Studies* (London, 1967), George Morgan, *The Human Predicament* (Providence, R.I., 1968), Otto Friedrich Bollnow, *Philosophie der Erkenntnis* (Stuttgart, 1970), and Charles Taylor, "Interpretation and the Sciences of Man," *Review of Metaphysics* 25 (1971):3–51. The remarkably contemporary quality of Dilthey's thought in the light of current theory of knowledge and scientific discovery is stressed in Peter Krausser, *Kritik der endlichen Vernunft* (Frankfurt am Main, 1968). Rudolf Makkreel's recent study, *Dilthey: Philosopher of the Human Studies* (Princeton, 1975), stresses the centrality of Dilthey's aesthetics to his theory of the *Geisteswissenschaften*.

   The crucial German term *Geisteswissenschaft(en)* will be translated here as "human science(s)." It has often been noted that the term has no precise counterpart in English: neither *Geist* (mind, spirit) nor *Wissenschaft* (science, discipline) has an exact equivalent, and the difficulty is compounded in their combination. These terms are deeply rooted in the German intellectual tradition—indeed, they almost epitomize that tradition: "It is hardly too much to say that a valuable and comprehensive intellectual history of Germany could result from a history-of-ideas study of what makes these two words peculiarly German. The chief philosophic difficulty which they present anyone attempting an English translation is that their possible meanings are more various and, at the same time, more unified than are those of their English equivalents" (C. S. Howe, foreword to Ernst Cassirer, *The Logic of the Humanities* [New Haven, 1960], pp. viii–ix). The German term includes both the social sciences and humanities and has been translated as "human studies." The term "human sciences," however, is preferable for several reasons. The rather flaccid "human studies" fails to convey Dilthey's concern for methodical rigor, general validity, and critical self-consciousness; thus it perpetuates the notion of this group of disciplines as somehow edifying and worthwhile but largely inchoate and vague in character. Indeed, "human studies" seems more appropriate for describing the condition of these disciplines *before* Dilthey set about his task of providing their theoretical-critical foundation. The German *Wissenschaft* is certainly broader than the English "science," but it is decidedly more adamant than the looser term "study." It is noteworthy that Dilthey's reservations about the term *Geisteswissenschaft* centered upon the problematic connotations of *Geist* rather than *Wissenschaft*: he rejected such alternatives as "social sciences," "moral sciences," "historical sciences," and "cultural sciences," as too narrow and found the original term to be "least inappropriate." As this study hopes to show, it is arguable whether Dilthey's conception of the *Geisteswissenschaften* "seems to imply an Idealistic approach to the humanistic disciplines for which it stands" (Fritz Ringer, *The Decline of the German Mandarins* [Cambridge, Mass., 1969], p. 96). All things considered, the translation "human sciences" seems most in keeping with his intent—or "least inappropriate." The term "human sciences" has recently been employed by Joseph Kockelmans, *Contemporary European Ethics* (New York, 1972), p. 219, and by Ernest Becker, *The Denial of Death* (New York, 1973), p. ix and passim.

2. Jose Ortega y Gasset, *History as a System* (New York, 1961), p. 216; see also "A Chapter from the History of Ideas: Wilhelm Dilthey and the Idea of Life," *Concord and Liberty* (New York, 1946), p. 131. The more extravagant assessment is found in Hellmut Diwald, *Wilhelm Dilthey: Erkenntnistheorie und Philosophie der Geschichte* (Göttingen, 1963), p. 7. In a book which brought Dilthey to the attention of the English-speaking world H. A. Hodges noted that Dilthey "is recognized as one of the most significant figures in the intellectual world since Hegel" (*Wilhelm Dilthey: An Introduction* [London, 1949], p. 10). More recently, Ulrich Herrmann has termed Dilthey "one of the most universal and influential minds of his time" (*Die Pädagogik Wilhelm Diltheys* [Göttingen, 1971], p. 61).

3. Marx Horkheimer, "Psychologie und Soziologie im Werk Wilhelm Diltheys," *Kritische Theorie*, 2 vols. (Frankfurt a. M., 1968), 2:273.

4. Ortega, *Concord*, p. 138.

5. Ulrich Herrmann, *Bibliographie Wilhelm Dilthey* (Weinheim, Berlin, and Basel, 1969).

6. Georg Misch, *Vom Lebens- und Gedankenkreis Wilhelm Diltheys* (Frankfurt a. M., 1947), p. 20.

7. Bernhard Groethuysen, "Gedächtnisrede auf Wilhelm Dilthey," *Deutsche Rundschau* 39, no. 4 (1913):69.

8. Patrick Gardiner, *Theories of History* (Glencoe, Ill, 1959), p. 212.

9. Letter of 29 June 1911 to Husserl from "Der Briefwechsel Dilthey-Husserl" published, with an introduction by Walter Biemel, in *Man and World* 1 (1968):435.

10. Jonas Cohn, in a review in *Logos* 12 (1923–24):297.

11. Wilhelm Dilthey, *Gesammelte Schriften*, 18 vols. (Leipzig, Stuttgart, and Göttingen: Teubner, 1914–77).

12. Karlfried Gründer, foreword to *GS* 15:vii–ix; also Ulrich Herrmann, "Zum Stand der Ausgabe der Gesammelten Schriften Wilhelm Diltheys," *Zeitschrift fur Pädagogik* 16, no. 4 (1970):531–36.

13. For a description of the Nachlass, see Ulrich Herrmann, "Zur Quellenlage und den Voraussetzungen der Dilthey-Forschungen," *Die Pädagogik Wilhelm Diltheys* (Göttingen, 1971), pp. 20 ff.

14. Ringer, *Decline*, p. 336.

15. The image of Dilthey as a bridge or stepping-stone predominates in recent interpretations: "Dilthey, we have said, forms a bridge over the chasm of positivism, leading from absolute idealism to the phenomenology of our century...Dilthey can be considered only a transitional figure"; "In the influence he had on Husserl, Scheler, and Heidegger, his work was preparatory to great things" (E. Gilson, T. Langan, and A. Maurer, *Recent Philosophy: Hegel to the Present* [New York, 1966], pp. 99–100, 688. Hans Meyerhoff refers to "the transitional place which Dilthey occupies

in recent intellectual history between the Hegelian tradition and the existentialist breakthrough" (*The Philosophy of History in Our Time* [New York, 1959], p. 37). William Barrett repeats the conventional judgment: "Dilthey is thus a link between Hegel and Heidegger" (*What is Existentialism?* [New York, 1964], p. 24). Manfred Riedel sees Dilthey as "one of the great forerunners of contemporary philosophy," stressing his affinities with Heidegger and Husserl ("Das erkenntnistheoretische Motiv in Diltheys Theorie der Geisteswissenschaften," in *Hermeneutik und Dialektik*, 2 vols. edited by Rüdiger Bubner [Tübingen, 1970], 1:243, 247).

16. H. S. Hughes, *Consciousness and Society* (New York, 1958), p. 192. Hughes finds Dilthey "so old fashioned that by the end of his life he had become a modern" (ibid.).

17. Dilthey was a founder of the very archive in which his Nachlass is preserved.

18. Hughes, *Consciousness*, p. 7.

19. See Franco Bianco, *Dilthey e la genesi della critica storica della ragione* (Milan, 1973); "Wilhelm Dilthey: Persönlichkeit und Werk," in Hans-Hermann Groothoff and Ulrich Herrmann, eds., *Wilhelm Dilthey: Schriften zur Pädagogik* (Paderborn, 1971), pp. 334–65; Otto Friedrich Bollnow, "Wilhelm Dilthey" in *Neue deutsche Biographie*, 10 vols. to date (Berlin, 1953—), 3:723–26; Herman Nohl, "Wilhelm Dilthey," in *Die grossen Deutschen: Deutsche Biographie*, 5 vols. (Berlin: 1957), 4:193–204; Albert Dietrich, "Wilhelm Dilthey: in *Die grossen Deutschen: Neue deutsche Biographie*, 5 vols. (Berlin: 1937), 5:439–49; Laura Koepp, *Die Familie Dilthey* (Wiesbaden, 1906); and Walter Schmied-Kowarzik, "Wilhelm Dilthey," in *Biographisches Jahrbuch und Nekrolog 17* (1915):227–32.

20. Karol Sauerland, *Diltheys Erlebnisbegriff* (Berlin, 1972), p. 112.

21. H. J. Schoeps, foreword to *Das wilhelminische Zeitalter* (Stuttgart, 1967), p. 8.

22. Maurice Merleau-Ponty, *Signs*, trans. Richard McCleary (Evanston, 1964), p. 151.

Chapter 1

The source of the first epigraph is Goethe, *Maximen und Reflexionen* (Weimar, 1907), no. 419; the second is from *BDY* 140.

1. See also *GS* 9:237 ff., where Dilthey calls upon the human sciences to prevent a "fall into the abyss of anti-cultural destruction."

2. Karl Joël, *Wandlungen der Weltanschauungen*, 2 vols. (Tübingen, 1928), 2:182.

3. See Ernst Cassirer, *The Problem of Knowledge* (New Haven, 1950), and Maurice Mandelbaum, *History, Man, and Reason* (Baltimore, 1971), for probing analyses of this basic dichotomy.

4. See the following passages: *GS* 1:ix; *JD* 79–80, 92, 120, 124; *GS* 5:9. He also referred to it as a "critique of social reason" (*GS* 18:228).

5. Dilthey's statement is unmistakably akin to Schleiermacher's premise in the *Dialektik*: "We are earthbound. . .all operations of thought, even our whole systematic effort of the formation of concepts, must have its roots in the earth" (*Sämmtliche Werke*, 12 vols. [Berlin, 1835–64], 4:333).

6. See also *GS* 9:7. In a loose page in the Nachlass from the 1860s, Dilthey cited as "incisive" Guizot's remark that "de nos jours l'homme veut faiblement, mais il désire immensément" (*BNL* 210/157).

7. See Hans Rosenberg, *Rudolf Haym und die Anfänge des klassischen Liberalismus* (Berlin, 1953), p. 44.

8. Fritz Ringer, *The Decline of the German Mandarins: The German Academic Community, 1890–1933* (Cambridge, Mass., 1969). See esp. chapter 6. In his polemical work on the "enemies of Bismarck" the conservative Otto Westphal has rightly perceived that Dilthey's thought was deeply conditioned by the social question. Westphal finds that Dilthey's reflections on history were sustained by a "great social-reformatory urge" toward the progressive betterment of the life of society and the individual person: "It is totally erroneous to place Dilthey among the contemplative thinkers of the times." An archtraditionalist and staunch defender of Bismarck, Westphal finds Dilthey's ultimate purposes to be "extra-scientific." Westphal's book traces the connection between ideal-realism and liberalism in terms of "the primacy of the ethical-active principle over the harmonious-contemplative principle" (Westphal, *Feinde Bismarcks* [Munich, 1930], p. 94. See pp. 153–65).

9. Albert Glaser, foreword, *WM* (1856) 1:v.

10. "Briefe an Rudolf Haym 1861–1873." Edited by Erich Weniger. *Abhandlungen der preussischen Akademie der Wissenschaften*, phil.-hist. Klasse, 9 (1936):46.

11. For a systematic overview of these reviews, see Ulrich Herrmann, *Bibliographie Wilhelm Dilthey*, pp. 109–17.

12. See Ulrich Herrmann, "Introduction," *GS* 15:xviii.

13. "Briefe an Haym," p. 18.

14. See G. Calabro, *Dilthey e il diritto naturale* (Napoli: 1968).

15. Rosenberg, *Rudolf Haym*, pp. 207–8.

16. Kant, "Was ist Aufklärung?" in *Gesammelte Werke*, 27 vols. (Berlin, 1902–72), 8:36.

17. See also *GS* 13/1:64–65. For a more comprehensive investigation of this attitude, see Andrew Lees, *Revolution and Reflection* (The Hague, 1974).

18. Quoted in Felix Staehelin, "Burckhardt und Dilthey," *Museum Helveticum* 8 (1950): 304.

19. William James, *The Letters of William James*, 2 vols. (Boston, 1920), 1:109–10.

20. Rudolf Haym, *Zur deutschen Philosophie und Literatur: Klassiker der Kritik* (Zurich, 1963), pp. 182–85.

21. *Logos* 12 (1923–24):297.

22. Georg Misch, *Vom Lebens- und Gedankenkreis Wilhelm Diltheys* (Frankfurt a. M., 1947), p. 12 and BNL 71/275.

23. Misch, *Vom Lebens- und Gedankenkreis*, p. 56.

24. Ibid., pp. 54–55. Dilthey had been thinking on these problems for some time as a practical aspect of pedagogical theory and university and school reform. The Berlin Nachlass contains an important memorandum of 7 April 1904 to the Minister of Culture and Education, Friedrich Althoff, in which Dilthey registered his view of the function of the state in relation to culture and scientific research. Dilthey argued that the "great cultural coherences" (*Kulturzusammenhänge*) of religion, art, and science are independent and supranational entities (*Selbständigkeiten*) which live from their own powers and must stand in an autonomous relation to the state: the state should be prepared to support them on their own terms, not for its purposes. The state, however, stands in a different relation to the basic instructional institutions (*Unterrichtswesen*) which are more directly linked to the purposes of the nation. Dilthey insisted that this "double relation" is best served by the separation of the Ministry into two: one of culture and one of education (*BNL* 37/33).

25. "Aus dem Nachruf Wilhelm Dilthey von Hugo von Hofmannsthal," *VDM* x. In his study of Schiller, Dilthey had said: "Every great work of man has as its tragic element that it cannot reach adequate fulfillment. So it was with Kant and Hegel. They limited themselves in order to finish. Philosophical thought is a singular kind of tragedy. Life is too short and its flame too weak to reach the truly great" (ibid., p. 332). The conventional view of Dilthey, however, as a resigned old philosopher who was "rescued" from suprahuman tasks only by death stands in need of revision. Shortly before his death he wrote to his son-in-law, Georg Misch: "It's going so well with me, it's as if I should live to be 110 years old" (Misch, *Vom Lebens- und Gedankenkreis*, p. 11).

26. George Morgan, "Wilhelm Dilthey," *Philosophical Review* 42 (1933):351.

27. Theobald Ziegler, *Die geistigen und sozialen Strömungen des neunzehnten Jahrhunderts* (Berlin, 1901), p. 4.

28. Friedrich Heer, *The Intellectual History of Europe* (Cleveland, 1966), p. 448.

29. Friedrich Meinecke, *Werke*, 4 vols. (Munich, 1957–62), 4:359.

30. H. A. Hodges, *The Philosophy of Wilhelm Dilthey* (London, 1952), p. xviii. Hodges' excellent study, in aligning Dilthey with "the progeny of Locke and Hume," correctly underlines Dilthey's empiricism, but fails to locate him in the indigenous German tradition of empirical and "immanent" idealism or *Idealrealismus*. It has been argued that "in answer to the challenge of idealism by naturalism, Dilthey remained wholly, though critically, within the traditional [idealist] camp" (William Kluback, *Wilhelm Dilthey's Philosophy of History* [New York, 1956], p. 51). How one can be in a camp "wholly" and "critically" is problematic; the crucial point of *Idealrealismus* is that it was not a "traditional" camp nor a latter-day *Ersatz* for idealism.

31. Dilthey's exegesis of Kant was exceedingly sensitive to the inner paradoxes which drove Kant's thought beyond itself, though he was far from viewing Hegel as the "logical" consummation of transcendental idealism; Kant's real meaning pointed toward a new view of experience.

32. Dilthey was not indulging himself in a bit of self-serving hyperbole. From a later perspective Heer notes that Schleiermacher "fascinated the whole nineteenth century" (*Intellectual History*, p. 468).

33. Quoted in Misch, *Vom Lebens- und Gedankenkreis*, p. 22; see also *JD*, p. 103 and *GS* 15:xxxvi.

34. In the final analysis Dilthey judged Schleiermacher "ein ganz unhistorischer Kopf" (*GS* 13/2:155).

35. Rudolf Haym, *Hegel und seine Zeit*, 2d ed. (Hildesheim, 1962), p. 107.

36. Quoted in Erich Rothacker, *Einleitung in die Geisteswissenschaften* (Tübingen, 1930), p. 7.

37. Ibid., p. 65.

38. Haym, *Hegel*, pp. 4–5. See also Hans Rosenberg, "Zur Geschichte der Hegelauffassung" in *Politsche Denkströmungen im deutschen Vormärz* (Göttingen, 1972), pp. 69–96.

39. See Karl Löwith, *From Hegel to Nietzsche* (New York, 1964), for an incisive portrayal of these developments. See also *GS* 13/2:81.

40. L. von Ranke, "Vom Einflusse der Theorie," *Sämtliche Werke*, 50 vols. (Leipzig: 1867–90), 49/50:243–46. The Historical School shared Goethe's disdain for theory: "Theories are usually premature formulations of an impatient way of thinking which

wants to set itself above and apart from the phenomenon and wants to put in its stead images, concepts, and words" (*Maximen*, no. 428).

41. Ranke, *Sämtliche Werke*, 49/50:659.

42. "Das politische Gespräch," in Ranke, *Sämtliche Werke*, 49/50:337.

43. This point was made by Dilthey and has been more strongly stated by Erich Rothacker, *Einleitung*, pp. 75 ff., and Georg Iggers, *The German Conception of History* (Middletown, Conn., 1968).

44. Quoted in Misch, *Vom Lebens- und Gedankenkreis*, p. 20.

45. Trendelenburg, *Logische Untersuchungen*, 2 vols. (Leipzig, 1870), 1:1; 2:522.

46. Ibid., 2:531.

47. Ibid., 2:443.

48. Karl Rosenkranz, preface to *Hegels Leben* (Berlin, 1844), pp. xii–xiii.

49. Henri-Fréderic Amiel, *Private Journal* (London, 1885), p. 11.

50. Quoted in Rothacker, *Einleitung*, p. 131.

51. Dilthey, *Grundriss der allgemeinen Geschichte der Philosophie*. 6th ed. rev. and enlgd. by Hans-Georg Gadamer (Frankfurt: 1949), p. 231.

52. G. S. Hall, *Aspects of German Culture* (Boston, 1881), pp. 119, 295. Hall observed that "in Germany philosophy has expressed and moulded character scarcely less than Puritanism in the United States. Admirers of Kant, Hegel, and Schopenhauer are as different and marked individualities as thorough-going Methodists, Episcopalians, or Presbyterians" (p. 300).

53. Löwith, *From Hegel*; Rothacker, *Einleitung*, pp. 103 ff.

54. Quoted in Harald Höffding, *History of Modern Philosophy*, 2 vols. (New York, 1955), 2:507.

55. Haeckel, *Die Welträtsel*, 7th ed. (Bonn, 1901), p. vii.

56. Ibid., p. 3

57. "Comte and Mill had formed their views before 1830, but they became influential only after 1860" (W. Tartarkiewicz, *Nineteenth Century Philosophy* [Belmont, Calif., 1973], p. 234).

58. Masur, *Prophets of Yesterday* (New York, 1961), p. 56. A more diversified and qualified picture is presented in Walter Simon, *European Positivism in the Nineteenth Century* (Ithaca, N.Y., 1963).

59. Hughes, *Consciousness*, p. 188.

60. Cassirer, *Problem of Knowledge* (New Haven, 1950), p. 10.

61. Willson Coates and Hayden White, *The Ordeal of Liberal Humanism: An Intellectual History of Western Europe* (New York, 1970), pp. 112–13.

62. Haym, *Hegel*, p. 464.

63. Hughes, *Consciousness*, p. 189.

64. Wilhelm Windelband, *Die Philosophie im deutschen Geistesleben des XIX. Jahrhunderts* (Tübingen, 1909), p. 1.

65. Windelband, *Präludien: Aufsätze und Reden zur Philosophie und ihrer Geschichte*, 9th ed., 2 vols. (Tübingen, 1924), 1:291–92.

66. Quoted in Ziegler, *Die geistigen und sozialen Strömungen*, p. 672.

67. Ibid.

68. Windelband asserted that "Nietzscheanism" was the catchworld of the age (*Die Philosophie*, p. 109).

69. Hughes, *Consciousness*, p. 112.

70. This has been suggested by Masur, *Prophets*, p. 263.

71. Hughes, *Consciousness*, p. 35.

72. See Rudolf Eucken, *Geistige Strömungen der Gegenwart* (Leipzig, 1909), p. 5.

73. Dilthey, "Festrede," *Deutsche Revue* 103 (1900):416–17.

74. Karl Joël, "Die Gefahren modernen Denkens," *Logos* 1 (1911–12):257.

Chapter 2

The source of the first epigraph is *ED* 213; that of the second is *LS* 189.

1. Erich Rothacker, *Logik und Systematik der Geisteswissenschaften* (Bonn, 1947), pp. 10–17; Joachim Ritter, *Historisches Wörterbuch der Philosophie* (Basel, 1974), vol. 3, pp. 211–15.

2. Fritz Ringer, *The Decline of the German Mandarins* (Cambridge, Mass., 1969), p. 97.

3. Dilthey's formulation suggests that we experience reality "originally" as a unity, but this reality is "accounted" along two divergent lines: on the one side toward sensory properties and "sense data," on the other toward psychic meanings. This contrast is conveyed in the two different meanings of the word "sense": sense as sheer sensation (which for Dilthey is not equivalent to experience or perception, but is an abstract construction), and sense as meaning, which is not reducible to physical correlates. One might say that sensory experience *sensu strictu* is "senseless," whereas lived experience is both sensible and significant. The growing cleavage between these two notions of experience has been seen as the real root of the intellectual "crisis of modernity" by a follower of Dilthey and Husserl: see Ludwig Landgrebe, "The Phenomenological Conception of Experience," *Philosophy and Phenomenological Research* 34 (1973):1–13. Merleau-Ponty has provided a perfect summary of Dilthey's position: "Philosophy is indeed and always a break with objectivism and a return from *constructa* to lived experience, from the world to ourselves.... The 'interior' it brings back to us is not a 'private life' but an intersubjectivity that gradually connects us ever closer to the whole of history" (*Signs*, p. 112). It is noteworthy that the philosopher of science Georg von Wright has recently insisted upon the heuristic necessity of the inner-outer distinction—while at the same time pointing out that this does not prejudice the question of the nature of the "inner" (*Explanation and Understanding* [Ithaca, 1971], p. 91).

4. The relevant passage is Husserl, *Logische Untersuchungen*, 2 vols. (Halle, 1900–1901), 2:339.

5. See also *GS* 1:416; 7:119, 130. Dilthey's concept of "relative independence" must be contrasted with the manner in which it has been interpreted: "From then on [after Dilthey's efforts] the human studies were split off from the natural sciences; the two halves of man's cognitive effort were divorced from each other.... It was the first time in the history of Western civilization that such a separation had occurred." (Gerhard Masur, *Prophets of Yesterday* [New York, 1961], p. 171).

6. See Wilhelm Wundt, *Logik*, 3 vols. (Stuttgart, 1906–8), 3:81.

7. Von Wright has illuminated this crucial point in showing that the same "object" can be grasped in different ways—and that the mode of attending in fact conditions the object. There is a difference between explaining why *he* moves parts of his body (having to do with aims, values, cultural setting) and explaining why parts of his body move (having to do with neural conduction, synapses, etc.). The first is the province of human science, the latter of natural science—and yet both can have the same "phenomenal" object. See Von Wright, *Explanation and Understanding*, p. 119.

8. Dilthey's concept of life might loosely be equated with Kant's *Ding an sich*, especially in light of its quality of perpetually alluring mystery. This connection gains some plausibility in light of a passage in which Dilthey discusses the implications drawn from Kant's concept: "It was the deep insight of Solomon Maimon that the thing in itself is the irrational limit of rational knowledge. It is prescribed to knowledge that empirical facticity cannot be wholly subsumed under the power of rational consciousness" (*GS* 4:267). Kant's denial of any cognitive validity to the "inner sense," however, runs counter to Dilthey's position, for it is this "inner sense" which enables us to understand life.

9. The immediate "reality" of *Erlebnis*, as Dilthey conceived it, has been an exceedingly contested issue; its critics have regarded it as either unforgiveably mystical or else as an a priori construct, thus hoisting Dilthey with his own petard. One critic has accused Dilthey of using *Erlebnis* in much the same speculative way that nineteenth-century physicists used the concept of "ether":

> The *Erlebnis* is endowed with just those attributes which will allow belief in the notion of uniquely human characteristics. It would seem that Dilthey surreptitiously smuggled *Erlebnis* into his investigative method and then "discovered" it in order to justify a value assumed before he had ever begun his inquiry. In short, *Erlebnis* appears as a meaningful concept only if one holds a conception of the world that requires the qualitative differentiation of levels of being (Coates, *Ordeal*, p. 259).

It is true that life is Dilthey's "a priori," just as "experience" is the a priori of all empiricism. Dilthey would point out that the argument is circular. He insisted that *Erlebnis* cannot be fully defined or grasped logically: *GS* 7:70; 8:74.

10. See also *GS* 1:384–86, where Dilthey rules out "metaphysics as science" but insists that "the metaphysical dimension of our life [*das Meta-Physische unseres Lebens*] as personal experience remains. . . . Metaphysical science is a historically limited phenomenon, but the metaphysical consciousness of the person is eternal."

11. Humboldt, *Gesammelte Schriften*, 17 vols. (Berlin, 1903–68), 1:391.

12. Dilthey appears to have adopted the concept of *Realdialektik* from Kuno Fischer and Rudolf Haym rather than from the more notorious Left Hegelians. The concept was also brought into currency by the eccentric philosopher Julius Bahnsen; Dilthey found Bahnsen's ideas "stimulating" at points, but also excessively turgid (*WM* 52 [1885]:291). See also Yorck von Wartenburg, *Bewusstseinsstellung und Geschichte* (Tübingen, 1956), p. 41.

13. Ibid., p. 145.

14. Karl Pfannkuch neglects this later qualification and speaks of "Dilthey's sharp opposition of lived experience and knowledge. . . . Lived experience means for him not a form of consciousness which is susceptible to discursive thought and dependent upon a process of rationalization, but nevertheless still a form of cognition which is not bound by laws but rather speaks in 'life' and to 'life.' This realm is only open

to feeling" ("Weltanschauung um die Jahrhundertwende" in H. J. Schoeps, *Das wilhelminische Zeitalter*, pp. 75–76).

15. Haym, *Hegel*, p. 243.

16. Goethe, *Maximen*, no. 691.

17. Quoted in Richard Dobel, *Lexikon der Goethe-Zitate* (Zürich, 1968), p. 1065.

18. Since Kant's *Critique of Judgment*, aesthetics for many German thinkers was more than what is conventionally designated as the theory of art. It tended to become a theory of the creative synthetic relation between subject and object and thus a new form of epistemology, which had hitherto (including for Kant himself) been dominated by natural scientific models of knowing. Reflection upon art demonstrated with particular efficacy that the mind perceives actively not passively, thus providing a kind of incarnate "proof" of its transcendental function. Obviously Dilthey's aesthetics was "historically conditioned" by the actual art he knew. (He constantly pointed out that aesthetics was interpretive and not an eternal canon of judgment.) The art he referred to was not the highly abstract "conceptual" art of today.

19. Quoted in Dobel, *Lexikon*, 952.

20. Heinrich Rickert, "Lebenswerte und Kulturwerte," *Logos* 2 (1911):132 and 157.

21. Gerhard Masur's observation that "the old Dilthey had become along with Nietzsche and Bergson the prophet of Life" (*Prophets*, p. 105) is the kind of indistinct generalization which has dogged the interpretation of his thought.

Chapter 3

The source of the first epigraph is *BDY* 8; the second is *BA* 94.

1. It is clear from the passage in which the analogy appears (*GS* 7:116–17) that Dilthey no longer subscribed fully to this position: he cites it as one possible position in a spectrum of views. Wundt, too, put psychology at the foundation of the human sciences: *Logik* (Stuttgart, 1906–8), 3:8, 17.

2. The fundamental role Dilthey assigned to psychology in the system of the human sciences is closely analogous to the function Schleiermacher ascribed to "dialectic" in the system of the specific *Realwissenschaften*: "Strictly speaking, no scientific discipline can claim perfection for itself as long as it stands by itself. Perfection in science is only conceivable if each discipline is related to every other one and all are united under the umbrella of a single, highest discipline, which contains within itself their common ground of existence and each confirmed by virtue of its connection with all the others." Schleiermacher insisted that while this discipline is the "ground" of the sciences, it is not an a priori ground nor a substitute for their specific inquiry—it is rather a kind of "emergent ground": "No one will dare assert that he has actually found this highest discipline before all other disciplines, or that the other disciplines are produced by it, or even that the subordinate disciplines move simultaneously and by the same rules toward the perfection of their form and content and thereby originate gradually the idea of the highest discipline." See "Grundlinien einer Kritik bisherigen Sittenlehre" in *Sämtliche Werke* (Berlin, 1846), 1:339–40. Given this special conception of "grounding discipline," it is small wonder that Dilthey wavered in its precise designation.

3. H. S. Hughes, *Consciousness and Society* (New York, 1958), p. 196.

4. "Hegelfragment," *Hegelstudien* 1:19.

5. Hegel, *The Phenomenology of Mind* (London, 1931), pp. 414–38.

6. For Schelling in particular, see Dilthey, *GS* 14/1:468–69.

7. Humboldt, *Gesammelte Schriften* (Berlin, 1963–68), 1:257 and 4:49.

8. J. G. Droysen, *Historik*. Edited by R. Hübner (München, 1937), pp. 341–42.

9. H. Rickert, *Kulturwissenschaft und Naturwissenschaft* (Tübingen, 1921), p. x.

10. Like Dilthey, Wilhelm Wundt designated psychology as the most basic of the human sciences. He noted that many researchers in the human sciences, especially that of history, tried to do without psychology or any explicit theory of mind in the hopes of attaining a "purely historical grasp of things." But such an attempt is bound to end in skepticism: "Without psychology, theory of knowledge, and ethics, the historical human sciences remain a rudderless craft, tossed to and fro by the accidental opinions of the day" (*Logik* 3:517, also 523; see also *BDY*, 188–89 for Dilthey's view of Wundt). Nietzsche, too, wanted to establish psychology as the "queen of the sciences," for it was the true pathway to "fundamental problems." With a play on words, he called it the "unnatural science"—to contrast it with natural science, but also to stress the implicit mental resistances to it (*Jenseits von Gut und Böse* [Kröner ed. Stuttgart, 1953], pp. 32, 74, and 257). Nietzsche attacked existing psychology because it was dominated by morality, whereas Dilthey found it dominated by natural scientific models.

11. Siegfried Kracauer, *Geschichte: Vor den letzten Dingen* (Frankfurt, 1971), p. 30; F. Copleston, *History of Modern Philosophy*, vol. 7, part 2, 142.

12. H. A. Hodges asserts that "his [Dilthey's] spirit was not the Kantian spirit" (*The Philosophy of William Dilthey* [London, 1952], p. 28). In his last seminar Dilthey asserted: "We must go beyond Kant; the [formal] Kantians are dead; the living ones are those who carry his method further" (*LK* 5).

13. Kuno Fischer, *Logik und System der Metaphysik als Wissenschaftslehre* (Stuttgart, 1852), p. 382.

14. Hodges finds that "his approach to philosophy was not logical and to logic proper he made no contribution whatever. He was more at home in exploring the prelogical levels of experience, whether in sense-perception or in our awareness of our own and other selves" (*Philosophy*, p. 316). Gardiner is more caustic: "The temptation to dismiss or ignore Dilthey is admittedly great: he was a poor logician and impossible stylist" (*Theories of History*, p. 212). These evaluations clearly hinge upon what is meant by "logic proper"—by no means a simple or uncontested matter (not unlike "style," one could say).

15. For his conception of an "analytic logic," see *GS* 5:86; 1:117; *BDY* 222; *LK* 22, 26–29. (In this last reference, Dilthey relates his analytic logic to Husserl).

16. Johannes Hennig, *Lebensbegriff und Lebenskategorie* (Aachen, 1934), p. 28, maintains that Dilthey owed his conceptions in part to Charles Renouvier. This contention is difficult to substantiate, but Dilthey left a record of his positive opinion of Renouvier (*Grundriss* 238, 249). It is more likely that Dilthey took his idea from Trendelenburg's basic notion of "real categories": "Real categories are those that thought uses to express the essential character of things, as opposed to model categories, which have as their content only elements of knowing activity itself" (*Logische Untersuchungen* [Leipzig, 1870], 1:336). Dilthey praised Schleiermacher and Hegel for conceiving "Weltkategorien" of existence rather than mere "Konstruktionsbegriffe" (*GS* 14/2:540).

17. Goethe, *Maximen*, no. 1214.

18. *Zeitschrift für Völkerpsychologie*, 1:70.

19. This latter reference contains a list of the "social bonds." Dilthey's proposed extensions for the scope of psychology did not proceed merely in the direction of history or social psychology. He also demanded that psychology forge links with biology as well. In a series of notes written after the *Einleitung*, he asserted: "A biological extension of the inquiry is now needed in order to disclose the structure of life. I strived earlier to establish a psychological foundation for the human sciences in opposition to a one-sided intellectualism. This point of view has increasingly drawn more and more adherents. But after recognizing the basis of all thought and knowledge in the structure of life, I must expand and deepen the psychological standpoint into a biological one" (*BNL* 209/77). Dilthey appeared to be moving from "psychologism" to "biologism" in the late '80s and early '90s. But this "biological" extension was supplanted by a more distinctly cultural-historical one. See *GS* 9:73.

20. Eduard Spranger, *Berliner Geist* (Tübingen, 1966), p. 151.

21. Dilthey's relation to Brentano has surprisingly been neglected. Herbert Spiegelberg has asserted that Dilthey's knowledge of Brentano came late and through Carl Stumpf in the 1890s, after Dilthey had formed his program of description (*The Phenomenological Movement* [The Hague, 1960], 1:122–23). This is not the case. His essay of 1875 contains a reference to Brentano (*GS* 5:55) and the "Breslauer Ausarbeitung" contains extensive references (*BA* 109–15, 123, and passim). Both men had been students of Trendelenburg and Dilthey's correspondence suggests that they were friends. (See *BDY* 2, 35–37.) Husserl asserted that Dilthey was not influenced by Brentano (*Husserliana* 9:33).

22. Goethe, *Maximen*, nos. 1221 and 1222. See also no. 1165.

Chapter 4

The source of the first epigraph is *BNL* 167/319; see *GS* 5:434 and 18:224. The emphasis is Dilthey's. It could be said that the paradox in this statement is the dialectical element in Dilthey's "immanent critique" of all psychology. The second epigraph also comes from the Nachlass: *BNL* 237/76.

1. The following passages are particularly relevant to Dilthey's theoretical concerns: *GS* 2:314; 4:28; 9:68. On Bolzano, see *BNL* 209/274; 195/102; 85/55.

2. Ebbinghaus, "Über erklärende und beschreibende Psychologie," *Zeitschrift für Psychologie und Physiologie der Sinnesorganen* 9 (1895):161–205.

3. Ibid., p. 193.

4. Ibid., p. 205.

5. See *BDY* 38 and 205; Cassirer, *The Problem of Knowledge* (New Haven, 1944), p. 243; *Husserliana* 9:34; Hermann, *Bibliographie*, pp. 121–23.

6. An extensive correspondence concerning the article exists at Berlin: *BNL* 170/31–85; *BDY* 207.

7. Theodor Elsenhans, *Lehrbuch der Psychologie*, 2d ed. (Tübingen, 1912), p. 49. Surprisingly, Elsenhans had previously published a short book *Die Aufgabe einer Psychologie der Deutung als Vorarbeit für die Geisteswissenschaften* (Giessen, 1904) which repeated Dilthey's position almost exactly.

8. Windelband, "Genetische und kritische Methode," *Präludien*, 9th ed. (Tübingen, 1924), 1:120.

9. Windelband, *Präludien* 2:101.

10. Windelband, "Die Philosophie des 19. Jahrhunderts" in *Die Kultur der Gegenwart* (Leipzig, Berlin, 1923), p. 585.

11. Windelband, *Präludien* 1:18.

12. Ibid., 144–49.

13. Ibid., 160.

14. Ibid., 2:21.

15. Rickert, *Die Grenzen der naturwissenschaftlichen Begriffsbildung* (Tübingen, 1902), p. 228.

16. Ibid., p. 138.

17. Ibid., pp. 489–90.

18. Ibid., p. 230.

19. Ibid., p. 301.

20. Ibid., p. 766.

21. Ibid., p. 300. One might recall Goethe's "court" image in reference to Kant.

22. Ibid., p. 688.

23. Ibid., p. 325.

24. H. Rickert, "Vom Begriff der Philosophie," *Logos* 1 (1910/1911):19, 24–25. Rickert insisted that transcendental philosophy is "prior" to all psychology, metaphysics, and history (*Kant*, p. 4). He seemed to depart from strict methodological formalism in granting that history is "closer to reality" [*wirklichkeitsnah*] than natural science, but went on to insist that this experiential "closeness" does not in any sense permit a Diltheyan "Erleben" (*Grenzen*, p. 502). Caricaturing Dilthey's "nonmethodical 'method'," he insisted "mere lived experience is not science and it cannot be constituted in a generalized manner in the service of historical cognition." The experientially immediate remains "dumb." (*Kulturwissenschaft und Naturwissenschaft* [Freiburg, 1899], p. 64).

25. Rickert, *Kulturwissenschaft*, p. 26.

26. Rickert, preface to 3d ed., *Die Grenzen der naturwissenschaftlichen Begriffsbildung* (Tübingen, 1929), p. xii; cf. E. Troeltsch, *Der Historismus und seine Probleme* (Tübingen, 1922), p. 520.

27. Franz Brecht, "Edmund Husserl" in *Die grossen Deutschen*, 5 vols. (Berlin, 1957), 5:437; Misch's comments, *GS* 5:CXVII; and Joachim Wach, *Das Verstehen*, 3 vols. (Tübingen, 1926–33), 1:28; and Ludwig Landgrebe, *Phänomenologie und Metaphysik* (Hamburg, 1949), p. 18. Dilthey's reaction was strikingly different from that of William James, who when presented with a translation, maintained "nobody in America would be interested in a new and strange German work on logic" (Spiegelberg, *The Phenomenological Movement* [The Hague, 1960], 1:112).

28. Spiegelberg, *Phenomenological Movement* 1:89–90. Spiegelberg aptly refers to the "legends" which have arisen around this relationship (ibid., 122).

29. Stephan Strasser, "Phenomenological Trends in European Psychology," *Philosophy and Phenomenological Research* 18 (1957):20.

30. T. K. Oesterreich, "Die philosophischen Strömungen der Gegenwart," in *Kultur der Gegenwart* 5:374. Oesterreich concluded: "one could almost say that phenomenology has dissolved neo-Kantianism" (p. 376).

31. Husserl, *Logische Untersuchungen*, 2 vols. (Halle, 1901), 2:353.

32. Ibid. 2:152.

33. Ibid. 1:68.

34. Ibid. 2:655.

35. Ibid. 1:175.

36. Ibid. 2:9–10.

37. Ibid. 1:13, 190; 2:467, 569.

38. Ibid. 2:101, 483.

39. Ibid. 2:513.

40. See Herman Nohl, "Wilhelm Dilthey über Friedrich Paulsens Nachfolge," *Eduard Spranger: Zum 75. Geburtstag*, edited by Hans Wenke (Heidelberg, 1957), pp. 438–40. In a letter of 5 October 1911 to Frau Dilthey after her husband's death, Husserl describes Dilthey as "one with whom I felt united in the struggle for a new philosophy" (*GNL* 15b ["Beileidsbriefe"]/2).

41. H. A. Hodges, *The Philosophy of Wilhelm Dilthey* (London, 1952), p. xxi.

42. In 1925 Husserl reported from personal experience that Dilthey regarded the *Logische Untersuchungen* "with great joy" as the first concrete execution of his idea for a descriptive psychology. Husserl added: "The more I have progressed in the formation of the phenomenological method and the phenomenological analysis of mental life, the more I must acknowledge that Dilthey was in fact correct in his judgment about the inner unity of phenomenology and descriptive-analytical psychology, a judgment which put me off at the time. His writings contain a genial preview and preliminary stage of phenomenology" (*Husserliana* 9:34–35).

43. Schleiermacher *Gesammelte Werke* 3:584 ff.

44. For example *BNL* 243/154; 208/39; see also *GS*, 6:301; 7:296; 8:37.

45. G. Misch, afterword in *Lebensphilosophie und Phänomenologie* (Stuttgart, 1967), pp. 327–28. Fritz Heinemann reports on a meeting which he had with Husserl at Untermainquai in Frankfurt in 1931:

> After publication of his *Logical Studies* in 1900, he visited Dilthey in 1905, who told him that this book represented the first fundamentally new departure in philosophy since the days of Mill and Comte, and that he, Dilthey, regarded the fifth and sixth essays, "On Intentional Experiences and Their Contents," and "Elements of a Phenomenological Elucidation of Knowledge," i.e., the return to the subject and its inner experiences, as most fruitful. This, combined with the fact that Dilthey was holding a seminar on that book, made a deep impression on him. I do not say that Dilthey was the cause for Husserl's subsequent turn to the subject, but he confirmed his conviction that this way was worth going" (*Existentialism and the Modern Predicament* [New York, 1958], p. 52).

46. W. H. Boyce Gibson, "From Husserl to Heidegger," *The Journal of the British Society for Phenomenology* 2 (1971):68–82.

47. "Philosophie als strenge Wissenschaft," *Logos* 1 (1911):289–314. This article is widely recognized as a decisive turning point in the evolution of phenomenology towards a transcendental form.

48. "Der Briefwechsel Dilthey-Husserl," *Man and World* 1 (1968):428–46. This exchange has been reported by Walter Biemel, who provides a valuable set of introductory remarks.

49. Ibid., 434.

50. Ibid., 438–41.

51. Ibid., 442.

52. By 1928 Husserl had perceived very clearly that the content of Dilthey's descriptive psychology was not merely the inner experience of the individual person: "The theme [of Dilthey's psychology] concerns not an inwardly encapsulated person, but the combined unity of all these individualities in the totality of their personal psychic life and in the higher totality of the all-embracing historical life" (*Husserliana,* 9: 355–56). Nevertheless, Husserl continued to fault Dilthey for a residual naturalism and a failure to fathom the "radical problem of the objectivity of mental products [*Gebilde*]." These products are objective-ideal and transcendent to the "stream of experience" [*Erlebnisstrom*]; they have a "lasting identity" (ibid., 359; Husserl's judgment was based upon the "Ideen" not the later "Aufbau" studies, in which Dilthey confronted precisely this problem). Husserl concluded that Dilthey achieved an "inductive typology of the forms of mental life" but not "universal description of essence" or the "ideal, in the light of which the empirical is an approximation" (ibid., 13, 17). Nevertheless, Husserl described Dilthey's "Ideen" as the first attack on naturalistic psychology and therefore "unforgettable" (ibid., 6).

53. William Stern, *Die psychologische Arbeit des neunzehnten Jahrhunderts, inbesondere in Deutschland* (Berlin, 1900).

54. Husserl, *Logische Untersuchungen* 2:11.

55. Ibid., 704–5.

56. Wilhelm Wundt, *Logik* (1st ed., 1883), 3:482–500; *Logik* (3rd ed., 1906–8), 3:28, 164–69.

57. William James, *The Principles of Psychology,* 2 vols. (New York, 1890), 1:230–34.

58. Ibid., 255.

59. Ibid., 196.

60. Ibid., 244.

61. Ibid., 191.

62. Wilhelm Schuppe, "Begriff und Grenzen der Psychologie" *Zeitschrift für immanente Philosophie* 1 (1895):37–76. See *BNL* 169 and *BNL* 195/24–31. These latter references to Schuppe are combined with fragments on Lipps and Bolzano on "Psychology of Objects."

63. Schuppe, "Begriff," p. 38.

64. Ibid., pp. 50–51.

65. Ibid., pp. 69–73.

66. Ibid., p. 57.

67. Wundt, *Logik* 3:v, 1, 18–19, 23, 51–53, 57.

68. Ibid., 9.

69. Georg Simmel, *Soziologie* (Berlin, 1908), p. 21.

70. Also quoted in Arthur Stein, *Der Begriff des Verstehens bei Dilthey* (Tübingen, 1926), p. 32.

71. Compare *GS* 5:212 and 223 with 7:16–19.

72. Bollnow observed even before "structuralism" that this word was in danger of becoming an "empty fashion-phrase" (*Einführung*, p. 151).

73. Howard Tuttle, *Wilhelm Dilthey's Philosophy of Historical Understanding* (Leiden, 1969), p. 16. The two most influential English commentators have failed to comprehend the difference between the reflected character of *Lebenserfahrung* and the immediate character of *Erlebnis*. Thus R. G. Collingwood asserts in *The Idea of History* (Oxford, 1946):

> But a problem still remains, because life for Dilthey means immediate experience, as distinct from reflection or knowledge; and it is not enough for the historian to *be* Julius Caesar or Napoleon, since that does not constitute a knowledge of Julius Caesar or Napoleon any more than the obvious fact that he *is* himself constitutes a knowledge of himself.

Collingwood goes on to assert that Dilthey tried to solve the gap between immediate experience and knowledge by means of psychology, which for Collingwood reveals Dilthey's implicit "positivism":

> To say that history becomes intelligible only when conceived in terms of psychology is to say that historical knowledge is impossible and that the only kind of knowledge is scientific knowledge: history by itself is mere life, immediate experience, and therefore the historian as such merely experiences a life which the psychologist as such and he alone understands. Dilthey has come up against the question which Windelband and the rest had not the penetration to recognize: the question how there can be a knowledge, as distinct from an immediate experience, of the individual. He answered that question by admitting that there cannot be such a knowledge, and falling back on the positivistic view that the only way in which the universal (the proper object of knowledge) can be known is by means of natural science or a science constructed on naturalistic principles. Thus, in the end he, like the rest of his generation, surrenders to positivism [pp. 173–74].

Not only has Collingwood failed to grasp the nature of Dilthey's psychology, he has also overlooked the distinction between immediately personal *Erlebnis* and historically-mediated *Lebenserfahrung*. H. A. Hodges, otherwise a far more discerning interpreter of Dilthey than Collingwood, commits a similar mistake:

> His conception of lived experience as the undifferentiated unity, in which subject and object, appearance and reality, substance and attribute are not yet distinguished, an experience prior to all thought, and lit up by a certitude of its own reality which is peculiar to itself—this conception remains unchanged (*Philosophy*, pp. 217–18)

To my knowledge only Mircea Eliade has perceived the intended mediating function of Dilthey's "allgemeine Lebenserfahrung," but he goes on to find it inadequate as a final means of overcoming the problem of relativism (*The Myth of Eternal Return* [Princeton, 1950], p. 150).

74. There is a certain affinity (and perhaps direct ancestral link) between Dilthey's *Lebenserfahrung* and J. S. Mill's notion of a "general and enlarged experience" or "whole unanalyzed experience of the human race" which constitutes "the accumulated wisdom of all former ages embodied in traditional aphorisms" (Mill, "Benthan" and Prof. Sedgwick's Discourse," *Dissertations and Discussions*, 5 vols. [Boston, 1864–67], 1:146 and 351). Dilthey's concept seems very close to C. S. Peirce's "experience in the course of life" and G. H. Mead's "communicative-interactive experience." All stress—in opposition to both Cartesian tradition of "self-intuition" and conventional empiricism—that experience is constituted in intercourse and discourse with others.

One can find precedents in Bacon's *"experientia literata"* and recent counterparts in the "floating dicta" and "practical syllogisms" of some contemporary analytic philosophers. With clear reference to Dilthey, Wundt spoke of the conflict mounting after the turn of the century between those who wanted to found the human sciences upon "scientific psychology" and those who founded them upon "general experience of life" (*allgemeine Lebenserfahrung*) (*Logik* 3:18). In this same vein, Isaiah Berlin speaks of "a knowledge of life" or "natural wisdom" deriving from direct experience and not formulable in psychological science, yet entirely free of metaphysical overtones: "I mean by this not introspection, but knowledge of life—something that springs from interaction with others and with the surrounding environment and constitutes the sense of reality" ("The Concept of Scientific History," *History and Theory* 1 (1960–61):24 ff; the similarity with Diltheyan conceptions is patent here).

75. Dilthey explicitly separated *Erlebnis* and *Lebenserfahrung* in a late essay on Schiller (*VDM* 359) and in a later revision of an earlier essay he changed "Erlebnis" to "lebendige Erfahrung" (*GS* 9:173).

76. Hodges, *Philosophy*, pp. 80, 96. For Dilthey's objections to the purely psychological derivation of value see *GS* 7:241.

77. Troeltsch, *Historismus*, p. 523n. The shift from *Erlebnis* to *Lebenserfahrung* effectively counters the charge that in Dilthey "immediate vital experience is deeply individual" (e.g., Jacques Kornberg, "Dilthey on the Self and History," *Central European History* 10 [1973]:297). The importance of this later adaptation lies precisely in the move beyond the subjective "individualism" of experience to an emphasis upon its shared and mediated qualities. Such experience is the source of the common world of meaning within the medium of language. Dilthey's theory of mind undergoes what might be called a historical "deepening." The net result is to diminish the distinction between individual mind and its inalienable matrix of common meanings, or "objective mind." Although there appears to be no direct relation, the concept of *Lebenserfahrung* is comparable to Ernst Mach's "inherited psychological truths." As deeply historical and social, such a concept of experience is incompatible with any such science as Husserl's "egology" or ego-psychology. The science of consciousness becomes a historical "phenomenology of mind" or *Geistesgeschichte* "with philosophical intent." Kornberg has held that "Dilthey's approach to history must be understood in the light of his view of personality" (ibid., 309). In the light of Dilthey's later reflections, it would be more accurate and illuminating to say just the reverse: that his theory of personality, of the individual life, and of psychology itself must be understood in the light of his view of history. Philip Rieff posits a non-psychologistic notion of experiential meaning which is similar to Dilthey's: "By extending the psychological beyond itself into the social, the meaning of the psychological is totally changed" ("History, Psychoanalysis, and the Social Sciences," *Ethics* 63 (1952):113).

78. Hodges, *Introduction*, p. 49.

79. In a rectoral address, Dilthey's brother-in-law Hermann Usener called for "an anthropology in the higher sense" which would embrace the special disciplines (*Vorträge und Aufsätze* [Bonn, 1907], p. 13).

80. The conceptual dilemma Dilthey faced at the level of "foundations" has, if anything, been exacerbated rather than mitigated. Albert Hofstadter has posed the question "what mode of thinking makes intelligible the concrete subject in his life?" and then elaborates:

This is tantamount to asking what is the principle of the form of life of an individual person so far as that life exhibits form, and it is obviously one of the most difficult questions facing human knowledge, if we expect as an answer to it a concrete and particularized account of the principle of life-form. Hence the temptation is to escape from the challenge of dealing with it by handing it over to the psychologist as the putative expert in understanding the forms of life. Unfortunately psychology is today hardly in a position to get very far with this question, for in order to answer it the psychologist would have to have mastered the dynamic principles involved in all the forms of human activity, e.g., sexual, economic, social, political, legal, artistic, cognitive, religious, philosophical. Does any form of contemporary psychology even begin to approach the beginnings of a scientific treatment of this subject?" ["The Philosophy in History" in *Philosophy and History: A Symposium*, ed. Sidney Hook [1963], pp. 232–33].

J. Barzun makes the point in a different way, concluding that history and psychology are "preliminary to each other" ("History: The Muse and Her Doctors," *American Historical Review* 77 [1972]:63–64).

81. Bollnow, *Einführung*, pp. 212–16; H. Tuttle, *Wilhelm Dilthey's Philosophy of Historical Understanding* (Leiden, 1969), pp. 21, 26; K. Müller-Vollmer, *Towards a Phenomenological Theory of Literature* (The Hague, 1963), Antoni insists that hermeneutics as Dilthey conceived it must lead back to descriptive psychology (*From History to Sociology*, p. 23).

82. Cassirer, *An Essay on Man* (New Haven, 1944), p. 195.

Chapter 5

The two epigraphs of Dilthey are found in *GS* 7:205 and 5:334. Trendelenburg's statement appears in the *Logische Untersuchungen* 2:443.

1. H. S. Hughes, *Consciousness and Society* (New York, 1958), p. 187. Alfred Schütz maintains that "he [Dilthey] opposes to rational science another so-called 'interpretive' science based upon metaphysical presuppositions and incorrigible 'intuition' " (*The Phenomenology of the Social World* (Evanston, 1967), p. 240). Masur sees it as "sympathetic intuition" (*Prophets of Yesterday* [New York, 1961], p. 166); Tillinghast as "sympathetic and empathetic imagination . . . a special form of empathetic, inside knowledge that all humans share" (*Specious Past*, p. 147). Fritz Ringer has aptly observed that *Verstehen* was "a much more formal and empirically controlled procedure than the word empathy would suggest" (*The Decline of the German Mandarins* [Cambridge, Mass., 1969] p. 319).

2. Compare J. S. Mill, *Philosophy of Scientific Method* (New York, 1950), pp. 307–8.

3. J. Wach, *Das Verstehen*, 3 vols. (Tübingen, 1926–33).

4. Paul Ricoeur has observed that "there is no question that the problem of hermeneutics has to a great extent been constituted within the boundaries of the interpretation of Holy Scripture" (*Freud and Philosophy: An Essay on Interpretation* [New Haven, 1970], p. 24). Dilthey tried to reconstitute it beyond these boundaries, while still preserving some of the symbolic force of its original ambit. Like Dilthey, Ricoeur poses the question of whether there can be a *science* of symbolic meaning which retains meaning itself: "For the logician the word "symbol" means precisely the opposite of what it means for us" (ibid., p. 48).

5. Only if one assumes dialectic in its Hegelian sense of an *Idealdialektik* can it be said that Dilthey's hermeneutical method is "undialectical" (as does Rudolf Makkreel in "Wilhelm Dilthey and the Neo-Kantians," *Journal of Philosophy* 7 [1969]:437).

H. A. Hodges claims that Dilthey's hermeneutic is largely an elaboration of Schleiermacher's (*Wilhelm Dilthey* [London, 1949], p. 26). This assertion neglects very substantial differences, especially the historical *Realdialektik* of experience and ideas which Dilthey put at the foundation of his hermeneutic. See *GS* 11:ix.

6. For a complete overview of the directions, see H. Henrichs, *Bibliographie der Hermeneutik und ihrer Anwendungsbereich seit Schleiermacher* (Düsseldorf, 1968). See also Christofer Zöckler, *Dilthey und die Hermeneutik* (Stuttgart, 1975).

7. This distinction corresponds closely to William James' discrimination of "knowledge-of" and "knowledge-about"; the former derives from acquaintance or use and is more perceptual in character, while the latter is more conceptual—the result of sustained, systematic study and the application of logic and abstraction (*The Principles of Psychology* [New York, 1890] 1:122). James pursued the same point elsewhere, differentiating between "knowledge as acquaintance" and "knowledge as conception and proposition." Like Dilthey, James sees a relation in this difference: "In such pieces of knowledge-of-acquaintance all our knowledge-about must end, and carry a sense of this possible termination as part of its content. These percepts, these *termini*, these sensible things, these mere matters of acquaintance, are the only realities we ever directly know, and the whole history of our thought is the history of our substitution of one of them for another, and the reduction of the substitute to the status of conceptual sign. Condemned as they be by some thinkers, these sensations are the mother-earth, the anchorage, the stable rock, the first and last limits, the *terminus a quo* and the *terminus ad quem* of the mind" ("The Function of Cognition" in *Pragmatism* (New York, 1965), pp. 209–10, 223). The dependence of methodical understanding upon a "participating" pre-reflective understanding derived from the subject's embeddedness in a social context and set of social rules has been stressed by Peter Winch:

> I do want to say that any more reflective understanding must necessarily presuppose, if it is to count as genuine understanding at all, the participant's unreflective understanding—and this in itself makes it misleading to compare it with the natural scientist's understanding of his scientific data. Similarly, although the reflective study of society, or of a particular mode of social life, may find it necessary to use concepts which are not taken from the forms of activity which he is investigating, but which are taken rather from the context of his own investigation, still these technical concepts of his will imply a previous understanding of those other concepts which belong to the activities under investigation. (*The Idea of a Social Science and Its Relation to Philosophy* [London, 1958], p. 89).

8. G. von Wright has carried this view further in maintaining that there are different layers and orders of understanding (*Explanation and Understanding* [Ithaca, 1971], p. 132). Wright's view is exceedingly close to Dilthey's.

9. Dilthey acclaimed Vico's New Science as "one of the greatest triumphs of modern thought" (*GS* 14/2:698). Cassirer has pointed out that the transcendental turn in German thought postulates understanding through the "Werk" to the "Wirken" (*Freiheit und Form*, p. 12 ff.).

10. For similar pronouncements see also *GS* 9:201; 4:97; 14/2:619. Hegel provided a version of this same view in the early writings which Dilthey brought to light: "This feeling of life, which finds itself again in other life, is love.... Life finds itself again in love" (*Theologische Jugendschriften* [ed. H. Nohl], pp. 283, 289). George Morgan insists: "The climax of his [Dilthey's] philosophical insight was a feeling rather than a theory, something personal and private, hardly communicable at all." Thus, his thought represents "a kind of Fabian retreat into irrationalism"

("Wilhelm Dilthey," pp. 377, 380). It should be noted that feeling in German thought was far from mere "subjective affect." Husserl referred to the "feeling of evidence"; Meinong spoke of "value-feelings," "judgment-feelings," and "cognitive-feelings." Cassirer, following in this tradition, distinguished between intellectual sympathy and emotional sympathy: the former rests upon an "objective anthropomorphism" and does not entail concurrence or agreement (*An Essay on Man* [New Haven, 1944], p. 191). The student closest to Dilthey in his last period, Bernhard Groethuysen, installed a similar distinction at the basis of his notion of "cognitive sympathy." Insisting that this concept had not yet found its rightful place in logic, epistemology, and psychology, Groethuysen stipulated that the form of knowledge concerns not the quality of a psychic act but its symbolic content. Such empathic knowledge has nothing whatever to do with agreement, approval, or the transpiring of identical mental processes. "When I sympathize with you for having a toothache, I do not have a toothache because you have one." Indeed, the greater the degree of empathic comprehension, the less one refers to any specific identity of processes; we do not sympathize less with a hungry person after we have had a good meal. Such cognitive empathy is directed to an objective state of affairs [*Sachverhalt*], not to a set of psychological facts ("Das Mitgefühl," *Zeitschrift für Psychologie und Physiologie der Sinnesorgane* 34 [1904]:161–270. See esp. 234). In *Idea of a Social Science*, Peter Winch argues that *Verstehen* is not merely a feeling but an ability to participate in the "rules" of a form of life. This formulation comes close to Dilthey's notion of the structures of objective mind. Von Wright claims that *Verstehen* is distinct from *Einfühlen* and is more properly considered a semantic rather than psychological category (*Explanation and Understanding*, p. 30).

11. *Verstehen* is frequently regarded as inherently a-logical, involving false analogy, tautology, or *petitio principii*. Max Weber complained that it rested upon a "logic of emanation" which presumed an identity of minds and provided no formal criteria of knowledge. This same objection was carried much further by the positivist critique of Otto Neurath, Ernest Nagel, and Theodore Abel, who exclude it altogether as knowledge. H. S. Hughes finds *Verstehen* both pertinent and problematic, bordering on the empty tautology "we understand because we understand" (*History as Art and as Science*, pp. 10–11). Arthur Danto observes: "*Verstehen* is, after all, understanding, not knowledge. Knowledge entails the truth of what is known, whereas understanding entails nothing so far as concerns the truth or falsity of what is understood. Understanding, however it is achieved, gives us entry into the world of another in the sense that it opens up the beliefs of others. But to understand the world of another is not to understand the world, unless those beliefs are also our beliefs, at which point they become transparent" ("Historical Language and Historical Reality" *Review of Metaphysics* 27 [1973]:258). Dilthey is often criticized for restricting *Verstehen* to a kind of private "communion of souls" which excludes publicly observable behavior (Wolfgang Metzger, "The Historical Background for National Trends in Psychology: German Psychology" *Journal for the History of the Behavioral Sciences* 1 [April, 1965]:112; Ralf Dahrendorf, "The German Idea of Truth" in *Society and Democracy in Germany* [New York, 1969], pp. 142–55; Jürgen Habermas, *Erkenntnis und Interesse* [Frankfurt a. M., 1968], p. 226 ff.). Gordon Leff sees in *Verstehen* an "excessive reliance upon the autonomy of individual conduct" (*History and Social Theory* [New York, 1971], pp. 19–26).

12. A similar position has been advanced by Michael Polanyi in *The Tacit Dimension* (New York, 1966).

13. Hegel had defined knowledge as a circle and science as "a circle of circles";

Geist is "the circle which returns into itself, that presupposes its beginning and reaches this beginning only in the end" (*Sämtliche Werke* 5:351). It is likely that Dilthey's intensive study of Hegel in his last years brought him to a heightened sensitivity to the problem of the circular structure of all knowledge. But he had examined it much earlier: see *GS* 13/1:252.

14. Humboldt, *Gesammelte Schriften* 4:47.

15. R. Aron, *Essai sur la théorie de l'histoire dans l'Allemagne contemporaine: La philosophie critique de l'histoire* (Paris, 1938), p. 79. Elsewhere Aron makes the sàme point: "In his writings, Dilthey juxtaposed rather than united the two contradictory ideas that one understands what one has experienced or might have experienced in life, and that one understands the other person" (*Introduction to the Philosophy of History* [Boston, 1961], p. 334).

16. Cassirer observes "an analogy is not an identity and a model is not the object itself" (*The Problem of Knowledge* [New Haven, 1950], p. 182). Freud held a similar view: "analogies, it is true, decide nothing, but they can make one feel more at home" (*New Introductory Lectures*, p. 72). Goethe observed that "analogy has the advantage that it does not foreclose and aspire to some ultimate formulation; induction, on the contrary, is harmful because it always holds a pre-established aim in mind" (*Maximen*, no. 1247).

17. Paul Ricoeur, "Interpretation Theory" (privately printed; University of Chicago, 1969), p. 20.

18. Sartre has furnished the clearest concrete statement of this crucial doctrine of ideal objects:

> Phenomenology has come to teach us that *states* [of consciousness] are objects, that an emotion as such (a love or a hatred) is a transcendent object and cannot shrink into the interior unity of a 'consciousness.' Consequently, if Paul and Peter both speak of Peter's love, for example, it is not true that the one speaks blindly and by analogy of that which the other apprehends in full. They speak of the same thing. Doubtless they apprehend it by different procedures, but these procedures are equally intuitional. And Peter's emotion is no more *certain* for Peter than for Paul. (*The Transcendence of the Ego* [New York, 1957], p. 95).

19. Husserl, *Logische Untersuchungen* 2:483.

20. See Hodges, *The Philosophy of Wilhelm Dilthey* (London, 1952), p. 123. Polanyi insists that "Dilthey taught that the mind of a person can be understood only by reliving its workings" (*Tacit Dimension*, p. 16). The term "workings" is highly problematic here, for it suggests psychological processes not mentally objective products.

21. After Rickert, this charge was made by Arthur Stein, Othmar Spann, Max Scheler, and more recently by Jürgen Habermas and Hans-Georg Gadamer. Lester Kolokowski insists that Dilthey's *Verstehen* is "the imitative reproduction of intentions, objectified in signs" and is flawed by its "obvious psychologism" ("Historical Understanding and the Intelligibility of History," *Tri-Quarterly* [1971], p. 104).

22. See also Yorck, *Bewusstseinsstellung und Geschichte: Ein Fragment aus dem philosophischen Nachlass* (Tübingen, 1956), p. 208.

23. Husserl, *Logische Untersuchungen* 2:173.

24. Alfred Schütz has given a concise description of this typification:

> The actual world of our experience . . . is experienced from the outset as a typical one. Objects are experienced as trees, animals, and the like, and more specifically

as oaks, firs, maples, or rattlesnakes, sparrows, and dogs. This table I am now perceiving is characterized as something recognized, as something foreknown and, nevertheless, novel. What is newly experienced is already known in the sense that it recalls similar or equal things formerly perceived. But what has been grasped once in its typicality carries with it a horizon of possible experiences with corresponding references to familiarity, that is, a series of typical characteristics still not actually experienced but expected to be potentially experienced (*Collected Papers* [The Hague, 1966], 1:281).

25. In 1901 Otto Ritschl called for a third term to mediate between Rickert's polarity of *Gesetz* and *Individuum*. Reasoning on lines quite similar to Dilthey, he found this middle term in the concept of type, which shares the generality of law and the specificity of the individual (*Die Kausalbetrachtung in den Geisteswissenschaften* [Bonn, 1901]).

26. "Briefe von und an Hegel," *Archiv für Geschichte der Philosophie* 1 (1888):291.

27. There is a pervasive misconception stretching from Rickert onward that Dilthey, in founding *Verstehen* upon lived experience, thereby made history and the human sciences dependent upon introspective psychology or some fuzzy version thereof. His critique of historical reason becomes merely an outwardly projected self-intuition, a colossally solipsistic effort to turn the world outside in and collapse history into the self. He is often linked with Novalis' view that "true history" is possible only through "genial self-observation" (*Schriften* [ed. Minor, 1923], p. 2, 134 ff.) and Droysen's statement that "the outside world can only be grasped by way of an analogy with what goes on in us ourselves" (*Historik*, p. 74). His full treatment of *Verstehen*, however, proceeds along the more objective line of Humboldt, Schleiermacher, and Hegel. Thus he notes that "the grasping of our own inner states is termed 'understanding' only in a spurious sense" (*GS* 5:318).

28. Kant had insisted upon the same point: "We must distinguish judgments pertaining to metaphysics from metaphysical judgments properly so called" (*Prolegomena to Any Future Metaphysics* [New York, 1950], p. 18).

29. Von Wright observes: "Dilthey's development from a more 'subjectivist-psychologistic' towards a more 'objectivist-hermeneutic' position was at the same time an increased orientation towards Hegel and the Hegelian tradition" (*Explanation*, p. 174). See also G. Misch, *Lebensphilosophie und Phänomenologie* (Stuttgart, 1967), p. 128. Dilthey's treatment of Hegel stressed two factors germane to his own philosophy: the notion of the experiential foundation of all theoretical thinking and the notion of objective mind. Dilthey saw Hegel's greatest contribution in the doctrine of "the real as life"—an insight he then tried to establish as the content of logic (*BNL* 77/236). Dilthey reminded his contemporaries of "something lastingly valuable in the new position of Hegel," which was best expressed in his *Phenomenology*. But even his *Logic*, though largely discredited by Trendelenburg's critique, nevertheless "retained an enduring meaning" (*BNL* 85/14–18, 81–83). As Lichtheim, Rosenberg, and others have perceived, Dilthey rehabilitated Hegel by enlarging his lopsided image as a pure logocrat. Hegel is conceived to be pointing toward a "concrete idealism" (see *GS* 15:305, 346–47).

30. Wundt too spoke of language, morality, and belief as "a mental atmosphere surrounding every person, without which he could not exist in his own mental individuality" (*Logik* [Stuttgart, 1906–8] 3:34); "The mental development of the single person is everywhere conditioned by his mental environment and the reciprocal relations in which he stands with his environment are as primordial and originary as individual existence itself" (ibid., 226). The originary and fundamental role of

hermeneutics had been stressed by Schleiermacher: "Every child arrives at the meaning of words only through hermeneutics" (*Hermeneutik* [Heidelberg, 1959], p. 40).

31. "Briefe Wilhelm Diltheys an Bernhard und Luise Scholz 1859–1864," *Sitzungs-berichte der preussischen Akademie der Wissenschaften* 10 phil.-hist. Kl (19733): 435–71.

32. Dilthey's literary efforts show that, despite his own conviction, great thinkers are not necessarily great poets (*GS* 11:49).

33. Yorck, *Bewusstseinsstellung*, pp. 84–85. This theme was also pursued by Bergson and Fritz Mauthner in a conspicuously radical manner.

34. Also quoted by A. Stein, *Der Begriff des Verstehens bei Dilthey* (Tübingen, 1926), p. 46.

35. Hegel, *Sämtliche Werke* 10:355. Kuno Fischer may also have provided an impetus toward this later position: "This outer aspect does not stand over against the inner aspect, but arises directly from it. . . . The inner must be thought as a productive activity and only as such productive activity: it *is* only insofar as it is effective [*wirksam*]" (*Logik*, Section 131, pp. 377–80). See also J. G. Droysen, *Historik* (Darmstadt, 1958), pp. 221–33.

36. For some telling examples and criticisms of this "unhistorical" reason see *GS* 8:46, 65–66, 129; 2:113; *LS* 374.

37. Tillinghast, *Specious Past*, p. 148. Masur asserts that because of "indecision" Dilthey "never answered the question of whether the material or spiritual elements were to be considered the decisive factors in the progress of culture" ("Dilthey and the History of Ideas," p. 106). The whole point of his *Idealrealismus*, and of the specific notion of a *Realdialektik*, was to mediate this abstract conceptual polarity in experience.

38. Discussing Hegel's conflation of consciousness and history, Dilthey stressed that "history cannot be construed out of this kind of inwardness [*Innerlichkeit*]. Every-thing in history has a mental aspect [*Bewusstseinsseite*], but nothing is intelligible solely on this basis" ("Diltheys Hegel-Fragment" *Hegelstudien* 1 [1961]:134).

39. Frank Manuel, "The Use and Abuse of Psychology in History," *Freedom from History* (New York, 1971), pp. 29–30. This view is underlined by others: "None of the perceptions of modern psychoanalysis which seek the sources for adult behavior in early experiences and which make sexual development central are used by Dilthey" (George Kren and Leon Rappaport, "Clio and Psyche," *History of Childhood Quarterly* 1 [1973]:152). H. S. Hughes observes "Dilthey himself tried to grapple with psychology of the more speculative sort. But in this openness of mind his successors among the neo-idealists refused to follow him" (*History as Art and as Science*, p. 44).

40. Ringer, *Decline*, p. 329. Masur insists that Dilthey saw ideas as "the core of world history" ("Wilhelm Dilthey," p. 96), whereas Gunter Remmling finds him "already very susceptible to materialistic interpretations of history and human life" (*Road to Suspicion: A Study of Modern Mentality and Sociology of Knowledge* [New York, 1967], p. 83).

41. *Zeitschrift für Völkerpsychologie* 10 (1878):48. See also *GS* 11:119.

42. Georg Lukacs, *Die Zerstörung der Vernunft* (Neuwied am Rhein, 1962), p. 394. Hajo Holborn, "Wilhelm Dilthey and the Critique of Historical Reason," *Journal of the History of Ideas* 11 (1950):117. Hodges has asserted that Marx's name appears

only once in Dilthey's writings (*Wilhelm Dilthey*, p. 63); Masur says Dilthey "never referred to Marx" (*Prophets*, p. 164); Henri Irénée Marrou repeats the same misconception in a review (*History and Theory* 2 [1962]:200).

43. For further references to Marx, see *GS* 15:321; 4:256; 10:15; also *Archiv für Geschichte der Philosophie* 3 (1890):141; 4 (1891):706; 12 (1899):334.

44. Ernst Troeltsch has suggested a direct connection: *Der Historismus und seine Probleme* (Tübingen, 1922), p. 511.

45. Like Lukacs, Westphal argues that Dilthey's own theories carry an "antirevolutionary accent" (*Feinde Bismarcks* [Munich, 1930], p. 157). Riedel finds that his theory of knowledge was determined by "the general bourgeois antirevolutionary tradition of German philosophy" ("Einleitung" in *Der Aufbau*, p. 17).

46. Hodges, *Wilhelm Dilthey*, pp. 56, 61.

47. Hodges, *Philosophy*, p. 340.

48. Such statements address the charge of "psychologism" and "methodological individualism" made by the theorist of "corporatism" Othmar Spann, who charged that Dilthey's *Verstehen* reduced society to a collection of "atomic individualities" and neglected the "whole" (*Tübinger Zeitschrift für Staatswissenschaften* 59 [1903]:216). Dilthey had made the same charge against Bentham and the Mills. Otto Westphal saw Dilthey's primary aim as the analysis of the social relations which mediate between the "old-liberal" dichotomy of state and individual. Dilthey inaugurated an "era of social liberalism in science" whose principles were "Seele und Gesellschaft anstelle von Geist und Staat" (*Feinde Bismarcks* pp. 164–70).

49. More circumstantial evidence of Dilthey's interest in sociology comes from his conversations with Kurt Breysig, who as a follower of Lamprecht, was condemned by traditional historians for his attempt to ally history with sociology. While cautioning Breysig against weakly founded generalizations, Dilthey concurred with his effort to isolate regularities (*Gesetzmässigkeiten*) in social behavior and organizations (H. Diwald, *Wilhelm Dilthey* [Göttingen, 1963], p. 14). Dilthey's endorsement of Simmel for a chair at Berlin also included a brief defense of sociology and sociological methods. (*GNL* 7/1–3).

50. The point has been extensively examined in Iggers and Ringer. Kren and Rappaport find "the concern for individuality and uniqueness by German historians was a defensive reaction to a perceived threat to conservative values. By emphasizing the constant flux of historical movement and seeing all values as relative to time and place, they maintained a philosophic posture opposed to the democratic premises of the Enlightment" ("Clio and Psyche," *History of Childhood Quarterly* 1 [1973]:152).

51. Winch, *Idea of Social Science*, p. 138.

52. S. Kracauer, *Geschichte: Vor den letzten Dingen* (Frankfurt a. M., 1971), p. 60.

53. Cassirer, *Problem*, p. 241; Ernest Becker, *The Structure of Evil* (New York, 1968), p. 124.

54. Von Wright makes a similar point: "To say that the concept of causation presupposes the concept of freedom seems to me to be right, in the sense that it is only through the idea of doing things that we come to grasp the idea of cause and effect" (*Explanation*, p. 81).

55. The concept of *Steigerung* had been stressed by Goethe, Trendelenburg, and K. Fischer (see the latter's *Logik*, pp. 410–11).

56. Dilthey's anticipation seems to be fulfilled in von Wright's notion of "teleonomy"

or "quasi-teleological explanation" which is both causal and purposeful (*Explanation*, pp. 59–61). Dilthey has been specifically invoked in Ludwig von Bertalanffy, *Problems of Life* (New York, 1960).

57. Von Wright makes the same point (*Explanation*, pp. 7–8).

58. Kurt Breysig, *Aus meinen Tagen und Träumen* (Berlin, 1962), p. 107.

59. Karl Mannheim distinguished interpretation (*Deutung*) and explanation (*Erklärung*) and found them complementary only "in turn":

> Interpretation does not make causal explanation superfluous. It refers to something quite different, and consequently there is no rivalry between the two. Interpretation serves for the deeper understanding of meanings; causal explanation shows the conditions for the actualization or realization of a given meaning. At any rate there can be no causal, genetic explanation of meanings—not even in the form of an ultimate theory superadded to the interpretation. Meaning in its proper sense can only be understood or interpreted.... Causal explanation and interpretation will both be applied in turn (but not in the same breath!) in order to give as good an idea as possible of the full, concrete variety and "vitality" of the historical process in question. ("On the Interpretation of World-Views," *From Karl Mannheim* [ed. Kurt Wolff, New York, 1971], pp. 56–57.

This distinction might best be viewed in Kant's sense of the two "interests" of reason, that is, as "regulative" but not "constitutive" and objective. Only if taken as an objective principle are the two interests contradictory or mutually exclusive. While maintaining the distinction, Kant saw the possibility of adjustment—"In reality reason has one interest only" (*CPR*, Muller II, 571).

61. Hegel, *Phenomenology of Mind*, trans. by Baillie, p. 112.

62. Ibid., pp. 70, 117.

63. Ibid., p. 85.

64. Hegel, *Sämtliche Werke* 5:ii. Karl Rosenkranz later promoted the view that Hegel's method was "immanent critique" (*Hegel als deutscher Nationalphilosoph* [Leipzig, 1870] p. 230.

65. Fischer, *Logik*, p. 200.

66. Wundt, *Logik* 3:116–17.

67. R. G. Collingwood, *The Idea of History* (New York, 1946), pp. 215–16.

68. Cassirer, *Problem*, p. 149 ff.; F. Meinecke, *Die Enstehung des Historismus* (Munich-Berlin, 1946), p. 496 ff.

69. Quoted in R. Haym, *Hegel und seine Zeit* (Hildesheim, 1962), p. 420. See Hegel, *Sämtliche Werke* 3:222–23; 7:43–45; 16:400.

70. Cassirer, *Problem*, p. 226.

71. Nietzsche's attitude toward history was as paradoxical as the rest of his thought; by most of his contemporaries it was interpreted as wholly negative and critical ("Vom Nutzen und Nachteil der Historie für das Leben," *Sämtliche Werke* 71:95–195).

72. Windelband, *Die Philosophie*, pp. 104–5.

73. Max Nordau, *The Interpretation of History* (New York, 1910), especially pp. 7, 12, 22–30, 43, 396.

74. Ludwig Wittgenstein, *Notebooks 1914–1916* (Oxford, 1961), p. 82e. As Ernst Troeltsch observed, the war and its aftermath only confirmed the process of histor-

ical disillusionment and magnified the call for new "creative" myths (*Historismus*, pp. 3–4).

Chapter 6

The source of the epigraph is *GS* 5:406.

1. Ricoeur, *Freud*, p. 33.

2. Karl Mannheim observed that Dilthey showed "great critical reserve and theoretical acumen in treating world-views" (*From Karl Mannheim* [New York, 1971] p. 50). Werner Brock attaches an important caution: "The phenomenon of *Weltanschauung*, as elaborated by Dilthey—it was he who also settled the meaning of this term—is, of course, not to be identified with the conceptions of *Weltanschauung* which occur in the widespread and often misunderstood popularisation of Dilthey's thought" (*Contemporary German Philosophy* [Cambridge, 1935], p. 24).

3. H. A. Hodges, *Wilhelm Dilthey* (London, 1949), p. 85. Schopenhauer had spoken of "an absolute need for the interpretation of life" (*Essays and Aphorisms* [Baltimore, 1970], p. 96). Explicitly invoking Schopenhauer, Einstein added: "Man tries to make for himself in the fashion that suits him best a simplified and intelligible picture of the world; he then tries to some extent to substitute this cosmos of his for the world of experience, and thus to overcome it. This is what the painter, the poet, the speculative philosopher, and the natural scientist do, each in his own fashion. Each makes this cosmos and its construction the pivot of his emotional life, in order to find in this way the peace and security which he cannot find in the narrow whirlpool of personal experience" (*Ideas and Opinions* [New York, 1954], pp. 220–21).

4. In somewhat different form this critical distinction can be found in Kant, Trendelenburg, Brentano, Husserl, Mannheim and others; it concerns the difference between thought at the first and second intentions (*intentio recta* and *intentio obliqua*). The intrinsic and extrinsic levels are combined in what Dilthey called "partial transcendence." Both Schleiermacher and Trendelenburg had maintained that predications claiming absolute truth within a system of beliefs could not attain the status of knowledge, but that one could make valid cognitive judgments *about* these predications. Husserl observed: "To make a judgment about a judgment is something quite different from making a judgment about an objective state of affairs" (*Logische Untersuchungen* [Halle, 1900–1901], 2:431).

5. Dilthey's typology has been widely interpreted as inimical to his whole project: "But it is clear that any attempt at creating such a typology implies the adoption of a standpoint outside of history from which these types can be actualized and contemplated. In other words, the wholesale development of a historical typology—if taken seriously—would completely undermine the very foundations of the entire Diltheyan position.... Once Dilthey embarked upon this course, most scholars agree, he actually sacrificed the integrity of his original stance. For now, no longer convinced that certainty would develop naturally out of our experience and participation in the creative forces of life, Dilthey, in effect, attempted to impose certainty upon history. And since the natural sciences constituted the only nontheological certainty available, this meant he was forced to adapt their procedures to the cultural sciences. But thereby Dilthey could not avoid implying that science was somehow superior to history and even the superiority of the cultural sciences which he had established earlier was again suspect" (Berthold Riesterer, *Karl Löwith's View of*

History [The Hague, 1969], pp. 6–7). Carlo Antoni regards his typology as "historical crystallography," that is, as incompatible with a truly historical conception of development. (*From History to Sociology* [Detroit, 1959], p. 30; see also W. Kluback, *Wilhelm Dilthey's Philosophy of History* [New York, 1958], pp. 93–97: 'The naturalistic concept of type not only renders historiography schematic, but reduces it to sociology"). Landgrebe maintains that Dilthey's concept of type changes after 1900 from a quasinaturalistic, morphological one to an "artistic" one ("Wilhelm Diltheys Theorie," pp. 277–78, 284). F. Rodi makes the same point: *Morphologie und Hermeneutik* (Stuttgart, 1969).

6. E. Troeltsch, *Der Historismus und seine Probleme* (Tübingen, 1922), pp. 28 ff., 247 ff.

7. As in O. F. Bollnow, *Einführung* (Stuttgart, 1968), p. 17.

8. Dilthey has gone down as the archrelativist, but even here, it seems, there is a question of relative degrees. Masur proclaims flatly that Dilthey was an "avowed relativist" (*Prophets of Yesterday* [New York, 1961], p. 167). Tillinghast finds "Dilthey's theory turns historical understanding toward existentialism and even more toward relativism" (*Specious Past*, p. 87); likewise Ferguson: "It is clear that the whole of Dilthey's philosophy of history tended toward an inescapable relativism. Yet he always maintained that positive historical knowledge was possible, that we may achieve an 'understanding' " (*Renaissance in Historical Thought*, p. 217). Kluback finds: "He had neither Herder's belief in humanity, nor Hegel's faith in the progress of the consciousness of liberty, nor Comte's conviction of the triumph of science. He was a relativist" (*Philosophy*, p. 106). Lichtheim finds "historical relativism" and "radical historicism" (*Concept of Ideology*, pp. 30, 35). Diwald asserts that the theory of world-views leads inexorably to relativism, inescapable aporias, and anarchy of values (*Das historische Erkennen*, p. 17). Mandelbaum is more cautious and perceptive, noting that Dilthey did not consider himself a relativist (*The Problem of Historical Knowledge* [Baltimore, 1971], p. 58).

9. In a similar vein Ortega observed: "Perspective is one of the component parts of reality. Far from being a disturbance of its fabric, it is its organizing element. A reality which remained the same from whatever point of view it was observed would be a ridiculous conception" (*The Modern Theme* [New York, 1933], p. 90). This same point was made by Karl Mannheim:

> Human consciousness can grasp a landscape *as a landscape* only from various perspectives; and yet the landscape does not dissolve itself into its various possible pictorial representations. Each of the possible pictures has a "real" counterpart and the correctness of each perspective can be controlled from the other perspectives. This implies, however, that history is only visible from within history and cannot be interpreted through a "jump" beyond history, in occupying a static standpoint arbitrarily occupied outside history. The historicist standpoint, which starts with relativism, eventually achieves an absoluteness of view, because in its final form it posits history itself as the absolute; this alone makes it possible that the various standpoints, which at first appear to be anarchic, can be ordered as component parts of a meaningful overall process" (*From Karl Mannheim*, p. 97).

10. R. Aron, *Introduction to the Philosophy of History* (Boston, 1961), p. 297.

11. Mannheim later made the same point:

> The functionalization of an intellectual phenomenon with respect to an underlying meaningful existential order bestows new meaning on the phenomenon. It is the miracle of historical thinking that we are able to look back and thus, in retrospect, to grasp a past intellectual content or idea as ideology, that is, to

functionalize it by reference to an existence that now becomes meaningful to us—to see new meaning in past content. Indeed, our historical thinking does not progress in the sense that we simply immanently accept or reject past contexts of meaning. Essentially it progresses in the sense that, being pushed on by history, we gain a certain distance from past contents and grasp them "from without," where earlier we understood them "from within." Once they have become visible to us in their contours, we functionalize them with respect to a social-existential totality that we conceive of as a context of meaning. (*From Karl Mannheim*, p. 124).

12. Karl Heussi, *Die Krisis des Historismus* (Tübingen, 1932), p. 74. Mannheim distinguished between existential relativity and epistemic relativism:

At this point it is, so to speak, still open whether the "existential relativization" of thought is to be combined with epistemological relativism or not. In any case, however, we would like to go on record at this point that we cannot share the present widespread fear of relativism. "Relativism" has become a catchword which, it is believed, will instantly annihilate any adversary against whom it is used. But as for us we definitely prefer a "relativism" which accentuates the difficulty of its task by calling attention to all those moments which tend to make the propositions actually discoverable at any given time, partial and situationally conditioned—we prefer such a "relativism" to an "absolutism" which loudly proclaims, as a matter of principle, the absoluteness of its own position of "truth in itself," but is in fact no less partial than any of its adversaries—and, still worse, is utterly incapable of tackling with its epistemological apparatus the problems of temporal and situational determination of any concrete process of thought, completely overlooking the way in which this situational conditioning enters into the structure and evolution of knowledge" (*From Karl Mannheim*, p. 62).

13. This theme is very explicitly developed in Cassirer, *Freiheit und Form*; Meinecke denies that the recognition of the relativity of values entails a wholesale relativism (*Werke* 4:83 ff.).

Conclusion

The epigraph is from Hegel, *Early Theological Writings*, edited by T. M. Knox (Chicago, 1948), p. 254.

1. J. S. Mill, "Coleridge," in *Essays on Politics and Culture* (New York, 1967), p. 124.

2. W. Wundt, *Logik* (Stuttgart, 1906–8), 3:7.

3. Karl Jaspers, *Vernunft und Widervernunft in unserer Zeit* (Heidelberg, 1950), p. 68; Joseph Derbolav, "Dilthey and das Problem der Geschichtlichkeit," in *Rationalität, Phenomenalität, Individualität* (Bonn, 1966), p. 239.

4. H. Diwald, *Wilhelm Dilthey* (Göttingen, 1963), p. 21; F. Rodi, *Morphologie und Hermeneutik* (Stuttgart, 1969), p. 9.

5. *Husserliana* 9:6.

6. G. Masur, "Wilhelm Dilthey and the History of Ideas," p. 94.

7. E. Troeltsch, *Der Historismus und seine Probleme* (Tübingen, 1922), pp. 517–18.

8. Scheler, *Vom Umsturz der Werte* (Leipzig, 1923) 2:146.

9. Ortega, *Concord and Liberty* (New York, 1946), p. 140.

10. Coates, *Liberal Humanism*, p. 256; Horkheimer, *Kritische Theorie* (Frankfurt, 1968) 2:283.

11. H. S. Hughes, *Consciousness and Society* (New York, 1958), p. 199.

12. Egon Friedell, *Kulturgeschichte der Neuzeit* (Munich, 1927), pp. 50–51.

13. Troeltsch, *Historismus*, p. 512.

14. Ibid., p. 47.

15. Quoted in Julian Marias, *Ortega y Gasset* (Norman, Okla., 1970), p. 339.

16. Sartre, *Search for a Method* (New York, 1963), p. 111.

17. Michael Landmann, *Philosophische Anthropologie* (Berlin, 1969), p. 111.

18. Cassirer, *Logik*, p. 9.

19. G. Morgan, "Wilhelm Dilthey," p. 371.

20. Maurice Merleau-Ponty, "Phenomenology and the Sciences of Man," in *The Primacy of Perception* (Evanston, 1964), p. 95.

21. Cassirer, *An Essay on Man* (New Haven, 1944), p. 191. Cf. *GS* 11:21 and 68.

22. See Georg Lukács, *Die Zerstörung der Vernunft* (Neuwied, 1962). Lukács had been a student of Dilthey's at Berlin and had employed Diltheyan conceptions in his early studies in literary and cultural criticism. His conversion to Marxism brought the repudiation of Dilthey's "subjective idealism" and the notion of *Erleben* (George Lichtheim, *Georg Lukács* [London, 1970], pp. 13–21). A recent study repeats Lukács' allegations: Gustav Schmidt, "Wilhelm Dilthey," in *Deutsche Historiker* (Göttingen, 1972), pp. 58–63. Wladyslaw Tatarkiewicz alleges that "the consequence of Dilthey's view of human reality was irrationalism" (*Nineteenth Century Philosophy*, p. 192). "Dilthey represented irrationalist skepticism. . . . Instead of actually providing a world-view, philosophy becomes a doctrine of world-views. Its final word is skepticism" (T. K. Oesterreich, "Die philosophischen Strömungen der Gegenwart" in *Systematische Philosophie* 3d ed. [Berlin, 1921], pp. 378, 280).

23. On the multiple meanings of the term, cf. Dwight Lee and Robert Beck, "The Meaning of 'Historicism,' " *American Historical Review* 59 (1953–54):568–77. Georg Iggers, "Historicism" *Dictionary of the History of Ideas* 2:456–64. Maurice Mandelbaum, "Historicism," *Encyclopedia of Philosophy* 4:22–25. G. Scholtz, "Historismus," *Historisches Wörterbuch der Philosophie* 3: 1142–47.

24. Heussi, *Die Krisis des Historismus* (Tübingen, 1932), p. iv. Cf. also Thomas Nipperdey, "Historismus und Historismuskritik Heute" in *Gesellschaft, Kultur, Theorie* (Göttingen, 1976), pp. 59–73.

25. Troeltsch, *Historismus*, pp. 527–58; Kracauer, *Geschichte*, pp. 30, 223; Tillinghast, *Specious Past*, pp. 9, 146.

26. Georg Iggers, *The German Conception of History* (Middletown, 1968), pp. 128–29.

27. Karl Löwith, "Mensch und Geschichte," in *Gesammelte Abhandlungen zur Kritik der geschichtlichen Existenz* (Stuttgart, 1960), pp. 152–53. Kolowkowski finds that "Every view of history as something intelligible moves beyond history and is antihistorical. . . . History is not intelligible as a meaningful structure unless an extrahistorical essence which embodies itself in its temporal course is accepted as a matter of principle. It is necessary to posit a pre-empirical (transcendental or transcendent) world of the possible to which empirical history gives body and which it transforms into history. It is necessary in short to admit the distinction between the possible and the actual in the Leibnizian sense" ("Historical Understanding," pp. 115–16). Protagonists of the "new metaphysics" of the early twentieth century saw Dilthey's thought as "merely historical" (*nur historisch*), incapable of genuine philosophical truth. By 1911 the journal *Logos*, devoted to the systematic philosophy of culture, announced that "the flood of historicism is ebbing everywhere" (*Logos* 2 [1911]:129).

Jonas Cohn, a student of Rickert, wrote in the same journal: "Because he does not see the real objective core of metaphysical issues, Dilthey denies altogether the possibility of truly objective confrontation with them. From this attitude arises his antimetaphysical position, which is simply the reflection of his merely historical mode of seeing" (*Logos* 12 [1923–24]:296).

28. *London Times Literary Supplement*, September 15, 1972, p. 1047.

29. Mannheim, *Essays on the Sociology of Knowledge* (ed. Keksmeti), pp. 84–85.

30. Cassirer, *The Problem of Knowledge* (New Haven, 1950), p. 325.

31. The term "transcendental historicism" was first used by Ludwig Landgrebe, "Wilhelm Diltheys Theorie der Geisteswissenschaften," *Jahrbuch für Philosophie und phänomenologische Forschung* 9 (1928):327–66. It has subsequently been applied to R. G. Collingwood; Rubinoff characterizes Collingwood by means of the tradition of "transcendental historicism according to which philosophic truth, while admittedly grounded in history, is nevertheless not entirely historical in character" (*Collingwood and the Reform of Metaphysics* [Toronto, 1970], p. 24). This position has been defined best by Merleau-Ponty:

> Since we are all hemmed in by history, it is up to us to understand that whatever truth we may have is to be gotten not in spite but through our historical inherence. Superficially considered, our inherence destroys all truth; radically considered, it founds a new idea of truth. As long as I cling to the ideal of an absolute spectator, of knowledge with no point of view, I can see my situation as nothing but a source of error. But if I have once recognized that through it I am grafted onto every action and all knowledge which can have a meaning for me, and that step by step it contains everything which can *exist* for me, then my contact with the social in the finitude of my situation is revealed to me as the point of origin of all truth, including scientific truth. And since we have an idea of truth, since we are in truth and cannot escape it, the only thing left for me to do is to define a truth in the situation (*Signs* [Evanston, 1964], p. 109).

Klibansky observes: "Though the objectivity of history only grows from a subjective basis, this cannot imperil its value as a form of knowledge. To say that the attempt to reach an absolute *Always* must forever start from a relative *Now* and *Here*, can betoken a depreciation only in the eyes of one who fancies himself standing, like a dogmatist of the old learning, in a space without time; or to an intelligence suspended *in vacuo* which considers itself to be bound by neither space nor time" ("The Philosophic Character of History" in *Philosophy and History*, pp. 336–37). The concept "transcendental historicism" has been called a "contradiction in terms" by Theodor Litt, Hellmut Diwald, and others.

32. Karl Löwith, *Gesammelte Abhandlungen*, p. 175; Fritz Wagner, *Moderne Geschichtswissenschaft* (Freiburg, 1951), pp. 341 ff.; Leonard Krieger, "History and Existentialism in Sartre," in *The Critical Spirit* (Boston, 1967), pp. 241–42.

33. Dilthey has rightly been termed "a defender of liberal humanism" by Wilson Coates, *The Ordeal of Liberal Humanism*, p. 449.

34. *Logos* 1 (1910–11):286.

Selected Bibliography

Bibliographies

Diaz de Cerio, Franco. "Bibliographia de W. Dilthey." *Pensamiento* 24 (1968):195–258.

Herrmann, Ulrich. *Bibliographie Wilhelm Dilthey: Quellen und Literatur.* Weinheim, Berlin, and Basel: Julius Beltz, 1969.

Weniger, Erich. "Verzeichnis der Schriften Wilhelm Diltheys von den Anfängen bis zur *Einleitung in die Geisteswissenschaften.*" In *Gesammelte Schriften* 12:208–13.

Zeeck, Hans. "Im Druck erschienene Schriften von Wilhelm Dilthey." *Archiv für Geschichte der Philosophie.* New series 25 (1912):154–61.

Dilthey's Works

Gesammelte Schriften

Gesammelte Schriften. 18 vols. Stuttgart: B. G. Teubner; Göttingen: Vandenhoeck & Ruprecht, 1914–77.

> *GS* 1: *Einleitung in die Geisteswissenschaften: Versuch einer Grundlegung für das Studium der Gesellschaft und der Geschichte.* Edited by B. Groethuysen. 4th ed., 1959.
> *GS* 2: *Weltanschauung und Analyse des Menschen seit Renaissance und Reformation.* Edited by G. Misch. 5th ed., 1957.
> *GS* 3: *Studien zur Geschichte des deutschen Geistes: Leibniz und sein Zeitalter. Friedrich der Grosse und die deutsche Aufklärung. Das achtzehnte Jahrhundert und die geschichtliche Welt.* Edited by P. Ritter. 2d ed., 1959.
> *GS* 4: *Die Jugendgeschichte Hegels und andere Abhandlungen zur Geschichte des deutschen Idealismus.* Edited by H. Nohl. 2d ed., 1959.
> *GS* 5: *Die geistige Welt: Einleitung in die Philosophie des Lebens. Erste*

Hälfte: Abhandlungen zur Grundlegung der Geisteswissenschaften. Edited by G. Misch. 2d ed., 1957.

GS 6: Die geistige Welt: Einleitung in die Philosophie des Lebens. Zweite Hälfte: Abhandlungen zur Poetik, Ethik und Pädagogik. Edited by G. Misch. 3d ed., 1958.

GS 7: Der Aufbau der geschichtlichen Welt in den Geisteswissenschaften. Edited by B. Groethuysen. 2d ed., 1956.

GS 8: Weltanschauungslehre: Abhandlungen zur Philosophie der Philosophie. Edited by B. Groethuysen. 2d ed., 1960.

GS 9: Pädagogik: Geschichte und Grundlinien des Systems. Edited by O. F. Bollnow. 2d ed., 1960.

GS 10: System der Ethik. Edited by H. Nohl. 1st ed., 1958.

GS 11: Vom Aufgang des geschichtlichen Bewusstseins: Jugendaufsätze und Erinnerungen. Edited by E. Weniger. 2d ed., 1960.

GS 12: Zur preussischen Geschichte: Schleiermachers politische Gesinnung und Wirksamkeit. Die Reorganisatoren des preussischen Staates. Das allgemeine Landrecht. Edited by E. Weniger. 2d ed., 1960.

GS 13: Leben Schleiermachers. Auf Grund des Textes der 1. Auflage von 1870 und der Zusätze aus dem Nachlass. Edited by Martin Redeker, 1970.

GS 14: Leben Schleiermachers. Zweiter Band: Schleiermachers System als Philosophie und Theologie. Edited by Martin Redeker, 1966.

GS 15: Zur Geistesgeschichte des 19. Jahrhunderts: Portraits und Skizzen. Quellenstudien und Literatur berichte zur Theologie und Philosophie im 19. Jahrhundert. Edited by Ulrich Herrmann, 1970.

GS 16: Zur Geistesgeschichte des 19. Jahrhunderts: Aufsätze und Rezensionen aus Zeitungen und Zeitschriften 1859–1874. Edited by Ulrich Herrmann, 1972.

GS 17: Zur Geistesgeschichte des 19. Jahrhunderts: Aus Westermanns Monatsheften: Literaturbriefe, Berichte zur Kunstgeschichte, verstreute Rezensionen 1867–1884. Edited by Ulrich Herrmann, 1974.

GS 18: Die Wissenschaften vom Menschen, der Gesellschaft und der Geschichte: Vorarbeiten zur Einleitung in die Geisteswissenschaften (1865–1880). Edited by Helmut Johach and Frithjof Rodi, 1977.

Other Published Writings

Von deutscher Dichtung und Musik, 2d ed. Stuttgart: B. G. Teubner; Göttingen, Vandenhoeck & Ruprecht, 1957.

"Diltheys Kant-Darstellung in seiner letzten Vorlesung über das System der Philosophie." In Dietrich Bischoff, *Wilhelm Diltheys geschichtliche Lebensphilosophie,* pp. 46–63. Leipzig: Teubner, 1935.

Das Erlebnis und die Dichtung: Lessing. Goethe, Novalis, Hölderlin. 13th ed. Stuttgart: B. G. Teubner: Göttingen: Vandenhoeck & Ruprecht, 1957.

"Fragmente aus Wilhelm Diltheys Hegelwerk." Edited by F. Nicolin and O. Pöggeler. *Hegelstudien* 1 (1961):103–34.

Die grosse Phantasiedichtung und andere Studien zur vergleichenden Literaturgeschichte. Edited by H. Nohl. Göttingen: Vandenhoeck & Ruprecht, 1954.

Grundriss der allgemeinen Geschichte der Philosophie. 6th rev. ed. Edited and supplemented by H-G. Gadamer. Frankfurt a.M.: Klostermann, 1949.

Grundriss der Logik und des Systems der philosophischen Wissenschaften: Für Vorlesungen. Berlin: Mittler, 1865.

Leben Schleiermachers. Vol. 1. Edited and supplemented by H. Mulert. 2d ed. Berlin: de Gruyter, 1922.

Aus Schleiermachers Leben: In Briefen. 4 vols. Berlin: G. Reimers, 1858–63. (Vols. 3 and 4 edited by Dilthey.)

Diaries and Correspondence

"Briefe Wilhelm Diltheys an Bernhard und Luise Scholz, 1859–64." Edited by Sigrid von der Schulenburg. *Sitzungsberichte d. preuss. Akad. d. Wiss., Phil-hist. Kl.* 10 (1933):416–71.

"Briefe Wilhelm Diltheys an Rudolf Haym, 1861–73." Edited by E. Weniger. *Abhandlungen der preuss. Akad. d. Wiss.* 9 (1936):2–48.

"Der Briefwechsel Dilthey-Husserl." With an introduction by Walter Biemel. *Man and World* 1 (1968):428–46.

Briefwechsel zwischen Wilhelm Dilthey und dem Grafen Paul Yorck von Wartenburg. 1877–97. Edited by Sigrid von der Schulenburg. Halle a.d.S.: Niemeyer, 1923.

Der junge Dilthey: Ein Lebensbild in Briefen und Tagebüchern, 1852–1870. Edited by Clara Misch, née Dilthey. 2d ed. Stuttgart: B. G. Teubner; Göttingen: Vandenhoeck & Ruprecht, 1960.

Unpublished Manuscripts

"Der Berliner Entwurf." Nachlass Dilthey, no. 179. Literatur-Archiv der deutschen Akademie der Wissenschaften, Berlin.

"Die Breslauer Ausarbeitung." Nachlass Dilthey. Cod. Ms. W. Dilthey, no. 2. Niedersächsische Staats- und Universitätsbibliothek, Göttingen.

"Diltheys letztes Kolleg über das System der Philosophie." Nachlass Dilthey. Cod. Ms. W. Dilthey, no. 9. Niedersächsische Staats- und Universitätsbibliothek, Göttingen.

Manuscripts from the Berlin Nachlass. Literatur-Archiv der deutschen Akademie der Wissenschaften, Berlin.

392 SELECTED BIBLIOGRAPHY

Manuscripts from the Göttingen Nachlass. Niedersächsische Staats- und Universitätsbibliothek, Göttingen.

Selections in Translation

Emery, S. A., and W. T. *The Essence of Philosophy*. New York: AMS Press, 1969.

Gardiner, P. *Theories of History*. New York: Free Press, 1969.

Gay, P., and Cavanaugh, G. *Historians at Work*, vol. 4: *Dilthey to Hofstadter*. New York: Harper & Row, 1975.

Hodges, H. A. W. *Dilthey: An Introduction*. London: Routledge & Kegan Paul, 1949.

Rickman, H. P. *Pattern and Meaning in History*. New York: Harper & Row, 1962.

————. *W. Dilthey: Selected Writings*. Cambridge, Eng.: at the University Press, 1976.

Selected Secondary Works

Abel, Theodore. "The Operation Called *Verstehen*." *American Journal of Sociology* 54 (1948):211–18.

Antoni, Carlo. *From History to Sociology*. Detroit: Wayne State University Press, 1959.

Apel, Karl-Otto. "Das Verstehen." *Archiv für Begriffsgeschichte* 1 (1955): 142–99.

Aron, Raymond. *Essai sur la théorie de l'histoire dans l'Allemagne contemporaine. La philosophie critique de l'histoire*. Paris: J. Vrin, 1938.

————. *Introduction to the Philosophy of History*. Boston: Beacon Press, 1961.

Bergstraesser, Arnold. "Wilhelm Dilthey and Max Weber: An Empirical Approach to Historical Synthesis." *Ethics* 57 (1947):92–110.

Betti, Emilio. *Die Hermeneutik als allgemeine Methode der Geisteswissenschaften*. Tübingen: J. C. B. Mohr, 1962.

Bianco, Franco. *Dilthey e la genesi della critica storica della ragione*. Milan: Marzorati, 1971.

Bischoff, Dietrich. *Wilhelm Diltheys geschichtliche Lebensphilosophie. Mit einem Anhang, eine Kantdarstellung Diltheys*. Leipzig and Berlin: B. G. Teubner, 1935.

Bollnow, Otto Friedrich. *Das Verstehen: Drei Aufsätze zur Theorie der Geisteswissenschaften*. Mainz: Kirchheim, 1949.

————. *Dilthey: Eine Einführung in seine Philosophie*. 3d rev. ed. Stuttgart: W. Kohlhammer, 1968.

————. *Die Methode der Geisteswissenschaften*. Mainz: Gutenberg, 1950.

———. "Die Lehre von den Typen der Weltanschauung." *Neue Jahrbücher für Wissenschaft und Jugendbildung* 8 (1932):234–44.

———. "Diltheys Pädagogik." *Neue Jahrbücher für Wissenschaft und Jugendbildung* 9 (1933):289–301.

Brentano, Franz. *Psychologie vom empirischen Standpunkt.* Leipzig: Duncker Verlag, 1874.

Cassirer, Ernst. *An Essay on Man.* New Haven: Yale University Press, 1944.

———. *The Logic of the Humanities.* New Haven: Yale University Press, 1960.

———. *The Problem of Knowledge: Philosophy, Science, and History since Hegel.* New Haven: Yale University Press, 1950.

Collingwood, R. G. *The Idea of History.* New York: Oxford University Press, 1946.

Coates, Willson, and White, Hayden. *An Intellectual History of Western Europe.* 2 vols. New York: McGraw-Hill, 1966–70.

Dietrich, Albert. "Wilhelm Dilthey." *Die grossen Deutschen: Neue deutsche Biographie* 5 (Berlin, 1937):439–49.

Diwald, Hellmut. *Wilhelm Dilthey.* Göttingen: Musterschmidt Verlag, 1963.

Droysen, Johann Gustav. *Historik: Vorlesungen über Enzyklopëdie und Methodologie des Geschichte.* Edited by Rudolf Hübner. 3d ed. Darmstadt: Wissenschaftliche Buchgesellschaft, 1958.

Ebbinghaus, Hermann. "Über erklärende und beschreibende Psychologie." *Zeitschrift für Psychologie und Physiologie der Sinnesorgane* 9 (1895): 161–205.

Engel-Janosi, Friedrich. *The Growth of German Historicism.* Johns Hopkins University Studies in Historical and Political Science. Baltimore, 1944.

Friess, H. L. "Wilhelm Dilthey: A Review of His Collected Works." *Journal of Philosophy* 26 (1929):5–25.

Frischeisen-Koehler, Max. "Wilhelm Dilthey als Philosoph." *Logos* 3 (1912):25–58.

Gadamer, Hans-Georg. *Kleine Schriften.* Vol. I: *Philosophie/Hermeneutik.* Vol. II: *Interpretationen.* Tübingen: J. C. B. Mohr, 1967.

———. *Wahrheit und Methode: Grundzüge einer philosophischen Hermeneutik.* Tübingen: J. C. B. Mohr, 1965.

Gierke, Otto. "Eine Grundlegung für die Geisteswissenschaften." *Preussische Jahrbücher* 53 (1884):104–44.

Glock, Carl Theodor. *Wilhelm Diltheys Grundlegung einer wissenschaftlichen Lebensphilosophie.* Berlin: Junker und Dünnhaupt, 1939.

Groethuysen, Bernhard. "Wilhelm Dilthey." *Deutsche Rundschau* 39 (1913):69–92, 249–70, 283–304.

———. "Idée et Pénsee: Reflexions sur le Journal de Dilthey." *Recherches Philosophiques* 4 (1934–35):371–76.

———. *Introduction a la pensée allemande depuis Nietzsche*. Paris: Stock, 1926.

———. *La philosophie allemande au XIX Siècle*. Paris: Alcan, 1912. Chapter on "Dilthey et son école," pp. 1–23.

Gründer, Karlfried. *Zur Philosophie des Grafen Paul Yorck von Wartenburg*. Göttingen: Vandenhoeck & Ruprecht, 1970.

Gusdorf, G. *Introduction aux sciences humaines*. Paris: Les Belles Lettres, 1960.

Gutmann, James. "Wilhelm Dilthey." *Journal of Philosophy* 64 (October, 1947):609–12.

Habermas, Jürgen. *Erkenntnis und Interesse*. Frankfurt a.M.: Suhrkamp, 1968.

Haym, Rudolf. *Ausgewählter Briefwechsel Rudolf Hayms*. Stuttgart: Deutsche Verlagsanstalt, 1930.

———. *Gesammelte Aufsätze*. Berlin: Weidmannsche Buchhandlung, 1903.

———. *Hegel und seine Zeit*. 2d ed. Hildesheim: G. Olms, 1962.

Hegel, Georg Wilhelm Friedrich. *The Phenomenology of the Mind*. Translated by J. B. Baillie. London: Allen Unwin, 1931.

———. *Sämtliche Werke*. Edited by H. Glockner. Stuttgart: Frommann Verlag, 1927–40.

Heidegger, Martin. *Sein und Zeit*. 9th ed. Tübingen: M. Niemeyer, 1960.

Heinemann, Fritz. *Existentialism and the Modern Predicament*. New York: Harper and Row, 1958.

Herrmann, Ulrich. *Die Pädagogik Wilhelm Diltheys*. Göttingen: Vandenhoeck & Ruprecht, 1971.

Heussi, Karl. *Die Krisis des Historismus*. Tübingen: J. C. B. Mohr, 1932.

Hirsch, E. D., Jr. *Validity in Interpretation*. New Haven: Yale University Press, 1967.

———. *The Aims of Interpretation*. Chicago: University of Chicago Press, 1976.

Hodges, Herbert A. *Wilhelm Dilthey: An Introduction*. 2d ed. London: Routledge & K. Paul, 1949.

———. *The Philosophy of Wilhelm Dilthey*. London: Routledge & K. Paul, 1952.

Holborn, Hajo. "Wilhelm Dilthey and the Critique of Historical Reason." *Journal of the History of Ideas* 11 (1950):93–118.

Horkheimer, Max. *Kritische Theorie*. 2 vols. Frankfurt a.M.: S. Fischer, 1968.

Hughes, Henry Stuart. *Consciousness and Society: The Reorientation of European Social Thought, 1890–1930*. New York: Knopf, 1958.

Humboldt, Wilhelm von. *Gesammelte Schriften.* 17 vols. Berlin: de Gruyter, 1903–68.

Hünermann, Peter. *Der Durchbruch geschichtlichen Denkens im 19. Jahrhundert.* Frieburg: Herder Verlag, 1967.

Husserl, Edmund. *Logische Untersuchungen.* 2 vols. Halle a.d.S.: Niemeyer, 1900–1901.

———. "Philosophie als strenge Wissenschaft." *Logos* 1 (1911):289–341.

———. *Husserliana.* 16 vols. Edited by Walter Biemel. The Hague: Martinus Nijhoff, 1950–73.

Iggers, Georg. *The German Conception of History.* Middletown: Wesleyan University Press, 1968.

Imaz, Eugenio. *El Pensamiento de Dilthey: Evolucion y Sistema.* Mexico D. F.: El Colegio de Mexico, 1946.

Ineichen, Hans. *Erkenntnistheorie und geschichtlich-gesellschaftliche Welt: Diltheys Logik der Geisteswissenschaften.* Frankfurt a.M.: Klostermann, 1975.

James, William. *The Principles of Psychology.* New York: Henry Holt, 1890.

———. *The Letters of William James.* Boston: Atlantic Monthly Press, 1920.

Jaspers, Karl. *Die Psychologie der Weltanschauungen.* 3d ed. Berlin: J. Springer, 1935.

Joël, Karl. *Wandlungen der Weltanschauung.* 2 vols. Tübingen: J. C. B. Mohr, 1928–34.

Johach, Helmut. *Handelnder Mensch und objektiver Geist: Zur Theorie der Geistes- und Sozialwissenschaften bei Wilhelm Dilthey.* Meisenheim: Hain, 1974.

Kamerbeek, J. "Dilthey versus Nietzsche." *Studia Philosophica* 10 (1950): 52–84.

Kant, Immanuel. *Gesammelte Schriften.* 27 vols. Akademie-Ausgabe. Berlin: Reimer/de Gruyter, 1902–72.

Kaufmann, Fritz. "Die Philosophie des Grafen Paul Yorck von Wartenburg." *Jahrbuch für Philosophie und phänomenologische Forschung* 9 (1928):1–235.

Kluback, William. *Wilhelm Dilthey's Philosophy of History.* New York: Columbia University Press, 1956.

Kornberg, Jacques. "Wilhelm Dilthey on the Self and History: Some Theoretical Roots of *Geistesgeschichte.*" *Central European History* 5 (1973): 295–317.

Krausser, Peter. "Diltheys philosophische Anthropologie." *Journal of the History of Philosophy* 1 (1963):211–21.

———. "Dilthey's Revolution in the Theory of the Structure of Scientific

Inquiry and Rational Behavior." *Review of Metaphysics* 22 (1968): 262–80.

———. *Kritik der endlichen Vernunft: Diltheys Revolution der allgemeinen Wissenschafts- und Handlungstheorie.* Stuttgart: Kohlhammer, 1969.

Kremer-Marietti, Angèle. *Wilhelm Dilthey et la anthropologie historique.* Paris: Seghers, 1971.

Landgrebe, Ludwig. *Philosophie der Gegenwart.* Frankfurt a.M.: Ullstein Verlag, 1958.

———. "Wilhelm Diltheys Theorie der Geistwissenschaften: Analyse ihrer Grundbegriffe." *Jahrbuch für Philosophie und phänomenologische Forschung* 9 (1928):238–366.

———. "Vom geisteswissenschaftlichen Verstehen." *Zeitschrift für philosophische Forschung,* 6 (1951):3–16.

Lee, Dwight E., and Beck, Robert. "The Meaning of Historicism." *American Historical Review* 59 (1954):568–77.

Lieber, Hans-Joachim. "Geschichte und Gesellschaft im Denken Diltheys." *Kölner Zeitschrift für Soziologie und Sozialpsychologie* 17 (1965):703–42.

———. *Kulturkritik und Lebensphilosophie: Studien zur deutschen Philosophie der Jahrhundertwende.* Darmstadt: Wissenschaftliche Buchgesellschaft, 1974.

Liebert, Arthur. *Wilhelm Dilthey: Eine Würdigung seines Werkes zum 100. Geburtstage des Philosophen.* Berlin: Mittler, 1933.

Lorenz, H. "Das Bewusstsein der Krise und der Versuch ihrer Überwindung bei Wilhelm Dilthey und Paul Graf Yorck von Wartenburg." *Zeitschrift für Religions- und Geistesgechichte* 11 (1959):59–68.

Löwith, Karl. *Gesammelte Abhandlungen: Zur Kritik der geschichtlichen Existenz.* Stuttgart: Kohlhammer, 1960.

———. *Meaning in History: The Theological Implications of the Philosophy of History.* Chicago: University of Chicago Press, 1949.

———. *From Hegel to Nietzsche: The Revolution in Nineteenth-Century Thought.* New York: Holt, Rinehart and Winston, 1964.

Lukács, Georg. *Die Zerstörung der Vernunft: Der Weg des Irrationalismus von Schelling zu Hitler.* Neuwied am Rhein: Luchterhand, 1962.

Makkreel, Rudolf. *Dilthey: Philosopher of the Human Studies.* Princeton: Princeton University Press, 1975.

———. "Wilhelm Dilthey and the Neo-Kantians." *Journal of the History of Philosophy* 7 (1969):423–49.

Mandelbaum, Maurice. *History, Man and Reason: A Study in Nineteenth-Century Thought.* Baltimore: Johns Hopkins University Press, 1971.

———. *The Problem of Historical Knowledge: An Answer to Relativism.* New York: Harper and Row, 1967.

Mannheim, Karl. *From Karl Mannheim.* Edited with an introd. by Kurt Wolff. New York: Oxford University Press, 1971.

Marini, Guiliano. *Dilthey e la comprensione del mondo umano*. Milan: Guiffrè, 1965.

Masur, Gerhard. *Prophets of Yesterday. Studies in European Culture, 1890-1914*. New York: Macmillan Co., 1961.

———. "Wilhelm Dilthey and the History of Ideas." *Journal of the History of Ideas* 13, no. 1 (1952):94–107.

———. "Wilhelm Dilthey und die europäische Geistesgeschichte," *Deutsche Vierteljahreshefte für Literaturwissenschaft und Geistesgeschichte* 12 (1934):479–505.

Meinecke, Friedrich. *Die Entstehung des Historismus*. 2d ed. Munich-Berlin: R. Oldenbourg, 1946.

Merz, J. T. *A History of European Thought in the Nineteenth Century*. 4 vols. Edinburgh and London: Blackwood, 1907–14.

Mill, John S. *A System of Logic, Ratiocinative and Inductive*. 8th ed. New York: Harper & Bros., 1874.

Misch, Georg. "Dilthey versus Nietzsche." *Die Sammlung: Zeitschrift für Kultur und Erziehung* 9 (1952):378–96.

———. "Die Idee der Lebensphilosophie in der Theorie der Geisteswissenschaften." *Kant-Studien* 33 (1926):536–48.

———. "Vorbericht des Herausgebers." In Dilthey, *Gesammelte Schriften* 5:7–117.

———. *Lebensphilosophie und Phänomenologie: Eine Auseinandersetzung der Diltheyschen Richtung mit Heidegger und Husserl*. Stuttgart: B. G. Teubner, 1967.

———. *Vom Lebens- und Gedankenkreis Wilhelm Diltheys*. Frankfurt a.M.: Schulte-Bulmke, 1947.

Morgan, George. "Wilhelm Dilthey." *Philosophical Review* 42 (1933): 351–80.

———. *The Modern Predicament*. Brown University Press: Providence, R. I., 1968.

Müller-Vollmer, Kurt. *Towards a Phenomenological Theory of Literature: A Study of Wilhelm Dilthey's "Poetik."* Stanford [University] Studies in Germanics and Slavics. The Hague: Mouton, 1963.

Nietzsche, Friedrich. *Sämtliche Werke*. Stuttgart: Kröner, 1964.

Nohl, Herman. "Der junge Dilthey." *Germanisch-romanische Monatschrift* 22 (1934):139–44.

———. "Theologie und Philosophie in der Entwicklung Wilhelm Diltheys." *Die Sammlung* 14 (1959):19–23.

———. "Zur Neuausgabe der Werke Wilhelm Diltheys." *Die Sammlung* 12 (1957):618–25.

Ortega y Gasset, Jose. "History as a System." *Philosophy and History*. Ed. by R. Klibansky and H. J. Paton. New York: Harper & Row, 1963.

———. *History as a System*. New York: Norton, 1961.

——. "Wilhelm Dilthey and the Idea of Life." *Concord and Liberty.* Translated by Helene Weyl. New York: W. W. Norton & Co., 1946.

Outhwaite, William. *Understanding Social Life: The Method Called Verstehen.* New York: Holmes & Meier, 1976.

Palmer, Richard. *Hermeneutics.* Evanston: Northwestern University Press, 1969.

Philipson, Morris. "Dilthey on Art." *Journal of Aesthetics and Art Criticism* 17 (1958):72–76.

Ranke, Leopold von. *Sämtliche Werke.* Leipzig: Duncker und Humblot, 1867–90.

Renthe-Fink, Leonhard. "Geschichtlichkeit." *Abhandlungen der Akademie der Wissenschaften in Göttingen,* phil.-hist. Kl. 59 (1964).

Rickert, Heinrich. *Die Grenzen der naturwissenschaftlichen Begriffsbildung.* Tübingen: J. C. B. Mohr, 1902.

——. *Kulturwissenschaft und Naturwissenschaft.* Freiburg: J. C. B. Mohr, 1899.

——. *Die Philosophie des Lebens.* Tübingen: J. C. B. Mohr, 1929.

Rickman, H. P. *Understanding and the Human Studies.* London: Heinemann, 1967.

Ricoeur, Paul. *The Conflict of Interpretations: Essays in Hermeneutics.* Evanston: Northwestern University Press, 1974.

Riedel, Manfred. "Einleitung," in Wilhelm Dilthey, *Der Aufbau der geschichtlichen Welt in den Geisteswissenschaften.* Frankfurt a.M.: Suhrkamp, 1970, pp. 9–80.

——. "Das erkenntnistheoretische Motiv in Diltheys Theorie der Geisteswissenschaften," in Rüdiger Bubner (ed.), *Hermeneutik und Dialektik* 1 (Tübingen: J. C. B. Mohr, 1970):233–55.

——. "Wilhelm Dilthey und das Problem der Metaphysik." *Philosophisches Jahrbuch* 76 (1968/69):332–48.

Ringer, Fritz. *The Decline of the German Mandarins: The German Academic Community 1890–1933.* Cambridge, Mass.: Harvard University Press, 1969.

Rodi, Frithjof. *Morphologie und Hermeneutik: Zur Methode von Diltheys Aesthetik.* Stuttgart: Kohlhammer, 1969.

Rossi, Pietro. *Lo storicismo tedesco contemporaneo.* Turin: Einaudi, 1956.

Rothacker, Erich. *Die dogmatische Denkform in den Geistewissenschaften und das Problem des Historismus.* Mainz: Verlag der Akademie der Wissenschaften und der Literatur, 1954.

——. *Einleitung in die Geisteswissenschaften.* 2d ed. Tübingen: J. C. B. Mohr, 1930.

——. *Logik und Systematik der Geisteswissenschaften.* Bonn: Bouvier, 1947.

———. "Wilhelm Dilthey." *Deutsche Vierteljahresschrift für Literaturwissenschaft und Geistesgeschichte* 16 (1938):101–7.

Sauerland, Karol. *Diltheys Erlebnisbegriff*. Berlin: de Gruyter, 1972.

Schlegel, Wolfgang. "Der Standort Diltheys und Yorcks von Wartenburg." *Zeitschrift für Religions- und Geistesgeschichte* 12 (1960):45–59.

Schleiermacher, F. E. D. *Hermeneutik*. Edited and with an introduction by Heinz Kimmerle. Heidelberg: Carl Winter, Universitätsverlag, 1959.

———. *Sämmtliche Werke*. Berlin: G. Reimer, 1835–64.

Schmoller, Gustav. *Zur Literaturgeschichte der Staats- und Sozialwissenschaften*. Chapter "Die Schriften von K. Menger und W. Dilthey zur Methodologie der Staats- und Sozialwissenschaften." Leipzig: Duncker und Humblot, 1888.

Simmel, Georg. *Die Probleme der Geschichtsphilosophie*. Leipzig: Duncker und Humblot, 1892.

Spiegelberg, Herbert. *The Phenomenological Movement*. 2 vols. The Hague: Nijhoff, 1960.

Spranger, Eduard. *Lebensformen: Geisteswissenschaftliche Psychologie und Ethik der Persönlichkeit*. Halle: Niemeyer, 1937.

———. "Zur Theorie des Verstehens und zur geisteswissenschaftliche Psychologie." In. *Festschrift für Johannes Volkelt*. Munich: Beck, 1918, pp. 357–403.

Staehelin, Fleix. "Burckhardt und Dilthey." *Museum Helveticum* 51 (1951): 299–304.

Strasser, Stephan. *Phenomenology and the Human Sciences*. Pittsburg: Duquesne University Press, 1963.

Stein, Arthur. *Der Begriff des Verstehens bei Dilthey*. 2d rev. ed. Tübingen: J. C. B. Mohr, 1926.

Stenzel, Julius. "Dilthey und die deutsche Philosophie der Gegenwart," *Vorträge der Kant-Gesellschaft*, no. 33 (Berlin, 1934).

———. "Über Diltheys Verhältnis zu Hegel: Ein Beitrag zum Begriff der Geschichtsphilosophie," *De Idee: Orgaan van het Bollandgenootschap voor Zuivre Rede*, vol. 12, no. 1 (n.d.).

Suter, Jean-Francois. *Philosophie et histoire chez Wilhelm Dilthey*. Basel: Verlag für Recht und Gesellschaft, 1960.

Tapper, Bonno. "Dilthey's Methodology of the Geisteswissenschaften." *Philosophical Review* 34 (1925):332–49.

Trendelenburg, Friedrich Adolf. *Logische Untersuchungen*. 3 vols. Leipzig: S. Hirzel, 1870.

Troeltsch, Ernst. *Der Historismus und seine Probleme*. Tübingen: J. C. B. Mohr, 1922.

Tuttle, Howard. *Wilhelm Dilthey's Philosophy of Historical Understanding: A Critical Analysis*. Leiden: Brill, 1969.

Vicentini, Claudio. *Studio su Dilthey*. Milan: Mursia, 1974.

Vuillemin, Jules. "Le Monde de l'Esprit selon Dilthey." *Revue Philosophique* 140 (1950):508–19.

Wach, Joachim. *Das Verstehen: Grundzüge einer Geschichte der hermeneutischen Theorie im 19. Jahrhundert*. 3 vols. Tübingen: J. C. B. Mohr, 1926–33.

———. *Die Typenlehre Trendelenburgs und ihr Einfluss auf Dilthey*. Tübingen: J. C. B. Mohr, 1926.

Weber, Max. *Gesammelte Aufsätze zur Wissenschaftslehre*. Tübingen: J. C. B. Mohr, 1922.

Westphal, Otto. *Feinde Bismarcks: Geistige Grundlagen der deutschen Opposition, 1848–1918*. Munich: R. Oldenbourg, 1930.

Winch, Peter. *The Idea of a Social Science and Its Relation to Philosophy*. New York: Humanities Press, 1962.

Windelband, Wilhelm. *Präludien: Aufsätze und Reden zur Philosophie und ihrer Geschichte*. 9th ed., 2 vols. Tübingen: Mohr Verlag, 1924.

Windelband, Wilhelm, and Heimsoeth, Heinz. *Lehrbuch der Geschichte der Philosophie*. 15th ed. Tübingen: J. C. B. Mohr, 1957.

Wright, Georg von. *Explanation and Understanding*. Ithaca: Cornell University Press, 1971.

Wundt, Wilhelm. *Logik*. 3 vols. 3d rev. ed. Stuttgart: F. Enke, 1906–8.

Yorck von Wartenburg, Graf Paul. *Bewusstseinsstellung und Geschichte Ein Fragment aus dem philosophischen Nachlass*. Introduced and edited by Iring Fetscher. Tübingen: Niemeyer, 1956.

Ziegler, Theobald. *Die geistigen und sozialen Strömungen des neunzehnten Jahrhunderts*. Berlin: B. Bendi, 1901.

Zöckler, Christofer. *Dilthey und die Hermeneutik*. Stuttgart: Metzler Verlag, 1975.

Index

physiological psychology, 76; on return to Kant, 74

Hennig, Johannes, 368n

Heraclitus, 115, 331, 356

Herbart, Johann F., 75, 77, 173, 175, 184, 332; "Realen" in, 170–71; world-view as subjective idealist, 330

Herder, Johann Gottfried von, 292, 330; belief as metacritique, 154; immediate intuition in, 57; language as constitutive of world-view, 278; as romantic idealist, 47; *Verstehen* in, 243, 315

hermeneutic circle, 132, 228, 233, 251–53, 276, 290; in foundation of human sciences, 94; at work in Dilthey's thought, 10

hermeneutic standpoint, 211, 238–39, 346–48

hermeneutics, 4, 5, 7, 375n, 380n; double direction of depth and breadth, 245, 263, 268, 375n; "Die Entstehung der Hermeneutik," 255; extended beyond textual meaning, 303; as fundamental science, 236–39; life as hermeneutical, 346, 356; logical vs. ontological form of, 139, 242, 347; model for theory of knowledge, 232–37; psychology distinct from, 232–33, 236–39, 328, 346; sacralization of world in, 243, 375n; Schleiermacher as "Kant of," 244; solves antinomy of psychology, 211. *See also* reflection; understanding

"Das hermeneutische System Schleiermachers in der Auseinandersetzung mit der älteren protestantischen Hermeneutik" ("Schleiermacher's Hermeneutic System in the Confrontation with the Older Protestant Hermeneutic"), 22, 183, 243–45, 258, 268, 278, 281

Herrmann, Ulrich, 4, 360n

Hertz, Heinrich, 309

Herz, Henriette, 270

Heussi, Karl, 336

His, Wilhelm, 31

historical consciousness: critique of, 317–19, 386n; ethical function of, 320; in Hegel, 49, 318; key to understanding man, 319–21; as organ of sight, 324, 337–38; and philosophical consciousness, 25, 355–56; in Schleiermacher, 46,

363n; and transcendentalism, 22, 337, 352, 355–56, 386n

Historical School, 25, 27, 52, 55–58, 134, 363n; Dilthey's critique of, 58; individuality in, 263. *See also* Ranke

historicism, 7, 30, 60, 335–38, 351–57; Dilthey rejects attribution of, 207, 352; Dilthey's transcendental historicism, 355–57, 387n; Husserl attacks, 206–7; modern critique of, 353–54, 357; multiple meanings of, 351–53; Rickert attacks, 192. *See also* historical consciousness

historicity: in Historical School, 58; life and, 115–17, 285–86, 352, 356–57; Schleiermacher's lack of, 46, 244, 363n; Yorck's form of "absolute," 115, 356

history: causal laws in, 26, 190, 266, 303–10; causality and value in, 120–21, 308–9; class in, 296–97; doing and knowing in, 250; existing forms of, inadequate, 25–26; experience as primordial cell, 97; facticity in, 291–94; Hegel's revaluation of, 49; historical a priori, 117, 157–58, 253, 279–80, 324, 344; human nature in, 120, 284–86, 319; ideal subjects in, 266; irony of, 337; life as historical, 112–15, 125, 177; most complex of human sciences, 175, 289; as objectivation, 271; "with philosophical intent," 25, 58, 152, 165, 182, 313, 344, 356; presentism in, 289–90; progress in, 289; psychology and, 177; purpose and motive in, 225, 288; as relative but valid knowledge, 289–91, 336–38, 387n; as structure of intersecting coherences, 121–23, 266, 308; substantive philosophy of, impossible, 144; 298; *Zeitgeist* in, 266. *See also* human sciences; psychology; sociology

Hobbes, Thomas, 330

Hodges, H. A., 202, 232, 298, 325, 360n, 362n, 368n; on Dilthey's hermeneutics, 376n; *Erlebnis* as undifferentiated, 373n; on Marx and Dilthey, 380n

Hoffmannsthal, Hugo von, eulogy for Dilthey, 36

Hofstadter, Albert, 374–75n

Holborn, Hajo, 293

Hölderlin, Friedrich, 40, 84, 134

Horkheimer, Max, 4, 343

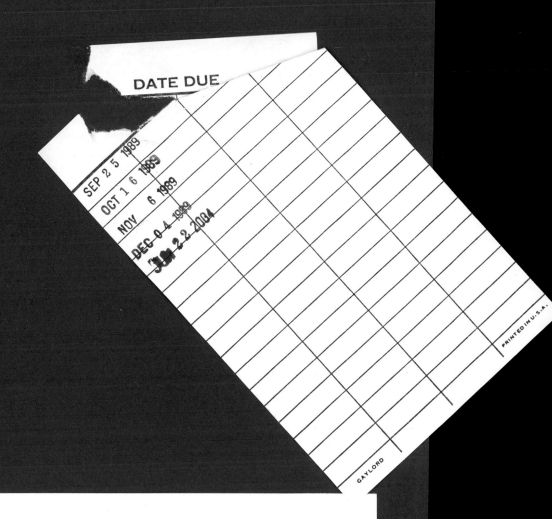

 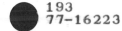